Treatises on Solvency II

Meinrad Dreher

Treatises on Solvency II

Springer

Meinrad Dreher
Johannes Gutenberg University
Mainz
Germany

ISBN 978-3-662-46289-8 ISBN 978-3-662-46290-4 (eBook)
DOI 10.1007/978-3-662-46290-4

Library of Congress Control Number: 2015935187

Springer Heidelberg New York Dordrecht London

Printed on acid-free paper

Springer-Verlag GmbH Berlin Heidelberg is part of Springer Science+Business Media (www.springer.com)

Preface

“Treatises on Solvency II” collects 13 articles on the new European insurance supervisory regime under the Solvency II Directive and the EIOPA Regulation, viewed predominantly from a legal standpoint. The articles treat the basis of the European insurance supervisory regime and its three pillars of solvency, governance, and disclosure. As background and by way of example, the treatise describes the German insurance supervisory regime and the efforts of the German legislator to implement the Solvency II system into this German insurance supervisory regime.

These articles were written in the period from 2009 to 2014, the time frame within which the Solvency II system was being created. They were first published in German and reflect the states and stages of the European and German insurance supervision at the time of their particular publication.

Although the insurance supervisory system is now definitively marked by European standards, there has been no thoroughgoing debate and consideration of this system with respect to theory and practice. In only a few Member States has there been public discussion of the issues implicated by the new European insurance supervisory regime. This book is intended to contribute to such a European debate by making the collected articles accessible in English. The intended addressees consist of, i.a., European and national insurance supervisory authorities, insurance undertakings, legislators dealing with insurance supervision, interested associations, financial auditors, courts, and above all insurance academics.

This book would not have been possible without contributions from various persons. First of all, the articles rendered from German into English by specialized translators had to be refined and harmonized. In this regard, my thanks go to attorney-at-law Ms. Julia Körner, research assistant to my academic chair at Mainz University, for her commitment, dedication, and input. For their dedicated support in producing, editing, and finalizing the indexes, I gratefully acknowledge my assistants: Ms. Judith Kreher, law clerk; Mr. Benjamin Franz, law clerk; Mr. Tobias Gerigk, cand. jur.; and Ms. Sarah Gillenberg, stud. jur. Significant contribution in the form of generous financial support for translating and printing was provided by the Dr. Paul-Otto Faßbender Stiftung für Bildung und

Wissenschaft [Foundation for Education and Science] of Düsseldorf, and I take this opportunity to express my particular thanks to the Foundation. Finally, I thank the publishers, editors, and co-authors involved with the initial appearance in print of these articles for their permission to publish these writings in English in the form of this book.

Mainz, Germany
1 October 2014

Meinrad Dreher

List of Abbreviations

AG	Die Aktiengesellschaft (Zeitschrift), **The Journal of Corporation Law**
AktG	Aktiengesetz, **German Stock Corporation Act**
ALM	**Asset-Liability Management**
art.	**Article**
BaFin	Bundesanstalt für Finanzdienstleistungsaufsicht, **Federal Financial Supervisory Authority**
BaFin-Journal	Bundesanstalt für Finanzdienstleistungsaufsicht-Journal, **Federal Financial Supervisory Authority-Journal**
BB	Betriebs-Berater (Zeitschrift), **The Journal of Management Consultant, Law, Tax & Economics**
BDSG	Bundesdatenschutzgesetz, **German Federal Data Protection Act**
BGB	Bürgerliches Gesetzbuch, **German Civil Code**
BGHZ	Entscheidungen des Bundesgerichtshofes in Zivilsachen, **Decisions of the Federal Court of Justice in Civil Matters**
BGBl.	Bundesgesetzblatt, **German Federal Law Gazette**
BJR	**Business Judgement Rule**
BR-Drucks.	Bundesrat-Drucksache, **Document of the German Bundesrat**
BT-Drucks.	Bundestag-Drucksache, **Document of the German Bundestag**
BVerwG	Bundesverwaltungsgericht, **Federal Administrative Court**
BVerwGE	Bundesverwaltungsgerichts-entscheidungen, **Federal Administrative Court Decisions**
CCZ	Corporate Compliance (Zeitschrift), **Journal of Corporate Compliance**
CEIOPS	**Committee of European Insurance and Occupational Pensions Supervisors**
CFL	Corporate Finance Fachportal (Zeitschrift), **Journal of Corporate Finance**
CMLRev	**Common Market Law Review**
COF	**Classification of Own Funds**

COM	**European Commission Documents**
DB	Der Betrieb (Zeitschrift), **Journal of Business, Tax and Economic Law**
DÖV	Die Öffentliche Verwaltung (Zeitschrift), **Journal of Public Administration**
DCGK	Deutscher Corporate Governance Kodex, **German Corporate Governance Code**
DRS	Deutsche Rechnungslegungsstandards, **German Accounting Standards**
DVO	Durchführungsverordnung, **Draft Implementing Measures Solvency II**
ECB	**European Central Bank**
ECJ	**European Court of Justice**
ed	**Edition**
ed., eds.	**Editor, editors**
e.g.	**Exempli gratia**
EIOPA	**European Insurance and Occupational Pensions Authority**
EOF	**Eligibility of Own Funds**
EU	**European Union**
EuR	Europarecht (Zeitschrift), **European Law Journal**
EuZW	Zeitschrift für Europäisches Wirtschaftsrecht (Zeitschrift), **Journal of European Business Law**
EWiR	Entscheidungen zum Wirtschaftsrecht – Kurzkommentare (Zeitschrift), **Decisions in the Field of Economic Law – short commentaries**
FAZ	Frankfurter Allgemeine Zeitung, **Frankfurt General Newspaper**
f., ff.	**Following page, following pages**
FMA	**Financial Market Authority (Austria)**
FinDAG	Gesetz über die Bundesanstalt für Finanzdienstleistungsaufsicht, **Financial Services Supervisory Act**
FinStabGEG	Gesetz zur Stabilisierung der deutschen Finanzaufsicht, **Act to Strengthen German Financial Supervision**
FIW	Forschungsinstitut für Wirtschaftsverfassung und Wettbewerb, **Research Institute for Economic Constitution and Competition**
FS	Festschrift, **Publication in Honor**
GDV	Gesamtverband der Deutschen Versicherungswirtschaft, **German Insurance Association**
GenTG	Gentechnikgesetz, **Genetic Engineering Act**
GG	Grundgesetz, **German Constitution**
GmbHR	Gesellschaft mit beschränkter Haftung Rundschau (Zeitschrift), **Journal of Limited Liability Companies**
GWG	Geldwäschegesetz, **German Money-Laundering Act**
HGB	Handelsgesetzbuch, **German Commercial Code**

i.a.	**Inter alia**
IAS	**International Accounting Standard**
IASB	**International Accounting Standards Board**
i.e.	**Id est**
ICS	**Internal Control System**
id.	**Idem**
IFRS	**International Financial Reporting Standard**
Inc.	**Incorporation**
IR	**Implementing Regulation**
JECLAP	**Journal of European Competition Law and Practice**
Jite	**Journal of Institutional and Theoretical Economics**
JZ	Juristenzeitung (Zeitschrift), **Jurists' Journal**
KSzW	Kölner Schrift zum Wirtschaftsrecht (Zeitschrift), **Cologne Journal of Economic Law**
KWG	Kreditwesengesetz, **German Credit Service Act**
MaComp VA	Mindestanforderungen an die Compliance Funktion (Versicherungsaufsicht), **Minimum Requirements for the Compliance Function (Insurance Supervision)**
MaComp WA	Mindestanforderungen an die Compliance Funktion (Wertpapieraufsicht), **Minimum Requirements for the Compliance Function (Securities Supervision)**
MaRisk BA	Mindestanforderungen an das Risikomanagement (Bankenaufsicht), **Minimum Requirements for Risk Management (Banking Supervision)**
MaRisk VA	Mindestanforderungen an das Risikomanagement (Versicherungsaufsicht), **Minimum Requirements for Risk Management (Insurance Supervision)**
MCR	**Minimum Capital Requirement**
n.	**Number**
no.	**Numero**
NJW	Neue Juristische Wochenschrift (Zeitschrift), **New Weekly Journal of Law**
NZBau	Neue Zeitschrift für Baurecht (Zeitschrift), **New Journal of Building Law**
NZG	Neue Zeitschrift für Gesellschaftsrecht (Zeitschrift), **New Journal of Company Law**
OECD	**Organisation for Economic Cooperation and Development**
OFT	**Office of Fair Trading**
OJEU	**Official Journal of the European Union**
ORSA	**Own Risk and Solvency Assessment**
öOGH	Österreichischer Oberster Gerichtshof, **Austrian Supreme Court**
para.	**Paragraph**
pp.	**Paginae**
QIS	**Quantitative Impact Study**
ref.	**Reference**

RegE	Regierungsentwurf, **Government's Draft**
RSR	**Regular Supervisory Report**
RTS	**Report to Supervisors**
SCR	**Solvency Capital Requirement**
sec., secs.	**Section, sections**
sent.	**Sentence**
SFCR	**Solvency and Financial Condition Report**
SGG	Sozialgerichtsgesetz, **Social Court Act**
SRP	**Supervisory Review Process**
StGB	Strafgesetzbuch, **German Criminal Code**
StrlSchV	Strahlenschutzverordnung, **German Regulation on Protection against Harm from Ionizing Radiation**
subpara.	**Subparagraph**
TFEU	**Treaty on the Function of the European Union**
TKG	Telekommunikationsgesetz, **Telecommunication Act**
TP	**Technical Provision**
TSIM	**Tests and Standards for the Use of an Internal Model**
UFR	**Ultimate Forward Rate**
VAG	Versicherungsaufsichtsgesetz, **German Insurance Supervision Act**
VersR	Versicherungsrecht (Zeitschrift), **Journal of Insurance Law**
VersVergV	Versicherungsvergütungsverordnung, **German Remuneration Regulation for the Insurance Industry**
VGH	Verwaltungsgerichtshof München, **Munich High Administrative Court**
viz.	**Videlicet**
VuR	Verbraucher und Recht (Zeitschrift), **Journal of Consumer and Law**
VVG	Versicherungsvertragsgesetz, **Insurance Contracts Act**
VW	Versicherungswirtschaft (Zeitschrift), **Journal of Insurance and Economy**
VwGO	Verwaltungsgerichtsordnung, **Code of Administrative Court Procedure**
WiSt	Wirtschaftswissenschaftliches Studium (Zeitschrift), **Journal of Economic Studies**
WM	Wertpapiermitteilungen – Zeitschrift für Wirtschafts- und Bankenrecht (Zeitschrift), **Securities Review – Journal of Commercial and Banking Law**
WpDVerOV	Verordnung zur Konkretisierung der Verhaltensregeln und Organisationsanforderungen für Wertpapierdienstleistungsunternehmen, **German Investment Services Conduct of Business and Organization Regulation**
WPg	Die Wirtschaftsprüfung (Zeitschrift), **Journal of Accounting**
WpHG	Wertpapierhandelsgesetz, **German Securities Trading Act**

WuW	Wirtschaft und Wettbewerb (Zeitschrift), **Journal of German and European Competition Law**
WuW/E	Wirtschaft und Wettbewerb – Entscheidungssammlung, **Decisions collected in the Journal of German and European Competition Law**
ZBB	Zeitschrift für Bankrecht und Bankwirtschaft (Zeitschrift), **Journal of Banking Law and Finance**
ZfV	Zeitschrift für Verwaltung (Zeitschrift), **Journal of Administrative Law**
ZGR	Zeitschrift für Unternehmens- und Gesellschaftsrecht (Zeitschrift), **Journal of Business and Company Law**
ZHR	Zeitschrift für das gesamte Handels- und Wirtschaftsrecht (Zeitschrift), **Comprehensive Journal of Commercial and Economic Law**
ZIP	Zeitschrift für Wirtschaftsrecht (Zeitschrift), **Journal of Economic Law**
ZIR	Zeitschrift Interne Revision (Zeitschrift), **Journal of Internal Revision**
ZVersWiss	Zeitschrift für die gesamte Versicherungswissenschaft (Zeitschrift), **German Journal of Risk and Insurance**
ZWeR	Zeitschrift für Wettbewerbsrecht (Zeitschrift), **Journal of Competition Law**

Contents

Part I Basics

1 Harmonization of Insurance Supervisory Law 3
1.1 Introduction 4
1.2 The Typology of Harmonization Methods 5
1.3 The European Law Sources for Harmonization of the Insurance Supervisory Regime 8
1.3.1 The Solvency II Framework Directive 8
1.3.2 The Implementing Regulations for the Solvency II Framework Directive 12
1.3.3 The EIOPA Regulation 14
1.3.4 Interim Result 15
1.4 Consequences for the Future Insurance Supervisory System in Germany 16
1.4.1 The Impact of Full Harmonization on the Insurance Supervision Act 16
1.4.2 Supervision According to the Principle of Abusiveness with Regard to Primary Insurance Undertakings 17
1.4.3 The Effect of Full Harmonization in Certain Areas . . . 21
1.5 Conclusions 23

2 Supervisory Review Process 27
2.1 Introduction 28
2.2 Principles of Insurance Supervision Under Solvency II 29
2.3 Objective and Concept of the Supervisory Review Process . . . 30
2.3.1 Objective 30
2.3.2 Art. 36 of the Solvency II Directive and Its Implementation in Sec. 289, Paras. 2–4 of the VAG Reg-E [Government's Draft of a Tenth Act Amending the German Insurance Supervision Act] 31
2.3.3 The CEIOPS Advice on Procedures for Supervisory Authorities 36

2.4 The Subjects of the Supervisory Review Process 37
2.4.1 Subject of the Investigation and Investigatory Standard 37
2.4.2 The Governance System as Examination Subject . . . 41
2.4.3 Capital Requirements as Examination Subject 44
2.5 Powers of Supervisory Authorities to Remedy Weaknesses and Deficiencies 53
2.5.1 "Weaknesses or Deficiencies" as Legal Terms 53
2.5.2 The Role of Art. 36, Para. 5 of the Solvency II Directive in the Classification of Intervention Powers 58
2.5.3 Non-compliance with Capital Requirements 60
2.5.4 Non-compliance with Requirements on Governance 61
2.6 Summary 63

3 Insurance Supervisory Law and Consumer Protection 67
3.1 Introduction 68
3.2 Consumer Protection Provisions of the New Insurance Supervisory Regime 69
3.2.1 The EIOPA Regulation 69
3.2.2 The Solvency II Directive 71
3.2.3 The Draft Regulation on Key Information Documents and the Draft Directive on Insurance Mediation 72
3.2.4 The Second and Third Regulatory Levels of the Solvency II System 72
3.2.5 The VAG-RegE [Government's Draft of a Tenth Act Amending the German Insurance Supervision Act] 73
3.2.6 The BaFin [Federal Financial Supervisory Authority] 74
3.3 The Role of Consumer Protection in the Supervision of Insurance Undertakings 75
3.3.1 The Objective of Supervision 75
3.3.2 Further Implications 77
3.4 Summary 94

Part II Solvency

4 Solvency Requirements 99
4.1 Introduction 100
4.2 The Solvency System Under Supervisory Law 101
4.2.1 The Economic Balance Sheet (Solvency Statement) . . . 101
4.2.2 Own Funds Under Supervisory Law 102
4.2.3 Capital Requirements Under Supervisory Law 103
4.2.4 The Supervisory Review Process 107

4.3 Complexity, Volatility and Procyclicality of the Solvency Requirements: Implications for Solvency Supervision 109
4.3.1 The Problems 109
4.3.2 Complexity 111
4.3.3 Volatility 115
4.3.4 Procyclicality 121
4.4 The New Roles of the Managing and Supervisory Boards, Supervisory Authorities, Courts and Insurance Academics in the Solvency Supervision of Insurance Undertakings 124
4.4.1 The Managing and Supervisory Boards of Insurance Undertakings 124
4.4.2 The Supervisory Authorities 133
4.4.3 Competent Courts in the Insurance Supervisory Regime 146
4.4.4 Insurance Academics 148
4.5 Summary 149

Part III Governance

5 Own Risk and Solvency Assessment 157
5.1 Introduction 158
5.2 Subject-Matter and Objective of the ORSA 160
5.3 The Solvency II Legal Principles Applicable to the ORSA . . . 161
5.4 The ORSA and the Risk Management System 162
5.4.1 The European Law Framework 162
5.4.2 Present Law: The Relationship of the ORSA to Sec. 64 a, Para. 1, 2 of the VAG [German Insurance Supervision Act] and the MaRisk VA [Minimum Requirements for Risk Management (Insurance Supervision)] 164
5.4.3 Future Law: Sec. 28 of the VAG [German Insurance Supervision Act] in the Version of the Ministerial Draft 167
5.5 ORSA, Actuarial Function, Standard Formula and Internal Model 170
5.6 The ORSA, the Compliance Function, and the Internal Audit Function 172
5.7 Individual Issues Concerning the ORSA 173
5.7.1 The ORSA and Free Enterprise 173
5.7.2 The Relationship of the ORSA to Capital Add-Ons 179
5.7.3 The Own Assessment of Interest Rate Risk 180
5.7.4 Significant Deviation from the Assumptions Underlying the Calculation of the Standard Formula and the Internal Model 181

5.8 Documentation and Publication of the ORSA 186
5.8.1 Addressees and General Principles of the ORSA Information 186
5.8.2 The Internal Report 187
5.8.3 Requirements for Reporting to the Supervisory Authorities 187
5.8.4 Requirements for Reporting to the Public 190
5.9 Supervisory Powers with Respect to the ORSA 191
5.10 Summary 192

6 Fitness of Members of Supervisory Board 195
6.1 Introduction 196
6.2 General Requirements of Company Law Applicable to the Qualification of Supervisory Board Members 197
6.2.1 The Federal Court of Justice-Ruling in *Hertie* 197
6.2.2 The German Corporate Governance Code 199
6.3 The Insurance Supervisory Regime Requirements for the Qualification of Supervisory Board Members 200
6.3.1 The Statutory Rules on the Expertise Requirement . . . 200
6.3.2 The BaFin [Federal Financial Supervisory Authority] Bulletin of 22 February 2010 204
6.3.3 Amendments in the Process of Implementing Solvency II 206
6.4 Individual Expertise of the Supervisory Board Members and the Overall Qualification of the Supervisory Board 211
6.4.1 Requirements for the Individual Supervisory Board Member 211
6.4.2 Overall Qualification of the Supervisory Board 212
6.5 Summary 214

7 Definition and Holders of Key Functions 217
7.1 Introduction 218
7.2 The Term "Key Function" 219
7.2.1 The Key Functions 219
7.2.2 Terminological Dual-Tracking and the Irrelevance of the Difference Between "Key Function" and "Key Task" 220
7.2.3 The Term "Key Functions": Exhaustive or Open? . . . 223
7.3 The Key Function Holders and Their Subordinate Staff Members in Key Functions 227
7.3.1 The Solvency II System 227
7.3.2 The Equalization of Key Function Holders and Persons Who Effectively Run the Undertaking 228
7.3.3 Factual Distinctions in the Duty of Notice 231
7.3.4 Factual Distinctions in Qualification Requirements . . . 231

7.3.5 Determination of Each Key Function Holder and the Staff Members Subordinate to Them 232
7.4 Summary 241

8 Supervisory Review of Key Functions 243
8.1 Introduction 244
8.2 The "Fit" Requirement for Key Function Holders and Their Subordinate Staff Members in Key Functions 245
8.2.1 The Two-Tier Qualification Structure in General . . . 245
8.2.2 The Special Rules 247
8.2.3 The Fitness of Key Function Holders 249
8.2.4 The Fitness of Subordinate Staff to Key Function Holders 257
8.3 The "Proper" Requirement for Key Function Holders and Their Subordinate Staff Members in Key Functions 258
8.3.1 The Two-Tier Structure of the Proper Requirement and the Proceduralization of the Proper Requirement as Starting Point 258
8.3.2 The Proper Requirement of Key Function Holders 259
8.3.3 The "Proper" Requirement for Staff Members Subordinate to Key Function Holders 264
8.4 The Remuneration of Key Function Holders 264
8.5 The Duties of Notice and Public Disclosure for Key Function Holders 265
8.5.1 The Duties of Notice to Supervisory Authorities . . . 265
8.5.2 The Duties of Public Disclosure 268
8.6 Supervisory Recall and Prohibition of Exercise of Function for Key Function Holders in Cases of Fit-and-Proper Deficiencies and Supervisory Right to Direct Information from Key Function Holders 268
8.6.1 Solvency II 268
8.6.2 VAG-RegE [Government's Draft of a Tenth Act Amending the German Insurance Supervision Act] 269
8.7 Summary 271

9 'Senior Management' of Insurance Undertakings 275
9.1 Introduction 275
9.1.1 The Normative Rules 276
9.2 'Senior Management' in the Solvency II System 277
9.3 Summary 281

10 Definition, Tasks and Legal Nature of the Compliance Function 283
10.1 Introduction 284
10.2 The Legal Bases of Compliance Under the Insurance Supervisory Regime 286

10.2.1 The Relationship of Compliance Under the Insurance Supervisory Regime to Compliance Under General Company Law 286
10.2.2 The Solvency II Directive 287
10.2.3 The Draft of the Solvency II Implementing Regulation 288
10.2.4 The CEIOPS Guidelines on the System of Governance 290
10.2.5 The EIOPA Guidelines on the System of Governance 291
10.2.6 The VAG-RegE [Government's Draft of a Tenth Act Amending the Insurance Supervision Act] 292
10.2.7 The Government's Draft of the German Banking Ringfencing Act 293
10.2.8 MaRisk BA [Minimum Requirements for Risk Management (Banking Supervision)] 294
10.2.9 MaComp VA [Minimum Requirements for the Compliance Function (Insurance Supervision)]? 294
10.3 The Definition of "Compliance Under the Insurance Supervisory Regime" 296
10.4 The Task of Compliance Under the Insurance Supervisory Regime and the Compliance-Related Requirements 299
10.4.1 Underlying Principles 299
10.4.2 General Legal Monitoring 306
10.4.3 Advising the Managing Board 313
10.4.4 Evaluation of Risks from Changes in the Legal Environment 316
10.4.5 Evaluation of the Compliance Risk 317
10.5 The Legal Nature of Compliance Under the Insurance Supervisory Regime 318
10.5.1 The Long Arm of the Insurance Supervisory Authority? 318
10.5.2 Company Officials? 319
10.5.3 Statutorily Prescribed and Designed Functions of Undertakings 321
10.6 Summary 322

11 Integrating the Compliance Function into the Legal Department 325
11.1 Introduction 326
11.2 Combining the Legal Department and the Compliance Function as a Legal Problem 327
11.3 Combining the Legal Department and the Compliance Function in Light of Their Respective Responsibilities 328
11.3.1 Crossover in Tasks 328

11.3.2 Advisement of Insurance Undertakings' Staff Members as an Area of Potential Conflict 330
11.3.3 Advisement of an Insurance Undertaking's Managing Board as an Area of Potential Conflict 331
11.3.4 Formation of Law by the Legal Department as an Area of Potential Conflict 333
11.4 Combining the Legal Department and the Compliance Function in Light of the Special Rules Aimed at the Compliance Function as a Key Function 334
11.4.1 Particular Competencies 334
11.4.2 Special Qualifications 335
11.5 Combining the Legal Department and the Compliance Function in Light of the Principle of Functional Segregation 336
11.6 Combining the Legal Department and the Compliance Function in Light of the Principle of Functional Independence 337
11.7 Combining the Legal Department and the Compliance Function in Light of the Principles of Freedom of Internal Organization and of Proportionality 338
11.8 Summary 340

Part IV Disclosure

12 Supervisory Reporting 345
12.1 Introduction 346
12.2 The Obligations to Notify Based on Formal Grounds 347
12.2.1 The Term "Obligations to Notify Based on Formal Grounds" 347
12.2.2 Obligations to Notify Based on Formal Organizational Grounds 348
12.2.3 Reporting Duties Related to Tariffs and General Policy Conditions 351
12.3 The Disclosure Obligations of Financial Reporting 352
12.3.1 The Disclosure Obligations for Financial Reporting Based on Formal Organizational Grounds 352
12.3.2 The Disclosure Obligations for Substantive Financial Reporting 357
12.4 The Disclosure Obligations for Risk Reporting 364
12.5 Disclosure Obligations at the Group Level 366
12.5.1 The Obligations to Notify Based on Formal Grounds at the Group Level 366
12.5.2 The Disclosure Obligations of Financial Reporting at the Group Level 368
12.5.3 The Disclosure Obligations of Risk Reporting at the Group Level 371
12.6 The Disclosure Obligations for Financial Conglomerates 372

12.7 Further Implications . . . 373
12.7.1 The Function of the Reporting and Disclosure Obligations . . . 373
12.7.2 The Scope of the Reporting and Disclosure Obligations . . . 375
12.7.3 The Relationship Between the VAG [German Insurance Supervision Act] and Solvency II Directive Regarding Reporting and Disclosure Obligations . . . 377
12.7.4 The Concretization and Practical Management of Reporting and Disclosure Obligations . . . 380
12.8 Summary . . . 382

13 Public Disclosure . . . 385
13.1 Introduction . . . 386
13.2 The Objectives and Addressees of the Duties of Public Disclosure . . . 388
13.3 Minimum Content of the Report on Solvency and Financial Condition . . . 391
13.3.1 Overview . . . 391
13.3.2 Financial Reporting . . . 392
13.3.3 Information Related to Formal Organizational Aspects . . . 397
13.3.4 The Information on Risk Reporting . . . 398
13.4 The Duty to Update in the Event of Significant Changes to Published Information . . . 400
13.5 The Duty of Disclosure for Direct Insurance and Reinsurance Undertakings in the National Context . . . 401
13.5.1 Disclosure Duties Under Capital Market Law . . . 401
13.5.2 Disclosure Duties Under Commercial Law . . . 404
13.6 Comparison of the Report on Solvency and Financial Condition Under Solvency II and Publication Required Under National Commercial and Capital Market Law . . . 407
13.6.1 The Equal Rank of the Disclosure Duties of Solvency II and Disclosure Duties Under Capital Market and Commercial Law . . . 407
13.6.2 Content Overlap Between the Report on Solvency and Financial Condition Under Solvency II and the Annual Financial Statement and Management Report . . . 408
13.6.3 Content Overlap Between the Report on Solvency and Financial Condition Under Solvency II and Publications Under Capital Market Law . . . 410
13.7 Disclosure Duties at Group Level . . . 410
13.7.1 Disclosure Duties at Group Level Under Solvency II . . . 410
13.7.2 Disclosure Duties at Group Level in National Context . . . 412

13.7.3 Content Overlap Between the Report on Solvency and Financial Condition at Group Level Under Solvency II and the Annual Financial Statement, Management Report, and Financial Reports Under Capital Market Law 413
13.8 Form of Disclosure in the Report on Solvency and Financial Condition 414
13.9 Protection of Business and Trade Secrets in Public Disclosure Duties 415
13.10 Further Conclusions 416
13.10.1 Regulatory Approach in Public Disclosure Duties 416
13.10.2 Potential Synergies in Fulfillment of Public Disclosure Duties 418
13.10.3 Selection of Publication Date for the Report on Solvency and Financial Condition 419
13.10.4 Relief at Group Level and the Principle of Proportionality 420
13.10.5 Less Favorable Protection of Confidentiality Interests for Direct Insurance and Reinsurance Undertakings Compared to Basel II 421
13.11 Summary 423

List of Rules 425

Index 473

Part I
Basics

Chapter 1
Harmonization of Insurance Supervisory Law

Contents

1.1 Introduction ... 4
1.2 The Typology of Harmonization Methods ... 5
1.3 The European Law Sources for Harmonization of the Insurance Supervisory Regime ... 8
1.3.1 The Solvency II Framework Directive ... 8
1.3.2 The Implementing Regulations for the Solvency II Framework Directive ... 12
1.3.3 The EIOPA Regulation ... 14
1.3.4 Interim Result ... 15
1.4 Consequences for the Future Insurance Supervisory System in Germany ... 16
1.4.1 The Impact of Full Harmonization on the Insurance Supervision Act ... 16
1.4.2 Supervision According to the Principle of Abusiveness with Regard to Primary Insurance Undertakings ... 17
1.4.3 The Effect of Full Harmonization in Certain Areas ... 21
1.5 Conclusions ... 23

Abstract This chapter addresses the fundamental issue of what degree of harmonization applies in the Solvency II system. Distinguishing among the several degrees of harmonization—minimum harmonization, maximum harmonization, and full harmonization—leads to the conclusion that the Solvency II Directive has full harmonization as its objective. This has two important ramifications: First, the Solvency II Directive requires that any insurance supervisory regime implementation by the respective national legislators must completely align with the European insurance supervisory regime. Second, a system of full harmonization prohibits national legislators from unilaterally enacting additional measures not provided for in European law. A pertinent example in the German insurance

First published as "Die Vollharmonisierung der Versicherungsaufsicht durch Solvency II" [in English: Full Harmonization of Insurance Supervision under Solvency II], VersR (2011), 825 ff. with *Martin Lange* as coauthor. *Martin Lange* was at that time a research assistant at the law school of Johannes Gutenberg University in Mainz.

M. Dreher, *Treatises on Solvency II*, DOI 10.1007/978-3-662-46290-4_1

supervisory regime is the previously extant general supervision according to the principle of abusiveness, where now the Solvency II system allows only supervision of legality.

1.1 Introduction

The adoption of the Solvency II Framework Directive,[1] the impending passage of the implementing regulations, and the implementation of these European law provisions in the national supervisory systems of EU Member States together constitute decided progress toward fully establishing the internal insurance markets of the European Union. Decades have gone into integrating the internal insurance market; and these efforts have reached their highest point yet, placing the insurance supervisory regime on radically changed footing. Solvency II will consolidate and expand the previously existing EU directives in the area of insurance[2] and align that policy more clearly with the goal of creating a regulatory framework for primary insurance and reinsurance that achieves the greatest possible uniformity throughout Europe. Consequently, the Solvency II Framework Directive demands the creation of uniform conditions in the conduct of the insurance business throughout the internal market. This uniformity is to be achieved by eliminating the most extreme differences among the supervisory systems of EU Member States. In setting this demand, the Directive enunciates the fundamental legislative objective of Solvency II for Europe.[3]

Against the background of this goal, however, there still remain to be settled the issues of the degree of the intended pan-European harmonization of the insurance supervisory regime and of the practical implications flowing from changes to the existing supervisory system.[4] This article addresses these issues. At the outset, this

[1] Directive 2009/138/C of the European Parliament and of the Council of 25 Nov. 2009 on the taking-up and pursuit of the business of Insurance and Reinsurance (Solvency II), OJEU L 335, 17 Dec. 2009, 1 ff.

[2] For an overview of the European directive policy to this point, see *Rittner/Dreher*, Europäisches und deutsches Wirtschaftsrecht [in English: European and German Economic Law] (3rd ed. 2008), sec. 31, ref. 4 ff.

[3] On this point, see Recital 2 of Directive 2009/138/EU, n. 1 above and also in further detail below, at 1.3.1.2.

[4] The only examination and discussion found on the subject are in *Bürkle*, "Die aufsichtsbehördlichen Eingriffsbefugnisse nach Solvency II" [in English: Supervisory Intervention Powers under Solvency II] in: Dreher/Wandt, eds., Solvency II in der Rechtsanwendung [in English: Solvency II in Legal Application] (2009), 191 (208 ff.) on the issue of continuing the prevailing practice in supervision according to the principle of abusiveness; see on this point in further detail 1.4.2.2 below; further, there are merely apodictic references that the Solvency II legislation presupposes full harmonization – see, e. g., *Wandt/Sehrbrock*, "Solvency II – Rechtsrahmen und Rechtsetzung" [in English: Solvency II – Legal Framework and Legislation] in: Dreher/Wandt,

article looks at the classification of harmonization methods under European law (1.2, below). Next, the European provisions of Solvency II legislation are examined with regard to the intensity of the intended harmonization within the insurance supervisory regime (1.3, below). Finally, this article discusses basic issues of European law in consideration of the preexisting design of insurance supervision in Germany, draws conclusions about how the supervisory system will be configured in the wake of Solvency II, and illustrates outcomes using particular real-world areas of supervision (1.4, below).

1.2 The Typology of Harmonization Methods

The methods of legal harmonization across Europe via secondary law directives can be divided into three variants, identified under the criterion of how much discretionary power is left to the national legislator in the field of implementation. The three variants are generally distinguished as minimum harmonization, maximum harmonization, and full harmonization.

In the case of minimum harmonization, the Directive by law sets a minimum level of regulatory intensity, which the national legislator must at least meet but is allowed to exceed. Thus, the minimum harmonization scheme allows a higher degree of regulatory intensity and stricter legal requirements than designated in the Directive. On the other hand, implementation as national law must at least meet the minimum level of harmonization. Accordingly, an implementation that exceeds the stated minimum level under European law does not violate the secondary law provisions of the given directive, even if the implementation should contribute to a fragmentation of the law. A supererogatory implementation, however, must be evaluated against the criterion of possible restrictions on fundamental European economic freedoms in cross-border commerce and the concomitant distortions of competition.[5] In addition, the provisions of national constitutional law, particularly those provisions relating to basic rights of the persons affected, can set limits on reverse discrimination implicit in stricter treatment of nationals. Over the course of a long period, minimum harmonization by means of directives has been the established method in the European legal harmonization process.[6]

eds., *id.*, n. above, at 1, 23; likewise in the publications of practitioners, as, e.g., Reorganisation and Sitzverlagerung in der europäischen Versicherungswirtschaft [in English: Reorganization and Relocation in the European Insurance Industry] (KPMG: 2008), 17, downloadable at www.kpmg.de/docs/Reorganisation.pdf.

[5] Of many relevant voices on the point of the regularly attendant blocking effect of European directives when applied to basic rights, see *Riesenhuber*, "System und Prinzipien des Europäischen Vertragsrechts" [in English: System and Principles of European Contract Law] (2003), 222 ff.

[6] Thus, especially in the first consumer protection directives; see Directive 85/577/EEC of the Council of 20 Dec. 1985 to protect the consumer in respect of contracts negotiated away from business premises, OJEEC L 372 of 31 Dec. 1985, 31 ff.; Directive 93/13/EC of 5 Apr. 1993, on abusive terms in consumer contracts, OJEEC L 95 1993, 29 ff.; Directive 97/7/EEC of the

In contrast to minimum harmonization, the standard of maximum harmonization sets the specified harmonization level according to European law at the upper rather than at the lower limit. Consequently, where a directive prescribes a system aimed at maximum harmonization, implementation by the national legislator is not allowed to exceed the degree of harmonization set under European law. The legislator may, however, prescribe a lower standard. Maximum harmonization is rare and primarily occurs when required to prevent distortions of competition in a certain area, where the distortions result from overly broad national regulatory provisions, in the nature, perhaps, of national legislation seeking to outbid with respect to a given level of legal protection and regulation.[7]

We come then to full harmonization, which combines the devices of both minimal and maximum harmonization[8] and, by virtue of the legal rules contained in the Directive, represents the broadest form of harmonization. Full harmonization has as its object complete legal harmonization. Thus, in implementing a Directive, the national legislator cannot deviate from the Directive, whether up or down, when the Directive is aimed at full harmonization. This is so because full harmonization by legal rules contained in a Directive has as its end absolute sectoral harmonization of national rights among the Member States.[9] The difference between a directive aimed at full harmonization and a regulation—besides being acts of law in different

European Parliament and of the Council of 20 Apr. 1997, on the protection of consumers in respect of distance contracts, OJEC L 144, 4 Jun. 1997, 19 ff.; 1997 Directive 1999/44/EC of the European Parliament and of the Council of 25 May 1999, on certain aspects of the sale of consumer goods and associated guarantees, OJEC L 171, 7 Jul. 1999, 12 ff.

[7] Thus, for example, in the area of deposit insurance in the lending sector, where the level of protection was established by law at a maximum of 100,000 euros in art. 1, no. 3 a of Directive 2009/14/EC of the European Parliament and of the Council of 11 Mar. 2009, amending Directive 94/19/EC on deposit-guarantee schemes as regards the amount insured and payout delay, OJEU L 68, 13 Mar. 2009 at 3 ff. by inserting new paragraph 1 a of art. 7 of the original Directive; see most notably on the point of the otherwise threatened distortions of competition also Recital 3 of Directive 2009/14/EC ibid.

[8] The concept of full harmonization as used here is sometimes designated as maximum harmonization, making it difficult to construct legally rigorous demarcations among the several harmonization tools; see, e.g., *Knops*, "Der Verbraucherkredit zwischen Privatautonomie und Maximalharmonisierung" [in English: Consumer Credit between Private Autonomy and Maximum Harmonization] in: Habersack/Mülbert/Nobbe/Wittig, eds., Die zivilrechtliche Umsetzung der Zahlungsdiensterichtlinie/Finanzmarktkrise und Umsetzung der Verbraucherkreditrichtlinie – Bankrechtstag 2009 – 2010 [in English: Civil Law Implementation of the Payment Services Directive/Financial Market Crisis and Implementation of the Consumer Credit Directive – Banking Conference 2009 – 2010], 195 ff.; on this point see also *Schürnbrand*, "Vollharmonisierung im Gesellschaftsrecht" [in English: Full Harmonization in the Law of Associations] in: Gsell/Herresthal, eds., Vollharmonisierung im Privatrecht [in English: Full Harmonization in Private Law] (2009), 273 (74); *Mülbert*, ZHR 172 (2008), 170 (179 ff.).

[9] On the issue of any discretionary power remaining to the national legislator in implementation, see, e.g., *Riehm*, "Umsetzungsspielräume der Mitgliedstaaten bei vollharmonisierenden Richtlinien" [in English: Member States' Discretion in Implementation under Directives of Full Harmonization] in: Gsell/Herresthal, eds., Vollharmonisierung im Privatrecht [in English: Full Harmonization in Private Law] (2009), 83 ff.

form—is simply that the regulation requires no implementing legislation at the Member State level but is immediately effective. In their legal effect, the methods are interchangeable, distinguished only on the basis of their designations.[10] By different paths, both methods lead to the same result: complete unification of the given areas of law throughout the European Union. Directives intended to bring about full harmonization in given areas thus limit disparate regulatory intensity and by the same token limit distortions of competition among EU Member States. Accordingly, by guaranteeing a level playing field in the legal environment throughout Europe, directives represent the most effective tool for market integration. Directives are thus the most appropriate device—with respect to their given subject-matter—for achieving the completion of the internal markets. It is primarily this characteristic that is occasioning increased application of the Directive as a tool aimed at full harmonization.[11]

---

[10] See already *Köndgen*, in: Riesenhuber, ed., Europäische Methodenlehre [in English: European Methodology] (2nd ed. 2010), sec. 7, ref. 34; *Bast*, in: v. Bogdandy/Bast, eds., Europäisches Verfassungsrecht [in English: European Constitutional Law] (2nd ed. 2009) 526; thus the problem of a possible abuse of form arises when a directive rather than a regulation is used to establish full harmonization.

[11] Above all in the area of consumer protection law; see, e.g., the notice of the Commission on consumer policy strategy of 7 May 2002 (COM (2002) 208 final), OJEU C 137, 8 Jun. 2002, at 2; subsequently, consumer protection provisions were largely reoriented towards full harmonization; for example, the notion of full harmonization is explicit in Recital 10 f. and art. 22 of Directive 2008/48/EC of the European Parliament and of the Council of 23 Apr. 2008, on credit agreements for consumers and repealing Council Directive 87/102/EEC, OJEU L 133 of 22 May 2008, at 66 ff.; see further Recital (EG) 13, Directive 2002/65/EC of the European Parliament and of the Council of 23 Sep. 2002, concerning the distance marketing of consumer financial services and amending Council Directive 90/619/EEC and Directives 97/7/EC and 98/27/EC, OJEU L 271, 9 Oct. 2002, at 16 ff. and also RegE [government's draft] of the implementation act, BR-Drucks. [Document of the German Bundesrat] 84/04 at 23 ff.; Directive 2007/64/EC of the European Parliament and of the Council of 13 Nov. 2007 on payment services in the internal market amending Directives 97/7/EC, 2002/65/EC, 2005/60/EC, and 2006/48/EC and repealing Directive 97/5/EC, OJEC L 319 of 5 Dec. 2007, at 1 ff.; see also the recommendation of the Commission for a comprehensive directive on consumer rights of 8 Oct. 2008 KOM [Commission] (2008), 614 (final); for a detailed treatment of the entire development, see *Welter*, "Vom Anerkennungsprinzip zur Vollharmonisierung" [in English: From the Principle of Recognition to Full Harmonization] in publication in honor of Uwe H. Schneider (2011), 1412 ff.; *Gsell/Herresthal*, in: Gsell/Herresthal, eds., Vollharmonisierung im Privatrecht [in English: Full Harmonization in Private Law] (2009), introduction at 1 ff., *Dickert*, "Politische Implikationen der Vollharmonisierung" [in English: Political Implications of Full Harmonization] in: Gsell/Herresthal, eds., Vollharmonisierung im Privatrecht [in English: Full Harmonization in Private Law] (2009), 177 (178 f.).

1.3 The European Law Sources for Harmonization of the Insurance Supervisory Regime

1.3.1 The Solvency II Framework Directive

1.3.1.1 The Legislative Process

The overriding determinants in establishing the intensity of the desired pan-European harmonization of the supervisory system are the Framework Directive provisions themselves. Indeed, the entire Solvency II legislation makes use of the legislative process[12] such that the Framework Directive is but the first of altogether four regulatory levels. Further steps will see implementing regulations (Level 2 and Level 3) adopted based on the Framework Directive and greater harmonization undertaken. The Level 2 implementing regulations as well as further measures in the regulation levels will be adopted by the European Commission, which is empowered with their implementation, but without the participation of the primary lawmaking bodies of the EU. Pursuant to the reservation of materiality, initially developed by the European Court of Justice[13] and codified in art. 290, para. 1, AEUV [Treaty on the functioning of the European Union] since the effective date of the Treaty of Lisbon, fundamental provisions must be already addressed in the Framework Directive. But an express and generally applicable provision for the harmonization level sought is not to be found in the Solvency II Framework Directive legislative text. Thus, to determine what measure of harmonization is intended by the Framework Directive one must look primarily to the provisions of the Directive—not those generally directed to the degree of harmonization—and to their telos and classification.

1.3.1.2 The Recitals

First resort for enlightenment as to the harmonization level sought may be the Solvency II Framework Directive Recitals. Recital 2 of the Directive sets forth as the basic objective: "In order to facilitate the taking-up and pursuit of the activities of insurance and reinsurance, it is necessary to eliminate the most serious differences between the laws of the Member States as regards the rules to which insurance and reinsurance undertakings are subject."[14] At the same time, the Recital refers to the provision of a "legal framework for insurance and reinsurance

[12] See also *Rittner/Dreher*, *id.*, n. 2 above, sec. 32 ref. 7, following with further references.

[13] See already ECJ [European Court of Justice], 17 Dec. 1970, E.C.R. case no. 25/70 Köster (1970), 1161, pnt. 6; 27 Oct. 1992, case no. C-240/90 (Germany/Commission), E.C.R 1992 I-5383, pnt. 35 ff.; 13 Jul. 1995, case no. 156/93 (Parliament/Commission).

[14] See Recital 2 of Directive 2009/138/EU, n. 1 above, at 3.

undertakings to conduct insurance business throughout the internal market." Upon first reading, the terminology of Recital 2—especially the use of "most serious differences" and "legal framework"—seems to belie the objective of full legal harmonization and merely to indicate an amelioration of cross-border business activities and removal of serious differences among supervisory systems. The word "eliminate" in reference to "differences between the . . . laws of the Member States" does, however, demonstrate that the Solvency II Directive, even in its first substantive Recital, is asserting the objective of an essentially unitary system of supervisory systems of EU Member States. In like manner, Recital 11, which also refers to the Directive as "an essential instrument for the achievement of the internal market," expresses the objective "to bring about such harmonization as is required" to realize a consistent country of origin supervision of insurance undertakings.

Relating to certain regulatory sectors, there are further indications for a harmonization as comprehensive and extensive as possible. For example, Recital 16 provides for enhanced harmonization of regulation for evaluation of claims and liabilities with reference to risk management. Also, Recitals 46 and 54 state that insofar as possible valuation standards for supervisory purposes should be compatible with international provisions. Similarly, Recital 75 regards "community-wide harmonization to the extent possible" as "critical" for supervisory assessment of a proposed purchase of shares.

Recital 40 of the Solvency II Framework Directive sets forth a clear indication for the objective of unifying supervisory systems of EU Member States in expressly stating that "supervisory convergence" is an objective of the Directive. Pursuant to the wording of the Recital, convergence is to apply not only to the supervisory rules and tools, but also in like manner to the diverse "supervisory practices" among the Member States. The Committee of European Insurance and Occupational Pensions Supervisors,[15] created in 2009 and since replaced by the European Insurance and Occupational Pensions Authority (EIOPA),[16] is to make key contributions in this area to harmonization and convergence of, above all, the diverse supervisory practices in the Member States. And further, Recitals 113, 114, and 115 provide for the creation of an additional College of Supervisors in the area of group supervision.

---

[15] Decision 2009/79/EU of the Commission of 23 Jan. 2009 establishing the Committee of European Insurance and Occupational Pensions Supervisors, OJEU L 25 (29 Jan. 2009) 28 ff., abbreviated as AEAVBA in the German version, but uniformly known by the English-language designation CEIOPS.

[16] Therefore in the following only EIOPA will be used; on the establishment of previous committees by EIOPA, see Regulation 1094/2010/EG of 24 Nov. 2010 establishing a European Supervisory Authority (European Insurance and Occupational Pensions Authority), amending Decision No 716/2009/EC and repealing Commission Decision 2009/79/EC, OJEU L 331 (15 Dec. 2010), 48 ff. The necessary amendments to the Solvency II Framework Directive and insertion of the EIOPA concept will proceed under a provision known as the Omnibus II Directive; see the proposal of the Commission for a Directive amending Directives 2003/71/EC and 2009/138/EC in respect of the powers of the European Insurance and Occupational Pensions Authority and the European Securities and Markets Authority (19 Jan. 2001, COM (2011) 8 (final)).

Both the supervisory authorities in the Member States where undertakings belonging to a group are located and also the EIOPA are to be represented in the College of Supervisors to ensure an adequate exchange of information in order to secure effective group supervision.

Convergence of this nature in supervisory rules and tools and in the diverse supervisory practices of the Member States of the EU is not possible without an extensive pan-European, legally harmonized insurance supervisory regime. In the Recitals, the Directive sets out as its objective the convergence of the supervisory systems all the way to the actual supervisory practices, whereby prerequisites of this objective are unified legal principles, harmonized bases for intervention, and congruent legal design of the supervisory tools. The objective of supervisory convergence, however, conflicts in principle at the level of the Directive with the changeover from a rule-based to a principles-based approach to supervision, this latter approach being the one pursued by the Directive.[17] If in following the principles-based approach, one grants to supervisory authorities under application of undefined legal terms[18] a broadened discretionary power for flexible, individually tailored evaluations of supervisory circumstances, this will tend to lead to fragmentation and increasing unpredictability in supervisory practices for undertakings subject to these rules. This result would precisely run counter to the objective of supervisory convergence. Rather, this objective can be attained only by application of a principles-based regulatory structure such as the Solvency II Framework Directive if in turn at the level of the implementing regulations rule-based law is created, such as will lead to uniformity of legal principles and consequently to convergence of supervisory practice.

Indeed, the Recitals to the Solvency II Directive introduce the relationship of rule to exception for complete harmonization and the powers of deviation and self-regulation belonging to the Member States. This relationship is treated in fuller detail in the legislative part of the Directive. Numerous Recitals have as their objective the most complete harmonization possible. Among these are Recitals 2, 11, 75, 87, and 93. Besides these, a total of eleven Recitals—numbers 6, 9, 53, 75, 81, 83, 85, 86, 96, 99, and 127—cede to the Member States a choice among several supervisory schemes or the determination of the regulatory intensity.

1.3.1.3 The Legislative Text

While no general full harmonization of the supervisory system is expressly mandated in the legislative text or in the Recitals of the Directive, one finds the idea of supervisory convergence via legal harmonization set forth in different places

[17] *Wandt/Sehrbrock*, ZVersWiss (2011), 193 (205 f.) correctly point out that the objective of supervisory convergence is to a great extent incompatible with the "principles-based" approach to supervision under the Solvency II system at the level of the Directive.

[18] On this aspect of the principles-based approach, see *Dreher*, VersR (2008), 998 (1000).

among the rules of the Solvency II Framework Directive. Above all, this idea of supervisory convergence via legal harmonization is present in legal bases that grant the Commission the right to adopt more extensive implementing regulations at the second regulatory level (Level 2). Examples are art. 35, para. 4 of the Directive on reporting by supervisory authorities and art. 50, para. 2 of the Directive on establishing a governance system specifically pertaining to risk and stability assessment. These contain the directive to ensure extensive convergence within the designated areas by the adoption of implementing regulations.[19] In addition, in order to ensure the reorganization and financing of insurance undertakings, art. 143 of the Directive allows for enabling powers for implementing regulations with the objective of guaranteeing supervisory convergence. Further still, art. 71 in chapter 5 of the Directive includes a stand-alone provision placing the Member States under an explicit duty to hold their supervisory authorities in line with the convergence principle.

This duty further extends to close cooperation with European institutions, especially with the EIOPA, which has the additional authority to issue non-binding guidelines and recommendations.

The objective of full harmonization in the supervisory scheme is also seen in that the Solvency II Framework Directive expressly grants to the Member States and further down the line to the national supervisory authorities scope for deviation in but a few areas. These areas are group supervision under art. 213 ff., Recital 99, and duration under art. 304.[20] Accordingly, in negotiations over the Solvency II Framework Directive, it was not possible to achieve uniform mandatory group supervision by the supervisory authority of the Member State in which the parent company is headquartered. Consequently it is difficult under supervision law to shape pan-European group support for subsidiaries when own funds are concentrated at the top management level.[21] In principle, under art. 213, para. 1, subchapter 2, the rules relating to supervision of independent insurance undertakings also will be applied to insurance undertakings that belong to a group, to the extent that Title III of the Directive on group supervision does not expressly provide otherwise. Furthermore, in a range of situations, the Member States and the supervisory authorities are empowered objectively to determine on their own the areas where group

---

[19] The proposal of the Commission for an Omnibus II Directive on Solvency II, *id.*, at n. 16, above, envisions, for example, new art. 35, para. 6 and a new version of art. 50, which are intended to provide additional assurance of convergence.

[20] See on this point the comments of *Karel van Hulle*, Head of the Insurance and Pensions Unit, to the Commission (reproduced in *Lansch/Friedrich*, VW (2011), 266), where he states that Solvency II aims at a more far-reaching harmonization than Basel III, even in fact at full harmonization, and that differences among the Member States are acceptable only in areas of group supervision and in the duration approach: to quote van Hulle in this connection: "With Solvency II we will be creating for the first time a unified supervisory system." Similarly, *id.*, 3 VersRdsch. (2007), 28 (31).

[21] The original draft of the Solvency II Framework Directive proposed correspondingly extensive regulation aimed at uniform European standards for group supervision; on this point, see *Krämer*, ZVersWiss (2008), 319 (329 ff.); *Sehrbrock*, ZVersWiss (2008), 27 (30 ff.).

supervision will be applied.[22] The supervision of insurance undertakings that belong to groups based on the criteria applied to independent insurance undertakings, resides as before and by virtue of express decision with the individual national supervisory authorities, despite its harmonization under the Directive.

There are a total of 46 rules touching Member State options in the Directive. The fact that deviations from the provisions of the Directive in the nature of a relationship of rule to exception have been allowed in individual expressly designated areas, whereas the Directive overall seeks to craft uniform regulation, shows that in the remaining areas the Directive assumes complete legal harmonization, and thus full harmonization of the supervisory system. So explicit a grant to the national legislator of power to deviate in implementing the Directive, a power restricted to certain regulatory sectors, in itself allows the contrary inference for the objective of full harmonization in all areas comprised by the Directive and requiring implementation under art. 310, para. 1, sent. 1 of the Directive. Through the use of the phrase "at least" in a significant number of its provisions, the Directive indicates that a great number of discretionary legislative areas are granted to the Member States within the prescribed harmonization approach, and this without expressly denoting the Member States as subjects of the rules.[23] This is further supported by the closed system of rule and exception because these differentiations and distinctions would be superfluous in a system of minimum harmonization.

1.3.2 The Implementing Regulations for the Solvency II Framework Directive

The adoption of implementing regulations for Solvency II is imminent. Up to this point there have been only internal drafts of the implementing regulations for the second regulatory level (Level 2) as well as official preparatory announcements and documents emerging from ongoing consultation proceedings.[24] It is conceivable that as binding acts the second level implementing regulations will entail a departure from principles-based rules and fill the undefined legal terms of the Solvency II Framework Directive with rules-based content. To this extent, one can no longer on

[22] See art. 214, para. 2 of the Solvency II Framework Directive establishing criteria for including undertakings belonging to groups within group supervision by the appropriate national supervisory authority.

[23] See, e.g., art. 35, para. 1, sent. 1 of the Solvency II Directive and also *Dreher*, ZVersWiss (2009), 187 (215) (Chap. 12, below, at 12.7.3).

[24] See, e.g., the "List of Policy Issues and Options for the Level 2 Impact Assessment of Solvency II" in the paper "CEIOPS' Advice for Level 2 Implementing Measures on Solvency II: System of Governance" (CEIOPS-doc. 29/09 (Oct. 2009)) and the "Consultation Document on the Level 2 implementing measures for Directive 2009/138/EC on the taking-up and pursuit of the business of Insurance and Reinsurance (Solvency II)", http://ec.europa.eu/internal_market/consultations/2010/solvency-2_en.htm.

the whole speak of legislation in the Solvency II area as a principles-based approach. This is so because a solid conceptual understanding of principles-based law presupposes an equivocal departure, both de jure and de facto and likewise consistent, from rules-based standards on all regulatory levels.[25] Only by attention to form and separately examining the regulatory principles of the individual levels can one arrive at the supposition of a partially principles-based regulatory approach at the highest regulatory level in the Solvency II Framework Directive.[26]

The preparatory documents and working papers for the impending adoption of the implementing regulations already suggest a regulatory intensity and a high degree of detail, leading to the conclusion that the anticipated standards will be rules-based.[27] By the same token, a rules-based design of the implementing regulations points to the objective of complete harmonization of supervisory provisions and anticipates convergence of supervisory practice, since uniform regulatory provisions throughout the EU will be achieved by employing a consistent rules-based approach. Precisely on account of the anticipated legal nature of the implementing regulations at the second level as directly and equally applicable regulations in all Member States, a design of that nature will lead to a level playing field for regulatory standards and will significantly reduce the discretionary scope of the national supervisory authorities in applying the law below the level of discretion that these authorities would have under a consistently applied principles-based approach. To the extent that the implementing regulations are enacted as regulations as anticipated, the European legislator will prefer the objectives of complete harmonization of the regulatory provisions and extensive convergence of supervisory practice to principles-based design of the implementing regulations, such as might tend to lead to fragmentation of the law and its application.

According to a ruling of the ECJ, the fact that the implementing regulations—as might be expected—will exceed the provisions of the basic legal act of Level 1 as to their regulatory intensity and with respect to degree of legal harmonization sought does not contravene the reservation of materiality and the fundamentally principles-based approach of the Solvency II Framework Directive. Thus, the ECJ early on ruled that the implementing regulations are permitted to exceed a purely technical implementation of the basic legal act and to allow for a higher degree of detailed and novel rules.[28]

---

[25] Along these lines see, *Dreher*, VersR (2008), 998 (1000).

[26] For the difference, see *Wandt/Sehrbrock*, ZVersWiss (2011), 193 (203) and *id.*, n. 4 above, at 1, 16.

[27] As to the result, also *Wandt/Sehrbrock*, ZVersWiss (2011), 193 (204); *Bürkle*, VersR (2009), 866 (873), and *Weber-Rey*, AG-Report (2007), para. 396.

[28] See e.g. – though not with reference to the Lamfalussy process introduced later – as to sanctions foreseen by the Commission only at the level of the implementing regulations, ECJ, 27 Oct. 1992, case no. C-240/90 (Commission/Germany), E.C.R. 1992 I-5383, pnt. 30 ff.; on the Markets in Financial Instruments Directive (MiFID) and the pertinent implementing regulations likewise *Mülbert*, ZHR 172 (2008), 170 (182f.).

1.3.3 The EIOPA Regulation

The regulation establishing a European insurance supervisory authority will strengthen the effort toward extensive harmonization that already exists in substantive law sources.[29] The stated objective of the regulation in establishing the EIOPA is "to contribute . . . ensuring a high, effective and consistent level of regulation and supervision" in order to establish a European system of financial supervision and thereby to improve the functioning of the internal market.[30] It is further the task of the EIOPA in applying European law[31] to prevent regulatory arbitrage within the EU, which could occur as a result of disparate supervisory levels within the individual Member States. In so doing, the EIOPA by promoting "supervisory convergence" would be ensuring a level playing field for all supervised insurance undertakings.[32] The idea of a level playing field is made explicit in relation to the alignment of the technical regulatory standards.[33] In essence, "greater harmonisation and the coherent application of rules for financial institutions and markets across the Union should also be achieved."[34] Accordingly, the objective is a coherent and effective application of basic principles of European law and thus the creation of a "common Union supervisory culture."[35]

The special emphasis on the need for extensive harmonization of the supervisory systems of EU Member States is above all attributable to the fact that the establishment of the uniform European supervisory authority, EIOPA, came about in the course of overcoming the recent financial crisis. This crisis, in the view of the European legislator, exposed "shortcomings in the areas of cooperation, coordination, consistent application of Union law and trust between national supervisors."[36] As a consequence, to ensure "correct and consistent application of Union law," EIOPA was equipped in particular with the power to adopt enforcement measures in the form of decisions with respect to individual supervised insurance undertakings, to the extent a national supervisory authority has not complied with a previous—equally binding—settlement decision of EIOPA.[37]

---

[29] Regulation 1094/2010/EU of 24 Nov. 2010, establishing a European Supervisory Authority (European Insurance and Occupational Pensions Authority), amending Decision No 716/2009/EC and repealing Commission Decision 2009/79/EC, OJEU L 331 (15 Dec. 2010), 48 ff.

[30] See Recitals 7, 8, 10, and 66 of Regulation 1094/2010/EU, *id.*, n. 29 above.

[31] The legal scope of the EIOPA is set forth in art. 1 of Regulation 1094/2010/EU, *id.*, n. 29 above; see especially para. 2 and the expansion in para. 3, under which EIOPA also acts in regard to issues that stand "in relation to" legal acts under para. 1.

[32] See Recitals 10 and 21 of Regulation 1094/2010/EU, *id.*, n. 29 above.

[33] Recital 21 of Regulation 1094/2010/EU, *id.*, n. 29 above.

[34] Recital 8 of Regulation 1094/2010/EU, *id.*, n. 29 above.

[35] Art. 8, para. 1b, art. 29 of Regulation 1094/2010/EU, *id.*, n. 29 above.

[36] As specifically set forth at the end of Recital 1 of Regulation 1094/2010/EU, *id.*, n. 29 above.

[37] On the legal powers of the EIOPA, see art. 8 ff. of Regulation 1094/2010/EU, *id.*, n. 29 above; on the enforcement measures in particular, see art. 17, para. 6 and Recital 31 of the same Regulation.

In establishing the EIOPA, the European legislator's top priorities were thereby to ensure a uniform supervisory level in the EU, to guarantee uniform application of the substantive provisions, to create a level competitive playing field, and thus to bring about complete harmonization of the EU supervisory systems. If this concept of full harmonization of the supervisory systems had not already been inherent in the basic substantive legal provisions, most especially in the Solvency II Framework Directive, it would not have been legally possible to create such an objective in the establishment of the EIOPA. To this extent, the fact that the objective of the EIOPA is the complete alignment of supervisory systems leads to inferences about the intended and achieved codification of the full harmonization principle in the Solvency II Framework Directive. Thus, the EIOPA is designed only to consistently carry out the substantive provisions of the Solvency II Framework Directive, provisions that must be understood as overwhelmingly directed at full harmonization.

1.3.4 Interim Result

Solvency II legislation has as its goal the full harmonization of supervisory systems in the EU Member States. On the basis of the reservation of materiality under art. 290, para. 1, of the AEUV, the primary reference for the objective of harmonization is the Solvency II Framework Directive. The teleological and systematic interpretation of the Recitals and the legislative text of the Solvency II Framework Directive lead one to the conclusion that the intended result is a complete alignment of the insurance supervisory provisions and a maximally extensive convergence of supervisory practices in the EU Member States. At the least, the specific exceptions in the Directive, namely group supervision and duration approach, where scope has been left to the Member States in implementation, compel by implication the inference of a harmonization design in all other areas.

This conclusion comports with the principle of complete supervisory convergence via legal harmonization.

In addition, the preparatory working papers and drafts on implementing regulations for the second regulatory level (Level 2) show the objective of complete harmonization of the supervisory systems. In their detailed specificity, the planned rules of the implementing regulations are appropriately designed to fill out the principles-based and undefined legal terms, of the Solvency II Framework Directive with well-defined, rules-based content. By virtue of the anticipated legal nature of the implementing measures as regulations, these rules should immediately be applicable throughout the EU.

With respect to full harmonization, the efforts of the European legislator ultimately will be supported and reinforced by the establishment of a European insurance supervisory authority. The work of the EIOPA will lead to establishment of a European system of financial oversight and will ensure coherent, efficient, and effective application of the basic European legal principles in the field of insurance supervision. In this, the goal of complete harmonization of the supervisory systems within the EU should primarily serve the objective of ensuring a uniform level of supervision and thus a level playing field for insurance undertakings throughout the European internal insurance market.

1.4 Consequences for the Future Insurance Supervisory System in Germany

1.4.1 The Impact of Full Harmonization on the Insurance Supervision Act

The full harmonization flowing from the Solvency II Framework Directive will require a complete alignment of the German Insurance Supervision Act with the requirements of European law. The objective of a level regulatory playing field throughout Europe should be pursued with consistency in implementing the Framework Directive in national law. This means that in implementing the Directive, the German legislator shall not create any supervisory provisions or requirements that deviate from the Framework Directive, except as noted earlier in the particular areas of group supervision and duration approach. The Solvency II Framework Directive rules must be entirely incorporated in the German Insurance Supervision Act.[38] Extant provisions of national law that are stricter and exceed the supervisory standard of the Framework Directive cannot persist, or at least must be adjusted to the Directive. In like manner, rules not yet in existence but henceforward required by Solvency II will have to be integrated into the Insurance Supervision Act. Additionally, any supervisory regulation, tools, and practices not represented in the provisions of the Directive must be eliminated and not replaced.[39] Along the same lines, legal mechanisms must be provided to ensure convergence of German supervisory practice with the application of the law in the other EU Member States. At the same time, it must not be overlooked that the directly applicable implementing regulations and other related measures adopted in the future by the European Commission will have a substantial effect on application of the law and supervisory practice. This is so because, although the German legislator is entrusted solely with technical implementation and clarification in national law of the principles-based rules of the Solvency II Framework Directive, the rules-based and therefore ultimately determinative provisions will be in the implementing regulations of Level 2. As a result, for this reason and despite the reservation of

[38] In this context, the pending Insurance Supervision Act amendment must address the question of whether to enact laws duplicating the directly applicable rules of the implementing regulations. In view of the merely declaratory effect of such an adoption into the Insurance Supervision Act, which additionally might require substantial future amendment, it would be advisable to avoid altogether such duplicative superimposition.

[39] See on this point 1.4.2.2, below.

materiality applicable to the Framework Directive,[40] transfer of responsibility and authority to the European Commission is seen to have been made. In connection with the principles-based and thus flexible requirements of the Solvency II Framework Directive, the Commission will be entrusted in the future with creating essential regulatory provisions directly binding on the national supervisory authorities and, because of directly applicable European law, requiring compliance by insurance undertakings.

1.4.2 Supervision According to the Principle of Abusiveness with Regard to Primary Insurance Undertakings

1.4.2.1 The Existing System of Supervision According to the Principle of Abusiveness Under the General Clause

The third generation of insurance contract law Directive, implemented in national law in 1994,[41] provided for only minimum harmonization and thus granted to the national legislators the authority to enact stricter requirements for supervision under national law of primary insurance undertakings headquartered domestically than for primary insurance undertakings headquartered in another EU Member State. This situation allowed the German legislator to maintain the outdated system of supervision according to the principle of abusiveness with regard to domestic primary insurance undertakings, based on the general clause of sec. 81, para. 1, sent. 2, of the Insurance Supervision Act. Indeed as a result of the third Directive, the German supervisory authorities had to abandon the concept of comprehensive, substantive national supervision. Despite nearly universal rejection in the literature,[42] based above all on European and constitutional law, supervisory authorities

[40] See on this point 1.3.1, above.

[41] Council Directive 92/49/EEC of 18 Jun. 1992 (third non-life insurance Directive); Council Directive 92/96/EEC, 10 Nov. 1992 (third life assurance Directive); implementation in German law was accomplished by the Drittes Gesetz zur Durchführung versicherungsrechtlicher Richtlinien des Rates der Europäischen Gemeinschaften, 21 Jul. 1994 BGBl I 1630.

[42] See *Dreher*, VersR (1993), 1443; WM (1995), 509; *id.*, Die Konkretisierung der Mißstandsaufsicht nach § 81 VAG [In English: Practical Application of Supervision According to the Principle of Abusiveness under sec. 81 of the Insurance Supervision Act] (1997), 9 ff.; *Miersch*, Versicherungsaufsicht nach den dritten Richtlinien [in English: Insurance Supervision under the Third Directives] (1996), 107 ff.; *Zischka*, Bundesversicherungsaufsichtsamt (BAV) – Aufgaben und Kompetenzen – [in English: Federal Insurance Supervisory Office – Tasks and Competencies –] (1997), ref. 451; *Braumüller*, Versicherungsaufsichtsrecht [in English: Insurance Supervisory Law] (1999), 553; *Korinek*, Rechtsaufsicht über Versicherungsunternehmen [in English: Legal Supervision over Insurance Undertakings] (2000), 197 f.; *Bähr*, Das Generalklausel- und Aufsichtssystem des VAG im Strukturwandel [In English: The General Clause and Supervisory System of the Insurance Supervision Act: Structural Transformation] (2000), 230 ff.; generally, *Rittner/Dreher*, *id.*, n. 2. above, sec. 31, ref. 25 ff. with further references.

nevertheless succeeded in pursuing the concept of supervision according to the principle of abusiveness not restricted to infringements of the law. This activity was based on an extremely broad interpretation of the general clause and on self-generated administrative practices developed in circulars.

In the past this system of supervision according to the principle of abusiveness under the broad interpretation given by the supervisory authorities has met with insuperable legal objections as to its foundation. Today it represents to that extent a disadvantage for German primary insurance undertakings in the European market. The system can be explained only from a historical perspective and it stands as a comparatively rigid and intensely regulatory structure[43] of a kind not to be found in any other EU Member State. This presents a classic case of reverse discrimination, since it is thus in many areas only the German insurance undertakings that are subject to regulatory restrictions that greatly hamper their business development.[44] This discrimination toward German insurance undertakings in the European market arises also from the fact that the intended broadening of supervision according to the principle of abusiveness into the area of supervision by the country of operations overinsurance undertakings of other EU countries contravenes European law. Insurance undertakings conducting business in Germany pursuant to the European freedoms to establish enterprises and for movement of services should be treated under sec. 81, para. 1, sent. 2–4, and para. 2 Insurance Supervision Act through sec. 110 a, para. 4, no. 3a Insurance Supervision Act according to the standards of German supervision according to the principle of abusiveness. By this reference, the German legislator in implementing the third Directive has disregarded the European law threefold prescription restricting supervision by the county of operations to (1) monitoring the legal field, (2) monitoring "applicable law" and, on this point, (3) only such as are in the public interest.[45,46] Consequently, supervision according to the principle of abusiveness, in an intensity comparable to that previously applicable to domestic primary insurance undertakings, cannot in principle be valid for primary insurance undertakings in other EU countries. This in turn gives such undertakings a competitive advantage for business activities in Germany.

---

[43] The general clause of sec. 81, para. 2, sent. 1 Insurance Supervision Act tracks almost word for word the provision of sec. 64, para. 2 Insurance Supervision Act of 1901, which allowed the Imperial Supervisory Office for Private Insurance a legal basis for intervention.

[44] The following observers also detect reverse discrimination here: *Bürkle*, *id.*, n. 4 above, at 191, 200 f.; *Winter*, VersR (2005), 145 (158 ff.); *Bähr*, VersR (2001), 1185 (1192 ff.); for actual effect in, for example, product design, see *Dreher/Lange*, VersR (2010), 1109 (1113) on the regulatory impermissibility of variable annuities in Germany.

[45] On the restrictive concept of the public interest, see Commission Interpretive Communication 2000 C 43/03, of 16 Feb. 2000, "Use of free movement of services and the general good in the insurance sector".

[46] See in detail *Rittner/Dreher*, *id.*, n. 2 above, sec. 31 ref. 28, 95, with further references; in the context of offering variable annuities through insurance undertakings with headquarters in another EU Member State, see also *Dreher/Lange*, VersR (2010), 1109 (1114).

1.4.2.2 The End of Supervision According to the Principle of Abusiveness and Reverse Discrimination

The implementation of the Solvency II Framework Directive in German law will spell the end for a situation that in multiple points of view contravenes European law and raises concerns under constitutional law. This situation includes reverse discrimination, the substantial expansion of supervision by the country of operations and supervision according to the principle of abusiveness in general, which in part is based on a definition of the concept "abusiveness" defined by the supervisory authorities themselves and thus goes beyond mere legal control.

Thus, the very far-reaching, pan-European full harmonization of supervisory systems of EU Member States will lead to both elimination of reverse discrimination through stricter regulatory provisions for German insurance undertakings and by the same token elimination of any expansion of these stricter national law regulations to insurance undertakings in other EU countries. This is most especially true for regulatory requirements that go further with respect to insurance undertakings of other EU countries than they do for domestic companies, when these requirements up to this point have already been prohibited in the insurance industry by specific provisions of secondary law and generally by the criterion of basic economic freedom. Full harmonization will bring about for the first time uniform regulatory standards throughout the EU, thus ensuring uniform market conditions in the sense of a fully harmonized level playing field in the internal market for insurance with respect to the regulatory environment. Thus, supervisory standards, tools, criteria, and powers relating to the country of origin and country of operations supervision for the first time will be fully uniform throughout Europe in the area where full harmonization is applied. In implementing the Directive, national legislators will not be permitted to deviate and thus will not be allowed to retain the attendant diverse levels of regulatory intensity with the resultant prospect of regulatory arbitrage and ultimately to perpetuate the existing distinctive national features of supervisory systems of EU Member States. Further, full harmonization of the supervisory systems will be ensured by the increased convergence of regulatory practice in the EU Member States.[47] This increased convergence is intended to prevent disparate application of the uniform basic principles under Solvency II and thereby additionally prevent actions of national supervisory authorities amounting to an application of the law contrary to the objective of full harmonization of the European regulatory system.

With the application of Solvency II, the previous supervision according to the principle of abusiveness practice will not be allowed to continue, a practice based on a broad construction of the general clause and self-created by means of circulars and announcements. On the basis of European law alone, implementation of the Solvency II Framework Directive in German law at the national level requires without exception the creation of provisions having the nature of a legal norm; That

[47] On this point see 1.3.1.2 and 1.3.1.3, above.

means at least the adoption of regulations ranking below the level of formal legislative laws but constituting laws in a substantive sense.[48] From the outset, the use of supervisory circulars, announcements, and other such "opinions" from supervisory authorities—such as the MaRisk VA [Minimum Requirements for Risk Management (Administrative Order)]—will be excluded with regard to the application of future legal basics and powers for intervention. The implementation of European law through measures of administrative practice will also be foreclosed.

As a result of all these factors, the supervisory authority cannot continue to usurp the legislative function by the existing practice of expanding its discretionary power on its own by substantively defining, expanding, or contracting the undefined legal requirement of "abusiveness" in general announcements.[49] The establishment of regulatory powers of intervention only in the case of legal infringements arises not only from the previously noted necessity to implement the provisions of European law by means of legal norms, but even more so in the fact that the Solvency II Framework Directive itself demands the narrowing of scope for regulatory interventions to cases involving actual legal infringement. With regard to the future design of supervisory powers, art. 34, para. 1, sent. 1 of the Solvency II Framework Directive obliges the Member States to provide "that the supervisory authorities have the power to take preventive and corrective measures to ensure that insurance and reinsurance undertakings comply with the laws, regulations and administrative provisions with which they have to comply in each Member State." In this regard, the Solvency II Framework Directive differs from the rules on supervisory powers in the third Directive. Along with monitoring compliance with provisions of the law, under the third Directive supervisory authorities were expressly permitted to counter other "improprieties" beyond actual legal infringements.[50] The Solvency II Framework Directive deliberately restricts the supervisory standard to pure control of legality.[51] An indication of this scheme is shown in the fact that the concept of "abusiveness"—as distinguished from the text of the draft Directive[52]—is nowhere to be found in the final version of the Solvency II Framework Directive.

---

[48] General European principle; see, ECJ, 24 Jun. 2004, case no. C-212/02, and *Dreher*, JZ (2002), 1101 (1102); EuZW (1997), 522 (523 f.).

[49] See, e.g., in reference to MaRisk VA, *Dreher*, "Die BaFin geriert sich als Ersatzgesetzgeber", [in English: The Federal Financial Supervisory Authority is usurping the legislative function], FAZ, no. 216, 17 Sept. 2009, at 22; in reference to the self-generated supervisory principle banning cross-subsidization, see *Dreher*, ZVersWiss (1996), 499; in reference to the likewise self-generated supervisory principle banning managing board and supervisory board membership for relatives, see *Dreher*, WM (1995), 509 (511 f.).

[50] See, e.g., art. 13, para. 3b of Directive 2002/83/EC of the European Parliament and of the Council of 5 Nov. 2002 on life insurance (comprehensive Directive on life insurance), OJEU L 345, p. 1; and see also *Bürkle*, *id.*, n. 4 above, at 191, 203 f.

[51] Likewise, *Bürkle*, *id.*, at n. 4 above, at 191, 204; to the same effect also, *Korinek*, VersRdsch (2010), 27 (29), noting "substantive state supervision" in Austria already is confined to matters of law.

[52] See *Bürkle*, VersR (2007), 1595 (1598); *Präve*, VW (2007), 1380 (1383).

1.4.2.3 Summary

In the event, two conditions are telling: on the one hand, the Directive's full harmonization concept, combined with the adjustment of the Solvency II Framework Directive to the supervisory standard of pure control of legality; and on the other hand, the general requirement of European law that the provisions of the Solvency II Framework Directive are to be implemented in national law through provisions having the nature of a legal norm. The effect of these two factors is such that the previously existing supervision according to the principle of abusiveness for primary insurance undertakings cannot be maintained. The future supervisory system of the Insurance Supervision Act will rather be characterized by the supervisory standard of pure legal control, a necessity for consistent transfer into legal form of existing regulatory areas thus far solely based on supervisory practice, to the extent they comply with the requirements of the Directive. Further, this future supervisory system will be marked by a completely level legal and practical playing field with respect to equivalent regulatory rules applicable to both German insurance undertakings and those of other EU countries. This, however, does not conflict with publication by BaFin [Federal Financial Supervisory Authority] of administrative principles binding only on itself.

In such publications, the supervisory authority does not impose new requirements on the supervised undertakings, but rather renders its anticipated actions discernible, foreseeable, and transparent. This process, too, serves the interests of the insurance undertakings subject to supervision.[53]

1.4.3 *The Effect of Full Harmonization in Certain Areas*

1.4.3.1 The Requirements for Members of Supervisory Boards

The Solvency II Framework Directive exceeds the present qualification requirements of sec. 7a, para. 4 of the Insurance Supervision Act, with respect to the requirements for members of supervisory councils for insurance undertakings belonging to groups and for insurance holding companies. Specifically, while the provisions of art. 42, para. 1 of the Solvency II Framework Directive, by virtue of express reference in the provisions on group supervision, apply fully and directly to the supervisory and monitoring boards for these undertakings, the Directive does not prescribe any direct qualification requirements for supervisory council members of insurance undertakings not belonging to a group because they do not fulfill the

[53] This is the case above all where only explanation of formal supervisory standards is concerned, such as in clarification of the requirements on the CV to be submitted in BAV R [Federal Insurance Supervisory Office Circular] 6/97.

criteria of "persons with key functions" within the meaning of art. 42, para. 1 of the Solvency II Framework Directive.[54] Thus, the qualification requirements of the Directive will have only indirect and mediated effect on members of the supervisory and monitoring boards of insurance undertakings not belonging to a group.

Thus, in the course of implementing the Solvency II Framework Directive, the provisions relating to the qualification requirements of the supervisory council members will have to be newly drafted and further differentiated. This is so because the Solvency II objective of full harmonization means that the national provisions on monitoring by supervisory council members must duplicate and not deviate from the provisions of the Directive. In future, it will be necessary that specific provisions be designed for the qualifications of supervisory council members of insurance undertakings belonging to groups; and these provisions will have to implement the rules of art. 42, para. 1 of the Solvency II Framework Directive fully in national law. And in contrast to existing sec. 7a, para. 4 of the Insurance Supervision Act, these new provisions must set higher requirements for supervisory council members, in compliance with the Directive. Existing sec. 7a, para. 4 of the Insurance Supervision Act, which gives equal treatment to all supervisory council members, at best will be able to stay in its current form for members of the supervisory and monitoring boards of insurance undertakings not belonging to a group, and then only to the extent this section fully takes into account the indirect effects of the qualification requirements of art. 42, para. 1 of the Solvency II Framework Directive as well as of the governance requirements of chapter 2 of the Solvency II Framework Directive. At the least then, sec. 7a, para. 4 of the Insurance Supervision Act must be construed and applied with consideration for European law provisions for supervisory council members of insurance undertakings not belonging to a group, and perhaps also its contents should be rendered more precisely in terms of increased European influence.[55]

1.4.3.2 The Prohibition on Borrowing

The prior prohibition on borrowing for primary insurers was deduced by the supervisory authorities from the prohibition on conducting non-insurance business. In 2009, however, in the Act to Strengthen the Financial Market and Insurance Supervision[56] the prohibition was codified in sec. 7, para. 2, sent. 3, clause 1 of the Insurance Supervision Act as an independent provision.[57] Indeed, the prohibition on conducting non-insurance business, as provided in sec. 7, para. 2, sent. 1 of the

---

[54] For a detailed treatment, see *Dreher/Lange*, ZVersWiss (2011), 211 (220 ff.) (Chap. 6, below, at 6.3.3).

[55] On the subject as a whole, see *Dreher/Lange*, ZVersWiss (2011) 211 (223 f.) (Chap. 6, below, at 6.3.2).

[56] Act to Strengthen the Financial Market and Insurance Supervision, 29. Jul. 2009, BGBL [Federal Law Gazette] I, 2305.

[57] For background, see, e.g., *Eilert,* in: Bähr, ed., Handbuch des Versicherungsaufsichtsrechts [in English: Manual of Insurance Supervision Law] (2011), sec. 5, ref. 59 ff.

Insurance Supervision Act in Germany, is represented as well in art. 18, para. 1a and b of the Solvency II Framework Directive. Thus even under Solvency II, insurance undertakings are restricted to conducting insurance business and other business directly connected with the insurance business. The Solvency II Framework Directive does not, however, expressly impose a blanket prohibition on receipt of outside funds by insurance undertakings.

Full harmonization of the European supervisory system entails the future codification in Germany of only the Solvency II Framework Directive provisions and thus also the prohibition on conducting non-insurance business. As to the application of such European-based prohibition, both the autonomous interpretation of the European requirements and the handling of a corresponding prohibition by the supervisory authorities of the other EU Member States in light of the objective of supervisory practice convergence will be crucial. German insurance supervision for decades has tended toward interpreting the provision as a complete prohibition on borrowing. This interpretation cannot be the criterion for future interpretation and application of the prohibition on non-insurance business. The German legislator's recent codification of the prohibition on borrowing will not alter anything in this area.

In view of the fact that a blanket prohibition on receiving outside funds—so far as can be seen—has not existed up to this point in any other EU Member State and that borrowing comports with the business objective and business type[58] of insurance undertakings, it may be presumed that supervisory practice throughout Europe will develop in the direction of a less restrictive interpretation of the prohibition. With regard to the objective of creating a level playing field in the entire internal market for insurance, one may assume that the prohibition on borrowing—which in its dogmatic approach alone, but also not least in view of its unrealistic management practice has essentially missed the mark—will not be perpetuated in the upcoming new version of the Insurance Supervision Act and at the least will not be retained in the course of the pan-European convergent application of the Directive provisions by supervisory authorities in Germany.

1.5 Conclusions

I. In the Solvency II Framework Directive, the European legislator is pursuing the objective of full harmonization for insurance supervision in Europe. One may read directly in both the legislative text and the Recitals of the Directive the intent to bring about a complete alignment of regulatory provisions and the desire for the greatest possible convergence of supervisory practice in the EU Member States.

This intent is reinforced in the full harmonization set forth in the Framework Directive by the expected implementing measures at Level 2, which in part will fill

---

[58] See for the difference, e.g., *Rittner/Dreher*, *id.*, n. 2 above, sec 9 ref. 56 ff.

the principles-based standards of the Directive with exhaustive rules-based content and—in the form of a European regulation—will apply directly throughout the entire EU. In addition, the newly created European insurance supervisory authority EIOPA, equipped with effective enforcement powers, is responsible for a coherent and maximally effective application of the European provisions.

II. In the course of implementing the Directive, the German legislator must effect a complete alignment of the German Insurance Supervision Act with the provisions of the Solvency II legislation. The Framework Directive itself allows the national legislator to deviate only where express Member State reservations exist and in the areas of group supervision and duration approach. Consequently, in all other areas national legislators must ensure that they are in alignment with the European regulations. In creating the new version of the Insurance Supervision Act, all current provisions therefore must be examined as to whether they exceed or fall short of the rules of the Solvency II Framework Directive, whether a corresponding section in the Directive exists, or whether they are in fact directly prescribed. These are the criteria to be applied in determining which new provisions to insert into the Insurance Supervision Act, which provisions to strike, and which to adapt so that they comport with the level of the Directive provisions as to type and intensity.

III. The extant system of supervision according to the principle of abusiveness for primary insurance undertakings, for which the supervisory authorities essentially relied on the general clause of sec. 81, para. 2, sent. 1 of the Insurance Supervision Act, will not survive the implementation of the Solvency II Framework Directive in German law. In the area of supervision by the country of operations, such supervision according to the principle of abusiveness exceeding pure legal control has already proven contrary to European law. Further, full harmonization of supervision will lead to the abolition of the current reverse discrimination, which has resulted from a stricter treatment of primary insurance undertakings headquartered in Germany vis-à-vis their competitors in other European countries. This is so because on the one hand, the implementation of European Directive provisions in German law by the creation of legal norms will be incompatible with a self-generated administrative practice arising out of circulars and announcements, as has been done in the past with the broadening of supervision according to the principle of abusiveness. On the other hand, the concept of supervision in the Solvency II Framework Directive is aligned solely with the criterion of actual legal infringement. This orientation prohibits any and every form of supervision according to the principle of abusiveness exceeding this standard.

IV. Moreover, full harmonization in the new version of the Insurance Supervision Act will have an impact on regulatory provisions in all those areas where the regulatory level of the previous rules does not reflect exactly the Directive provisions. For example, this is the case with the statutory requirements for qualifications of supervisory council members under sec. 7a, para. 4 of the Insurance Supervision Act and under the recent codification of the prohibition on borrowing in sec. 7, para. 2, sent. 3, clause 1 of the Insurance Supervision Act. Pursuant to the Directive provisions, the Insurance Supervision Act qualification requirements for members of the supervisory and monitoring boards will be further differentiated; in particular, the level of requirements for members of supervisory councils for insurance companies belonging to groups will be different from the requirements for such members in the case of companies not belonging to groups. On the other hand, the express codification of the prohibition on borrowing concerning insurance undertakings in the Insurance Supervision Act does not comport with the Solvency II Framework Directive provisions, which provide only the European law prohibition on conducting non-insurance business, a law subject to purely autonomous interpretation. Not least because of the desired objective to converge supervisory practice within the EU, the German specific prohibition on borrowing concerning insurance undertakings will not survive.

Chapter 2
Supervisory Review Process

Contents

2.1 Introduction 28
2.2 Principles of Insurance Supervision Under Solvency II 29
2.3 Objective and Concept of the Supervisory Review Process 30
2.3.1 Objective 30
2.3.2 Art. 36 of the Solvency II Directive and Its Implementation in Sec. 289, Paras. 2–4 of the VAG Reg-E [Government's Draft of a Tenth Act Amending the German Insurance Supervision Act] 31
2.3.3 The CEIOPS Advice on Procedures for Supervisory Authorities 36
2.4 The Subjects of the Supervisory Review Process 37
2.4.1 Subject of the Investigation and Investigatory Standard 37
2.4.2 The Governance System as Examination Subject 41
2.4.3 Capital Requirements as Examination Subject 44
2.5 Powers of Supervisory Authorities to Remedy Weaknesses and Deficiencies 53
2.5.1 "Weaknesses or Deficiencies" as Legal Terms 53
2.5.2 The Role of Art. 36, Para. 5 of the Solvency II Directive in the Classification of Intervention Powers 58
2.5.3 Non-compliance with Capital Requirements 60
2.5.4 Non-compliance with Requirements on Governance 61
2.6 Summary 63

Abstract This chapter addresses the legal outlining of the supervisory review process. There is an apparent contradiction between principles-based insurance supervision on the one hand and, on the other hand, legal certainty along with foreseeability of supervisory action under art. 36 of the Solvency II Directive.

First published as "Das aufsichtliche Überprüfungsverfahren nach Art. 36 Solvency II-Richtlinie und § 289 VAG-RegE" [in English: The Supervisory Review Process under Art. 36 of the Solvency II Directive and Sec. 289 of the VAG-RegE [Government's Draft of a Tenth Act Amending the German Insurance Supervision Act]], in: Dreher/Wandt, eds., Solvency II in der Rechtsanwendung [in English: Solvency II in Legal Application], Frankfurt Edition, Volume 26, Karlsruhe (2012), 73 ff. with *Christoph Ballmaier* as coauthor. *Christoph Ballmaier* was at that time a research assistant at the law school of Johannes Gutenberg University in Mainz.

M. Dreher, *Treatises on Solvency II*, DOI 10.1007/978-3-662-46290-4_2

With this in view, the chapter next examines the objectives and subject matter of the supervisory review process, with particular scrutiny given to requirements relating to solvency and governance. The powers of supervisory authorities to remedy weaknesses and deficiencies are then taken up.

2.1 Introduction

The principles-based approach of the Solvency II regulatory scheme presents new challenges for insurance supervision. The new supervisory scheme for insurance undertakings has been made dynamic and flexible. These changes put supervision into conflict with legal certainty and foreseeability of official actions.[1] Paradoxically, these changes also increase the intensity of scrutiny by supervisory authorities. These authorities are primarily charged with concern for the actual risk status of the supervised undertakings.[2] Consequently, they must collect and evaluate large amounts of information from the insurance undertakings.[3] Occasionally they must even evaluate the adequacy of measures taken by insurance undertakings' management. This places the supervisory authorities in a position where they must make extensive evaluations and give substance to undefined legal terms. It is, therefore, all the more important to have a clear legal structuring of the Supervisory Review Process, now widely known as SRP.

The preceding is the background to the points addressed in this chapter: First, this article provides an explanation of the general principles of insurance supervision under Solvency II (2.2, below). Then, a detailed account is given of the objective and concept behind the review process under art. 36 of the Solvency II Directive and the VAG RegE [Government's Draft of a Tenth Act Amending the German Insurance Supervision Act][4] (2.3, below).[5] Next, the subject areas involved are set forth (2.4, below). Finally, this article addresses in detail the regulatory intervention powers in the context of the Supervisory Review Process (2.5, below).

[1] See already *Wandt*, "Solvency II – Wird die Aufsicht zum 'Mitunternehmer'?" [in English: Solvency II – Will the Supervisory Authority Become a 'Partner'?], VW (2007), 473 (475).

[2] See art. 29, para. 1 of Directive 2009/138/EC of the European Parliament and of the Council on the taking-up and pursuit of the business of insurance and reinsurance (Solvency II), OJEU, 17 Dec. 2009, no. L 335, 1–155 (hereafter, Solvency II Directive).

[3] Any mention of insurance undertakings in this chapter includes reinsurance undertakings.

[4] See the Government's Draft of a Tenth Act Amending the VAG [German Insurance Supervision Act], 15 Feb. 2012, BT-Drucks. [Document of the German Bundestag] 17/9342, also found at BR-Drucks. [Document of the German Bundesrat] 90/12, cited as VAG-RegE [Government's Draft of a Tenth Act Amending the German Insurance Supervision Act] in this chapter.

[5] The particulars of the group supervisory review process under arts. 218, para. 4 and 247 ff. of the Solvency II Directive are outside the scope of the matters addressed in this chapter.

2.2 Principles of Insurance Supervision Under Solvency II

As prescribed by the Solvency II Directive, the Supervisory Review Process, in its function as a part of insurance supervision, tracks the general principles of the new insurance supervisory scheme.[6] One such principle is first of all the risk-oriented character of supervision, a quality that requires supervision to align with the actual risk status of insurance undertakings. This principle is designed to guard against orthodoxy of statistical models. A further principle requires that the individual circumstances of an insurance undertaking be taken into account in evaluating whether it meets supervisory requirements (the principle of proportionality).[7] Similarly, the principle of materiality ensures that supervisory activities and regulatory requirements are dictated only by material circumstances. For example, immaterial information does not fall under the regulatory duties to report.[8] Immaterial risks do not figure into the evaluation of the individual risk status of an insurance undertaking.

When put into the regulatory mix along with undefined legal terms as to matters of fact and with discretionary schemes as to legal consequences, these principles allow discretionary scope in assessment (assessment orientation) to the supervisory authorities.[9] The new insurance supervisory scheme also displays an increased orientation to the modalities and processes of insurance undertaking activities and does not focus on results alone (process orientation). Further, the supervisory scheme increasingly incorporates models and methods from the field of economics into its tool kit (economization). This applies to assessment of compliance with the qualitative as well as the quantitative requirements.[10]

[6] See in detail *Dreher*, "Solvenzanforderungen in der Versicherungsaufsicht nach Solvency II und künftigem VAG" [in English: Solvency Requirements in Insurance Supervision under Solvency II and the Future German Insurance Supervision Act], ZVersWiss (2012), 381 (388 f.; 410 ff.) (Chap. 4, below, at 4.2.4 and 4.4.2).

[7] The European law principle of proportionality applies automatically to the VAG RegE [Government's Draft of a Tenth Act Amending the German Insurance Supervision Act] pursuant to interpretation in conformity with the Directive, even if the VAG RegE [Government's Draft of a Tenth Act Amending the German Insurance Supervision Act] is not expected to expressly adopt the Directive.

[8] *CEIOPS*, CEIOPS' Advice for Level 2 Implementing Measures on Solvency II: Supervisory Reporting and Public Disclosure Requirements (2009), no. 3.2.5.

[9] On whether this manner of assessment is accompanied by restrictions on judicial review, see 2.5.1.3, below and *Dreher*, n. 6 above, at 422.

[10] See in detail as to the principles noted, *Dreher*, n. 6 above, at 410 ff.

2.3 Objective and Concept of the Supervisory Review Process

2.3.1 Objective

Art. 36, para. 1, subpara. 1 of the Solvency II Directive directs the Member States to ensure that "the supervisory authorities review and evaluate the strategies, processes and reporting procedures which are established by the insurance and reinsurance undertakings to comply with the laws, regulations and administrative provisions of this Directive". Art. 36, para. 1, subpara. 2 provides further detail to the effect that certain requirements on the system of governance are matters for investigation, namely those requirements addressing the risk profile. Also subject to such investigation is the ability of the undertakings to identify those risks. The Supervisory Review Process is modeled on the Supervisory Review Process (SRP) adopted as part of Basel II in the banking sector,[11] which process itself will in turn be modified by Basel III along the lines of the Solvency II Directive.[12]

Supervisory authorities must determine whether insurance undertakings in their strategies, processes, and reporting procedures are achieving the prescribed supervisory objectives. They do not, however, consider the modalities of attaining these objectives, to the extent these are violations of the law for reasons not based on the insurance supervisory regime. The objective of regularly conducted Supervisory Review Processes is to ensure timely intervention by supervisory authorities when the Solvency II Directive objectives on supervision are threatened. Protection of insureds and beneficiaries under insurance contracts thus stands front and center in the Supervisory Review Process as the main objective under Recital 16 and arts. 27 and 28 of the Solvency II Directive.[13] Against this background, the Supervisory

[11] See on this point, BaFin [Federal Financial Supervisory Authority], Präambel Aufsichtsrichtlinie [in English: Preamble to Supervisory Directive], in the version of 21 Feb. 2008.

[12] See esp. arts. 92 ff., Proposal for a Directive of the European Parliament and of the Council on the access to the activity of credit institutions and the prudential supervision of credit institutions and investment firms and amending Directive 2002/87/EC of the European Parliament and of the Council on the supplementary supervision of credit institutions, insurance undertakings and investment firms in a financial conglomerate, COM (2011) 453 final, also found at BR-Drucks. [Document of German Bundesrat] 424/11.

[13] Protection of insureds and insurance beneficiaries is the primary objective of Solvency II. At a secondary level, the objectives are fair and stable markets and financial stability. On this subject see Recital 16 of the Solvency II Directive; on the objectives of insurance supervision, see also, *Dreher/Häußler*, "Die Aufsicht über Versicherungsunternehmen durch die BaFin und die Überwachungsaufgabe des Aufsichtsrats" [in English: Supervision of Insurance Undertakings by BaFin [Federal Financial Supervisory Authority] and the Monitoring Task of the Supervisory Board], ZGR (2011), 471, (485); *Wandt/Sehrbrock*, "Regelungsziele der Solvency II-Rahmenrichtlinie" [in English: Regulatory Objectives of the Solvency II Framework Directive], ZVersWiss (2011), 193 (195 ff.); *Dreher*, n. 6 above, at 384; all with further references.

Review Process supports the supervisory authorities in their tasks of appraising and monitoring risks so that necessary measures may be taken.[14]

The Supervisory Review Process is an ongoing process. This status is not contradicted by art. 36, para. 6 of the Solvency II Directive and sec. 289, para. 3, sent. 2 of the VAG-RegE [Government's Draft of a Tenth Act Amending the German Insurance Supervision Act], which provide that the Supervisory Review Process is to be conducted "regularly". The terms of art. 36, para. 6 of the Solvency II Directive and sec. 289, para. 3, sent. 2 of the VAG RegE [Government's Draft of a Tenth Act Amending the German Insurance Supervision Act] provide that an assessment of the strategies, processes, and reporting procedures is to be done on a periodical basis and that the supervisory authorities are to establish the minimum frequency of the assessments. In sum, the Supervisory Review Process constitutes a comprehensive process conducted by the insurance supervisory authorities applying an individualized, risk-oriented scrutiny to assess compliance with regulatory requirements.[15] To this extent, the Supervisory Review Process mirrors the extensively required self-review imposed on insurance undertakings for the first time by Solvency II with regard to regulatory requirements,[16] for example by instituting an internal review process and an ORSA.[17]

2.3.2 Art. 36 of the Solvency II Directive and Its Implementation in Sec. 289, Paras. 2–4 of the VAG Reg-E [Government's Draft of a Tenth Act Amending the German Insurance Supervision Act]

2.3.2.1 The Terms of Art. 36 of the Solvency II Directive

Art. 36, para. 1, subpara. 1 of the Solvency II Directive provides that the supervisory authorities shall review insurance undertakings' compliance with legal and administrative provisions adopted on the basis of the Directive. The immediately following subpara. 2 along with paras. 2 through 4 supply detail concerning the areas to be examined. Paragraph 2 recites a non-exhaustive list, including system of governance, technical provisions, own capital requirements, investment rules,

[14] See, *CEIOPS*, Issues Paper – Supervisory Review Process and Undertakings' Reporting Requirements, 2008 (hereafter: Issues Paper), no. 1.1.

[15] See Issues Paper, no. 1.3. On the examination criteria, see 2.4.1, below.

[16] To the same effect: *Bürkle*, in: Fahr/Kaulbach/Bähr/Pohlmann, eds., "Versicherungsaufsichtsgesetz" [in English: Insurance Supervision Act] (5th ed. 2012), Solvabilität II [in English: Solvency II] ref. 62.

[17] See in detail *Dreher/Ballmaier*, "Die unternehmenseigene Risiko- und Solvabilitätsbeurteilung (ORSA) nach Solvency II und VAG 2012" [in English: Risk and Solvency Evaluation by Undertakings under Solvency II and the German Insurance Supervision Act 2012], VersR (2012), 129 ff (Chap. 5, below).

quality and quantity of own funds, and where applicable the correctness of an internal model. Paragraph 3 imposes upon the Member States a duty to deploy tools adapted to continuous supervision in order to identify "deteriorating financial conditions" and to monitor the remedy of that deterioration.

Paragraph 1, subpara. 2 goes on to specify that the Supervisory Review Process shall comprise the assessment of the system of governance and of the risks that insurance undertakings are or could be exposed to. In art. 36, para. 6, subpara. 2, the Solvency II Directive instructs the supervisory authorities to determine, based on the principles of proportionality, how often they will subject an insurance undertaking to the periodic supervisory processes of review, evaluation, and assessment. The supervisory authority may thus also determine the appropriate subject-matter scope of the supervisory process, based on the risk profile of the insurance undertaking. Article 36, para. 5, of the Solvency II Directive prescribes that the Member States shall provide their insurance supervisory authorities with such intervention powers as will enable these authorities to demand that insurance undertakings remedy weaknesses or deficiencies discerned by the authorities.

In art. 36, para. 1, subpara. 2, the Solvency II Directive provides for assessment of risks that an insurance undertaking faces or may face. This assessment is the conceptual counterpart to the own-risk and solvency assessment (ORSA). Article 36, para. 4 of the Solvency II Directive requires supervisory authorities to assess the adequacy of the "methods and practices" of insurance undertakings designed to identify and withstand future or possible risks arising from economic conditions of the insurance undertakings.

Article 36 of the Solvency II Directive contains some overlapping provisions. For example, para. 2 (a) and para. 1, subpara. 2 both identify the system of governance as a matter for review. Since an insurance undertaking must incorporate risks attending economic conditions into its risk management system[18] and—pursuant to paragraph 1, subpara. 2—the SRP includes risk assessment, paragraph 4 is in part superfluous. Furthermore, the non-exhaustive nature of art. 36, para. 1 of the Solvency II Directive is important with regard to the application of the law. This nature leads to art. 36, para. 4 of the Solvency II Directive, also not exhaustive,[19] which sets forth further matters for review.[20]

Article 36, para. 3 of the Solvency II Directive prescribes that the supervisory authorities shall have in place appropriate monitoring tools to enable them to

[18] At least this is so when these risks are viewed as part of the operational risks as set forth in art. 44, para. 2, subpara. 2 (e) of the Solvency II Directive, as suggested by the definition of operational risk in art. 13, no. 33 of the Solvency II Directive: "risk of loss arising[. . .]from external events".

[19] See the wording of this provision ("in particular").

[20] Besides the listing of provisions addressed, it is proper, for example, to review insurance undertakings as to whether they are complying with the sector demarcation rule under art. 73 of the Solvency II Directive. Overall, however, the regulatory scheme set forth in art. 36, para. 2 of the Solvency II Directive covers the important supervisory areas. The subject-matter scope of a detailed supervisory review process, however, rests in the hands of the supervisory authorities, within the general limits set for the process.

identify deteriorating financial conditions in insurance undertakings and to monitor the pertinent remedies. This prescription comports with Recital 17 of the Solvency II Directive in imposing on the Member States the regulatory task of sufficiently equipping and establishing the administrative processes of their authorities. This provision is irrelevant in relation to the supervised undertakings because in other places the Solvency II Directive establishes intervention powers for the purpose of monitoring financial condition. Monitoring tools are procedures to collect information pertaining to insurance undertakings. Information comes to the supervisory authorities on the one hand in the Report to Supervisors (RTS),[21] in the Solvency and Financial Condition Report (SFCR),[22] and by virtue of the insurance undertakings' ad hoc reporting duty. In addition, however, information is gained from on-site investigations authorized under art. 34, para. 5. And further yet, in some instances the Solvency II Directive imposes an information and reporting duty on third parties.[23] Still further, the supervisory authorities have access to generally available sources and they observe the insurance markets. These activities enable them to form conclusions pertaining to individual insurance undertakings.[24] This information-gathering is aimed at identifying risks to insureds and beneficiaries, among such risks being deterioration of financial conditions.[25]

2.3.2.2 The Implementation in the VAG-RegE [Government's Draft of a Tenth Act Amending the German Insurance Supervision Act]

The implementation of art. 36 of the Solvency II Directive in German law on the one hand is complete with the RegE [Government's Draft] but from another view exceeds its mandate and thus misses the mark. The Supervisory Review Process is defined in sec. 289, para. 3, sent. 2 of the VAG RegE [Government's Draft of a Tenth Act Amending the German Insurance Supervision Act]. Pursuant to this definition, the process consists in assessing the "strategies, processes, and reporting procedures established by insurance undertakings to comply with the legal and administrative

[21] Bericht an die Aufsicht [in English: Report to Supervisors] under Art. 35 the Solvency II Directive and sec. 43 VAG RegE [Government's Draft of a Tenth Act Amending the German Insurance Supervision Act]; see *Dreher*, "Die Veröffentlichungspflichten von Versicherungsunternehmen gegenüber der BaFin" [in English: Insurance Undertakings' Duty of Disclosure to the BaFin [Federal Financial Supervisory Authority]], ZVersWiss (2009), 187 ff (Chap. 12, below).

[22] Bericht über die Solvabilität und Finanzlage [Solvency and Financial Condition Report] under art. 51 the Solvency II Directive and sec. 50 VAG-RegE [Government's Draft of a Tenth Act Amending the German Insurance Supervision Act]; see *Dreher/Schaaf*, "Die Veröffentlichungspflichten gegenüber der Allgemeinheit nach Solvency II" [in English: Duty of Disclosure to the Public under Solvency II], in: Dreher/Wandt, eds., Solvency II in der Rechtsanwendung [in English: Solvency II in Legal Application] (2009),129 ff (Chap. 13, below).

[23] See arts. 35, para. 2 (c) and 72, para. 1 of the Solvency II Directive.

[24] See Issues Paper, no. 4.35. ff.

[25] To the same effect, Issues Paper, no. 4.4.

provisions adopted by Directive 2009/138/EC". It is inapposite to incorporate this definition into the paragraph on "financial supervision", which is distinguished from "legal supervision" also in the VAG-RegE [Government's Draft of a Tenth Act Amending the German Insurance Supervision Act]. Financial supervision is a part of legal supervision. This is so because the Supervisory Review Process, for example as regards the system of governance and the ORSA expressly noted in art. 36, para. 2 (a) of the Solvency II Directive, includes "legal supervision" under sec. 289, para. 2 of the VAG-RegE [Government's Draft of a Tenth Act Amending the German Insurance Supervision Act] along with "business activities" in the same manner as "financial supervision" along with "business organization" captured in the following paragraph. In view of the exclusive supervision under the laws of the country of origin only in the area of financial supervision under art. 30, para. 1 of the Solvency II Directive, the assignment of the Supervisory Review Process to the financial supervision area entails significant legal consequences. In addition, art. 30, para. 2, subpara. 1 of the Solvency II Directive defines the factual scope of financial supervision without including the requirements as to the business organization. A further inconsistency is seen in the separation of the legal definition from the description of the object of the Supervisory Review Process, a description appearing in paragraph 4.

In this paragraph 4, along with paragraph 3, the RegE [Government's Draft] integrates the terms of art. 36, paras. 1 and 6 of the Solvency II Directive. But without explanation, RegE [Government's Draft] fails to include the list of examples in art. 36, para. 2 of the Solvency II Directive. This feature needlessly hampers application of the law but does not create an incomplete implementation that is contrary to law. The draft act also declines to grant special powers for the remedy of weaknesses or deficiencies established in the supervisory process.[26] Consequently, the statement of grounds for RegE [Government's Draft] envisions no such requirement. Under this statement of grounds, a weakness or deficiency satisfies the conditions of sec. 289, para. 1 of the VAG RegE [Government's Draft of a Tenth Act Amending the German Insurance Supervision Act] and constitutes abusiveness within the meaning of sec. 292 para. 1, sent. 3 of the VAG-RegE [Government's Draft of a Tenth Act Amending the German Insurance Supervision Act].[27] In opposition to this stance, however, is the general view that supervision according to the principles of abusiveness is not consistent with the Solvency II Directive, which contemplates only legal supervision.[28] Finally, sec. 289, paras. 2–4 of the

[26] But see particularly as to group supervision sec. 257, para. 2, sent. 5 of the VAG-RegE [Government's Draft of a Tenth Act Amending the German Insurance Supervision Act].

[27] RegE [Government's Draft] at n. 4, statement of grounds for sec. 289, p. 322; see on this point 2.5.1.2, below.

[28] On the incompatibility of supervision according to the principles of abusiveness with Solvency II, see in the present context 2.5.1 und 2.5.2, below, and generally in detail *Dreher/Lange*, "Die Vollharmonisierung der Versicherungsaufsicht durch Solvency II" [in English: Full Harmonization of Insurance Supervision through Solvency II], VersR (2011), 825 ff. (Chap. 1, above); *Bürkle*, "Die Zukunft der materiellen Missstandsaufsicht in Deutschland" [in English: The Future

VAG-RegE [Government's Draft of a Tenth Act Amending the German Insurance Supervision Act] does not mention the monitoring tools for determining deterioration of the financial foundations of an insurance undertaking (art. 36, para. 3 of the Solvency II Directive).[29]

Further, a certain easing of BaFin [Federal Financial Supervisory Authority] supervision in the government's draft of the VAG-RegE [Government's Draft of a Tenth Act Amending the German Insurance Supervision Act] is not congruent with the Solvency II requirements. On this point, sec. 45, para. 2 of the VAG-RegE [Government's Draft of a Tenth Act Amending the German Insurance Supervision Act] provides for auditors' review of the solvency statement under sec. 69 of the VAG-RegE [Government's Draft of a Tenth Act Amending the German Insurance Supervision Act],[30] resulting in a separate report on the result. The same applies to the insurance undertakings' obligation under sec. 47, para. 2 of the VAG-RegE [Government's Draft of a Tenth Act Amending the German Insurance Supervision Act] in each case "to submit promptly" to the supervisory authority "the reviewed solvency statement and the review report on the solvency statement". No legal basis for this scheme appears in the Solvency II Directive. In its response on this point, the Bundesrat [German Federal Council] thus explained[31]: "The solvency statement is a key element of the new Solvency II rules. Its review cannot be assigned to an external auditor. This is to be accomplished as a core task of insurance supervision, not least because responsibility for this area rests with insurance supervisory authorities". In its response, the German federal government noted[32] "providing for audit of the solvency statement will make reviewing the content substantially easier for the supervisory authority". This approach, however, contradicts core requirements of the Solvency II Directive. Namely, art. 27 of the Directive requires "that the supervisory authorities are provided with the necessary means and have the relevant experience [and] capacity... ". Similarly, under art. 36, para. 3, "[t]he supervisory authorities shall have in place appropriate monitoring tools... ". And in reference to auditors, art. 35, para. 2 (c) and art. 72, para. 1 of the Solvency II

of Substantive Supervision According to the Principles of Abusiveness in Germany], VersR (2011), 1469 ff.; *Bürkle/Grote*, "Die aufsichtsbehördlichen Eingriffsbefugnisse nach Solvency II" [in English: Supervisory Intervention Powers under Solvency II], in: Dreher/Wandt, n. 22 above, at 191 ff., 225 ff.; *Kaulbach*, "Die laufende Rechts- und Finanzaufsicht nach § 81 VAG – Grundlegung" [in English: Ongoing Legal and Fiscal Supervision pursuant to § 81 VAG – Basics] in: Bähr, ed., Handbuch des Versicherungsaufsichtsrechts [in English: Manual of Insurance Supervision Law] (2011) sec 8, ref. 46, at the end.

[29] The table of corresponding sections at the end of the statement of grounds of the government's draft, however, indicates that sec. 289, para. 2 of the VAG-RegE [Government's Draft of a Tenth Act Amending the German Insurance Supervision Act] implements art. 36, para. 3 of the Solvency II Directive. A recitation of the required tools is not set forth there, however. But see also, RegE [Government's Draft], n. 4 above, at 322.

[30] See on this point *Dreher*, n. 6 above, at 383.

[31] BT-Drucks. [Document of the German Bundestag] 17/9342, at 7; also BR-Drucks. [Document of the German Bundesrat] 90/12.

[32] BT-Drucks. [Document of the German Bundestag] 17/9342, 7.

Directive provide only for a right of information regarding the findings from the statutory audit, and do not anticipate use of these findings for further purposes such as a relaxation of supervision for the insurance supervisory authorities.

2.3.3 *The CEIOPS Advice on Procedures for Supervisory Authorities*

The Supervisory Review Process is a continuing process. CEIOPS recommended dividing this process into four components,[33] placing particular value—but incorrectly only—on a realistic risk-profile assessment of an insurance undertaking by the supervisory authorities. Primarily with information on an insurance undertaking based on the RTS[34] and the SFCR,[35] the supervisory authority shall first perform a preliminary assessment of the risk profile. Criteria particularly pertinent to this assessment are the business organization, the quantitative requirements, the business performance, and the external business environment.[36] Having thus formed a first opinion of the risk profile, supervisory authorities shall use this opinion to determine the scope of appropriate measures.[37] In a step identified as Follow-up Assessment, the assessment of the risk profile shall be updated on a continuous basis.[38] Appropriate supervisory actions are put into play once the authority has completely assessed the risk profile. The authority shall make full use of the information available and employ further clarification measures if necessary.[39]

[33] See Issues Paper, no. 4.9 ff.

[34] Report to Supervisors, see n. 21, above.

[35] Solvency and Financial Condition Report, see n. 22 above.

[36] See Issues Paper, no. 4.12.

[37] See Issues Paper, no. 4.22. CEIOPS emphasized that supervisory authorities should consider the following principles in selecting measures: Every policyholder should be afforded the same level of protection; the proportionality principle must be followed; the supervisory review process should be preventive and future-looking; supervisory authorities must be able to react quickly with appropriate measures. See Issues Paper, no. 4.25.

[38] See Issues Paper, no. 4.27.

[39] See Issues Paper, no. 4.29 f. Some possibilities are information gathering at the site of the undertaking or requiring information from third parties. See art. 34, para. 5 and art 35, para. 2 (c) of the Solvency II Directive and also sec. 300, para. 1 and sec. 299 of the VAG-RegE [Government's Draft of a Tenth Act Amending the German Insurance Supervision Act].

2.4 The Subjects of the Supervisory Review Process

2.4.1 Subject of the Investigation and Investigatory Standard

2.4.1.1 Subject of the Investigation

The starting point for the Supervisory Review Process is art. 36, para. 1, subpara. 1 of the Solvency II Directive and, in like manner, sec. 289, para. 3, sent. 2 of the VAG-RegE [Government's Draft of a Tenth Act Amending the German Insurance Supervision Act]. Under these provisions, the Supervisory Review Process shall review and evaluate the "strategies, processes, and reporting procedures" established by insurance undertakings to comply with the provisions of the insurance supervisory regime. The new supervisory regime endeavors to identify processes. The deficiencies of these processes may be manifested in the form of inadequate provision of capital, which in itself is also an indicium of weaknesses and deficiencies in insurance undertakings. In other words, the new orientation of the supervisory regime is not merely on the results of business, but also on the modalities and procedures employed therein.[40]

The term "process" appears to have been adopted from the field of business management. Thus, the science of business management can provide insight into the legal term "process", as it appears in art. 36, para. 1, subpara. 1 of the Solvency II Directive. A process is the convergence of material and human resources to accomplish an objective.[41] The express listing of the reporting procedure as a matter for review highlights the importance of a functioning communications structure and culture. This emphasis, however, is superfluous in view of the broad scope of the term "process", as presented here. The identification of strategy as a matter for review ultimately does not raise concerns here under art. 16 of the Charter of Fundamental Rights of the European Union (CFREU) or under art. 12 of the GG [German Basic Law][42] because it is compliance strategy alone and not business strategy that is subject to supervisory evaluation.

In contrast, under art. 36, para. 2 of the Solvency II Directive, "compliance" with subsequently named requirements is subject to the Supervisory Review Process. In contradistinction to art. 36, para. 1, subpara. 1 of the Solvency II Directive, art. 36, para. 2 is not restricted by its terms to "strategies, processes, and reporting procedures". Whether an insurance undertaking satisfies the regulatory capital requirements is of course indirectly an issue relating to investment strategies and other processes. But separate from procedural approaches, the issue is one directly

[40] See for more detail, *Dreher*, n. 6 above, at 412 f.

[41] See Gabler Verlag, ed., Gabler Wirtschaftslexikon [in English: Gabler's Dictionary of Business and Economics], Stichwort: Prozess [Entry: Process]; online on the Internet: http://wirtschaftslexikon.gabler.de/Archiv/12416/prozess-v10.html.

[42] See for the relevant risks of supervisory review of ORSA, *Dreher/Ballmaier*, n. 17 above, at 135 ff., 143 and generally, *Dreher*, n. 6 above, at 411 f.

related to purely result-oriented matter. With reference to the scheme set forth in art. 36 of the Solvency II Directive, one might assume that art. 36, para. 2 of the Solvency II Directive is restricted at the outset to review of compliance with requirements that address "strategies, processes, and reporting procedures". This is so because art. 36, para. 2 clearly refers to art. 36, para. 1 of the Directive. The language of art. 36, para. 2 of the Solvency II Directive by its own terms clearly contradicts this interpretation. This passage addresses "compliance" with requirements and is not restricted to the "strategies, processes, and reporting procedures" as noted in art. 36, para. 1, subpara. 1 of the Solvency II Directive. Moreover, the scheme of art. 36, para. 2 of the Solvency II Directive bears on art. 36, para. 1, subpara. 2 of the Solvency II Directive. This latter provision in turn provides for the "assessment of the qualitative requirements relating to the system of governance" and for its part is not restricted to strategies, processes, and reporting requirements.

2.4.1.2 Investigatory Standard

The review criteria to be applied by the supervisory authorities arise from art. 36 of the Solvency II Directive and from sec. 289, para. 3, sent. 2 and para. 4, sent. 1 of the VAG-RegE [Government's Draft of a Tenth Act Amending the German Insurance Supervision Act]. The "review", "evaluation", and "assessment" provided for here relate to whether the insurance undertakings have in place strategies, processes, and reporting procedures to ensure that they comply with the "laws, regulations, and administrative provisions adopted pursuant to this Directive". In contrast, art. 34, para. 1 of the Solvency II Directive provides further that supervisory authorities shall have the power "to ensure that insurance and reinsurance undertakings comply with the laws, regulations and administrative provisions with which they have to comply in each Member State". Against this background, the Supervisory Review Process accords with art. 34, para. 1 of the Solvency II Directive as a procedure to establish infringements.[43] In a departure from the suggestion in the title to the rule, this provision contains an assignment not only of task but also of power.[44] And in accord, for example, with art. 40, art. 71, para. 2, and art 72, para. 1, subpara. 1 (a) of the Solvency II Directive, art. 36, para. 1, subpara. 1 of the Solvency II Directive relates exclusively to compliance with "the laws, regulations and administrative provisions adopted pursuant to this Directive". These are the respective national implementation rules based on the Solvency II Directive, i.e., in Germany the rules of the VAG-RegE [Government's Draft of a Tenth Act Amending the German Insurance Supervision Act] and the rules of the implementing regulation. The corresponding EIOPA Guidelines are not

[43] On this point see in detail 2.5.1.2, below.

[44] On the examination subject under art. 34, para. 1 of the Solvency II Directive, see n. 109 below; for another view, see *Bürkle*, n. 28, 1474.

part of this scheme because they are not legally binding and, because of the *comply or explain* approach, have only a de facto binding effect. Nevertheless, the supervisory authorities resort to the Guidelines to construe the rules they elucidate. Thus, review, evaluation, and assessment as to insurance undertakings can lead to no more than the conclusion that an infringement of the identified rules exists or not. A more extensive supervision of insurance undertakings is not possible on this basis.[45]

The undefined legal terms "review and evaluation" must be given definite content, also in the context of the principle of proportionality.[46] The Solvency II Directive is largely silent as to this definite content. Article 31, para. 2, subpara. 1 (b) of the Directive, implemented in sec. 312, para. 2, no. 2 VAG-RegE, provides that the Member States shall disclose "the general criteria and methods. . .used in the Supervisory Review Process as set out Article 36". Upon this basis, the BaFin [Federal Financial Supervisory Authority] could publish further explanatory notices, circulars, and the like. With such disclosure, however, the supervisory authorities restrict their discretionary power under the general principle that administrative authorities are bound by the very rules they lay down. It remains a mystery how these "criteria and methods" are to be developed and applied throughout Europe, in view of the objective of full harmonization, which according to Recital 40 of the Solvency II Directive includes "supervisory convergence. . .also in respect of supervisory practices".[47] As a result, only the EIOPA by use of appropriate guidelines can forestall the obvious danger of supervisory divergence and thus also regulatory arbitrage.[48]

2.4.1.3 Review, Assessment, Evaluation, and Report of Results

"Evaluation" within the Supervisory Review Process allows the supervisory authority to assess the insurance undertaking internally with respect to its development and the risk that it might not be able to comply with the requirements of the law in the future. Evaluation does not depend solely on whether infringements by the insurance undertaking have occurred, but also on the prospect of infringements. In this process, all foreseeable circumstances should enter into the evaluation. Evaluation, then, is the result of the review process.

Article 36, para. 1, subpara. 2 of the Solvency II Directive establishes the supervisory evaluation of risks, of qualitative requirements relating the system of governance and of the ability of insurance undertakings to assess those risks. Article 36, para. 4 of the Solvency II Directive expands the scope for assessment to the adequacy of the methods and practices of the insurance undertakings designed to identify and withstand future unfavorable changes. The English-language version

[45] Likewise, *Bürkle*, n. 28 above, 1475.

[46] On the values-based character of the supervisory regime, see *Dreher*, n. 6 above, at 416 ff.

[47] See *Dreher/Lange*, n. 28 above, at 827 f.

[48] CEIOPS has emphasized this risk in Issues Paper, no. 3.6.

of the Solvency II Directive uses the term "assessment" in this context. "Assessment" can be translated as "Einschätzung". Following the natural literal interpretation, "Bewertung" [assessment] might be distinguished from "Beurteilung" [evaluation] on the criterion of intensity of appraisal. An "Einschätzung" or "Bewertung" according to its ordinary unforced meaning has a stronger appraisal imprint than "Beurteilung". Despite this (minimal) difference in the appraisal-based character, the difference between "Beurteilung" [evaluation] and "Bewertung" [assessment] is of purely academic interest. From the legal point of view, this situation presents a pleonasm as often occurs in European law because of the compromise nature of many European legal acts. The same situation often arises both within[49] and outside insurance law[50] and is of no significance in the application of the law.

If the authority discerns an infringement by an insurance undertaking, the undertaking—in Germany—will be subject to an administrative measure requiring remedy of the infringement. If the evaluation determines that the insurance undertaking is in compliance with the supervisory requirements, the supervisory authority likewise must disclose this result to the insurance undertaking subject to the procedure. Initial support for communicating the results of the Supervisory Review Process is found in that such information serves to prevent infringements by confirmation of conduct that previously was unobjectionable.[51] In addition, in no. 3.70 CEIOPS' Advice for Level 2-Implementing Measures on Solvency II: Supervisory Reporting and Public Disclosure,[52] CEIOPS took it as given that the insurance undertakings would be aware of their evaluation by the supervisory authority. Otherwise, CEIOPS would not emphasize that the result of the Supervisory Review Process should not be the subject of public reports by insurance undertakings. In addition, the concept of notice of results of the Supervisory Review Process to the affected insurance undertaking is a basis for Issues Paper, no. 4.43, where it is stated that in certain cases discussions between the supervisory authority and the insurance undertaking should be held. Ultimately, however, this result is attributable above all to the principle of transparency of the supervisory process, as set forth in art. 31, para. 1 of the Solvency II Directive.

Thus, the supervisory authority can confirm the compliance of an insurance undertaking with the legal provisions to be met by means of determinative administrative measure. This is so because this determination would be sought by the affected insurance undertaking such that adoption of an administrative measure

[49] But compare art. 36, para. 5 of the Solvency II Directive with the paired terms "weaknesses and deficiencies" and in detail on this point 2.5.1, below.

[50] But see the phrase "restriction or distortion" in art. 101, para. 1 AEUV [Treaty on the Functioning of the European Union].

[51] See art. 29, para. 1 of the Solvency II Directive, according to which supervision is based on a prospective approach.

[52] No. 3.70 CEIOPS' Advice for Level 2 Implementing Measures on Solvency II: Supervisory Reporting and Public Disclosure Requirements, 2009.

would be possible in this instance.[53] In the absence of a legal basis for a claim, insurance undertakings have no claim to a notice in the form of an administrative measure. In particular, such a measure is not inferable from the construction of sec. 289, paras. 3 and 4 of the VAG-RegE [Government's Draft of a Tenth Act Amending the German Insurance Supervision Act]. In principle, a private individual has no claim to a determinative administrative measure in the absence of a corresponding provision of law.[54] Therefore, the form of the report of results in an instance of full compliance, which as such is mandatory, is consigned to the decision of the supervisory authority.

2.4.2 *The Governance System as Examination Subject*

2.4.2.1 The System of Governance as Source of Risk and as Structural Framework for Adequate Risk Management

The evaluation whether governance requirements[55] have been met is a core area of the Supervisory Review Process. Articles 41 ff. of the Solvency II Directive and secs. 24 ff. of the VAG-RegE [Government's Draft of a Tenth Act Amending the German Insurance Supervision Act] contain the governance requirements. Based

---

[53] See *U. Stelkens*, in: Stelkens/Bonk/Sachs, eds., Verwaltungsverfahrensgesetz [in English: Administrative Procedures Act] (7th ed. 2008), sec. 35, ref. 220 with further references at n. 12.

[54] *U. Stelkens*, in: Stelkens/Bonk/Sachs, eds., n. 53 above, at sec 35, ref. 220 with further references at n. 13.

[55] The Solvency II Directive provides for a risk management system with a risk management function as an imperative component of corporate governance, to which is added a compliance system with a compliance function. Also required is an internal review function. And under art. 48 of the Solvency II Directive and sec. 31 of the VAG-RegE [Government's Draft of a Tenth Act Amending the German Insurance Supervision Act] an actuarial function is to be embedded in insurance undertakings. Under art. 42 of the Solvency II Directive and sec. 25 of the VAG-RegE [Government's Draft of a Tenth Act Amending the German Insurance Supervision Act] persons with key functions must be "fit" and "proper." On this point see in detail *Dreher*, "Begriff und Inhaber der Schlüsselfunktionen nach Solvency II und VAG 2012" [in English: Concept and Holders of Key Functions under Solvency II and the German Insurance Supervision Act 2012], VersR (2012), 933 ff. (Chap. 7, below); *id.*, "Die aufsichtsbehördliche Kontrolle der Inhaber von Schlüsselfunktionen nach Solvency II und künftigen VAG" [in English: Review by Supervisory Authorities of the Holders of Key Functions under Solvency II and the Future German Insurance Supervision Act], VersR (2012), 1061 ff (Chap. 8, below). With regard to the requirements for corporate governance from the European and national point of view, see for an overview, e.g., *Lüttringhaus*, "Neue Governance- und Aufsichtsregeln für die europäische Versicherungswirtschaft nach Solvency II" [in English: New Governance and Supervisory Rules for the European Insurance Industry under Solvency II], EuZW (2011), 856 ff.; *Grote/Schaaf*, "Zum Referentenentwurf der 10. VAG-Novelle zur Umsetzung der Solvency II Richtlinie in deutsches Recht – eine erste Analyse" [in English: On the Consultants' Draft of the Tenth German Insurance Supervision Act for the Implementation of the Solvency II Directive in German Law – A First Analysis], VersR (2012), 17 (19 ff.).

on the general principles for corporate governance found in art. 41, para. 1 of the Solvency II Directive and in sec. 24 of the VAG-RegE, arts. 42 ff. of the Solvency II Directive and secs. 25 ff. of the VAG-RegE [Government's Draft of a Tenth Act Amending the German Insurance Supervision Act] contain specific details with respect to the requirements for personnel with key functions, for the risk management system, for internal monitoring (including the compliance function), for the internal review function, for the actuarial function and for outsourcing. The implementing regulation[56] at Level 2 of the delegated legislative process supplies detail to the basic legal requirements. The Guidelines[57] at Level 3, by contrast, are not legally binding.[58]

Article 41, para. 1 of the Solvency II Directive and sec. 24 of the VAG-RegE [Government's Draft of a Tenth Act Amending the German Insurance Supervision Act] require insurance undertakings to have an "effective system of governance" in place as well as, respectively, an effective and proper "business organization", adequate to their individual circumstances. Under the risk-based approach of Solvency II, the aim is a system of governance that for its part entails the fewest risks possible and at the same time identifies and adequately deals with the risks arising from business activities and in the organizational area. Governance is effective when it examines its own nature as a source of risk and handles risks without endangering the objectives of supervision. In this manner it will be assured that insurance undertakings meet the primary objective[59] of insurance supervision.

Four supervisory criteria arise from arts. 41 ff. of the Solvency II Directive and secs. 24 ff. of the VAG-RegE [Government's Draft of a Tenth Act Amending the German Insurance Supervision Act]. One of these criteria is that an effective communications system must exist,[60] which above all shall be directed toward exchange of information about risks. Another criterion is sufficient internal review within the insurance undertaking, a review that takes into account the nature of the system of governance as a source of risk. Also essential is the transparency directive, which for example requires clear lines of responsibility and the issuance of guidelines in the areas of the business organization. Finally, Solvency II is concerned with an appropriate allocation of competencies. Thus, art. 42 of the Solvency II Directive, implemented in sec. 25 of the VAG-RegE [Government's Draft of a Tenth Act Amending the German Insurance Supervision Act], sets forth

---

[56] Up to the present available only in draft: *European Commission*, Draft Implementing measures Solvency II, 2011 (hereafter, DVO).

[57] *CEIOPS*, Draft Proposal for Level 3 Guidelines on the System of Governance, 2011; see also: *CEIOPS*, Consultation Paper EIOPA-CP-14/017, of 2 June 2014.

[58] See on this point *Dreher*, n. 55 above "Begriff und Inhaber" [in English: Concept and Holders] at 935 f.

[59] See on this point n. 13, above.

[60] See art. 41, para. 1, subpara. 2 of the Solvency II Directive ("an effective system for ensuring the transmission of information" and sec. 24, para. 1, sent. 2, at the end, of the VAG-RegE [Government's Draft of a Tenth Act Amending the German Insurance Supervision Act]).

"fit" and "proper" requirements for personnel having key functions.[61] And a component of competence allocation is that, under art. 48, para. 1 (i) and sec. 31 para. 2, sent. 2 of the VAG-RegE [Government's Draft of a Tenth Act Amending the German Insurance Supervision Act], the actuarial function is to be incorporated into the risk management system. Most of the deeply ramified requirements for the components of the governance system can be comprehended within one of these criteria.

2.4.2.2 The Complex Governance Concept in Application of the Law

Especially in the area of governance supervision, it is as difficult as it is sensitive to draw a hard and fast line between the supervision of legality set down under art. 34, para. 1 of the Solvency II Directive and an ill-defined, "back door" supervision according to the principles of abusiveness[62] not provided for in the new Solvency II system. But even if, contrary to European law, supervision according to the principles of abusiveness is retained, as is the case under the current VAG-RegE [Government's Draft of a Tenth Act Amending the German Insurance Supervision Act], still its predictability should be ensured so far as possible. To this extent, then, a dilemma arises, for example, that the assessment of whether an insurance undertaking has in place an "effective risk-management system" (art. 36, para. 2 (a) and art. 44, para. 1, subpara. 1 of the Solvency II Directive and sec. 27, para. 1, sent. 1 of the VAG-RegE [Government's Draft of a Tenth Act Amending the German Insurance Supervision Act]) presupposes an assessment of a chiefly economic nature on the part of the insurance supervisory authorities: The evaluation of what is "effective" proceeds de facto under commercial and thus theoretical concepts. This leads to a not inconsiderable scope for unpredictable assessment by supervisory authorities and thus also to the problem of uncertainty in the law.[63]

This is so because even a literal interpretation of the legal requirements at issue becomes difficult due to their abstract nature. They require judgmental detail.

Nevertheless, despite these difficulties one may ascertain the natural sense of such complex concepts as "risk-management system" and "internal control". In this, one finds assistance in business concepts and findings which are widely accepted by scholars.[64] It is especially noteworthy here that the Solvency II legal requirements prescribe merely a minimum level of precautions for an operating business organization. This condition gives rise at the same time to a prohibition on

---

[61] See on this point *Dreher*, n. 55 above ("Die aufsichtsbehördliche Kontrolle" [in English: Review by Supervisory Authorities]).

[62] See n. 28 above and *Dreher*, n. 6 above, at 420 ff.

[63] See for more detail, *Dreher*, n. 6 above, at 420 ff. and 422 f.

[64] Known in competition law as statements of sound economic principles; see on this point *Dreher*, "Die Zukunft der Missbrauchsaufsicht in einem ökonomisierten Kartellrecht" [in English: The Future of Supervision According to the Principles of Abusiveness in Economized Competition Law], WuW (2008), 23 (27).

optimization for supervisory authorities with respect to the supervised insurance undertakings.[65] By contrast, economic principles generally align with the business organization best suited to maximize profit. For a business policy autonomously oriented thereon, this would signify a de facto order on optimization. Further, the law does not aim for the highest level of individual complexity; rather it seeks an application that is both abstract and of lesser complexity. In distinction to the economic sciences, the law is based upon general values and weighing of interests.[66] This should be taken into account when applying art. 36 of the Solvency II Directive. Further, the teleological interpretation of the Solvency II provisions and their concretion have a key role to play, a role that must take account of the principle of proportionality. The risk-based approach of Solvency II requires that the supervised undertakings shall have a risk status that is always within their power to control.

Early on, CEIOPS announced several pertinent criteria in order to provide insurance undertakings and supervisory authorities with non-binding guidelines. Much in this material is to be affirmed.[67] CEIOPS, however, proposed among other things handling the problem by creating groups of comparable undertakings in order to identify where each undertaking stands in this group.[68] Such a comparison cannot, for example, disclose whether a risk-management system is effective because a determination of effectiveness requires absolute, not relative, criteria. This is particularly so, because arts. 41 ff. of the Solvency II Directive and secs. 24 ff. of the VAG-RegE [Government's Draft of a Tenth Act Amending the German Insurance Supervision Act] prescribe a supervisory minimum standard as to governance which, as a practical matter, insurance undertakings will mostly exceed, in view of the economic advantages of a good business organization. Indeed, a further difficulty is presented by the depth of detail in the proposals, which do not strike a proper balance between certainty in the law and principles-based supervision.

2.4.3 Capital Requirements as Examination Subject

2.4.3.1 General Assessment Requirements

Under art. 75, para. 1 of the Solvency II Directive and sec. 69 of the VAG-RegE [Government's Draft of a Tenth Act Amending the German Insurance Supervision Act], liabilities and assets are to be valued at market value. This valuation is to be based on the amount for which they could be exchanged between "knowledgeable willing parties in an arm's length transaction". Title 1, Chapter II of the draft of the

[65] On this point see 2.5.1.2, below.

[66] *Dreher*, n. 64 above, at n. 23.

[67] Issues Paper, no. 5.27 ff.

[68] See, e.g., Issues Paper, no. 5.27.

proposed implementing regulation is addressed to concretizing these requirements. Both insurance undertakings and supervisory authorities must make use of complex models in order to correctly set market value. The requirements of art. 75 of the Solvency II Directive and sec. 69 of the VAG-RegE [Government's Draft of a Tenth Act Amending the German Insurance Supervision Act] lead to difficult assessments based on the assumption of a hypothetical contractual party.[69]

2.4.3.2 Compliance with Requirements on Technical Provisions

Overview of the Rules on Technical Provisions

The calculation of the technical provisions arises from the principles of market orientation,[70] of prudence, of dependability, and of objectivity.[71] Article 77, para. 1 of the Solvency II Directive specifies that the value of the technical provisions shall be equal to the sum of a best estimate and a risk margin. According to art. 77, para. 4 of the Solvency II Directive, insurance undertakings are to value these factors separately. The calculation of the best estimate is to be based on valid data,[72] adequate methods,[73] and realistic assumptions.[74] Under art. 77, para. 2, subpara. 1 of the Solvency II Directive and sec. 72, para. 1 of the VAG-RegE [Government's Draft of a Tenth Act Amending the German Insurance Supervision Act], the best estimate results from the probability-weighted average of future cash-flows, with the insurance undertakings taking account of the relevant time value of money and the risk-free interest rate term structure. Under art 77, para. 3 of the Solvency II Directive and sec. 73, para. 1 of the VAG-RegE [Government's Draft of a Tenth Act Amending the German Insurance Supervision Act], the risk margin must ensure that the reserves are equivalent to the amount the insurance undertaking would require in order to assume and meet the insurance obligations.

---

[69] See, *Dreher*, n. 6 above, at 394 f.

[70] See art. 76, paras. 2 and 3 of the Solvency II Directive and sec. 70 paras. 3 and 4 VAG-RegE [Government's Draft of a Tenth Act Amending the German Insurance Supervision Act], which provide that the value of the technical provisions must be established in line with the market and must conform to what the insurance undertakings would have to pay the substituted obligor for an immediate assumption of the liabilities; for a comprehensive look at market-oriented assessment, see *Dreher*, n. 6 above, at 394 f.

[71] Art. 76, para. 4 of the Solvency II Directive and sec. 70, para. 2, sent. 2 of the VAG-RegE [Government's Draft of a Tenth Act Amending the German Insurance Supervision Act].

[72] More detailed provisions on data quality are set forth in art. 82 and art. 83 of the Solvency II Directive and secs. 77 f. of the VAG-RegE [Government's Draft of a Tenth Act Amending the German Insurance Supervision Act].

[73] Art. 77, para. 2, subpara. 2 of the Solvency II Directive and sec. 72, para. 2 of the VAG-RegE [Government's Draft of a Tenth Act Amending the German Insurance Supervision Act].

[74] Art. 77, para. 2, subpara. 2 of the Solvency II Directive and sec. 72, para. 2 of the VAG-RegE [Government's Draft of a Tenth Act Amending the German Insurance Supervision Act].

Further, when calculating technical provisions, insurance undertakings must consider among other things: inflation, all expenses pertaining to servicing insurance obligations, all payments to policy holders (including for example future discretionary bonuses),[75] future choices to be made by policy holders about exercising contractual options, the value of any financial guarantees given,[76] and amounts recoverable from reinsurance contracts and special purpose vehicles.[77] Under art. 84 of the Solvency II Directive and sec. 79, para. 1 of the VAG-RegE [Government's Draft of a Tenth Act Amending the German Insurance Supervision Act], upon request from the supervisory authorities insurance undertakings must demonstrate the appropriateness of their methods, the adequacy of the data employed, and the appropriateness of their technical provisions. Under art. 85 of the Solvency II Directive and sec. 79, para. 2 of the VAG-RegE [Government's Draft of a Tenth Act Amending the German Insurance Supervision Act], in some cases the supervisory authority may require an increase in the amount of the technical provisions, if the insurance undertakings do not meet the requirements of arts. 76 ff. of the Solvency II Directive and secs. 70 ff. of the VAG-RegE [Government's Draft of a Tenth Act Amending the German Insurance Supervision Act].

Concretizing the Principle of Proportionality

Supervision of the technical provisions presents a great challenge both for insurance undertakings and supervisory authorities. The requirements of arts. 76 ff. of the Solvency II Directive[78] and their implementing rules are complex and to a great degree "technical" in nature. Specifics appear above all in relation to the principle of proportionality and the look into the distant future which both insurance undertakings and supervisory authorities must take.

In arts. 47 TPS1 ff. of the DVO [Level-2-Durchführungsverordnung [in English: Draft Implementing Measures Solvency II]], great detail is devoted to the principle of proportionality. That principle is echoed in art. 47 TPS1, para. 1 of the DVO, which prescribes that the method for calculating provisions should be proportionate to the nature, scale, and complexity underlying the insurance contract obligations. Paragraphs 2 through 5 of the provision set forth the specifics for determining whether the methods employed are proportionate to the risk status. In so doing, paragraphs 4 and 5 of the provision set up legal presumptions. Insurance

---

[75] See art. 78 of the Solvency II Directive and sec. 74 of the VAG-RegE [Government's Draft of a Tenth Act Amending the German Insurance Supervision Act] for these three requirements.

[76] See art. 79 of the Solvency II Directive and sec. 75 of the VAG-RegE [Government's Draft of a Tenth Act Amending the German Insurance Supervision Act] for the latter two factors.

[77] Art. 81 of the Solvency II Directive and sec. 76 of the VAG-RegE [Government's Draft of a Tenth Act Amending the German Insurance Supervision Act].

[78] Expected to be concretized in arts. 12 TP [Technical Provision] 1 through 50 quater of the DVO.

undertakings may simplify their methods of calculation to the extent the risk status permits. This applies to amounts recoverable from reinsurance contracts and special purpose vehicles, to the risk surcharge, to the best estimate of contractual premium adjustment clauses, for counter-party default, and for the matching premium. In such manner, the principle of proportionality undergoes a concrete legal formation.

Future-Looking Approach

With its risk-based approach, the new supervisory architecture has been conceived to include future events and developments.[79] It is, however, almost impossible to avoid some degree of significant unpredictability to the extent models and extrapolations are employed. One example of this is the extrapolation relating to interest rate structure under art. 39 IR [Implementing Regulation]4 and art. 40 IR5 of the DVO projected over a period of several decades. The predictive value of such prognoses is dubious.[80]

The limited possibility to take account of future developments in calculation of provisions appears also when art. 19 TP [Technical Provision] 6, para. 1 of the DVO is considered. Under this clause, assumptions concerning future insurance undertaking activities are to be taken into account in calculating technical provisions. Succeeding paragraphs 2 through 7 set forth in detail the requirements for assessing these future activities. In part, they go so far as to establish requirements for the projected business decisions themselves.[81] The draft of the DVO clearly is based on the legal requirement of "realistic assumptions" in art. 77, para. 2, subpara. 2 of the Solvency II Directive. It is certain that business activities can be planned "realistically". The question arises, however, as to how far into the future the planning should or even can extend. Supervisory authorities and insurance undertakings face the same difficulties with respect to the unpredictability of future developments. There is a question here concerning how deeply interventions may go into such insurance undertakings' positions as are protected under basic rights. To answer this question requires above all a sensitive handling of the principles of proportionality and commensurability.

---

[79] See especially Art. 19 TP [Technical Provision] 6 ff. and 38 IR [Implementing Regulation] 2 ff. of the DVO, which set forth the requirements for the assumptions meant to undergird the technical provisions and for the calculation of the risk-free interest rate structure.

[80] See in detail, *Dreher*, n. 6 above, at 3.3.4 and 4.2.5.3.

[81] See, e.g., art. 19 TP [Technical Provision] 6, para. 4 of the DVO, under which the projected future business activities must be consistent. See n. 42 above, on the principle of supervisory freedom of insurance undertakings' management.

2.4.3.3 Compliance with the Minimum and Solvency Capital Requirements

The calculation of the Solvency Capital Requirement is accomplished under the principles set forth in art. 101 of the Solvency II Directive and sec. 88 of the VAG-RegE [Government's Draft of a Tenth Act Amending the German Insurance Supervision Act] on the assumption that the undertaking will pursue its business as a going concern and adjusted to the risk status of the insurance undertaking. In this process, art. 101, para. 3, subpara. 1 of the Solvency II Directive and sec. 88, para. 2, sent. 1 of the VAG-RegE [Government's Draft of a Tenth Act Amending the German Insurance Supervision Act] require that all quantifiable risks be taken into account. The Solvency Capital Requirement must be calculated so that the Value-at-Risk equals 99.5 % over a one-year period. Insurance undertakings can use the statutorily provided standard formula or an internal model approved by the supervisory authority. Calculation of the Minimum Capital Requirement proceeds under the requirements of arts. 129 ff. of the Solvency II Directive and secs. 86 and 113 of the VAG-RegE [Government's Draft of a Tenth Act Amending the German Insurance Supervision Act]. Solvency II focuses on the actual risk status of insurance undertakings and signifies a departure from solvency calculation based on book value to a calculation based on market value.[82]

Article 36, para. 3 of the Solvency II Directive requires supervisory authorities to have in place appropriate monitoring systems, such as will enable them to identify deteriorating financial conditions in insurance undertakings. These authorities may make use of all sources available to them, which may include the economic environment of the insurance undertakings as well as the insurance undertakings themselves. Supervisory authorities can acquire information about insurance undertakings from the Report to Supervisors (RTS) and the Solvency and Financial Condition Report (SFCR) to the public.[83] Both of these reports will contain indicia of deterioration, if any such exist. Thus, the SFCR[84] should contain "any material change to the [business] and performance",[85] including especially "any significant . . .events that have had a material impact on the undertaking".[86] Under art. 288, PDS7 of the DVO, insurance undertakings are obligated to disclose highly detailed statements on their capital management. Pursuant to art. 293, PDS 13, para. 1 of the DVO, the SFCR must be updated whenever there is a "major development" affecting the relevance of the SFCR.

[82] See section "Overview of the Rules on Technical Provisions", above. On the advantages and disadvantages of the Solvency I regime compared to the new rules, see *Wiesemann*, "Solvency II: Einführung in die neuen Eigenmittelregeln für Versicherungen" [in English: Solvency II: Introduction to the new Own Funds Rules for Insurance Companies], WiSt (2011), 338 (344).

[83] See on this point n. 21 f., above.

[84] And also of the RTS, via art. 294, SRS1, para. 1 (a) of the DVO.

[85] Art. 283, PDS2, para. 2 of the DVO.

[86] Art. 284, PDS3, para. 1 (g) of the DVO.

The RTS contains, among other things, more extensive statements on the business performance,[87] the capital management,[88] and the solvency status of the undertaking. With regard to this last category, the notice of ORSA results plays a significant role.[89] This is so because ORSA requires insurance undertakings to assess their overall solvency needs as well as to assess whether they are at all times in compliance with the solvency requirements. Results from an ad hoc ORSA[90] must be reported pursuant to sec. 44 no. 8 of the VAG-RegE [Government's Draft of a Tenth Act Amending the German Insurance Supervision Act]. Auditors have a duty to report in the event that an insurance undertaking does not meet the SCR or MCR requirements. This duty is set forth in sec. 45, para. 4, no. 4 of the VAG-RegE [Government's Draft of a Tenth Act Amending the German Insurance Supervision Act] as provided for in Article 72, para. 1 of the Solvency II Directive.

CEIOPS provides that discussions should take place between insurance undertakings and supervisory authorities before any regulatory capital requirements are breached, when indications of financial deterioration appear.[91] The regulatory assessment as to when they are appropriate, should be based on an early warning system on both a quantitative[92] and qualitative[93] level.

2.4.3.4 Compliance with the Investment Provisions

The Solvency II requirements on capital investment continue the prior division into rules on the investment spectrum and qualitative rules, such as those on processes tied to capital investment.[94] The rules on capital investment seek to strike a balance between the principle of freedom of investment, on the one hand, as set forth in art. 133, para. 1 of the Solvency II Directive and the mandated prudent person principle on the other hand, as found in art. 132, para. 1 of the Solvency II Directive and sec.

[87] Art. 296, SRS3 of the DVO.

[88] Art. 300, SRS7 of the DVO.

[89] On the obligation to report to the supervisory authority and the obligations of public disclosure in connection with ORSA, see *Dreher/Ballmaier*, n. 17 above, at 140 f.

[90] Art. 45, para. 5 of the Solvency II Directive and sec. 28, para. 1, sent. 1 of the VAG-RegE [Government's Draft of a Tenth Act Amending the German Insurance Supervision Act].

[91] Issues Paper, no. 4.38.

[92] In Issues Paper, no. 4.39, CEIOPS identifies among other early warning indicators: rapid growth, declining profitability, sudden increase (also, dramatic decrease) in technical provisions, and high expenses coupled with low profitability.

[93] See Issues Paper, no. 4.40, which lists among other indicators: change in strategy, failure to implement supervisory requirements, non-cooperation with the supervisor, and vulnerability to legal or fiscal changes.

[94] See on this division under prior law, *Berger/Varain*, "Solvabilität, Kapitalanlage und Rechnungslegung" [in English: Solvency, Capital Investment and Accounting] in: Bürkle, ed., Compliance in Versicherungsunternehmen [in English: Insurance Undertakings' Compliance] (2009), 140, ref. 47.

115, para. 1 of the VAG-RegE [Government's Draft of a Tenth Act Amending the German Insurance Supervision Act]. The "prudent person principle" applies to "all. . .assets". This is attributable to the integrated, risk-based approach of Solvency II. Accordingly, all insurance undertakings' assets must be secure, of sufficiently high quality, liquid, profitable, and localized such that they are available. In addition, art. 132, para. 2, subpara. 3 of the Solvency II Directive and sec. 115, para. 1, no. 3 of the VAG-RegE [Government's Draft of a Tenth Act Amending the German Insurance Supervision Act] require that assets held to cover the technical provisions must be invested in a manner appropriate to the nature and duration of the (re)insurance liabilities, and in particular must be sufficiently fungible to meet contractual obligations to policy holders and insureds. What the Directive emphasizes here is the necessity of a sufficient asset-liability management system (ALM).[95]

Derivative instruments may be used insofar as they are directly or even indirectly employed to reduce risks through "facilitat[ing] efficient portfolio management".[96] Investments traded outside regulated financial markets should be resorted to only conservatively ("kept to a prudent level"), pursuant to art. 132, para. 4, subpara. 3 of the Solvency II Directive together with sec. 115, para. 1, no. 6 of the VAG-RegE [Government's Draft of a Tenth Act Amending the German Insurance Supervision Act]. Insurance undertakings must avoid concentrating risks.[97] Also, the supervisory authorities will pay particular attention in their evaluation to risk management in connection with capital investment. Only such investments are permitted as the undertaking "can appropriately identify, measure, monitor, manage, control and report". This limitation appears in art. 132, para. 2 of the Solvency II Directive, implemented in sec. 115, para. 1, no. 1 of the VAG-RegE [Government's Draft of a Tenth Act Amending the German Insurance Supervision Act]. A precondition for compliance with this standard is an adequate ALM. Investment in tradable securities and other repackaged financial instruments is subject to special regulatory intensity by arts. 244, RL2 ff. of the DVO, which proceeds on the basis of art. 135, para. 2 of the Solvency II Directive. There is also a difference between requirements that address the characteristics of the investments themselves, such as art. 244, RL2, paras. 1 and 2 of the DVO and requirements addressed to the

[95] The ALM consists of "all strategical and tactical partial procedures of insurance undertakings that promote the objective of controlling the interaction between assets and liabilities in order to eliminate the time lag ("mismatch"). See *"DIIR-Arbeitskreis 'Interne Revision in der Versicherungswirtschaft'"* [in English: German Institute for Internal Revision Working Group 'Internal Review in the Insurance Industry'], ZIR (2009), 270 for this definition and on a possible practical implementation by insurance undertakings; see further on the ALM, *Dreher*, n. 6 at 4.1.1.3.

[96] Art. 132, para. 4, subpara. 2 of the Solvency II Directive together with sec. 115, para. 1, no. 5, clause 1 of the VAG-RegE [Government's Draft of a Tenth Act Amending the German Insurance Supervision Act].

[97] Art. 132, para. 4, subpara. 4 of the Solvency II Directive together with sec. 115, para. 1, nos. 7 and 8 of the VAG-RegE [Government's Draft of a Tenth Act Amending the German Insurance Supervision Act].

investment process, including due diligence and potential reporting duties, such as art. 244, RL2, paras. 3 and 4, and art. 247, RL5, para. 1 of the DVO.

With respect to the undefined legal terms relating to the investment process, such as "appropriate" risk management, the previously addressed fundamental problem arises also in this context: the employment of complex concepts in the application of the law.[98] The provisions addressing the characteristics of investment vehicles contain on the one hand clear rules (see the 5 % rule of art. 244, RL2, para. 1 of the DVO) and undefined legal terms on the other hand. In this area, perhaps the principles set forth above[99] could become a fertile field with consideration given to the criteria of prudent business management. The crucial question here is whether the investments on behalf of the policy holders and insureds facilitate the continuing business activities of the insurance undertaking and the timely satisfaction of all liabilities from (re)insurance contracts. Investment strategy, especially in life insurance undertakings, enjoys particular protection through the basic freedoms relating to undertakings.[100] Therefore, supervision must above all be attentive to evaluation of capital investment management and for reasons of commensurability intervene first and foremost on this level.

2.4.3.5 Compliance with the Requirements on the Quality and Quantity of Own Funds

In contradistinction to prior law, available own funds include asset and liability reserves and are not balance-sheet items.[101] Article 93 of the Solvency II Directive and sec. 82 of the VAG-RegE [Government's Draft of a Tenth Act Amending the German Insurance Supervision Act] classify own funds into three tiers according to quality.

The main classification criteria are permanent availability and subordination; additional criteria are sufficient duration and the absence of incentives to redeem, of mandatory costs, and of other encumbrances.[102] The Solvency II Directive and the VAG-RegE [Government's Draft of a Tenth Act Amending the German Insurance Supervision Act] distinguish between basic own funds items[103] and ancillary own

[98] See 2.4.2.2, above.

[99] See 2.4.2.2, above.

[100] See 2.4.1.1, above.

[101] See, e.g., *Wiesemann*, n. 82 above, at 340.

[102] All criteria are defined in art. 93, para. 1 (main criteria) and para. 2 (additional criteria) of the Solvency II Directive and sec. 82 VAG-RegE [Government's Draft of a Tenth Act Amending the German Insurance Supervision Act].

[103] Under art. 88 of the Solvency II Directive and sec. 80, para. 3 of the VAG-RegE [Government's Draft of a Tenth Act Amending the German Insurance Supervision Act], these include "the excess of assets over liabilities" (excluding own shares) and subordinated liabilities.

funds items.[104] The determinative inquiry as to classification in Tier 1 is whether the own funds "substantially possess" the characteristics of permanent availability and subordination. The features relating to sufficient duration and the absence of incentive to redeem, of mandatory servicing costs, and of encumbrances are to be taken into consideration under art. 94 of the Solvency II Directive and sec. 83 of the VAG-RegE [Government's Draft of a Tenth Act Amending the German Insurance Supervision Act].

The principle of proportionality has but indirect application to the requirements relating to own funds. It is of course true that the individual situations of insurance undertakings will be relevant to the assessment of capital investment. An example appears in the consideration given to "sufficient duration" in art. 93, para. 2, subpara. 1, sent. 2 of the Solvency II Directive. Classification in a Tier, however, relies on the characteristics of the capital investment and not on the characteristics of the assets of the insurance undertaking making the investment. Nevertheless, one is surprised by the markedly detailed and in part almost impenetrable tangle of rules in the draft of the implementing regulation, which are based on art. 97 of the Solvency II Directive. The problematic arts. 58 COF [Classification of Own Funds]1 ff. of the DVO, for example, employ the legal device of presumptions for classification in the Tiers. For the purpose of legal review of requirements on the quality of own funds, supervisory authorities have a detailed legal scheme at their disposal.

Article 98 of the Solvency II Directive, implemented in secs. 85 f. of the VAG-RegE [Government's Draft of a Tenth Act Amending the German Insurance Supervision Act], prescribes the eligible amounts of Tier 2 and Tier 3 items required to comply with the Solvency Capital Requirement. Thus, the Tier 3 assets must constitute less than one third of the total amount of eligible own funds, while Tier 1 assets must constitute more than one third of eligible own funds. To comply with the Minimum Capital Requirement, Tier 1 basic own-fund items must constitute more than one half of the total amount of basic own-fund items. Tier 1 own funds can be combined with eligible Tier 2 and Tier 3 own funds to meet the Solvency Capital Requirement. To comply with the Minimum Capital Requirement, only Tier 1 amounts and eligible Tier 2 amounts may be considered. Detailed rules on compliance with the Solvency Capital Requirement and the Minimum Capital Requirement are to be found in art. 72, EOF [Eligibility of Own Funds]1 of the DVO, adopted pursuant to art. 99, sent. 1 (a) of the Solvency II Directive. The requirements on the quantitative makeup of own funds give supervisory authorities clear rules to rely on in this area.

[104] Art. 89, para. 1, subpara. 1 of the Solvency II Directive and sec. 80, paras. 4 and 5 of the VAG-RegE [Government's Draft of a Tenth Act Amending the German Insurance Supervision Act]: The ancillary own funds items consist of items not counted toward basic own funds which can be called up on demand to absorb losses. Under art. 90 of the Solvency II Directive and sec. 81 of the VAG-RegE [Government's Draft of a Tenth Act Amending the German Insurance Supervision Act] they are subject to approval. See in detail, arts. 51 AOF [Ancillary Own Funds]1 through 57 AOF7 of the DVO.

2.4.3.6 Compliance with the Requirements on the Internal Model

The requirements for compliance with an internal model arise from Title 1, Chapter VI, Section 4, Subsection 3 of the Solvency II Directive. These too are to be incorporated into the Supervisory Review Process. Under these requirements, supervisory authorities review whether insurance undertakings are in compliance with arts. 120 ff. of the Solvency II Directive and secs. 106 ff. of the VAG-RegE [Government's Draft of a Tenth Act Amending the German Insurance Supervision Act]. These provisions, for example, prescribe integration of the internal model into the risk-management system, establish statistical quality standards along with standards on calibrating the internal model, on the capacity of the internal model (validation standards), and on documenting the internal model. These rules are qualitative in nature and partake of the previously mentioned difficulties in legal application attendant upon this form of rule-making.[105] Articles 211 TSIM [Tests and Standards for the Use of an Internal Model]1 ff. of the DVO contain further, more concrete requirements.

2.5 Powers of Supervisory Authorities to Remedy Weaknesses and Deficiencies

2.5.1 "Weaknesses or Deficiencies" as Legal Terms

2.5.1.1 "Weaknesses or Deficiencies" as Uniform Legal Requirement

Under art. 36, para. 5 of the Solvency II Directive, supervisory authorities are to have all powers necessary to require insurance undertakings to remedy weaknesses and or deficiencies identified in the Supervisory Review Process. The term "weakness" appears in only one other place in the Solvency II Directive.[106] The same is true for the term "deficiency", which the Directive specifies as a condition for a governance capital add-on in art. 37, para. 1, sent. 2 (c). The terminology employed in art. 36, para. 5 of the Solvency II Directive raises legal issues.

To begin with, its wording could be wrongly understood as assigning to supervisory authorities the power to exercise a form of supervision according to the principles of abusiveness. This is so because it does not explicitly address non-compliance with legal requirements, as does art. 34, para. 1 of the Solvency II Directive, but only "weaknesses or deficiencies". Such a reading, however, would be incompatible with the general view that the Solvency II Directive on this basis is strict in allowing only supervision of legality, and not any manner of further-reaching general supervision according to the principles of abusiveness.[107]

[105] See 2.4.2.2, above.

[106] See Recital 28 of the Solvency II Directive.

[107] See on this point 2.3.2.2, above and 2.5.1.2, below.

A further question is whether there is any difference between the legal terms "weakness" and "deficiency" or whether the language of art. 36 para. 5 of the Solvency II Directive on this point is merely editorial pleonastic piling-on of synonyms.[108] Support for this view appears in the examination subjects mentioned in art. 36, para. 1 of the Solvency II Directive, namely, strategies, processes, and reporting procedures, which from the point of view of language usage could be "deficient" and "weak" at the same time—and vice versa. In addition, in its statement of legal consequences, art. 36, para. 5 of the Solvency II Directive does not distinguish between these two words being used in the realm of fact. Any possible gradation derived from this language, to the effect that a weakness may become a deficiency at a certain level, is thus rendered superfluous due to systematic reasons.

2.5.1.2 "Weaknesses or Deficiencies" as Non-compliance with Legal Requirements

Evaluation and review of strategies, processes, and reporting procedures may disclose that they are weak and deficient within the meaning of art. 36, para. 5 of the Solvency II Directive. Under the Solvency II Directive system, however, this is not necessarily the case when an insurance undertaking fails to follow a best practice, for instance, with respect to risk management. Article 34, para. 1 of the Solvency II Directive prescribes legal supervision, in that it confers upon supervisory authorities the power to employ preventive or corrective measures to ensure compliance with legal and administrative provisions.[109] Under art. 36, para. 1 of the

[108] On the frequent use of this "method" in European law, see 2.4.1.3, above.

[109] See in detail 2.5.1.2 and 2.5.2. The questionable legal and administrative provisions under art 34, para. 1 of the Solvency II Directive are those rules designed to implement the objectives of insurance supervision. When such is the case, they should be construed by objective interpretation. For the criteria of such interpretation, applicable also in the present circumstances, see *Dreher*, Die Konkretisierung der Missstandsaufsicht nach § 81 VAG [in English: Concretizing Supervision According to the Principles of Abusiveness under sec. 81 of the German Insurance Supervision Act] (1997), 24 ff.; Art. 29, para. 1 of the Solvency II Directive, in reference to supervision of insurance undertakings by supervisory authorities, stipulates "continuous verification of the proper operation" of insurance undertakings and review of "compliance with supervisory provisions" by insurance undertakings. By this language, it narrows the scope of art. 34, para. 1 of the Solvency II Directive to rules which serve the purpose of supervision over insurance undertakings. For a different view, see *Bürkle*, n. 16 above, ref. 54 f., interpreting art. 34, para. 1 of the Solvency II Directive so that the "activities of supervisory authorities are in service only of compliance with the revamped European insurance supervisory regime." But the very language of art. 34, para. 1 of the Solvency II Directive contradicts this, because in contrast to art. 36, para. 1 of the Solvency II Directive, it does not mention this restriction. Further, on the implementation of the Solvency II Directive rules addressing compliance with legal requirements, see also *Bürkle*, "Berliner Sprachverwirrung im RegE des 10. VAG-Änderungsgesetzes" [in English: The Berlin Tower of Babel in the Government's Draft of the Tenth German Insurance Supervision Act], VersR (2012), 829 f.

Solvency II Directive, a process is not weak and deficient unless the supervisory authority identifies a breach of the "laws, regulations and administrative provisions adopted pursuant to this Directive", such as a breach of a qualitative requirement on governance. Supervisory authorities in the Solvency II system are subject to a prohibition on optimization, as has been the case in the German insurance supervisory regime since the D. A. S. judgment of the Federal Administrative Court.[110]

The architecture of the rules on powers demonstrates also in another place that Solvency II does not attempt to treat supervision according to the principles of abusiveness. If insurance undertakings fail to meet the regulatory capital requirements, arts. 138 ff. of the Solvency II Directive provide for a process that may run the gamut from minimally intensive to highly intrusive interventions in the activities of the undertakings. Article 141 of the Solvency II Directive grants supervisory authorities all powers necessary to safeguard "the interests of policy holders". The same applies—restricted to these specific cases—to the legal supervision, albeit with far-reaching intervention powers. These powers are activated only when "the solvency position of the undertaking continues to deteriorate", thus requiring observation of solvency over time. In addition, art. 141 of the Solvency II Directive, relying on reasons of proportionality,[111] posits that the "interests of policy holders" cannot otherwise be safeguarded. Thus art. 141 of the Solvency II Directive contains an intervention power contoured in the matter of fact. This power is rather far-reaching in its legal requirement of the interests of policy holders and in its legal consequence of "all measures necessary". Thus also there is no basis for assuming supervision according to the principles of abusiveness restricted in its content to the situations contemplated by art. 141 of the Solvency II Directive. It follows further from this that, in confirmation of the previously and independently arrived general view that supervision according to the principles of abusiveness is impermissible,[112] sec. 292, para. 1, sent. 3 and sec. 289, para. 1, sent. 2 of the VAG-RegE [Government's Draft of a Tenth Act Amending the German Insurance Supervision Act], in specifying supervision according to the principles of abusiveness, contravene European law as expressed in art. 34, para. 1 and art. 36, para. 5 of the Solvency II Directive.

---

[110] See 2.4.2.2, above; *Bürkle*, n. 28 above, 1476 f.; BVerwG ["Federal Administrative Court"], VersR (1981), 222 (223) on identical sec. 8, para. 1, sent. 1, no. 3, VAG [German Insurance Supervision Act] in the current version; and addressing same, *Rittner*, "Die Versicherungsaufsicht nach dem D.A.S.-Urteil des Bundesverwaltungsgerichts" [in English: Insurance Supervision Following the D. A. S. Judgment of the Federal Administrative Court], VersR (1982), 205 ff. and *Dreher*, Die Versicherung als Rechtsprodukt [in English: Insurance as a Legal Product] (1991), 215 ff.

[111] Also *Bürkle*, n. 16 above, ref. 40 emphasizes in connection with art. 141 of the Solvency II Directive the relation between means of intervention and failure to meet the Solvency Capital Requirement.

[112] See the references at n. 28, above.

This result is in accord with the basic posture of CEIOPS[113] on the Supervisory Review Process, which assumes that it belongs within the system of legal supervision. Thus, no. 4.43 of the Issues Paper clarifies that supervisory authorities should require insurance undertakings to remedy a situation if their governance is in breach of Directive requirements. And no. 4.45 of the Issues Paper is similarly targeted in its prescriptions for when capital requirements are breached ("if a regulatory solvency level…is breached"). Along the same lines, no. 4.42 of the Issues Paper, states: "Therefore, the supervisor needs the appropriate powers to require the undertaking to take the appropriate action to remedy any areas of non-compliance with the Directive".

2.5.1.3 Scope of Judicial Review Over Decisions of Supervisory Authorities

The assessment of complex economic contexts is the condition precedent of supervisory assessment as to whether the strategies, processes, and reporting procedures of an insurance undertaking are weak or deficient. In the area of competition law, the European Court of Justice has conferred upon the Commission when applying European law a scope for judgment evaluation that can only be judicially reviewed to a limited extent in cases where the Commission may be compelled to make difficult evaluations of economic or technical facts. The Court ruled that judicial review must be restricted to examining the facts underlying a decision with regard to correctness[114] and to analyzing whether the subsumption of these facts under applicable law constitutes a clear evaluation error.[115] A similar restriction on judicial review of official decisions in economically and technically complex contexts appears in European law on intangible property[116] and public procurement law.[117] This restriction rests on the assumption that such evaluations require certified expertise and special expert knowledge.[118] In several areas, the European courts have themselves disavowed possessing such qualities. To the

[113] Somewhat contradictory, however, is no. 4.45. of the Issues Paper: "Where necessary, the supervisor may require undertakings to remedy weaknesses or deficiencies identified in the SRP." This may also be the case if the capital requirements have been met. Presumably this refers to a situation where the insurance undertaking has met the regulatory capital requirements but other breaches of legal requirements are found. On this point see also 2.5.3, below.

[114] Beginning with ECJ, 13 Jul. 1966, case nos. 56/64 and 48/64, E.C.R. 1966, 321, 396 (Consten und Grundig).

[115] See most recently ECJ., 8 Dec. 2011, case no. C-389/08 P, also, WuW (2012), 281 (KME). See also ECJ., 25 Oct. 1977, 26/76, E.C.R. 1977, 1875 (Metro/SABA).

[116] See, e.g., EGC, 19 Nov. 2008, case no. T-187/06, E.C.R. 2008, II-3151 (Schräder/CPVO [SUMCOL1]), headnote 1.

[117] See on this point *Dreher*, in: Dreher/Stockmann, eds., Kartellvergaberecht [in English: Competition Law and Public Procurement Law] (2008), sec. 97, refs. 140 ff., 223 ff. with further ref.

[118] EGC, n. 116 above, at headnote 1 and ref. 59 f.

extent that courts thereby acknowledge a scope for judgment evaluation, this term is congruent with its use in German administrative law, but is not based on the affiliated dogmatics and systematic. European courts prefer to use the term "discretion" as a synonym for "scope for judgment evaluation". In applying this usage, they do not distinguish between the factual area and the legal area, as is done under German legal principles. Rather, by using these terms, and other terms such as "scope for assessment," they establish, in the sense of a unified design, an executive scope immune to review.[119] Examination of this process reveals that in recent times—also in reference to the procedural guarantees of art. 6 of the European Convention on Human Rights—there has been a clear change of course from the earlier jurisprudence to substantially increased scrutiny of regulatory decisions in the pronouncements of the European Court of Justice.[120]

This jurisprudence addresses first of all the conduct of European regulators and thus also the activities of EIOPA and has indirect significance for measures of the national insurance supervisory authorities. This is so because these measures implement fully harmonizing European law. In Germany this primarily takes the form of the VAG-RegE [Government's Draft of a Tenth Act Amending the German Insurance Supervision Act].[121] Retention of German administrative law doctrine without due consideration would not be correct in this environment. Thus, the ECJ criteria on rendering certain executive areas immune to review will necessarily influence scrutiny of decisions by national regulators. There is, however, an issue of prior import: whether the ECJ will recognize, in the circumstances underlying review of insurance supervision, a complexity comparable to the previously mentioned situations in the legal areas of competition, public procurement law, and intangible property law. Essentially, this is a matter of proper functioning of courts: If a court, even with the help of expert opinions, cannot incorporate the fact situation in the same manner as the regulatory authorities, i.e., cannot consistently reach the same decision as regulatory authorities, then in that case there would appear to be a restriction on the scrutiny of such a decision.[122] Certain criteria have been mentioned above, which are to be applied with restraint for the adoption, in exceptional circumstances, of a complex regulatory decision subject to narrow judicial review. These criteria militate against a wholesale transfer of the practice of judicial self restraint into the insurance supervisory regime.

---

[119] See in detail, e.g., *Adam*, Beurteilungsspielraum und Legalausnahme im Europäischen Kartellrecht [in English: Scope for Evaluation and Legal Exception in European Competition Law] (2007), 21 ff.

[120] But see ECJ, 8 Dec. 2011, case no. C-272/09 P (KME Germany/Commission), ref. 94 and ECJ, 8 Dec. 2011, case no. C-386/10 P (Chalkor AE Epexergasias Metallon/Kommission), ref. 54; also in EuZW (2012), 190; and in journals, e.g., *Nazzini*, "Administrative enforcement, judicial review and fundamental rights in competition law," CMLRev. (2012), 971 (1005).

[121] To the same effect generally, i.e., not in the context of the insurance supervisory regime, see also *Sachs*, n. 53 above, at sec. 40, refs. 164, 235.

[122] See for an overview, *Dreher*, n. 6 above, at 416 f. and 422 f.

In rare cases, German administrative law recognizes a scope for judgment evaluation by the authorities not subject to judicial review.

This scope for evaluation is permissible as an exception to art. 19, para. 4 of the GG [German Basic Law] only if the presiding court would otherwise come up against the limit of its ability to function. The statutory empowerment of the regulatory authorities is a condition precedent.[123] It may be appropriate for a court to adopt the scope of judgment evaluation principle if the court would otherwise be called upon to step in for the regulatory authorities to decide matters and assess risks in areas requiring special expertise, where the regulatory authorities are better equipped because of the tools at their disposal.[124] With regard to case types in German jurisprudence,[125] the only ones that might come into consideration are those dealing with risk and prognosis assessment in especially complex circumstances. The German courts have accorded regulatory authorities scope for judgment evaluation in certain areas. Among these are investment approval under the Gentechnikgesetz [Genetic Engineering Act],[126] market analysis and market definition of the Bundesnetzagentur [Federal Network Agency] under the Telekommunikationsgesetz [Telecommunications Act],[127] and compiling and evaluating types of environments in the context of review of flora-fauna-habitat compatibility.[128]

Even if one allows a comparable complexity, the relationship of German administrative law to that of Europe must be considered. The grant of scope for evaluation, which is based on national administrative law, contrasts with European provisions, while these do not impose the same conditions on the restriction of judicial scrutiny. To the extent that German administrative law has created categories of cases, these should be examined against the criteria laid down in ECJ rulings to determine whether they conform to European law. In the area of insurance supervision, therefore, there is no warrant for a judicially unreviewable scope for evaluation originating in the principles of German administrative law.

2.5.2 The Role of Art. 36, Para. 5 of the Solvency II Directive in the Classification of Intervention Powers

Article 36, para. 5 of the Solvency II Directive must be distinguished from the basic rule of art. 34, paras. 1 and 2 of the Solvency II Directive on the one hand and from the rules on special powers on the other hand. The heading to art. 34, para. 1 of the

[123] BVerwGE [Federal Administrative Court Decisions] 92, 340 (348).

[124] BVerwGE [Federal Administrative Court Decisions] 72, 300 (316 ff) (Wyhl).

[125] Compare to these, *Sachs*, n. 121 above, at ref. 107 ff., with references to the rulings noted thereafter.

[126] BVerwG [in English: Federal Administrative Court] NVwZ (1999), 1232 (1233).

[127] BVerwGE [Federal Administrative Court Decisions] 131, 41.

[128] BVerwGE [Federal Administrative Court Decisions] 130, 299.

Solvency II Directive is "General supervisory powers" and that provision functions to institute the rules relating both to tasks to be performed as well as to the powers to perform those tasks.[129] This latter function is evident from the plain language of the provision; the former from the fact-based phrasing that powers should be given to the supervisory authorities "to ensure that... ". Thus, the functional context for instituting tasks (securing compliance with legal requirements) and for conferring powers becomes clear. In its capacity as a rule concerning powers, art. 34, para. 1 of the Solvency II Directive prescribes that regulatory authorities shall have the power to remedy insurance undertakings' breaches. Article 34, para. 2 provides that the supervisory authorities are empowered "to take any necessary measure...with regard to insurance or reinsurance undertakings" with respect to insurance undertakings and the members of their administrative, management, or supervisory bodies. Thus, this paragraph affects supervisory tools[130] and the addressees of the measures. The prescriptive scheme of art. 34, para. 1 makes manifest that a measure is required if insurance undertakings fail to comply with laws, regulations, and administrative provisions.

This raises the question as to what sort of independent content art. 36, para. 5 of the Solvency II Directive has.[131] To begin with, it contains the components of a rule establishing powers and to this extent is comparable to art. 34, para. 1 of the Solvency II Directive. Then it also treats intervention tools and thus builds a link to art. 34, para. 2 of the Solvency II Directive. In contrast to art. 34, paras. 1 and 2 of the Solvency II Directive, art. 36, para. 5 based on its wording is subject to a factually restricted field of application because it applies only when the Supervisory Review Process identifies "weaknesses or deficiencies". The supervisory authority, however, can limit the supervisory process both as to scope and frequency, under the authority of art. 36, para. 6, subpara. 2 of the Solvency II Directive. Furthermore, from a time-determinative point of view, art. 36 of the Solvency II Directive applies only to ongoing supervision and does not apply to supervision of licensing or approval. Accordingly, art. 36 of the Solvency II Directive is *lex specialis* with respect to art. 34, para. 1 and 2 of the Solvency II Directive.

And in turn, the supervisory powers of art. 36 of the Solvency II Directive for ongoing proceedings have been concretized in part in other rules as *leges*

[129] Most probably of a different view concerning the tasks of the supervisory authorities *Bürkle*, n. 28 above, 1474, according to which art. 34 "is not a general rule for tasks, but stipulates in particular the intervention possibilities available to the national supervisory authorities".

[130] *Bürkle*, n. 28, 1475.

[131] Thus in *Grote*, n. 28 above, at 228, only art. 34 and not art. 36, para. 5 of the Solvency II Directive is identified as a rule relating to intervention powers.

speciales.[132] If the applicable conditions precedent are not met, then resort to one of the demands on insurance undertakings arising under art. 36 of the Solvency II Directive is not available. For example, if the conditions precedent for a capital add-on under art. 37 of the Solvency II Directive are not present, no capital add-on is permissible, even if it would not reach the level to be calculated under art. 37 of the Solvency II Directive. A subsidiary recourse to art. 36 of the Solvency II Directive or to its counterpart in the law of the Member States would otherwise cause the special intervention powers to become inoperable. This would contradict the scheme of the Directive and also the intent of the European legislator, who otherwise would have restricted himself to the general clauses.

2.5.3 Non-compliance with Capital Requirements

In the context of financial supervision the CEIOPS Issues Paper emphasizes the principle of proportionality, which indeed is applicable also in areas outside financial supervision. It lays out the various levels of possible regulatory intervention (Supervisory Ladder). Under this CEIOPS scheme,[133] the first stage addresses actions by the regulatory authorities in the area of compliance with capital requirements (Level A). This activity is restricted to monitoring future potential issues concerning the insurance undertaking. If necessary, supervisory authorities nevertheless may take action, such as if weaknesses or deficiencies in the internal model are discovered.[134]

The CEIOPS Issues Paper specifies that Level B is reached where an undertaking is in compliance with the Minimum Capital Requirement but not with the Solvency Capital Requirement, or if there is a foreseeable risk of non-compliance with the Solvency Capital Requirement within the coming 3 months. (Compare art. 138, para. 1 of the Solvency II Directive and sec. 125, para. 1 of the VAG-RegE [Government's Draft of a Tenth Act Amending the German Insurance Supervision Act]). Article 138 of the Solvency II Directive provides that the supervisory authority shall require the insurance undertaking to effect a remedy. This does

[132] This applies in the case of the capital add-on under art. 37 of the Solvency II Directive or for the requirement of a (partial) internal model under art. 119 of the Solvency II Directive, in the event that the standard model is not adequate for the risk status of the insurance undertaking. It does not apply, however, to the rules concerning powers to investigate a situation such as the basis to intervene for an on-site review, mentioned in art. 34, para. 5 of the Solvency II Directive, or to obtain information from third parties pursuant to art. 35, para. 2 of the Solvency II Directive. Nor does it apply to the powers of the regulatory authorities under art. 62 of the Solvency II Directive regarding natural or legal persons, who have taken a decision to acquire a qualifying holding and hence could have a negative influence on the "prudent management" of an insurance undertaking.

[133] Issues Paper, no. 4.45.

[134] Issues Paper no. 4.45: "Where necessary, the supervisor may require undertakings to remedy weaknesses or deficiencies identified in the SRP".

not apply, however, at least not directly, to the recovery plan of art. 138, para. 2 of the Solvency II Directive and sec. 125, para. 2 of the VAG-RegE [Government's Draft of a Tenth Act Amending the German Insurance Supervision Act] nor to the progress report of art. 138, para. 4, subpara. 2 of the Solvency II Directive and sec. 125, para. 4, sent. 2 of the VAG-RegE [Government's Draft of a Tenth Act Amending the German Insurance Supervision Act]. It does, however, apply to the requirement to re-establish own funds or to adjust the risk profile and to the prohibition or restriction on disposal of assets of the undertaking under art. 138, paras. 3 and 5 of the Solvency II Directive and sec. 125, para. 3, sents. 1 and 5 of the VAG-RegE [Government's Draft of a Tenth Act Amending the German Insurance Supervision Act]. The Issues Paper provides for further measures at Level B, such as the engagement of third parties to provide the supervisory authorities with information about the insurance undertaking.[135]

Level C is implicated when there is a shortfall with respect to the Minimum Capital Requirement or if such is foreseeable within the next 3 months. The measures provided for in art. 139 of the Solvency II Directive and sec. 126 of the VAG-RegE [Government's Draft of a Tenth Act Amending the German Insurance Supervision Act] are largely congruent with those that can be employed only in the case of a shortfall with respect to the Solvency Capital Requirement. The intensity of such measures may increase, however, without running afoul of the principle of proportionality. In addition, the conditions of art. 141 of the Solvency II Directive and sec. 128 of the VAG-RegE [Government's Draft of a Tenth Act Amending the German Insurance Supervision Act] are often met as well. According to these provisions, "where the solvency position of the undertaking continues to deteriorate" the supervisory authorities shall have the power to take all measures to safeguard the interests of policy holders and to ensure the obligations arising out of reinsurance contracts.

Also, in other places, Solvency II provides for special rules on intervention powers with respect to non-compliance with quantitative requirements. Thus, under art. 85 of the Solvency II Directive as implemented in sec. 79, para. 2 of the VAG-RegE [Government's Draft of a Tenth Act Amending the German Insurance Supervision Act], the supervisory authority may require an increase in the amount of the technical provisions if the calculations of insurance undertakings do not comply with legal provisions.

2.5.4 Non-compliance with Requirements on Governance

Under art. 36, para. 5 of the Solvency II Directive, weaknesses and deficiencies in the system of governance of insurance undertakings must be remedied.

[135] Issues Paper, no. 4.45. This power is conferred by art. 35 para. 2 (c) of the Solvency II Directive.

The determination that such weaknesses and deficiencies exist must be limited to the effect that a minimum standard provided by the Solvency II Directive has not been met.[136] The power of the supervisory authorities is limited to restoring this minimum standard. There is a particular issue in regard to supervision of governance as to the specific permissible content of regulatory demands. Insurance undertakings are required only to keep their system of governance above a minimum level and need not examine it with a fine-tooth comb, insofar as they meet the prescribed standards. The supervisory authorities, on the other hand, whose supervisory measures must be determinable and are subject to the principle of proportionality, must make a perfect "three-point landing" with their measures, since they must determine these within the parameters of minimum standards. The rule of law prohibits supervisory authorities from employing measures to restore legal requirements in "at least" merely abstract form. Consider the notion that they might have a scope of mandate that is unreviewable or reviewable only to a limited extent. In German administrative law this would be a discretion in the area of legal consequences. This notion would be conceivable if at all in the area of implemented European insurance supervisory regimes and then only under the authority of the previously described[137] proviso that relevant ECJ rulings are applicable to the insurance supervisory regime. Until such determination, however, the principle applies that the supervisory discretion is fully reviewable by the courts regarding its misuse. Further, the principle of proportionality requires that for any instance the most moderate appropriate measure shall be imposed to remedy weaknesses or deficiencies. Other means would not be required and thus would be disproportionate.

In the practical application of the law, however, this ideally precise definition of a minimum standard cannot be achieved. But this must be taken into account in that supervisory authorities must pay particular attention to the principles of supervisory transparency[138] in art. 31, para. 1 of the Solvency II Directive and sec. 312, para. 2, no. 2 of the VAG-RegE [Government's Draft of a Tenth Act Amending the German Insurance Supervision Act] and to the proportionality of a measure. An obvious example in this area is the capital add-on because of an insufficient system of governance under art. 37, para. 1, sent. 2 (c) of the Solvency II Directive and sec. 295 para. 1, sent. 1, no. 3 of the VAG-RegE [Government's Draft of a Tenth Act Amending the German Insurance Supervision Act]. The capital add-on of art. 37, para. 1, sent. 2 (a) and sec. 295, para. 1, sent. 1, no. 1 of the VAG-RegE [Government's Draft of a Tenth Act Amending the German Insurance Supervision Act] is a supervisory tool that takes into account the potential discrepancy between the actual risk status and the assumptions underlying the calculation of the Solvency Capital Requirement. The supervisory authority likewise can prescribe a capital add-on to the extent that the system of governance of an insurance undertaking is

---

[136] Compare to the prohibition on optimization above, at 2.5.1.2.

[137] See 2.5.1.3, above.

[138] *Bürkle*, n. 28 above, 1476.

substantially deficient. The capital add-on is a tool of last resort,[139] but this does not rule out lesser measures.[140] Such measures would be those that address violations with means other than imposition of a capital add-on. In order to impose a capital add-on, the supervisory authority must convert a qualitative deficiency into a quantitative measure,[141] thus, in a manner of speaking, squaring the circle.

2.6 Summary

1. The new scheme of insurance supervision under Solvency II adheres to the principles of risk orientation, assessment orientation, economization, and process orientation. Under Solvency II, supervisory authorities monitor in increased measure the activities of insurance undertakings and not merely their results.
2. The Supervisory Review Process is an ongoing procedure, which serves to establish whether insurance undertakings have in place adequate strategies, processes, and reporting procedures to achieve the prescribed supervisory objectives. The Supervisory Review Process is designed to facilitate timely supervisory intervention in the event of a legal infringement by an insurance undertaking. Supervisory authorities conduct the supervisory procedure on an individual, risk-based footing.
3. Pursuant to CEIOPS advice, the Supervisory Review Process takes place in four stages. Using the Report to Supervisors (RTS) and the Solvency and Financial Condition Report (SFCR), supervisory authorities can undertake an initial assessment of the risk profile in order to limit potential supervisory measures. There should be ongoing follow-up to the assessment of the risk profile. As soon as the supervisory authority learns of a weakness or deficiency, it can take appropriate remedial measures.
4. The supervisory authority's evaluation of whether the strategies, processes, and reporting procedures of an insurance undertaking are in compliance with the governance requirements of art. 36, paras. 1 and 2 (a) of the Solvency II Directive and sect 289, para. 3, sent. 2 and para. 4 of the VAG-RegE [Government's Draft of a Tenth Act Amending the German Insurance Supervision Act]

[139] Recital 27 and art. 37, para. 1, sent. 1 of the Solvency II Directive and sec. 295, para. 1 of the VAG-RegE [Government's Draft of a Tenth Act Amending the German Insurance Supervision Act].

[140] See *Sehrbrock*, "Rechtsprobleme des Kapitalaufschlags" [in English: Legal Problems of the Capital Add-on], ZVersWiss (2010), 665 (669).

[141] Thus on point, *Sehrbrock*, n. 140 above, at 679, which points out that the Directive contains an inherent contradiction. This is so because it contains qualitative provisions because some risks cannot be quantified. This is precisely the objective of the governance capital add-on under art. 37, para. 1, sent. 2 (c) of the Solvency II Directive and sec. 295, para. 1, sent. 1, no. 3 of the VAG-RegE [Government's Draft of a Tenth Act Amending the German Insurance Supervision Act].

requires that numerous undefined legal requirements be given judgmental content. In the areas involving economic fact situations, if any, the supervisory authority may align itself with findings of experts in the field of economics. In this regard, the limitation must be accounted for that Solvency II prescribes only legal minimum standards for the governance, capitalization, and other regulated areas of insurance undertakings. This is the case insofar as a supervisory prohibition on optimization applies while the autonomously operating insurance undertaking, oriented toward findings in the field of economics, adheres to an order on optimization. By contrast, the CEIOPS suggestion to create groups of comparable undertakings, in order to identify where each undertaking stands in the group and possibly thereafter to institute measures, constitutes an incorrect approach.

5. Assignment of the Supervisory Review Process to the realm of financial supervision in sec. 289, para. 3, sent. 2 of the VAG-RegE [Government's Draft of a Tenth Act Amending the German Insurance Supervision Act] is incorrect and entails substantial legal consequences.
6. The future-looking approach of supervision over technical provisions will encounter legal obstacles because of the long time periods this approach must take into account.
7. In order to make the supervisory evaluation whether the strategies, processes, and reporting procedures are sufficient to ensure that capital requirements are identified and met, supervisory authorities require detailed information on the risk status of the supervised insurance undertakings. In this process, the ORSA findings of the insurance undertakings play a prominent role. In addition, supervisory authorities will employ quantitative and qualitative early warning indicators of potential non-compliance with capital requirements.
8. By considering the capital investment spectrum and the processes conjoined with the investments, supervisory authorities will evaluate whether an insurance undertaking is complying with the permissible investment provisions. Successful inclusion of the investment process in the risk management system of the insurance undertaking is a key factor in compliance with provisions.
9. The phrase "weakness or deficiencies" within the meaning of art. 36, para. 5 of the Solvency II Directive constitutes a uniform legal requirement, whose criteria are met if the strategies, processes, and reporting procedures of an insurance undertaking fail to meet a legally prescribed minimum standard and thus a legal requirement is violated. Accordingly, art. 36, para. 5 of the Solvency II Directive is a part of supervision of legality under the Solvency II Directive.
10. The implementation of art. 36, para. 5 of the Solvency II Directive, under which supervisory authorities must have the intervention powers necessary to require insurance undertakings to remedy weaknesses or deficiencies, has missed the mark and contravenes European law, in that secs. 289 and 292 of the VAG-RegE [Government's Draft of a Tenth Act Amending the German Insurance Supervision Act] retain supervision according to the principles of abusiveness.

11. The general intervention powers in art. 36, para. 5 of the Solvency II Directive have been specified in part in other rules as *leges speciales*. A measure is not permissible when the conditions precedent for the special basis for intervention are not present.
12. In practice, regulatory interventions into the area of compliance with regulatory capital requirements proceed by stages. In this process, intensity of intervention increases as capital strength decreases.
13. Pursuant to the principle of proportionality, supervisory authorities must thoroughly examine the minimum standard to be met by insurance undertakings in their governance, their capitalization, and the other Solvency II requirements. An insurance undertaking's non-compliance with such legal rules does not confer a supervisory mandate to restore "at least" the minimum standard.

Chapter 3
Insurance Supervisory Law and Consumer Protection

Contents

3.1 Introduction 68
3.2 Consumer Protection Provisions of the New Insurance Supervisory Regime 69
3.2.1 The EIOPA Regulation 69
3.2.2 The Solvency II Directive 71
3.2.3 The Draft Regulation on Key Information Documents and the Draft Directive on Insurance Mediation 72
3.2.4 The Second and Third Regulatory Levels of the Solvency II System 72
3.2.5 The VAG-RegE [Government's Draft of a Tenth Act Amending the German Insurance Supervision Act] 73
3.2.6 The BaFin [Federal Financial Supervisory Authority] 74
3.3 The Role of Consumer Protection in the Supervision of Insurance Undertakings 75
3.3.1 The Objective of Supervision 75
3.3.2 Further Implications 77
3.4 Summary 94

Abstract This chapter discusses the relationship between insurance supervisory law and consumer protection within the ambit of Solvency II and the EIOPA system. To this, the article focuses on existing laws, with particular regard given to European rules on insurance supervision. The Solvency II Directive takes as its exclusive objective the protection of insureds and insurance beneficiaries. Solvency II does not address consumer protection. Nevertheless, consumer protection is a significant by-product of the Solvency II rules, in the sense of collective consumer protection. The EIOPA Regulation provisions, too, address consumer protection solely in the realm of collective consumer protection. The applicable profile is that of the mature and discerning consumer. The consumer protection guidelines of EIOPA on handling of complaints have no legal basis in the EIOPA Regulation.

First published as "Versicherungsaufsichtsrecht und Verbraucherschutz im Solvency-II- und EIOPA-System" [in English: The Insurance Supervisory Regime and Consumer Protection in the Solvency II and EIOPA System], VersR (2013), 401 ff.

M. Dreher, *Treatises on Solvency II*, DOI 10.1007/978-3-662-46290-4_3

3.1 Introduction

The concept of consumer protection in insurance immediately brings to mind insurance contract law. But the subject matter of insurance contract law is not consumer protection but solely protection of the policy holder.[1] At the same time, consumer protection constitutes one of the main subjects of legal policy and thus encompasses the insurance supervisory regime. In fact, under art. 1, para. 6, subpara. 1 sent. 2 f of the EIOPA Regulation,[2] one of the objectives of EIOPA, the European insurance supervisory authority, is "enhancing customer protection."

Against this background, the first issue to be addressed concerns what existing legal provisions on the subject consumer protection the EIOPA Regulation and the Solvency II Framework Directive contain,[3] taking note of their equally ranked and successive regulatory levels. Attention must also be given to the provisions appearing in the government's draft of the new VAG [German Insurance Supervision Act][4] (3.2, below). It is upon this basis then that the role of consumer protection in the supervision of insurance undertakings must be determined. Particular attention in the following remarks will then be directed to the supervision objective (3.3.1, below) and consequences relating to the insurance supervisory regime's existing prohibition on optimization (3.3.2.1, below), to the indirect consumer protection function of insurance supervisory regime (3.3.2.2, below), to EIOPA activities in the set of consumer and policy holder protections in the form of guidelines on complaints-handling (3.3.2.3, below), and to collecting consumer trends (3.3.2.4, below). Above all and finally, some questions on the future relationship of consumer protection and the insurance supervisory regime will be addressed (3.3.2.5, below).

---

[1] See in more detail, *Brand*, "Verbraucherschutz im Versicherungsrecht" [in English: Consumer Protection in Insurance Law], in: E. Lorenz, ed., Karlsruher Forum 2011: Verbraucherschutz – Entwicklungen und Grenzen [in English: Karlsruher Forum 2011: Consumer Protection – Developments and Limits] (2012), 55 (59 f.).

[2] Regulation (EU) No 1094/2010 of the European Parliament and of the Council of 24 Nov. 2010, OJEU L 331 [Official Journal of the EU], 15 Dec. 2010, 48.

[3] Directive 2009/137/EC of the European Parliament and of the Council of 25 Nov. 2009, OJEU L 335, 17 Dec. 2009,1.

[4] RegE eines Zehnten Gesetzes zur Änderung des VAG [Government's Draft of a Tenth Act Amending the German Insurance Supervision Act] of 15 Feb. 2012, BT-Drucks. [Document of the German Bundestag] 17/9342, also found at BR-Drucks. [Document of the German Bundesrat] 90/12 (hereafter VAG-RegE).

3.2 Consumer Protection Provisions of the New Insurance Supervisory Regime

3.2.1 The EIOPA Regulation

The EIOPA Regulation forms the foundation of the relationship between the insurance supervisory regime and consumer protection. Under art. 1, para. 6, subpara. 1, sent. 2 f. of the EIOPA Regulation, "the Authority" expressly "contributes to enhancing customer protection." This contribution, although the last-named of six areas of "contributing", is incorporated into the objective of art. 1, para. 6, subpara. 1, sent. 1 of the EIOPA Regulation. Under this provision, "The objective of the Authority shall be to protect the public interest by contributing to the short, medium and long-term stability and effectiveness of the financial system, for the Union economy, its citizens and businesses."[5]

The objective of "enhancing customer protection" will be achieved only if EIOPA in addition receives concrete tasks and powers. These are to be found in art. 8, para. 2 i and art. 9 of the EIOPA Regulation. First of all, in art. 8, para. 1 j, the EIOPA Regulation directs that the Authority shall "fulfil any other specific tasks set out in this Regulation... ." Thus, this mandate includes the "Tasks related to consumer protection and financial activities," as set forth in the heading of art. 9. Paragraph 1 of Article 9 addresses consumer protection[6] as does all of art. 9, contrary to its somewhat unclear heading. The introduction of Paragraph 1 states:

> The Authority shall take a leading role in promoting transparency, simplicity and fairness in the market for consumer financial products or services across the internal market.

Four such tasks are then enumerated by way of example, viz.: collecting, analyzing, and reporting on consumer trends; mediating financial literacy and education initiatives[7]; developing training standards; and contributing to the development of the common disclosure rules. Thus, the transparency mentioned at the outset of the Article is of prime importance within these tasks. In view of the tasks and powers delegated to the EIOPA in the area of consumer protection, one may see at once that the issues concern only collective consumer protection and do not (also) touch individual consumer protection matters.

---

[5] Compare also Recital 10, sent. 3 of the EIOPA Regulation, under which the EIOPA is to "strengthen international supervisory coordination, for the benefit of the economy at large, including....consumers" with Recital 66 of the EIOPA Regulation enumerating the "objectives of this Regulation" but not naming consumer protection.

[6] See Recital 2, EIOPA Board of Supervisors, EIOPA procedures for issuing warnings, temporary prohibitions and restrictions of 12 Nov. 2012.

[7] See on this point EIOPA Report on Financial Literacy and Education Initiatives by Competent Authorities of 16 Dec. 2011.

EIOPA powers arise both from special provisions and also generally from art. 8, para. 2 of the EIOPA Regulation. Article 8 states that "the Authority shall have the powers set out in this Regulation... ." Letter i of this paragraph names particularly the power to "develop common methodologies for assessing the effect of product characteristics and distribution processes on the financial position of institutions and on consumer protection... ." This power is fleshed out in art. 32, para. 2, sent. 2 c of the EIOPA Regulation. Under this provision,

> the Authority shall develop for application by the competent authorities: "...(c) common methodologies for assessing the effect of particular products or distribution processes on an institution's financial position and on policyholders, pension scheme members, beneficiaries, and customer information."

Further, art. 9 of the EIOPA Regulation assigns the Authority special powers pertaining to consumer protection. Among these are the very far-reaching powers under para. 3 to issue "warnings in the event that a financial activity poses a serious threat to the objectives laid down... ." Moreover, under para. 5, the EIOPA can go so far as to "temporarily prohibit or restrict certain financial activities... ." Of course, narrow and specifically defined conditions must be met for the application of these powers.[8]

In addition, art. 37, para. 2, sent. 1 of the EIOPA Regulation addresses consumer organizations. The Insurance and Reinsurance Stakeholder Group is to include "consumers" "in balanced proportions" to the other groups included.[9] And finally, consumer protection under the EIOPA Regulation is also significant in connection with a Member State's recourse to the safeguard clause of art. 38 of the EIOPA Regulation to fend off a perceived interference in its fiscal responsibilities. Art. 38, para. 5 of the EIOPA Regulation bars Member States from "abuse" of the safeguard clause, "in particular in relation to a decision by the Authority which does not have a significant or material fiscal impact... ." Particulars substantiating this provision are set forth in Recital 50, sent. 4 of the EIOPA Regulation. As examples of such EIOPA decisions, the Recital adduces—in somewhat awkward language—such impacts "as a reduction of income linked to the temporary prohibition of specific activities or products for consumer protection purposes." The EIOPA possesses the prohibitory power implicit in this provision under the already noted art. 9, para. 5 of the EIOPA Regulation pertaining to consumer protection.

Based on art. 9, para. 4 of the EIOPA Regulation, the EIOPA ultimately considers itself warranted in setting up a Committee on Consumer Protection and Financial Innovation (CCPFI). This Committee has the special characteristic that it also comprises national authorities that do not belong to the EIOPA as national insurance supervisory authorities but that do, however, fulfill certain functions in

[8] See in general EIOPA Board of Supervisors, *id.*, n. 6, above.

[9] See similarly Recital 47, sent. 3 of the EIOPA Regulation.

the area of supervising insurance mediation.[10] This Committee is to contribute to the work of the EIOPA in the areas of consumer protection and financial innovation. A part of this contribution is to be the presentation of draft technical standards, policies, and advice. Despite the absence of pertinent legislation, the CCPFI members remarkably have awarded themselves extensive tasks and powers with the express objective "to complement the provisions in the EIOPA Regulation".[11]

3.2.2 *The Solvency II Directive*

The Solvency II Directive contains the phrase "consumer protection" only in Recital 79, where it is stated: "In an internal market for insurance, consumers have a wider and more varied choice of contracts." In order for consumers to benefit from that diversity and the results of competition,

> consumers should be provided with whatever information is necessary before the conclusion of the contract and throughout the term of the contract to enable them to choose the contract best suited to their needs.

The Solvency II Directive, however, sets forth its fundamental objectives without any reference to consumer protection. Recital 16 and arts. 27 and 28 of the Solvency II Directive identify the protection of policy holders and beneficiaries of indemnity payments as the main objective. Of lesser importance are financial stability and fair and stable markets, which are of equal weight.[12] As may be seen also in Recital 17, the Solvency II Directive rules on solvency are not directed so much toward consumers as toward policy holders.[13] In those places where the Directive does distinguish among persons, the distinctions are nevertheless not oriented toward the concept of the consumer. For example, the duty to inform set forth in the non-life insurance provisions of art. 183, para. 2 of the Solvency II Directive applies only when the policy holder is a "natural person." A further example is seen in art. 186, para. 2 b of the Solvency II Directive, which allows Member States to omit a cancellation provision,

[10] See EIOPA CCPFI Mandate of 29 Mar. 2012, sent. 1.

[11] EIOPA, CCPFI Mandate, *id.*, n. 10 above, at 2.

[12] See in detail, *Dreher/Häußler,* "Die Aufsicht über Versicherungsunternehmen durch die BaFin und die Überwachungsaufgabe des Aufsichtsrat" [in English: Supervision of Insurance Undertakings by BaFin [Federal Financial Supervisory Authority] and the Monitoring Task of the Supervisory Board], ZGR (2011), 471 (485); *Wandt/Sehrbrock,* "Regelungsziele der Solvency II-Rahmenrichtlinie" [in English: Regulatory Objectives of the Solvency II Framework Directive], ZVersWiss (2011), 193 (195 ff.).

[13] See *Dreher,* "Solvenzanforderungen in der Versicherungsaufsicht nach Solvency II und künftigem VAG" [in English: Solvency Requirements in Insurance Supervision under Solvency II and the Future German Insurance Supervision Act], ZVersWiss (2012), 381 (384) (Chap. 4, below, at 4.2.2).

where, because of the status of the policy holder or the circumstances in which the contract is concluded, the policy holder does not need special protection.

3.2.3 The Draft Regulation on Key Information Documents and the Draft Directive on Insurance Mediation

In like manner, the new plans under European law to introduce a regulation on "information documents for investment products" are divorced from any concept relating to consumers.[14] Under art. 2 (a), the regulation shall apply also to the marketing of certain insurance products. The key information document, however, is not intended especially for consumers; rather, under art. 4 (c) of the proposed regulation, it targets "retail investors." These are defined as "retail clients" within the meaning of the Markets in Financial Instruments Directive (MIFID, hereafter: MIFID Directive), i.e., as non-professional clients, and as "customers" within the meaning of the Directive on Insurance Mediation. The proposal for a new directive on insurance mediation is also tied in with the concept of the "customer."[15]

3.2.4 The Second and Third Regulatory Levels of the Solvency II System

The draft of an implementing regulation [DVO][16] for the second regulatory level of the Solvency II Directive does not contain any provisions on consumer protection.

For Level 3, the CEIOPS Consultation Paper, *Draft Proposal for Level 3 Guidelines on the System of Governance*, of December 2010,[17] mentions consumer protection law in refs. 3.46 and 3.48 in relation to the inquiry into repute and integrity within the meaning of art. 42, para. 1 b of the Solvency II Directive. This mention occurs in the explanations to Guideline 13. Under this authority, breaches of consumer protection law would be taken into consideration in the inquiry into repute and integrity.[18]

---

[14] See the Proposal for a Regulation, COM (2012) 352 (final); also at BR-Drucks. [Document of the German Bundesrat] 388/12 of 4 Jul. 2012.

[15] See the Proposal for a Directive, COM (2012) 360 (final); also at BR-Drucks. [Document of German Bundesrat] 389/12, 4 Jul. 2012.

[16] The abbreviation DVO-E when used here and after in reference to the Level 2 DVO signifies the EU Commission draft known as *Draft Implementing Measures Solvency II*, 31 Oct. 2011.

[17] Hereafter: Governance Guidelines.

[18] For a critical view, see *Dreher*, "Die aufsichtsbehördliche Kontrolle der Inhaber von Schlüsselfunktionen nach Solvency II und künftigem VAG" [in English: Review by Supervisory Authorities of the Holders of Key Functions under Solvency II and the Future German Insurance Supervision Act], VersR (2012), 1061 (1067) (Chap. 8, below, at 8.3.2.1).

3.2.5 The VAG-RegE [Government's Draft of a Tenth Act Amending the German Insurance Supervision Act]

The VAG-RegE [Government's Draft of a Tenth Act Amending the German Insurance Supervision Act] addresses consumer protection only to note that earlier VAG [German Insurance Supervision Act] rules, such as secs. 10,10 a, 157, para. 1, sent. 2 of the superseded version, are now "obsolete" due to enhancements of insurance contract law, in particular with regard to consumer information.[19] In addition, sec. 319, para 2, sent. 2 of the VAG-RegE [Government's Draft of a Tenth Act Amending the German Insurance Supervision Act] denotes representatives of consumer organizations as persons who should be a part of the Insurance Advisory Council to be assembled by the BaFin [Federal Financial Supervisory Authority]. Likewise, the primary provision on legislative intent, found in sec. 1, para. 1 of the VAG-RegE [Government's Draft of a Tenth Act Amending the German Insurance Supervision Act] relates not to consumers but generally to the "protection of insureds."

At the same time, secs. 1 and 292 of the VAG-RegE [Government's Draft of a Tenth Act Amending the German Insurance Supervision Act] propose to continue the undefined general supervision according to the principles of abusiveness, a practice that contravenes European law and German constitutional law, this despite the fact that the Solvency II Directive expressly allows only supervision of legality.[20] As pertaining to the present subject matter under investigation, this result follows from other rules, which have not been considered in relation to the only legal supervision that will be permissible in the future. Initially, this applies in the case of art. 181, para. 1, subpara. 2, sent. 1 of the Solvency II Directive to review by supervisory authorities of general policy conditions in the area of life insurance. Under this provision,

> Member States may require non-systematic notification of those policy conditions and other documents only for the purpose of verifying compliance with national provisions concerning insurance contracts.

Further support for the proposition that only legal supervision is possible may be found in art. 182, para. 2, sent. 1 of the Solvency II Directive. That provision concerns life insurance and allows the Member State of origin to

---

[19] VAG-RegE [Government's Draft of a Tenth Act Amending the German Insurance Supervision Act], *id.*, n. 4 above, Begründung [Statement of Reasons], 258, 311.

[20] See on this point *Dreher/Lange*, "Die Vollharmonisierung der Versicherungsaufsicht durch Solvency II" [in English: Full Harmonization of Insurance Supervision under Solvency II], VersR (2011), 825 (Chap. 1, above); *Bürkle*, "Die Zukunft der materiellen Missstandsaufsicht in Deutschland" [in English: The Future in Germany of Substantive Supervision According to the Principles of Abusiveness], VersR (2011), 1469; *Bürkle/Grote*, "Die aufsichtsbehördlichen Eingriffsbefugnisse nach Solvency II" [in English: Supervisory Intervention Powers under Solvency II] in: Dreher/Wandt, eds., Solvency II in der Rechtsanwendung [in English: Solvency II in Legal Application] (2009), 191 ff.(225 ff.); *Kaulbach* in: Bähr, ed., Handbuch des Versicherungsaufsichtsrechts [in English: Manual of Insurance Supervisory Regime] (2011) sec. 8, end of ref. 46.

> require systematic communication of the technical bases used in particular for calculating scales of premiums technical provisions.

This passage provides, however, that this requirement may be imposed

> for the sole purpose of verifying compliance with national provisions concerning actuarial principles.

Previously there has existed within the environment of supervision according to the principles of abusiveness a prohibition on limited coverage insurance,[21] a prohibition that lacked a basis in law. This prohibition will not survive.

3.2.6 The BaFin [Federal Financial Supervisory Authority]

The consumer protection rules of the EIOPA Regulation also have an influence on the national insurance supervisory regime,[22] although in fact consumer protection has not thus far been mentioned in the legal bases of BaFin [Federal Financial Supervisory Authority] activity. Nevertheless, according to the BaFin [Federal Financial Supervisory Authority], the general clause on supervision in the VAG [German Insurance Supervision Act] should encompass the objective of consumer protection.[23] And in line with this view, the Gesetz zur Stärkung der deutschen Finanzaufsicht [Act to Strengthen German Financial Supervision] has created a new Consumer Advisory Council at BaFin [Federal Financial Supervisory Authority].[24] In fact, the policy argument is being made that consumer protection should

---

[21] See criticizing, e.g., the asserted danger of misleading and the innovation-inhibiting effect, *Dreher*, Die Versicherung als Rechtsprodukt [in English: Insurance as a Legal Product] (1991), 223 f.; for still another view, *Präve* in: Prölss, VAG [German Insurance Supervision Act] (12th ed. 2005) sec. 8, ref. 25.

[22] On the parallel issue for credit institutions, see the answer of the German Federal Government to a parliamentary question: Aufsichtspraxis der BaFin und finanzieller Verbraucherschutz [in English: Supervisory practices of the BaFin [Federal Financial Supervisory Authority] and financial consumer protection], BT-Drucks. [Document of the German Bundestag] 17/8889, 6 Mar. 2012 and specifically from the consumer protection point of view, *Reifner*, "Europäische Finanzaufsicht und Verbraucherschutz – wie kann der Schutz der Verbraucherinteressen in die BaFin integriert werden?" [in English: European Financial Supervision and Consumer Protection – How Can Protection of Consumers' Interests be Integrated into the Federal Financial Supervisory Authority?] *VuR* (2011), 410 and the articles in *Keßler/Micklitz/Reich*, eds., "Institutionelle Finanzmarktaufsicht und Verbraucherschutz" [in English: Institutional Financial Market Supervision and Consumer Protection] (2010).

[23] See BaFin-Journal (Oct. 2011) 3; see on the earlier critical corresponding BAV [German Insurance Supervisory Agency] position, *Dreher*, *id*., n. 21 above, at 213 ff., 232.

[24] RegE [Government's Draft] BT-Drucks. [Document of the German Bundestag] 17/10040; see also the answer of the German Federal Government to a parliamentary question on "Verbraucherorganisationen und ihre Marktwächterfunktion als Teil der systematischen verbraucherorientierten Beobachtung des Finanzmarkts" [in English: Consumer organizations and market monitoring functions as part of the consumer-oriented supervision of the financial markets] BT-Drucks. [Document of the German Bundestag] 17/11751.

be fixed as a proprietary supervisory objective for the BaFin [Federal Financial Supervisory Authority].[25] Apart from the development of legal bases, the national insurance supervisory authorities are also compelled to attend to consumer protection issues if the EIOPA produces applicable guidelines and advice.

3.3 The Role of Consumer Protection in the Supervision of Insurance Undertakings

3.3.1 The Objective of Supervision

As has been seen in the systematic collection of references concerning consumer protection law in the future European insurance supervisory regime,[26] consumer protection has no role to play in supervision of insurance undertakings under the Solvency II Directive. A different situation obtains in reference to the EIOPA Regulation. Herein there appears to be a conflict between the European insurance supervision regime and European law as it relates to insurance supervisory authorities. In point of fact, however, this is not the case.

The determinative factors demonstrating the absence of a conflict are the objectives of the two legal acts and their rules on tasks and powers. It has been noted above that the main objective of the Solvency II Directive is the protection of insureds and of beneficiaries of indemnification payments, without regard to whether they are consumers. The subsidiary objectives of financial stability and of fair and stable markets do not touch upon consumer protection in any case. This is so because the concept of fairness, which also appears in the EIOPA Regulation, is not peculiarly the province of consumer issues.

These objectives of the Solvency II Directive do not alter any aspect of the EIOPA Regulation. To the contrary, art. 1, para. 6, subpara. 1, sent. 2 of the EIOPA Regulation denotes the prime objective of the Authority to be "contributing to the short, medium, and long-term stability and effectiveness of the financial system" in the "public interest." This comports with the subsidiary objective of the Solvency II Directive. And the EIOPA's "task" under art. 8, para. 1 h of the EIOPA Regulation to foster "the protection of policyholders, pension scheme members, and beneficiaries" corresponds precisely with the main objective of the Solvency II Directive.

Under art. 1, para. 6, subpara. 1, sent. 2 f of the EIOPA Regulation, the Authority shall contribute to "enhancing consumer protection." To the extent the Authority does so, such action nevertheless does not affect the objectives of the Solvency II Directive and the role of the EIOPA in the application of this Directive. This conclusion follows i. a. directly from the fact that according to art. 1, para. 6, subpara. 1, sent. 2 of the EIOPA Regulation the Authority shall ensure the purposes within the

[25] According to the Partei Bündnis 90/Die Grünen [German green party] per a report in VW 17 (2011), 1207: "Verbraucherschützer wollen Finanzmarktwächter werden" [in English: Consumer Protection Watchdogs Seek to Become Financial Market Guardians].

[26] See 3.2.2 and 3.2.4, above.

meaning of art. 1, para. 6, subpara. 1, sent. 2 a through f of the EIOPA Regulation, by way of "efficient and effective application of the acts referred to in paragraph 2." There are 19 legal acts in the paragraph referred to here. Along with the Solvency II Directive itself, these include not only the 13 acts repealed since 1 Nov. 2012 by art. 310 of the Solvency II Directive, but also, e.g., the Directive on Insurance Mediation, 2002/92/EC. According to Recital 8 of this Directive "the coordination of national provisions on professional requirements" for insurance brokers is meant to contribute "both to the completion of the single market for financial services and to the enhancement of customer protection in this field." In line with this objective, the consumer frequently appears as the addressee of regulations in this Directive.[27] Against this background, it becomes clear that the consumer protection functions of the EIOPA under art. 1, para. 6, subpara. 1, sent. 2 f. art. 8, para. 2 i, and art. 9 of the EIOPA Regulation do not pertain to the responsibility of the EIOPA in connection with applying the Solvency II Directive. Rather, these functions relate solely to legal acts directed toward consumer protection.

This result is seen also when the adoption of the EIOPA Regulation on the one hand and the Solvency II Directive on the other are examined with a view to areas of responsibility. The legal basis of Solvency II Directive is the regulation of the free movement of services, formerly art. 47, paras. 2 and 55 of the EGV [Treaty on the European Community]. By contrast, the EIOPA Regulation is based on art. 114 of the Treaty on the Functioning of the European Union (TFEU), the rule governing competence for provisions "which have as their object the establishment and functioning of the internal market." Consumer protection is not addressed in this rule, but in art 169, para. 1 of the TFEU. The relevant means are mentioned in art. 169, para. 2 of the TFEU, including measures adopted pursuant to art. 114 of the TFEU. Thus, the EIOPA Regulation comes full circle. To the extent the Regulation pursues consumer protection concerns, measures pursuant to art. 169, para. 2 a of the TFEU are involved. In contrast, the Solvency II Directive does not serve the purposes of consumer protection, but rather the implementation of basic freedoms for the purpose realizing the internal market for insurance.[28]

In the final analysis, this assignment and determination of competence is congruent with the substantive regulatory content of the EIOPA Regulation. This is so because the consumer protection tasks and powers set forth in art 8, para. 2 i and art. 9 of the EIOPA Regulation are essentially independent of supervision over the licensing and activities of insurance undertakings and others to whom the rule is directed, as subject matter of the Solvency II Directive. In substance, the EIOPA Regulation is concerned with developments and trends, assessments, and transparency with regard to consumer protection.

[27] See Recitals 17, 18, 22, and 23. This point is continued in Recitals 5 ff.: Proposal for a Directive of the European Parliament and of the Council on Insurance Mediation (recast) COM (2012) 360 (final); also at BR-Drucks. [Document of the German Bundesrat] 389/12, 4 Jul. 2012.

[28] See for more details on the internal insurance market in relation to basic freedoms, *Rittner/Dreher*, "Europäisches und deutsches Wirtschaftsrecht" [in English: European and German Economic Law] (3rd ed. 2008), sec. 31, ref. 1 ff.

3.3.2 *Further Implications*

3.3.2.1 The Prohibition on Optimization in the Supervisory Review Process Under Solvency II and the European Law "High Level of Protection" in Consumer Protection

As shown by Recital 16, the Solvency II Directive as a whole pursues "adequate protection of policy holders and beneficiaries" as the "main objective of insurance and reinsurance regulation and supervision."[29] This objective is also served by the supervisory review process (SRP) under art. 36 of the Solvency II Directive. This process is designed to "ensure that the supervisory authorities review and evaluate the strategies, processes, and reporting procedures which are established by the insurance and reinsurance undertakings to comply with the laws, regulations, and administrative provisions adopted pursuant to this Directive."[30] Art. 36, para. 2 of the Solvency II Directive identifies the subject matter of this process, the core of which comprises the governance, capital, and risk-related requirements of the Solvency II Directive. Consumer protection is not a part of this core group, nor is it part of the objective of the process under art. 36, para. 1 of the Solvency II Directive. Further, consumer protection is not a concern in the rules on supervisory authority powers in this process.

Pursuant to the Solvency II Directive's wording and scheme, a prohibition on optimization applies to the SRP.[31] This is so because the Directive's requirements for insurance undertakings and the provisions on licensing and activities establish only the required supervisory level, i. e., the minimum level. With regard to insurance undertakings, which are the ones toward whom the insurance supervisory regime is directed, supervisory authorities can therefore enforce compliance only with what is legally required. And thus the future legal situation under art. 36 of the Solvency II Directive and sec. 289 of the VAG-RegE [Government's Draft of a Tenth Act Amending the German Insurance Supervision Act] corresponds to the legal situation under the hitherto existing VAG [German Insurance Supervision Act].[32]

---

[29] For example, Recital 98 of the Solvency II Directive refers to an "adequate level of protection" in relation to group supervision.

[30] See in detail *Dreher/Ballmaier*, "Das aufsichtliche Überprüfungsverfahren nach Art. 36 Solvency II-Richtlinie und § 289 VAG-RegE" [in English: The Supervisory Review Process under Art. 36 of the Solvency II Directive and Sec. 289 of the Government's Draft of a Tenth Act Amending the German Insurance Supervision Act] in: Dreher/Wandt, eds., Solvency II in der Rechtsanwendung [in English: Solvency II in Legal Application] (2012), 73 ff. (Chap. 2, above).

[31] See for more detail *Dreher/Ballmaier*, *id.*, n. 30 above, at 95, 109, 117.

[32] See on this point BVerwG [Federal Administrative Court], VersR (1981), 221 (223) on sec. 8, para. 1, sent. 1, no. 3. of the VAG [German Insurance Supervision Act]; *Rittner*, "Die Versicherungsaufsicht nach dem D.A.S.- Urteil des BVerwG" [in English: Insurance Supervision Following the D. A. S. Judgment of the Federal Administrative Court], VersR 1982, 205; *Dreher*, n. 21 above, at 215 ff.

While thus a prohibition on optimization applies to insurance company supervision under the Solvency II Directive, the TFEU, which is the legal basis of the EIOPA Regulation, in art. 114, para. 3 requires a "high level of protection" in the field of consumer protection.[33] This wording does not mean, however, that the Authority may seek the "highest" or "highest possible" level of protection in the field of consumer protection. According to a widespread view, even the so-called safeguard clause and extended safeguard clause for Member States in art 114, paras. 4 through 6, 9, and 10 and art. 169, para. 4 of the TFEU clarify that the phrase "high level of protection" signifies simply a minimum harmonization.[34]

The phrase "high level of protection," however, is also found in the EIOPA Regulation itself. Under art. 8, para. 1 i of the EIOPA Regulation, the Authority shall "contribute"

> to the consistent and coherent functioning of colleges of supervisors, the monitoring, assessment and measurement of systemic risk, the development and coordination of recovery and resolution plans, providing a high level of protection to policy holders, to beneficiaries and throughout the Union, in accordance with Articles 21 through 26.

In this passage, then, the criterion of a "high level of protection" does not relate to the consumer protection activities of the EIOPA, but rather to protection of policy holders and beneficiaries, as targeted by the Solvency II Directive.

Nevertheless, no conflict arises with the prohibition on optimization that applies to the SRP according to the Solvency II Directive. On the one hand, in the place at issue, art. 8, para. 1 i of the EIOPA Regulation, by pointing to arts. 21 through 26 of the Regulation, restricts its application to risk-oriented supervision by colleges of supervisors within the meaning of art. 212, para. 1 e and art. 248 para. 2 of the Solvency II Directive in cases of groups active across borders and in consideration of possible systemic risks and of development of a network of national guarantee schemes. Thus, the rule on the level of protection does not constitute for the SRP a standard in the nature of a general clause. Rather, they provide that the EIOPA, in consideration of the risk-oriented rules of the Solvency II Directive, also shall "contribute" to the protection of policy holders and beneficiaries. This objective is enunciated and pursued in numerous corresponding rules of the Solvency II Directive. In other words, the issue in this respect is solely the realization of the Solvency II Directive's goals through insurance supervision. The issue is not establishment of additional supervisory standards. Additional support for this point is seen in the wording of the level of protection for group supervision in

[33] See also art. 38 of the Charter of the Fundamental Rights of the European Union (CFREU): "Union policies shall ensure a high level of consumer protection".

[34] See, e.g., *Kahl*, in: Callies/Ruffert, eds., TFEU [Treaty on the Functioning of the European Union] (4th ed. 2011) art. 114, para. 35, and see with a partially different view, *Krebber*, in: Callies/Ruffert, eds., TFEU [Treaty on the Functioning of the European Union] (4th ed. 2011) art. 169, para. 14, each with further references.

Recital 98 of the Solvency II Directive, where the objective is stated as an adequate level of protection for policy holders and a level playing field between groups.

On the other hand, it is no contradiction to the foregoing that Recital 141 of the Solvency II Directive in reference to group supervision denotes the criterion of a "high level of policy holder (and beneficiary) protection" for the advice that CEIOPS may render for insurance and occupational pension matters. This is so because the Solvency II Directive defines the intended level of protection through the respective substantive content of the individual provision or set of provisions. Since the Directive's nature leans toward full harmonization, except in the places where wording such as "at least" appears or in the areas where Member States have a right of election,[35] EIOPA, too, is tied into achieving the regulatory content—and only this content—of the given standard as to the level of protection intended by the exhaustive provisions of the Directive. Thus, for insurance undertakings as the addressees of this regulation, this constitutes the level required by supervisory law in the sense of a minimum level, a level which the undertakings may voluntarily exceed; and it leads to the prohibition on optimization by the supervisory authorities. Ultimately then, the level of protection provided by the Directive flows from the Directive provisions themselves and not from the Solvency II Recitals. Recitals 16 and 98, noted above, merely characterize the established level of protection as "adequate," while Recital 141, also noted above, employs the word "high" to describe the level of protection in the regulatory area at issue there.

[35] See in detail *Dreher/Lange,* n. 20 above, at 825; *Bürkle,* n. 20 above, at 1469 (1472 f.); *Wandt/Sehrbrock,* n. 12 above, at 200; *Vogelgesang,* "Die Aufsicht über Rückversicherungsunternehmen nach Solvency II" [in English: Supervision of Reinsurance Undertakings under Solvency II], ZVersWiss (2011), 233 (243); *Saria,* "Compliance nach Solvency II" [in English: Compliance under Solvency II], VersRdsch 11 (2011), 21 (22); *Bürkle,* "Vorgaben der Richtlinie Solvabilität II für die Compliance in Versicherungsunternehmen" [in English: Requirements of the Solvency II Directive for Compliance in Insurance Undertakings] in: Looschelders/Michael, eds., Düsseldorfer Vorträge zum Versicherungsrecht 2010 [in English: Dusseldorf Lectures on Insurance Law], (2011) 1, 5. Unclear as to its basis – "The Directive does not provide full harmonization in all areas" – and inconsistent with the continuation of the existing VAG [German Insurance Supervision Act] provisions, VAG-RegE [Government's Draft of a Tenth Act Amending the German Insurance Supervision Act] 2012 *id.*, n. 4 above, at 255. Full harmonization is also the presumption of the Bundesrat [German Federal Council], as expressed in the Empfehlungen der Ausschüsse zu dem Entwurf eines Zehnten Gesetzes zur Änderung des VAG [Committee Advice on the Draft of a Tenth Act Amending the German Insurance Supervision Act] BR-Drucks. [Document of the German Bundesrat] 90/12, 16 Mar. 2012, Begründung [Statement of Reasons] for no. 15, at 14, thus: "not compatible with the 'full harmonization approach' of the Solvency II Directive"; these recommendation require – *id.*, no. 2, at 3: "a 1: 1 implementation of the Solvency II Directive." Also supporting full harmonization, *Wagner,* "Solvabilität II und VAG neu: Was bleibt, was ändert sich?" [in English: Solvency II and the New German Insurance Supervision Act: What is Unchanged? What is Changed?], VersRdsch 9 (2010), 23 (24, 26) and recently FMA [Financial Market Authority (Austria)– Österreichische Finanzmarktaufsicht Solvency II Handbuch [in English: Austrian Financial Market Authority Solvency II Manual] (2012), 1, 5 in reference to the "new rules" under Solvency II.

3.3.2.2 The Indirect Consumer Protection Function of the Insurance Supervisory Regime

Even though the Solvency II Directive neither is a consumer protection directive nor even has consumer protection as an objective, consumer protection effects indirectly arise from its individual rules. These effects are indirect, inasmuch as the rules do not especially apply to consumer protection—by whatever definition, a topic not addressed here,[36]—but apply only generally to policy holders and beneficiaries under insurance contracts.[37]

Perhaps the most important area where the insurance supervisory regime indirectly effects consumer protection is the realm of solvency supervision.[38] Even if the objective of solvency supervision[39] does not focus on the consumer, but, as expressed in Recital 17, on "better protection for policy holders" as a whole, protection of solvency through insurance supervision results in the best consumer protection.[40]

Also important in connection with this objective is the regulation on the Solvency and Financial Condition Report (SCFR), a completely new regulation in the area of the insurance supervisory regime following Solvency II. The SFCR is provided for in art. 51 of the Solvency II Directive and in sec. 50 of the VAG-RegE [Government's Draft of a Tenth Act Amending the German Insurance

[36] See for the definition frequently applied in European law, e.g., art. 2 d of Directive 2002/65/EC on the distance marketing of consumer financial services, OJEC L 271 of 9 Oct. 2002, at 16: "every natural person who...is acting for purposes which are outside his trade, business or profession." On the term "consumer" in European law, see *Dreher*, "Der Verbraucher – Das Phantom in den opera des europäischen und deutschen Rechts?" [in English: The Consumer – Phantom of the Opera in German and European Law?], JZ (1997), 167; and on the more recent view, *H. Roth*, "Verbraucherschutz – Entwicklungen und Grenzen" [in English: Consumer Protection – Developments and Limits] in: E. Lorenz, ed., Karlsruher Forum 2011: Verbraucherschutz – Entwicklungen und Grenzen [in English: Karlsruher Forum 2011: Consumer Protection – Developments and Limits], (2012), 5 (15 ff.).

[37] See, e.g., on group supervision Recital 105 of the Solvency II Directive: "All policy holders and beneficiaries should receive equal treatment[...]."

[38] On this point correctly, *König*, BaFin Journal 4 (2012), 13 (17) and in the context of Solvency II, *Romeike*, "Auswirkungen von Solvency II auf Verbraucher" [in English: Effects of Solvency II on Consumers] in: Brömmelmeyer/Heiss, et al., eds., Pflegeversicherung, Risikosteuerung und Versicherungsaufsicht, Europa, Versicherungsvertragsrecht [in English: Long-term Care Insurance, Risk Management, Insurance Supervision, Europe, Insurance Contract Law] (2009), 114 (130) (137).

[39] See in detail on this point, *Dreher*, n. 13 above, at 381.

[40] See, e.g., the response of the German Federal Government to the position of the German Federal Council on the Gesetz zur Stärkung der deutschen Finanzaufsicht [Act to Strengthen German Financial Supervision] BT-Drucks. [Document of the German Bundestag] 17/10252, 4. Jul. 2012, to no. 5: "Ensuring the solvency of the institutions and functioning of the financial markets is a basic cornerstone of overall investor and consumer protection."

Supervision Act][41] The objective of the SFCR is to increase transparency in the insurance market[42] and remove informational imbalances. There remains, however, the insoluble contradiction that the legal and economic requirements of solvency for policy holders and insureds, in particular for the consumers among them, are on the whole intransparent[43] by reason of their complexity, and perhaps even incomprehensible.

Insureds and beneficiaries are the true intended addressees of the public report,[44] since protection of these parties accords with the main objective of the Solvency II Directive.[45] Many policy holders and beneficiaries are also consumers, however that term may be defined. With respect to the contractual information under the Solvency II scheme, the SFCR can function as an additional source of information and thereby as an indirect and factual tool for consumer protection. On the issue of who is the primary addressee of the SFCR it has been argued[46] that the capital market fulfills this role. According to this view, the creation of market discipline constitutes the focus of the duty to inform with respect to the public. In other words, disclosure would occur with the objective of allowing market participants to make assessments. The result of these assessments would be, in some circumstances, corrective action by the market with regard to insurance undertakings.[47] This view contradicts not only the tiered objectives of the Solvency II Directive, but also the existence of additional very extensive duties to disclose imposed upon insurance undertakings by virtue of capital market and commercial law.[48] Further and not least significantly, the special pre-contractual duty to inform imposed upon insurance undertakings toward policy holders under art. 185, para. 2 d of the Solvency II Directive shows who the European legislator intended the main addressees of the report to be. That

---

[41] See in detail on this point, *Dreher/Schaaf*, "Die Veröffentlichungspflichten gegenüber der Allgemeinheit nach Solvency II" [in English: Duty of Disclosure to the Public under Solvency II] in: Dreher/Wandt, eds., Solvency II in der Rechtsanwendung [Solvency II in Legal Application] (2009), 129 ff. Chap. 13, below, and on the function of the SFCR in connection with the regulatory review process, *Dreher/Ballmaier id.*, n. 30 above, at 101 f. and on the duty of public disclosure related to ORSA, *Dreher/Ballmaier*, "Die unternehmenseigene Risiko- und Solvenzbeurteilung (ORSA) nach Solvency II und VAG 2012" [in English: Risk and Solvency Evaluation by Undertakings under Solvency II and the German Insurance Supervision Act 2012], VersR (2012), 129 (141 f.) (Chap. 5, below, at 5.8.4).

[42] See generally on the transparency principle, *Wandt*, "Transparency as a General Principle of Insurance Law" in: Wandt/Ünan, eds., Transparency in Insurance Law (2012) 9 ff.

[43] See in detail on this point, *Dreher*, n. 13 above, at 390.

[44] See 3.2.2, above.

[45] See in detail, *Dreher/Schaaf, id.*, n. 41 above, at 136 ff. The CEIOPS' Advice for Level 2 Implementing Measures on Solvency II: Supervisory Reporting and Public Disclosure Requirements of October 2009, no. 3.62. at 3.3.3: Disclosure audience (p. 26) is restricted to listing the potential readers of the report as exhaustively as possible, without hierarchical rating.

[46] See *Sehrbrock/Gal*, "Solvency II – Europäischer Rechtsrahmen einer neuen Versicherungsaufsicht" [in English: Solvency II – European Legal Framework of a New Insurance Supervision], CFL (2012), 140 (147).

[47] See, however, *Dreher/Schaaf, id.*, n. 41 above, at 138.

[48] See in detail, *Dreher/Schaaf, id.*, n. 41 above, at 153 ff.

provision requires a concrete reference to the report on the solvency and financial condition…, allowing the policy holder easy access to this information.

3.3.2.3 EIOPA in Between Consumer Protection and Insured Protection: The EIOPA Guidelines on Complaints-Handling as an Example

On 27 June 2012, EIOPA presented guidelines on complaints-handling by insurance undertakings.[49] The Guidelines are based on art. 16 of the EIOPA Regulation. A Best Practices Report and an Impact Assessment were issued along with the Guidelines.[50] The EIOPA Guidelines are aimed at the national supervisory authorities[51] and require these authorities to carry out the tasks listed below with regard to the undertakings they supervise, with appropriate subsidiary standards in individual cases:

- to put in place, publish, and implement a written complaints management policy, for which the undertaking's senior management is responsible,
- to create a complaints management function in the insurance undertakings,
- to ensure that insurance undertakings register complaints internally,
- to issue regular reports on complaints to the competent national authorities or ombudsman,
- to ensure that undertakings conduct internal analysis of complaints-handling and
- to put in place internal procedural rules for complaints-handling with regard to complainants, including the obligation to adhere to specific response and follow-up time lines.

Detailed further requirements are found in the introduction and in the epilogue to the EIOPA Guidelines. In this respect, the Guidelines direct attention to the Best Practices Report.

The issuance of the EIOPA Guidelines initially raises the basic issue of whether EIOPA has the requisite competence. On this point, it is indeed debatable whether a consumer protection measure or an insurance supervisory measure unrelated to consumer protection is at issue. The Impact Assessment[52] justifies the issuance of the EIOPA Guidelines as follows:

> In order to steer a harmonized approach to consumer outcomes and to mitigate regulatory discrepancies due to varying national provisions, EIOPA suggests the introduction of the guidelines.

In this context, the Impact Assessment explains that the process of creating the Guidelines included discussion of whether the Guidelines should cover only

---

[49] Hereafter: EIOPA Guidelines.

[50] All documentation is available on the EIOPA homepage under Consultation 2011.

[51] Inexplicably, EIOPA considered focusing the Guidelines directly on the supervised undertakings. See, Impact Assessment, *id.*, n. 50 above, at 3, point 4.

[52] Impact Assessment, *id.*, n. 50 above, at 3, point 4.

consumers' complaints or complaints from all customers. The EIOPA Report on Best Practices by Insurance Undertakings in handling complaints states the purpose as follows:

> Their purpose is to contribute to "enhancing customer protection" as described in the underlying statutory objectives of EIOPA.

This language cites (inaccurately) for authority "art. 1, para. 6 f. EIOPA Regulation", the regulation on consumer protection. The voice of BaFin [Federal Financial Supervisory Authority] was heard thus: "In consideration for the great importance of consumer protection, Germany has agreed to the Guidelines in the Board of Supervisors."[53] Both the Impact Assessment and the Best Practices Report expressly invoke consumer protection to justify issuance of the EIOPA Guidelines. And consumer protection was telling for the decision in the EIOPA Board of Supervisors. Yet consumer protection is not mentioned in the EIOPA Guidelines themselves. To the contrary, the Guidelines do not expressly refer to the proffered legal bases,[54] but to art. 16 of the EIOPA Regulation "taking into account Recital 16 and arts. 41, 46, 183, and 185" of the Solvency II Directive and the "adequate protection of policy holders and beneficiaries" of Recital 16.[55]

Under art. 16, para. 1 of the EIOPA Regulation, however, issuance of guidelines by the Authority shall be restricted to ensuring the "common, uniform, and consistent application of Union law. . . ." But there is no such Union law for the field of complaints-handling. With regard to the Guidelines, EIOPA itself explained in a 27 June 2012 press release:

> The guidelines in question cover complaints-handling by insurance companies and seek to address two current areas of concern.

Objections to this obvious deficiency[56] had already been lodged on various occasions in the public hearing phase of the draft EIOPA Guidelines. EIOPA responded in a working paper as follows:

> EIOPA is issuing these Guidelines under art. 16 of its empowering Regulation, with a view to "ensuring the common, uniform and consistent application of Union law" and not on the basis of Solvency II, given that EIOPA may also act under its empowering Regulation in the field of insurance undertakings even

[53] BaFin-Journal (Aug. 2012), 12.

[54] See EIOPA Guidelines, 2, point 1.

[55] *Bernadino*, "How EIOPA is 'taking the lead' in consumer protection," address of 23 Mar. 2012, commends the EIOPA Guidelines on complaints-handling nevertheless as the main portion of EIOPA's consumer protection achievements up to now.

[56] See *Sasserath-Alberti/Hartig*, "EIOPA-Verordnung: Herausforderungen für die Praxis" [in English: EIOPA Regulation: Challenges for Practitioners], VersR (2012), 524 (531).

> where Solvency II is not directly concerned provided that action ensures effective and consistent application of Solvency II [Article 1 (3), EIOPA Regulation ...]. These Guidelines take inspiration from Solvency II and are considered complementary to Solvency II. *EIOPA considers the notion of a "complaints management function" to be capable of clear differentiation from the notion of a "key function" under Solvency II.*[57]

Thus, EIOPA views art. 1, para. 3 of the EIOPA Regulation as the core legal basis for competence for the EIOPA Guidelines on complaints-handling. Nevertheless, this provision is not mentioned in the EIOPA Guidelines among the statements addressing legal bases. This omission is somewhat surprising in light of, for example, the rather stringent requirements for justifying legal acts, in the context of transparency and protection of rights considerations under art. 296 of the TFEU.[58] But further and more importantly, the rule of art. 1, para. 3 of the EIOPA Regulation contains the following necessity clause pertaining to competence ancillary, as it is called: "provided that such actions by the Authority are necessary to ensure the effective and consistent application of those acts." Where the Solvency II legal act is concerned, however, the "effective and consistent application" can relate only to the terms of the regulation and cannot exceed them. Otherwise, this would not be an "application" of the law, but a supplement or expansion. But this is exactly the case in the present situation.

EIOPA itself perceives "an existing regulatory gap – a current lack of EU rules on complaints-handling by insurance companies."[59]

And when one looks at the legal bases proferred by EIOPA in the introduction to the complaints-handling guidelines, namely arts. 183 and 185 of the Solvency II Directive, one sees why EIOPA reached the conclusion that there currently was no EU law on complaints-handling by insurance undertakings. This is so because art. 183, para. 1, subpara. 2 and art. 185, para. 3 l of the Solvency II Directive address only the insurance undertakings' information duty vis-à-vis policy holders about provisions concerning the handling of complaints and, where appropriate, information about the complaints body. Only with respect to non-life insurance, the scope is restricted to "natural persons" as policy holders, i.e., not to consumers.[60] Thus, EIOPA correctly recognizes on the one hand that there is no EU legislation on complaints-handling, such that the EIOPA Guidelines on complaints-handling could "ensure" its "effective and consistent application." Nevertheless, EIOPA considers itself on the other hand empowered to adopt guidelines for complaints-handling based on art. 16 in conjunction with art. 1, para. 3 of the EIOPA

---

[57] EIOPA, Public Consultation on the Guidelines and Best Practices Report on Complaints-Handling by Insurance Undertakings – Summary of the responses received, 14 Jun 2012, 5 (emphasis by EIOPA).

[58] See in more detail, *Callies*, in: Callies/Ruffert, eds., TFEU [Treaty on the Functioning of the European Union] (4th ed. 2011), art. 296 ref. 11 ff.

[59] EIOPA, EIOPA Newsletter, 27 Jun. 2012.

[60] See 3.2.2, above.

Regulation. This view and the course of action based on it are, however, to be rejected. The current insurance supervisory regime grants EIOPA no such authority.[61]

Even if complaints-handling by insurance undertakings does not constitute a focus of corporate governance ("Unternehmensführung" in the German version of art. 1, para. 3 of the EIOPA Regulation), strict observance is still required as to justification and scope of authority at Level 3. Ultimately and regardless of the subject matter, exceeding the scope of the rule defining competence always concerns supervisory intervention into basic rights without a legal basis. The core issue in every instance then is whether the EIOPA Guidelines address the permissible area of the application of defined legal acts at Levels 1 and 2 or whether they address the impermissible supplementing or expansion of such legal acts.[62] The EIOPA Regulation holds these areas separate not only by a clear formulation of the rules defining competence as explained above. But in addition, Recital 10 of the Regulation indicates both the fact that and the extent to which in the legislative area, beyond mere application of the law, EIOPA is to act as an advisory board for

> the Union institutions in the area of insurance, reinsurance and occupational retirement provision regulation and supervision, and related corporate governance, auditing and financial reporting issues.

This mandate also includes submission of draft regulatory and implementing technical standards under arts. 10 and 15 of the EIOPA Regulation. With this background in mind, separation must be strictly maintained between the two spheres: on the one hand, application of the law along with EIOPA's power to issue guidelines and advice; on the other hand, legislation with EIOPA power to advise.

A close reading of the EIOPA Guidelines on complaints-handling yields the further insight that the extremely detailed provisions and requirements of the Guidelines effect a deep incursion into the entrepreneurial administrative freedom of insurance undertakings. This, in effect, sacrifices the maxim of principles-based insurance supervision also in the general governance area of Pillar 2 of Solvency II.[63] The self-organization principle for key functions of undertakings is set down in Recital 31 of the Solvency II Directive as the central element of corporate governance. This principle must then apply even more so to complaints-handling by insurance undertakings, which is of somewhat lesser importance. Under the principle of the part standing for the whole, along with the requirement for an in-house

---

[61] Accord, *Sasserath-Alberti*/*Hartig*, VersR (2012), 524 (532).

[62] See for a parallel in supervisory monitoring of those exercising key functions under the draft of corresponding governance guidelines, *Dreher*, "Begriff und Inhaber der Schlüsselfunktionen nach Solvency II und VAG 2012" [in English: Concept and Holders of Key Functions under Solvency II and the German Insurance Supervision Act 2012], VersR (2012), 933 (936) (Chap. 7, below, at 7.2.3).

[63] See on the mandatory abandonment of the principle in the area of solvency supervision, *Dreher*, ZVersWiss (2012), 381 (391 f.) (Chap. 4, below, at 4.3.2.2).

"complaints-handling function" for insurance undertakings,[64] this is supported by the EIOPA Guidelines provision that "senior management"—which is not more specifically defined[65]—or a corresponding "management level" of the insurance undertaking should be responsible to put in place, publish, and implement the Guidelines on complaints-handling. However, beyond the provisions, of the Solvency II Directive, the future DVO, and general company law, the division of responsibility is in the hands of an insurance undertaking's managing board, which has the sole responsibility for the undertaking's activities. As a proprietary function of the undertaking's management, this task is not subject to supervision.[66]

In the final analysis, the EIOPA Guidelines on complaints-handling disclose that the boundaries between consumer protection and policy holder protection can fluctuate. Further, the Guidelines show that EIOPA resolves the classification of a measure on the basis of where it deems competence to lie. Here, however, it appears that in each of the areas a precise regard for the factual premises of competence provisions is called for. This is so because a deviation from the finely crafted competence framework prescribed under European law will override the mandatory rules on the attribution of competence in the tri-level system of Solvency II and the EIOPA Regulation.

Although the Guidelines themselves do not address consumer protection either on their legal basis or on the basis of their terms, it is the express objective of the Best Practices Report "to contribute to 'enhancing customer protection' as described in the underlying statutory objectives of EIOPA." This is followed by a citation to art. 1, para. 6 f. of the EIOPA Regulation.[67] The very first instance where

EIOPA adopted Guidelines reveals astonishing contours: The Guidelines themselves purportedly were based on EIOPA's supervisory authority over the insurance industry. Yet no such authority exists, as will be shown presently. Meanwhile, the Best Practices Report complementing[68] the Guidelines draws on EIOPA's

---

[64] See as a further example of the BaFin [Federal Financial Supervisory Authority] view, BaFin-Journal (Aug. 2012),12: "The undertaking must have a neutral body to receive and analyze the complaints." Yet in Guideline 2 – Complaints management function – of the EIOPA Guidelines there is no mention of neutrality. Rather, the emphasis is on a fair method of investigating complaints along with identifying and mitigating possible conflicts of interest.

[65] See on this point *Dreher*, "Das senior management der Versicherungsunternehmen und das künftige Versicherungsaufsichtsrecht" [in English: Senior Management of Insurance Undertakings and Future Insurance Supervisory Regime], VersR (2013), 35 (Chap. 9, below). The German version of the Guidelines speaks of "der Führungsebene, die auch für die Umsetzung und die Überwachung der Einhaltung dieser Maßnahmen zuständig ist" [senior management, who should also be responsible for [this policy's] implementation and for monitoring compliance with it].

[66] See in more detail, *Dreher/Ballmaier,* n. 41 above, at 135 ff., 143 with reference to the relationship between supervisory ORSA review and business strategy; *Dreher*, n. 13 above, at 411 with reference to supervisory risk consideration and business strategy.

[67] Best Practices Report, 2; a reference to art. 1, para. 6, subpara. 1, sent. 2 f of the EIOPA Regulation would be pertinent from a legal standpoint.

[68] Accord, Best Practices Report, 2.

consumer protection role. The legal basis for the Best Practices report is asserted to be art. 29, para. 2 of the EIOPA Regulation.[69] Under this provision,

> the Authority may, as appropriate, develop new practical instruments and convergence tools to promote common supervisory approaches and practices.

This is the first instance of EIOPA's citation of the new legal basis; and Point 9 in the introduction the Guidelines on complaints-handling reads less like a "practical tool" of a new supervisory culture than like a directive from a command culture. The following verbatim passage makes this clear:

> Please note that more detailed provisions on insurance undertakings' internal controls when handling complaints are contained in a. . .Best Practices Report.[70]

Beyond even this, the citation to art 29, para. 2 of the EIOPA Regulation as a legal basis is dubious. In its language, telos, and systematic position this provision is clearly concerned only with insurance supervisory regime and not with consumer protection. Yet, as noted already, in the Best Practices Report, EIOPA identifies consumer protection as the sole objective of the measure.

3.3.2.4 Collecting Consumer Trends Under Art. 9, Para. 1 a of the EIOPA Regulation

One consumer protection activity has been completed by EIOPA up to this point; and it provides the first overview of consumer trends in the EU.[71] In this overview, EIOPA sees three key consumer trends, which call for future attention: consumer protection issues around payment protection insurance, increased focus on unit-linked life insurance policies, and increased use of comparison websites by consumers. By collecting and analyzing such trends, EIOPA is performing its function under art. 9, para. 1 a of the EIOPA Regulation. In the present situation, however, the question arises whether the trends identified by EIOPA are truly consumer trends or if they rather constitute problem areas for consumers conceived by EIOPA, and thus a failure of the purpose of this particular function. The collection of consumer trends in and of itself does not raise any particular issues in relation to insurance supervisory regime. No such issues should arise unless EIOPA uses the trends to draw conclusions concerning the insurance supervisory regime. Up to this point, however, EIOPA, has announced its intention to do no more than use the consumer trends information to derive key consumer protection subjects.[72]

---

[69] Best Practices Report, 2.

[70] EIOPA Guidelines, 4, point 9.

[71] *EIOPA*, EIOPA's Initial Overview of Key Consumer Trends in the EU, 1 Feb. 2012.

[72] See EIOPA, Methodology Report for Collecting, Analysing and Reporting on Consumer Trends, November 2012, point 1.1. at end of section.

3.3.2.5 Future Issues in the Relationship of Insurance Supervisory Regime and Consumer Protection

Collective Consumer Protection as a Point of Reference

Beyond all of this, there are still some basic issues requiring legal clarification in the area of the relationship of insurance supervisory regime and consumer protection. These must be examined against the fact that consumer protection is rooted in the EIOPA Regulation and against the background of the first EIOPA measures in the gray area between policy holder protection and consumer protection. The need for a clear separation of responsibility and for a competence-based rationale for appropriate measures has already been addressed. Besides these points, there are basic issues concerning which consumers the EIOPA Regulation has in mind and what kind of consumer profile underlies the consumer protection scheme of the EIOPA Regulation.

The EIOPA Regulation does not define the legal requirement "consumer" either in its art. 4 definitions or in its rules on function and enabling laws relating to consumers. Indeed, art. 1, para. 6, subpara. 1, sent. 1 of the EIOPA Regulation states:

> The objective of the Authority shall be to protect the public interest by contributing to the short, medium and long-term stability and effectiveness of the financial system, for the Union economy, its citizens and businesses.

It follows directly from this assertion that EIOPA's mandate is directed only toward collective and not toward individual consumer protection. EIOPA itself has described its role to this effect.[73] In assuming this stance, the EIOPA is merely following a view held by the European Court of Justice concerning not EIOPA itself but the secondary law of financial services in general. With regard to financial market supervision, the Court had long since ruled that secondary law does not impose a duty on "the competent authorities" to "engage in supervisory measures" in the interest of individuals.[74]

On the parallel issue in German insurance supervisory regime, the applicable criterion likewise is the public interest. This orientation is found in sec. 81, para. 1, sent. 3 of the VAG [German Insurance Supervision Act] and correspondingly in sec. 1, para. 2 of the VAG RegE [Government's Draft of a Tenth Act Amending the

[73] EIOPA, EIOPA Work Program 2013, 13, n. 1, although lacking rationale and with the somewhat pallid formulation: "EIOPA considers the needs of consumers as a whole rather than as individuals."

[74] ECJ, 12. 10. 2004, case no. C-222/02 (Peter Paul/Germany), VersR (2005), 101; also at EuZW (2004), 689 pnt. 30 together with 25, with reference to protecting investors only in the public interest.

German Insurance Supervision Act] as well as in sec 4, para. 4 of the FinDAG [Financial Services Supervisory Act]. Therefore, the general opinion always has been that the insurance supervisory regime has but an indirect effect in the sense of collective consumer protection, not least on account of the absence of statutory rules on consumer protection.[75] In any case, official individual-centered consumer protection would not be conceivable in a market-based economic system, such as that underlying Union and German law,[76] and in the economic supervision attending that system. Protection for the individual consumer, then, arises solely as a "by-product of supervision."[77]

To the extent that the BaFin [Federal Financial Supervisory Authority] receives and handles individual consumer complaints, it does so in reliance on the general right to petition towards competent authorities, as set forth in art. 17 of the GG [Basic Law].[78] The BaFin [Federal Financial Supervisory Authority] is the competent authority in this area on account of its assigned function to supervise insurance undertakings.

Still to resolve, however, is the issue of when the collective consumer interest is concerned, presuming the legally required consideration of consumer protection by an insurance supervisory authority.

On this point, the statement of reasons for the RegE des Gesetzes zur Stärkung der deutschen Finanzaufsicht [Government's Draft of an Act to Strengthen German Financial Supervision] sets forth the following fundamentally sound definition, which may be applied generally to EIOPA actions concerning undertakings:

> if an undertaking breaches legal provisions protecting consumers, such that the seriousness and significance of the breach goes beyond the individual case and a general determination appears required.[79]

---

[75] See recently *König*, BaFin-Journal (Apr. 2012), 13 (18); (June 2012), 3 (4) and now also RegE Gesetz zur Stärkung der deutschen Finanzaufsicht [Government's Draft of an Act to Strengthen German Financial Supervision] BT-Drucks. [Document of the German Bundestag] 17/10040, 19 Jun. 2012, 13.

[76] See *Dreher/Lange*, "Die europäische Wirtschaftsverfassung nach dem Vertrag von Lissabon" [in English: The European Economic Constitution under the Treaty of Lisbon] in Publication in Honor of 50 Years, FIW (2010), 161 ff.; *Rittner/Dreher*, n. 28 above, sec. 2.

[77] See on this point RegE zum Gesetz zur Stärkung der deutschen Finanzaufsicht, [Government's Draft of an Act to Strengthen German Financial Supervision], *id.*, n. 75 above, at 13.

[78] See, e.g., *Keßler*, in: Keßler/Micklitz/Reich, eds., "Institutionelle Finanzmarktaufsicht und Verbraucherschutz" [in English: European Financial Supervision and Consumer Protection] (2010), 31.

[79] RegE zum Gesetz zur Stärkung der deutschen Finanzaufsicht [Government's Draft of an Act to Strengthen German Financial Supervision], *id.*, n. 75 above, at 13.

Consumer Profile

There is a further and more fundamental issue: What is the consumer profile underlying the EIOPA Regulation? The Regulation itself provides no information on this point. The European Court of Justice has addressed this issue somewhat by refraining from issuing numerous rulings eroding basic freedoms secured by European law. In the European Court of Justice rulings on consumer-oriented secondary law,[80] it correctly adjudicates on the basis of "the average consumer who is reasonably well-informed and reasonably observant and circumspect."[81] There is no support for the proposition that the EIOPA Regulation intended to deviate from this profile by encouraging a paternalistic portrait of an immature consumer. To the contrary, by focusing on creating transparency vis-à-vis consumers, the EIOPA Regulation demonstrates that it views consumers as capable of handling information even in complex matters. The same is true for the Solvency II Directive with respect to all policy holders, i.e., even those who would be categorized as consumers under any definition of the term. This follows from the fact that the Directive views policy holders as the main addressees of the Solvency and Financial Condition Report.[82]

It has long been recognized, however, that rationality is limited in economic situations, even when people are dealing with significant matters.[83] The relatively new branch of the field known as behavioral economics[84] has but enlarged upon and

[80] See Recital 18 of Directive 2005/29/EC concerning unfair business-to-consumer practices in the internal market (UCP Directive).

[81] See ECJ (1998), case no. I-4657 (Gut Springenheide und Tusky) pnt. 31; 1999, case no. I-513 (Verbraucherschutzverein/Sektkellerei Kessler) pnt. 36; *Glöckner,* in: Harte-Bavendamm/ Henning-Bodewig, eds., UWG [Unfair Competition Act] (2nd. ed. 2009) intro. B, ref. 143 ff.; *Dreher,* n. 36 above, at 170 ff.; *Krebber, id.,* n. 34 above, art. 169, ref. 7; *Micklitz*, "Brauchen Konsumenten und Unternehmen eine neue Architektur des Verbraucherrechts?" [in English: Do Consumers and Undertakings Need a New Architecture of Consumer Law?] in 69th DJT [German Jurists' Forum] – Gutachten [Report] – Part A (2012), *passim*; *Gsell*, "Verbraucherrealitäten und Verbraucherrecht im Wandel" [in English: Consumer Realities and Rights in Transition], JZ (2012), 809 (810 f., 813), each with further references; and in presentation to the ECJ, case no. C-51/11, on the restrictive interpretation of a ban on advertising of the BGH [Federal Court of Justice],13. Jan. 2011 – I ZR 22/09 – pnt. 3: "Query: whether a statement in view of the average consumer who is reasonably well-informed and reasonably observant and circumspect is to be applied to the consumer under Recital 15 of Regulation (EU) 1924/2006." See further OLG Naumburg [Naumburg Higher Regional Court], VersR (2012), 1034 (1037) on restricting the meaning of the terms broker and agent by sec. 11, para. 1 no. 3, VersVermV [Insurance Mediation Regulations]; on the discernment of the average consumer and on the consumer profile in pronouncements in insurance law, to differing effect, *Präve,* VersR (2012), 1159 (1163) (remarks to BGH [Federal Court of Justice], 25 Jul. 2012, – IV ZR 201/10 – VersR (2012), 1149).

[82] See 3.2.2, above.

[83] See *H. Simon*, Models of Bounded Rationality (1982).

[84] See on this point from the legal perspective, e.g., the articles in: Fleischer/Zimmer, eds., Beitrag der Verhaltensökonomie zum Handels- und Wirtschaftsrecht [in English: Contribution of Behavioral Economics to Business and Economic Law] (2011); and OFT [Office of Fair Trading (UK)], What does Behavioral Economics mean for Competition Policy? (March 2010), also with particular focus on consumer protection.

made finer distinctions in the category of behavioral anomalies, as they are called. Given the likewise limited rationality of national and European legislation, it is doubtful that this incipient convergence of theory and reality provides a basis for protecting consumers from themselves whether in specific and appropriate situations or even as a whole with broad-based legislation. And before all this, there is the consideration that the field of behavioral economics, on account of consumers' limited rationality, challenges the now-predominant efforts[85] to increase the amount of information and transparency vis-à-vis consumers. Beyond this, however, there remains as a consumer protection measure the already noted comprehensive regulation through dictates and prohibitions in the form of mandatory law,[86] i.e., a paternalistic approach with less competition and even narrower freedom of choice for consumers[87]; and this approach is not all compatible with a profile of the consumer as mature and discerning. Every few years, consumers are relieved of this self-inflicted immaturity and accepted as mature and discerning voters, only to be immediately relegated to the role of immature objects of comprehensive legislative and official ministration.

More recent approaches in consumer law policy, especially in Europe, have tended to draw distinctions in the heretofore essentially uniform portrait of consumers. On the one hand, the "responsible consumer," in line with the concept of the European Court of Justice, who is considered capable of making responsible decisions.[88] On the other hand, the "vulnerable consumer", who is viewed as overwhelmed by the demands of the legal system and the attendant responsibility. These consumers are supposedly in need of protection, particularly with respect to partaking of the benefits of public services. Under this view, this need for protection must be addressed by compensating consumer protection measures, such as mandatory insurance on deposit account contracts in the lending sector. A further example, one already in place, is protection against attachment under sec. 167 of the VVG [Insurance Contracts Act] in the insurance field.[89]

---

[85] See, e.g., *Inderst*, Consumer Protection and the Role of Advice in the Market for Retail Financial Services, Journal of Institutional and Theoretical Economies (JITE) (2011), 4 (18).

[86] See for an appraisal that, however, ultimately refers only to the effect of the era on legal policy, *Schön*, "Zwingendes Recht oder informierte Entscheidung – zu einer (neuen) Grundlage unserer Zivilrechtsordnung" [in English: Mandatory Law or Informed Decision: Toward a (New) Basis of Our Civil Law System] in: Publication in Honor of Claus-Wilhelm Canaris on his 70th birthday (2007), 1191 ff.; differing, *Koch*, "Grenzen des informationsbasierten Anlegerschutzes" [in English: Limits on Information-based Investor Protection], BKR (2012), 485 (493): "when the concept of paternalism loses the negative connotation that many associate with it".

[87] See *Saint-Paul*, The Tyranny of Utility – Behavioral Social Science and the Rise of Paternalism (2011); and for the view according to constitutional law jurisprudence, see *Volkmann*, Darf der Staat seine Bürger erziehen? [In English: Should the State Be a Parent to its Citizens?] (2012).

[88] See *Micklitz*, *id.*, n. 81 above, at A 39.

[89] See *Kohte*, "Der verletzliche Verbraucher" [in English: The Vulnerable Consumer], VuR (2012), 338; *Micklitz*, n. 81 above, at A 40 ff.; LG Erfurt [Erfurt District Court], 8. May 2007 – 1 HK O 28/07 – point of law 37 on the other hand, employing a different approach, attributes the vulnerability of consumers to the fiduciary relationship arising from earlier consultation and advice in the financial advice sector.

In the area under discussion, vulnerable consumers have at best a completely subordinate role to play, and then only by means of future law. The concern in private insurance law is namely to achieve the broadest possible personal autonomy. In social insurance law, on the other hand, the concern is to allow participation in the social services that are indispensable for everyone. And where private insurance serves as a substitute for social insurance, such as by substitute health insurance, the policy holder and thus all consumers are protected under existing law, e.g., by mandatory election of a different rate[90] and by the insurer's inability to terminate the contract. In reference to taking part in the automotive traffic, the same applies in the field of liability insurance through the obligation to contract and numerous other more extensive rules imposed to protect all policy holders. Thus it may be seen that in the societal aspects of private insurance the concept of the vulnerable consumer, even if in the guise of a policy holder, has long been recognized. And what is more, the challenges arising from this recognition have been surmounted.

Combining the Roles of Insurance Supervision and Consumer Protection in One Authority

Consumer protection addresses contractual safeguards. Insurance supervision, on the other hand, addresses the administration and monitoring of business activities. As explained earlier, consumer protection is but an indirect by-product of insurance supervision. In view of this posture, it is ultimately quite appropriate to question whether the two clearly different and distinguishable tasks of insurance supervision and collective consumer protection should be combined in a single insurance supervisory authority such as EIOPA. This question is most particularly appropriate in view of the fact that the respective groups addressed by insurance supervision and consumer protection are distinct and may indeed have conflicting interests.[91]

[90] Thus the BVerfG [Federal Constitutional Court], VersR (2009), 957, pnt. 171 and also BVerfG [Federal Constitutional Court], VersR (2009), 1057, approved mandatory insurance in the base rate schedule by reference to the societal principle of art. 20, para. 1, GG [German Basic Law] as well as on the basis of the dual phases of statutory and private health insurance; see also, *Rittner/ Dreher*, "60 Jahre Grundgesetz und das Wirtschaftsrecht" [in English: Sixty Years of the Basic Law and Economic Law], in: Jahrbuch des öffentlichen Rechts [Yearbook of Public Law], updated version, vol. 59 (2011), 59 (93 f.).

[91] See to the same effect the statement of principle at the beginning of the RegE Gesetz zur Stärkung der deutschen Finanzaufsicht [Government's Draft of an Act to Strengthen German Financial Supervision], n. 75 above, at 1 (likewise at 11, 13): "Consumer protection: The supervisory activities of the Federal Office in the future shall devote greater attention to consumer issues, provided, however, that this shall not impair the supervisory objectives directed toward ensuring solvency of the supervised institutions and the ability of the financial markets to function".

Insurance supervision revolves around protecting the interests of policy holders and insureds, whereas consumer protection is directed toward protecting the interests of consumers, however one defines "consumer."

Not all policy holders and insureds are simultaneously consumers with respect to any particular form of insurance, except perhaps in certain specialty insurance areas such as travel cancellation insurance. Therefore, promoting the interests of one class will necessarily come into conflict with the interests of the other class at some point. The very conflicts that arise with essentially homogeneous classes demonstrate this inevitability. In fact, just such a conflict already has arisen within the class of policy holders and insureds. The conflict centered on termination notice and settlement provisions for life insurance.[92] And in the class of consumers, conflicts have arisen between protection of the individual consumers and protection of the class as a whole. One example is the betterment of individual policy holders by relief from obligation, under the rubric of consumer or policy-holder protection. This has been seen in the case of negligent, intentional, or even fraudulent actions of policy holders.[93] EIOPA already serves a consumer protection function along with its insurance supervision task. At present, BaFin [Federal Financial Supervisory Authority] is in many cases called upon to do the same. To then ask insurance supervisory authorities to exercise a consumer protection function is no wiser than the plan to grant extensive supervisory authority over lending institutions to the European Central Bank, when that would create a partial conflict with ECB's established responsibility for monetary stability.

There are, in addition, systemic considerations. These considerations involve the numerous supervised or even regulated economic fields beyond the scope of financial services.[94] Here, too, consumer protection has a significant role to play; and for that reason, other supervisory and regulatory authorities operate pursuant to principles and rules of consumer protection. Moreover, some EU Member States have their own consumer protection authorities or have assigned the consumer protection function to an authority other than the one responsible for supervising financial services.[95] Hence, assigning consumer protection tasks exclusively to supervisory authorities in the financial services sector will not yield a consistent

[92] See BGH [Federal Court of Justice], VersR (2012), 1149 and on this point *Armbrüster*, "Konsequenzen des Urteils zu unwirksamen Klauseln" [in English: Consequences of the Judgment on Ineffective Clauses], VW 19 (2012), 1434; *id.*, "Kehrtwende des BGH bei der AGB-Kontrolle in der Lebensversicherung" [in English: The Federal Court of Justice Makes an About-face in Monitoring of Standard Terms and Conditions for Life Insurance], NJW (2012), 3001; *Präve*, n. 81 above, at 1163; *id.*, "Individualrechte zulasten des Versichertenkollektivs?" [in English: Individual Rights at the Expense of the Insured Class?], VersR (2012), 657.

[93] See *Brand, id.*, n. 1 above, at 70 (84 ff.), and *Dreher*, "Die "bedingungsgemäße Entschädigung" des arglistig täuschenden Versicherungsnehmers" [in English: The 'Conditional Indemnification' of the Fraudulently Deceptive Policy Holder], VersR (1998), 539; JZ (1992), 926 (Comments to the BGH [Federal Court of Justice] of 25. Mar. 1992 – IV ZR 55/91 – VersR (1992), 603).

[94] See on this particular segment of economic law in detail, *Rittner/Dreher*, n. 28 above, secs. 29 ff.

[95] For example in Ireland, in a move with little reason to recommend it, the present consumer protection authority is about to be merged with the competition authority.

regulatory system. Rather what is required is delegation based on a consistent allocation of responsibility for consumer protection with consideration and harmonized balancing of all consumer protection tasks.

3.4 Summary

1. According the EIOPA Regulation, EIOPA shall contribute to the enhancement of consumer protection. The EIOPA Regulation gives substance to this standard with specific allocation of tasks and powers.
2. On the basis of consumer protection regulations, EIOPA can issue guidelines or advice on insurance supervisory regime for national insurance supervisory authorities. In such a case, consumer protection will become a matter also for BaFin [Federal Financial Supervisory Authority], although the law applicable to BaFin [Federal Financial Supervisory Authority] does not yet mention consumer protection and BaFin [Federal Financial Supervisory Authority] is not a consumer protection authority.
3. The main objective of the Solvency II Directive is the protection of insureds and insurance beneficiaries. Consumer protection is not a matter addressed in the Solvency II Directive. The same is true for regulatory levels 2 and 3 and for the VAG RegE [Government's Draft of a Tenth Act Amending the German Insurance Supervision Act].
4. The proposals for a regulation on key information documents and for a new directive on insurance mediation likewise do not tie into the concept of consumer, but relate to "retail investors" and "customers."
5. The rules on consumer protection in the EIOPA Regulation make no changes in the objective of insurance supervisory regime under Solvency II, which is not directed at consumer protection. Rather, they relate to other insurance sector legal acts intended to apply to consumer protection.
6. Under the Solvency II Directive and the VAG RegE, a prohibition on optimization applies to the supervisory review process (SRP). Even if European law presupposes a "high level of protection" in the field of consumer protection, this essentially means only minimum harmonization. The specific level of protection sought to be achieved by a regulation depends furthermore completely upon the substantive content of the regulation. Thus, there is no conflict between the standards for the supervisory review process under insurance supervisory regime on the one hand and the standards for measures seeking to protect consumers under consumer protection law on the other hand.
7. Though not required by law, the insurance supervision regime indirectly protects consumers in many areas in the sense of a collective consumer protection. Aside from solvency supervision as a whole, this indirect effect is seen in transparency attained in the public Solvency and Financial Condition Report.
8. Under EIOPA measures, the boundaries between insured protection and consumer protection can fluctuate. The EIOPA Guidelines on complaints-handling

furnish one such example. Ultimately, the EIOPA adduces competence regulations only on insured protection. But EIOPA goes on to announce that the measures evince the spirit of consumer protection.

9. EIOPA adopted the Guidelines on complaints-handling, despite the fact that in the presentation the Authority itself noted the absence of European law on complaints-handling and thereby the failure to satisfy the factual basis of the existence of "Union law" for EIOPA guidelines and advice. That factual basis would require a showing of the need for a "uniform and consistent application of Union law" under art. 16, para. 1 of the EIOPA Guidelines. This provision, therefore, could not be the legal basis for the EIOPA Guidelines on complaints-handling.
10. Seen against this background, the submission of the EIOPA Guidelines on complaints-handling without regard to their consumer protection nature raises the question of how far EIOPA's competence ancillary extends in the area of corporate governance under art. 1, para. 3, keeping in mind that this competence is mentioned by EIOPA in the consumer protection context but not proferred as a legal basis in the Guidelines.

    a) The competence ancillary under art. 1, para. 3. of the EIOPA Regulation expressly exists only for the "application" of Union legal acts at Levels 1 and 2. This restriction comports with the finely crafted allocation of responsibility in the three-tiered Solvency II system. There is no such competence, however, if an EIOPA measure moves outside this scope and supplements or expands existing legal acts. Viewed in this light, the EIOPA Guidelines on complaints-handling lack a legal basis, because there is no European legal act which EIOPA can merely apply.
    b) Furthermore, the EIOPA Guidelines on complaints-handling abandon a principles-based approach by adopting very detailed regulations and, in so doing, intrude into a proprietary business management area not subject to supervision.

       An example of this incursion is assigning responsibility to certain persons in insurance undertakings for putting in place, publishing, and implementing the in-house guidelines on complaints-handling mandated by EIOPA and for the creation of an in-house complaints-handling function.
    c) Under the EIOPA Regulation, EIOPA is obligated to provide the legal bases for any measures it adopts. The failure to mention the competence ancillary of art. 1, para. 3 of the EIOPA Regulation in the Guidelines on complaints-handling constitutes a serious want of transparency, even without regard to the fact that the legal conditions of the provision establishing competence are not met.

11. EIOPA employs art. 29, para. 2 of the EIOPA Regulation as a legal basis for the first time in the Best Practices Report accompanying the Guidelines on complaints-handling. The associated objective of enhancing consumer protection according to art. 1, para. 6 of the EIOPA Regulation experiences here a double conflict: on the one hand with the legal basis for the later EIOPA

Guidelines, based as it is on supervision law alone; and on the other hand again with a legal basis pertaining only to insurance supervisory regime, namely art. 29, para. 2 of the EIOPA Regulation.

12. In its first appraisal, EIOPA collected and analyzed consumer trends under art. 9, para. 1 a of the EIOPA Regulation. Such an appraisal essentially does not affect the insurance supervisory regime.
13. At the same time, EIOPA's assigned objective "to protect the public interest" means that its consumer protection tasks involve exclusively collective and not individual consumer protection.
14. The EIOPA Regulation makes no pronouncements concerning the relevant consumer profile. From the legal point of view, especially that of European law, the predominant characterization has been that of a mature and discerning consumer. The EIOPA Regulation confirms this with its focus on transparency and information, a focus that presupposes a consumer capable of handling information. The economic view, however, highlights the limits of rational consumer actions, but also the limits of compensating information and transparency.
15. Beyond these areas, where consumer protection is the indirect result of insurance supervision, conflicts may arise between the objectives of the insurance supervisory regime and consumer protection law. Combining consumer protection tasks with the task of insurance supervision in one insurance supervisory authority, whether EIOPA or the BaFin [Federal Financial Supervisory Authority], thus does not constitute a reasonable and sound regulatory model for the long term.

Part II
Solvency

Chapter 4
Solvency Requirements

Contents

4.1 Introduction 100
4.2 The Solvency System Under Supervisory Law 101
  4.2.1 The Economic Balance Sheet (Solvency Statement) 101
  4.2.2 Own Funds Under Supervisory Law 102
  4.2.3 Capital Requirements Under Supervisory Law 103
  4.2.4 The Supervisory Review Process 107
4.3 Complexity, Volatility and Procyclicality of the Solvency Requirements: Implications for Solvency Supervision 109
  4.3.1 The Problems 109
  4.3.2 Complexity 111
  4.3.3 Volatility 115
  4.3.4 Procyclicality 121
4.4 The New Roles of the Managing and Supervisory Boards, Supervisory Authorities, Courts and Insurance Academics in the Solvency Supervision of Insurance Undertakings 124
  4.4.1 The Managing and Supervisory Boards of Insurance Undertakings 124
  4.4.2 The Supervisory Authorities 133
  4.4.3 Competent Courts in the Insurance Supervisory Regime 146
  4.4.4 Insurance Academics 148
4.5 Summary 149

Abstract Solvency II imposes upon insurance undertakings a new system of solvency requirements based on a risk-oriented approach. Risks must be covered by own funds of the insurance undertakings. This chapter systematically analyzes the new insurance-related solvency system in terms of the Solvency II Directive, the proposed Level 2-Regulation, and the proposed new VAG [German Insurance Supervision Act]. It focuses then on the three problem areas under the new solvency regime: complexity, volatility, and procyclical effects. Finally it turns to the new roles which the boards of directors and supervisory boards of insurance

First published as "Solvenzanforderungen in der Versicherungsaufsicht nach Solvency II und künftigem VAG" [in English: Solvency Requirements in Insurance Supervision under Solvency II and the Future German Insurance Supervision Act], ZVersWiss (2012), 381 ff.

M. Dreher, *Treatises on Solvency II*, DOI 10.1007/978-3-662-46290-4_4

undertakings, the supervisory authorities, the courts, and the academics will play in the Solvency II process.

4.1 Introduction

With the replacement of the current Solvency I system by Solvency II, the solvency requirements for insurance undertakings are striking off in a new direction.[1] The sometimes overworked term "paradigm shift" finds appropriate application in this case in light of the fundamental new legal conditions that define the solvency of insurance undertakings.[2,3] This is so because Solvency II also subjects the solvency of insurance undertakings to the new risk focus. The standards for capital requirements are no longer related mainly to the amount of premiums as before,[4] but rather to the magnitude of the risks.

This fundamental change in the criteria for required capitalization of insurance undertakings—or "Solvency Capital Requirement", in the terminology of the Solvency II Directive[5]—and the requirements for determining the individual components of own funds are accompanied by a corresponding radical change to insurance supervision. The supervisory authorities will need to conduct supervision not only on the basis of new legal provisions. Rather, the very content of their tasks will change, as the following two examples demonstrate: With the admission of internal models under art. 112 of the Solvency II Directive or sec. 102 of the VAG [German Insurance Supervision Act] 2012,[6] insurance supervision is already involved in establishing the criteria under which insurance undertakings determine their Solvency Capital Requirement. Furthermore, individual components of own funds must now be classified, with supervisory approval, into particular "tiers" of capital based on qualitative criteria. This individualization and the orientation on

---

[1] Any mention of insurance undertakings in this chapter includes reinsurance undertakings.

[2] Regarding the developments in solvency supervision of credit institutions, see recently *Körnert*, "Paradigmenwechselin der deutschen Bankenregulierung – Zur Evolution eigenkapitalorientierter Solvabilitätsnormen in Theorie und Praxis seit 1850" [in English: Paradigm Shift in German Banking Regulation – The Evolution of Equity-based Solvency Standards in Theory and Practice since 1850], ZHR 176 (2012), 96 ff.

[3] Separately, there is the question of whether a paradigm shift also arises in the basic transition stipulated in Solvency II from rules-based to principles-based supervisory law.

[4] See sec. 53c of the VAG [German Insurance Supervision Act] and its attendant regulations.

[5] Directive 2009/138/EC of the European Parliament and of the Council of 25 Nov. 2009, OJEU L 335, p. 1, of 17 Dec. 2009.

[6] References to the provisions of VAG [German Insurance Supervision Act] 2012 in this chapter refer to the "RegE eines Zehnten Gesetzes zur Änderung des VAG" [Government's Draft of a Tenth Act Amending the German Insurance Supervision Act] of 15 Feb. 2012, BT-Drucks. [Document of the German Bundestag] 17/9342; also, BR-Drucks [Document of the German Bundesrat] 90/12.

qualitative criteria combined with market value calculations will produce a complexity, volatility, and procyclicality never before seen in the solvency system. This may trigger extensive discussion and potential disputes in the relationship between insurance undertakings and supervisory authorities regarding the external or internal origins of this complexity, volatility, and procyclicality faced by the insurance undertaking and its consequences under supervisory law.

Against this background, the following article encompasses the regulation of the new solvency system from a conceptual and systemic standpoint (below, 4.2). Based on this, it then analyzes the new problems of complexity, volatility, and procyclicality that emerge in solvency supervision (below, 4.3), followed by a discussion of the new roles in insurance supervision assumed by the managing and supervisory boards of insurance undertakings, the supervisory authorities, the courts, and insurance academics (below, 4.4). Thus, this article treats the supervisory review process under art. 36 of the Solvency II Directive (also in the VAG [German Insurance Supervision Act] 2012 in secs. 289 and 292[7]) to the extent that it discusses the new solvency-related responsibilities of the supervisory authorities[8] and particularly their new role under risk-focused solvency supervision.[9] The issue of specific supervisory powers such as mandating a capital add-on[10] or a recovery plan and finance scheme is beyond the scope of this article.

4.2 The Solvency System Under Supervisory Law

4.2.1 The Economic Balance Sheet (Solvency Statement)

The principle for determining the "solvency requirement", according to Recital 45 of the Solvency II Directive, is "an economic valuation of the whole balance sheet". Meant here is not the balance sheet in the accounting sense, but rather a

[7] See in detail, *Dreher/Ballmaier*, "Das aufsichtliche Überprüfungsverfahren nach Art. 36 of the Solvency II Directive und § 289 VAG-RegE" [in English: The Supervisory Review Process under art. 36 of the Solvency II Directive and Sec. 289 of the Government's Draft of a Tenth Act Amending the Insurance Supervision Act] in: Dreher/Wandt, eds., Solvency II in der Rechtsanwendung [in English: Solvency II in Legal Application] (2012) (Chap. 2, above).

[8] See 4.2.3, below.

[9] See 4.4.2, below.

[10] See on this point briefly, 4.2.4 and 4.3.3.3. The assessment of a capital add-on for an individual undertaking proceeds in accordance with art. 37 of the Solvency II Directive (sec. 295 of the VAG [German Insurance Supervision Act] 2012), or for groups in accordance with art. 232 or art. 233, para. 6, subparas. 2 and 3 of the Solvency II Directive (secs. 250 and 251, para. 6 of the VAG [German Insurance Supervision Act] 2012) – depending on the standard chosen for the calculation of group solvency. See in more detail on the supervisory order for a capital add-on, *Sehrbrock*, "Rechtsprobleme des Kapitalaufschlags" [in English: Legal Problems of the Capital Add-on], ZVersWiss (2010), 665 ff.

separate "economic balance sheet".[11] The term has undergone extensive legal refinement in the VAG [German Insurance Supervision Act] 2012, but not in the Solvency II Directive,[12] under the overarching term "solvency statement". Thus the solvency statement must be submitted "in addition to . . . the balance sheet prepared for accounting purposes".[13] Through a calculation of assets in excess of liabilities, the solvency statement shows the total amount of own funds.[14] Under sec. 69, para. 1, sent. 1 of the VAG [German Insurance Supervision Act] 2012, insurance undertakings must "prepare a comparison of assets to liabilities for the purpose of determining available own funds (solvency statement)". Therefore, the German legislator goes no further than the requirements in the Directive that also provide for this manner of stating business affairs.[15]

4.2.2 *Own Funds Under Supervisory Law*

The Solvency II Directive requires insurance undertakings to maintain specific own funds.[16] It is only by this means that the basic objectives of the insurance supervision can be achieved. Recital 16 and arts. 27 and 28 of the Solvency II Directive provide for this as European law. Protection of insureds and insurance beneficiaries is the primary objective. Of lesser importance are financial stability and fair and

---

[11] Accord, RegE VAG [Government's Draft of a Tenth Act Amending the German Insurance Supervision Act], at n. 6, statement of grounds p. 287.

[12] Occasionally, however, there is reference to the balance sheet in this sense, such as in arts. 24, 163 and 142 of the Solvency II Directive. But this is not centrally governed.

[13] RegE VAG [Government's Draft of a Tenth Act Amending the German Insurance Supervision Act], at n. 6, statement of grounds for sec. 69, p. 287.

[14] RegE VAG [Government's Draft of a Tenth Act Amending the German Insurance Supervision Act], at n. 6, ibid.

[15] Nevertheless, the VAG [German Insurance Supervision Act] 2012 regulates some of the legal consequences in connection with the solvency statement – for example the auditor's review of the statement as well as the preparation and submission of a corresponding report under secs. 45, para. 2, and 47, para. 2 of the VAG [German Insurance Supervision Act] 2012 [Government's Draft of a Tenth Act Amending the German Insurance Supervision Act] – without basis in the Solvency II Directive and thus improperly excessive, also according to Bundesrat [German Federal Council], Empfehlungen der Ausschüsse zu dem Entwurf eines Zehnten Gesetzes zur Änderung des VAG [Advice of the Committee on the Draft of a Tenth Act Amending the German Insurance Supervision Act], BR-Drucks. [Document of the German Bundesrat], 90/1/12 of 16 Mar. 2012, p. 6 f.

[16] See on this point overview by *Schüller/Mitzner*, "Die neuen Eigenkapitalanforderungen für (Rück)Versicherungsunternehmen nach Solvency II" [in English: The New Own Funds Requirements for (Re)insurance Undertakings under Solvency II], ZHR 175 (2011), 338 (341 ff.); *Lüttringhaus*, "Die neuen Eigenkapitalanforderungen für (Rück)Versicherungsunternehmen nach Solvency II" [in English: The New Own Funds Requirements for (Re)insurance Undertakings under Solvency II], EuZW (2011), 822 ff.; *Bürkle*, in: Fahr/Kaulbach/Bähr/Pohlmann, VAG [in English: The German Insurance Supervision Act] (5th ed. 2012), Appendix 1, Ref. 33 ff.

stable markets, which are of equal weight.[17] Specifically, according to Recital 17 of the Solvency II Directive, "the solvency regime laid down in this Directive is expected to result in even better protection for policyholders". Consequently, the legislator must determine which resources can be recognized under supervisory law as own funds to ensure attainment of the objective. This is found at the first level of the norm hierarchy in arts. 87 to 99 of the Solvency II Directive. Further specification of "own funds" is provided at Level 2, namely in arts. 51 to 72 of the DVO-E,[18] and the numerous drafts of own funds regulations issued by CEIOPS (now EIOPA). The German legislator finally implements these requirements at the fourth regulatory level in secs. 80 to 86 of the VAG [German Insurance Supervision Act] 2012.

The supervisory provisions for own funds distinguish between basic own funds and ancillary own funds, each defined in more detail. All own funds are further classified into three tiers. The allocation of own funds to each tier is based both on their character as basic or ancillary own funds and on the extent to which the criteria of "permanent availability" and "subordination" apply.[19] The own funds classification is the basis for determining the extent to which the risk-related capital requirement under supervisory law can be met in terms of the "coverage quota" by "eligible own funds". Thus the insurance undertaking's capital requirements under supervisory law must be established in parallel with its own funds under supervisory law.

4.2.3 Capital Requirements Under Supervisory Law

4.2.3.1 The Solvency Capital Requirement (SCR)

For the insurance undertaking's capital requirement under supervisory law, the solvency capital it is required to maintain must first be calculated.[20] The relevant

[17] See in detail, *Dreher/Häußler*, "Die Aufsicht über Versicherungsunternehmen durch die BaFin und die Überwachungsaufgabe des Aufsichtsrats" [in English: Supervision of Insurance Undertakings by BaFin [Federal Financial Supervisory Authority] and the Monitoring Task of the Supervisory Board], ZGR (2011), 471, 485; *Wandt/Sehrbrock*, "Regelungsziele der Solvency II-Rahmenrichtlinie" [in English: Regulatory Objectives of the Solvency II Framework Directive], ZVersWiss (2011), 193 (195 ff.).

[18] The rules of the implementing measures – "Draft Implementing Measures Solvency II" of 31 Oct. 2011 – cited in this chapter with the designation DVO-E.

[19] See art. 93 of the Solvency II Directive and sec. 82 of the VAG [German Insurance Supervision Act] 2012.

[20] This must be distinguished from the "economic capital" referred to in Recitals 64 and 65 as well as art. 120, para. 1 (b) of the Solvency II Directive – or in the Statement of Reasons for sec. 87 of the government's draft of the VAG [German Insurance Supervision Act] (n. 6), p. 291, but not in sec. 106 para. 1, no. 2 of VAG [German Insurance Supervision Act] 2012 as the implementation rule for art. 120, para. 1 (b) of the Solvency II Directive. Economic capital is the risk capital of an

provisions are found in arts. 100 to 127 of the Solvency II Directive,[21] arts. 75 to 235 of the DVO-E, some Level 3 papers, and secs. 87 to 112 of the VAG [German Insurance Supervision Act] 2012. Here, the VAG [German Insurance Supervision Act] 2012 replaces the term "Solvenzkapitalanforderung" found in the German-language version of the European law—and generally rendered in English as "Solvency Capital Requirement" or "SCR"—by the alternate term "Solvabilitätskapitalanforderung" [in English: Solvability Capital Requirement]. These provisions also govern the use of the "standard model" and the partial or fully internal model according to which the relevant Solvency Capital Requirement is determined. The calculation of required capital is no longer centered on business volume as measured by premium income but rather on the risk exposure of the insurance undertaking. The insurance supervisory regime specifies individual risk modules for this purpose which must be considered when determining the Solvency Capital Requirement. In order to ensure the most uniform procedure possible for all insurance undertakings in the EU and European Economic Area,[22] highly detailed requirements in this respect appear in all three levels of the Solvency II system.

The connection between the Solvency Capital Requirement with own funds is established in arts. 100, para. 1, 102, para. 1, subpara. 2 of the Solvency II Directive—and reflected in sec. 80, para. 1, sent. 1 of the VAG [German Insurance Supervision Act] 2012—according to which all insurance undertakings must "hold eligible own funds covering the Solvency Capital Requirement". In other words, an

insurance undertaking needed for the long-term financial viability of the business. The term thus belongs to the category of risk management and therefore to Pillar II of Solvency II. Solvency capital, in contrast, is the actuarial amount of own funds held by an insurance undertaking appropriate to its risk within the meaning of insurance supervisory regime requirements under Pillar I of Solvency II. Due to a largely similar calculation of the two amounts, solvency capital will approximate economic capital, according to, for example, *Romeike/Müller-Reichart*, Risikomanagement im Versicherungsunternehmen [in English: Risk Management in the Insurance Undertaking], (2nd ed. 2008), p. 145 ff.

[21] See on this point in overview, *Lüttringhaus*, n. 16, 825 ff.

[22] On the principle of full harmonization in the Directive, see *Dreher/Lange*, "Die Vollharmonisierung der Versicherungsaufsicht durch Solvency II" [in English: Full Harmonization of Insurance Supervision under Solvency II], VersR (2011), 825 ff. (Chap. 1, above); *Bürkle*, "Die Zukunft der materiellen Versicherungsaufsicht in Deutschland" [in English: The Future of Substantive Insurance Supervision in Germany], VersR (2011), 1469 (1472 f.); *Wandt/Sehrbrock*, n. 17, 200. Unclear as to basis – "The Directive does not prescribe full harmonization in all areas . . ." – and inconsistent with continuing the VAG's [German Insurance Supervision Act's] existing law in RegE VAG [German Insurance Supervision Act] 2012 [Government's Draft of a Tenth Act Amending the German Insurance Supervision Act], n. 6, p. 255. Full harmonization is also the presumption of the Bundesrat [German Federal Council], n. 6, statement of reasons for no. 15, p. 14, thus: "not compatible with the 'full harmonization approach' of the Solvency II Directive"; these recommendation require – id., no. 2, at 3: "a 1:1 implementation of the Solvency II Directive". Also in support of full harmonization – even in confusing the terms full harmonization and maximum harmonization – staff member of the Austrian Federal Ministry of Finance *Wagner*, "Solvabilität II und VAG neu: Was bleibt, was ändert sich?" [in English: Solvency II and the New German Insurance Supervision Act: What is Unchanged? What is Changed?], VersRdsch 9/2010, 23(24), (26).

insurance undertaking is no longer in compliance with its Solvency Capital Requirement when the ratio of own funds to the Solvency Capital Requirement, referred to here as the "solvency ratio", is below 100 %.

The Solvency Capital Requirement must be calculated and reported to the supervisory authorities at least once a year according to arts. 100, para. 1, subpara. 1, 102, para. 1 subpara. 1 of the Solvency II Directive, or sec. 89, para. 1 of the VAG [German Insurance Supervision Act] 2012. Under art. 101 of the Solvency II Directive or sec. 88 of the VAG [German Insurance Supervision Act] 2012, the calculation assumes the undertaking is a going concern, and all quantifiable risks to which the undertaking is exposed must be accounted for.

4.2.3.2 The Minimum Capital Requirement (MCR)

In addition to the Solvency Capital Requirement, supervisory law also requires the calculation of a Minimum Capital Requirement for an insurance undertaking. While the German-language version of the Solvency II Directive provides the term "Mindestkapitalanforderung" in art. 128, it is often replaced by the English "Minimum Capital Requirement" (MCR) in practice. Details on the Minimum Capital Requirement are found in arts. 128 to 131 of the Solvency II Directive, arts. 226 to 242 of the DVO-E, and draft regulations at Level 3. The VAG [German Insurance Supervision Act] follows the terminology of the German-language version of the European law in this case—unlike with the Solvency Capital Requirement—in secs. 213 f. of the VAG [German Insurance Supervision Act] 2012.

The Minimum Capital Requirement draws a line in the sand for capital resources held by insurance undertakings. If the line is crossed, "policyholders and beneficiaries are exposed to an unacceptable level of risk were insurance and reinsurance undertakings allowed to continue their operations"—as stated in art. 129, para. 1 (b) Solvency II Directive, with the equivalent in sec. 113, para. 1 of the VAG [German Insurance Supervision Act] 2012. The Minimum Capital Requirement can be met only with eligible basic own funds, meaning the highest class of own funds.[23] There are also numerous additional rules—such as quantitative floors and a low confidence level for the determination—intended to ensure that an insurance undertaking covers the Minimum Capital Requirement. Unlike the Solvency Capital Requirement, the Minimum Capital Requirement must be calculated and reported to the supervisory authority each quarter.[24]

[23] See 4.2.3.1, above.

[24] See art. 129, para. 4, subpara. 1 of the Solvency II Directive and sec. 114, para. 1 of the VAG [German Insurance Supervision Act] 2012 [Government's Draft of a Tenth Act Amending the German Insurance Supervision Act].

4.2.3.3 Special Solvency Requirements for Groups Under Supervisory Law

The Solvency II Directive governs "The Supervision of Insurance and Reinsurance Undertakings in a Group" separately, under Title III with arts. 212 to 266. Art. 212, para. 1 (c) of the Solvency II Directive defines the term "group". Under art. 213, para. 1, subpara. 2 of the Solvency II Directive—and correspondingly in sec. 231, para. 1, sent. 2 of the VAG [German Insurance Supervision Act] 2012—the "provisions of this Directive which lay down the rules for the supervision of insurance and reinsurance undertakings taken individually" generally apply to undertakings that are part of a group. The extent to which the group is subject to special supervision as an insurance group can be found in art. 213, para. 2 of the Solvency II Directive or. sec. 231, para. 2 of the VAG [German Insurance Supervision Act] 2012. This provision provides a detailed delineation on which group supervision rules apply to various types of group structure. Accordingly, the rules for solvency supervision in arts. 218 ff. of the Solvency II Directive and likewise in secs. 236 ff. of the VAG [German Insurance Supervision Act] 2012 apply to only two types of groups. The first are groups where the parent undertaking is an insurance or reinsurance undertaking[25] that participates in any insurance or reinsurance undertaking. The second are groups where the parent is an insurance holding company[26] with a head office in the Community and that, again, participates in any insurance or reinsurance undertaking.

Art. 218, para. 1 of the Solvency II Directive mandates supervision of the "solvency of the group" and provides the rules governing this in arts. 218 to 243 of the Solvency II Directive. The DVO-E expands on these in arts. 321 to 334. The VAG [German Insurance Supervision Act] 2012 seeks to implement the Directive's rules in secs. 236 ff. Many of the rules on solvency supervision at the group level correspond to the solvency supervision rules at the level of the individual undertaking. This is true, to start with, for eligible own funds and the Solvency Capital Requirement at the group level according to arts. 218, paras. 2 and 3; 230, paras. 1, subpara. 2 (a); 233, para. 1 (a), para. 2 of the Solvency II Directive, or secs. 236, paras. 2 and 3; 247, para. 1, sent. 2; 251, para. 1, no. 1, and para. 2 of the VAG [German Insurance Supervision Act] 2012. Other examples include the annual calculation frequency for the Solvency Capital requirement at group level in art. 219, para. 1, subpara. 1 of the Solvency II Directive, or. sec. 237, para. 1, sent. 1 of the VAG [German Insurance Supervision Act] 2012; the basis for a supervisory review process of group solvency requirements in art. 218, para. 4, 247 ff. of the Solvency II Directive or secs. 236, para. 1 and 261 ff.

[25] These are insurance undertakings that hold a participation pursuant to the definitions in art. 212, para. 1 (a) of the Solvency II Directive or sec. 8, no. 6 of the VAG [German Insurance Supervision Act] 2012.

[26] See definition in art. 212, para. 1 (f) of the Solvency II Directive or sec. 8 no. 24 of the VAG [German Insurance Supervision Act] 2012 [Government's Draft of a Tenth Act Amending the German Insurance Supervision Act].

of the VAG [German Insurance Supervision Act] 2012 as well as in individual regulations such as art. 244 f. of the Solvency II Directive or secs. 259 f., of the VAG [German Insurance Supervision Act] 2012; or the establishment of reporting duties on the part of the undertaking when the solvency capital requirement is not met for the group in art. 218, para. 5 of the Solvency II Directive or sec. 266, para. 3 of the VAG [German Insurance Supervision Act] 2012; and for the valuation of assets and liabilities in arts. 224, and 75 of the Solvency II Directive or sec. 69 of the VAG [German Insurance Supervision Act] 2012.

Additional supervisory requirements specifically for the solvency of groups, however, are evident because many special issues related to solvency emerge when undertakings are combined into a group. They include issues such as which of the combined undertakings to include in the solvency calculation at the group level, and to what extent (art. 221 of the Solvency II Directive or sec. 239 of the VAG [German Insurance Supervision Act] 2012); the prevention at the group level of "double gearing" in which the same eligible own funds are counted multiple times when calculating solvency capital (art. 222 of the Solvency II Directive or sec. 240 of the VAG [German Insurance Supervision Act] 2012); and the exclusion in the group solvency calculation of capital created internally through reciprocal financing of group undertakings (art. 223 of the Solvency II Directive or sec. 241 of the VAG [German Insurance Supervision Act] 2012). Added to this are detailed rules on the calculation methods for group solvency (arts. 220 and 221 ff. of the Solvency II Directive or secs. 238 and 239 ff. of the VAG [German Insurance Supervision Act] 2012). Essentially, there are two calculation methods available: a calculation based on a consolidated financial statement, referred to as the "standard method", and the deduction and aggregation method, or "alternative method".[27] These are applicable based on the criteria of art. 220, para. 2 of the Solvency II Directive or sec. 238 of the VAG [German Insurance Supervision Act] 2012. A few additional provisions on monitoring group solvency for groups with a centralized risk management function (arts. 236 ff. of the Solvency II Directive or secs. 253 ff. of the VAG [German Insurance Supervision Act] 2012) complete the series of rules governing the solvency requirements for groups. Nevertheless, there are still unanswered questions that emerge from the Directive's rules on the solvency requirements for groups, primarily with respect to determining eligible own funds in light of the two different calculation methods for group solvency.[28]

4.2.4 The Supervisory Review Process

The rules on own funds, the Solvency Capital Requirement, and the Minimum Capital Requirement form the coordinates of the solvency requirements of

[27] See on this point for more detail *Schüller/Mitzner*, n. 16, 350 ff.

[28] See *Schüller/Mitzner*, n. 16, 353 ff.

insurance supervision. The supervisory approach to monitoring whether an insurance undertaking is in compliance with these requirements is found in the regulations for the supervisory review process in art. 36 of the Solvency II Directive or in secs. 289, para. 2 and 292 of the VAG [German Insurance Supervision Act] 2012. Under this provision, "member States shall ensure that the supervisory authorities review and evaluate the strategies, processes and reporting procedures which are established by the insurance and reinsurance undertakings to comply with the laws, regulations and administrative provisions adopted pursuant to this Directive". To this end, "the supervisory authorities shall in particular review and evaluate compliance with the following: (...) the capital requirements (...)[29]; the quality and quantity of own funds (...); (...) on-going compliance with the requirements for full and partial internal models (...)".

Thus, in the list of areas to be reviewed in art. 36, para. 2 of the Solvency II Directive, which is not presented in this manner in sec. 289 of the VAG [German Insurance Supervision Act] 2012, three of the six points pertain to the solvency requirements for insurance undertakings. Added to this as items for review are the system of governance including the ORSA,[30] the technical provisions, and the investment rules. In other words, and not surprisingly, the solvency requirements incumbent upon insurance undertakings stand at the center of the supervisory review process. In the VAG [German Insurance Supervision Act] 2012, the detailed requirements for the supervisory review process are presumed to be replicated in the brief rules of secs. 289, para. 2, and 292, para. 1 sent. 3, para. 2, no. 3.[31] And sec. 1 of the VAG [German Insurance Supervision Act] 2012 even connects the solvency requirements to the very "purpose(s) of the law". According to this passage, the purpose of the VAG [German Insurance Supervision Act] encompasses "protection of insured persons, particularly against the solvency risks of insurance undertakings".

Art. 36 of the Solvency II Directive also governs the competence of the supervisory authorities. Under paragraph 3, they are required to have "appropriate monitoring tools that enable them to identify deteriorating financial conditions in an insurance or reinsurance undertaking and to monitor how that deterioration is remedied". If, on this basis of such monitoring, the supervisory authorities should determine that an insurance undertaking has deviated from the solvency requirements, they would need further authority in the area of legal consequences. This is the subject matter of art. 36, para. 5 of the Solvency II Directive: "The supervisory

---

[29] The Directive is referring here to the Solvency Capital Requirement and the Minimum Capital Requirement.

[30] See in detail *Dreher/Ballmaier*, "Die unternehmenseigene Risiko- und Solvabilitätsbeurteilung (ORSA) nach Solvency II und VAG 2012" [in English: Risk and Solvency Assessment by Undertakings (ORSA) under Solvency II and the German Insurance Supervision Act 2012], VersR (2012), 129 ff. (Chap. 5, below).

[31] See the table of corresponding sections in the annex to the government's draft (n. 6) in which sec. 292, para. 2, no. 3 of the VAG [German Insurance Supervision Act] 2012 is absent; and in detail as a whole *Dreher/Ballmaier* (n. 7).

authorities shall have the necessary powers to require insurance and reinsurance undertakings to remedy weaknesses or deficiencies identified in the supervisory review process." Sec. 292, para. 1 sent 3, and para. 2 no. 3 of the VAG [German Insurance Supervision Act] 2012 embeds the implementation in supervision based on the principle of abusiveness, which is not provided for in European law and ultimately not permissible.[32]

One of the particularly expansive powers of the supervisory authority is regulated in direct connection with the supervisory review process and explicitly refers to it: the assessment of a capital add-on for an insurance undertaking.[33] The remaining responsibilities and competences in the area of solvency requirements are spread across numerous individual rules governing own funds, the Solvency Capital Requirement and the Minimum Capital Requirement. Other important supervisory responsibilities and competences are included in the chapter on "Insurance and reinsurance undertakings in difficulty or in an irregular situation" in arts. 136 to 144 of the Solvency II Directive (or secs. 123 to 128 of the VAG [German Insurance Supervision Act] 2012), which corresponds to art. 36, para. 3 of the Solvency II Directive, in this respect not implemented in the VAG [German Insurance Supervision Act] 2012.

4.3 Complexity, Volatility and Procyclicality of the Solvency Requirements: Implications for Solvency Supervision

4.3.1 The Problems

The new solvency requirements in the Solvency II system also bring a new set of problems to solvency supervision. Three realities that will shape them in the future can be identified as complexity, volatility, and procyclicality, which are the subject of closer analysis below. A few additional problems arise which cannot be addressed in detail in the present context.

The substantial lack of transparency of the solvency requirements and their supervision can be counted among these additional problems. The melange of legal requirements and economic assessment found in the solvency requirements are entirely intransparent, if not incomprehensible, even for economists and legal experts who are not constantly involved with it, not to mention the policyholders

[32] See on this point 4.4.2.5, below, as well as *Dreher/Lange*, n. 22, 831 f.; *Bürkle*. n. 22, 1472 ff.; *Bürkle* and *Grote*, "Die aufsichtsbehördlichen Eingriffsbefugnisse nach Solvency II" [in English: Supervisory Intervention Powers under Solvency II], in: Dreher/Wandt, eds., Solvency II in der Rechtsanwendung [in English: Solvency II in Legal Application] (2009), 191 ff. and 225 ff.

[33] See n. 10, above.

and insured persons beyond that.[34] This regulatory farrago stands in striking contrast to the simultaneous requirement of insurance undertakings under arts. 51 and 256 of the Solvency II Directive or secs. 50 and 269 of the VAG [German Insurance Supervision Act] 2012 to provide public information on the details of their own capital requirement and its coverage with own funds in a "report on solvency and financial condition".[35] The lack of transparency is compounded by the decoupling of the solvency requirements from accounting requirements. The economic balance sheet or the solvency statement on which it is based[36] is to be prepared,[37] audited,[38] and submitted to the supervisory authority independently from the balance sheet for accounting purposes.[39] The only link to accounting in this economic balance sheet is the market-based valuation of assets and liabilities.[40] To confuse matters further, there is the additional requirement that insurance undertakings submit yet a third "solvency assessment", distinct from both the economic balance sheet and the accounting balance sheet, which assesses as part of the ORSA the "overall solvency needs" and "compliance, on a continuous basis, with the capital requirements", among other things—this according to art. 45, para. 1 of the Solvency II Directive or sec. 28, para. 2 VAG [German Insurance Supervision Act] 2012.[41] And none of this includes the balance sheet prepared for tax purposes.

Aside from lack of transparency, there is the further problem of path dependence[42] in the Solvency Capital Requirement, which is not discussed in depth.

[34] The BaFin [Federal Financial Supervisory Authority] provides a good example in its "Ergebnisse der fünften quantitativen Auswirkungsstudie zu Solvency II (QIS 5)" [in English: Results of the Fifth Quantitative Impact Study on Solvency II (QIS5)], (2011), p. 22 where, among 27 undertakings participating in the QIS 5 with respect to the solvency calculation using internal models, "most undertakings expect to apply to use a fully internal model even though, for example, this model omits operational risk".

[35] On this point see *Dreher/Schaaf*, "Die Veröffentlichungspflichten von Versicherungsunternehmen gegenüber der Allgemeinheit" [in English: Insurance Undertakings' Duty of Disclosure to the Public], in Dreher/Wandt, eds., Solvency II in der Rechtsanwendung [in English: Solvency II in Legal Application] (2009), 129 ff. (Chap. 13, below).

[36] See 4.2.1, above.

[37] See 4.2.1, above, and explicitly sec. 69, para. 1, sent. 2 of the VAG [German Insurance Supervision Act] 2012 [Government's Draft of a Tenth Act Amending the German Insurance Supervision Act].

[38] See sec. 45, para. 2 of the VAG [German Insurance Supervision Act] 2012 [Government's Draft of a Tenth Act Amending the German Insurance Supervision Act], and above, n. 15.

[39] [39] See sec. 47, para. 2 of the VAG [German Insurance Supervision Act] 2012 [Government's Draft of a Tenth Act Amending the German Insurance Supervision Act], and above, n. 15.

[40] See 4.3.3.1, below.

[41] See in detail on this point *Dreher/Ballmaier*, n. 30, passim and 134 specifically on the relationship of ORSA to the solvency requirement as it pertains to the economic balance sheet.

[42] See on this point generally and not from a legal perspective, in lieu of multiple citations, and with further references, for example, *Ackermann*, Pfadabhängigkeit, Institutionen und Regelungen, [in English: Path Dependence, Institutions and Regulations] (2001).

Insurance undertakings have numerous choices for the solvency requirement, and this for good reasons inherent to the system—namely, to enable the determination of required solvency capital based on the individual risk status. At the forefront is the choice from among the standard model, the standard model with individual parameters, the partial internal model, and the full internal model. Once this choice is made, or another of the numerous options selected, any subsequent change entails supervisory notifications and approvals, possibly with the necessity of making unpleasant declarations—including to the public. It can also involve high material and staff costs. Moreover, with this sort of change, comparability to earlier calculations is lost and thus the problem of lack of transparency in the Solvency Capital Requirement surfaces once again. From the perspective of the undertaking and the supervisory authority, this sort of path dependence is essentially neutral and—as is often argued in economics—a natural consequence of the systemic right to choose. It can mutate into a risk, however, if the required path corrections are not actually made or not made in time.

4.3.2 *Complexity*

4.3.2.1 The Flood of Regulations

Holding first place on the list of the problems brought on by solvency supervision is complexity. Highlighted in this regard pars pro toto are the detailed supervisory requirements for own funds and their valuation at market price under art. 75 of the Solvency II Directive or sec. 69 of the VAG [German Insurance Supervision Act] 2012 for individual undertakings and under art. 224 of the Solvency II Directive or again sec. 69 of the VAG [German Insurance Supervision Act] 2012 for groups; also, the qualitative and quantitative criteria for eligibility, which are found for individual undertakings in arts. 93 ff. and 98 ff., respectively, of the Solvency II Directive or secs. 82 ff. and 85 f., respectively, of the VAG [German Insurance Supervision Act] 2012, and for groups in arts. 222 and 223 of the Solvency II Directive or secs. 240 f. of the VAG [German Insurance Supervision Act] 2012.[43] This also applies to the different rules for the Solvency Capital Requirement and the Minimum Capital Requirement. The complexity of the provisions in these three areas, with 59 articles in the Solvency II Directive at the first level alone, increases many times over at the second and third regulatory levels. At the second level alone, the draft implementing measures contains 183 articles covering own funds, the Solvency Capital Requirement and the Minimum Capital Requirement.

[43] See on this point *Schüller/Mitzner*, n. 16, 356.

4.3.2.2 The Failure of the Principles-Based Approach in Solvency Supervision

In the existing laws, the fundamental principles-based approach has been abandoned. It was the starting point for the Solvency II idea[44] and is still given lip service in Brussels today. Regardless of the level of normative detail, however, the problem in the relationship between a basis in principles and solvency requirements is not so much in the scope and depth of the solvency provisions. Instead, it lies in the all too programmatic requirement for the principles-based approach as a general theme of Solvency II. For the new risk-focused solvency supervision, however, such a requirement was a poor fit from the outset. This is so because the capital resources crucial to the existence of the insurance undertaking and therefore to the rise and fall in the claims of the policyholders and insureds as creditors, cannot be handled simply with indefinite supervisory requirements such as "adequacy" and "self-assessment". Required in this area instead are additional normative requirements with the greatest possible definitiveness. Their complexity and sophistication mirrors that of modern life.

Thus a failure of the proposed conversion from a system of binding rules to a system based on expansive principles is unavoidable in this area. As a significant factor in the internal market for insurance, the capital charges necessitate essentially unified solvency rules for all insurance undertakings. The solvency discretion provided in the system can apply only to the individual risk exposure of each insurance undertaking and not to the basic issue of required solvency and its determination. Anything else would mean regulatory arbitrage, inefficient allocation proceedings, and, from a legal perspective in particular, contestable unequal treatment.[45] This is why the Solvency II Directive emphasizes the principle of equivalent treatment of all insurance undertakings as a basis for solvency supervision directly in the solvency provisions of arts. 77, para. 5, subpara. 2, 104, para. 5, 106, para. 2 and 111, para. 1.

[44] See on this point in more detail *Dreher*, "Das Risikomanagement nach § 64 a VAG und Solvency II" [in English: Risk Management under Sec. 64 1 of the German Insurance Supervision Act and Solvency II], VersR (2008), 998 (999 ff.); *Wandt/Sehrbrock*, n. 22, 203 ff.; *Bürkle*, n. 22, 1476 f.; *Schaaf*, Risikomanagement und Compliance in Versicherungsunternehmen – aufsichtsrechtliche Anforderungen und Organverantwortung [in English: Risk Management and Compliance in Insurance Undertakings – Supervisory Requirements and Institutional Responsibility] (2010), 25 f.

[45] See also government's draft, n. 5, Statement of Reasons, p. 258. *Bürkle*, n. 22, 1477 concludes differently: "[D]etailed provisions at Level 2 in the Lamfalussy process would generally not conform to the Directive" and who should on this basis reach the conclusion that wide parts of the DVO-E are inconsistent with European law – in particular, the extensive 128 articles with solvency provisions.

4.3.2.3 Equivalent Treatment of Insurance Undertakings in Solvency Supervision

The principle of equivalent treatment[46] highlights a matter brought on by the complexity of the solvency requirements. An initial aspect of this is seen in a problem facing small and medium sized undertakings[47]: The new risk-focused solvency requirements offer the possibility, at the group or individual level of the undertaking, to use parameters specific to that undertaking via internal models in the interest of obtaining better, meaning lower, solvency requirements. But these models are only appropriate for a few insurance undertakings because of their complexity and the associated cost, which is widely acknowledged to be very high. Currently in Germany the number of such models planned, as indicated by pre-applications at the BaFin [Federal Financial Supervisory Authority], is said to be in the single digits. For small and medium sized insurance undertakings which are nevertheless broadly diversified, the option is de facto unavailable for the most part.

This raises the issue of equivalent treatment of insurance undertakings under supervisory law, given that, in line with a de facto restriction on access, only large insurance undertakings are likely to be able to use internal models while small and medium sized insurance undertakings are blocked from doing so because of the expense it entails.[48] It has also been heard from large insurance undertakings in the process of pre-applying for internal models that the expense is very high, even for them. Further, they question whether it will be of any ultimate benefit to their solvency requirements.

Against this background, the supervisory consequence of the equivalent treatment problem can only be that the supervisory authorities for now have a responsibility to monitor whether the use of full or partial internal models leads, on average, to marked improvement in the solvency of the relevant undertakings. Supervisory authorities will be aided in this respect by their power under art. 112, para. 7 of the Solvency II Directive or sec. 102, para. 7 of the VAG [German Insurance Supervision Act] 2012 to require insurance undertakings to submit an alternative estimate of the Solvency Capital Requirement based on the standard model after their internal model has been approved. If a clear solvency advantage for insurance undertakings using an internal model is revealed,[49] the supervisory authorities are required to introduce this overall by means of future law in a review

[46] See 4.3.2.2, above.

[47] See *Dreher*, n. 44, 1000.

[48] See in general on the mandate for "proportionate application of this Directive, in particular to small insurance undertakings", art. 29, para. 4 of the Solvency II Directive and Recitals 5, 19, 32, 59 and 66 of the Solvency II Directive.

[49] EIOPA has determined, in its "Report on the fifth quantitative impact study" (QIS 5) for Solvency II (14 Mar. 2011, e.g. p. 7) that insurance groups applying an internal model need to hold just 80 % of the solvency capital that would be required under the standard model. The BaFin [Federal Financial Supervisory Authority], n. 34, p. 22 summarizes the solvency calculation of

of solvency supervision under the Solvency II system. Most significantly, however, the effect with respect to substantive realization of equivalent treatment under supervisory law that already ensues in the present law from the de facto block on the use of internal models for small and medium sized insurance undertakings with broad insurance operations[50] is that the supervisory authorities will liberally approve their use of undertaking-specific parameters in the standard model according to art. 104, Abs. 7 of the Solvency II Directive or sec. 100, para. 2 of the VAG [German Insurance Supervision Act] 2012 based on the principle of proportionality[51] just as liberally as they allow the option of a simplified calculation when justified by the absence of risk complexity under art. 109 of the Solvency II Directive or sec. 100, para. 1 of the VAG [German Insurance Supervision Act] 2012.[52]

The second aspect of potential unequal treatment in the context of complex solvency requirements affects the "monoline" insurer. These are specialty insurance undertakings in such areas as legal defense insurance, animal insurance, and weather insurance for agriculture. Because of their focused risk position[53] the standard model is clearly not suitable.[54] Therefore, regardless of their size within the competitive arena over the long term, they are de facto forced to choose a partial internal model or make extensive use of deviations from the standard formula that are specific to their undertaking. Alternatively the supervisory authorities can require that such undertakings apply parameters specific to the undertaking for certain risk modules in accordance with art. 110 of the Solvency II Directive or sec. 101 of the VAG [German Insurance Supervision Act] 2012, or use an internal model in accordance with art 119 of the Solvency II Directive or sec. 87, para. 2 of the VAG [German Insurance Supervision Act] 2012. In terms of supervision, the effect once again is that these types of applications must be liberally approved based on the principle of proportionality. Conversely, however, the supervisory

---

27 undertakings from 10 groups using internal models as follows: "The results reported are between 25 % and 250 % of SCR calculated under the standard formula, with a median of 85 %".

[50] On potential "competitive disadvantages for insurers that apply the standard formula", see also the motion of the CDU/CSU and FDP factions, BT-Drucks. [Document of the German Bundestag], 17/6456, p. 3, statement of reason to no. 5.

[51] See Recital 19 of the Solvency II Directive: "This Directive should not be too burdensome for small and medium sized insurance undertakings. One of the tools by which to achieve that objective is the proper application of the proportionality principle".

[52] See Recital 66 of the Solvency II Directive: "In order to reflect the specific situation of small and medium sized undertakings, simplified approaches to the calculation of the Solvency Capital Requirement in accordance with the standard formula should be provided for".

[53] See on this example of a legal defense insurer *Faßbender*, "Europäische Ordnungspolitik im Umbruch: Auswirkungen auf ein international tätiges Familienunternehmen" [in English: The Transformation of European Regulatory Policy: Effects on a Family Business with International Operations], in: Insurance law institute at the university of Düsseldorf, ed., Perspektiven der Deutschen Versicherungswirtschaft im europäischen Wettbewerb [in English: Perspectives on the Insurance Business in Germany in European Competition] (2011), 1 (7 f.).

[54] See also Recital 26, sent. 4 of the Solvency II Directive.

authorities should use restraint in exercising their discretion when faced with a contrary decision by insurance undertakings, even in mandating the use of company-specific parameters in the standard model or the internal model instead of the standard model.

4.3.3 Volatility

4.3.3.1 The Market-Consistent Valuation of Assets and Liabilities (Fair Value)

Recital 54 of the Solvency II Directive states that the calculation of technical provisions should be, i.a., "in line with international developments in accounting and supervision". Further, under arts. 88, no. 1 and 224 of the Solvency II Directive in combination with. art. 75 of the Solvency II Directive or under sec. 69, paras. 2, 3 of the VAG [German Insurance Supervision Act] 2012, both assets and liabilities must be valued at market value at the group level and the level of the individual undertaking. Thus, under art. 75, para. 1 of the Solvency II Directive assets and liabilities are "valued at the amount for which they could be exchanged between knowledgeable willing parties in an arm's length transaction" or "transferred or settled" under the same terms. This definition of fair value is based on the definition from the International Financial Reporting Standards (IFRS) in International Accounting Standard (IAS) 39.9. Unlike other insurance undertakings, this is nothing new in the consolidated financial statements for insurance undertakings based in the capital markets within the meaning of sec. 264d of the HGB [German Commercial Code] due to the market valuation principles in IFRS accounting that apply to many of the assets in accordance with secs. 290 and 315a of the HGB [German Commercial Code]. What is new, however, is the definition's extension to all assets and all insurance undertakings.

Arts. 5 to 11 of the DVO-E contain further details. Art. 7 V3, para. 1 of the DVO-E presumes a valuation according to market prices in active markets as basic policy. If such market price is not available, para. 2 refers to modeling based on active markets that exist for similar assets and liabilities. If values cannot be determined in this way either, then paras. 4 and 5 provide for alternative valuation methods that make maximum use of relevant market inputs and rely as little as possible on undertaking-specific inputs.

Thus the objective pursued by Solvency II is essentially a market-consistent valuation of assets and liabilities. But market values fluctuate constantly and sometimes considerably. This can generate considerable uncertainties and disparities for the solvency-related requirements on the asset side of the insurance undertaking's economic balance sheet and solvency statement,[55] which are

[55] See 4.2.1, above.

definitive in this regard. This high volatility is further exacerbated by the extensive use of models to determine unavailable prices on both sides of the balance sheet, but particularly on the liability side.[56]

4.3.3.2 The Confidence Level

Of particular interest for application of the law are the liabilities side and the confidence level prescribed in the Solvency II system for fulfillment of obligations. The intent of the Directive is to "ensure that ruin occurs no more often than once in every 200 cases or, alternatively, that those undertakings will still have at least a 99.5 % probability of meeting their obligations to policyholders and beneficiaries arising over the following 12 months."[57] Accordingly, the 99.5 % confidence level for a year is mandated in arts. 101, para. 3, subpara. 2; 104, para. 4, subpara. 1; 122, paras. 1 and 2; and 129, para. 1 (c) of the Solvency II Directive—likewise in secs. 88, para. 2, sent. 4; 91, para. 3, sent. 1; and 109, para. 2, sent. 2 of the VAG [German Insurance Supervision Act] 2012.[58] The same applies at the group level under arts. 218, para. 2, 3; 230, para. 1, subpara. 2 (a); 233, para. 1, (a), and para. 2 of the Solvency II-Directive or secs. 236, 247, and 251 of the VAG [German Insurance Supervision Act] 2012.

Calibrating the Solvency Capital Requirements on this "200-year event" is unsubstantiated and cannot be derived as statistically "right". This criterion shares that trait with almost all quantitative limits established by the law.[59] And the legislator is given a great deal of latitude in setting commercial law under the constitution. The legislator may "pursue all appropriate economic policy as long as it complies with the constitution, and fundamental rights in particular (. . .). The legislator has a large degree of freedom in formulating (the law)."[60] Since this also includes the "law on politico-economic failure",[61] questionable models other than

[56] A critical view to such fair value analyses: *Deutsche Prüfstelle für Rechnungslegung e.V.* [in English: Financial Reporting Enforcement Panel], Activity Report 2011, p. 9; and in detail, *id.*, Comments with regard to the IASB Consultation Paper "Agenda Consultation 2011", 28 Nov. 2011.

[57] Recital 64 of the Solvency II Directive.

[58] See on this point the listing for 200-year events by country in European Commission, "Annexes to the QIS5 Technical Specifications", 5 Jul. 2010, p. 42, Annex L.5.

[59] See on this point essentially, *Rittner*, "Quantitative Legaldefinitionen im Wirtschaftsrecht" [in English: Quantitative Legal Definitions in Economic Law] in: Gedächtnisschrift Rödig [in English: Publication in Memory of Jürgen Rodig] (1978), 74 ff.

[60] See, in German law, BVerfGE 50, 290, 238 [German Federal Constitutional Court Decisions] – co-determination and generally, *Rittner/Dreher*, Europäisches und deutsches Wirtschaftsrecht [in English: European and German Economic Law] (3rd ed. 2008), sec. 4, ref. 10 and sec. 6 ref. 12 f. The same applies in the European law.

[61] BVerfGE [German Federal Constitutional Court Decisions], n. 60, ibid.

irrational excesses with no relevance in the present context must be accepted as an exercise of the legislative prerogative to estimate.

4.3.3.3 The Zero-Risk Weighting of Government Bonds

This applies as well to "zero-risk weighting", i.a., of bonds issued by EU/European Economic Area Member States, referring to their acceptance at nominal value without additional coverage by own funds in the market risk models according to arts. 13, no. 31 and 105, para. 5, subpara 2 (d) of the Solvency II Directive or secs. 8, no. 26 and 95, para. 2, sent. 1, no. 4 VAG [German Insurance Supervision Act] 2012 regardless of whether the government bonds in question are issued by Germany, Italy, or Greece. Insurance undertakings should correct this obvious distortion—which arose with the QIS 5 study[62] and is now expressly provided for in Art. 163 SR7, para. 3 (b) of the DVO-E[63]—of the Solvency Capital Requirements of Pillar I of Solvency II, and indeed at the level of the Own Risk and Solvency Assessment (ORSA) in Pillar II.[64] This discrepancy is partially to be corrected in the exercise of solvency supervision in that a capital add-on cannot be ordered by the authorities[65] based on these ORSA evaluations.[66]

4.3.3.4 The Interest Rate Yield Curve, or: Systems Competition in Supervisory Clothing

Another example of volatility of the Solvency Capital Requirements arises with the interest rate yield curve in life insurance. Under art. 77, para. 2, of the Solvency II Directive or sec. 72, para. 1 VAG [German Insurance Supervision Act] 2012, this determination is the basis for the valuation of technical provisions according to a hypothesis that a default-free investment is possible at this interest rate. An interest rate reduction requires higher technical reserves under the market-based valuation and thus additional own funds coverage is required.[67] In view of the long-term nature of the life insurance business and the assumption of corresponding interest guarantees, even small changes in the yield curve have significant impact on the

---

[62] European Commission, QIS5 Technical Specifications, 05 Jul. 2010, p. 123 at SCR.5.88.

[63] Likewise for credit institutions, art. 109, para. 4 of the proposal for regulation on prudential requirements for credit institutions and investment firms, COM(2011) 452 final. (Capital Requirements Directive IV).

[64] German Federal Government, Answer to parliamentary question, BT-Drucks. [Document of the German Bundestag] 17/8225, 19 Dec. 2011, p. 10.

[65] See on this point n. 10 above.

[66] See *Dreher/Ballmaier*, n. 30, 134, 142.

[67] See art. 76, para. 3 of the Solvency II Directive or sec. 70, para. 3 of the VAG [German Insurance Supervision Act] 2012.

solvency requirements.[68] German life insurance undertakings are particularly sensitive to this. They hold large amounts of fixed-interest bonds whose average terms do not correspond to those of the average interest guarantees, which results in “duration mismatch”. In contrast, foreign EU life insurances pass the risk of changing interest rates to the policyholder with investment risk by focusing on fund-linked life insurance.

For liquid investment securities beyond the 20-year limit that are not—at least not sufficiently traded on the market, a future projection of interest rates is required. In the current state of discussions, the projection is obtained through an extrapolation in accordance with art. 39 IR4 of DVO-E which begins, according to Recital 20 of the DVO-E, after 20 years. On the basis of the “Forward Rate” in national economies,[69] this extrapolated interest yield curve transitions in the 60th year[70] to the “Ultimate Forward Rate” (UFR) in accordance with art. 40 IR5 of the DVO-E.[71] Ultimately, the yield curve amounts to an assumed development of interest rates that provides insurance undertakings with a specific interest rate for future decades that they can apply as the assumed risk-free rate under supervisory law. It is based on hypothetical scenarios in the absence of actual market data. After a few earlier divergent drafts, the approach on which the Level 2 rules are based still appears more politically motivated than based in economics when one considers the transition methodology applied for years 20 through 60 and the resulting determination of the Ultimate Forward Rate after that in the amount of 4.2 %,[72] which consists of 2 % inflation and 2.2 % real interest in accordance with the criteria of art. 40 IR5, para. 2 of the DVO-E.[73] Relatively small changes in the actual assumptions raise or lower the capital requirements for insurance undertakings by up to several 100 % factors. Based on the assumed market situation, the same undertaking is considered over-capitalized at one point and under-capitalized at another.

This method of determining the interest rate yield curve and, above all, its individual elements by means of a delegated legal act of the EU Commission leads to a fundamental legal question. Art. 290 of the Treaty on the Functioning of the European Union (TFEU) expressly provides for such legal acts and art. 86 (a) of the Solvency II Directive even assigns determination of the “relevant risk-free interest rate term structure” to the Commission. European primary law sets the following restriction for all such delegation in art. 290, para. 1, subpara. 2, sent. 2 of the TFEU: “The essential elements of an area shall be reserved for the legislative

---

[68] See, for example, BaFin [Federal Financial Supervisory Authority], n. 34, p. 14 ff. with data on the specific changes to the solvency requirements in life insurance based on QIS 5.

[69] See EIOPA (European Insurance and Occupational Pensions Authority), QIS5: Relevant risk-free interest rate term structures, 6 Jul. 2010.

[70] See. art. 39 IR4, para. 4 of the DVO-E.

[71] See European Commission, Annexes to the QIS5 Technical Provisions, 5 Jul. 2010, p. 20, n. 2 and p. 23 at 8. iv).

[72] European Commission, n. 71, p. 20. In currencies other than the euro, the interest rate deviates to some extent.

[73] See CEIOPS, Paper on extrapolation of risk-free rates, 02 Aug. 2010, p. 3.

act and accordingly shall not be the subject of a delegation of power". This is to prevent the adoption of binding legislation without formal legislative procedure, in alignment with art. 289, para. 3 of the TFEU. On the other hand, delegation provides relief to the EU legislator from the need to overload formal EU law with technical details.[74] However, the three elements of the yield curve provided are not simply technical details. They play a critical role in deciding on market admission or exit and determining the competitive position of insurance undertakings in the internal market by establishing the criteria for required solvency resources.

Especially in view of the various conceptions of cash-value life and pension insurance with fixed guarantees in Germany and fund-linked life and pension insurance without such guarantees in many other Member States of the European Union, particularly the United Kingdom and Ireland, what emerges as a matter of fact and a matter of law is clear: not the determination of technical details at all, but rather systems competition in supervisory clothing. While with cash-value life insurance the capital costs for insurance undertakings in the context of future interest rate trends become the decisive competitive factor,[75] the risks in fund-linked insurance arising from capital investments—which include interest rate development risk—are essentially passed to the policyholder. Thus the content of the interest rate yield curve and the determination of methodology for its calculation is not just a matter of insignificant technical detail that can be regulated without formal legislative action by the EU. It is a central element of the normative system, and specifically, of supervisory law for insurance undertakings. Since this element of the capital charges of insurance undertakings also controls the pricing of insurance protection for private pensions,[76] the object of these material determinations of the interest rate yield curve is not the insurance supervision regime alone, but the functioning of private group pensions in Germany.

4.3.3.5 Economic Pluralistic Methodology and Openness in Respect of Results Versus Legally Compliant Discretionary Powers in Prognosis and Evaluation for Solvency Requirements

The Solvency II legislator is, in fact, aware of the problem of volatility. But the result is mainly that the volatility of individual risk factors is supposed to have explicit influence on the calculation of solvency requirements. This is seen for example in art. 105, para. 3, subpara. 2 (a) to (f); para. 4, subpara. 2 (a); and para.

[74] See *Gellermann* in: Streinz, ed., EUV/AEUV [Treaty on European Union/Treaty on the Functioning of the European Union] (2nd ed. 2012), art. 290 AEUV [Treaty on the Functioning of the European Union], ref. 2; *Bueren*, "Grenzen der Durchführungsrechtssetzung im Unionsrecht" [in English: Limits on Adoption of Implementing Law in EU Legislation], EuZW (2012), 167 ff., each with further references.

[75] According to the QIS 5 study, 10 % of the participants from Germany still report coverage quotas below 100 %, see BaFin [Federal Financial Supervisory Authority], n. 34, p. 13.

[76] See also motion of the CDU/CSU and FDP factions, n. 50, p. 2 at no. 3.

5 of the Solvency II Directive or sec. 93 of the VAG [German Insurance Supervision Act] 2012, and thus in particular for the market risk defined in art. 13, no. 31 of the Solvency II Directive or sec. 8, no. 26 of the VAG [German Insurance Supervision Act] 2012. With rules of this nature, however, the European legislator is attempting only to integrate the volatility of individual risk factors into the solvency capital calculation. These rules are not concerned with confronting the volatility of the Solvency Capital Requirement as such from a supervisory perspective. This goal is pursued by the Directive only marginally, such as with the so-called shock absorbers under art. 106, para. 3 of the Solvency II Directive or sec. 97, para. 3 of the VAG [German Insurance Supervision Act] 2012 or at the level of general supervisory authority.[77]

The extent to which the calculation methodology determines the solvency requirements for insurance undertakings is revealed, for example, in the three tiers of the qualitative classification system of own funds under art. 93 of the Solvency II Directive or sec. 82 of the VAG [German Insurance Supervision Act] 2012.[78] In the QIS 5 study, German insurance undertakings assigned 97 % of their own funds to Tier 1. This has definite consequences—positive for insurance undertakings—on the quantitative own-funds limits in the form of Tier limits under art. 98 of the Solvency II Directive secs. 85 f. of the VAG [German Insurance Supervision Act] 2012. Without further explanation, the BaFin [Federal Financial Supervisory Authority] commented on this as part of its QIS 5 study as follows: "The BaFin is unconvinced of the validity of these results".[79] Two sides of the same coin, two completely different views: while the qualification of own funds by insurance undertakings generally anticipates no relevant market effects, the BaFin finding suggests the opposite. Both views relate to the same insurance supervisory regime requirements and implementation in actuarial assumptions.

How much the solvency of insurance undertakings can fluctuate overall under the proposed Solvency Capital Requirements is further proven by example in the solvency calculation according to the QIS 5 study of the EU Commission. For this recent impact study, the BaFin [Federal Financial Supervisory Authority] referred to a "volatility of the approach to determining coverage overall" in its assessment of the solvency requirement for life insurance.[80] In concrete terms, this means that for one and the same undertaking in the context of the QIS 5 study solvency cover could be anywhere between 80 % and 300 % in modeling based on various parameters used.[81]

---

[77] See on this point 4.3.4.4, below.

[78] See on this point 4.2.4, above.

[79] BaFin [Federal Financial Supervisory Authority], n. 34, p. 14.

[80] BaFin [Federal Financial Supervisory Authority], n. 34, p. 14; see also EIOPA, n. 49, pp. 8 and 17.

[81] See *Pfeifer* according to a report in VW (2011), 1593 and concerning the ability of individual undertakings to influence solvency in using an internal model, for example *Höppner*, "Unternehmenssteuerung durch Solvency II weiterentwickeln" [in English: To further develop corporate management through Solvency II] VW (2012), 280 (281).

Rules that enable such a range of results that have serious regulatory consequences can hardly be the legal basis for supervisory action consistent with basic rights. Therefore, after the final determination of the solvency rules on the three levels, it would be necessary to review, first and foremost, whether the supervisory requirements with the individual criteria are entirely indeterminate or if it is only in their method of implementation that these types of varying determinations emerge due to justifiable differences of actuarial opinion. If the first case turns out to be true, it would be difficult under current administrative and constitutional law to find in such effective legal bases for administrative action. If the second case holds true, the pluralistic methodology would need supervisory containment on a factually convincing basis that is then written into the laws. In both cases, therefore, as all of the examples show, some follow-up work and fine tuning with respect to this problem of volatility from the legal perspective must still be performed for a legally certain implementation, no matter what the concrete solvency requirements are. From a legal perspective two topics have particular significance to these as yet outstanding corrections, namely the valuation and projection discretion of the legislator and the supervisory authorities who implement the legislative requirements.[82]

4.3.4 *Procyclicality*

4.3.4.1 Distortions of Reality

Closely associated with the volatility of the solvency requirements and even partly inherent in them is a corresponding procyclicality. This is already clear in the relationship between external ratings to capital investments and supervisory solvency requirements. If the ratings of investments, equities, or other capital investments of the insurance undertaking decline, their solvency requirements increase while investment conditions simultaneously deteriorate. The same applies to the relationship between falling interest on capital and the actuarial interest commitments for cash-value life and pension insurance, which leads not only to higher solvency requirements but also to a deterioration of new business. The procyclicality within this means an even stronger impact from economic trends that affect the solvency requirements of insurance undertakings.[83] The same holds

[82] See 4.4.2.5, below at *Undefined Legal Terms* and 4.4.2.5 at *Projection Focus and Proportionality*.

[83] See in general on the procyclicality of risk management systems in financial crises *Müller/ Brackschulze*, "Prozyklische Effekte von Risikomanagementsystemen nach KonTraG den in Finanz- und Vertrauenskrisen" [in English: Procyclical Effects of Risk Management Systems under the Corporate Control and Transparency Act (KonTraG) in Financial and Confidence Crises], DB (2011), 2389 ff.

true for the rigid 99.5 % value-at-risk confidence level,[84] which is specifically based on current fair value.[85] In fluctuating economic cycles, the respective worst- or best-case scenarios follow, distorting reality in a procyclical way.[86]

For long-term contracts, the solvency capital system of Solvency II attempts to partially soften the negative effects unleashed by distortions in the financial markets on the solvency of insurance undertakings. Behind this is the assumption that policyholders will largely maintain their contracts even during financial market distortions. In these cases and under certain conditions a temporary release of insurance undertakings from the solvency requirements seems reasonable.

4.3.4.2 The Matching Premium

An instrument for this is the "matching premium" under Recital 24 ff. and arts. 37 IR1, para. 1, (c), 42bis and 42ter of the DVO-E. This constitutes a premium to the risk-free interest rate, with the result that the discounted obligations of the regulation's addressee to the policyholder are lower and are therefore subject to lower requirements for own funds. The same is supposed to happen as a type of symmetrical adjustment through a reduction to the yield curve if capital investments perform well, with the result that the value of obligations rises. Due to the numerous conditions for applicability of the premium according to the DVO-E—for example, portfolios of obligations and assets that are separately held, hedged, and separately managed—these premiums are likely to yield little significance for insurance undertakings in Germany, unlike for other Member States, based on the current draft regulations.

4.3.4.3 The Counter-Cyclical Premium

A significant contribution to dampening procyclical effects could be made, however, by the "counter-cyclical premium" (CCP) under arts. 37 IR1 no. 1 (b) and 41 IR6 of the DVO-E. This is the successor instrument to the illiquidity premium that had been the subject of the QIS 5 study.[87] Like the matching premium, this premium is supposed to moderate excessive capital requirements resulting from long-term guarantees made by insurance undertakings.

The counter-cyclical premium faces considerable legal reservations[88] from several perspectives. To begin with, it is not provided for in the primary law,

[84] See on this point 4.3.3.2, above.

[85] See 4.3.3.1, above.

[86] See *Höppner*, n. 81, 281.

[87] See BaFin [Federal Financial Supervisory Authority], n. 34, p. 11 f.

[88] On economic doubt see *Gründel/Schmeiser*, "Langzeit-Garantien und 'antizyklische Prämie'" [in English: Long-term Guarantees and 'Anti-cyclical' Premiums'], VW (2011), 1595.

which is also true of the matching premium. The rule then cedes two critical decisions to a single authority alone, namely EIOPA, through a delegated legal act of the EU Commission. Since the premium is expressly "zero" under normal conditions, it takes effect, according to art. 41 IR6, para. 1 of the DVO-E, only in "periods of stressed markets".[89]

The first critical decision, namely as to whether such a period is present and its duration, is made solely by EIOPA. The DVO-E provides three criteria for this, each of which depends on a number of undefined legal terms. Thus one criterion is whether there is a "fall in financial markets which is unforeseen, sharp and steep".[90] If EIOPA determines that this situation exists, it alone also makes the second critical decision, that concerning the starting level of the premium. It likewise determines, on its sole authority, reductions to the premium each quarter after the first year of introduction, and on any increases to it each quarter immediately after introduction.

All of these rules and the decisions based on them are central to insurance supervisory regime determinations. They specifically affect the criteria for the Solvency Capital Requirement itself and other measures taken by insurance undertakings. Under art. 41 IR6, para. 6 of the DVO-E, for example, insurance undertakings are required to submit solvency capital calculations to the supervisory authority under the hypothetical assumption of an anti-cyclical premium of zero, and in cases where the solvency capital is insufficient, to submit a corresponding recovery plan. While the former burdens the undertaking with expense and represents a measure of supervisory relief, the latter is eyebrow-raising and inconsistent with the intent of the anti-cyclical premium. If its specific intention is to provide adjustment to Solvency Capital Requirements in turbulent financial markets, EIOPA cannot simultaneously demand that undertakings submit plans for a restoration of the solvency capital requirement assuming stable financial market conditions—and all of this in the guise of technical rules without any formal supervision legislation from the EU and thus without any influence of the Member States on the resulting material legislation. Such legislation, therefore, has no democratic legitimacy.

4.3.4.4 The "Exceptional Movements in the Financial Markets" as Supervisory Criterion

A general starting point for the consideration of procyclical effects, as well as the volatility of own funds, in the supervision of insurance undertakings is actually found in art. 28, para. 2, of the Solvency II Directive or sec. 289, para. 1, sent. 4 of the VAG [German Insurance Supervision Act] 2012, which states the following: "In

[89] In this connection, Recital 22 of the DVO-E adverts to illiquid markets or excess credit spreads "particularly with respect to government bonds".

[90] Art. 41 IR6, para. 1, sent. 2 (c) of the DVO-E.

times of exceptional movements in the financial markets, supervisory authorities shall take into account the potential procyclical effects of their actions".

The Statement of Reasons for sec. 289, sent. 4 of the VAG [German Insurance Supervision Act] 2012, which implements the regulation, presumes the following, which is very restrictive and hardly definable: "The exceptional movements in the financial markets mentioned in sentence 4 refer to situations that are graver than the normal lows of an economic cycle but that do not necessarily occur with the same crisis-like intensity and dynamic of an exceptional fall in financial market within the meaning of 125, para. 4". The passage referred to, sec. 125, para. 4 of the VAG [German Insurance Supervision Act] 2012 implements art. 138, para. 4 of the Solvency II Directive which contains the regulation for situations where the solvency capital requirement is not covered. Based on the prior determination of an "exceptional fall in financial markets", once again by EIOPA,[91] the supervisory authority can "extend by an appropriate period of time" the deadline prescribed for implementation of the recovery plan in these specific cases. On the other hand, art. 28, para. 2 of the Solvency II Directive or sec. 289, para. 1, sent. 4 VAG [German Insurance Supervision Act] 2012 provides a general rule applicable to all supervisory actions in the scope of solvency supervision. This general rule must therefore be observed in the context of supervisory discretion and the proportionality of supervisory intervention.

4.4 The New Roles of the Managing and Supervisory Boards, Supervisory Authorities, Courts and Insurance Academics in the Solvency Supervision of Insurance Undertakings

4.4.1 The Managing and Supervisory Boards of Insurance Undertakings

4.4.1.1 Solvency Management as a Core Function of the Entire Managing Board of Insurance Undertakings

The Solvency II requirements According to art. 40 of the Solvency II Directive, the managing board has "the collective responsibility for the compliance, by the undertaking concerned, with the laws, regulations and administrative provisions adopted pursuant to this Directive" in the context of the principle of legality. The German legislator does not intend to implement this regulation into the VAG [German Insurance Supervision Act] 2012 but rather to stipulate only the applicability of the BGB [German Civil Code], HGB [German Commercial Code] and

[91] See also on this point Government's Draft, n. 6, Statement of Reasons for sec. 125, p. 300.

AktG [German Stock Corporation Act].[92] Additionally, as part of the governance system and under arts. 41, para. 1, subpara. 2, and 44 of the Solvency II Directive—or sec. 27 of the VAG [German Insurance Supervision Act] 2012—the managing board must also institute an "effective risk-management system". Under art. 44, para. 2 of the Solvency II Directive—and in this respect not reflected in sec. 27, para. 3 of the VAG [German Insurance Supervision Act] 2012—this in turn encompasses, inter alia, "the risks to be included in the calculation of the Solvency Capital Requirement as set out in Article 101(4)". In addition, all insurance undertakings must conduct an ORSA process at regular intervals as part of the risk management system in accordance with art. 45 of the Solvency II Directive or sec. 28 VAG [German Insurance Supervision Act] 2012.[93] Part of this process is an assessment of "overall solvency needs" and "compliance, on a continuous basis, with the capital requirements" as laid down in the Solvency Capital Requirement and the Minimum Capital Requirement. In other words, the managing board of an insurance undertaking bears the responsibility of monitoring the solvency of the undertaking and managing it with respect to solvency requirements under supervisory law[94] as an integral part of the basic governance requirements in Pillar II of the Solvency system.[95]

There are, in addition, numerous detailed requirements within the three key elements of the new solvency system (the rules on own funds, on the Solvency Capital Requirement, and the Minimum Capital Requirement). Meeting these requirements is essentially also the responsibility of the managing board. With respect to the application and use of an internal model, the responsibility of the managing board appeared so important to the European legislator that it was expressly emphasized multiple times, specifically in arts. 116 and 120, para. 3 of the Solvency II Directive, with references to a "responsibility" of the managing board. The Governments Draft of the VAG [German Insurance Supervision Act] implements this in sec. 104 VAG [German Insurance Supervision Act] 2012.

The collective responsibility of the managing board for managing the capital resources of the insurance undertaking With this as background, the management of the capital resources of the insurance undertaking must be viewed as an essential component of responsibility assigned to the managing board in connection with the strategic management of own funds. This has specific consequences for the role of the managing board and its members relating to the solvency of the insurance undertaking. For one thing, the managing board has collective responsibility under corporate law for this important task by virtue of an explicit set of obligations under

---

[92] According to the table of corresponding sections between the Solvency II Directive and the VAG [German Insurance Supervision Act] 2012, with respect to art. 40 of the Solvency II Directive.

[93] On this point see in detail *Dreher/Ballmaier*, n. 30.

[94] See, by way of example only, the solvency-related decision to operate in individual Member States of the EU through subsidiaries, where separate capital requirements apply, or through local offices.

[95] But Pillar I also refers explicitly to the system of governance in connection with solvency requirements, namely in arts. 120, para. 1 and 121, para. 4 subpara. 2 of the Solvency II Directive.

the Solvency II Directive. This means a minimum level of obligation on the part of each managing board member to work toward upholding and fulfilling the duties incumbent on the entire managing board.[96] Thus, responsibility for capital resources can no longer be assigned to a single managing board member as a sole departmental responsibility. However, the entire managing board retains management responsibility when it assigns, as a horizontal delegation,[97] to an individual managing board member from within the entire managing board the preparation, execution and follow-up for decisions made in this area by the managing board as a whole.

To be sure, the solvency of an insurance undertaking is already a core issue of management. However, the Solvency II requirements expand the scope of the management responsibilities at issue. The subject matter of the managing board's collective responsibility is no longer only the fulfillment of supervisory solvency requirements in the sense of deciding on results. In the future, the entire managing board of an insurance undertaking will also be required to engage in the processes and conditions on which basic solvency-related management decisions are based. For the conception of the managing board's role with respect to solvency, this switch from solvency management based primarily on results to management based on both process and results according to the principle of collective responsibility is a particularly important caesura brought on by Solvency II.

In meeting this responsibility under Solvency II, however, the danger arises that this independent management of solvency now required of the entire managing board could dissipate into an accumulation of technical processes that is not straightforward or understandable even by the managing board members, accompanied by an ensuing unreflected dependency on it. The pseudo-accuracy of calculations and faith in models underlying Solvency II can compound this situation and likewise diminish the managerial function of the entire managing board, which has an additional significance in the future. The calculation by individual undertakings of their Solvency Capital Requirements based on risk favors the use of the most complex model possible—namely, an internal model.[98] This also has implications for the solvency-related fitness requirements of managing board members, which are highly significant in the present context.[99]

Capital investment, asset liability management, the internal model, and segment orientation as components of solvency management under the collective responsibility of the managing board of an insurance undertaking

---

[96] See *Dreher*, "Die persönliche Verantwortlichkeit von Geschäftsleitern nach außen und die innergesellschaftliche Aufgabenteilung" [in English: The Personal Responsibility of Managing Directors under External and Internal Division of Tasks], ZGR (1992), 22 (49 ff.); *id.*, "Nicht delegierbare Geschäftsleiterpflichten" [in English: Non-delegable Duties of Management], in Publication in Honor of Hopt (2010), pp. 517, 524, 529, each with further references.

[97] See on this point *Dreher*, n. 96, p. 529.

[98] See on this point 4.3.2, above.

[99] See on this point 4.4.1.2, below.

The assignment of solvency management to the collective responsibility of the managing board has specific consequences. To begin with, it means that capital investment is part of the collective responsibility of the managing board. It is the key element on the asset side of the balance sheet. At the same time, capital investment must sufficiently and risk-appropriately reflect the strategy of the insurance undertaking and the resulting obligations on the liabilities side. As vividly expressed in sec. 69, para. 1 of the VAG [German Insurance Supervision Act] 2012 in a rather modified implementation of art. 75, para. 1 of the Solvency II Directive using the term "solvency oversight",[100] a comparison of "assets and liabilities must be prepared for the purpose of determining current own funds" under such oversight. And technical provisions must be formed—according to art. 76, para. 1 of the Solvency II Directive and similarly sec. 70, para. 1 of the VAG [German Insurance Supervision Act] 2012—"with respect to all of their insurance and reinsurance obligations towards policyholders and beneficiaries". The capital investments of an insurance undertaking also represent a significant portion of its own funds. Thus, the basic issues as to which capital investments the insurance undertaking holds and how these are adjusted in terms of scope, type, duration, etc. in response to internal and external influences are part of the core area of management that constitutes the responsibility of the entire managing board of an insurance undertaking according to sec. 76 of AktG [German Stock Corporation Act].[101] The external influences include in particular the Solvency II requirements on capital resources as well as the coverage capacity of individual investments. The more volatile a capital investment is, the more solvency capital it ties up under supervisory law.[102] And the less it can contribute to covering solvency requirements, the more it adversely impacts, depending on its size, the strategy of the particular insurance undertaking.

However, the assignment of capital investment to the collective responsibility of the managing board of an insurance undertaking, does not necessarily mean that key elements of capital investment cannot continue to be assigned to a department of the managing board under an allocation of responsibilities in the organization. Collective responsibility means, as discussed earlier, only that the full managing board must decide on the critical issues that fall within the respective department, and that each individual member of the managing board shall share the obligation to

---

[100] See on this point 4.2.1, above.

[101] See on such characterization of management responsibility earlier *Dreher*, n. 96/1992, 60 as well as *Fleischer*, "Zur Leitungsaufgabe des Vorstands im Aktienrecht" [in English: Management Responsibility of the Managing Board in the Law on Stock Companies], ZIP (2003), 1 (2); *Schneider/Brouwer*, "Die Verantwortlichkeit der Gesellschaft und ihrer Geschäftsleiter bei Delegation öffentlich-rechtlicher Pflichten" [in English: The Responsibility of Companies and their Management in the Delegation of Public Duties under Law] in Publication in Honor of Priester (2007), pp. 713, 720.

[102] A particularly high capital coverage of 30 % to 60 % for shares and 25 % for real estate demonstrates the problem of an investment strategy based on solvency under the current government draft.

uphold and fulfill the associated duties. Therefore, should there be a case of liability based on a fundamental defect in a capital investment, no managing board member of an insurance undertaking can argue that one particular member of the managing board was exclusively responsible for the capital investment. Beyond the limits of possible horizontal delegation, capital investment is thus the affair of the entire managing board. Managing board members bear personal responsibility for decisions in connection with their capital investment duties, but they can delegate other elements of these non-delegable duties.[103] These elements primarily include preparation, implementation, and follow-up work associated with decisions that fall under collective responsibility. Decisions within this area can be ceded to a the sole responsibility of a managing board member at the outset.

The particular limits of horizontal delegation, and thus subsequent vertical delegation, cannot be determined in the abstract.[104] This is so because the situation for a small mutual insurance company is different from that for an insurance group operating internationally. However, it can be said in accord with the principles of materiality and proportionality that significant decisions, a category including any decision involving clear risk for the insurance undertaking, fall under the collective responsibility of the managing board. The same applies, for example, to the question of whether and to what extent derivatives are used, whether to invest in asset classes such as real estate, and what the maximum and minimum equity ratios should be. Thus the collective responsibility of the managing board with respect to capital investment always includes any circumstances marked as decisions fundamental or material in the context of specific cases and which previously have triggered the managing board's duty to report to the supervisory board.[105]

With the transition to the new solvency system, the requirements for capital investments by insurance undertakings also change. Art. 132 of the Solvency II Directive essentially grants freedom in capital investments.[106] The result of this needs to be that, in order to perform its duties with respect to finance, the entire

---

[103] See *Dreher*, n. 96, p. 527 f. with further references.

[104] See on the options and limits of internal and external delegation using the example of risk management under insurance supervisory law for the present collective responsibility of the managing board, *Dreher*, "Ausstrahlungen des Aufsichtsrechts auf das Aktienrecht" [in English: Effects of Supervisory Law on Corporation Law], ZGR (2010), 496 (523 ff.); *Dreher/Schaaf*, "Versicherungsunternehmensrecht und Risikomanagement – Gesamtverantwortung der Geschäftsleitung, Outsourcing des Risikomanagements und konzernweites versicherungsaufsichtsrechtliches Risikomanagement" [in English: Insurance Undertaking Law and Risk Management – the Collective Responsibility of Management, Outsourcing of Risk Management, and Group-wide Risk Management under Insurance Supervisory Law], WM (2008), 1765 (1768 ff.) and *Schaaf*, n. 44, p. 167 ff.

[105] See for example sec. 90, para. 1, sent. 1, no. 1 of the AktG [German Stock Corporation Act]: "fundamental matters regarding the future conduct of the company's business (in particular plans regarding financing, investment and personnel)... " and sec. 90, para. 1, sent. 1, no. 4 of the AktG [German Stock Corporation Act]on individual transactions "that may have a material impact upon the profitability or liquidity of the company".

[106] See for example as an exception art. 111, para. 2 of the Solvency II Directive.

managing board of an insurance undertaking must become still more involved than it currently is with the basic issues of capital investment, and that it issue relevant guidelines.

Risk management, which is part of the governance system under the collective responsibility of the managing board according to the Solvency II rule presented above, also encompasses "asset-liability management" under Art. 44, para. 2, subpara. 2 (b) of the Solvency II Directive. This is already known to insurance undertakings as technical asset-liability management (ALM).[107] ALM is based on the practice of recording the capital investments of an insurance undertaking on the asset side with the risk-related obligations on the liability side together so that a stable, risk-appropriate financial structure results. This practice is used in particular for avoiding asset-liability mismatch risk[108] resulting from long-term obligations of insurance undertakings and significantly shorter investment periods for the assets intended to cover them.[109]

Sec. 27 of the VAG [German Insurance Supervision Act] 2012, which is intended to implement art. 44 of the Solvency II Directive, uses the term "Asset-Liability-Management" in para. 3, sent. 1, no. 2 rather than the term "Aktiv-Passiv-Management" used in the German language version of the Solvency II Directive. The term "Asset-Liability-Management" had already been in use in the MaRisk VA [Minimum Requirements for Risk Management (Insurance Supervision)].[110] The renewed emphasis on the concept behind this economic tool for insurance through the new risk management requirements demonstrates the significance the legislator ascribes to it for the future. Since risk management as a whole falls under the collective responsibility of the managing board of an insurance undertaking, within the meaning of responsibility for decisions as discussed previously, the same applies to its six key areas listed under art. 44, para. 2, subpara. 2 of the Solvency II Directive or sec. 27, para. 3, sent. 1, nos. 1 through 6 of the VAG [German Insurance Supervision Act] 2012.

Finally, the internal model, if used by an insurance undertaking, is also part of the solvency management of the undertaking and thus the collective responsibility of the managing board. For the "use test", art. 120, para. 1 of the Solvency II Directive requires that the internal model is "widely used" and plays "an important role" in the governance system. Para. 3 addresses the responsibility of the managing board for the internal model. Sec. 106, para. 1 of the VAG [German Insurance

---

[107] See *Farny*, Insurance Business Management Theory, (5th ed. 2011), p. 882.

[108] See on this point *Nguyen*, Handbuch der wert- und risikoorientierten Steuerung von Versicherungsunternehmen [in English: Handbook of Value and Risk-focused Management of Insurance Undertakings] (2008), p. 441.

[109] German Federal Government, Answer to parliamentary question, BT-Drucks. [Document of the German Bundestag] 17/8225, p. 7 sees the risk under Solvency I "limited due to the requirements of the investment regulations, the minimum requirements for risk management under supervisory law, and the traditional, conservative investment policies of German insurers".

[110] See MaRisk VA [Minimum Requirements for Risk Management (Insurance Supervision)] under 7.2.2 at 2.

Supervision Act] 2012 appropriately emphasizes that the internal model must "be used extensively in managing the undertaking and play an important role in the business organization".

In this context, the new segment orientation also has considerable importance in the use of an internal model. As previously discussed,[111] the legislator explicitly stresses the "responsibility" of the managing board in establishing and implementing the internal model. Full or partial internal models could be applied for the whole business or only to one or more major business units, according to art. 112, para. 2, subpara. 2 of the Solvency II Directive or sec. 103, para. 1, sent 2 of the VAG [German Insurance Supervision Act] 2012. Nevertheless, art. 123 of the Solvency II Directive or sec. 110 VAG [German Insurance Supervision Act] 2012 requires the insurance undertaking to review "at least annually, the causes and sources of profits and losses for each major business unit" in each case where an internal model is used. Also to be reviewed is "how the categorisation of risk chosen in the internal model explains the causes and sources of profits and losses". The special acceptance of duty on the part of the managing board in using an internal model signifies—in addition to numerous other duties emphasized in corresponding rules—its collective responsibility which is explicitly standardized in the law for the first time—even under segment-based management.

Why such segment orientation is assigned only to users of internal models cannot be derived from the telos of the rule. It is supposed to sharpen the risk-awareness of the managing board, thereby drawing its attention to the causes and sources of profits and losses for each major business. But such awareness has significance for the managing board of any insurance undertaking, regardless of the use of an internal model.[112]

4.4.1.2 The Suitability of Managing and Supervisory Board Members of Insurance Undertakings from a Solvency Perspective

Under art. 42 of the Solvency II Directive, certain fit-and-proper requirements apply for all "persons who effectively run the undertaking or have other key functions". Independent of the disputed matter of whether supervisory board members also hold key functions as meant here and are thus subject to the rule,[113] the German legislator keeps the fit-and-proper requirements already recog-

---

[111] See 4.4.1., above at *The Solvency II Requirements*.

[112] See on this point for example *Höppner*, n. 81, 280 f.

[113] See in detail *Dreher/Lange*, "Die Qualifikation der Aufsichtsratsmitglieder von Versicherungsunternehmen nach VAG und Solvency II" [in English: Qualifications of Supervisory Board Members of Insurance Undertakings under the German Insurance Supervision Act and Solvency II] ZVersWiss (2011), 211 ff. (Chap. 6, below).

nized for managing board members[114] and supervisory board members,[115] and adds the requirements for so-called key function holders,[116] in a somewhat arguable implementation of art. 42 of the Solvency II Directive.[117] Notwithstanding the regulatory discrepancies at the EU level and the implementation in national law, which continues to be highly problematic,[118] the present context is concerned solely with the fit and proper requirements of managing and supervisory board members of insurance undertakings from a solvency perspective. The former executive director for insurance supervision at the BaFin [Federal Financial Supervisory Authority] and chairman of CEIOPS at that time, Thomas Steffen, made the following comment on this matter in 2009 in the Journal of the Federal Financial Supervisory Authority, even referring to the internal model: "(...) it would not be helpful if we had a perfect system that only a few specialists understand. Collectively, the managing board should decide accordingly and the supervisory board should be able to review the decisions".[119] In other words, all managing board members should be required as a minimum condition of suitability to possess the ability to understand the basic solvency issues that arise for insurance undertakings and to assess them with their own expertise. To start with, this includes all of the topics that were discussed in the previous section in connection with the collective responsibility of the managing board. It also includes all other basic issues raised in this chapter with respect to own funds, the Solvency Capital Requirements, and the management of the solvency of the insurance undertaking.

For members of the supervisory board, the situation with respect to the scope and subject matter of duties is essentially the same. Only on the basis of one's own basic knowledge of the system of solvency requirements and the solvency management of insurance undertakings can the supervisory board fulfill its responsibility to monitor and advise the managing board on solvency matters. The depth of the knowledge that can be expected in this area from the average supervisory board member, however, could lag quite considerably behind the requirements that apply to managing board members. On one hand, this could be attributed to the

---

[114] See *Dreher*, "Die Kontrolle der Geschäftsleiter von Versicherungsunternehmen" [in English: The Monitoring of Managers of Insurance Undertakings], ZVersWiss (2006), 375 ff. (Supplement, Annual Conference 2006).

[115] See *Dreher/Lange*, n. 113.

[116] See on this point in detail *Dreher*, "Die aufsichtsbehördliche Kontrolle der Inhaber von Schlüsselfunktionen nach Solvency II and künftigem VAG 2012" [in English: Review by Supervisory Authorities of the Key Function Holders under Solvency II and the Future German Insurance Supervision Act 2012], VersR (2012), 1061 (Chap. 8, below).

[117] See on this point in overview *Dreher*, "Solvency II auf Deutsch – so nicht" [in English: Solvency II in German – not this way], Frankfurter Allgemeine (FAZ) No. 243, 19 Oct. 2011, p. 18.

[118] The problems newly created by this are amplified as a consequence of the failure to take further account in sec. 25 VAG [German Insurance Supervision Act] 2012 of the concretization of art. 42 of the Solvency II Directive by art. 263 of the DVO-E.

[119] *Steffen*, Journal of the Federal Financial Supervisory Authority 05/09, pp. 8, 9.

heterogeneity of supervisory board members and the nature of supervisory board activities as part-time work that does not allow for great depth from each individual supervisory board member, let alone with respect to all the important governance matters that affect insurance undertakings. On the other hand, however, this is offset by the requirement that the supervisory board be composed in such a manner that the overall qualifications needed are met as a whole through the combination of the in-depth and complementary knowledge of the individual members on the significant issues facing insurance undertakings.[120]

4.4.1.3 Solvency-Related Issues in the Compensation of the Managing and Supervisory Boards of Insurance Undertakings

The Solvency II Directive itself does not address the matter of compensation of the managing and supervisory boards. Detailed specifications on this are first seen in art. 265 of the DVO-E. Their expansion and specification are set forth at the third regulatory level.[121] Compensation has already been the subject matter of detailed rules in secs. 64b and 81b, para. 1a of the VAG [German Insurance Supervision Act] and in the VersVergV [German Remuneration Regulation for the Insurance Industry]. This is carried forward in the VAG [German Insurance Supervision Act] 2012 in secs. 26 and 125, para. 3, sent. 3 without waiting for or considering the detailed rules of art. 265 of the DVO-E or Level 3 rules. Added to this is also the power to adopt regulations in the future in sec. 34, para. 1 of the VAG [German Insurance Supervision Act] 2012, so that a VersVergV [German Remuneration Regulation for the Insurance Industry] can also be expected to exist in the future.

It is not surprising in light of this that the VAG [German Insurance Supervision Act] 2012 in sec. 125, para. 3, sent. 3 again provides for a solvency-related block or restriction on the payout of the variable component of compensation to members of the managing and supervisory boards as well as "employees". The precondition is that the applicable solvency capital requirement for the insurance undertaking is "no longer covered" or "this situation is imminent within the next three months". Non-compliance with the solvency capital requirement can therefore have direct effects on the compensation of managing board members. The same applies to the supervisory board members in the rare case they receive variable compensation.

Restricting the variable compensation of managing and supervisory board members based on solvency raises numerous legal questions. However, these are beyond the subject matter of this article. There is the question, for example, of how a block or restriction on payout affects the deferred payment of variable compensation. Art.

---

[120] See on this point *Dreher*, "Die Gesamtqualifikation des Aufsichtsrats" [in English: The Overall Qualification of the Supervisory Board], in: Publication in Honor of Hoffmann-Becking (2013), p. 313 ff.

[121] See CEIOPS, Draft Proposal for Level 3 Guidelines on the System of Governance, December 2010, ref. 2.10 and 3.2.8 f.

265, para. 2 (c) of the DVO-E specifically mandates that a substantial portion of variable compensation include such deferral, with a minimum deferral period of 3 years. In this mandate, no compensation accrues for periods in which the solvency capital requirement is not covered. When the payout is actually due, however, the preconditions for a block or restriction on payout generally no longer exist. Based on the telos of the rule, which is capital maintenance, the block would no longer be in effect on the later payout date. Thus, it becomes superfluous.

4.4.2 The Supervisory Authorities

4.4.2.1 From Quantitative to Qualitative Supervision

As with managing and supervisory boards of insurance undertakings, supervisory authorities also see their role changing under Solvency II, and specifically under the new solvency rules. The three European regulatory levels not only assign numerous new tasks, responsibilities, and authority to the supervisory body.[122] They change the way it functions, and mainly in a qualitative sense.[123] The change is aptly summarized in the phrase "from quantitative to qualitative supervision". This change with its four-part systematization described in the following essentially applies to all of the activities of supervisory authorities under Solvency II. As a consequence of the aptly named solvency orientation of the new qualitative supervision, it comes into play in particularly impressive fashion in solvency supervision. The examples given at the beginning[124] are representative.

4.4.2.2 Risk Focus

A primary characteristic of the new supervision under Solvency II is its risk focus.[125] This means an individualization of supervisory activities in two respects. First, insurance supervision will be concerned with the risk position of individual insurance undertakings rather than the general risks of insurance undertakings that

[122] See the first-time "supervision" of the full balance sheet of an insurance undertaking, appropriately emphasized in *Faßbender*, n. 53, p. 8.

[123] See Recital 29, sent. 1 of the Solvency II Directive: "Some risks may only be properly addressed through governance requirements rather than through the quantitative requirements reflected in the Solvency Capital Requirement".

[124] See 4.4.1, above.

[125] See Recital 15 of the Solvency II Directive: "(...) an economic risk-focused approach should be adopted which provides incentives for insurance and reinsurance undertakings to properly measure and manage their risks"; Recital 67 of the Solvency II Directive: "the new risk-focused approach (...)" and Recital 68 of the Solvency II Directive: "In accordance with the risk-oriented approach to the Solvency Capital Requirement (...)". See on this approach *Dreher*, n. 44, 1001.

are presumed to exist and regulated accordingly, as is currently the case.[126] Second, within the risk position of the individual insurance undertaking, the supervisory authority must determine certain principal risks under Solvency II—defined in art. 13, nos. 30 to 35 of the Solvency II Directive or sec. 8, no. 25 to 30 of the VAG [German Insurance Supervision Act] 2012—preferably on an individualized basis. This is demonstrated for example by the rules that empower supervisory officials to require the use of parameters specific to the undertaking in the standard model—as set forth in art. 110 of the Solvency II Directive or sec. 101 of the VAG [German Insurance Supervision Act] 2012—or even the use of an internal model—as set forth in art. 119 of the Solvency II Directive or sec. 87, para. 2 of the VAG [German Insurance Supervision Act] 2012. Thus the core of the new solvency supervision focuses on the risk of each individual insurance undertaking it supervises.

This new risk focus in insurance supervision has tangible consequences. For one thing, it forces the supervisory authority to become more involved than ever before with each insurance undertaking. In a departure from the past, insurance supervision must now take even the undertaking's business model or strategy into consideration. Yet also the individualized focus on risk by insurance supervision excludes supervision of the actual business model or the strategy pursued by the insurance undertaking. This is so because the business model or strategy is a core entrepreneurial activity of an insurance undertaking. It is the sole responsibility of the management bodies. The management direction and determination of the object of the undertaking are not subject to supervision. These are a proprietary function of the management bodies. To the extent they are indirectly the object of insurance supervision, the supervisory functions involved require particular sensitivity and restraint.[127]

Another consequence of the new individualized risk focus is a corresponding decline in legal certainty.[128] Qualitative supervision and legal certainty in the sense of predictable application of the law can hardly be reconciled. For insurance undertakings, this leads to an expensive economic and legal self-assessment of numerous scenarios that is ultimately of but limited meaning with regard to the supervisory authority.[129] For the supervisory authorities, the same essentially

---

[126] Sec. 64a VAG [German Insurance Supervision Act] and the MaRisk VA [Minimum Requirements for Risk Management (Insurance Supervision)] have already introduced risk-focused insurance supervision to a certain extent in anticipation of the Solvency II implementation; see in detail *Dreher,* n. 44, 998 ff.; *Dreher/Schaaf,* n. 104, 1765 ff.; *Dreher/Schaaf,* "Inhalt und Organisation des Risiko- sowie des Revisionsberichts" [in English: Content and Organization of the Risk Report and Internal Audit Report], VersR (2009), 1151 ff.; *Schaaf,* n. 44, 59 ff.

[127] See in detail *Dreher/Ballmaier,* n. 30, 135 ff., 143 on the relationship of the ORSA review in supervision and the business strategy of the insurance undertaking.

[128] Also in *Korinek,* "Veränderung der österreichischen Versicherungsaufsicht durch Solvabilität II: Paradigmenwechsel oder Evolution"? [in English: The Change to Austrian Insurance Supervision through Solvency II: Paradigm Shift or Evolution], VersRundsch (9/2010), 27.

[129] See, as parallels, the self-assessment of undertakings in competition law, under arts. 101 and 102 TFEU in the wake of the new Council Regulation 1/2003 on competition, and on this point, for example, *Rittner/Dreher,* n. 60, sec. 14, ref. 28 f. with further references.

applies to the review of these self-assessments as applies to original supervisory assessments based, for example, on duties of notice or approval. In particular, the supervisory action is of limited persistence in relation to the courts when considering the widespread economic assessments[130] specifically for risk-focused supervisory measures and the final referral of legal questions to the European Court of Justice[131] in the Solvency II system.

4.4.2.3 Process Focus

Another significant characteristic of the new orientation in supervision under the Solvency II Directive is a stronger focus on process in supervisory activities. This results from comprehensive involvement by the supervisory authority with the processes within the insurance undertaking, particularly those relating to solvency requirements and the system of governance. According to Recital 31 of the Solvency II Directive, undertakings essentially have the freedom to determine how they are organized with respect to the four governance functions.[132] But they must observe numerous mandatory conditions set forth under arts. 41 ff. of the Solvency II Directive. The supervisory authorities in turn review the resulting governance system of the insurance undertaking. Under art. 41, sent. 5 of the Solvency II Directive, the supervisory authorities are required to "evaluate emerging risks identified by those undertakings which may affect their financial soundness".

This simultaneously creates a bridge from the supervision of the governance system to the supervision of solvency. One is at least as process-focused as the other.[133] The calculation of the solvency capital requirement and the Minimum Capital Requirement as well as the determination of the own funds supporting them form a process that is governed by content on one hand but shaped by procedure and method on the other. For this reason, numerous reporting and approval requirements are found in arts. 87 to 131 of the Solvency II Directive or secs. 80 to 114 of the VAG [German Insurance Supervision Act] 2012—supplemented by detailed Level 2 rules and later by the corresponding requirements at Level 3. Most importantly, with the standard and internal models and their numerous individual components, they also determine the methods by which the relevant calculations take place.

And the new insurance supervision focus on process now also in the area of solvency means more formalization. Currently, a results-focus and proceduralization can be said to represent key points of potential supervisory philosophies. While proceduralization has compliance with supervisory procedure as its primary

---

[130] See on this point 4.4.2.4, below as well as 4.4.2.5.

[131] See on this point 4.4.3.2, below.

[132] See on the freedom to organize the undertaking, government's draft of the VAG [German Insurance Supervision Act], n. 6, Statement of Reasons for sec. 24, p. 271.

[133] Likewise for capital investment *Korinek*, n. 128, 27.

object, results-focus aims mainly to secure the supervisory objective of protecting policyholders and insured persons. Upon close examination of the legal environment in Europe, both manifestations can be found in the practice of supervisory authorities, even if not in pure form. In the future, Solvency II requires considerable emphasis on process for all supervisory bodies. More precisely, this will lead to a formalization by means of numerous new notification duties incumbent on insurance undertakings and approval powers of the supervisory authorities. All of these will be subject to specific procedures. The methods chosen are either required or designated by the undertaking and accepted by the supervisory authority through an administrative procedure.

Closely associated with formalization under Solvency II is the expanded role of documentation in supervisory matters. Supervisory authorities will receive numerous reports from undertakings with greater frequency and larger scope.[134] Added to this is the report to the public on solvency and financial condition under art. 51 of the Solvency II Directive or sec. 50 of the VAG [German Insurance Supervision Act] 2012.[135] All of these reports are based on extensive documentation kept by insurance undertakings. Supervisory authorities will access this documentation in cases where closer examination is called for. For the internal model, extensive "documentation standards" are even required according to arts. 44, para. 5 (c), and 125 of the Solvency II Directive—or sec. 112 of the VAG [German Insurance Supervision Act] 2012. However, the principle of self-organization by insurance undertakings in the exercise of their entrepreneurial freedom,[136] as embedded in Recital 31 of the Solvency II Directive, must be remembered with respect to the organization of the four governance functions in order to satisfy the mandate of proportionality under Recital 19 and art. 29, para. 3 of the Solvency II Directive and sec. 290 of the VAG [German Insurance Supervision Act] 2012,[137] as well as the principle of materiality.[138]

4.4.2.4 Economization

Most significantly, the new risk focus in insurance supervision brings with it a significantly stronger economization. This arises from the fact that risks are now calculated according to economic specifications and models in the same way that solvency requirements are. The new focus on process is also closely related to this. Risk-oriented solvency supervision is based on numerous stochastic mathematical models and procedures. But, as already discussed,[139] such models and procedures

[134] See on the risk and internal audit report *Dreher/Schaaf*, n. 126; *Schaaf*, n. 44, p. 100 ff., 117 ff.

[135] See on this point *Dreher/Schaaf*, n. 35.

[136] In detail on this point *Rittner/Dreher*, n. 60, sec. 9, ref. 47 ff.

[137] See 4.4.2.5, below.

[138] See 4.4.2.5, below.

[139] See 4.3.3.4, above, on the interest rate yield curve.

can degenerate into speculation in some cases. The economization of insurance supervision is model-based, and thus grounded in science. On the other hand, with its integration of very distant horizons—200-year events[140] and yield curves[141] are referred to in this respect—it generates a certain pseudo-accuracy and faith in modeling. The expectations this brings are not, or at least not completely, supportable simply because of the divergence between the reality of the future and today's economic assumptions. It must be noted in this respect that the new solvency supervision supports intervention by the supervisory authorities on substantive and temporal risk assumptions—for example, in the area of economic, climatic, and geological developments—that lack validity and have in contrast led to the rejection of private coverage for many major risks because there is no basis for calculation. Thus the models as well as their use and results always require the application of good business judgment.[142]

A business assessment of the significant solvency related findings that result from such use of economic models, under the collective responsibility of the managing board, leads to rationalizing, even though the models and the results they generate appear to embody rationality. Specifically, the limited rationality of models,[143] which lies at their very foundation, remains concealed. The results from the use of a model correlate with the depiction of limited rationality, and convey only pseudo-accuracy in this respect. Such results must be examined continuously with a view to the appropriateness and timeliness of the criteria on which the model is based. The solvency requirements in the Solvency II Directive demand nothing less. These include, for example, art. 120, para. 3 of the Solvency II Directive or sec. 104, para. 1 of the VAG [German Insurance Supervision Act] 2012, which requires that the managing board of an insurance undertaking continuously review adequacy of the internal model with use tests; art. 121, para. 2, subpara. 3 of the Solvency II Directive or sec. 107, para. 2 of the VAG [German Insurance Supervision Act] 2012, according to which the insurance undertaking must be able to justify the assumptions underlying its internal model to the supervisory authority; and art. 124, subpara. 2 of the Solvency II Directive or sec. 111, para. 2 of the VAG [German Insurance Supervision Act] 2012, from which a duty to provide justification also arises with respect to the adequacy of any capital requirement generated by the model, as well as art. 45 of the Solvency II Directive or sec. 25 of the VAG [German Insurance Supervision Act] 2012 with the duty to conduct an ORSA process.

The economization of solvency supervision is an example of an increasing tendency by the EU Commission to pursue a more economic approach to making

[140] See 4.3.3.2, above.

[141] See 4.3.3.4, above.

[142] Thus *Perlet* demands, for example, "an additional qualitative risk assessment, every time, without naive faith in models", see *Sehrbrock*, discussion report in: Dreher/Wandt, eds., Solvency II in der Rechtsanwendung [in English: Solvency II in Legal Application] (2009), p. 58.

[143] See on this point *H. Simon*, Models of Bounded Rationality (1982).

and applying the law. This approach was established for European competition law.[144] The EU Commission then applied it to the law on state aid.[145] And now in its essence it has reached the insurance supervisory regime, though not labeled as such. The "more economic approach" is based on the proposition that making and applying law in matters affected by the economy should be more strongly predicated on economic criteria. The reasoning is that formal but legally abstract "mandate or ban" rules—often called per se rules—would not be adequate to deal correctly with a complex economic situation. What must emerge in their place are rules based on economic analysis and effects-based decisions by supervisory authorities with focus on individual cases. This highly disputed approach necessarily leads to matters that are crucial even in the present context, such as growing uncertainty in the law, the lack of economic information at the time of decision, and problems of documentation and burden of proof.[146]

For the supervisory authorities the economization through Solvency II therefore means—as it does for insurance undertakings—that many supervisory questions will have an economic character, sometimes considerably so. Economic expert opinions will take on added significance for supervisory authorities as well as undertakings—following the trend in other legal areas where the more economic approach is already pervasive.[147] Supervision of insurance undertakings, however, ultimately involves official administrative actions with respect to those who are subject to the law in the vertical relationship between the state and the undertaking. With regard to supervision, the insurance economics will therefore always grade over into application of the law. Aside from the dominant European law, other provisos including those of both general administrative and, especially, basic law must be observed in consideration of the preconditions and limits on intervening in entrepreneurial freedom.[148,149] Monocausal derivations of legal intervention based on economic models are forbidden in any case under the present consideration. However, an examination of supervisory actions in conformance with the law—particularly in the area of solvency supervision—must take account of the autonomy of the law with numerous other requirements regardless of the inherent limits of model-based supervisory findings. These include, for example, the principles of materiality and proportionality, an appropriate allocation of the burden of

---

[144] See from among many treatments, *Rittner/Dreher,* n. 60, sec. 14, ref. 56, sec. 15, ref. 43 and sec. 19, ref. 7, each with further references.

[145] See *Rittner/Dreher,* n. 60, sec. 26, ref. 61, with further references.

[146] See *Dreher*, "Die Zukunft der Missbrauchsaufsicht in einem ökonomisierten Kartellrecht" [in English: The Future of Supervision According to the Principles of Abusiveness in Economized Competition Law], WuW (2008), 23 ff. on the relationship between economics and competition law.

[147] In competition law, an arguable practice of providing economic expert opinion emerged as a result of this approach causing European and German antitrust officials to publish standards for acceptable scientific economic opinions recently.

[148] See above on this point in this part.

[149] On the assessment focus and its consequences, see 4.4.2.5, above.

presentation and proof as well as conformance with constitutional and European law. In the relationship between economics and the insurance supervisory regime, the law serves not as a tool for implementation but rather as a formative creative force.[150]

4.4.2.5 Assessment Orientation

Undefined Legal Terms This autonomy of the law also has implications for the considerable focus on assessment found in the insurance supervisory regime. Indeed, the idea of principles-based regulation must be set aside when it comes to solvency supervision.[151] Nevertheless, the new insurance supervisory regime provisions are generally characterized by undefined legal terms which need to be interpreted and assessed. To start with, this applies to key terms such as "adequacy" or "suitability". It also affects other legal terms that are frequently used in the Directive such as "the nature, scale and complexity of the risks", the "prudent person", the "completeness" or "accuracy" of data or information, or the parameters that are "relevant" or "specific" to an insurance undertaking. The use of these terms reflects the new risk-focused and qualitative approach to solvency supervision.[152,153]

It is generally accepted in European and German legislation that the legislator may use undefined legal terms—even those that refer to other disciplines such as economics[154]—and general clauses. As such terms are applied in practice, they undergo refinement and specification, which are then subject to judicial review. The case law of the European courts, which admittedly grants wide discretionary powers to the Commission in terms of legal consequences,[155] fully reviews the interpretation and application of undefined terms in legal provisions. The use of undefined legal terms such as "adequacy"[156] or "suitability"[157] necessarily comes with discretionary scope in assessment. But this, too, is part of the application of

[150] See on this point *Dreher*, n. 147, 23.

[151] See 4.3.2.2, above.

[152] See Part 4.4.2.1, above.

[153] In the German implementation, for example, a few sentences in sec. 295, paras. 1 and 2 of the VAG [German Insurance Supervision Act] 2012 on the capital add-on in accordance with art. 37 of the Solvency II Directive contain – sometimes more than once – the words "significantly", "(in) appropriate", "insufficiently", "better", "likely", "proportionally" and "material".

[154] See on this point for example *Rittner/Dreher,* n. 60, sec. 6, ref. 22.

[155] See *von Danwitz*, Europäisches Verwaltungsrecht [in English: European Administrative Law] (2008), p. 363 with further references.

[156] The Solvency II Directive uses this in the Recitals 16 times and in the text of the Directive 107 times, of which 24 instances are in connection with own funds, the solvency capital requirement, or the Minimum Capital Requirement.

[157] The Solvency II Directive uses this 8 times in the Recitals and 14 times in the text of the Directive.

law that is subject to judicial review—mainly with a view to a substantive determination of actual conditions and subsumption of the circumstances of the case.

The European courts even extend their control to "complex economic circumstances". This is demonstrated, for example, by judicial review in matters of competition law that rely to a large extent on economic assessments and—primarily in merger control—are based on projections.[158] In this case, however, there is no full review. Rather, the European Court of Justice concedes to the Commission, on one hand, "a margin of discretion with regard to economic matters" and on the other, it reviews the Commission's actions to establish "whether the evidence relied on is factually accurate, reliable and consistent, (...) also whether that evidence contains all the information which must be taken into account in order to assess a complex situation, and whether it is capable of substantiating the conclusions drawn from it".[159]

Against this background, many new methodological questions of enormous practical significance will arise in the future within the insurance supervisory regime. The literature readily presumes that the traditional categories of German administrative law, namely, "undefined legal term", "scope for evaluation", and "discretion" are also used in the Solvency II system due to the validity of the VAG [German Insurance Supervision Act]. But this is incorrect. If the degree of freedom of the undertaking or the supervisory authority when formulating the substance for undefined legal terms and the scope of subsequent review of such (self-) assessments depended on national standards, the path to a unified European supervisory law would be blocked. The effet utile would be meaningless. In light of this, such questions will need to be evaluated in all Member States according to European law to the extent the European Court of Justice has provided for this. As seen in other areas of law, such as competition law discussed above, the European Court of Justice develops these standards in the context of responding to the substantive legal questions brought before it.

Materiality The directive appropriately proceeds in its assessment orientation with the principle of materiality. It expresses this principle through multiple uses of another undefined legal term, "material". To start, the term is found in Recital 38 and then 19 times in this sense of materiality in the text of the directive. For example, there are "material risks" within the meaning of art. 37, para. 2, subpara. 2 of the Solvency II Directive or sec. 295, para. 2 of the VAG [German Insurance

[158] See recently with the tendency toward more judicial scrutiny, European Court of Justice, 8 Dec. 2011, case no. C-272/09 P – KME Germany/Commission, ref. 94 and European Court of Justice, 8 Dec. 2011, case no. C 386/10 P – Chalkor AE Epexergasias Metallon/Kommission, ref. 54 = EuZW (2012), 190 and generally on case law of the European courts *Adam*, Beurteilungsspielraum und Legalausnahme im Europäischen Kartellrecht [in English: Scope for Evaluation and Legal Exception in European Competition Law] (2007), p. 21 ff. and passim; *Pohlmann*, "Verfahrensrecht für ein ökonomisiertes Kartellrecht: Der Beurteilungsspielraum der Kommission" [in English: Procedure for an Economized Competition Law: The Scope for Evaluation of the Commission], in: Publication in Honor of Möschel (2011), p. 471 ff.

[159] See for example the European Court of Justice, n. 159/KME Germany, ref. 94.

Supervision Act] 2012; "material changes" in arts. 41, para. 3, subpara. 2, and 45, para. 5 of the Solvency II Directive or secs. 24, para. 3, sent. 3 and 28, para. 1, sent. 1 of the VAG [German Insurance Supervision Act] 2012; the matter of "materially impairing the quality of the system of governance of the undertaking concerned" in art. 49, para. 2 (a) of the Solvency II Directive or sec. 42, para. 3 of the VAG [German Insurance Supervision Act] 2012 or "any significant non-compliance with the Solvency Capital Requirement" in arts. 51, para. 1, subpara. 2 (e)(v), and 54, para. 1 subpara. 2 (b) and subpara. 4 of the Solvency II Directive or secs. 50, para. 4, and 52, para. 1, sent 2, no. 2 and para. 2, sent. 1, no. 2 of the VAG [German Insurance Supervision Act] 2012.

Whether the legal requirements linked to the term "materiality" are fulfilled requires an overall analysis and assessment in each case with consideration of the supervisory interests on one hand and the individual interests of the relevant insurance undertaking on the other. But this could become a probatio diabolica for an insurance undertaking if—as in art. 118, para. 1 of the Solvency II Directive or sec. 105, para. 1 of the VAG [German Insurance Supervision Act] 2012—it must itself submit "the evidence" to the supervisory authority related to, for example, an internal model and compliance with arts. 120 to 125 of the Solvency II Directive or secs. 106 to 112 of the VAG [German Insurance Supervision Act] 2012 that "the effect of non-compliance is immaterial". The same applies when an insurance undertaking—according to art. 121, para. 2, subpara. 3 of the Solvency II Directive—must "be able to justify the assumptions underlying its internal model to the supervisory authorities". This is even supposed to lead, under sec. 107, para. 2 of the VAG [German Insurance Supervision Act] 2012, to a reversal of the burden of presentation and proof, where the insurance undertaking must "at all times be able to prove the plausibility of the assumptions underlying the internal model to the supervisory authority". With respect to the use test under art. 120 of the Solvency II Directive, the implementation rule of sec. 106, para. 3 of the VAG [German Insurance Supervision Act] 2012 expressly states: "The insurance undertaking bears the burden of proof that the requirements of paragraphs 1 and 2 are fulfilled".

The vast amount of proof that insurance undertakings must produce under the Solvency II Directive and the VAG [German Insurance Supervision Act] 2012 presents a novel situation for the law on intervention in which the uncertainty of facts is essentially borne byte administration.[160] It shows clearly how the European law overlays principles of national administrative law and indirectly shapes areas of the law in an autonomous European way.

Projection focus and proportionality A particular problem arises with respect to projections. This is so because there is a decisive precondition for the appropriateness of legal intervention in that the intervention increases the likelihood that the aimed result will occur. If the intervention is based on speculation, however, no causal link is forged between supervisory intervention and increased likelihood of

[160] The Solvency II Directive alone contains 14 articles with sometimes multiple requirements of proof to be provided by insurance undertakings for approvals or ongoing business operations.

the desired result. And it cannot be argued that projections are part of the nature of legislation.[161] In fact, a projection need only be reasonable to suffice. This is however precisely at issue in the present case. "Rules for the unknown" applied on a speculative basis such as with the long-term assumptions for the interest yield curve are ultimately not a matter of prognostic but rather speculative lawmaking.[162] How are interest and inflation expectations supposed to be projectable over 100 years, when just before reunification economists assessed the value of total GDR assets as positive, thereby completely over-projecting, or when the financial crisis of 2008 was entirely under-projected?[163] Against this background it is hardly surprising that many consider "quantitative projections with a time horizon of more than 10 years to be scientifically dubious".[164] Thus, even in merger control under European and German competition law, which is largely based on projected criteria (namely, significant impediment of competition or the creation or strengthening of a dominant market position), it is acknowledged that the projection horizon is limited to 3–5 years.[165]

In light of this, solvency requirements could prove to be unsuitable or at least inadequate, depending on their final structure and the supervisory rules established to avoid distortions in the model assumptions and calculations. This is so because under these conditions the impediment of the legally protected entrepreneurial freedom could be disproportionate to the desired goal. Solvency requirements that are built on sand and that for some insurance undertakings could even mean exiting the market would no longer be reasonable from a legal perspective. In the end, however, these questions can only be answered on the basis of the fully accomplished regulatory system of Solvency II and in the interaction between insurance supervisory assessment and economic assessment.

---

[161] See BVerfGE 106, 62, 151 – Altenpflege [in English: Elder Care]; *Meßerschmidt*, Gesetzgebungsermessen [in English: Legislative Discretion] (2000), p. 946 ff., *Lepsius*, "Prognose als Problem von Wissenschaft und Politik" [in English: Projection as Problem in Science and Policy] in: Dreier/Willoweit, eds., Wissenschaft und Politik [in English: Science and Policy] (2010), pp. 181, 194.

[162] See 4.3.3.4, above.

[163] For numerous additional examples of erroneous assessments in economics, even in the short and medium term, see *Lepsius,* n. 162, p. 182 ff.

[164] *Lepsius*, n. 162, p. 185 with reference to *Borchardt*, "Produktions- und Verwertungsbedingungen von Langfristprognosen in historischer Perspektive" [in English: Production and Assessment Conditions of Long-term Projections in Historical Perspective], Allgemeines Statistisches Archiv [in English: Journal of the German Statistical Society], 63 (1979), p. 1 ff. with further references.

[165] See in detail *Schroeder*, "Der Prognosezeitraum in der Fusionskontrolle" [in English: The Projection Time Horizon in Merger Control] in: Publication in Honor of Säcker (2011), p. 985 ff. and with reference to outliers with a maximum of 8–15 years in merger control cases in the energy markets, which are relatively quite stable for the purpose of projections.

Clearly, the entirely evident intent of the issuers of the Solvency II Directive that "the solvency regime laid down in this Directive is expected to result in even better protection for policyholders" must be weigh heavily in this assessment.[166] Protection of policyholders includes their protection with respect to extremely long-term contracts. But quantifiable projections based on current facts are possible for a limited period of up to 20 years into the future, at the most. Their regular review as part of an iterative process, with appropriate consequences for solvency requirements, protects policyholders for the full length of a contract, even beyond this limit. Meanwhile there remains the current expectation gap of guaranteed solvency protection over the entire term of each risk, which the Solvency II system for now attempts to close through an extrapolated and then speculative forward projection of the yield curve as Forward Rate, or UFR,[167] for a period of time that is not foreseeable.

A middle way that would have been conceivable would be the requirement for legitimately calculated solvency capital for the time period in which verifiable economic projections are available and a declining capital add-on for increasing uncertainty in more remote years as a safety margin for the subsequent period. But since the die has been cast in European law with respect to long-term solvency requirements, it becomes solely a matter of methodological integrity under the Solvency II system in that a distinction is now made between the discretion in projections that lawmakers are entitled to and the speculative assumptions when such projections are extended into the future. Which consequences will emerge with the supervisory measures based on such speculative assumptions cannot yet be foreseen in the absence of corresponding parallel scenarios in the law. In operating on such an uncertain footing, however, it is advisable that the special emphasis given to the principles of materiality and proportionality by the Solvency II legislator be given great weight in the practical application of the law.

Added to this is the applicability of the principle of proportionality to the entire Solvency II system.[168] The Directive even emphasizes this principle in Recitals 19 to 21, and it is also explicitly mentioned multiple times in the text of the Directive itself. This is seen in arts. 29, para. 4, 41, para. 4 and 141, para. 2 of the Solvency II Directive. Though insufficient, an implementation of the general principle of proportionality under art. 29, para. 4 of the Solvency II Directive is to be found in sec. 290 of the VAG [German Insurance Supervision Act] 2012. The "proportionality" mentioned explicitly in art. 41, para. 4 and art. 141, para. 2 of the Solvency II Directive is reflected in the implementation rule sec. 24, para. 4 of the VAG [German Insurance Supervision Act] 2012 with the word "adequacy" and in sec. 128 of the VAG [German Insurance Supervision Act] 2012 the words

[166] According to Recital 17 of the Solvency II Directive, see 4.2.2, above.

[167] See 4.3.3.4, above.

[168] On the special emphasis of the principle of proportionality with respect to small and medium sized insurance undertakings, see 4.3.2.3, above.

"suitability, necessity, and adequacy", but employed in a deficient and inconsistent manner.

Implications The consequence of this legislative technique is that supervision will be largely assessment-oriented. Unlike in a system of quantitative supervision, a monocausal, somewhat mechanistic derivation of legal consequences through simple subsumption of a circumstance under an assessment-based supervisory rule is not possible in a system of qualitative supervision. The text of the Directive reflects this position in numerous places. Examples can be seen in the facts discussed earlier, according to which the supervisory authorities must "take into account"[169] the procyclical effects of their actions or even "evaluate"[170] potential risks.

With this assessment-based subsumption of insurance supervisory regime facts leading up to discretion-based supervisory measures, the interpretation of insurance supervisory rules and of their individual conditions takes on special significance. As a result of the Solvency II requirements, interpretation must be in conformity with European law. Thereupon—and most importantly—qualitative supervision yields a new turn in the direction of functional interpretation of the insurance supervision rules empowering intervention. This affects solvency supervision in a special way, but it also applies to the other areas of qualitative insurance supervision. The functional interpretation of the rules under the insurance supervisory regime means that, due to the inevitably assessment-based formulation of the requirements, the interpretation must carry out the policy of the European insurance supervisory regime.

The strict adherence to the law by the insurance supervision is also reflected in a subsumption of the legal requirements that cannot be replaced by an insurance-economics approach, meaning a specific insurance-related manifestation of the "economic approach" sometimes proposed for the application of commercial law requirements.[171] Thus, in particular, the wording is also the starting point for the interpretation of the rules of the insurance supervisory regime. In relation to the overall legal system, the wording must be viewed independently and as autonomous under European law. However, its openness and especially the general methodology[172] under European law will necessitate the use of additional interpretation methods on a regular basis. Teleological interpretation has special importance in this process because it is especially well suited for realizing the goals of the Solvency II system—ultimately, the goal of the single insurance market and the

[169] See 4.3.4.4, above.

[170] See Part 4.4.2.3, above.

[171] See on this point *Rittner/Dreher*, n. 60, sec. 6 ref. 20, sec. 14 ref. 86, each with further references.

[172] See in more detail on the case law of the European Court of Justice *Riesenhuber*, in: id., ed., Europäische Methodenlehre [in English: European Methodology] (2nd ed. 2010), sec. 11, ref. 13 ff.; *Neuner*, ibid, sec. 13, ref. 17 and based on the example of European public procurement law *Dreher* in: Dreher/Stockmann, Kartellvergaberecht [in English: Competition Law and Public Procurement Law] (2008), before sec. 97, ref. 95 ff. each with numerous further references.

protection of policyholders and claimants within it[173]—and the individual rules. The insurance supervisory regime rules gain practical effectiveness, or effet utile, through the specific functional interpretation of laws under the insurance supervisory regime approaching these goals. The goals are specified in particular in the Recitals of the Solvency II Directive and the DVO-E.

As is customary in European law, historical interpretation is subordinate, but not entirely insignificant. Aside from the wording and telos of a rule, interpretation still continues to be based on the systematic of the relevant legal rule. Lastly, there are the general rules of interpretation under European law, including the narrow interpretation of exemption clauses. This specific rule of interpretation under European law has thus far been unknown in the application of the German insurance supervisory regime, which is based solely on German administrative law.[174]

At the level of legal consequences, the principle of equivalent treatment of insurance undertakings in the context of the principle of proportionality must also be taken into account when exercising discretionary power.[175] To be given substantial effect, it must be supplemented by special emphasis on the proportionality principle with respect to small and medium sized insurance undertakings.[176] In particular, if quantitative determinations by the supervisory authorities are also based on qualitative elements, then consideration of a security mark-up [Sicherheitszuschlag] when establishing the facts and a substantiality mark-up [Erheblichkeitszuschlag] concerning the supervisory measures should be envisaged regardless of the size of the relevant insurance undertaking. The reason for this is the immense uncertainty of quantitative determinations based on economic methods and models and on probabilities and projections. A model for such a procedure is competition law, where it is also not part of the statute but considered necessary in case law for constitutional reasons. In this area, the courts have allowed prohibitory orders against prices considered to be abusively inflated due to extremely difficult establishment of the legitimate price level only when there is a "substantial deviation" from the competitive price.[177]

---

[173] See on objective of supervision under Solvency II, 4.2.2, above.

[174] The extent to which exemption clauses are also narrowly construed in German administrative law – see for example BVerwG [Federal Administrative Court], DÖV 1974, 133; BVerwG [Federal Administrative Court] DÖV 1988, 381; *Ehlers*, in: Schoch/Schmidt-Aßmann/Pietzner, VwGO [in English: Administrative Court Procedures Code], 22. Supplement 2011, sec. 40, ref. 520 with further references – is not generally attributable to the single market objective as in European law, but rather to the specific purpose of each law.

[175] See on this point 4.3.2.2 and 4.3.2.3, above.

[176] See 4.3.2.3, above.

[177] See BGH [German Federal Court of Justice], 28 Jun. 2005, WuW/E DE-R 1513, 1519 – Stadtwerke Mainz; BGH [German Federal Court of Justice], 16 Dec. 1976, WuW/E BGH 1445, 1452 – Valium; KG [Higher Regional Court] Berlin, 12 Feb. 1982 – Kart. 4/82, WuW/E OLG 2616, 2617; KG [Court of Appeal], 10 Dec. 1990 – Kart. 19/90, WuW/E OLG 4640, 4644 – Hamburger Benzinpreise; OLG [Higher Regional Court] Düsseldorf, 11 Feb. 2004, WuW/E DE-R 1239, 1244 – TEAG.

Additionally, the assessment orientation of the new insurance supervision proves once again that the current factually loose supervision based on the principles of abusiveness of the VAG [German Insurance Supervision Act] can no longer survive in the Solvency II system, which is based on rules.[178]

And finally, due to the assessment-based character of the conditions for mandates and bans in the new insurance supervisory regime, its enforcement under criminal and administrative fines law as provided for in secs. 326 and 327 of the VAG [German Insurance Supervision Act] 2012 can have no significant meaning against the background of the constitutional requirements that apply to such laws.[179]

4.4.3 Competent Courts in the Insurance Supervisory Regime

4.4.3.1 The Scope of Control

The new realities in solvency supervision also affect the activities of the courts that review the acts of intervention by the supervisory authorities. As has been established in connection with the extensive use of undefined legal terms in the new solvency requirements,[180] these terms and their subsumption are in principle fully subject to judicial review,[181] and the insurance supervisory regime case law of the European Court of Justice yet to be made is still open to influence on this matter. Thus undefined legal terms in the insurance supervisory regime do not actually provide a scope for evaluation to the supervisory authorities on the requirements side that is exempt from judicial control after their implementation in the national insurance supervisory regime. Missing in this respect is both the legal authority required—according to the prevailing opinion including case law[182]—for such scope for evaluation as well as—despite complex decisions of judgment—fulfillment of the criterion required by the minority opinion on the justification for scope

[178] See 4.2.4, above with n. 30. *Korinek,* n. 128, 29 again sees "substantive state supervision", even if it is completely different from what is currently understood, due to the numerous undefined legal terms and the resulting scope of the material control in the new Solvency II system. The continuation of such term under Solvency II, understood differently at least in Germany, provides no added value to the legal systematic and results only in terminological confusion.

[179] Nevertheless, the recommendations of the Bundesrat [German Federal Council], n. 15, no. 17, p. 15 f., require supplementation of the offenses in the VAG [German Insurance Supervision Act] in the government's draft.

[180] See 4.4.2.5 above.

[181] See on such scrutiny of undefined legal terms BVerwGE [Decisions of the German Federal Administrative Court] 15, 207, 208 and 109, 59, 65 ff.

[182] See BVerwGE 92, 340, 348.

of evaluation for interpretation of facts.[183] Essentially, decisions on projections are included among those decisions subject to full judicial review.[184] Nevertheless it is still an open matter as to whether the European Court of Justice will take up specific limitations for the reviewability of business or supervisory (self-)assessments as in the complex economic situations in competition law[185] already discussed or in the likewise complex award decisions in cartel procurement law[186] which, like the VAG [German Insurance Supervision Act], is implemented European law.

Concerning legal consequences, there is in fact the limitation under sec. 114 of the VwGO [Administrative Court Procedures Code] that excludes judicial review of the appropriateness of the administrative act. Nevertheless, a wide scope of review in this respect for the acts with discretion has been established based on the doctrine of abuse of discretion.[187] Of particular significance is the principle of proportionality, which is accentuated in the European insurance supervisory regime in particular ways.[188] However it remains to be seen what consequences emerge from a scrutiny under European law in the event of abuse of discretion, a scrutiny that is ultimately less intensive than under German administrative procedure law.[189]

In sum, the actions of insurance supervisory authorities are largely subject to the control of the courts, even with respect to solvency supervisory measures under Solvency II.

4.4.3.2 The Responsibility for Control

Among the courts that exercise this control the European Court of Justice has special significance. Judicial control for supervisory measures by German supervisory authorities is exercised through the jurisdiction of the administrative court. But its courts may, or rather, must submit all questionable matters of European law to the European Court of Justice depending on art. 267 of the TFEU, and thus to the interpretation and application of the Solvency II Directive and DVO. Due to the breadth and depth of the Solvency II provisions, the European Court of Justice assumes the role of "insurance supervisory regime court of last resort". Any unresolved legal questions in the Solvency II system are ultimately referred to

---

[183] See as a whole, in detail and with numerous further references *Wolff,* in: Sodan/Ziekow, eds., VwGO [in English: Administrative Court Procedures Code] (3rd ed. 2010), sec. 114, ref. 306 ff.

[184] *Wolff,* n. 184, sec. 114, ref. 317 ff. with further references.

[185] See 4.4.2.5, above.

[186] See references at *Dreher*, in: Dreher/Stockmann, Kartellvergaberecht [in English: Competition Law and Public Procurement Law] (2008), sec. 97, ref. 223 ff.

[187] See *Wolff,* n. 184, sec. 114, ref. 59 ff. with further references.

[188] See 4.4.2.5, above at *Projection focus and proportionality.*

[189] See *von Danwitz,* n. 156, p. 366 with further references.

it.[190] This is the only way to ensure the uniform interpretation of EU law targeted in art. 267 of the TFEU.

In legal disputes pertaining to the insurance supervisory regime, orders for reference from national courts will occur often, even in the area of solvency supervision, due to the current absence of case law. This duty to refer for the German administrative courts is enforceable. This is so because a violation in this area also implies a violation of due process under art. 101, para. 1, sent. 2 of the GG [German Basic Law].[191]

The new role of the European Court of Justice as the "supreme insurance supervisory regime court" is also seen in art. 61 of the EIOPA-VO.[192] According to this authority, the European Court of Justice has exclusive responsibility under art. 263 of the TFEU for all challenges to decisions rendered by the EIOPA Board of Appeal or by EIOPA itself if there is no right of appeal. Such complaints may be lodged by the Member States or by affected insurance undertakings, among other entities.

4.4.4 Insurance Academics

The new orientation of solvency supervision also shapes the insurance sciences. Aside from the rising influence of actuarial science within that particular business function[193] and the use of its scientific methods,[194] it is primarily seen as relevant to the relationship between insurance economics and the insurance supervisory regime. Understanding and appreciation could be the themes for future closer collaboration of the two disciplines.

Understanding in this sense means recognition and acceptance by one discipline of the findings of the other. Considering the breadth and depth of each field, this places no small demand on the corresponding other party that lacks the expertise. At the same time, each is further called upon to explain its own findings to the opposite discipline in the overlapping area with language and methodology that can be understood by the other.

If many solvency-related insurance supervisory regime situations will require a significantly closer integration of insurance economics and the insurance

[190] See 4.4.2.2, above.

[191] See BVerfGE 73, 339, 366 ff.; BVerfGE 82, 159, 192.

[192] Regulation (EU) No. 1094/2010, OJ 2010, no. L 331, p. 48 ff.

[193] See on the actuarial function, art. 48 of the Solvency II Directive or sec. 31 of the VAG [German Insurance Supervision Act] 2012.

[194] See on their new significance, for example art. 77, para. 2, subpara. 2 of the Solvency II Directive (similarly, sec. 72, para. 2, sent. 2 of the VAG [German Insurance Supervision Act] 2012) on technical provisions: "... be performed using adequate, applicable and relevant actuarial and statistical methods".

supervisory regime in the future,[195] then surely a mutual appreciation for respective abilities and boundaries will be a precondition for this integration. Part of this is the maxim that the law achieves a "proper rule" based on democratic legitimacy with abstract applicability. The rule is concretized through the decisions of a supervisory authority meeting the aspect of justice in individual cases. However, economic approaches, even the solvency capital calculation in the Solvency II system, aim for the most "correct assessment" possible of the actual situation. Thus, while they attempt to depict its complexity, the necessarily abstract legal rules require that complexity be reduced.[196] Nevertheless, the rules must be based to the greatest extent possible on economic rationality.

4.5 Summary

1. The new risk-based solvency requirements for insurance undertakings represent a paradigm shift. According to the Solvency II Directive, the primary objective of the future solvency supervision is "even better protection for policyholders".
2. The solvency supervisory system encompasses three elements: own funds, the Solvency Capital Requirement (SCR) and the Minimum Capital Requirement (MCR). The latter draws a line in the sand for the capital resources an insurance undertaking is required to maintain.
3. All three elements of the solvency supervisory system are the subject matter of highly detailed provisions at the three levels of European legislation and rules formation. For this, a distinction must be made between the solvency requirements at the level of the individual undertaking and those at the group level.
4. The solvency requirements for insurance undertakings stand at the center of a new supervisory review process.
5. The new solvency requirements for insurance undertakings give rise to three particularly significant new problems—complexity, volatility, and procyclicality—with considerable effects on solvency supervision.
6. The complexity of the solvency requirements is readily seen in the flood of rules in the Solvency II system, which brings in its train an abandonment of principles orientation. This requirement for the Solvency II system had to be set aside in the area of solvency requirements because of the unified solvency protection for policyholders in the internal market for insurance and because of the capital charges as a significant factor in the operations of an insurance undertaking. This leads to a mandate of equivalent treatment of insurance undertakings. To put actual equivalent treatment into practice as a concrete

[195] See for a specific example 4.3.3.5, above.

[196] See on this point as an example of economization of competition law *Rittner/Dreher*, n. 60, sec. 4, ref. 56 and *Dreher*, n. 151, 23 and 27.

outcome of supervisory law, the applications of small and medium sized insurance undertakings as well as monoline insurers and others must be liberally granted supervisory approval based on the use of parameters specific to the individual undertaking and simplified risk calculations.

7.

(a) The volatility of solvency requirements is mainly the result of the market-consistent valuation of assets and liabilities combined with their determination on the basis of economic models and the 99.5 % confidence level by year. These types of requirements are legally allowable as an expression of the legislator's degree of freedom in formulating economic policy. But limits emerge in this respect for solvency-related supervisory actions. First, questionable quantitative economic determinations such as the zero-risk weighting of government bonds cannot be corrected by supervisory acts. In addition, the boundaries on delegated legal acts under European law are violated when—as with the determination of the interest rate yield curve—it is no longer a matter of technical details but rather competition in supervisory clothing, meaning substantive insurance supervisory law of considerable significance for insurance operations.

(b) The Solvency II Directive only marginally addresses the volatility of the solvency requirements. It integrates the volatility of individual risk factors into the solvency capital requirement and provides for a "shock absorber". From a legal perspective, the extent to which the results of calculations on the basis of models and quantitative assumptions can fluctuate is still much too large to justify serious supervisory consequences with regulations of such nature.

(c) The use of numerous undefined legal terms in the solvency supervision regime ultimately can indeed be contained through appropriate scrutiny. But this does not apply to rules for the unknown based on speculation. Supervisory intervention with relevance to basic law cannot be justified by looking at a crystal ball. This is relevant to supervisory action in connection with the long-term assumptions that are based on the yield curve and far exceed all projection horizons that are currently the norm in a legal context.

8. The procyclicality of the Solvency Capital Requirements is closely associated with the market-consistent valuation of assets and liabilities as well as with the significance of external ratings. To the extent the Solvency II Directive hopes to counteract procyclicality, the matching premium in the current version of the draft for German insurance undertakings omits the area of legal application; and this then runs into skepticism in terms of law and results for the anti-cyclical premium. Against this background, the general requirement of the Solvency II Directive that supervisory authorities take account of procyclical effects in their actions takes on particular significance.
9. With the new solvency supervision, there is a considerable transformation in the roles of the participating institutions and persons.

(a) Initially, this applies to the insurance undertakings, that is, primarily to their managing and supervisory boards. The Solvency II Directive itself repeatedly refers to the managing board's responsibility for solvency. The management of the capital resources of the insurance undertaking constitutes a significant component of the managing board's responsibility in the context of strategic management of own funds. It is therefore the collective responsibility of the managing board. The same applies to capital investment (the ALM), to the use of an internal model, and to the new segment-orientation based on that internal model. However, this hinders neither horizontal (within the managing board) nor further vertical delegation of numerous tasks. But the entire managing board must decide on the fundamental issues in these areas. The direct involvement of the managing board in the business is required here in order to prevent solvency mismanagement based on blind faith in models and calculations with only the appearance of accuracy.

(b) The new solvency requirements also influence the minimum requirements for fitness in solvency management—with a classification based on context—for managing and supervisory board members. All members of the managing board must be able to understand the basic solvency issues for which the managing board is collectively responsible, and to evaluate them from the standpoint of their own expertise, not necessarily in detail but in their fundamental points. The average minimum requirements for supervisory board members reflect this requirement in terms of subject matter but not content. The requirement is that the overall qualification of the supervisory board shall be constituted from the members' complementary individual expertise or relevant experience.

(c) Lastly, solvency supervision extends to matters of compensation. This is seen primarily in the blocks or restrictions on the payout of variable compensation when the solvency capital requirement has not been covered. But these blocks and restrictions are ultimately ineffective.

10.

(a) Outside of the effects on insurance undertakings, the new solvency requirements have their most extensive impact on the operations of the insurance supervisory authorities. Solvency supervision constitutes the core of the new supervisory review process. The supervisory authorities are facing a shift from quantitative to qualitative supervision. With this come numerous new tasks, responsibilities, and authority. Supervisory activity will be largely shaped by an environment where the focus is on risk, process, economization, and assessment.

(b) The risk focus forces the supervisory authorities to be deeply involved with each supervised insurance undertaking. However, this must not develop into control of the business model or strategy, which are not subject to supervision. A further consequence of the risk focus is heightened legal uncertainty and a call to the supervisory authorities to review the economic and legal self-assessments prepared by insurance undertakings.

(c) Thus the supervisory authorities will also be considerably more focused on processes than in the past. The Solvency II Directive strictly governs the internal business processes related to solvency, and these are the object of supervisory review. These processes are shaped by procedures and methods. As a result, solvency supervision will undergo considerable formalization. An expression of this can be seen in the numerous reporting duties, required approvals, and documentation requirements for insurance undertakings. In this context, too, the principles of proportionality and materiality as well as the freedom of internal organization must receive perceptible consideration.

(d) The risk focus of solvency supervision requires its economization. This is model-based. As such, the pseudo-accuracy of results thus obtained and any faith in models that suggests a presumed rationality of the model must be addressed by the supervisory authorities. In addition, solvency supervision based on economic modeling will always have implications in application of the law. There are specific legal categories for this. Thus the law takes on formative creative force even in the relationship between economics and the insurance supervisory regime.

(e) The assessment orientation in solvency supervision is a consequence of numerous undefined legal terms and requirements based on projections, as well as of the principles of materiality and proportionality. A mechanistic subsumption of solvency circumstances under the rules of the insurance supervisory regime is ruled out in this context. Instead, many insurance supervisory rules themselves need an assessment-based concretization. This will occur through a new functional interpretation under the insurance supervision regime for realization of the legal policy content of the Solvency II Directive and Level 2 DVO.

(f) Closely connected to this is the dominance of European law, particularly the rules of interpretation under European law with its particular emphasis on the regulatory objectives, that has thus far been absent in the insurance supervisory regime. Contrary to popular belief that application of the VAG [German Insurance Supervision Act] 2012 is fully accomplished exclusively with the traditional administrative law categories for "undefined legal term", "scope for evaluation", and "discretion", the stronger influence of European law in the future must be pointed out in this respect. This is particularly true in the question of the extent to which (self-) assessments by the undertaking or supervisory authorities are subject to supervisory and/or judicial control when they are conducted on the basis of undefined legal terms.

(g) With respect to legal consequences, the principle of equivalent treatment must be considered in addition to the traditional categories of discretion. Further, for solvency-related supervisory measures on the basis of even quantitative determinations, a substantiality mark-up in the context of the establishment of the facts, which has thus far gone unrecognized in the insurance supervisory regime, should also be considered as a consequence of the sometimes very uncertain derivation of results.

11. The role of the courts that must evaluate certain situations in relation to the insurance supervisory regime will also change with the new solvency requirements. An initial point of interest here is the scope of control. The requirements of solvency supervision contain an exceedingly high number of undefined legal terms that are essentially entirely subject to judicial control. This also entails a high level of scrutiny whenever there is discretion in the legal consequences. An additional issue in judicial review of solvency-related supervisory measures arises in the question of the jurisdiction to review. The breadth and—now primarily—depth of Europeanization of nearly the entire insurance supervisory regime gives the European Court of Justice a new role as "supreme insurance supervisory regime court", which results from the duty to refer on the part of the national administrative courts. Added to this is the direct legal recourse available in all EIOPA matters to the European Court of Justice.
12. Finally, Solvency II has an impact on insurance academics. This pertains in a specific sense to the increased importance of actuarial science and more generally to the relationship between insurance economics and insurance supervisory law. For the collaboration required of these two disciplines in the future, the themes of mutual understanding and appreciation apply. Under the insurance supervisory regime also insurance economics always face the application of law. But in solvency supervision, the application of law must always be based to the greatest extent possible on economic rationality.

Part III
Governance

Chapter 5
Own Risk and Solvency Assessment

Contents

5.1 Introduction 158
5.2 Subject-Matter and Objective of the ORSA 160
5.3 The Solvency II Legal Principles Applicable to the ORSA 161
5.4 The ORSA and the Risk Management System 162
5.4.1 The European Law Framework 162
5.4.2 Present Law: The Relationship of the ORSA to Sec. 64 a, Para. 1, 2 of the VAG [German Insurance Supervision Act] and the MaRisk VA [Minimum Requirements for Risk Management (Insurance Supervision)] ... 164
5.4.3 Future Law: Sec. 28 of the VAG [German Insurance Supervision Act] in the Version of the Ministerial Draft 167
5.5 ORSA, Actuarial Function, Standard Formula and Internal Model 170
5.6 The ORSA, the Compliance Function, and the Internal Audit Function 172
5.7 Individual Issues Concerning the ORSA 173
5.7.1 The ORSA and Free Enterprise 173
5.7.2 The Relationship of the ORSA to Capital Add-Ons 179
5.7.3 The Own Assessment of Interest Rate Risk 180
5.7.4 Significant Deviation from the Assumptions Underlying the Calculation of the Standard Formula and the Internal Model 181
5.8 Documentation and Publication of the ORSA 186
5.8.1 Addressees and General Principles of the ORSA Information 186
5.8.2 The Internal Report 187
5.8.3 Requirements for Reporting to the Supervisory Authorities 187
5.8.4 Requirements for Reporting to the Public 190
5.9 Supervisory Powers with Respect to the ORSA 191
5.10 Summary 192

First published as "Die unternehmenseigene Risiko-und Solvabilitätsbeurteilung (ORSA) nach Solveny II und VAG 2012" [in English: Own Risk and Solvency Assessment (ORSA) under Solvency II and the VAG 2012 [German Insurance Supervision Act 2012]], VersR (2012), 129 ff. with *Christoph Ballmaier* as coauthor. *Christoph Ballmaier* was at that time a research assistant at the law school of Johannes Gutenberg University in Mainz.

M. Dreher, *Treatises on Solvency II*, DOI 10.1007/978-3-662-46290-4_5
Published by Springer-Verlag Berlin Heidelberg 2015.

Abstract The own risk and solvency assessment under art. 45 of the Solvency II Directive forms the subject of this chapter. Initial attention is given to clarifying the role of ORSA in the insurance supervisory regime and the principles applicable to it. Then follows a discussion of the relationship of ORSA to the risk management function as well to the other key functions under the insurance supervisory regime. In conclusion, the chapter addresses, inter alia, the documentation, the public disclosure, and the supervisory powers involved in an ORSA procedure.

5.1 Introduction

Under art. 45 of the Solvency II Framework Directive,[1] each insurance undertaking will be required to conduct its Own Risk and Solvency Assessment in the future.[2] The ORSA process has been designed to be part of the risk management system of an insurance undertaking. Detailed rules on the ORSA process are not provided in the draft of the implementing regulation (Level 2).[3,4] In November 2011, however, the EIOPA[5] published a Consultation Paper on the design of Level 3 measures for the ORSA process.[6] This Consultation Paper largely excludes both the role of supervisory authorities and their power with respect to Own Risk and Solvency Assessment.[7] Many details on integration of the ORSA process into the

[1] Directive 2009/138/EC of the European Parliament and of the Council of 25 Nov. 2009, OJEU L 335, p. 1 ff., of 17 Dec. 2009, (the "Solvency II Framework Directive").

[2] Own Risk and Solvency Assessment (hereafter, ORSA).

[3] The introduction of the new Solvency II regime is based on the "Lamfalussy process" and will occur in four stages: At Level 1, there is the Solvency II Framework Directive itself. At Level 2, this Directive is concretized in an implementing regulation. Then, through further concretization and clarification, measures at Level 3 are intended to produce convergent supervision of insurance undertakings regardless of member-state borders. Finally, at Level 4, there is the implementation in national law. In Germany this will be accomplished through the VAG [German Insurance Supervision Act]. Monitoring of insurance undertakings falls to the responsibility of authorities in each Member State and of the EIOPA. In detail on the legislative process for Solvency II, *Wandt/ Sehrbrock*, "Solvency II – Rechtsrahmen und Rechtsetzung" [in English: Solvency II – Legal Framework and Legislation], in: Dreher/Wandt eds., "Solvency II in der Rechtsanwendung" [in English: Solvency II in the Application of Law], (2009), p. 1 ff.

[4] See, however, the enabling provisions under art. 50, para. 2 of the Solvency II Framework Directive and art. 2, para. 7 of the Proposal for an Omnibus II Directive dated 19 Jan. 2011 (COM (2011) 8 final) for delegated acts "to ensure appropriate convergence of the assessment referred to in Article 45(1)(a)" of the Solvency II Framework Directive.

[5] European Insurance and Occupational Pensions Authority (EIOPA).

[6] EIOPA, Consultation Paper on the Proposal for Guidelines on Own Risk and Solvency Assessment 2011 (Hereafter: Consultation Paper).

[7] According to no. 3.5 of the Consultation Paper, this is reserved for the Guidelines on the Supervisory Review Process, which have not yet been issued.

organizational structure and existing processes within the insurance undertakings remain to be clarified. The EIOPA's statements primarily center on the objectives of the ORSA and not on its implementation and execution.[8]

Insurance undertakings will enter unexplored legal territory with the introduction of the ORSA, and thus numerous legal questions arise. Due in part to the ambitious time frame for implementing Solvency II,[9] these questions must be addressed in order to ensure the proper conversion of art. 45 of the Solvency II Framework Directive into national law as well as swift and legally correct adoption of the ORSA process by insurance undertakings. A new sec. 28 of the VAG [German Insurance Supervision Act] will implement relevant paras. 1 through 5 of art. 45 of the Solvency II Framework Directive into national law[10]; and para. 6 on the reporting obligations of insurance undertakings to the BaFin [Federal Financial Supervisory Authority] will be implemented by a new sec. 44, no. 8 of the VAG [German Insurance Supervision Act], accompanied by implementation measures from the European Commission.[11] The declaratory paragraph 7 is not taken up in the ministerial draft of the law.[12]

The ORSA's origin from within the Solvency II system is important to understanding it from a legal point of view. The present article therefore begins with the role of the ORSA in the new Solvency II regime (5.2) as a precursor to illustrating the principles underlying an ORSA (5.3). The article then frames the ORSA more precisely within the risk management function of an insurance undertaking (5.4) and examines the relationship of the ORSA to both the actuarial function and the calculation of regulatory capital requirements (5.5). The roles of the compliance function and internal audit for the ORSA also are worthy of attention (5.6). A number of individual issues related to the ORSA are also addressed (5.7), along with documentation and duties of disclosure in connection with the ORSA (5.8). Finally, the powers of the supervisory authorities with respect to the ORSA are examined (5.9).

---

[8] See no. 3.2 of the Consultation Paper.

[9] In principle, the date of application for Directive 138/2009/EC (Solvency II Framework Directive) is supposed to be set at 1 Jan. 2013 according to the proposal for the Omnibus II Directive (COM(2011) 8 final) in art. 2, para. 72 and 74.

[10] See sec. 28 of the Referentenentwurf der Bundesregierung für ein Zehntes Gesetz zur Änderung des Versicherungsaufsichtsgesetzes [in English: Government's Ministerial Draft of a Tenth Act Amending the Insurance Supervision Act] of August 2011 (hereafter: VAG-E).

[11] Statement of grounds for sec. 28 of the VAG-E [Government's Ministerial Draft of a Tenth Act Amending the Insurance Supervision Act], p. 288, see below, at 5.8.3.

[12] Statement of grounds for sec. 28 of the VAG-E [Government's Ministerial Draft of a Tenth Act Amending the Insurance Supervision Act], p. 288, see below, at 5.4.3.

5.2 Subject-Matter and Objective of the ORSA

Recital 36 of the Solvency II Framework Directive emphasizes the prominent role of regular self-assessment of overall solvency needs with respect to the individual risk profile of each insurance undertaking. The ORSA is the logical consequence of the principles-based supervision that Solvency II targeted, however unsuccessfully, with the four-level system. Its intention is to confer more direct responsibility to insurance undertakings for meeting the requirements of financial supervision law.[13]

Thus, from the perspective of the undertaking, the ORSA is an internal tool for estimating the overall solvency needs expected in the short and long term. On the other hand, from the perspective of the supervisory regime, it is a source of information for the insurance supervisory authorities.[14] The Issues Paper on Own Risk and Solvency Assessment from CEIOPS defines the ORSA as the entirety of the processes and procedures employed to identify, assess, monitor, report, and manage short and long term risks, and to quantitatively determine and meet own funds requirements.[15] The ORSA is therefore composed of a qualitative and quantitative component.[16] In its analysis, the ORSA is also supposed to include risks that have not already been accounted for based on the requirements of the standard model or of any approved internal model used.[17]

Under art. 45, para. 5 of the Solvency II Framework Directive, the ORSA should be conducted on a regular basis—at least once a year or as otherwise appropriate based on the risk profile of the insurance undertaking, according to EIOPA[18] and the Statement of Grounds for the Ministerial Draft,[19]—and additionally "following

[13] See No. 11 CEIOPS, Issues Paper ORSA 2008 (IP ORSA). In more detail on the legal term of "principles-based supervision": *Wandt/Sehrbrock*, ZVersWiss (2011), 193 (203) and published in ZVersWiss 2010 special edition: "Solvency II in der Rechtsanwendung" [in English: Solvency II in Legal Application]. See in summary on the risks and opportunities of a principles-orientation *Boetius*, in: Ellenbürger/Ott/Frey/Boetius, eds., Mindestanforderungen an das Risikomanagement (MaRisk VA) für Versicherungen [in English: Minimum Requirements for Risk Management for Insurance Supervision (MaRisk VA)], 2009 p. 19; on further advantages, as well as problems in implementation, see *Schaaf*, "Risikomanagement und Compliance in Versicherungsunternehmen – aufsichtsrechtliche Anforderungen und Organverantwortung" [in English: Risk Management and Compliance in Insurance Undertakings – Supervisory Requirements and Institutional Responsibility] (2010), p. 25 f.

[14] See below, at 5.8.3 as well as No. 8 IP ORSA, *Gödeke*, VersR (2010), 10 (14) and the statement of grounds for sec. 28 of the VAG-E [Government's Ministerial Draft of a Tenth Act Amending the Insurance Supervision Act] p. 286.

[15] No. 9 IP ORSA.

[16] Not entirely clear, art. 45, para. 1, subpara. 2 (a) of the Solvency II Framework Directive. But according to Guideline 8 of the Consultation Paper.

[17] Art. 44, para. 2 of the Solvency II Framework Directive; see also no. 4.1 of the Consultation Paper ("all the risks").

[18] Guideline 15 of the Consultation Paper.

[19] Statement of grounds for sec. 28 VAG-E [Government's Ministerial Draft of a Tenth Act Amending the Insurance Supervision Act], p. 287.

any significant change in the risk profile". Whether a change is "significant" in this sense depends on the individual case.[20] With respect to the role of the ORSA in risk management, significance can be assumed if, based on prior evaluation, doubt exists that the ORSA conducted most recently still accomplishes its functions stated above.

5.3 The Solvency II Legal Principles Applicable to the ORSA

The ORSA is part of the new risk management system within the meaning of Solvency II. All of the principles underlying Solvency II therefore apply. The existence of the ORSA concept is chiefly the result of the principles-based approach to supervision.[21] This concept rests on the assumption that an increase in regulation does not facilitate the adequate recognition of risks nor can it keep pace with the dynamics of financial markets.[22]

The Solvency II Framework Directive is shaped in particular by the principles of materiality and proportionality. According to the former, only risks that are material to the risk status of the insurance undertaking should be considered in the risk analysis. The assessment as to which risks should be viewed as material is essentially left to the insurance undertaking.[23] This is consistent with the current concept in sec. 64a of the VAG [German Insurance Supervision Act] in conjunction with the explanatory MaRisk VA [Minimum Requirements for Risk Management (Insurance Supervision)][24] and the future secs. 27 ff. in the VAG-E [Government's Ministerial Draft of a Tenth Act Amending the Insurance Supervision Act]. The materiality principle entails regular review of the criteria that insurance undertakings apply to determining the significance of risks.

According to the principle of proportionality in art. 29, para. 3 and Recital 19 of the Solvency II Framework Directive, which in its partial implementation[25] is presumably reflected only in the context of the exercise of the supervisory authority in sec. 290 of the VAG-E [Government's Ministerial Draft of a Tenth Act

[20] The statement of grounds for sec. 28 VAG-E [Government's Ministerial Draft of a Tenth Act Amending the Insurance Supervision Act] is silent with respect to the determination of significant change to the risk profile.

[21] See above, n. 13.

[22] *Dreher*, VersR (2008), 998 (1000).

[23] The listing found in art. 44, para. 2 of the Solvency II Framework Directive denotes the minimum areas of coverage; see *Gödeke*, VersR (2010), 10 (13).

[24] BaFin Circular 3/2009 – Minimum Requirements for Risk Management in Insurance Undertakings (MaRisk VA), with later amendments.

[25] The Directive is based on the concept of double proportionality, meaning the relevance of proportionality both to the requirements imposed on insurance undertakings and to the exercise of supervisory authority.

Amending the Insurance Supervision Act]—and thus is not sufficiently anchored in the VAG-E [Government's Ministerial Draft of a Tenth Act Amending the Insurance Supervision Act] as far as the ORSA is concerned—the complexity of an ORSA must be aligned with the complexity of the business model and the risk status of the insurance undertaking.

CEIOPS emphasized that the principle of proportionality can have impact in two directions.[26] Undertakings with simple business models can conduct a simple ORSA. But with increasing complexity in the business model, a sufficiently comprehensive ORSA must be used.[27]

Under art. 45, para. 4 of the Solvency II Framework Directive, the results of an ORSA are to "be an integral part of the business strategy and shall be taken into account on an ongoing basis in the strategic decisions of the undertaking". The ORSA, therefore, cannot be divorced from the business strategy. If fulfillment of the requirements of art. 45, para. 4 of the Solvency II Framework Directive is subject to supervision, the business strategy is then indirectly also subject to review. Taken on its own, the coupling of a legally required ORSA with the business strategy impacts the proprietary function of all (insurance) undertakings in an economic and legal system based on entrepreneurial freedom. Added to this is a supervisory responsibility that includes this strategy-based ORSA. Against this background, a question requiring special emphasis concerns the boundaries between business autonomy and the outside influence of the state in determining, amending, and implementing the business strategy.[28]

5.4 The ORSA and the Risk Management System

5.4.1 The European Law Framework

In its legislative design, the ORSA is part of the risk management system classified under Pillar 2 of Solvency II.[29] But the ORSA also pertains to some measures that are attributable to Pillars 1 and 3 of Solvency II.[30] For example, according to art. 45, para. 6 of the Solvency II Framework Directive, the results of an ORSA must be disclosed to the supervisory authority in the report required under art. 35 of the Solvency II

[26] Indeed, this is already inherent in the very concept of proportionality, but was specifically mentioned in CEIOPS, Draft Proposal for Level 3 Guidelines on Own Risk and Solvency Assessment (Article 45), 2010, (hereafter: Level 3 Proposal), no. 3.7.

[27] See also on this point statement of grounds for sec. 28 of the VAG-E [Government's Ministerial Draft of a Tenth Act Amending the Insurance Supervision Act] p. 286.

[28] See in detail 5.7.1.3, below.

[29] See art. 45, para. 1 of the Solvency II Framework Directive.

[30] *Brinkmann/Bruhns,* VW (2011), 411 (413) speak of the ORSA in this regard as a "bracket around the three pillars of Solvency II"; similarly, *Axer/Kaya,* ZfV (2011), 543 (546) and *Riefl Bender,* VW (2011), 1493.

Framework Directive (Pillar 3). Quantitative matters, which are actually categorized under Pillar 1 of the three-pillar concept, must also be addressed in the ORSA process, particularly as the overall solvency requirements must be presented both quantitatively and qualitatively.[31] As Recital 36 and art. 45 of the Solvency II Framework Directive, as well as the papers published by CEIOPS and now EIOPA indicate, the ORSA is not simply a matter of documenting and communicating a result. The ORSA is designed in such a way that its implementation will also have a significant effect on the internal and external conduct of insurance undertakings.[32] This result flows not in the least from the obligation to assess whether the undertaking continuously ensures compliance with the solvency capital requirement in accordance with art. 45, para. 1, subpara. 2 b of the Solvency II Framework Directive.[33]

Under art. 45, para. 4 of the Solvency II Framework Directive, ORSA has considerable influence on the governance of an insurance undertaking. This is so because ORSA is presumed to be an integral component of the business strategy and must be taken into account in making strategic decisions.[34] Most importantly, a certain amount of interaction between the ORSA and the business strategy established by management is supposed to transpire: On one hand, the business strategy and the determination of risk appetite of an insurance undertaking defines the ORSA process, since the ORSA is based on their assessment.[35] On the other, business strategy is supposed to be based on the results of the ORSA.[36] Further the ORSA sets boundaries for asset management. Under art. 132, para. 2 of the Solvency II Framework Directive,[37] investment is permitted only in financial instruments that can be considered adequate to the undertaking's self-assessment of its risk profile and solvency. In November 2011, EIOPA published a Consultation Paper on implementation guidelines at Level 3. The guidelines therein reflect the understanding of the supervisory authority regarding art. 45 of the Solvency II Framework Directive. The purpose of the guidelines is to ensure convergent and effective insurance supervision in the member states, particularly with respect to the Level 2 implementing regulation. The guidelines must be gauged against

---

[31] See above, n. 16.

[32] Art. 45, para. 4 of the Solvency II Framework Directive; Nr. 9, 47 IP ORSA; see also sec. 28, para. 1, sent. 2 of the VAG-E [Government's Ministerial Draft of a Tenth Act Amending the Insurance Supervision Act]. On the impact of the ORSA on business strategy, see also 5.7.1.3, below.

[33] EIOPA understands art. 45, para. 1, subpara. 2 b of the Solvency II Framework Directive to mean that "continuous compliance" can be estimated with fundamentally "sufficient accuracy" and that constant recalculation is generally not required; No. 4.40 of the Consultation Paper. Nevertheless, EIOPA expects the insurance undertaking to be able to justify its preference of an estimate over a calculation.

[34] See n. 32 and below, under 5.7.1.3.

[35] Art. 45, para. 1, subpara. 2 a of the Solvency II Framework Directive.

[36] Art. 45, para. 4 of the Solvency II Framework Directive; see also Guideline 14, no. 4.69 ff. of the Consultation Paper.

[37] Implemented in sec. 115, para. 1, no. 1 of the VAG-E [Government's Ministerial Draft of a Tenth Act Amending the Insurance Supervision Act].

the implementing regulation on the one hand, and directly against art. 45 of the Solvency II Framework Directive on the other. Otherwise they would not be functional as guidelines for supervisory measures in the Member States. Although the guidelines at Level 3 are not legally binding,[38] due to the comply-or-explain approach and the disclosure obligation associated with it—for example, in art. 16 of the EIOPA regulation[39]—they have a de facto binding effect for national supervisory authorities and insurance undertakings. Not least for this reason, their density is questionable, a matter which the European Economic and Social Committee addresses head-on.[40] Nevertheless, Level 3 measures, unlike the Level 2 implementing regulations, may not exceed the requirements in the basic legal act at Level 1, or extend further than the implementing regulations at Level 2.[41] A condition of the multilevel supervisory regime is the delegation to the Commission for implementation at Level 1. The limit of the delegation at Level 2 is the principle of materiality in combination with the relevant delegation rule. At level 3, however, it is the terms of the law at Levels 1 and 2.

5.4.2 Present Law: The Relationship of the ORSA to Sec. 64 a, Para. 1, 2 of the VAG [German Insurance Supervision Act] and the MaRisk VA [Minimum Requirements for Risk Management (Insurance Supervision)]

Sec. 64 a of the VAG [German Insurance Supervision Act] was introduced to a certain extent in anticipation of the coming changes in Solvency II and thus to enable insurance undertakings to make a smooth transition to the Solvency II regime.[42] In Circular 3/2009 (MaRisk VA [Minimum Requirements for Risk

[38] See for example *Weber-Rey/Baltzer*, "Verlautbarungen der EU und der BaFin zur internen Governance von Banken" [in English: Pronouncements of the EU and BaFin (German Federal Financial Supervisory Authority) on the Internal Governance of Banks], in Hopt/Wohlmannstetter, eds., Handbuch Corporate Governance von Banken [in English: Handbook of Corporate Governance of Banks] (2011), p. 431 (447 f.).

[39] Regulation 1094/2010/EU of the European Parliament and of the Council of 24 Nov. 2010, establishing a European Supervisory Authority (European Insurance and Occupational Pensions Authority), amending Decision No 716/2009/EC and repealing Commission Decision 2009/79/EC of 24 Nov. 2010, OJEU L 331/48.

[40] Response of the European Economic and Social Committee to the "Proposal for a directive of the European Parliament and of the Council amending Directives 2003/71/EC and 2009/138/EC in respect of the powers of the European Insurance and Occupational Pensions Authority and the European Securities and Markets Authority", 2011/C 218/15.

[41] See on this point *Dreher/Lange*, VersR (2011), 825 (829) (Chap. 1, above, at 1.3.2), with n. 28.

[42] See statement of grounds of the 9th VAG [German Insurance Supervision Act] amendment, BT-Drucks. [Document of the German Bundestag] 16/6518 p. 15, 17 and *Dreher*, VersR (2008), 998.

Management—Insurance Supervision]), BaFin [Federal Financial Supervisory Authority] provides its legally non-binding interpretation of the application of sec. 64 a of the VAG [German Insurance Supervision Act] for the addressees of the law.[43] Because the ORSA process is part of the risk management system, many of its components have already been implemented in German law in advance, in particular in sec. 64 a, para. 1 sent. 4, no. 3 a of the VAG [German Insurance Supervision Act] with the obligation to generate a risk-bearing capacity concept. Some of the rules of the guidelines proposed by EIOPA on ORSA have counterparts in the MaRisk VA [Minimum Requirements for Risk Management (Insurance Supervision)], in particular concerning the own risk assessment.[44] In the new four-level system of Solvency II, however, there is no longer a place for the current MaRisk VA [Minimum Requirements for Risk Management (Insurance Supervision)]. This is so because it not only explains the practice—which may also continue under Solvency II—of BaFin [Federal Financial Supervisory Authority] in a purely descriptive way. Rather, it goes further in some respects, taking on the character of a normative system by justifying new and far-reaching legal obligations of insurance undertakings.[45] Here, the BaFin [Federal Financial Supervisory Authority] usurps the role of the legislator.[46] Add to this that supervisory circulars, whatever the substantive quality one may see in them, can never constitute the implementation act necessary under European law. Therefore, any remaining anticipatory implementation of Solvency II requirements by MaRisk VA [Minimum Requirements for Risk Management (Insurance Supervision)] are ruled out, including with respect to the ORSA.

The ORSA under Solvency II and the internal management and control system under the current VAG [German Insurance Supervision Act] start from the same assumption that undertakings should capture their overall risk profile based on an economic assessment. In the view of EIOPA[47] and the BaFin [Federal Financial Supervisory Authority][48] respectively, both the ORSA and risk management under

---

[43] There does exist, however, a legal obligation for the BaFin [Federal Financial Supervisory Authority] through the principle that an institution must itself comply with the rules it has made.

[44] Given as example are the principles of proportionality and materiality that underlie both sec. 64a of the VAG [German Insurance Supervision Act] and the MaRisk VA [Minimum Requirements for Risk Management (Insurance Supervision)] as well as the ORSA. The tailored-to-fit approach of Guideline 1 is also reflected in no. 4 (1) of the MaRisk VA [Minimum Requirements for Risk Management (Insurance Supervision)]. Guideline 2 of the Consultation Paper has its counterpart in no. 6 (1) of the MaRisk VA [Minimum Requirements for Risk Management (Insurance Supervision)].

[45] See in detail on the limits of lawmaking by institutions not appointed for that function and on the considerable difference in this area between normative systems and technical rules, *Rittner/Dreher*, Europäisches und deutsches Wirtschaftsrecht [in English: European and German Economic Law] (3rd ed. 2008), sec. 7, ref. 58 f.

[46] See *Dreher*, FAZ no. 216 of 17 Sep. 2009, p. 22.

[47] See above, at 5.2.

[48] See no. 7.3.2.2 (1) MaRisk VA [Minimum Requirements for Risk Management (Insurance Supervision)].

sec. 64 a, para. 1 and 2 of the VAG [German Insurance Supervision Act] should entail a qualitative and quantitative assessment of the risks. In a departure from sec. 64 a of the VAG [German Insurance Supervision Act], art. 48, para. 1 i of the Solvency II Framework Directive includes the actuarial function in the risk management process. In the current law under sec. 64 a of the VAG [German Insurance Supervision Act], it is left to insurance undertakings as to whether they even have an actuarial function at all.[49] The opposite applies under the Solvency II Framework Directive. A convergence of the VAG [German Insurance Supervision Act] with the requirements of Solvency II in this respect was actually proposed by the BaFin [Federal Financial Supervisory Authority],[50] but no requirement to install an actuarial function is present in current law.

The assessment of continuous compliance with regulatory capital requirements, as required in accordance with art. 45, para. 1, subpara. 2 a of the Solvency II Framework Directive, is also found in sec. 64 a, para. 1, sent. 3 and 4, no. 3 a of the VAG [German Insurance Supervision Act].[51] The same applies to art. 45, para. 2 of the Solvency II Framework Directive. Its counterpart in the current German law is sec. 64 a, para. 1, sent. 3 and 4, of the VAG [German Insurance Supervision Act]. The documentation requirement with respect to the methodology of risk recognition and risk evaluation[52] is included in sec. 64 a, para. 1, sent. 4, no. 3 a of the VAG [German Insurance Supervision Act].[53]

Art. 45, para. 1, subpara. 2 c of the Solvency II Framework Directive obligates insurance undertakings to review their risk profile for significant deviation[54] from the underlying assumptions in Solvency II for the calibration of solvency. Sec. 64 a of the VAG [German Insurance Supervision Act] is silent on this matter, and the MaRisk VA [Minimum Requirements for Risk Management (Insurance Supervision)] also makes no mention of such reviews. This can be explained in that the assumptions underlying Solvency II have thus far not been sufficiently transparent and the legislator was therefore unable to prescribe this sort of review. Should the rule, for which a draft already exists with sec. 24 VAG-E [Government's Ministerial Draft of a Tenth Act Amending the Insurance Supervision Act], not be replaced with a successor provision by the critical implementation date, one possibility for taking account of the questionable review requirement in sec. 64 a, para. 1 of the VAG [German Insurance Supervision Act] would be its interpretation in alignment with European law. That sec. 64 a of the VAG [German Insurance Supervision Act] is not technically an implementation act but rather an anticipation of the (expected)

[49] See *Schaaf* id., n. 13, p. 124.

[50] See *Schaaf* id., n. 13, p. 125.

[51] See also no. 7.3.1 (1) MaRisk VA [Minimum Requirements for Risk Management (Insurance Supervision)].

[52] See art. 45, para. 2, sent. 2 of the Solvency II Framework Directive.

[53] See also no. 7.3.1 (4) MaRisk VA [Minimum Requirements for Risk Management (Insurance Supervision)].

[54] On the term "significance" see below, at 5.7.4.

legislation upon enactment of the Directive is not a hindrance to such an interpretation at this time. An interpretation that aligns with the Directive is also possible absent an implementation act, or in the event one is adopted that has gaps.[55] The link would be sec. 64 a, para. 1, sent. 4, no. 3 b of the VAG [German Insurance Supervision Act]. Significant deviation of the individual risk profile from the calculation assumptions in Solvency II is itself a risk of defective or insufficient models, also known as parameter or model risk.[56] Recognition of this risk and managing it would be encompassed in an interpretation of sec. 64 a, para. 1, sent. 4, no. 3 b of the VAG [German Insurance Supervision Act] that aligns with the Directive, and in doing so the criteria for evaluating this risk would necessarily be the basic assumptions required by Solvency II.

Thus, in this respect, with sec. 64 a of the VAG [German Insurance Supervision Act], the German legislator has largely, but not completely, achieved his goal of early incorporation of Solvency II into German law. In particular, the actuarial function does not play the role in risk management under sec. 64 a VAG [German Insurance Supervision Act] that European law assigns to it. Moreover, the German "pre-implementation" in some partial rules, combined with the MaRisk VA [Minimum Requirements for Risk Management (Insurance Supervision)], has even overshot this goal. This is the case in particular if it specifically requires independence only for the risk-controlling function—as in sec. 27, para. 5 of the VAG-E [Government's Ministerial Draft of a Tenth Act Amending the Insurance Supervision Act]—rather than independence for all governance functions as required in art. 258 SG6 of the draft implementing regulation.

5.4.3 Future Law: Sec. 28 of the VAG [German Insurance Supervision Act] in the Version of the Ministerial Draft

The implementation of the European law ORSA requirements into the VAG [German Insurance Supervision Act], adverted to above, is intended to produce a new sec. 28 of the VAG [German Insurance Supervision Act].[57] In its wording, sec. 28 of the VAG-E [Government's Ministerial Draft of a Tenth Act Amending the Insurance Supervision Act] largely follows art. 45 of the Solvency II Framework Directive. But the Ministerial Draft is generally, and thus also in sec. 28, focused on preserving German legal terminology. This is seen, for example, in sec. 28, para.

---

[55] See in lieu of multiple citations *Wolf*, in: Grabitz/Hilf, eds., Das Recht der Europäischen Union [in English: The Law of the European Union] vol. IV (40th ed. 2009) A 1 V 2 ref. 29.

[56] On the term, see the draft of a new Insurance Core Principal [sic] of the IAIS (International Association of Insurance Supervisors), Insurance Core Principal [sic] 16 (Enterprise Risk Management) (2010), no. 16.1.10.

[57] See sec. 28 of the VAG-E [Government's Ministerial Draft of a Tenth Act Amending the Insurance Supervision Act].

2, no. 3 of the VAG-E [Government's Ministerial Draft of a Tenth Act Amending the Insurance Supervision Act], which employs the term "Wesentlichkeit von Abweichungen" [in English: materiality of deviations] while art. 45, para. 1, subpara. 2 c of the Solvency II Framework Directive uses "Signifikanz der Abweichung" [in English: significance of deviation]. This terminological unicum in the VAG-E [Government's Ministerial Draft of a Tenth Act Amending the Insurance Supervision Act] goes astray in both principle and specifics. In order to ensure the most unified possible application of the law within the scope of the Solvency II Framework Directive, it would be advisable to also use the term "significance" in the new sec. 28 of the VAG-E [Government's Ministerial Draft of a Tenth Act Amending the Insurance Supervision Act]. This is especially true in light of the fact that the language in the German version of the Solvency II Framework Directive in arts. 37, 45 and 119 also wrongly deviates and must itself be unified in a correct interpretation of the European law.[58]

Where art. 45, para. 2 of the Solvency II Framework Directive further speaks of "the risks [the insurance undertaking] faces in the short and long term and to which it is or could be exposed", sec. 28, para. 3 of the VAG-E [Government's Ministerial Draft of a Tenth Act Amending the Insurance Supervision Act] makes do with referring to "all risks".[59] This is all the more surprising since the VAG-E [Government's Ministerial Draft of a Tenth Act Amending the Insurance Supervision Act] actually employs the terminology of the Solvency II Framework Directive largely unaltered elsewhere in sec. 27, para. 1, sent. 2 of the VAG-E [Government's Ministerial Draft of a Tenth Act Amending the Insurance Supervision Act], requiring that risk management cover "risks to which the undertaking is exposed or could be exposed". What must be made clear for the interpretation of the legal requirement of "all risks" is, first of all, that the national legislator's use of this terminology does not invalidate the principles of materiality and proportionality,[60] as discussed above, and that only the material risks pertaining to the respective insurance undertaking can be meant. Thus here again, through a divergence in wording, the VAG-E [Government's Ministerial Draft of a Tenth Act Amending the Insurance Supervision Act] prompts an avoidable need for interpretation in alignment with the Directive. This is so because only such interpretation will ensure the necessary consideration of materiality and proportionality. Furthermore, this example once again underscores the criticism of what is currently only partial implementation of the principle of proportionality in the VAG-E [Government's Ministerial Draft of a Tenth Act Amending the Insurance Supervision Act].[61]

Further, sec. 28, para. 3 VAG-E [Government's Ministerial Draft of a Tenth Act Amending the Insurance Supervision Act] forgoes implementing the formulation "could be exposed" as found in art. 45, para. 2, sent. 1 of the Solvency II Framework

---

[58] See on this point in detail 5.7.4.1, below.

[59] See also in this respect, however, Consultation Paper (above, n. 17).

[60] See above, at 5.3.

[61] See above, at 5.3.

Directive in reference to the risks recognized. This does not ultimately appear to interfere with interpretation of sec. 28, para. 3 of the VAG-E [Government's Ministerial Draft of a Tenth Act Amending the Insurance Supervision Act] because hypothetical risks are also risks. Nevertheless, legal clarity is not well served by this type of defective implementation.

Conversely, sec. 28, para. 3, sent. 2 of the VAG-E [Government's Ministerial Draft of a Tenth Act Amending the Insurance Supervision Act] has no counterpart in the Solvency II Framework Directive. According to this passage, the ORSA process must "incorporate, in particular, the independent conduct of stress tests and scenario analyses". Based simply on the nature of the Directive as fully harmonizing,[62] a legal order for independent stress tests and scenario analyses is not allowable, absent a rule at Level 2 that is yet to be made. Moreover, it also breaks from the design of the ORSA in the European law, which gives free rein to insurance undertakings with respect to the modality of conducting an ORSA.[63] While insurance undertakings are free to decide the methodology of implementation, they are at the same time under an obligation to explain the method's adequacy under art. 45, para. 2, sent. 2 of the Solvency II Framework Directive. The national legislator is bound by this.

The Ministerial Draft then refrains from adopting art. 45, para. 7 of the Solvency II Framework Directive. In this passage, the European legislator makes clear, i.a., that the ORSA "shall not serve to calculate a capital requirement".[64] For this defective implementation, the statement of grounds for sec. 28 of the VAG-E [Government's Ministerial Draft of a Tenth Act Amending the Insurance Supervision Act] refers only to the declaratory nature of the rules[65] and views a counterpart in the new VAG [German Insurance Supervision Act] as superfluous. However, in view of the important role of ORSA in risk management, and particularly because the insurance industry thus far has no experience with Own Risk and Solvency Assessments, the determination made in art. 45, para. 7 of the Solvency II Framework Directive would be entirely reasonable in a new VAG [German Insurance Supervision Act]. Practitioners would assuredly find such a clarification a useful aid to interpretation.

Lastly, art. 45, para. 6 of the Solvency II Framework Directive, which governs the disclosure requirements in the report to supervisory authorities with respect to the ORSA, is implemented incompletely in sec. 44, no. 8 of the Ministerial Draft of the VAG [German Insurance Supervision Act] through the establishment of duties of notice.[66]

---

[62] *Dreher/Lange*, VersR (2011), 825 (Chap. 1, above).

[63] Art. 251 SG3, para. 3 of the draft implementing regulation provides for stress tests and scenario analyses as part of risk management only "where appropriate". Also in this area, No. 4.6 of the Consultation Paper mentions stress test as a methodology for the ORSA process only as an example.

[64] See on this point in detail, below, at 5.7.2.

[65] Statement of grounds for sec. 28 VAG-E [Government's Ministerial Draft of a Tenth Act Amending the Insurance Supervision Act], p. 288.

[66] On this point, see 5.8.3, below.

The ORSA is a highly complex process; and its associated costs may have a significant impact on insurance undertakings. In terms of cost, the Statement of Grounds of the VAG-E [Government's Ministerial Draft of a Tenth Act Amending the Insurance Supervision Act] refers only to those incurred in complying with the duties to inform. The draft identifies "the new risk and solvency assessment in sec. 44, no. 8 at 635,000 euros" as the "most expensive duty to inform".[67] To the extent the draft relies on mandatory EU law, the legal basis given is incorrect[68] and the amount given is incorrectly low. Sec. 44, no. 8 of the VAG-E [Government's Ministerial Draft of a Tenth Act Amending the Insurance Supervision Act] relates exclusively to the duty to inform the supervisory authority in the event of an extraordinary ORSA, and the table accompanying the Statement of Grounds[69] contains six additional ORSA-related duties, solely in consideration of art. 45 of the Solvency II Framework Directive or sec. 28 of the VAG-E [Government's Ministerial Draft of a Tenth Act Amending the Insurance Supervision Act], for which a total cost of 15,375,499 euros is indicated.

5.5 ORSA, Actuarial Function, Standard Formula and Internal Model

The ORSA requires—even if not directly stated in the wording of sec. 28 VAG-E [Government's Ministerial Draft of a Tenth Act Amending the Insurance Supervision Act]—to include the actuarial function into risk management since the overall solvency assessment is quantitative.[70] In this context, the actuarial function is part of the risk management system pursuant to the legislative concept.[71] Accordingly, it determines not only whether the Solvency Capital Requirements according to supervisory law are met, but also how high the overall solvency requirements are. Further, the actuarial function must assess the significance of deviation within the meaning of art. 45, para. 1, subpara. 2 c of the Solvency II Framework Directive,[72] or the materiality of deviations within the meaning of sec. 28, para. 2, no. 3 of the VAG-E [Government's Ministerial Draft of a Tenth Act Amending the Insurance Supervision Act].

[67] See the Statement of Grounds of the VAG-E [Government's Ministerial Draft of a Tenth Act Amending the Insurance Supervision Act], General Part, p. 255, 257.

[68] The draft refers to art. 102, para. 1 of the Solvency II Framework Directive rather than to art. 45 in conjunction with art. 35.

[69] See the Statement of Grounds of the VAG-E [Government's Ministerial Draft of a Tenth Act Amending the Insurance Supervision Act], General Part, p. 255 f.

[70] See statement of grounds for sec. 28 of the VAG-E [Government's Ministerial Draft of a Tenth Act Amending the Insurance Supervision Act], p. 287.

[71] See also art. 48 of the Solvency II Framework Directive and sec. 31, para. 2 of the VAG-E [Government's Ministerial Draft of a Tenth Act Amending the Insurance Supervision Act].

[72] See art. 48, para. 1 i of the Solvency II Framework Directive.

The standard formula and internal models are directed exclusively at the capital requirements according to supervisory law. The ORSA, on the other hand, examines the capital position of the insurance undertaking from the perspective of the overall solvency needs. This perspective encompasses, for example, the future-looking risk and overall solvency analysis in the ORSA over longer periods of time[73] and allows, consistently, that future sources of profit may also be considered in the ORSA along with all significant risks. Non-quantifiable risks must also be specifically included in the ORSA process.[74] It must also be emphasized that capital add-ons required under supervisory law shall not be automatically tied to the ORSA process.[75]

The ORSA is intended to enable insurance undertakings to assess whether the standard formula of Solvency II is sufficient to assure the solvency of the insurance undertaking.[76] If this sufficiency is in doubt, the undertaking must, according to the EIOPA, examine whether the development of an internal model would be more advantageous.[77] If the insurance undertaking already uses an internal model, the ORSA shall evaluate the adequacy of its functioning.[78] For example, the assumptions underlying the internal model and other data must be reviewed. Or an investigation is conducted to determine whether the risks depicted in the model are sufficient for an adequate projection of the true risk profile.[79] Such techniques and processes entail a great deal of crossover, which produces not only considerable redundancy but also the danger of accretion in technical processes that are no longer transparent or understandable by the management and supervisory bodies in the insurance undertaking, and a concomitant dependence on this structure.

Finally, questions arise when comparing the standard formula and the ORSA. The problem is that, on one hand, the insurance supervisory regime gives insurance undertakings instructions for calculating regulatory capital with the standard formula. On the other, with the requirements for the risk management system, it

---

[73] According to the statement of grounds for sec. 28 of the VAG-E [Government's Ministerial Draft of a Tenth Act Amending the Insurance Supervision Act], p. 287, "three to five years depending on the individual planning horizon of the undertaking" should be estimated for this. It is not sufficient to assume a one-year planning horizon such as that on which the standard formula is based.

[74] See above, 5.2 and 5.4.1 as well as *Axer/Kaya*, ZfV (2011), 543 (545).

[75] See on this point above, 5.4.3 at n. 65 and in detail at 5.7.2, below.

[76] See also the statement of reasons for sec. 28 of the VAG-E [Government's Ministerial Draft of a Tenth Act Amending the Insurance Supervision Act], p. 286.

[77] No. 4.3 of the Consultation Paper.

[78] Thus correctly, *Meyer*, "Anforderungen an das Governance System von Versicherungsunternehmen und -gruppen" [in English: Requirements for the Governance Systems of Insurance Undertakings and Groups], in: Bennemann/Oehlenberg/Stahl, eds., Handbuch Solvency II [in English: Solvency II Manual] (2011), p. 92, who views the ORSA in its "broadest sense as also a part of model validation".

[79] See also the statement of reasons for sec. 28 of the VAG-E [Government's Ministerial Draft of a Tenth Act Amending the Insurance Supervision Act], p. 286.

requires the undertaking's management to continuously question the standard formula in connection with any significant deviation within the meaning of art. 45, para. 1, subpara. 2 c of the Solvency II Framework Directive. This interpretation inverts the supervisory relationship, demanding that the supervised insurance undertaking continuously audit the usefulness of the standard formula provided in supervisory law. From a legal point of view, it cannot be the responsibility of those subject to supervision to conduct ongoing review of supervision rules with an eye out for necessary changes, and in so doing undergo yet another examination by the supervisory authority actually responsible for this.

This contradiction can be explained only by noting the strong emphasis on Pillar 2 in the architecture of Solvency II, which assigns a key role to risk management.[80] The legal bases for intervention under supervisory law in the event of violations of regulatory capital requirements (Pillar 1) are accordingly different from those related to violations of the requirements for risk management (Pillar 2). Thus the capital add-on under art. 37 of the Solvency II Framework Directive can be tied cumulatively to both defective corporate governance (art. 37, para. 1, sent. 2 c of the Solvency II Framework Directive) as well as to any significant deviation in the risk profile from the assumptions underlying the calculation of the standard formula (art. 37, para. 1 a and b of the Solvency II Framework Directive). The implementation proposal in sec. 295, para. 1, sent. 2 of the VAG-E [Government's Ministerial Draft of a Tenth Act Amending the Insurance Supervision Act] reflects this view.

5.6 The ORSA, the Compliance Function, and the Internal Audit Function

Under art. 46, para. 1, subpara. 2 of the Solvency II Framework Directive, the internal control system for all insurance undertakings includes a "compliance function". One of the requirements whose fulfillment is monitored by this function is the ORSA as prescribed under the supervision law. Thus, the compliance function is also involved with the ORSA.

Simply monitoring whether the regularly mandated ORSA is aligned with applicable requirements constitutes a significant challenge for a compliance function, particularly as it relates to the required expertise of the relevant compliance staff. The challenge is even more significant for two areas in which the duty to act on the part of the compliance function, based on the sweeping wording of the Solvency II Framework Directive alone—and made even more concise in the implementation proposal in sec. 29, para. 1 of the VAG-E [Government's Ministerial Draft of a Tenth Act Amending the Insurance Supervision Act]—leads to an unsound resolution.

[80] Stating the equivalent weight of Pillar 1 and Pillar 2 in Solvency II, for example, *Fopma/Klingeler*, VW (2007), 2045 (2046).

First, there is the nexus, discussed in detail below,[81] of the ORSA with the business strategy under art. 45, para. 4 of the Solvency II Framework Directive. If, as a proprietary function of the undertaking's management, business strategy is not only non-delegable but also exempt from supervision, as will be shown, the activity of the compliance function in connection with ORSA must also be excluded from the outset. Below this threshold, where a certain sensitivity to and restraint from influence by third parties is always mandated due to the close involvement with strategic decisions by management, it must be consistently restricted to verifying the exercise and subsequent consideration by management of the ORSA process and its results.

A further question arises with respect to the competence limits of the compliance function as to how it should monitor the requirement mandated in art. 45 of the Solvency II Framework Directive for an extraordinary ORSA. Under art. 45, para. 5 of the Solvency II Framework Directive, an extraordinary ORSA is required following any significant change to the risk profile of an insurance undertaking.[82] However, the result of this cannot be that the compliance function itself also monitors for changes to the risk profile. Rather, the compliance function is restricted to analyzing its findings from general compliance activities, which also includes monitoring risk management requirements, to determine whether cause for an extraordinary ORSA exists. Beyond this, the compliance function may observe risk management only to ascertain whether it properly responds to relevant changes in the risk profile by initiating an extraordinary ORSA.

Because the ORSA is part of the risk-management system, it is also within the scope of responsibility of the risk-management function, which monitors the risk-management system by virtue of art. 259 SG7, para. 1 b of the draft implementing regulation. In addition, internal audit is required to examine the "adequacy and effectiveness of . . . elements of the system of governance" in accordance with art. 47, para. 1, subpara. 2 of the Solvency II Framework Directive.[83]

5.7 Individual Issues Concerning the ORSA

5.7.1 The ORSA and Free Enterprise

5.7.1.1 The Problem

View of the very far-reaching requirements of the ORSA, there may be concern that the legal framework no longer permits sufficient freedom of management in

[81] See 5.7.1.3, below.

[82] See above, at 5.2.

[83] See on this point the implementation in sec. 30 of the VAG-E [Government's Ministerial Draft of a Tenth Act Amending the Insurance Supervision Act], which requires that internal audit review the "entire business organization".

business. From a legal perspective this would mean that the ORSA is not compatible with the fundamental freedom rights to conduct a business (see art. 16 of the EU Charter of Fundamental Rights (the Charter)[84] and art. 12, para. 1 of the German Basic Law).[85] Indeed, substantial interference with free enterprise flows from the requirement on insurance undertakings for a continuous ORSA. Also relevant is the prohibition on optimization in supervisory law. This principle means that supervisory law must not mandate business practices which would best fit the aims of economic supervision.[86]

Only legally binding rules can be employed to answer the question of proportionality of the ORSA requirements. The Level 3 measures do not—at least not generally[87]—belong here.[88]

5.7.1.2 The Justification of the ORSA as an Obligatory Responsibility of the Undertaking

Apart from the question of whether the guarantee of essential substance in art. 52 of the Charter stands on its own or must instead be systematically assigned to the examination of proportionality,[89] the quintessence of entrepreneurial freedom[90] is unaffected by the ordering of an ORSA in art. 45 of the Solvency II Framework Directive. In this case, art. 45 of Solvency II Framework Directive is appropriate for

---

[84] On the – disputed –relationship of European fundamental rights to the fundamental rights in the Charter, see *Ehlers,* in Ehlers, ed., Europäische Grundfreiheiten und Grundrechte [in English: European Basic Freedoms and Fundamental Rights] (3rd ed. 2009), sec. 14 I 6, ref. 24 ff. However, in the Test-Achats case of the European Court of Justice of 1 Mar. 2011 (case no. C-236/09 – VersR (2011), 377), the primacy of the Charter appears to be presumed (see *Kahler,* NJW (2011), 894 [897]). The European Court of Justice does not expressly take a position on this problem.

[85] See *Rittner/Dreher* id., n. 45 above, secs. 4 ref. 43, 8 ref. 1, 9 ref. 1, and 11 ref. 59 with further references.

[86] See on insurance supervision and its objectives, BVerwG [in English: Federal Administrative Court] VersR (1981), 221 (227) – DAS [German Legal Insurance (Automobile) Company] and on this point *Dreher*, Die Versicherung als Rechtsprodukt [in English: Insurance as a Legal Product] (1991), p. 215 ff.

[87] In case of a high level of de facto binding and simultaneous regulatory density, an alternative analysis may be necessary here.

[88] See above, at 5.4.1.

[89] See on this point *Ruffert,* in: Ehlers, ed., Europäische Grundfreiheiten und Grundrechte [in English: European Basic Freedoms and Fundamental Rights] (3rd ed. 2009), sec. 16.3 III 2, ref. 36.

[90] The freedom to conduct a business adds independent legal content to the freedom to choose an occupation in art. 15 of the Charter. Concerning the differences of opinion on this, in detail, *Schmidt*, Die unternehmerische Freiheit im Unionsrecht [in English: The Freedom to Conduct Business in the European Union] (2010), p. 184 ff.

the purpose of meeting the supervisory objectives.[91] But doubt as to proportionality could arise from the criterion of necessity. It must be considered, however, that there is no apparent recourse that would be milder than an ORSA and yet equally effective. In particular, an appraisal of risk and solvency situation by the supervisory authorities instead of an ORSA by the insurance undertaking would not be a viable alternative as it would lack comparable effectiveness and curtail entrepreneurial latitude. Lastly, with respect to maintaining the principles of materiality and proportionality, its adequacy must also be affirmed. With respect to the "how" of implementing the ORSA, insurance undertakings—at least according to the text of the Directive—are largely given free rein.[92]

In addition, in the evaluation under European law, the decision practice of the European Court of Justice on the proportionality of intervention in the freedom to conduct a business must also be noted. The European Court of Justice tends to allow the European legislators a wide scope for evaluation as to limitations of occupational and entrepreneurial freedom exempted from judicial review.[93] In view of the essential goals of Solvency II and under the assumption that Level 2 and Level 3 rules cannot be the basis for an alternative assessment, the requirements of the principle of proportionality as it relates to justification of an obligatory responsibility of the undertaking for ORSA are therefore met.

These considerations, however, do not speak to the individual questions concerning the ORSA and, most importantly, its supervisory review. This is so because a legally permissible justification for Own Risk and Solvency Assessment does not necessarily mean that far-reaching official supervision and control of this process is legally permissible. If it did, the title "own" would be effectively removed on the subordinate level of enterprise supervision, and thus the associated entrepreneurial freedom with respect to "how" and "how much" would be eliminated.

5.7.1.3 ORSA as an Integral Part of Business Strategy

The Task of the Managing Board and Monitoring of the ORSA by the Supervisory Authority

Intervention in the entrepreneurial freedom is delicate insofar as ORSA results are intended to be an integral component of business strategy and important individual

[91] According to Recital 16 and arts. 27, 28 of the Solvency II Framework Directive, the main objective is the protection of the insured and beneficiaries of indemnification payments. Subordinate to this and of equivalent weight are the objectives of financial stability and free, stable markets (see *Dreher/Häußler*, ZGR (2011), 471 [485] as well as *Wandt/Sehrbrock*, ZVersWiss (2011), 193 [195 ff.]).

[92] See above, at 5.1 and n. 8.

[93] See, briefly, *Ruffert* id., n. 89 above, sec. 16.3 III 2, ref. 38 with further references, mainly in the area of Common Agricultural Policy.

decisions. Limitations on the insurance undertaking's freedom to act may result thereof. In order to evaluate the legal justification for such intervention, the reach of the intervention must first be examined, meaning the extent to which ORSA results are required to be used in the business strategy and important individual decisions, and how much latitude then remains for operating the business.

In Guideline 14 of the Consultation Paper and the explanatory text associated with it, EIOPA explained its conception of art. 45, para. 4 of the Solvency II Framework Directive to the effect that ORSA results and findings must be included at least for the Governance System, including long-term capital management, capital investment, business planning, and even product design and development. This is a broad subject area. However, the intensity of inclusion is more limited, as suggested on first view by the formulation "integral part". Insurance undertakings are required only to "take (the ORSA) into account" in each of these areas.[94] Under this design, the ORSA "feeds into" the management of the business.[95] In this understanding, the awareness and serious consideration—including with respect to any consequences derived—of the ORSA results and other findings from the ORSA process are sufficient.[96]

The development of a business strategy and of the internal processes leading to it is a key task of the managing board, which is exercised under its own responsibility in accordance with sec. 76 of the AktG [German Stock Corporation Act].[97] Thus, this task cannot be delegated[98] and is not subject to supervision. A broader view of the ORSA as an integral part of the business strategy would result not only in all those practical difficulties on whose account the "business judgement rule" was incorporated into German law first through case law[99] and later in statutory form through sec. 93, para. 1, sent. 2 of the AktG [German Stock Corporation Act].[100]

---

[94] See Guideline 14 of the Consultation Paper: "The undertaking should take . . . into account . . . ".

[95] See no. 4.70 of the Consultation Paper: "Hence the ORSA feeds into the management of the business. . .". Correctly in this respect, the statement of grounds for sec. 28 of the VAG-E [Government's Ministerial Draft of a Tenth Act Amending the Insurance Supervision Act]: "[ORSA] must feed into the strategic decisions of the undertaking and be adequately taken account of in their context".

[96] Also in this sense, *Meyer* id., n. 78 above. In matters of business strategy, the undertaking must "comply" with the risk-bearing capacity and overall risk capital "at all times".

[97] This is also true for mutual insurance companies (see sec. 175, sent. 2 of the VAG-E [Government's Ministerial Draft of a Tenth Act Amending the Insurance Supervision Act]), insurers organized as a Societas Europaea (see. art. 39, para. 1, sent. 1 of the SE Regulation) and according to the establishment acts for public insurance undertakings in German federal state law.

[98] In detail, *Dreher*, in: Publication in Honor of Klaus J. Hopt on his 70th Birthday on 24 Aug. 2010 (2010), p. 517, 518 ff.

[99] BGHZ [Decisions of the Federal Court of Justice in Civil Matters] (Ger.) (hereafter, BGHZ) 135, 244 = VersR (1997), 886 = JZ (1997), 1074 with comments by *Dreher*.

[100] See on justification for the business judgement rule, for example, *Spindler*, in: Münch. Komm. zum AKtG [in English: Munich Commentary on the AktG (German Stock Corporation Act)], Vol. II (3rd ed. 2008), sec. 93, ref. 35.

Most importantly, such broader view would also be incompatible with principle of freedom to conduct business protected through art. 12, para. 1 of the German Basic Law, and more recently, art. 16 of the EU Charter of Fundamental Rights.[101] Then, too, the principle of proportionality must receive its due consideration.[102] Accordingly, business strategy must be freely determined by the responsible management bodies. Whether business strategy inclines toward risk or leans away from risk in the long term remains essentially a separate matter from the ORSA as long as consideration of the ORSA takes place as outlined earlier. Of course, the results of the ORSA must result in change to the business strategy if there is no other way to ensure solvency. But that is only as a last resort. As a tool of risk management, ORSA has no unmediated impact on the business strategy in the sense of a direct control function. Rather, ORSA indirectly influences the strategy to the extent that its results are indicative of the risk status and overall solvency of the insurance undertaking, and thus indispensable to the responsible—in the sense of relevant for the exclusion of liability—development of business strategy by the proper bodies of the insurance undertaking.

Even if the principle of supervisory exemption applies to the development and amendment of business strategy, this area is not entirely supervision-free. According to the statement of grounds for sec. 28 of the VAG-E [Government's Ministerial Draft of a Tenth Act Amending the Insurance Supervision Act],[103] the ORSA process fulfills "two functions". It forms an "internal assessment process within the undertaking" on one hand. And on the other, it provides important insight about the undertaking to the supervisory authorities, who must be informed as to the results of the internal assessment of the undertaking's risks and solvency. The supervisory authorities review the internal assessment as part of the Supervisory Review Process ... First, this enables an evaluation of the risks to which the undertaking is exposed or could become exposed; second, it provides information about the ability of the undertaking to evaluate these risks; and third, it enables an evaluation of the extent to which the undertaking is in a position to withstand potential events or future changes that could adversely impact the overall financial capacity of the undertaking.

Finally, the ORSA allows the supervisory authority to conduct "a review as to whether the undertaking ought to develop an internal model or adjust an existing internal model, or whether the imposition of a capital add-on is appropriate".

These imputations in the law of ORSA functions to the supervisory authority ignore the primary internal nature of ORSA by assuming two equally ranked functions. The terminology employed—"own" assessment—is indicative of this primary nature. The danger associated with such imputations is that supervisory

[101] See 5.3 and 5.7.1.1, above.

[102] See 5.3, above in the context of the principle of proportionality.

[103] Statement of grounds for sec. 28 VAG-E [Government's Ministerial Draft of a Tenth Act Amending the Insurance Supervision Act], p. 286.

authorities actually do exercise supervision of an insurance undertaking's strategy through this approach, however indirectly. The statement of grounds for sec. 28 of the VAG-E [Government's Ministerial Draft of a Tenth Act Amending the Insurance Supervision Act] expressly provides that "supervisory authorities shall review the internal assessment as part of the Supervisory Review Process". At the same time, the ORSA is also an "integral" or "fixed" "part of the business strategy and shall be taken into account on an ongoing basis in the strategic decisions of the undertaking" under art. 45, para. 4 of the Solvency II Framework Directive and sec. 28, para. 1, sent. 2 of the VAG-E [Government's Ministerial Draft of a Tenth Act Amending the Insurance Supervision Act]. The business strategy of an insurance undertaking thus becomes, to state it differently, the indirect subject-matter of supervisory review. In light of this, and in order to maintain the sole responsibility of the management bodies and the supervisory exemption of the management tasks of the managing board, the supervisory review of the ORSA requires particular sensitivity and restraint.

The Interaction of the ORSA as Part of and Input Factor to the Business Strategy

Art. 45, para. 4 of the Solvency II Framework Directive—and now also sec. 28, para. 1, sent. 1 of the VAG-E [Government's Ministerial Draft of a Tenth Act Amending the Insurance Supervision Act]—provides that the ORSA be an "integral part of the business strategy" and that it must at the same time "be taken into account on an ongoing basis in the strategic decisions of the undertaking". For normative purposes, this interaction[104] is not formulated with sufficient clarity. For its part, Guideline 14 at Level 3 repeats only the second part of the interaction, namely the consideration of ORSA in strategic decisions. The explanatory text to the Guideline provides no further information.[105]

The starting point is the customary definition of strategy. According to this, business strategy pertains to the actions of the business pursued to achieve its objectives.[106] It is self-evident that the ORSA as the fundamental process for risk and solvency assessment must be taken into account for decisions concerning achievement of objectives, as the first function indicates. The Level 3 explanatory text[107] provides that this is so for "any strategic or other major decisions that may materially affect the risk and/or own funds' position of the undertaking". But at the same time, it emphasizes that "this does not require a full performance of the ORSA" every time such a decision must be made. Rather—and this is also provided

[104] See also 5.4.1, above.

[105] See nos. 4.69 to 4.72 of the Consultation Paper.

[106] See for insurance business management theory, for example, *Farny*, Versicherungsbetriebslehre [in English: Insurance Business Management Theory] (5th ed. 2011), p. 511 ff.

[107] See No. 4.71 of the Consultation Paper.

for without such Level 3 rules under the principle of proportionality—it is sufficient to examine how the output of the last ORSA process would change in light of these new strategic decisions.

The extent to which Solvency II sees the integration of ORSA into the business strategy itself as its second function can be understood in the wider view of the business strategy in general. In each undertaking, this is divided into a number of sub-strategies. Among these are the financial, marketing, product, and pricing strategies. These areas of business strategy are not dissociated from the risk and solvency posture. Even these—and thus the ORSA and its results—are elements of the overarching business strategy either as discreet sub-strategies[108] or as subject-matter of other sub-strategies,[109] as in the case of own funds in the financial strategy. In this respect, the statement that the ORSA is "an integral part of the business strategy" is comprehensible. Further, the interaction with strategic decisions, a process that influences the ORSA, can be understood.

5.7.2 *The Relationship of the ORSA to Capital Add-Ons*

Cause for confusion emerged early in the relationship of the ORSA and its results to the capital add-ons that can be ordered by supervisory authorities under art. 37 of the Solvency II Framework Directive,[110] and whose implementation in the Ministerial Draft is provided for in sec. 295 of the VAG-E [Government's Ministerial Draft of a Tenth Act Amending the Insurance Supervision Act]. Art. 45, para. 7 and Recital 36 of the Solvency II Framework Directive indicates that ORSA should not be used to calculate additional capital requirements in addition to the MCR and SCR.[111] And CEIOPS emphasized precisely this view as early as 2008.[112] In the feedback statement that followed, CEIOPS noted that "the connection between the ORSA and a possible decision to set a capital add-on is not mechanistic".[113] From a legal perspective, these determinations are correct. However, justifiable concerns exists that, with the in-house ORSA processes, insurance undertakings will provide the BaFin [Federal Financial Supervisory Authority] with occasion and reason for setting capital add-ons. Viewed in this way, the ORSA would serve more as a

[108] Sec. 27, para. 2 of the VAG-E [Government's Ministerial Draft of a Tenth Act Amending the Insurance Supervision Act] – currently similar to sec. 64 a, para. 1, sent. 4, no. 1 of the VAG [German Insurance Supervision Act] – correctly includes "a risk strategy aligned with the management of the business" in this.

[109] See also Recital 36 of the Solvency II Framework Directive.

[110] See CEIOPS, Internal Governance, Supervisory Review and Reporting Expert Group Issues Paper on ORSA – Feedback Statement 2008 CEIOPS-IGSRR-26/08, p. 1.

[111] On the terms "Minimum Capital Requirement" (MCR) and "Solvency Capital Requirement" (SCR) see Recital 60 of the Solvency II Framework Directive.

[112] No. 3 b, IP ORSA.

[113] See CEIOPS, n. 110, p. 1 f.

supervisory convenience than a confirmation of risk and capital for the insurance undertaking.

Capital add-ons conform to art. 37 of the Solvency II Framework Directive. The ORSA report and its results assist the authorities in evaluating the solvency position of the supervised undertaking. However, in particular, the supervisory authorities must always make their own determination as to whether the conditions set forth art. 37, para. 1, sent. 2 a and b of the Solvency II Framework Directive are fulfilled. Based on the principle of proportionality, the imposition or adjustment of an internal model is preferred. This is also statutorily provided for by art. 37 of the Solvency II Framework Directive and in sec. 295, para. 1 of the VAG-E [Government's Ministerial Draft of a Tenth Act Amending the Insurance Supervision Act]. This legal situation thus conforms to the conception of the Directive issuer and of CEIOPS that no direct connection shall exist between the ORSA and capital add-ons. However, there is indirect causal linkage; and this is ultimately desired in the system of Solvency II.

Still, in supervisory practice, there is the danger that some sort of automatic capital add-on might be produced. This lies in the partial alignment of the review under the ORSA with the review by the supervisory authorities in reference to significant deviation of the risk profile from the basic assumptions of the standard formula or approved partial model in accordance with art. 37, para. 1, sent. 2 a and b of the Solvency II Framework Directive on one hand and art. 45, para. 1, subpara. 2 c of the Solvency II Framework Directive on the other.[114] If, in the context of the reporting duty under art. 35 of the Solvency II Framework Directive, the insurance undertaking affirms a significant deviation and reports it to the authority, the authority is, in fact, likely to order a capital add-on more or less "mechanically" if the imposition of an internal model would be inadequate or ineffective. Against this background, it becomes important in supervisory practice that any "conclusion" by the supervisory authority as required by the Framework Directive for capital add-ons can be shown not to be based solely on the results of the ORSA report by the insurance undertakings in question, but rather on a separate supervisory review and corresponding determinations. At the same time, this supervisory review requirement also clearly modifies the widespread conception that the ORSA, according to its name, is an internal matter of the insurance undertaking in the broadest possible sense.[115]

5.7.3 The Own Assessment of Interest Rate Risk

The basis of the capital requirements on risk actually assumed leads to particular problems with respect to interest guarantees. The attractiveness of a number of

[114] See above, at 5.4.3 and below, at 5.7.4.

[115] See above, section "The Task of the Managing Board and Monitoring of the ORSA by the Supervisory Authority" on the often-emphasized "primary internal nature of ORSA".

insurance products is highly dependent on such guarantees. ORSA requirements, however, make these difficult in practice. The main reason is the sensitivity of the interest structure model proposed by EIOPA. The model underlies the assessment of interest risk and has come under enormous criticism from the insurance industry.[116] Apart from the fundamental economic concerns as to the soundness of the assumptions on which the model is based, and the resulting legal concerns with respect to supervisory measures on speculative grounds, the efficiency of the ORSA and the associated insurance supervision in this context is questionable from the legal perspective.

The starting point in order to describe the problem is the volatility of the interest structure and thus the interest risk that makes an ORSA in compliance with supervisory requirements in this regard more difficult. The overall solvency needs could be sufficiently met within the shortest period of time on one day, but might not be covered on another day because of the sensitivity of the interest yield curve. An ORSA would have to be tuned to these constant fluctuations, which not only raises the question of functionality of this method of moderating volatility, but would also entail higher administrative expenses and, to a certain extent, be inconsistent with the principle of proportionality (see the commentary by CEIOPS that ORSA should not be "too burdensome").[117] Apart from the difficulties in the ORSA itself, a more stable interest yield curve would also be desirable because otherwise the same supervisory measure, particularly within the area of Pillar 1, might or might not be legal within the very short time intervals, depending on when it was mandated—ultimately in obedience to the law of chance rather than to the law of a rigorous supervisory regime. This could have adverse effects on the stability of financial markets and insurance interests and be counterproductive in the truest sense of the word.

5.7.4 Significant Deviation from the Assumptions Underlying the Calculation of the Standard Formula and the Internal Model

5.7.4.1 The Ambiguous Wording of the German Version of the Framework Directive

Whereas, for example, the English version of the Solvency II Framework Directive in arts. 37, 45 and 119 uses the term "significance" uniformly, the German version speaks of a "material" deviation in art. 119, a "considerable" deviation in art.

[116] See also the Journal of the BaFin [Federal Financial Supervisory Authority] 03/2011, p. 9; on other complications with interest guarantees, see *Linde/Kutz*, VW (2011), 409 (410).

[117] No. 3 c, IP ORSA.

is the legal basis for such requests for information by the supervisory authority? According to art. 35, para. 1, sent. 1 of the Solvency II Framework Directive, information that is "necessary for the purposes of supervision" must be provided. The listing that follows this is not exhaustive. Nevertheless, the very wording itself confirms that information can be required only when it is necessary for the exercise of supervisory duties. According to art. 36, para. 2 a of the Solvency II Framework Directive, the Supervisory Review Process is limited to reviewing and evaluating compliance with the ORSA requirements. The Level 3 Guidelines, however, may not exceed the regulatory terms in the Level 1 and 2 provisions.[162] Unless a corresponding Level 2 rule is issued in the future, there is no legal basis for the type of far-reaching reporting requirement for insurance undertakings to supervisory authorities, as envisioned by CEIOPS. Lastly, the principle of proportionality (see on this point sec. 290 VAG-E [Government's Ministerial Draft of a Tenth Act Amending the Insurance Supervision Act]) also sets limits on any information request by supervisory authorities.[163] This applies in particular to the scope and the frequency of such requests.

5.8.4 Requirements for Reporting to the Public

The ORSA reporting to the public takes place under art. 51, para. 1, subpara. 2 b of the Solvency II Framework Directive through the Solvency and Financial Condition Report (SFCR).[164] Implementation is provided in sec. 50 VAG-E [Government's Ministerial Draft of a Tenth Act Amending the Insurance Supervision Act]. The probable implementing regulation establishes rules for the SFCR with respect to the ORSA in art. 285 PDS4, para. 4. Solvency II was designed to create an extensive duty of public disclosure. In particular, art. 51, para. 1, subpara. 2 of the Solvency II Framework Directive mandates a remarkably thorough concordance of the information required for the supervisory authority and the information that is to be made public. The structure is established, subject to amendments, by art. 282 PDS1, para. 1 in conjunction with Annex PD1 of the draft implementing regulation.

In principle, the supervisory authority can make exceptions in public disclosure requirements upon request when disclosure would provide competitors with a significant undue advantage or when the undertaking is bound by confidentiality with respect to policyholders or other third parties.[165] But, under the general principles of European law, exceptions must be narrowly construed and may rarely

[162] See above, at 5.4.1.

[163] See on this point, 5.3 and 5.4.3, above.

[164] See art. 51, para. 1, subpara. 2 b of the Solvency II Framework Directive and art. 282 PDS1 ff. of the implementing regulation.

[165] Art. 53, para. 1 of the Solvency II Framework Directive, see also sec. 51 of the VAG-E [Government's Ministerial Draft of a Tenth Act Amending the Insurance Supervision Act].

37, and a "significant" deviation in art. 45. This is inappropriate because, according to the German version, there is presumably a factual difference in the interpretation of these various rules. However, the rules in question are systematically interwoven. They sometimes make explicit reference to one another and cannot be interpreted in isolation. This calls for a unified interpretation in the German version of the Directive for the terms "significant", "material", and "considerable", such as is suggested in the wording of the English and French versions[118] of the Directive. Unfortunately, the statement of grounds to the ministerial draft contains no explanation as to the term "materiality".[119] As undefined legal terms, "significance" and "materiality" are entirely subject to judicial review. Comparison to other sectors, such as the banking sector, offers no additional assistance in this matter.[120]

The assessment of significance in the context of art. 45 of the Solvency II Framework Directive[121] is focused on the extent to which the actual risk profile deviates from the assumptions underlying the calculations. Thus, according to the English version of art. 45, para. 1, subpara. 2 c of the Solvency II Framework Directive "the significance with which the risk profile ... deviates" is supposed to be assessed.[122] The insurance undertaking is supposed to be aware of the extent to which it deviates and not merely whether it exceeds the lower limit of significance. This also proceeds from the teleological concept of the ORSA, which is based on raising awareness of all material risks. In some circumstances, these risks also include shortcomings in the standard formula or relevant internal model. Only such assessment enables adequate handling of the risks that arise from deviations from the standard formula or an internal model. It is primarily a matter of assessing what is known as model and parameter risk, which refers to those risks arising from models that incorrectly depict reality or simplify it to an extent that is not representational.[123]

Ultimately, the German language version of art. 45, para. 1, subpara. 2 c of the Solvency II Framework Directive requires in consideration of the corresponding rules in art. 37 and 119 a harmonized interpretation in conformity with European law. According to the versions of the Directive that are unified in this respect in

[118] See arts. 37, 119 of the French version of the Solvency II Framework Directive: "significativement"; also, on the term "mesure" in art. 45 of the French version.

[119] It is not more fully addressed in the statement of grounds for secs. 28 and 101 of VAG-E [Government's Ministerial Draft of a Tenth Act Amending the Insurance Supervision Act].

[120] In fact, under sec. 25 a KWG [German Credit Services Act], an internal assessment of capital adequacy is to be conducted whose design intersects with the ORSA (Internal Capital Adequacy Assessment Process [ICAAP]). But the underlying Directive, 2006/48/EG (known as the banking directive), has no counterpart to art. 45, para. 1, subpara. 2 c of the Solvency II Framework Directive.

[121] But not, for example, in the context of arts. 119 and 37 of the Solvency II Framework Directive.

[122] Also compare the french wording ("la mesure dans laquelle le profil de risque ... s´écarte ... ").

[123] See 5.4.2 and n. 56, above.

other languages, the relevant term in the Directive for all of these rules—for the reasons stated, with the exception of art. 45, para. 1, subpara. 2 c in the French version—is "significance". To the extent arts. 37 and 119 of the Solvency II Framework Directive refer to a "considerable" or "material" deviation, the term "significant" deviation will take the place of these terms.

5.7.4.2 The Significance of a Deviation

Point of Reference and Rule for Significance

There are critical implications for the insurance undertakings as to whether a deviation is determined to be significant. The insurance undertaking must then take precautions to eliminate the risks that arise from this, which can be done through change to the risk profile or (where allowed) through the use of parameters specific to the undertaking, but also through the development of an internal model structured in alignment with the risk profile.[124] Otherwise, the supervisory authority can mandate an internal model in accordance with art. 119 of the Solvency II Framework Directive or, as a last resort, a capital add-on in accordance with art. 37, para. 1, sent. 2 a, b of the Solvency II Framework Directive or sec. 295 of the VAG-E [Government's Ministerial Draft of a Tenth Act Amending the Insurance Supervision Act].[125]

The point of reference for evaluating the significance of a deviation comes straight from the Solvency II Framework Directive itself: the assumptions underlying the calculations for the standard formula or internal model used. Still, the evaluation also requires a rule that is not evident in the Solvency II regulatory framework. Teleological and systemic considerations, in particular, lead to the determination of this rule. First, the telos of the Solvency II regulatory framework is of high importance. Protected property in the European insurance supervisory regime means the protection of policyholders and beneficiaries of indemnification payments as well as, secondarily, the stability of the financial markets and fair insurance markets.[126] The latter aspect is of little importance in connection with the ORSA process. The decisive point is that the solvency situation of an insurance undertaking must allow for its continuing existence as a business.[127] This is endangered when the capital requirements for continuing operations of the insurance undertaking are not met and solvency is threatened. It is also consistent if art.

[124] See No. 4.53 of the Consultation Paper.

[125] On this also, *Sehrbrock,* ZVersWiss (2011), 207 (special edition: Solvency II in der Rechtsanwendung) [in English: Solvency II in the Application of Law].

[126] See above, n. 91.

[127] See also No. 4.34 of the Consultation Paper.

119 of the Solvency II Framework Directive, in cases of significant deviation of the risk profile from the assumptions underlying Solvency II, provides that the supervisory authority can mandate an internal model, sometimes partially. The rule for the evaluation of significance is derived from these considerations.

The legal requirement for significance of a deviation from the calculations underlying the standard formula and internal model also plays an important role in the imposition of a capital add-on under art. 37, para. 1, sent. 2 a and b of the Solvency II Framework Directive.[128] In connection with this, the draft of the implementing regulation at Level 2 establishes a method for determining significance, with quantitative aspects having precedence, coupled with qualitative adjustments.[129] Under this method, a deviation is significant if the difference between the actual regulatory solvency requirement and a hypothetical solvency requirement (Modified Solvency Capital Requirement) exceeds 15 %.[130] Under art. 271 CA6 of the draft of the implementing regulation, the Modified Solvency Capital Requirement is the solvency requirement that would ensue if the standard formula or internal model had been modified in such a way that it would reflect the actual risk profile and enable the insurance undertaking to satisfy the requirements of art. 101, para. 3 of the Solvency II Framework Directive.[131] A difference of ≥ 10 % and ≤ 15 % leads to a rebuttable presumption of significance.[132] A potential rebuttal may come from an assessment of qualitative factors. On the other hand, the supervisory authority can assume a significant deviation based on qualitative criteria even in cases where a deviation is less than 10 %.[133] The evaluation of the significance in the context of the ORSA can be roughly based on these criteria. Thus, in the design of Solvency II, a deviation from underlying assumptions is deemed significant when the actual risk profile deviates from the underlying assumptions for the calculation of the regulatory capital requirement in such a way that the actual regulatory capital requirement is below the hypothetically necessary capital requirement, for the long term and by a relevant amount. The latter is a product of an appropriate hypothetical calculation model.

---

[128] On significance in this context, in detail *CEIOPS*, CEIOPS' Advice for Level 2-Implementing Measures on Solvency II: Capital Add-On, 2009 (hereafter: Level 2 Add-on Advice), no. 3.3.2.

[129] Art. 268 CA3 of the draft implementing regulation. The CEIOPS proposal in no. 3.50 of the Level 2 Add-on Advice already tends this way. In contrast, with respect to the ORSA for systemic reasons – the ORSA is part of Pillar 2 – a qualitative assessment must take precedence (see on this point below section "Systemic Restrictions").

[130] See art. 268 CA3, para. 3 in conjunction with art. 271 CA6 of the draft implementing regulation.

[131] According to this, all possible quantifiable risks must be covered by the standard formula or the internal model used.

[132] Art. 268 CA3, para. 1 of the draft implementing regulation.

[133] See art. 268 CA3, para. 2 of the draft implementing regulation. Art. 266 CA1 of the implementing regulation contains a list of these qualitative characteristics. See also CEIOPS in No. 3.58 of the Level 2 Add-on Advice.

Systemic Restrictions

This rule presents insurance undertakings with the practical problem of how to judge whether another calculation model would fit their risk profile better, and if so, which one. Strictly speaking, an insurance undertaking would first have to generate the Modified Solvency Capital Requirement for every ORSA, which in some cases would go far beyond the principle of proportionality. Therefore, in the context of the ORSA, a careful assessment must suffice for determining the rule.

The requirements for precision in the estimate are also restricted by their purpose. The primary purpose of the ORSA is to raise awareness of the risk profile. This distinguishes the assessment of significance in the ORSA context from the assessment of significance in the context of a capital add-on, which the system classifies in Pillar 1 of Solvency II. If the objective of conscious, critical engagement with the internal risk profile is achieved, the purpose of the review under art. 45, para. 1, subpara. 2 c of the Solvency II Framework Directive is largely satisfied. A careful estimate must therefore suffice in the assessment of the hypothetically necessary capital requirements as indicated in a Modified Solvency Capital Requirement, From a legally systematic perspective, this also brings up considerations that set boundaries for the teleological viewpoint. Solvency II essentially aims to provide insurance undertakings with the choice of using the standard model or an internal model. Thus, in the review of significant deviation from risk assumptions, an additional calculation model cannot be necessary for examining the justification of such assumptions, since this would mean going "through the back door".

The requirements for such estimations can be found in No. 4.49 ff. of the Consultation Paper. According to EIOPA's proposal, the assessment of deviation significance takes place in two levels. First, the deviation of the risk profile is assessed on a qualitative basis.[134] A quantification is necessary[135] only if a material[136] deviation is found. As discussed, the quantification must legally allow for a summary approach. Such material deviations can arise, for example, from non-compliance or from over- and under-estimates of risk in the standard formula.[137] For the assessment of significant deviation of the actual risk profile, EIOPA has announced that it will publish information on the assumptions underlying Solvency II.[138] The content that should be included in the assessment process in the opinion of EIOPA is presented in No. 4.52 of the Consultation Paper for users of the standard formula and in No. 4.64 of the Consultation Paper for users of an internal model.

---

[134] Guideline 13 of the Consultation Paper.

[135] Guideline 13 of the Consultation Paper.

[136] See Guideline 13 of the Consultation Paper ("materially"). For the reasons stated, insurance undertakings also have discretion in evaluation at this first step of the "material" deviation.

[137] See No. 4.52 of the Consultation Paper.

[138] No. 4.50 of the Consultation Paper.

5.8 Documentation and Publication of the ORSA

5.8.1 Addressees and General Principles of the ORSA Information

The documentation of the ORSA process and results is generated for three addressees. Under art. 45, para. 6 of the Solvency II Framework Directive, the ORSA results must be reported as part of the information transmitted to the supervisory authority (Regular Supervisory Reporting [RSR]) in accordance with art. 35 of the Solvency II Framework Directive.[139] The ORSA information must also be published in the Solvency and Financial Condition Report (SFCR) for the public, as provided for in art. 51 of the Solvency II Framework Directive and sec. 50 of the VAG-E [Government's Ministerial Draft of a Tenth Act Amending the Insurance Supervision Act].[140] Internally, the results of the ORSA and subsequent conclusions from it, at a minimum, must also be reported to the undertaking's management and supervisory body as well as to any staff for whom this information could be relevant.[141] It is expected that EIOPA will deem it allowable to compose the report to the supervisory authority based on the internal report.[142]

The ORSA strategy must be set forth in writing in the internal policies of the insurance undertaking.[143] The principle of materiality also applies to the transmission of information.[144] Documentation serves the purpose of enabling internal or external agents[145] to critically review the ORSA process.[146] The scope of the information is based on each group of addressees. At a minimum, the

[139] In detail on the RSR, *Dreher*, ZVersWiss (2009), 187 ff. (Chap. 12, below).

[140] See also the explanations of RSR and SFCR in CEIOPS' Advice for Level 2 Implementing Measures on Solvency II: Supervisory Reporting and Public Disclosure Requirements, (2009) (hereafter: CEIOPS Reporting Advice), no. 3.30 ff. Also instructive, the diagram at no 3.25 of CEIOPS Reporting Advice; in detail on the SFCR, see *Dreher/Schaaf*, "Die Veröffentlichungspflichten von Versicherungsunternehmen gegenüber der Allgemeinheit nach Solvency II" [in English: Insurance Undertakings' Duty of Disclosure to the Public under Solvency II] in: Dreher/Wandt, eds., Solvency II in der Rechtsanwendung, [in English: Solvency II in Legal Application], (2009), 129 ff. (Chap. 13, below).

[141] Guideline 6 of the Consultation Paper.

[142] No. 4.16. of the Consultation Paper.

[143] Art. 45, para. 2 of the Solvency II Framework Directive, Guideline 4 of the Consultation Paper.

[144] Art. 294bis SRS1bis, 282bis PDS1bis of the draft implementing regulation, according to which materiality is based on the addressee of the report. On the definition of materiality in consideration of the information requirements, see also No. 3.2.5 CEIOPS of the Reporting Advice with respect to the International Accounting Standards (IAS), Framework for the Preparation and Presentation of Financial Statements, available for download at http://www.iasb.org/NR/rdonlyres/578562B5-2303-4F51-8D02-382A7CBDBA7E/0/AP4Materialityobnotes.pdf.

[145] Review by the persons conducting the ORSA is not permitted.

[146] No. 3.15 and Guideline 5 of the Consultation Paper.

documentation of the ORSA must include the ORSA policies,[147] the record of each ORSA,[148] the internal documentation of the ORSA information, and the information to be provided to the supervisory authority and the public.[149]

5.8.2 *The Internal Report*

According to EIOPA, the results as well as the conclusions related to the assessment of overall solvency, compliance with supervisory capital requirements, and requirements for technical provisions must be communicated. This information must be provided to the managing board, the supervisory board, and staff for whom the information is relevant.[150] The level of detail for the internal report must be sufficient to enable consideration of the ORSA in the process of making and implementing strategic decisions.[151]

5.8.3 *Requirements for Reporting to the Supervisory Authorities*

The supervisory authority must be able to evaluate the ability of an insurance undertaking to assess its own solvency and risk profile.[152] Reporting on the implementation of the ORSA always takes place in the context of a regular report to the supervisory authority (art. 35, para. 1, sent. 2 a, para. 2 a and i of the Solvency II Framework Directive (ORSA Supervisory Report)). The ORSA result itself is named in art. 45, para. 6 of the Solvency II Framework Directive (art. 294, para. 1 c and 3 of the draft implementing regulation) as part of the regular report.[153] Other requirements as to content are governed in art. 297, para. 4 of the draft implementing regulation, according to which insurance undertakings must explain how they perform and document the ORSA process and ensure its integration into the management process.

The comparison of art. 35, para. 1, sent. 2 a to art. 45, para. 6 of Solvency II Framework Directive deserves closer analysis. The first provision requires the insurance undertaking to transmit all information necessary to "assess the system

[147] On their content see Guideline 4 of the Consultation Paper.

[148] Additional detail on their content in Guideline 5 of the Consultation Paper.

[149] Guideline 3 of the Consultation Paper.

[150] Guideline 6 of the Consultation Paper.

[151] No. 4.15 of the Consultation Paper; see on this point 5.7.1.3, above.

[152] No. 51 IP 2008, see also the statement of reasons for sec. 28 VAG-E [Government's Ministerial Draft of a Tenth Act Amending the Insurance Supervision Act], p. 286.

[153] Preparation of the regular report largely follows the SFCR; see art. 294 SRS1 of the draft implementing regulation.

of governance, . . . the risks faced and the risk management systems as well as [the] capital needs". The implementation of ORSA as part of the risk management and governance systems requires explanation. But in addition, each individual ORSA result is information that can be subsumed with a broad interpretation under art. 35, para. 1, sent. 2 a of the Solvency II Framework Directive. On first view, it appears that art. 45, para. 6 of the Solvency II Framework Directive does not have an independent content.

Legally, art. 45, para. 6 of the Solvency II Framework Directive could acquire separate significance if it were viewed as lex specialis with respect to art. 35, para. 1, sent. 2 a of the Solvency II Framework Directive for the ORSA reporting requirements. The consequence of this interpretation would be that submission of the results of the ORSA alone would be sufficient to satisfy the ORSA information requirement since the information related to the process of implementing the ORSA is not expressly prescribed in art. 45, para. 6 of the Solvency II Framework Directive. Such interpretation, however, is immediately countered by the fact that only partial overlap is present in the context of art. 45, para. 6 of the Solvency II Framework Directive and art. 35, para. 1 sent. 2 a of the Solvency II Framework Directive. In such cases, the principle of lex specialis derogat legi generali is not valid.[154]

The apparent dissonance in the rules can be resolved through teleological interpretation. The information required for a proper supervisory assessment with respect to the ORSA includes both its process as well as its results. The less severe supervisory intervention—with respect to the surrender of the ORSA information that is proprietary to the undertaking—is the obligation to disclose the ORSA process.

More severe is the disclosure of the results. Therefore, in order to avoid overlap with art. 45, para. 6 of the Solvency II Framework Directive, the interpretation of art. 35, para. 1, sent. 2 a of the Solvency II Framework Directive must be restricted to prescribing reporting obligations with respect to the ORSA process only. Viewed from a system perspective, art. 45, para. 6 of the Solvency II Framework Directive and its specifics in art. 294 SRS1, para. 1 c of the draft of the implementing regulation are an expansion of the requirements in art. 35, para. 1, sent. 2 a of the Solvency II Framework Directive on the reporting requirement for the ORSA results. The content required for the ORSA-related reporting obligation to the supervisory authority in regular reporting in accordance with arts. 35, para. 1, sent. 2 a, and 45, para. 6 of the Solvency II Framework Directive is more extensive than the requirement for the SFCR.[155] Art. 294 SRS1, para. 1 a, c of the draft of the implementing regulation requires detailed explanations of how the insurance undertaking fulfilled its ORSA requirements and requires reporting on the ORSA results. The latter may be omitted in the SFCR.[156] Art. 294 SRS1, para.

---

[154] See *Zippelius*, Juristische Methodenlehre [in English: Judicial Methodology] (8th ed. 2003), sec. 7 c, d.

[155] For these, see 5.8.4, below.

[156] Art. 285 PDS4, para. 4 of the draft implementing regulation does not specify the results as content of the SFCR.

3 of the draft implementing regulation catalogs the most important key points for the content of the report on the ORSA,[157] supplemented by art. 297 SRS4, para. 4 a of the draft regulation.

The Directive includes the reporting obligation both for the ORSA occurring as part of the regular cycle as well as the ORSA mandated ad hoc.[158] An ad hoc ORSA is one required "following any significant change in t[he] risk profile" of an insurance undertaking in accordance with art. 45, para. 5 of the Solvency II Framework Directive. For these cases, the earlier proposal for Level 3 implementing measures presumed a "predefined business event" within the meaning of art. 35, para. 2 a ii of the Solvency II Framework Directive that would trigger a reporting obligation.[159]

In contrast, in the draft of the new VAG [German Insurance Supervision Act], the reporting obligation for the regular ORSA is not regulated. Sec. 43, para. 1 of the VAG-E [Government's Ministerial Draft of a Tenth Act Amending the Insurance Supervision Act], which implements art. 35 of the Solvency II Framework Directive, refers only to the insurance undertaking's duty to inform the supervisory authorities "in accordance with this law". And sec. 44, no. 8 of the VAG-E [Government's Ministerial Draft of a Tenth Act Amending the Insurance Supervision Act] includes only "all risk and solvency assessments conducted due to a significant change in the risk profile". However, in contrast to this wording, the statement of reasons for the rule sets forth that "information about the result both for ordinary as well as extraordinary risk and solvency assessment must be reported without delay".

The supervisory authority can require information regarding the regularity of the ORSA in individual cases according to art. 35 para. 1 sent. 2 a, para. 2 a iii of the Solvency II Framework Directive. Sec. 299, para. 1, no. 1 of the VAG-E [Government's Ministerial Draft of a Tenth Act Amending the Insurance Supervision Act] provides a right to information for the BaFin [Federal Financial Supervisory Authority] "on all business affairs". Normally, the supervisory authority will receive all significant information on implementation and results as part of the regular report. CEIOPS has expressed the view that the supervisory authority has the right to receive the full internal ORSA report upon request and may also request any additional information about the ORSA results and process.[160] This extremely broad understanding of the scope of information must be rejected. To begin with, the principle of materiality means there is a limit on the scope of the reporting obligation incumbent on insurance undertakings.[161] If the ORSA takes into account, for example, even somewhat immaterial non-obligatory risks, the supervisory authority cannot demand information about them. The question then is: What

[157] For the objective of the report on the ORSA, see also No. 3.371 of the CEIOPS Reporting Advice.

[158] Art. 45, para. 6 of the Solvency II Framework Directive.

[159] See No. 3.25 of the Level 3 Proposal.

[160] No. 3.27 of the Level 3 Proposal.

[161] So also CEIOPS elsewhere in nos. 3.48, 3.315 of the CEIOPS Reporting Advice.

be applicable concerning the disclosure of information in connection with the ORSA.[166] For practitioners generally, relevant relief is provided in art. 53, para. 3 of the Solvency II Framework Directive or sec. 50, para. 7 of the VAG-E [Government's Ministerial Draft of a Tenth Act Amending the Insurance Supervision Act]. These provisions allow for reference to other, contextually identical, information for the public that has been disclosed under other publication requirements to the extent it is "equivalent in nature and scope".[167] Nevertheless, the reporting requirements with respect to the ORSA yield no notable relief since it appears no contextually identical information exists. The duty of public disclosure with respect to the ORSA primarily concerns its organizational integration into the risk management system. This is an area that is not touched upon in other publications, and specifically not in the management report under sec. 289 of the HGB [German Commercial Code], which comes closest in terms of its context.

Art. 293 PDS13 of the draft implementing regulation, which is intended to concretize art. 54, para. 1 of the Solvency II Framework Directive, establishes a supplemental reporting requirement for insurance undertakings in cases where a major development places the content of published data into question. The list of examples in art. 54 of the Solvency II Framework Directive also includes any significant shortfall of the Minimum Capital Requirement combined with the simultaneous incapacity on the part of the insurance undertaking to submit a short-term finance scheme. A "significant non-compliance with the Solvency Capital Requirement" is also a major development if a reasonable recovery plan is not submitted to the supervisory authority within 2 months. The Ministerial Draft provides for implementation of art. 54 of the Solvency II Framework Directive in sec. 52 VAG-E [Government's Ministerial Draft of a Tenth Act Amending the Insurance Supervision Act].

5.9 Supervisory Powers with Respect to the ORSA

Because of its dual nature[168] the ORSA presents two areas of interest with respect to supervisory powers. First, it is a tool for insurance supervision, and therefore supervisory measures can be tied to its results. Second, however, the ORSA process itself is the object of supervision if its proper implementation is in question.

If an undertaking conducts an ORSA in a defective manner or even not at all, the supervisory authority may issue mandates in order to ensure the proper conduct of the insurance undertaking (art. 36, para. 2 a, and para. 5 of the Solvency II Framework

---

[166] For a narrow construction, see also no. 3.71 of the CEIOPS Reporting Advice.

[167] Information obligations pursuant to commercial and capital market law are meant here. In detail on this point, particularly with respect to the congruency of the risk report with information pursuant to commercial and capital market law, *Dreher/Schaaf*, n. 140, p. 160 ff.

[168] See above, at 5.2.

Directive as well as the implementation proposals in sec. 292, para. 1 of the VAG-E [Government's Ministerial Draft of a Tenth Act Amending the Insurance Supervision Act] in conjunction with sec. 289, para. 4 of the VAG-E [Government's Ministerial Draft of a Tenth Act Amending the Insurance Supervision Act]).

Because ORSA is a source of information for the supervisory authority, it can use the ORSA result as the basis of a decision for official interventions, but this cannot be tied directly (e.g., monocausally) to the ORSA result.[169] The latter is only an aid to factual investigation and not a release from the principle of the ex officio investigation. Prior to ordering a partial model in accordance with art. 119 of the Solvency II Framework Directive—provided for in sec. 87, para. 2 of the VAG-E [Government's Ministerial Draft of a Tenth Act Amending the Insurance Supervision Act]—or a capital add-on in accordance with art. 37, para. 1, sent. 2 a, b of the Solvency II Framework Directive or sec. 295, para. 1, nos. 1 and 2 of the VAG-E [Government's Ministerial Draft of a Tenth Act Amending the Insurance Supervision Act], the supervisory authority must come to the conclusion that the risk profile or solvency position of the addressee demands such action. The ORSA is only one of several possible sources of information in this process.

5.10 Summary

1. The ORSA is the entirety of the processes employed within the undertaking to identify, assess, monitor, report, and manage short and long term risks, and to quantitatively determine and meet own funds requirements. In this role, the ORSA is part of the risk management system, according to the design of Solvency II. With the ORSA, the importance of the actuarial function in the risk management area increases. As part of the risk management system, all of the fundamental principles of Solvency II, and in particular the principles of materiality and proportionality, apply to the ORSA.
2. Sec. 64a of the VAG [German Insurance Supervision Act] and the MaRisk VA [Minimum Requirements for Risk Management (Insurance Supervision)] have anticipated the ORSA in some respects. This is not so, however, for the role of the actuarial function in risk management. Sec. 28 VAG-E [Government's Ministerial Draft of a Tenth Act Amending the Insurance Supervision Act] implements the requirements of the European law sometimes with gaps and sometimes to excess.
3. ORSA is also intended to enable insurance undertakings to assess whether use of the norm or internal model is sufficient to assure the solvency of the insurance

[169] See 5.7.2, above. No supervisory measure at all in the form of a capital add-on may be employed in cases where Solvency II itself knowingly negates a risk, such as in the zero-risk weighting of government bonds, which must then be accounted for in the ORSA framework – according to the German Federal Government, Response to a Parliamentary Question, BT-Drucks. [Document of the German Bundestag] 17/8225, 19 Dec. 2011, p. 10.

undertaking. If this is not the case, the insurance undertaking must develop an internal model or adjust the model used. Based on the results of the ORSA, the supervisory authority can mandate the use of an internal model if this is a suitable supervisory measure and—in the event this does not produce the desired results—the supervisory authority may impose a capital add-on. However, there is no automatic link between the ORSA and supervisory measures in general and the imposition of a capital add-on in particular. If the supervisory requirements related to ORSA are not complied with, the supervisory authority may take additional measures against an insurance undertaking.

4. The ORSA is a part of risk management, and as such, the ORSA process is the responsibility of the risk management function, which is therefore required to monitor the ORSA.
5. Similarly, the compliance function monitors the proper implementation of the ORSA. But, for reasons of competence, it must exercise restraint in evaluating the influence of the ORSA on business strategy. The compliance function need not determine the presence of the conditions calling for an ad hoc ORSA in the context of a particular assignment of tasks. The investigation of any significant change in the risk profile as part of its general compliance operations is sufficient.
6. The ORSA is also subject to review by the internal audit function.
7. The ORSA places very high organizational requirements on insurance undertakings. Despite the principles of materiality and proportionality, the ORSA process presents a significant challenge due to its complexity, which is difficult to manage in practice.
8. With a consistent alignment of supervisory requirements and measures on the principles of proportionality and materiality, interventions by the ORSA in the freedom to conduct business are essentially justified.
9. The ORSA is intended to be an integral part of business strategy and to be taken into account on an ongoing basis in the strategic decisions of the insurance undertaking. Therefore, since the business strategy of an insurance undertaking, as central to the freedom to conduct business, is thereby indirectly the subject matter of insurance supervision—even though, as the exclusive responsibility of the management bodies, it is not subject to direct supervision—the supervisory review of an ORSA requires a certain sensitivity and restraint as well as a rigorous adherence to the principle of proportionality in this respect.
10. The own assessment of interest rate risk in the course of an ORSA presents a significant problem for insurance undertakings due to the sensitivity of the interest rate yield curve currently under consideration. A less volatile yield curve would therefore be desirable in this respect.
11. As part of the ORSA, significant deviations in the individual risk profile from the standard formula or internal model calculations must be examined. Despite the somewhat different terminology in the German wording of the Solvency II Framework Directive, the relevant criterion for significance is derived from a systematic interpretation under European law. A deviation is significant if an objective summary assessment reveals that only a new calculation model adequately represents the actual risk profile in the long term.

12. Documenting an ORSA has a threefold function: It is intended to ensure the inclusion of the ORSA in the strategic direction of the undertaking and its implementation. It is also intended to aid the insurance supervisory authorities in adequately assessing the risk and solvency situation of the insurance undertaking. Last, publication of the relevant data is intended to provide market transparency. For the publication requirements, only the ORSA process has to be presented. The report to the supervisory authority is different in this respect and must include the information on both the ORSA process and its result.
13. The supervisory authorities may sanction deficiencies in the implementation of the ORSA arising from deviations from the requirements for the ORSA in European and German insurance supervisory law. The results of an ORSA are only one source of information for supervisory authorities that must be exhausted as part of the ex officio investigation prior to official intervention.

Chapter 6
Fitness of Members of Supervisory Board

Contents

6.1 Introduction 196
6.2 General Requirements of Company Law Applicable to the Qualification of Supervisory Board Members 197
 6.2.1 The Federal Court of Justice-Ruling in *Hertie* 197
 6.2.2 The German Corporate Governance Code 199
6.3 The Insurance Supervisory Regime Requirements for the Qualification of Supervisory Board Members 200
 6.3.1 The Statutory Rules on the Expertise Requirement 200
 6.3.2 The BaFin [Federal Financial Supervisory Authority] Bulletin of 22 February 2010 204
 6.3.3 Amendments in the Process of Implementing Solvency II 206
6.4 Individual Expertise of the Supervisory Board Members and the Overall Qualification of the Supervisory Board 211
 6.4.1 Requirements for the Individual Supervisory Board Member 211
 6.4.2 Overall Qualification of the Supervisory Board 212
6.5 Summary 214

Abstract This chapter deals with the fitness of members of supervisory boards. Since 2009, German insurance regulatory law has provided internal qualification standards for the supervisory board members of insurance companies. In accordance with Paragraph 7a, sec. 4, clause 1 of the VAG [German Insurance Supervision Act], the members of supervisory boards must be able to fulfill their tasks and supervisory functions in accordance with their level of expertise. This new requirement comports with the previous standards of German corporate law, established by the BGH [German Federal Court of Justice] in its "Hertie"-ruling. As such, this

First published as "Die Qualifikation der Aufsichtsratsmitglieder von Versicherungsunternehmen nach VAG und Solvency II" [in English: The Qualification of Supervisory Board Members of Insurance Undertakings under the VAG [German Insurance Supervision Act] and Solvency II], ZVersWiss (2011), 211 ff. with *Martin Lange* as coauthor. *Martin Lange* was at that time a research assistant at the law school of Johannes Gutenberg University in Mainz.

M. Dreher, *Treatises on Solvency II*, DOI 10.1007/978-3-662-46290-4_6

ruling will also serve as a basis to interpret the expertise requirements in German insurance regulatory law. Consequently, each supervisory board member must have a certain minimum level of general competencies, so that specialized expertise and advance knowledge are maintained on the board. Even if the supervisory board members are not "persons with key functions" within the meaning of the framework directive of Solvency II, nevertheless, on its own, the pending transformation of existing guidelines into national law will indirectly affect the qualification requirements of supervisory board members in the insurance industry.

6.1 Introduction

The Gesetz zur Stärkung der Finanzmarkt- und der Versicherungsaufsicht [German Act To Strengthen the Financial Market and Insurance Supervision] of 29 July 2009[1] intensified supervision over members of the supervisory bodies of direct insurance and reinsurance undertakings, pension funds, insurance and financial holding companies, and insurance special purpose vehicles.[2] Newly crafted sec. 7a, para. 4, sent. 1 of the VAG [German Insurance Supervision Act], which sec. 121a, para. 1, sent. 1 and sec. 121g, para. 2, sent. 1 of the VAG [German Insurance Supervision Act] make applicable also to reinsurance undertakings and insurance special purpose vehicles, prescribes that the supervisory board members must "be reliable and must possess the expertise required for performance of the monitoring function as well as for the assessment and monitoring of the business engaged in by the undertaking". Thus, the supervisory requirements applicable to supervisory board members have become more closely aligned with similar requirements for managers of insurance undertakings. Under the VAG [German Insurance Supervision Act], managers of insurance undertakings have long been subject to extensive fit-and-proper criteria established by European law.[3] In the area of supervision over members of the supervisory and monitoring bodies, absent specific autonomous European law requirements, the fit-and-proper criterion is in any case initially amenable to an interpretation that considers nationally developed principles of trade and supervisory law. By contrast, widespread uncertainty exists up to this point concerning the quality and scope of the expertise requirements.

Thus, the requirements arising from the criterion of expertise that apply to the supervisory board members of the supervised undertakings are treated in the following discussion. This discussion will begin with the general rules of company law that apply to the qualification of supervisory board members (6.2, below). Next,

[1] BGBl. [German Federal Law Gazette] 2009 I, p. 2305.

[2] Hereafter, direct insurance and reinsurance undertakings, pension funds, insurance and financial holding companies, and insurance special purpose vehicles – to the extent no distinction is noted – will be denominated "supervised undertakings".

[3] On this point in detail see *Dreher*, ZVersWiss (Supplement 2006), 375 ff.

this article will take a closer look at the specific insurance supervisory regime requirements of sec. 7a, para. 4 of the VAG [German Insurance Supervision Act] and amendments made in the course of implementing Solvency II in the context of the criterion of expertise (6.3, below). Finally, these requirements will be considered with respect to the qualification of each individual supervisory board member. The assessment of the qualification requirements will include the overall qualification of the supervisory board (6.4, below).

6.2 General Requirements of Company Law Applicable to the Qualification of Supervisory Board Members

6.2.1 The Federal Court of Justice-Ruling in Hertie

In the case of insurance corporations, sec. 100 of the AktG [German Stock Corporation Act][4] provides certain minimum requirements that supervisory board members must meet. The Act, however, explicitly addresses only personal prerequisites, such as, for example, being a natural person, the full legal capacity of the supervisory board member, as well as incompatibility with other interlocking functions.[5] Under sec. 100, para. 4 of the AktG [German Stock Corporation Act], more extensive requirements can be set forth in the articles and by-laws. Furthermore, in 1982 the BGH [German Federal Court of Justice] decided the *Hertie* case,[6] which addressed the qualifications for supervisory board members of a limited-liability company subject to qualified employee participation. The court in its opinion derived further statutory minimum qualifications for supervisory board members from the precept that exercise of the office must be personal and self-dependent. The BGH [German Federal Court of Justice] requires in this respect that, at a minimum, each member "must possess or acquire the minimum knowledge and abilities" required "to be able without outside assistance to understand and properly assess all matters arising in the normal course of business".[7] In its ruling, the court did not put emphasis on the special knowledge belonging to a specific sector or field. Nor did it focus on business experience. Rather, the Court simply set forth the

[4] For the special expertise of financial experts under sec. 100, para. 5 of the AktG [German Stock Corporation Act] for corporations focused on the capital markets, see OLG München [in English: Munich Higher Regional Court], AG (2010), 639 = ZIP (2010), 1082 and *Staake*, ZIP (2010), 1013 ff.

[5] See, e.g., *Hüffer*, Kommentar zum AktG [in English: Commentary on the German Stock Corporation Act] (9th ed. 2010) sec. 100, ref. 2 ff.; *Wirth*, ZGR (2005), 327 (331 f.).

[6] BGHZ [Decisions of the Federal Court of Justice in Civil Matters] (Ger.) (hereafter, BGHZ) 85, 293 ff.; for the similar Austrian view, öOGH [in English: Austrian Supreme Court], AG (2004), 45 (50).

[7] BGHZ 85, 293, 295 f.

minimum requirements sufficient to enable an individual supervisory board member to understand the ordinary processes of a business operation and to evaluate these processes to a degree sufficient for effective supervision.

With slight individual nuances, this ruling of the BGH [German Federal Court of Justice] has received near-universal approval by commentators.[8] And there is general agreement on the concrete criteria relating to undertakings pursuant to which a structural distinction is to be effected and the determination of the minimum requirements for supervisory board members under company law is to be made. This view holds the determinative factors for the requisite minimum qualification to be the type and size of the given undertaking, the nature and purpose of the undertaking, the actual volume of business, and the company structure. Assessment of this last factor includes the issue whether the supervised undertaking belongs to a group.[9]

For the insurance realm this means that under company law requirements themselves as concretized by the BGH [German Federal Court of Justice] in *Hertie*, members of the supervisory board must have a basic command of the insurance business, must be conversant with the basic structures of the business model of the given undertaking, and must be able to sufficiently evaluate the ordinary business processes without making use of outside assistance. These minimum requirements under company law apply in principle irrespective of an undertaking's legal form. While *Hertie* applied to the supervisory board of a co-managed limited liability company, the minimum qualification for supervisory board members nevertheless was derived from the precept that exercise of the office must be personal and self-

[8] See, e.g. *Hüffer*, n. 5 above, at sec. 116, ref. 2; *Rieder/Holzmann*, AG (2010), 570 (573); *Drygala*, in: Schmidt/Lutter, eds., Kommentar zum AktG [in English: Commentary on the German Stock Corporation Act] (2008), sec. 116, ref. 7; *Habersack*, in: Münchener Kommentar zum Aktiengesetz [in English: Munich Commentary on the German Stock Corporation Act], v. 2 (3rd ed. 2008) sec. 116, ref. 24; *Lutter/Krieger*, Rechte und Pflichten des Aufsichtsrats [in English: Rights and Obligations of the Supervisory Board] (5th ed. 2008) ref. 26; *Hoffmann-Becking*, in: Münchener Handbuch des Gesellschaftsrechts [in English: Munich Manual of Company Law] v. 4, Aktiengesellschaft [in English: The Corporation] (3rd ed. 2007) sec. 30, ref. 2a, sec. 33, ref. 61; *Hopt/Roth*, in: Hopt/Wiedemann, eds., Kommentar zum AktG [in English: Commentary on the German Stock Corporation Act] v. 4 (4th ed. 2006) sec. 100, ref. 29 f.; prior comprehensive discussion, *Dreher*, "Die Qualifikation der Aufsichtsratsmitglieder" [in English: The Qualification of Supervisory Board Members], in: FS [Publication in Honor of] Boujong (1996) 71, (75 ff.); *Schwark*, "Zum Haftungsmaßstab der Aufsichtsratsmitglieder einer AG" [in English: On the Standard of Liability for Supervisory Board Members of a Corporation], in: FS [Publication in Honor of] Werner (1984), 841 (847 f.); lesser requirements are considered sufficient, e.g., by *Möllers*, ZIP (1995), 1725 (1733 f.); and going beyond the requirements under *Hertie*, *Semler*, in: Münchener Kommentar zum Aktiengesetz [in English: Munich Commentary on the German Stock Corporation Act] (2nd ed. 2004) sec. 100, ref. 76 ff.; *id.*, "Anforderungen an die Befähigung eines Aufsichtsratsmitglieds" [in English: Requisite Capabilities of a Supervisory Board Member] in: FS [Publication in Honor of] K. Schmidt (2009), 1489 ff.

[9] See *Dreher*, n. 8 above, at 71, (76 f.); recently, e.g., *Hüffer*, n. 5 above, at sec. 116, ref. 3.

dependent. Irrespective of any given legal form, this precept obtains as a principle in carrying out the functions of seats on the supervisory and monitoring bodies. Thus it follows that monitoring body members of mutual insurance associations and public insurance undertakings are likewise included within the minimum qualification requirement, as, for example, supervisory board members of the larger insurance corporations are.[10]

6.2.2 *The German Corporate Governance Code*

For exchange-listed companies the company law requirements clarified in the Federal Court of Justice-ruling in *Hertie*, are supplemented by the requirements and principles of the German Corporate Governance Code (DCGK).[11] This code, of course, presents only an unofficial legal scheme but with its reference to sec. 161 of the AktG [German Stock Corporation Act] can nevertheless claim a certain binding force, even if there exists no enforcement mechanism under company law.[12] Provision 5.4.1 of the DCGK [German Corporate Governance Code] prescribes that the supervisory board shall be so constituted that "its members as a whole possess the knowledge, abilities, and practical experience required for the proper performance of their tasks". This guiding principle, viz., in the selection of supervisory board members to be attuned to the minimum knowledge and abilities adequate to the scope of business, is simply a confirmation of the minimum qualification requirements already existing and mandatory under company law.[13]

[10] In the case of mutual insurance associations, this result is explicit in the reference to sec. 100 of the AktG [German Stock Corporation Act] in sec. 35, para. 3 of the VAG [German Insurance Supervision Act].

[11] German Corporate Governance Code, in the version of 26 May 2010; the current version may be found at www.bmj.bund.de; on the most recent amendments, see *Ringleb/Kremer/Lutter/v. Werder*, NZG (2010), 1161 ff.

[12] On this type of "private" legislation and the objectives of corporate governance, see *Rittner/ Dreher*, Europäisches und deutsches Wirtschaftsrecht [in English: European and German Economic Law] (3rd ed. 2008) sec. 7, ref. 58 and sec. 9, ref. 75 ff.

[13] Likewise also *Ringleb/Kremer/Lutter/v.Werder*, NZG (2010), 1161 (1165); on the previous version of the Code provision, comparable as to the minimum qualification requirements, see *Kremer*, in: Ringleb/Kremer/Lutter/v.Werder, eds., Deutscher Corporate Governance Kodex [in English: German Corporate Governance Code] (4th ed. 2010), ref. 1015 ff.; see in this connection also the press release of the German Government Commission Deutscher Corporate Governance Kodex [German Corporate Governance Code], 10 Feb. 2010, to be found at http://www.corporate-governance-code.de/ger/download/Qualifizierung_von_Aufsichtsraeten_10_02_2010.pdf.

Consequently, this provision does not give rise to any further requirements for the individual qualification of supervisory and monitoring body members.[14]

6.3 The Insurance Supervisory Regime Requirements for the Qualification of Supervisory Board Members

6.3.1 The Statutory Rules on the Expertise Requirement

6.3.1.1 The Substantive Law Requirements of Sec. 7a, Para. 4 of the VAG [German Insurance Supervision Act]

The original legislative intent respecting the VAG [German Insurance Supervision Act] was to codify the requirement of "fitness" for supervisory board members of supervised undertakings and in so doing to go a long way toward bringing the qualification requirements for supervisory board members in line with those of management monitoring.[15] In the final version, however, sec. 7a, para. 4, sent. 1 of the VAG [German Insurance Supervision Act] only uses r the term "expertise".[16] The required expertise is deemed present according to the stated intent of the legislator if the members of the supervisory and monitoring bodies of the supervised undertakings are able to "understand the business conducted, assess the attendant risks for the undertaking, and if necessary implement management changes.[17] Accordingly, expertise requires at all times "that the individual concerned in case of doubt must demonstrate that he or she possesses the aptitude to understand the economic and legal processes of ongoing events".[18]

The expertise requirement in sec. 7a, para. 4, sent. 1 of the VAG [German Insurance Supervision Act] thus corresponds to the company law requirements

[14] In the meanwhile, the issue of the required qualification for members of supervisory and monitoring bodies and the resulting need for rules has also been recognized at the European level. On this point, see European Commission, ed., Green Paper: Corporate governance in financial institutions and remuneration policies, COM(2010) 284/3 at 3.3, first bullet point. On the issue of the qualification of the supervisory board as a whole, see 6.4.2, below.

[15] Accord, Statement of Reasons to the Government's Draft of the Gesetz zur Stärkung der Finanzmarkt- und der Versicherungsaufsicht [Act To Strengthen the Financial Market and Insurance Supervision] of 27 April 2009, BT-Drucks. [Document of the German Bundestag] 16/12783, pp. 8, 18; critical on this point, *Dreher*, ZGR (2010), 496 (510 f.).

[16] This amendment harks back to the Recommended Resolution and the Report of the Finance Commission of 01 July 2009, BT-Drucks. [Document of the German Bundestag] 16/13684, p. 43, referring at p. 41 to the Statement of Reasons for the parallel provision, sec. 36, para. 3 of the KWG [German Credit Services Act]; on the course of the legislative process, see *Dreher*, ZGR (2010), 496 (509 ff.); *Bürkle*, VersR (2010), 1005 f.

[17] Recommended Resolution and the Report of the Finance Commission, n. 16 above, at 43.

[18] Recommended Resolution and the Report of the Finance Commission, n. 16 above, at 43, referring at p. 41 to sec. 36, para. 3 of the KWG [German Credit Services Act].

developed and clarified in the Federal court of Justice-ruling in *Hertie*.[19] The legal requirement of expertise is to be conceived as the codification under supervisory law of the *Hertie* principles, especially since the legislator in sec. 7a, para. 4, sent. 2 of the VAG [German Insurance Supervision Act] expressly interpreted as applicable a structural distinction according to type and scope of the business conducted as well as to the size of the supervised undertaking also in the area of the supervisory law expertise requirement.[20] The codification under supervisory law of the minimum requirements for qualification for members of the monitoring and supervisory bodies of supervised undertakings undergoes a clarification in content only to the extent that the type of business conducted, to which business the knowledge and skills of the supervisory board members must pertain, arises from the insurance-related nature and purpose of the undertaking, that the insurance supervisory regime expertise requirement is in principle connected to knowledge of the given insurance business. An additional factor is the insurance-related predetermination of minimum qualification under supervision law. Thus, it may be derived from sec. 317, para. 4 of the HGB [German Commercial Code] in conjunction with sec. 91, para. 2 of the AktG [German Stock Corporation Act] that all supervisory board members must possess knowledge and skills in the area of risk management. Sec. 64a of the VAG [German Insurance Supervision Act], however, yields far more detailed and extensive requirements relating to risk management for the insurance industry. As a result, all members of an insurance undertaking's supervisory board must possess a basic understanding of these rules. At the least, within the meaning of qualification as a whole,[21] individual members must possess particular knowledge and skills with respect to risk management, such that they may be capable of adequately monitoring the managing board's compliance with statutory requirements.[22]

On the other hand, "diversity" of supervisory board members is not a subject of supervision law even under the amended version of sec. 7a, para. 4 of the VAG [German Insurance Supervision Act]. Yet it is true that Provision 5.4.1 of the DCGK [German Corporate Governance Code] prescribes that exchange-listed insurance undertakings in constituting their supervisory boards shall have regard for "variety (diversity)", for example, by appointment of women and foreign nationals to the board.[23] But no such corresponding statutory obligation can be

---

[19] See *Dreher*, ZGR (2010), 496 (511); *Hasse*, VersR (2010), 18 (23); on the parallel provision of sec. 36, para. 3 of the KWG [German Credit Services Act] likewise *Hingst/Himmelreich/Krawinkel*, WM (2009), 2016 (2019); arguably with another view, *Berger*, VersR (2010), 422 (423 f.), without, however, identifying any substantive concrete differences.

[20] Recommended Resolution and the Report of the Finance Commission, n. 16 above, at 43, 41; on the undertaking-oriented criterion of expertise, see in detail *Bürkle*, VersR (2010), 1005 (1007 ff).

[21] See 6.4.2, below.

[22] Thus *Dreher*, ZGR (2010), 496 (512 f.).

[23] A corresponding provision appears in the Green Paper of the European Union on corporate governance in financial institutions. See European Commission, ed., Green Paper: Corporate governance in financial institutions and remuneration policies, n. 14 above at 6.3.3, second bullet point.

derived from sec. 7a, para. 4 of the VAG [German Insurance Supervision Act]. In particular, the requirement of diversity is not comprehended within the term "expertise" and thus also is not an element of supervisory board member suitability.

6.3.1.2 Intervention Powers

The actual innovation of the codification under supervisory law of the expertise requirement, already required by company law, is thus that meeting the minimum requirements for the qualification of supervisory board members is no longer a matter limited to organizational and liability issues under company law. Rather, infringements of the qualification requirement will support application of the supervisory tools of the VAG [German Insurance Supervision Act]. Since the conventional supervisory powers under the VAG [German Insurance Supervision Act] allowed enforcement of general corporate and company law under an interpretation of intervention powers in conformance with European and constitutional law only within narrow limits,[24] the legislator by enacting the Gesetz zur Stärkung der Finanzmarkt- und der Versicherungsaufsicht [Act To Strengthen the Financial Market and Insurance Supervision] expanded the supervisory set of tools and thus brought them into accord with the new requirements of sec. 7a, para. 4 of the VAG [German Insurance Supervision Act].[25]

Consequently from now on, with reference to the expertise requirement of sec. 7a, para. 4, sent. 1 of the VAG [German Insurance Supervision Act], under sec. 87, para. 8, sent. 1, and sec. 121c, para. 6, sent. 1 of the VAG [German Insurance Supervision Act],[26] the supervisory authority has the power to issue a demand to the competent bodies of the supervised undertakings seeking recall of a member of the supervisory board or to prohibit such individual from the exercise of his or her office, if the

[24] On the mandatory narrow construction of intervention powers, especially of the general clause of the VAG [German Insurance Supervision Act], see *Rittner/Dreher*, Europäisches und deutsches Wirtschaftsrecht [in English: European and German Economic Law] (3rd ed. 2008), sec. 31, refs. 25 ff., 93 ff.; going too far is *Hasse*, VersR (2010), 18 (23), who, under former law before sec. 7a, para. 4 of the VAG [German Insurance Supervision Act] took effect, considered assertion of the company law minimum qualification requirement for supervisory board members feasible on the basis of sec. 81 of the VAG [German Insurance Supervision Act].

[25] An overview of the supervisory intervention powers is provided, e.g., by *Berger*, VersR (2010), 422 (425 ff.); in addition, the Jahressteuergesetz [Annual Tax Act] of 08 Dec. 2010, BGBl. [German Federal Law Gazette] I, 1768, expanded the power to adopt regulations as found in sec. 5, para. 6, of the VAG [German Insurance Supervision Act], so that henceforward statements relating to evaluating the qualification of supervisory board members are subject to the duties of notice set forth in sec. 5, para. 5, no. 9 and sec. 13d, no. 12 of the VAG [German Insurance Supervision Act].

[26] Sec. 121c applies also to insurance special purpose vehicles pursuant to sec. 121g, para. 2 of the VAG [German Insurance Supervision Act].

requisite expertise is demonstrably not present. To the extent the want of expertise is reflected in a breach of the duty of care in respect to exercise of office leading to the results specified in sec. 87, para. 8, sent. 2 and sec. 121c, para. 6, sent. 2 of the VAG [German Insurance Supervision Act] and thus displays its actual concrete effect, these provisions supply the supervisory authority with an additional power to recall and to demand cessation of the exercise of office. Under sec. 1b, para. 6 of the VAG [German Insurance Supervision Act] in conjunction with sec. 1b, para. 4, no. 3 of the VAG [German Insurance Supervision Act], there is further a direct empowerment to prohibit performance with respect to individual supervisory board members if the expertise requirement is not met. This power is not coordinated with the rest of the rules. Such an original power to prohibit performance, however, would have been required in sec. 87, para. 8 and sec. 121c, para. 6 of the VAG [German Insurance Supervision Act] to avoid conflicts with company law provisions, since a tool of pure performance prohibition does not exist in corporate and company law. A demand for such by the supervisory authority upon the competent bodies of the relevant undertaking would be to demand an impossible act.[27]

If the body of the supervised undertaking responsible for the recall under sec. 103 of the AktG [German Stock Corporation Act][28] does not comply with the recall demand, the supervisory authority also can file for a recall in court, under sec. 87, para. 8, sent. 3 and sec. 121c, para. 6, sent. 3 of the VAG [German Insurance Supervision Act], to the extent the supervisory board has authority under sec. 103, para. 3, sent. 1 of the AktG [German Stock Corporation Act] to pursue a judicial procedure for recall.[29] Likewise, the appointment of a special representative under sec 83a, para. 1, no. 4 in conjunction with sec. 7a, para. 4 of the VAG [German Insurance Supervision Act] may be considered. As a last resort, the supervisory authority can eventually revoke the supervised undertaking's license to operate if supervisory board members do not satisfy the expertise requirement. The authority for such action lies in sec. 87, para. 1, no. 1 of the VAG [German Insurance Supervision Act] in conjunction with sec. 8, para. 1, no. 5 of the VAG [German Insurance Supervision Act] and in sec. 121c, para. 2, no. 1 of the VAG

[27] See *Dreher*, ZGR (2010), 496 (513).

[28] Sec. 35, para. 3 of the VAG [German Insurance Supervision Act] makes the essential parts of this power to revoke applicable to mutual insurance associations.

[29] *Berger*, VersR (2010), 422 (427) apparently overlooks the fact that the filing power of the supervisory board under sec. 103, para. 3, sent. 1 of the AktG [German Stock Corporation Act] concerns the filing of applications in judicial proceedings for recall and thus arrives at flawed conclusions in reference to the systematic interpretation of sec. 87, para. 8, sent. 3 of the VAG [German Insurance Supervision Act] and sec. 121c, para. 6, sent. 3 of the VAG [German Insurance Supervision Act] (the latter provision at *Berger* also cited as sec. 121c, para. 6, sent. 4 of the VAG [German Insurance Supervision Act]); similarly, *Bähr*, VW (2009), 1401 (1404).

[German Insurance Supervision Act] in conjunction with sec. 121, para. 1, no. 4 of the VAG [German Insurance Supervision Act].

6.3.2 *The BaFin [Federal Financial Supervisory Authority] Bulletin of 22 February 2010*

6.3.2.1 The BaFin [Federal Financial Supervisory Authority] Interpretation of the Expertise Requirement

In a non-legally binding bulletin dated 22 February 2010,[30] the German federal authority supervising financial services clarified the expertise requirement. In particular, it named groups of individuals whom the supervisory authority would presume to possess the required expertise. To this extent, the bulletin supplies some information on the understanding of the supervisory authority as to the relevant provisions of the VAG [German Insurance Supervision Act] and may function in effect as a form of administrative self-limitation.[31] Thus, the BaFin [Federal Financial Supervisory Authority] explicitly considers company law requirements in refining the parameters of the expertise requirement. Then it applies the principles of company law to the expertise requirement under supervisory law, in particular using the Federal court of Justice-ruling in *Hertie*. One field of this application, for example, lies in structural distinctions based on the type of insurance business conducted and the size of the supervised undertaking.[32] In this process, the supervisory authority exhibits a tendency to set a very low bar for the supervisory expertise requirement, for example, if it assumes that the mere exercise of political office, such as chief administrative official of a regional administrative body,[33] generally occupations in the public administration, or even an occupation as a farmer or forester required to keep accounts—as if the generality of insurance undertakings would operate in the sector of hail and storm insurance for agriculture and forestry—would routinely be a sufficient basis for the expertise required in a supervisory and monitoring body.

---

[30] Merkblatt zur Kontrolle von Mitgliedern von Verwaltungs- und Aufsichtsorganen gemäß KWG und VAG [Guidance Notice on Vetting Members of Administrative and Supervisory Bodies in accordance with the German Credit Services Act and the German Insurance Supervision Act] of 22 Feb. 2010, downloadable at http://www.bafin.de/cln_179/nn_721290/SharedDocs/Veroeffentlichungen/DE/Service/Merkblaetter/mb__100222__Verwaltungs__und__Aufsichtsorgane.html?__nnn=true.

[31] On the potential impact see *Bürkle*, VersR (2010), 1005 (1010).

[32] Bulletin, n. 30 above, at 1 f.

[33] The BaFin [Federal Financial Supervisory Authority] specifically mentions mayors and regional administrators. See Bulletin, n. 30, above, at p. 3.

6.3.2.2 Special Attention to the Existence of Minimum Qualification upon Assuming Office

The expertise requirement under company law and supervisory law applies in equal measure to all supervisory board members, particularly for labor representatives.[34] Occupation of a seat on the supervisory board absent the relevant expertise constitutes in any case fault upon assuming office[35] and forms the basis for liability of the supervisory board member for resultant damages to the supervised undertaking. This holds irrespective of any assumption of obstacle to appointment, as set forth explicitly, for example, in sec. 6 para. 3, InvG [German Investment Act].[36] In themselves, the company law requirements tied to liability lead to the conclusion that the requisite expertise of the supervisory board member need not be present upon selection, but at the latest must be present upon the member's assumption of office.[37] The bulletin of the BaFin [Federal Financial Supervisory Authority] allowing the required knowledge and skills to be acquired even after assumption of office[38] contradicts the company law requirements tied to liability. Further, the provision is incompatible with supervisory assessments, which are geared toward immediate and effective action by the supervisory board to protect the interests of the policy holders and of the undertaking itself and to ensure the stability of the finance and insurance sector as a whole.[39]

[34] Long the prevailing view for company law, see BGHZ 85, 293, 295 f. and e.g., *Hüffer*, n. 5 above, at sec. 116, ref. 2 with further references.

[35] Thus also, e.g., the answer of the German Federal Government to a parliamentary question on the topic: "Wahrnehmung der Aufsichts- und Kontrollfunktion des Staats als Anteilseigner" [in English: Exercise of the Supervisory and Monitoring Function of the State as Shareholder], BT-Drucks. [Document of the German Bundestag] 16/11536, 29 Dec. 2008, p. 3.

[36] Without regard to supervision law, this follows from company law principles; see of many examples, *Habersack,* in: Münchener Kommentar zum Aktiengesetz [in English: Munich Commentary on the German Stock Corporation Act], n. 8 above, at sec. 100, ref. 11 and sec. 116, ref. 22.

[37] See *Hommelhoff,* ZGR (1983), 551 (574 f); *Dreher*, n. 8 above, at 71, (76); *Semler*, "Anforderungen an die Befähigung eines Aufsichtsratsmitglieds" [in English: Requisite Capabilities of a Supervisory Board Member] in: FS [Publication in Honor of] K. Schmidt (2009), 1489 (1499); see also *Habersack*, in: Münchener Kommentar zum Aktiengesetz [in English: Munich Commentary on the German Stock Corporation Act], n. 8 above, at sec. 116, ref. 24; with particular reference to the insurance industry, likewise *Hasse*, VersR (2010), 18 (24); for yet a different view, BGHZ 85, 293, 295 f.; and still, *Raiser/Veil*, Kapitalgesellschaften [in English: The Law of Corporations] (5th ed. 2010), sec. 15, ref. 114.

[38] Bulletin, n. 30 above, at 3 f., providing a six-month grace period to reach qualification and, in fact, allowing an extension when "existential requirements of the chief activity" in "seasonal occupations" call for it; *Bürkle*, VersR (2010), 1005 (1007) calls this period "clearly too long", thus paraphrasing a fundamentally incorrect posture with a vague and concessive formulation.

[39] In addition, the bulletin, n. 30 above, is internally inconsistent: On p. 3 f., post-hoc qualification by continuing education is viewed as sufficient. At the same time, however, on p. 6, point III, members of the supervisory and administrative bodies are unconditionally required to be able to "fulfill their obligations at all times".

6.3.3 *Amendments in the Process of Implementing Solvency II*

6.3.3.1 The Requirements of Art. 42, Para. 1, Art. 248, Para. 1 (d), and Art. 257 of the Solvency II Framework Directive

The impending implementation of the Solvency II Framework Directive[40] in German law could have an impact on the qualification requirements for members of the supervisory and monitoring bodies of supervised undertakings. The Directive, in fact, covers the supervisory board, a scope illustrated by numerous of its provisions, e.g., arts. 34, para. 2; 40, 41, 41, para. 3, subpara. 2, 46, para. 2, 47, para. 3; and 48, para. 1 (e). Starting points for a potential impact of the European legal scheme on national provisions respecting minimum qualification appear in arts. 42, 248, and 257 of the Solvency II Framework Directive as well as in its Recitals 33 through 35. Thus, art. 42, para. 1 from Section 2 of the Directive, which controls the requirements for the system of governance of insurance undertakings, includes all "persons who effectively run the undertaking or have other key functions". Under art. 42, para. 1 (a), such persons must be sufficiently fit "to enable sound and prudent management". Although the members of the supervisory and monitoring bodies of the supervised undertakings are not engaged in management tasks, they could in fact be viewed as persons having key functions.[41] Accordingly, relevant CEIOPS papers contain references to the view that supervisory board members indeed could be classified as "persons with key functions". As a result of such classification, they would be subject to the qualification requirements of art. 42, para. 1 of the Solvency II Framework Directive.[42] And in fact, in another context the BaFin [Federal Financial Supervisory Authority] for example explicitly numbers supervisory board chairpersons among those who hold "key positions" in an undertaking.[43] And the issuer of a regulation alludes to "executive staff exercising key functions" in its concretizing rule

[40] Directive 2009/138/EC of the European Parliament and of the Council of 25 Nov. 2009 on the taking-up and pursuit of the business of Insurance and Reinsurance (Solvency II), OJEU L 335, 17 Dec. 2009, 1 ff.

[41] Thus *Schaaf*, Risikomanagement und Compliance in Versicherungsunternehmen – aufsichtsrechtliche Anforderungen und Organverantwortung, [in English: Risk Management and Compliance in Insurance Undertakings – Supervisory Requirements and Institutional Responsibility], (2010), 242 f.; contra, *Hasse*, "Informations- und Offenlegungspflichten der Versicherungsunternehmen nach Solvency II" [in English: Information and Disclosure Obligations for Insurance Undertakings under Solvency II] in: Dreher/Wandt, eds., Solvency II in der Rechtsanwendung, [in English: Solvency II in Application of the Law] 61 (80 ff.).

[42] See CEIOPS, ed., Issue Paper "Risk Management and Other Corporate Issues" of 17 July 2007 at pnt. 2.2 ("fit and proper"); CEIOPS, ed., Issue Paper "Implementing Measures on System of Governance" of 03 Nov. 2008 at pnt. 5.; both papers are downloadable at www.ceiops.eu.

[43] See BaFin [Federal Financial Supervisory Authority], Issuer Guideline, IV.2.2.4. (p. 57) and IV.2.2.11. (p. 62).

Inhaberkontrollverordnung [Holder Control Regulation], a rule that expressly excludes supervisory board members.[44]

As a result, the expertise requirement of sec. 7a, para. 4, sent. 1 of the VAG [German Insurance Supervision Act] would have to be autonomously construed pursuant to the criterion of European requirements. This, then, would mean that the requirements for members of supervisory and monitoring bodies would not be determined pursuant to the criteria under national law. One may presume that application of art. 42, para. 1 of the Solvency II Framework Directive to supervisory board members would impede the pertinent qualification requirements with respect to ensuring a functioning system of governance, as detailed in Chapter 2 of the Solvency II Framework Directive. This is so because an effective system of governance pursuant to the requirements of the Solvency II Framework Directive comprises, i.a., areas such as comprehensive risk management, compliance requirements pertaining to internal monitoring and review, and requirements for actuarial and investment functions. Thus, as an essential component of functioning governance within insurance undertakings, the members of the supervisory and monitoring body would be subject to enhanced requirements in respect to the exercise of their monitoring tasks in these areas.

In its plain language, art. 42, para. 1 (a) further indicates three criteria superior to the previous statutory and supervisory interpretations of the expertise requirement in sec. 7a, para. 4 of the VAG [German Insurance Supervision Act]. Together, these constitute the qualifying requirement for supervisory board members to have adequate "professional qualifications, knowledge and experience". One effect of these qualification prerequisites is that the presumptions as to expertise in the BaFin [Federal Financial Supervisory Authority][45] bulletin must fall. Nor is it at all clear how the presence of labor representatives in the supervisory board should be treated in view of the increased qualification prerequisites. And again, there is the altogether new objective stated in art. 42, para. 1 (a), which in effect repeats the directive of art. 41, para. 1, subpara. 1 to "provide for sound and prudent management... ". As yet, there is no parallel provision to be found in the AktG [German Stock Corporation Act] or in sec. 7a, para. 4 of the VAG [German Insurance Supervision Act]. Under general company law, the managing board, which the supervisory board would have to monitor in reference to this objective, is not under an obligation of "prudent management". The managing board may, for example, pursue speculative transactions if these are in accord with the nature and purpose of the undertaking or in line with its interests. The very assumption of novel risks in the insurance area[46] demonstrates that the term "prudence" as a term in supervisory law would require an interpretation specifically tied to the insurance industry. Further, this interpretation would have to be conformed to company law

[44] Sec. 15, para. 1, sent. 6, no. 2 InhKontrollV [Holder Control Regulation].

[45] See 6.3.2.1, above.

[46] See for more detail on this term in the context of the Block Exemption Regulation in the insurance industry *Dreher/Baubkus*, VersR (2010), 1389 ff.

requirements. The phrase "at all times" in art. 42, para. 1 (a) applied to supervisory board members would finally end the debate whether supervisory board members must possess minimum qualification upon assuming office.[47]

In interpreting art. 42, para. 1 of the Solvency II Framework Directive on the issue whether this provision includes supervisory board members in its ambit, one must consider that the regulatory approach of the provision, from the point of view of company law, assumes the single-board system as known in Anglo-American law. It is typical of this monistic management and administrative system that the executive directors are both supported and monitored by independent non-executive directors in the unified governing body. The Anglo-American system does not employ a separate supervisory and monitoring body as found in the company law tradition of the continental Europe and as indeed is at the heart of the organizational structure of the corporation. Consequently, it may be assumed that in art. 42, para. 1 of the Solvency II Framework Directive the term "persons who...have...key functions" should be interpreted such that only persons of the management body, not those of the supervisory board in an undertaking shall be included. This view finds support in the posture of the European supervisory authorities, which take the position that the qualification requirements shall apply primarily to individuals who actually conduct the affairs of the business, i.e., to the managers.[48]

In addition, persons who have key functions shall be included. The relevant CEIOPS papers identify certain essential functions within areas of responsibility as examples of key functions: These areas are risk management, compliance, internal audit, and actuarial function.[49] The same applies for Recitals 30 ff. of the Solvency II Framework Directive, which refer only to "key functions". Thus they pertain to an area in the system of governance of the Directive that does not include the supervisory board.[50] These are namely functions committed originally to the managers' realm of responsibility. Like all management conduct, they are subject only to the oversight and monitoring power of the supervisory board.

From the point of view of the systematics of the legal rules, another factor militates against the classification of supervisory and monitoring board members as persons having key functions within the meaning of art. 42, para. 1 of the Solvency II Framework Directive. This is the fact that art. 248, para. 1 (d)[51] specifically directs, for group supervision, that members of the supervisory bodies of undertakings belonging to a group must fulfill the "requirements set out in Articles 42 and 257". Hence, members of the supervisory and monitoring bodies of undertakings

[47] See 6.3.2.2, above.

[48] On this point, CEIOPS specifically mentions "all persons who effectively run the undertaking". See references in n. 42, above.

[49] On this point, CEIOPS states: "The other 'key functions' are those considered important and critical in the system of governance and include risk management, compliance, internal audit and actuarial functions. Additional key functions may be relevant."; see references at n. 42 above.

[50] See *Dreher/Schaaf*, VersR (2009), 1151 (1164).

[51] The reference to art. 250 in art. 248, para. 1 (d) of the Solvency II Framework Directive is an editorial error. The correct reference is to art. 246.

belonging to groups are subject to the full range of the enhanced qualification requirements of art. 42 of the Solvency II Framework Directive. A rule stating explicitly that the qualification requirement of art. 42, para. 1 of the Solvency II Framework Directive applies to members of the supervisory body of a participating undertaking in the context of group supervision would not have been necessary if art. 42, para. 1 of the Solvency II Framework Directive already included supervisory board members ipso iure. For that reason, no support is furnished here by the initially apparent argument, with respect to supervisory board members of insurance holding companies also included under art. 257, that both art. 257—at least in the text if not in the heading—and art. 42 respectively apply only to persons who "effectively run" the business and "effectively run the undertaking" and thus are not aimed at members of the supervisory and monitoring bodies.

In sum, the members of a supervisory and monitoring body formed in the context of the dual system of continental Europe basically cannot be regarded as persons having key functions, within the meaning of art. 42, para. 1 of the Solvency II Framework Directive. The qualification requirements set by European law for managers and other persons having key functions can have indirect impact on the members of supervisory bodies only insofar as the exercise of their oversight and monitoring tasks involves areas of management responsibility as to which art. 42, para. 1 of the Solvency II Framework Directive deems certain minimum qualifications for managers as critical and which are part of the system of governance under Section 2 of the Solvency II Framework Directive. Specifically, to the extent effective oversight and monitoring of the implementation of these requirements by managers demand that supervisory board members have adequate if also graduated levels of knowledge and abilities compared to managers, the qualification requirement of art. 42, para. 1 of the Solvency II Framework Directive will have a mediated impact as well on the members of supervisory and monitoring bodies in the areas expressly covered by the Directive, such as risk management and compliance.[52] Thus, beyond the specially treated area of group supervision, members of supervisory and monitoring bodies are covered at least indirectly by the overall regulatory scheme of the Solvency II Framework Directive. This is so because this has consequences for the requirement of minimum qualification to the extent that in the covered areas the supervisory board must possess adequate expertise such that it can ensure sufficient monitoring and oversight of the management activities in the impacted areas.

[52] For a comprehensive discussion, see *Bürkle*, in: Bürkle, ed., Compliance in Versicherungsunternehmen [in English: Insurance Undertakings' Compliance] (2009), 1 ff.

6.3.3.2 The Consequences for the Implementation of the Solvency II Framework Directive in National Law

If one correctly considers that members of supervisory and monitoring bodies of insurance undertakings are not persons having key functions within the meaning of art. 42, para. 1 of the Solvency II Framework Directive, this has consequences for the pending implementation of the European requirements in national law. Specifically, a special law must be created for supervisory board members of undertakings belonging to groups and of insurance holding companies. This is so because, while the qualification requirements of art. 42, para. 1 of the Solvency II Framework Directive by virtue of explicit reference in the provisions on group supervision apply directly and completely to the members of the supervisory and monitoring bodies of these undertakings, the supervisory board members of such undertakings, which are not under group supervision or as insurance holding companies not being the head of a group, are only indirectly affected by the European regulatory requirements. This is the case, to begin with, because of the legal rules of the Directive on the qualification of individual managers, a feature broadened in the areas noted in art. 42, para. 1 of the Solvency II Framework Directive. In addition, this has an inevitable direct impact on the scope of the monitoring and oversight tasks of the supervisory board and thus also on the qualification requirements of the individual supervisory board members as well as on the qualification of the supervisory board as a whole. As a further point, the overall system of governance described in Section 2 of the Directive creates repercussions for the qualification requirement, since implementation and oversight of such a system erects correlative, if also graduated, requirements as to content for individual and overall qualification of the supervisory board. Thus, in fact the expertise requirement of sec 7a, para. 4, sent. 1 of the VAG [German Insurance Supervision Act] will be applied and interpreted as to members of the supervisory boards of undertakings not belonging to a group, in the context of this mediated application of the qualification requirements with regard for the requirements of art. 42, para. 1 of the Solvency II Framework Directive and of the overall system of governance. A consequence of this will be that qualifications in the areas noted in Section 2 of the Solvency II Framework Directive are to be demanded to the extent they are required for an understanding of and thus also for the oversight and monitoring of the governance functions set forth in the Directive. At the same time, however, in the context of implementing the Directive requirements for group supervision, there are additional particular expertise requirements to set forth. These would go beyond the expertise requirement of sec. 7a, para. 4, sent. 1 of the VAG [German Insurance Supervision Act] and exclusively cover the supervisory board members of supervised undertakings affected by the requirements. This will be needed to avoid disparate definitions for the uniform term "expertise" in sec. 7a, para. 4, sent. 1 of the VAG [German Insurance Supervision Act] with reference to the particular supervisory board member. Thus, the undesirable result of inconsistent interpretations of the rule controlling minimum qualification will be prevented.

6.4 Individual Expertise of the Supervisory Board Members and the Overall Qualification of the Supervisory Board

6.4.1 Requirements for the Individual Supervisory Board Member

The minimum qualification requirement is designed to ensure that each member of an insurance undertaking's supervisory body is fundamentally able to perform his or her oversight and monitoring tasks[53] effectively. To this end, it is at least required that each supervisory board member possess general knowledge of the insurance industry, understand the specific business model of the pertinent supervised undertaking, and be able to comprehend the commercial and legal import of managers' activity related to ordinary business processes.[54] This requires, for example, a basic understanding of how the insurance business works, of accounting and drawing up of balance sheets, of capital investment, of the basic forms of risk management, of human resources management, and of the legal framework[55] of the insurance business. It is not necessary, on the other hand, that each and every supervisory board member possess special knowledge of actuarial principles and cost estimation, the details of risk management, the principles of capital investment and capital strategies, or the legal areas pertinent to the supervisory board's activity, such as the insurance supervisory regime or the law relating to companies or group of companies. The individual expertise requirement shall rather ensure a minimum standard for knowledge and abilities, permitting monitoring of the ordinary business processes. Absent this standard, a position on the supervisory board is in principle not possible. Furthermore, expert knowledge is indispensable for the supervisory board as a whole and for the exercise of its duties. It is not, however, a component of the individual expertise requirement. Rather, expert knowledge of this nature is significant in evaluating the overall qualification of the supervisory board, which is also required.

---

[53] For the broad view on the oversight duties of the supervisory board, see, e.g. *Semler*, Leitung und Überwachung der Aktiengesellschaft [in English: Managing and Monitoring the Corporation] (2nd ed. 1996), 53 ff.

[54] See 6.3.2 and 6.3.1.2, above.

[55] For a detailed treatment of supervisory board monitoring of the legality of management activities and the requisite legal knowledge for supervisory board members, see *Bürkle*, VersR (2010), 1005 (1008) f.

6.4.2 Overall Qualification of the Supervisory Board

Along with the knowledge and abilities of each individual supervisory board member, which are the foundation of his or her expertise, effective performance of oversight and monitoring by the supervisory board as a joint body requires professional overall qualification of the supervisory board beyond the individual minimum requirements. This is so because, pursuant to the relevant company law provisions and the rules of the German Corporate Governance Code, the supervisory board as a whole bears, for example, the legal obligation to develop a competence profile for its individual undertaking and to propose suitable candidates for the position of manager.[56] Thus, the supervisory board as a whole is under the legal duty pursuant to sec. 124, para. 3, sent. 1 of the AktG [German Stock Corporation Act][57] to present an appropriate proposed resolution to the annual shareholder meeting. If, in so doing, the supervisory board fails to comply with its duty to ensure adequate overall qualification, a corresponding instance of fault in selecting a member may exist.

This has particular significance for insurance undertakings operating in the legal form of mutual insurance associations. This is so because often in this situation the desire of the representatives' meeting for representation on the supervisory board is thwarted by a highly restricted pool of candidates in respect to individual and overall qualification. Thus, the supervisory board may in fact be under a legal obligation to present the representatives' meeting with a proposed resolution in which several non-members are nominated.[58]

Large, exchange-listed insurance undertakings are subject to Provision 5.3.3 of the DCGK [German Corporate Governance Code], which advises creation of a nominating committee to "propose suitable candidates". Most of the relevant insurance undertakings do in fact follow this advice. Yet the company reports are intransparent as to the list of criteria used for determining suitable candidates. Examining the composition of supervisory boards in certain very large insurance undertakings reveals a distinct, unacceptable tendency toward general business qualifications instead of specific insurance-related qualifications for the nominated and elected "candidates". Further, one notes an unmistakable tendency to continue the prior practice of "Deutschland AG" ["Germany, Inc."] in the form of a new system one might call "Europa AG" ["Europe, Inc"].[59]

The already-existing company law overall responsibility of the supervisory board therefore always calls for concomitant overall qualification. With due consideration to the division of labor, this overall qualification can be assessed only by

[56] See 6.2, above.

[57] Under sec. 36 of the VAG [German Insurance Supervision Act], the provision applies also to mutual insurance associations.

[58] Thus specifically for "mutual insurers", OECD (Draft Revised), OECD Guidelines on Insurer Governance, (2010) 33.

[59] In the "non-technical sense" and not related to the SE [Societas Europaea].

including the diverse areas of expertise and competence possessed by the supervisory board members.[60] Corresponding declaratory requirements for the composition of the supervisory and monitoring bodies are found at all events also in the most recent version of Provision 5.4.1 of the DCGK [German Corporate Governance Code], which explicitly prescribes that the composition of the supervisory board must be such that "its members as a whole have the requisite knowledge, abilities, and experience for the proper performance of their duties".[61] The Bulletin of the BaFin [Federal Financial Supervisory Authority] of 21 February 2010[62] unfortunately completely ignores this topic, although, for example, the draft of the OECD Guidelines on Insurer Governance expressly addresses the subject of overall qualification.[63]

In this regard, the requirement of sufficient overall qualification of the supervisory board in its totality is clear at the outset by virtue of general considerations. Consider thus a supervisory board consisting exclusively of members who meet only the mandatory minimum requirements with regard to individual expertise. Such a board could not perform its oversight and monitoring tasks with regard to special supervisory subjects beyond the scope of ordinary business processes, such as implementing a risk management system,[64] reviewing underwriting and actuarial methods, or the corporate, supervisory, and taxation legal issues connected with corporate restructuring. The same would apply to a supervisory board composed of highly specialized risk experts, lawyers, or actuaries, even though in such case the qualification of each individual member would assuredly far exceed the company law and supervisory expertise requirement.

Consequently, in evaluating the sufficiency of overall qualification, the special expertise of the supervisory board members must be considered along with individual expertise requirements. Here, the supervisory board as a whole must offer the range of expertise necessary to correctly evaluate, oversee, and monitor such complex matters as the management of the supervised undertaking engages in.[65] This criterion of overall qualification for the supervisory board permits mutual

[60] Thus BGHZ 85, 293, 296; on this subject from the company law point of view, *Habersack*, in: Münchener Kommentar zum Aktiengesetz [in English: Munich Commentary on the German Stock Corporation Act], n. 8 above, at sec. 116, ref. 24 ff.; *Hopt/Roth*, in: Hopt/Wiedemann eds., n. 8 above, at sec. 116, ref. 44; see, e.g., also *Feddersen*, AG (2000), 385 (393 f.); *Frühauf*, ZGR (1998), 407 (414 ff.); *Möllers*, ZIP (1995), 1725 (1732 ff.); *Seibert*, ZBB (1994), 349 (352); *Scheffler*, ZGR (1993), 63 (71).

[61] See on this point, e.g., *Ringleb/Kremer/Lutter/v. Werder*, NZG (2010), 1161 (1164 f.).

[62] See 6.3.2, above.

[63] See OECD, n. 58 above, at 6 and 32.

[64] For detail on the requirements for oversight of risk management by the supervisory board of an insurance undertaking, see *Schaaf*, ZVersWiss (2009), 613 ff.

[65] Company law in fact provides for appointment of supervisory board members with particular expertise for certain supervisory tasks. See sec. 100, para. 5 of the AktG [German Stock Corporation Act]; for a current case on this point, see OLG München [in English: Munich Higher Regional Court], AG (2010), 639 f.; *Staake*, ZIP (2010), 1013 ff.

attribution of existing diverse expertise and special knowledge of the supervisory board members in such manner that the deficiencies of individual members in given sectors are compensated for by particular expertise of other members. Even beyond this, the supervisory board may readily enlist the aid of experts and consultants to offset deficits in certain areas of competence, pursuant to sec. 109, para. 1, sent. 2 of the AktG [German Stock Corporation Act].

6.5 Summary

1. The Gesetz zur Stärkung der Finanzmarkt- und der Versicherungsaufsicht [Act To Strengthen the Financial Market and Insurance Supervision] of 29 July 2009 led for the first time to original supervisory qualification requirements for members of the supervisory boards of insurance undertakings. Sec. 7a, para. 4, sent. 1 of the VAG [German Insurance Supervision Act] demands that members of the supervisory bodies must possess the requisite expertise to sufficiently perform their monitoring function.
2. With the adoption of the expertise requirement of sec. 7a, para. 4, sent. 1 of the VAG [German Insurance Supervision Act], the legislator codified as supervision law the already existing company law requirements with respect to minimum qualification for members of supervisory and monitoring bodies. The company law requirements for the qualification of supervisory board members previously found by the BGH [German Federal Court of Justice] in its *Hertie* decision in the precept that exercise of office by supervisory board members must be personal and self-dependent and also entered into the German Corporate Governance Code for exchange-listed businesses henceforward apply directly to supervised insurance undertakings by virtue of supervision law. A consequence of this is that further to the company law and liability provisions put in place to ensure minimum qualification of supervisory board members there will now be the possibility of supervisory enforcement with the intervention powers and tools of the VAG [German Insurance Supervision Act].
3. Consequently, the criteria developed under company law must be taken as a basis for interpreting the term "expertise" in sec. 7a, para. 4, sent. 1 of the VAG [German Insurance Supervision Act]. And further, the principles and statements of supervision law and supervisory authorities that have occurred in the meantime must be brought into the assessment. Consequently, the result is that for minimum qualification for members of supervisory and monitoring bodies the criterion of requisite expertise is met if the supervisory board members at the time of assuming office are already capable of comprehending the activities of management as to legal and commercial issues from the perspective of ordinary business processes, of understanding the activities of the particular insurance business, and of evaluating the attendant risks for the undertaking. In accordance with company law requirements, supervision law also permits a structural distinction in the requisite expertise, whose range is primarily determined by

the size of the supervised undertaking as well as by the type and scope of the activities of the particular insurance business.

4. Thus the individual supervisory board member must possess basic knowledge and abilities of how the insurance business works, of accounting and balance sheet preparation, of capital investment, of risk management, and of the legal framework of the insurance business. Particularized knowledge in certain areas is of course required for effective performance of the oversight and monitoring function of the supervisory board, but it is not a defining component of individual expertise pursuant to sec. 7a, para. 4, sent. 1 of the VAG [German Insurance Supervision Act]. Rather, the existence of the appropriate special knowledge and expertise is to be ensured by the operation of the criterion of overall qualification of the supervisory board, a criterion that allows for mutual attribution of the expertise on the supervisory board that exceeds the minimum requirements. With respect to nominations to the supervisory board, the supervisory board as a whole is under a duty to develop appropriate profile requirements and to conform the nominations to that profile.
5. At the very least, the pending implementation of the Solvency II Framework Directive will indirectly impact the requisite minimum qualification for supervisory board members of insurance undertakings. This is so even though the members of supervisory and monitoring bodies are not considered managers or persons having key functions, such as directly covered by the Directive. Solvency II and its accompanying new areas of regulation, particularly with reference to the mandatorily specified establishment of an effective system of governance in insurance undertakings, will nevertheless have indirect impact on the expertise requirement to the extent that supervisory board members for the exercise of their oversight and monitoring tasks must possess in the future—compared to managers—a graduated degree of knowledge in the areas directly controlled by the Directive. It is only in the areas of group supervision that the enhanced qualification requirements of art. 42, para. 1 of the Solvency II Framework Directive, by virtue of express reference, apply directly to the members of supervisory and monitoring bodies of undertakings belonging to groups and of insurance holding companies at the head of a group. The consequence of this is that, in the context of implementing the Solvency II Framework Directive, a special regulatory scheme is needed on the qualification of supervisory board members of undertakings that are under group supervision pursuant to the insurance supervisory regime, unless one intends to increase the requirements for minimum knowledge of all supervisory board members under a uniform regulatory scheme.

Chapter 7
Definition and Holders of Key Functions

Contents

7.1 Introduction 218
7.2 The Term "Key Function" 219
7.2.1 The Key Functions 219
7.2.2 Terminological Dual-Tracking and the Irrelevance of the Difference Between "Key Function" and "Key Task" 220
7.2.3 The Term "Key Functions": Exhaustive or Open? 223
7.3 The Key Function Holders and Their Subordinate Staff Members in Key Functions . 227
7.3.1 The Solvency II System 227
7.3.2 The Equalization of Key Function Holders and Persons Who Effectively Run the Undertaking 228
7.3.3 Factual Distinctions in the Duty of Notice 231
7.3.4 Factual Distinctions in Qualification Requirements 231
7.3.5 Determination of Each Key Function Holder and the Staff Members Subordinate to Them 232
7.4 Summary 241

Abstract This chapter takes up the four key functions established in the Solvency II Directive. In this vein, the significance of the key functions is highlighted first. Then follows the analysis of the terms "key function" and "key function holders", terms undefined in the Solvency II Directive. The next step points out the distinctions among key function holders and their subordinate staff members. A part of this breakdown is to examine in practice who exercises which function in an

First published as "Begriff und Inhaber der Schlüsselfunktionen nach Solvency II und VAG 2012" [in English: Concept and Holders of Key Functions under Solvency II and the VAG 2012 [German Insurance Supervision Act 2012]], VersR (2012), 933 ff. Note to the reader: Eventually, the VAG 2012 did not take effect, but was postponed. Therefore, in the following text, VAG 2012 must be read as "2012 Government's Draft of a Tenth Act Amending the German Insurance Supervision Act".

M. Dreher, *Treatises on Solvency II*, DOI 10.1007/978-3-662-46290-4_7

insurance undertaking. The chapter wraps up by looking at whether key functions are performed in a centralized or decentralized organization.

7.1 Introduction

The term "key function" has a generally positive connotation. It suggests responsibility and importance. But it has hardly seen use as a legal term.[1] This will change when the rules of Solvency II and their implementation in the new VAG 2012 [German Insurance Supervision Act 2012][2] take effect. This is so because the term "key function" is the starting point for numerous rules of the insurance supervisory regime. These are directed at both insurance and reinsurance undertaking[3] and their staff members in certain roles as well as at the insurance supervisory authorities. Also at issue are important elements in the governance of insurance undertakings and their monitoring by supervisory authorities.

Against this background, the present article aims first to clarify the term "key function" under European law and the employment of that term in the German insurance supervisory regime (below, 7.2). The discussion then turns to the question of which staff members are in key functions, and in what capacity (below, 7.3). Numerous other questions emerge from this concerning, for example, the requirements to ensure the expertise of such persons and that they are fit and proper for this role, their compensation, their duties of disclosure and notification with respect to the supervisory authority or the public, and whether the supervisory authority can recall certain persons or prohibit them to exercise the relevant duties. These questions will be the topic of a subsequent article.[4] Excluded or only touched

---

[1] See sec. 15, para. 1, sent. 7, no. 2 of the InhKontrollVO [Holder Control Regulation]: "as well as disclosure of material changes with respect to internal audit and the compliance function, and any change to members of senior management in key functions". The term "key position" is also widespread in the German legislation. On this point see, for example, sec. 2, para. 3, no. 5 of the MaKonV [Market Manipulation Definition Ordinance].

[2] RegE eines Zehnten Gesetzes zur Änderung des VAG [Government's Draft of a Tenth Act Amending the German Insurance Supervision Act] of 15 Feb. 2012, BT-Drucks. [Document of the German Bundestag] 17/9342; also, BT-Drucks. [Document of the German Bundestag] 90/12 (hereafter: VAG-RegE).

[3] Any mention of insurance undertakings in this chapter includes reinsurance undertakings.

[4] *Dreher*, "Die aufsichtsbehördliche Kontrolle der Inhaber von Schlüsselfunktionen nach Solvency II und künftigem VAG 2012" [in English: Review by Supervisory Authorities of the Key Function Holders under Solvency II and the Future German Insurance Supervision Act 2012], VersR (2012), 1061 (Chap. 8, below).

upon as the subject matter of either essay, however, are other issues associated with the topic of key functions, particularly the relationship of individual key functions to one another,[5] the independence and segregation of key functions,[6] and the effects of outsourcing on key functions.[7]

7.2 The Term "Key Function"

7.2.1 The Key Functions

7.2.1.1 Solvency II

At the first regulatory level of the new European insurance supervisory regime, the Solvency II Directive,[8] the term "key function" is initially found in Recital 33. In this provision, the European issuer of the Directive establishes that certain functions within an undertaking "are considered to be key functions".[9] In the view of the issuer, these are "consequently also important and critical functions". Recital 33 of the Solvency II Directive further clarifies which functions are key functions under the law: "The functions included in the system of governance are considered to be key functions". It thus refers to the four functions specified in art. 13, no. 29 of the Solvency II Directive, which are set forth as mandatory in art. 41 ff. of the Solvency II Directive concerning the "system of governance" for all insurance undertakings. The four functions are the risk-management function, the compliance function, the internal audit function, and the actuarial function.

7.2.1.2 VAG 2012 [German Insurance Supervision Act 2012]

Sec. 8 no. 11 of the VAG 2012 [German Insurance Supervision Act 2012] includes the four governance functions as found in art. 13, no. 29 of the Solvency II Directive. However, the overarching term here is not "governance", but "business organization". Also absent in the implementation is a section equivalent to Recital 33 of the Solvency II Directive. Thus, the VAG 2012 [German Insurance

---

[5] On this point see *Bürkle*, "Compliance und Revision im Versicherungssektor nach Solvency II" [in English: Compliance and Review in the Insurance Industry under Solvency II], CCZ (2012), 220.

[6] See, however, on the improper conflation of independence and independence of procedure, below, 7.3.5.3.

[7] On this point see *Dreher* id., n. 4 above, at II 2 b).

[8] Directive 2009/138/EU of the European Parliament and of the Council of 25 Nov. 2009, OJEU L 335, p. 1, of 17 Dec. 2009.

[9] A different form of "key function" is assigned under Recital 104 of the Solvency II Directive, but only "to a group supervisor" in a regulatory sense.

Supervision Act 2012] does not designate the governance functions as key functions. Given the primacy of the European law and the provisions found there, it may be said that this omission is essentially harmless. However, if the functions of the business organization are not coupled with the term "key functions", the regulatory system becomes needlessly intransparent for those who apply the law but are not familiar with the European insurance supervisory regime. Furthermore and most importantly, the legislator will be passing up the opportunity to mirror the central terminology of the European insurance supervisory regime in the national insurance supervisory regime at what is called the "fourth regulatory level" although this would be in the interest of a uniform classification. This means that an essential new term will already be missing in the definitional provision of sec. 8, no. 11 of the new VAG 2012 [German Insurance Supervision Act 2012], even though numerous later provisions within the VAG [German Insurance Supervision Act], are tied to it.

Hence, VAG 2012 [German Insurance Supervision Act 2012] makes reference to the key functions in sec. 8 no. 11 only as follows:

> the business organization includes the risk-management function, the compliance function, the internal audit function, and the actuarial function.

The rules for each key function follow, with the risk management function—to further semantic confusion, however, in its terminological use of "risk controlling function" deviating from European law—in sec. 27, para. 5 of the VAG 2012 [German Insurance Supervision Act 2012], the compliance function in sec. 29, paras. 1 and 2 of the VAG 2012 [German Insurance Supervision Act 2012], the internal audit function in sec. 30 of the VAG 2012 [German Insurance Supervision Act 2012], and the actuarial function in sec. 31 of the VAG 2012 [German Insurance Supervision Act 2012].

7.2.2 *Terminological Dual-Tracking and the Irrelevance of the Difference Between "Key Function" and "Key Task"*

7.2.2.1 Solvency II

In the German version of the Solvency II Directive, the term "Schlüsselaufgabe" [in English: key task] is seen in addition to the term "Schlüsselfunktion" [in English: key function]. The German "Schlüsselaufgabe" is found only in art. 42, paras. 1 and 2 of the Directive, where it is rendered as "key function" in the English language version. In para. 1, it concerns the fit-and-proper requirements for "all persons who effectively run the undertaking or have other key functions". In para. 2 however, it refers to the duty of notice on the part of the insurance undertaking with respect to the supervisory authority and applies to "any changes to the identity of the persons who effectively run the undertaking or are responsible for other key functions".

In numerous other official languages of the Solvency II Directive—such as the English, French, and Dutch versions—this terminological dual-tracking does not occur. In these versions, a single term—"key function" in the English—is used throughout, including in art. 42, paras. 1 and 2 of the Directive. While the Solvency II Directive does see dual-track terminological structures here and there—for example, in the Spanish and Italian language versions—they differ from those found in the German version. Specifically, in these cases, the Directive uses the term "fundamental function" (English equivalent) in both art. 42 as well as art. 44 of the Solvency II Directive while choosing a different term in Recitals 33 through 35 of the Directive.

Under the European methodology, as established in the jurisprudence of the European Court of Justice, the interpretation of secondary law, which starts with the wording, must take all language versions into consideration. Majority rule does not apply here. Instead, in cases where language divergence could result in divergence of content, an interpretation according to the context and purpose of the rule is required.[10] In the present context, there has been no apparent divergence in content. In the Solvency II Directive, some language versions proceed exclusively from the term "key function" in the relevant Recitals 33 f. and art. 42, paras. 1, 2 as well as 44 para. 1 subpara. 2 of the Directive—each in the German conception—and thus feature a terminological difference between the recitals and articles or—as in the German language version—between the recitals and art. 44 of the Directive on one hand and art. 42 of the Directive on the other. Ultimately, the broader picture that emerges is quite clear. In the Solvency II Directive, for these recitals and the relevant articles the matter at hand is not the diffusion of different content through different terminology. Rather, it is concerned with emphasizing specific functions. It achieves this emphasis in the majority of individual language versions with systematic uniformity and consistency. But for those language versions that deviate and incorporate linguistic dual-tracking, their apparent arbitrariness does not detract from the sole objective of emphasizing specific functions. It can therefore be presumed, in summary, that the terminological distinction between "key function" and "key task" in the German language version of the Solvency II Directive serves no larger contextual significance other than emphasizing the special importance of the respective function.

This equivalence of key function and key task provided by the European law is confirmed in provisions at Levels 2 and 3 of the Solvency system. The DVO[11] uses the term "key function" exclusively in five different articles and regulatory

---

[10] See, e.g., *Riesenhuber*, in: Riesenhuber (ed.), Europäische Methodenlehre [in English: European Methodology] (2nd ed. 2010), sec. 11 ref. 15 ff.; *Neuner*, in: Riesenhuber (ed.), Europäische Methodenlehre [in English: European Methodology] (2nd ed. 2010), sec. 13 ref. 17.

[11] The abbreviation DVO when used here and after in reference to the Level 2 DVO signifies the EU Commission draft known as Draft Implementing Measures Solvency II, 31 Oct. 2011.

statements. The same can be seen in the very frequent use of only this term in the draft of the CEIOPS Consultation Paper, Draft proposal for Level 3 Guidelines on the System of Governance of December 2010.[12] Under art. 71, para. 2, sent. 2 of the Solvency II Directive, the supervisory authorities of the Member States are required to "take [these guidelines] duly into account". But in sec. 324, para. 1, sent. 2 of the VAG 2012 [German Insurance Supervision Act 2012], the restriction imposed by the word "duly" is omitted.[13]

7.2.2.2 VAG 2012 [German Insurance Supervision Act 2012]

Sec. 25 VAG 2012 [German Insurance Supervision Act 2012], which is the provision concerned with the expertise and personal qualifications of certain representatives and staff members of the undertaking based on art. 42 of the Solvency II Directive, likewise refers to persons who effectively run the insurance undertaking "or perform other key tasks". In this respect, sec. 25, para. 1, sent. 1 of the VAG 2012 [German Insurance Supervision Act 2012] follows the wording in the requirement of art. 42 of the Solvency II Directive. Unlike the Solvency II Directive, however, the VAG [German Insurance Supervision Act] draft immediately obscures the difference between key function and key task in the German language version of the Solvency II Directive again. This transpires because, according to the Statement of Reasons for sec. 25 of the VAG 2012 [German Insurance Supervision Act 2012], "the four functions specified in this paragraph (the risk-controlling function, compliance function, actuarial function, internal audit), at a minimum, are considered to be other key tasks".[14]

This means that, while according to the German language version of the Solvency II Directive, the use of the different terms "key function" and "key task" is not particularly necessary, the VAG [German Insurance Supervision Act] draft asserts that the key functions of the Solvency II Directive "are considered" key tasks. Finding a reason for this approach becomes just as difficult as discerning a legally sound system in this sort of labyrinthine national regulation. All the same, "function" has a prior definition in sec. 8, no. 11 of the VAG 2012 [German Insurance Supervision Act 2012] as "an internal capacity within the business organization for the assumption of practical tasks". According to the Statement of Reasons for sec. 25 of the VAG 2012 [German Insurance Supervision Act 2012],

---

[12] Hereafter: Governance Guidelines.

[13] On this point see also *Sasserath-Alberti/Hartig*, "EIOPA-Verordnung: Herausforderungen für die Praxis" [in English: EIOPA Regulation: Challenges for Practitioners], VersR (2012), 524 (530).

[14] VAG-RegE [Government's Draft of a Tenth Act Amending the German Insurance Supervision Act], id. n. 2 above, at Statement of Reasons for sec. 25 VAG [German Insurance Supervision Act] at 272. Against the use of the term "key task", Bundesrat [German Federal Council], Response to the VAG-RegE [Government's Draft of a Tenth Act Amending the German Insurance Supervision Act], BR-Drucks. [Document of the German Bundesrat] 90/12 sent. 4.

then, the functions should themselves be considered key tasks. Even using a generous standard for the semantics of legislative bases, the addressee of the legal rule could expect from the implementing German legislator, in view of the already convoluted terminology in the Directive's provisions, consistency between the content of the law, namely, function as the capacity to assume a task, and the justification for the law, namely, function as task. Indeed, it should be presumed that Recital 33 of Solvency II Directive has some influence on the law's statement of reasons. But according to the Recital, the governance functions "are considered" to be "key functions". This coherent statement runs counter to the Statement of Reasons for sec. 25 of the VAG 2012 [German Insurance Supervision Act 2012] as it concerns substitution of the term "key function" with "key task". Because of the primacy of the European law, however, the only relevant terminology and content from a legal standpoint are found exclusively in the three levels of Solvency II. This ultimately leads us to the equivalence of the terms "key function" and "key task", which has already been established.[15]

7.2.3 The Term "Key Functions": Exhaustive or Open?

The Solvency II Directive provides for four governance functions as key functions.[16] Numerous legal questions arise when a function is classified as a key function.[17] Thus, from a legal point of view, under the sub heading of "the term of key function" lies the question of whether the term is exhaustively defined by the European insurance supervisory regime as the four governance functions or remains open to other applications. This is so because only in the latter case could key functions be expanded by national insurance supervisory law.

The Statement of Reasons for the VAG 2012 [German Insurance Supervision Act 2012] readily assumes but only indirectly states that the term "key function" is open and that application of the term is not exhausted with respect to content by the four governance functions. It offers the following on this point:

> The four functions specified in this paragraph (the risk-controlling function, compliance function, actuarial function, internal audit), at a minimum, are considered to be other key tasks. However, depending on the circumstances of the respective undertaking, additional areas can be viewed as key tasks if these have considerable importance to the business operations of the undertaking.[18]

---

[15] See above, at 7.2.2.1.

[16] See above, at 7.2.1.

[17] See list above, at 7.1.

[18] VAG-RegE [Government's Draft of a Tenth Act Amending the German Insurance Supervision Act], id. n. 2 above, at Statement of Reasons for sec. 25 VAG [German Insurance Supervision Act] at 272.

Based, then, on the equivalence previously discussed of the four key functions and the key tasks of the VAG 2012 [German Insurance Supervision Act 2012],[19] the catalog of key functions would not be exhaustive. On the other hand, all the Solvency II rules connected with the term "key function" and with the presence of key tasks would necessarily apply to any additional key functions or key tasks under the VAG 2012 [German Insurance Supervision Act 2012]. The criteria—which are entirely undefined—solely relevant to such expansion and its validity should, according to the Statement of Reasons for the VAG [German Insurance Supervision Act] draft, be the "considerable importance" of an "area" of an insurance undertaking "to business operations" according to "the circumstances of the respective undertaking".

The question then arises as to whether the Solvency II Directive itself has an open or closed conception of the key functions. The starting point for answering this question is Recital 33 of the Solvency II Directive. In the various language versions the Directive, the Recital consistently restricts the designation of key function to the four governance functions. There is nothing to indicate that additional key functions are possible. This is also true with respect to use of the term "key function" in the very text of the Directive, where only the governance functions and not core operating functions, of an insurance undertaking are counted as the key functions. Recitals 98 f. and the relevant articles of the DVO lead to the same conclusion. At both Level 1 and Level 2, the phrase "persons who effectively run the undertaking or have other key functions"[20] is found repeatedly. But nowhere do the texts suggest that there could be or even needs to be any additional key functions in an insurance undertaking, nor do they allude to which key functions those might be. The phrase is meant only to convey that key functions have a particularly significant role. This is the only interpretation of the phrase that is consistent with the special, legally far-reaching rules imposed on them.[21]

The notion that other key functions may exist beyond the four governance functions, is found only at Level 3 in the explanations to the Governance Guidelines.[22] It is found in the following text in the introduction:

> Persons having key functions include all persons performing tasks related to a key function. At least the functions included in the system of governance, risk management, compliance, actuarial and internal audit, are considered to be key functions and consequently also important and critical functions.

Thus the use of the words "at least" in the Statement of Reasons for sec. 25 of the VAG 2012 [German Insurance Supervision Act 2012] has an equivalent in the

---

[19] See above, at 7.2.2.2.

[20] In the German version: "Personen, die das Unternehmen tatsächlich leiten oder andere Schlüsselfunktionen innehaben".

[21] See in detail on this point below, at 7.3.2.

[22] Governance Guidelines ref. 1.10.

Solvency system only at Level 3, namely in the words "at least" in the Level 3 Governance Guidelines. In the explanation to Guideline 14, it is further presumed that insurance undertakings notify the supervisory authority as to which functions are deemed key functions, and on what basis.[23]

But nothing is yet indicated about the legal effect with respect to the more basic question. While, according to the jurisprudence of the European Court of Justice, Level 2 rules may indeed go beyond Level 1 provisions,[24] such a relationship does not apply between the essentially non-binding Level 3 guidelines and the regulations of Levels 1 and 2. In terms of timing, the Guidelines were created prior to the DVO draft. And they are non-binding.[25] To view it otherwise would legitimize wide-ranging requirements on insurance undertakings that involve supervisory intervention[26] into basic rights without a legal basis at Level 1 or 2 simply as a result of Level 3 Guidelines. The CEIOPS Governance Guidelines—for example, in Guideline 5[27]—extend the mandate of independence under art. 41, para. 1 of the Solvency II Directive and art. 258 SG6 of the DVO to all "key functions". If the definition of "key function" under the Guidelines were simultaneously open, it could no longer be the basis for insurance supervision in accordance with the rule of law by the principle of legal certainty in the supervision of legality under art. 34, para. 1 and art. 36 of the Solvency II Directive. Intensive supervisory monitoring, with the potential for severe sanctions, of persons and activities in additional key functions, not established by law, that exist under entirely undefined criteria would mean a step backward to the earlier general supervision according to the principles of abusiveness, which is no longer permissible[28] under Solvency II. In the end, even the BaFin [German Federal Financial Supervisory Authority] would designate individual business functions as key functions, thereby determining their own scope of supervision.

Furthermore, there is this: The provisions of the Solvency II Directive, except where the numerous rights of election afforded to the Member States and where

---

[23] See Explanation 3.57 (c) of the Governance Guidelines.

[24] See *Dreher/Lange*, "Die Vollharmonisierung der Versicherungsaufsicht durch Solvency II" [in English: Full Harmonization of Insurance Supervision under Solvency II] VersR (2011), 825 (829) (Chap. 1, above, at 1.3.2) with further references.

[25] See Governance Guidelines, 1 with further references.

[26] *Bürkle*, in: Fahr/Kaulbach/Bär/Pohlmann, VAG [in English: The Insurance Supervision Act] (5th ed. 2012) in Solvabilität II [in English: Solvency II], ref. 77 appropriately refers to the relevance of art. 12, para. 1 of the Grundgesetz für die Bundesrepublik Deutschland [in English: Basic Law for the Federal Republic of Germany] and art. 15, para. 1 of the Charter of Fundamental Rights of the European Union.

[27] Governance Guidelines, id., n. 12 above, at ref. 2.5.

[28] See on this point *Dreher/Lange*, VersR (2011), 825 (831 f.) (Chap. 1, above, at 1.4.2); *Bürkle*, "Die Zukunft der materiellen Versicherungsaufsicht in Deutschland" [in English: The Future of Substantive Insurance Supervision in Germany], VersR (2011), 1469 (1472 ff.); *Bürkle/Grote*, "Die aufsichtsbehördlichen Eingriffsbefugnisse nach Solvency II" [in English: Supervisory Intervention Powers under Solvency II] in: Dreher/Wandt, eds., Solvency II in der Rechtsanwendung [in English: Solvency II in Legal Application] (2009), 191 ff. and 225 ff.

only minimum standards are set,[29] lean toward full harmonization.[30] Any deviation from the term "key function" as it is understood in the Solvency II Directive by the insurance supervisory regime of Member States is no more provided for in the Directive than a Member State's right of election in relation to it. Regardless of the CEIOPS Governance Guidelines, the German legislator cannot expand the scope of sec. 25 of the VAG 2012 [German Insurance Supervision Act 2012] to the effect that "additional areas [. . .] of considerable importance" aside from the four governance functions must be viewed as key functions within the meaning of the insurance supervisory regime. The authors of the Statement of Reasons for sec. 25 of the VAG 2012 [German Insurance Supervision Act 2012] are apparently led astray by the word "other". This is evident in the statement that the four governance functions, at a minimum, should be considered as "other tasks". The statement completely misconstrues the telos of the phrase "persons who effectively run the undertaking or have other key functions", which was discussed previously in the article. Specifically, the phrase is meant to emphasize the significance of other key functions, meaning the four governance functions, in relation to the—staying with the terminology—key function of effectively running the undertaking. It is not intended to represent an opening or invitation within the term "key functions" to include other functions in the undertaking as key functions. Therefore, regardless of the undertaking's individual hierarchical structure, the heads of any legitimately or effectively prominent business function at the undertaking, other than the governance functions in insurance undertakings, are never, in this capacity, key function holders within the meaning of the insurance supervisory regime.[31] This applies, for example, to the actuary, the head of the legal department, the director of the department for prevention and control of money laundering as well as senior staff in the areas of investment, data security, capital investment, accounting, marketing/communications and IT.

---

[29] See the use of the term "at least" or "not less than" in the Solvency II Directive.

[30] In detail *Dreher/Lange,* VersR (2011), 825 (Chap. 1, above); *Bürkle,* VersR 2011, 1469 (1472 f.); *Wandt/Sehrbrock*, "Regelungsziele der Solvency II-Rahmenrichtlinie" [in English: Regulatory Objectives of the Solvency II Framework Directive], ZVersWiss 2011, 193 (200). On an unclear basis – "The Directive does not prescribe full harmonization in all areas" – and inconsistent with continuing the VAG's [German Insurance Supervision Act's] existing law in RegE eines Zehnten Gesetzes zur Änderung des VAG [Government's Draft of a Tenth Act Amending the German Insurance Supervision Act] of 15 Feb. 2012, BT-Drucks. [Document of the German Bundestag] 17/9342, p. 255. Contra, based on the principle of full harmonization, BR-Drucks. [Document of the German Bundesrat] 90/12 at 2 f. in substance and at 13 explicitly. Also in support of full harmonization – even in confusing the terms full harmonization and maximum harmonization – staff member of the Austrian Federal Ministry of Finance *Wagner*, "Solvabilität II und VAG neu: Was bleibt, was ändert sich?" [in English: Solvency II and the New German Insurance Supervision Act: What is Unchanged? What is Changed?], VersRdsch 9/2010, 23 (24, 26).

[31] The opposite can apply when such a person is properly assigned the leadership of a key function in addition.

7.3 The Key Function Holders and Their Subordinate Staff Members in Key Functions

7.3.1 The Solvency II System

The Solvency II Directive reveals a surprising multiplicity of terms in the areas that deal with persons engaged in key functions. The German language version speaks of "Wahrnehmen" (Recital 34), "Verantwortlichsein" (art. 42, para. 2), and "Innehaben" (Recitals 34, 35; art. 26, para. 3 and 42, para. 1 and 44, para. 1 subpara. 2). The English language version recognizes the terms "perform" (Recital 34), "holder" (Recital 34), "responsible" (art. 42, para. 2) and "have" (Recital 35; art. 26 para. 3 and 42, para. 1 and 44, para. 1 subpara. 2). The French version uses "exercent" (Recital 34), "titulaire" (Recital 34), "ont" (Recital 35), "ocupent" (art. 26, para. 3 and 42, para. 1 and 44, para. 1 subpara. 2) and "assument" (art. 42, para. 2). The Spanish language version has the terms "ejerzan" (Recital 34, art. 44, para. 1 subpara. 2), "titulares" (Recital 34), "empeñen" (Recital 35; art. 26 para. 3 and 42, para. 1) and "responsables" (art. 42, para. 2). In other official languages, the same picture emerges of inconsistent use across a great multiplicity of terms—the Italian language version alone recognizes five different words for the activities under discussion, appearing across just six rules.

The DVO is no different. It generally contains the term "have" (Recital 99; arts. 251 SG3, 263 SG11, para. 1, and 285, para. 2 a and b), but it also uses the words "responsible" (Recital 98 sent. 1 and art. 297 SRS4, para. 2 a), "perform" (art. 258 SG6, paras. 3 and 4)[32] and "holders" (art. 265 SG13, para. 1 c).

Faced with this multiplicity of terms, only the wording of the Level 1 and 2 texts can only give first hints for making further distinctions in a system of diverse legal requirements. It is then apparent from the start that the Directive and the DVO intend to distinguish between persons who "hold" a key function and are "responsible" for it and those who "perform" tasks that are part of a key function. This linguistic distinction, however, is not strictly respected in the text of the rules and it becomes further blurred by the excessive use of additional words that are somewhat synonymous.

In light of these circumstances, the definition of persons who are legally included in the Solvency II Directive and the DVO in various ways is in need of additional systematic and teleological clarity. The starting point is the substantive differences seen in the Solvency II provisions beyond simply the terminology.

[32] Although art. 258 SG6 of the DVO refers only to "functions" and not "key functions", the rules apply to the key functions because they have a legal basis that exclusively refers to key functions in art. 50, para. 1 b of the Solvency II Directive.

7.3.2 *The Equalization of Key Function Holders and Persons Who Effectively Run the Undertaking*

7.3.2.1 The Normative Point of Departure

The foundation for this systematic and teleological approach is the equalization of persons who hold "other" key functions with "persons who effectively run the undertaking". This equalization is evident in Recital 35 and in art. 26, para. 3 and 42, para. 1 and 42, para. 2 as well as 44, para. 1, subpara. 2 of the Solvency II Directive, and also in Recital 98, sent. 1 and 99, art. 251 SG3, 263 SG11, para. 1, 265 SG13, para. 1 c as well as 285 PDS4, para. 2 a and b of the DVO. The Solvency II Directive places special requirements on this type of management personnel because their actual management responsibilities with or even—and herein lies the special significance of rule—without their formal membership in management make them distinct in the risk-oriented nature of the Solvency II system.[33] In addition to management, meaning the managing board of an insurance undertaking operating under a dual structure, there are both general agents in the subsidiary offices of insurance undertakings[34]—at least according to the VAG 2012 [German Insurance Supervision Act 2012]—as well as the few de facto members of management body as laid down in company law.[35] At issue is whether and which of the staff members subordinate to management are included in this group of persons with special significance.

7.3.2.2 The System, Telos and Scope of Equalization

The word "other" preceding "key functions" in the text of the Solvency II rules is intended to establish equalization with the responsibilities assumed for the "effective running of the business". This is so because only through this word is the responsibility associated with a key function effectively elevated to the level of management of the undertaking, and thus it confers the necessary importance required for such equalization.[36] It is not, on the other hand, intended to expand the circle of key function holders. This conclusion can be drawn directly from the legal consequences associated with such classification. The far-ranging fit-and-proper requirements of Solvency II[37] can be justified only if a responsible person in the undertaking holds a

[33] See in detail *Dreher* "Die Solvenzanforderungen in der Versicherungsaufsicht nach Solvency II und VAG-RegE" [in English: Solvency Requirements in Insurance Supervision under Solvency II and VAG-RegE [Government's Draft of a Tenth Act Amending the German Insurance Supervision Act]], ZVersWiss (2012), 381 (Chap. 4, above).

[34] See sec. 25, para. 2, sent. 2 of the VAG 2012 [German Insurance Supervision Act 2012].

[35] See for more detail, e.g., *Schürnbrand*, Organschaft im Recht der privaten Verbände [in English: Governing Bodies in the Law of Private Associations] (2007), 294 ff.

[36] See above, 7.2.3.

[37] See on this point *Dreher* id., n. 4 above, at II and III.

position so distinct that it warrants essentially the same high requirements imposed on members of the managing board. This is consistently expressed in the Solvency II system at Levels 1 and 2 in that it distinguishes the management generally understood to be a core function in an insurance undertaking[38] from "other key functions" which—apart from the activities of supervisory board members, to be addressed presently—are understood to be the four governance functions only.[39] So called senior management, then, is also not part of this level.[40]

7.3.2.3 The Special Question of Equalization of Supervisory Board Members

While the activities in key functions other than management exhaustively restrict the addressees of the legislation and demarcate them from levels below, the question remains—at least in the dual governance system—as whether the supervisory board overseeing the managing board forms another key function in this sense. Even before the submission of the draft of the DVO for the Solvency II Directive and draft of the VAG 2012 [German Insurance Supervision Act 2012], some of the literature[41] had been including supervisory board members as key function holders, making reference to earlier papers from CEIOPS.[42] But this runs counter to both the wording and the system of the Solvency II Directive. This is so because arts. 248 and 257 extend the fit-and-proper requirements only to members of supervisory boards for undertakings that are members of a group or for insurance

---

[38] See on the significance of management responsibility in general and the associated limits on delegation authority from a corporate law view *Dreher*, "Nicht delegierbare Geschäftsleiterpflichten" [in English: Non-delegable Duties of Business Managers] in Festschrift für [Publication in Honor of] Klaus J. Hopt on his 70th Birthday on 24 August 2010 (2010), 517 (518 ff.) with further references, and concerning horizontal and vertical delegation under Solvency II, id., ZVersWiss (2012), at 4.1.1.3.

[39] See above, 7.2.3.

[40] See on this point *Dreher*, "Das senior management der Versicherungsunternehmen und das künftige Versicherungsaufsichtsrecht" [in English: Senior Management of Insurance Undertakings and the Future Insurance Supervisory Regime], VersR 2013, 35 (Chap. 9, below).

[41] See *Schaaf*, "Risikomanagement und Compliance in Versicherungsunternehmen – aufsichtsrechtliche Anforderungen und Organverantwortung", [in English: Risk Management and Compliance in Insurance Undertakings – Supervisory Requirements and Institutional Responsibility] (2010), 242 f.; refuting, *A. Hasse*, "Informations- und Offenlegungspflichten der Versicherungsunternehmen nach Solvency II" [in English: Information and Disclosure Obligations for Insurance Undertakings under Solvency II] in: Dreher/Wandt, eds., Solvency II in der Rechtsanwendung [in English: Solvency II in Legal Application] (2009), 61 (80 ff.).

[42] See CEIOPS, Issue Paper "New risk management and other corporate issues" (17 Jul. 2007) under 2.2; CEIOPS, Issue Paper "Implementing measures on systems of governance" (3 Nov. 2008) under 5.

holding companies.[43] However, art. 263 SG 11 para. 3 DVO, which was published only afterwards, contained not only—as in art. 249, no. 1 c of the DVO—a reference to the usual triad of "administrative body", "supervisory body", and "management body",[44] but also the two management body activities, "managed" and "overseen". This could be misunderstood as meaning that the rule intends to view even supervisory board members as being encompassed by the Solvency II Directive in art. 42, i.e. the underlying rule to be concretized.[45]

However, such a far-reaching question as the inclusion of all supervisory board members in fit-and-proper supervision under European law is not posed by a single word in the subject matter of the DVO. Rather, the choice of words can be explained quite simply by looking at either the monistic system of corporate entities in some Member States or, in the dual system, at the activities of the managing board that encompass organizational and supervisory duties in a company.[46] The new consultation paper of European Banking Authority for the fit-and-proper supervision of lending institutions distinguishes clearly between supervisory board members, managing board members and key function holders.[47]

Regardless of this, the German legislator expressly continues the current qualifications monitoring of sec. 7 a, para. 4 of the VAG [German Insurance Supervision Act][48] in sec. 25 of VAG 2012 [German Insurance Supervision Act 2012], referring to supervisory board members as "persons who hold other key functions".[49] In effect, this does only appear permissible from the view of the result but not based on the derivation in the European law of "other key functions"—even not on the basis of the view presented above, that the Solvency II Directive subjects only supervisory board members of certain undertakings to such monitoring and

---

[43] See in detail *Dreher/Lange*, "Die Qualifikation der Aufsichtsratsmitglieder von Versicherungsunternehmen nach VAG und Solvency II" [in English: Qualifications of Supervisory Board Members of Insurance Undertakings under the German Insurance Supervision Act and Solvency II], ZVersWiss (2011), 211 (220 ff.) (Chap. 6, above, at 6.3.3.1).

[44] This is overlooked by *Krauel/Broichhausen,* "Zu den Qualifikationsanforderungen an Aufsichtsräte in Versicherungsunternehmen vor dem Hintergrund von Solvency II" [in English: About Qualification Requirements for Board Members Against the Background of Solvency II], VersR 2012, 823 (824), who thus draw too far-reaching consequences from art. 249 DVO [Draft Implementing Measures Solvency II] and early CEIOPS papers.

[45] See legal basis in art. 50 para. 1 c of the Solvency II Directive.

[46] See in detail concerning the term "management" within the meaning of company law *Dreher* id., at n. 38 above, 518 ff.

[47] See European Banking Authority, "Consultation paper on draft Guidelines for assessing the suitability of members of the management body and key function holders of a credit institution" (18 Apr. 2012), and concerning this *Nikopoulos,* BaFin-Journal (May 2012), 17.

[48] See on this point for more detail *Dreher*, "Ausstrahlungen des Aufsichtsrechts auf das Aktienrecht" [in English: Effects of Supervisory Law on Corporation Law], ZGR (2010), 496 (508 ff.).

[49] VAG-RegE [Government's Draft of a Tenth Act Amending the German Insurance Supervision Act], id. n. 2 above, at Statement of Reasons for sec. 25 VAG [German Insurance Supervision Act] at 272.

that it leans toward full harmonization.[50] The qualifications required for supervisory board membership are based on a broader approach to company law in Germany for the type of qualifications monitoring currently applied to the supervisory board members of financial service undertakings, which will continue to be applied in the future. This, however, has no bearing on the question of which persons other than members of the management and supervisory boards are key function holders.

7.3.3 *Factual Distinctions in the Duty of Notice*

Insurance undertakings have duties of notice to the supervisory authority with respect to key function holders.[51] These duties are significant in the present context to the extent that they differentiate between the various persons who perform activities in the four key functions. According to the version consistent across numerous official languages, the duty of notice set forth in art. 42, para. 2 of the Solvency II Directive extends only to those who are "responsible" for the key functions.[52] The same is true at the DVO level under art. 297 SRS4, para. 2 a and at Level 3 under the Governance Guidelines.[53]

This choice of terms corresponds to the one used in the Solvency II provision presented previously concerning persons who effectively run the insurance undertaking. In addition, in Recital 34 of the Solvency II Directive there is an explicit distinction corresponding to art. 42, para. 2 of the Solvency II Directive made between those who hold key functions and all others who perform activities within the scope of a key function. This recital also states that the duty of notice to the supervisory authority applies only "to the key function holders". The same is reflected in Recital 98 of the DVO. Thus, the Solvency II Directive and the DVO attach special legal consequences to the position singled out. This, too, illustrates that key function holders occupy these positions from within the key functions themselves, which allows them to be distinguished from other staff members who perform tasks in the key functions.

7.3.4 *Factual Distinctions in Qualification Requirements*

The insurance undertaking's obligations under supervision law with respect to the fit-and-proper requirements for key function holders eventually lead to the same conclusion.[54] As with the duty of notice above, here, too, the Solvency II Directive

---

[50] See above, at 7.2.1.

[51] For detail on this point see *Dreher* id., n. 4 above, at V.

[52] See, e.g., the German, English, Spanish, and Italian language versions of the Solvency II Directive.

[53] See Governance Guidelines, id., n. 12 above, at ref. 1.11, sent. 2 and 3.57.

[54] See in detail on this point *Dreher* id., n. 4 above, at II and III.

makes the distinction between key function holders and all other persons who perform tasks in these areas—with equivalent distinctions appearing in the DVO and the CEIOPS Governance Guidelines. In sum, this follows from Recital 35 and art. 42 of the Solvency II Directive.[55] For the present analysis it suffices to see confirmation in the Solvency II rules on this legal question of the legally relevant distinction between key function holders and other staff members in key functions.

7.3.5 Determination of Each Key Function Holder and the Staff Members Subordinate to Them

7.3.5.1 The Restriction to Natural Persons

From the previously considered rules of the Solvency II system regarding key function holders,[56] it now follows that only natural persons and not legal persons or other groups of persons can be key function holders. This is suggested not merely by the terms used in connection with persons who perform activities within key functions. The conclusion is derived even more directly from the equalization with "persons" who effectively run the undertaking and from the duty of notice, as well as the fit-and-proper rules and the rules governing qualifications for key function holders, all of which quite obviously presume natural persons as the addressees of the rules.

7.3.5.2 Institutional and Functional Determination of Terms

The basis for determining which persons are key function holders in the legal sense is an institutional analysis. In this analysis, the key function holder is always a person in the undertaking's organization who—according to the criteria formulated below[57]—is responsible for a key function as a director or deputy director of such staff unit or department, or accountable for a material portion of a key function within the same, according to the individual policies of the undertaking mandated under art. 41, para. 3 of the Solvency II Directive or sec. 24, para. 3 of the VAG 2012. Therefore, the group of key function holders in a legal sense is already evident from the insurance undertaking's organization chart for the highest level in each of the four key functions. At the subordinate levels, however, it is derived only from the circumstances of each case or from a relevant determination—sometimes in relation with job descriptions—in the undertaking's policies

[55] See in detail *Dreher* id., n. 4 above, at II 4 and III 1.

[56] See above, at 7.3.1.

[57] See below, 7.3.5.3 through 7.3.5.5.

concerning the key functions.[58] This reveals that equating the key function holders with the director of the key function may not correctly identify the individuals at whom the rule is directed.

The institutional analysis must therefore always be supplemented by a functional view, apart from any responsibilities under organizational law. There may be cases, for example, where deficiencies in organizational law exist or the selected management structure is compatible with organization law but ill-suited to practice. In such cases, an institutional definition would fail of its objective pertaining to the insurance supervisory rules on functions due to its purely static approach based on the organization charts of the insurance undertaking. It must therefore be supplemented by a functional view.

This can be readily concluded from the wording in the relevant rules that refer to the "holder" or the person "responsible" and do not preclude "transfer" of key functions or key tasks. The functional perspective asks the question, which persons, regardless of their responsibilities under organization law, actually perform in a distinctive and accountable manner the tasks that legally constitute the core elements of a key function. On the basis of the criteria formulated below, which are at least partially transferable, such persons must always be viewed as key function holders under the law. The supplementary functional approach also forms the parallel to the functional view of management personnel at insurance undertakings as required by art. 42 of the Solvency II Directive, among other provisions. The parallel emerges because this analysis is presumed to include all "persons who effectively run the undertaking", which itself includes de facto members of management body.[59]

7.3.5.3 The Basic Question of Separate Departments (Centralized Organization) or an Integrated Management Structure (Decentralized Organization)

In general and especially at all larger undertakings, the key functions are centrally organized. In any event, the principle of functional segregation always applies to the internal audit function under art. 47, para. 2 of the Solvency II Directive and under art. 261 para. 1 DVO, or sec. 30 para. 2 VAG 2012 [German Insurance Supervision Act 2012]. The internal audit function must therefore always have its own separate department, apart from the issue of outsourcing by small undertakings. But the basic principle requiring the existence of different organizational units and responsible persons also applies for the other three key functions according to art. 41, para. 1 subpara. 2 of the Solvency II Directive and art. 258 SG6, para. 1 of the DVO, and/or sec. 24, para. 1, sent. 2 of the VAG 2012 [German Insurance

[58] See in more detail below section "Subordinate Staff Members of a Function Director as Key Function Holders".

[59] See above, at 7.3.2.1.

Supervision Act 2012] excluding "smaller and less complex undertakings"—as stated in Recital 32 of the Solvency II Directive and art. 258 SG6, para. 2 of the DVO, or sec. 24, para. 1, sent. 1, clause 1 of the VAG 2012 [German Insurance Supervision Act 2012].[60] Nevertheless, there is still the decision to be made by the managing board of an insurance undertaking as to whether the responsibilities of the key functions are performed in separate departments or in an integrated management structure, in accordance with the principle of freedom of internal organization in Recital 31, sent. 2 of the Solvency II Directive.[61] The only constraint is that, even in the latter case, the requirements set forth by the European insurance supervisory regime must be met, which are, namely, the principles of functional segregation and functional independence under the Solvency II Directive and DVO.

Under art. 47 para. 2 of the Solvency II Directive, Recital 97, sent. 2 and art. 258 SG6, para. 1 of the DVO the internal audit function must be "fully independent". By contrast, for the other key functions, Recital 97 sent. 1 and art. 258 SG6, para. 1 of the DVO stipulate merely the necessity of independence. The DVO provides more substance to the meaning of this independence, Unfortunately, the VAG 2012 [German Insurance Supervision Act 2012] does not fully implement this difference. Instead of "fully independent" as in Solvency II, internal audit under sec. 30, para. 2 of the VAG 2012 [German Insurance Supervision Act 2012] is merely "independent". Further, pursuant to sec. 27, para. 5 sent. 1 of the VAG 2012 [German Insurance Supervision Act 2012], insurance undertakings must also establish an "independent risk monitoring function". Nevertheless, based only on the primacy of European law, the differentiation in the types of independence found in the Solvency II system takes precedence to the independence stipulations in the VAG 2012 [German Insurance Supervision Act 2012]. The scope and content of the principle of functional independence cannot be exhaustively addressed in the present context, however.[62]

The government's draft of VAG 2012 [German Insurance Supervision Act 2012] appears too far-reaching, even to the extent that it seeks to replace the criterion for independence in the Solvency II Directive and DVO with the materially narrower criterion of independence of procedure, as laid down in a prohibition of simultaneous engagement with operating tasks.[63] This would make the decentralized organization of key functions in the sense presented earlier nearly impossible.

[60] In the implementation rule, however, there is a shift in that it is not based on the undertaking but rather on the activity, a posture that deviates from the Directive. The Statement of Reasons for the rule for business organization in the VAG-RegE [Government's Draft of a Tenth Act Amending the German Insurance Supervision Act], id., n. 2, sent. 271, includes even "small and medium-size businesses".

[61] VAG-RegE [Government's Draft of a Tenth Act Amending the German Insurance Supervision Act], id. n. 2 above, at Statement of Reasons at 271.

[62] This will be reserved for examination in its own right.

[63] VAG-RegE [Government's Draft of a Tenth Act Amending the German Insurance Supervision Act], id. n. 2 above, at Statement of Reasons for sec. 27 VAG [German Insurance Supervision Act] at 273.

The "cooperation of the operating areas (collection of input and inclusion of expert knowledge)",[64] which is all that the government's draft permits, is already somewhat assumed and does not address the underlying problem of the principle of independence. The Statement of Reasons for the government's draft goes on to explain exhaustively—and surprisingly only in connection with the key function of risk management—that it is "conceivable to have an integrated approach, in addition to the establishment of a separate department, if process independence is properly assured". To this extent, it contradicts the previous passages in the Statement of Reasons.

By referring to independence of procedure, the VAG [German Insurance Supervision Act] legislator attempts to retain the legal posture under sec. 64 a of the existing VAG [German Insurance Supervision Act] and the MaRisk VA [Minimum Requirements for Risk Management (Insurance Supervision)].[65] Thus the legislator extends the valid demand applicable to the director of the risk management function that responsibilities for the establishment and monitoring of risk positions must be separated with the objective of avoiding conflicts of interest,[66] incorrectly to the key functions as a whole using a more widely understood meaning of independence of procedure. Correctly understood, as in the European insurance supervisory regime there is ultimately only one concept of independence under European law. It precludes general substitution by a widely understood concept of independence of procedure, and is not compatible with the attempt to maintain the current German approach to an insurance supervisory regime by using the expression "reasonable protection" of independence of procedure.[67]

7.3.5.4 The Key Function Holders in a Centralized Structure of Key Functions

The Problem

If the key functions are centrally organized, meaning that all are placed under the responsibility of a single department, the question arises as to which staff members of the undertaking are "key function holders" as laid down in the insurance

[64] VAG-RegE [Government's Draft of a Tenth Act Amending the German Insurance Supervision Act], id., n. 2, ibid.

[65] VAG-RegE [Government's Draft of a Tenth Act Amending the German Insurance Supervision Act], id. n. 2 above, at Statement of Reasons at 271.

[66] See *Dreher*, ZGR (2010), 469 (537 f.); there, independence of procedure is understood in the sense of avoiding conflicts of interest and not in the broader sense of the VAG-RegE [Government's Draft of a Tenth Act Amending the German Insurance Supervision Act].

[67] A differing and uncritical view *Grote/Schaaf*, "Zum Referentenentwurf der 10. VAG-Novelle zur Umsetzung der Solvency-II-Richtlinie in deutsches Recht – eine erste Analyse" [in English: On the Consultants' Draft of the Tenth VAG Amendment Implementing the Solvency II Directive in German Law – An Initial Analysis], VersR (2012), 17 (20).

supervisory regime. The question is important because the designation brings on numerous legal consequences, extending from the fit-and-proper requirements in art. 42 of the Solvency II Directive and sec. 25 of the VAG 2012 [German Insurance Supervision Act 2012 to the special supervisory recall powers under art. 41, para. 5, subpara. 2 of the Solvency II Directive and sec. 297 of the VAG 2012 [German Insurance Supervision Act 2012]. The specific issue at hand is: How far out does the circle of persons extend in an insurance undertaking subject to supervisory requirements and possible sanctions? It is thus already presumed that key function holders as laid down in the insurance supervisory regime does not necessarily imply only a single person for each function but rather that several persons related to a key function "can be holders".[68]

The Director of a Function as Key Function Holder

To answer the question about key function holders, the proper starting point is the equalization of key function holders with "the persons who effectively run the undertaking".[69] It has already been inferred from this equalization that not all staff members in a department who assume the tasks of a key function are at the same time holders of the key function in a legal sense. Rather, this larger pool comprises only persons whose significance within the undertaking according to the purpose of the rule justifies the equalization for purposes of legal requirements and consequences.[70] These always include—as already explained[71]—the directors of the relevant departments.

Subordinate Staff Members of a Function Director as Key Function Holders

The extent to which persons subordinate to a director of a department are counted as key function holders cannot be established in abstract in advance. Decisive on this point are the circumstances characterizing the individual company and its activities, such as the size of the particular insurance undertaking or insurance group. A very

---

[68] To the same effect, VAG-RegE [Government's Draft of a Tenth Act Amending the German Insurance Supervision Act], id., n. 2 above, Statement of Reasons for sec. 29 at 275, though with unpersuasive provenance from the definition of "function" in art. 13, no. 29 of the Solvency II Directive rather than from the majority of persons upon whom the recitals and corresponding articles concerning the key functions of the Solvency II Directive are based. Also found in the Statement of Reasons for the duty of notice under sec. 44, no. 1 of the VAG 2012 [German Insurance Supervision Act 2012], is the following contradictory statement: "if a key task is performed by two or more persons, only the 'holder of the management role' is relevant for most tasks".

[69] See above, at 7.3.2.

[70] See on this point above, at 7.3.2.2 and 7.3.2.3.

[71] See above, at 7.3.5.2.

large insurance undertaking with multiple organizational levels and division of responsibilities within a single key function must consider the possibility that certain individuals may very well be key function holders under the law by virtue of their job description and decisional authority. How far this circle of persons extends is determined by an insurance undertaking's self-assessment, which is itself subject to supervisory review. The assessment is ultimately the responsibility of the managing board as a whole—as set down in general terms in art. 40 of the Solvency II Directive[72] and quite correctly in art. 258, para. 1 sent. 2 of the DVO.

The proper reference for the undertaking's internal determination of key function holders are the guidelines for each key function that must be adopted in any event under art. 41, para. 3 of the Solvency II Directive or sec. 24, para. 3 of the VAG 2012. By virtue of art. 41, para. 3 of the Solvency II Directive, these directly include the risk management function and the internal audit function. The compliance function is also included via art. 41, para. 3 in conjunction with art. 46, para. 1, subpara. 2 of the Solvency II Directive. And for all key functions including the actuarial function under art. 48 of the Solvency II Directive or sec. 31 VAG 2012 [German Insurance Supervision Act 2012], "documented policies" have to be adopted by the insurance undertakings according to sec. 263, para. 1 of the DVO, meaning again guidelines, among these guidelines for "fit and proper assessments" of key function holders. With this documentation, ideally together with the guidelines, the list of key function holders for an insurance undertaking can be exhaustively established with relative ease, at least from an institutional perspective.

The Deputy Director of a Function as Key Function Holder

Regardless of the individual undertaking's conception as to which staff members below the level of the department director for each key function are also to be viewed as key function holders under the insurance supervisory regime depending on the circumstances of the particular case, the deputy director of the respective department must be included.[73] This individual takes on the director's responsibilities in the event of a planned or unplanned absence or hindrance and must therefore have the same professional qualifications and be deemed fit and proper.

Managing Board Members as Key Function Holders

It is an open question whether a managing board member may also be key function holder. The Solvency II Directive draws a distinction between "persons who

[72] The VAG 2012 [German Insurance Supervision Act 2012] provides no implementation rule on this point. Rather, it simply refers to the applicability of general provisions, particularly sec. 76, para. 1 of the AktG [German Stock Corporation Act].

[73] See above, 7.3.5.2.

effectively run the undertaking" and holders of "other key functions". A per se prohibition on the dual role for a single person does not quite follow from this distinction since managing board members as managers of the business are subject to the requirements and legal consequences applicable to key function holders. Still, this incompatibility may arise from the special tasks of key function holders. To the extent that key function holders are under a specific prohibition on self-monitoring and that special standards of independence apply to them under law—for example, art. 47, para. 2 of the Solvency II Directive and art. 258 SG6, para. 1 of the DVO,— managing board members as the ultimate decision-makers for all operations in the insurance undertaking could be affected by these strictures.

It must also be considered that the key function holders, in accordance with the operational structure provided for under the Solvency II Directive, must report matters concerning their key functions to the managing board. The four governance functions report to the managing board or advise it on specific questions and in matters related to the functions generally according to art. 41, para. 1, subpara. 2 and 44, para. 5 e, 46 para. 2 and 47, para. 3 and 48 para. 1 e of the Solvency II Directive and, for example, art. 258 SG6, para. 4 of the DVO or secs. 24 para. 1 sent. 2, 27 para. 5, 29 para. 2, 30 para. 2, and 31 para. 1 no. 5 of the VAG 2012 [German Insurance Supervision Act 2012].[74] That a managing board member cannot, as a functional director, report to him or herself—not even under the auspices of membership on the management board as a body to whom the information is directed—appears to negate from the outset any possibility that a managing board member can simultaneously be the director of a governance function.

With the establishment of the governance functions the Solvency II rules further require, under art. 41, para. 1, subpara. 2 of the Solvency II Directive, "an adequate transparent organizational structure with a clear allocation and appropriate segregation of responsibilities and an effective system for ensuring the transmission of information". This organizational structure is based on the assumption that, beneath the managing board, a clearly compartmentalized management structure exists that preferably eliminates conflicts of interests, gathers information, and ensures a proper vertical flow of the information to the managing board. If a managing board member were to also assume the directorship of a governance function, the system would become unbalanced. Instead of unfiltered vertical information flowing to the entire management board, a horizontal information flow would arise in the form of one managing board member to the other managing board members.

Art. 258 SG6, para. 1 sent. 2 of the DVO therefore presumes segregation between functional directors and management with the following words:

[74] Note that the VAG 2012 [German Insurance Supervision Act 2012], with its obligation for only selective reporting, contradicts art. 258 SG6, para. 4 of the DVO, for example, which requires an immediate report about any major problem to the managing board as a management body. The same applies in the relationship concerning the minimum annual reporting duty under art. 262 SG10, para. 8 of the DVO.

> Each function shall operate under the ultimate responsibility of, and report to the administrative, management or supervisory body and shall, where appropriate, cooperate with the other functions in carrying out their roles.

Paragraph 4 repeats this once again specifically for the duty to inform the managing board with respect to any major problem within the key function. At the same time, the rules make clear that Solvency II is based on the idea that the four governance functions do not have a hierarchy, but rather rank equally.[75] Now if managing board members were to assume the directorship of particular functions while other functions were still directed by a non-member of the managing board, the horizontal cooperation among the functions which is based on their equal ranking would be compromised.

With respect to smaller and medium-size insurance undertakings in the context of the principle of proportionality, Recital 31, sent. 4 of the Solvency II Directive makes a corresponding presumption of three possibilities: "for those functions to be staffed by own staff, to rely on advice from outside experts or to be outsourced to experts within the limits set by this Directive". The Recital makes no mention of the fourth, debatable possibility, namely to assign functional directorship to a managing board member. The same applies to the corresponding text of the DVO in art. 258 SG6, para. 2. Against this background and in view of the deviation from an undertaking's freedom of internal organization under Recital 31, sent. 2 of the Solvency II Directive, if the Directive has "otherwise specified", the assumption of directorship of a key function by a managing board member is essentially impermissible.[76] Aside from the internal audit function,[77] an exception based on the principle of proportionality is conceivable for what are in all respects small insurance undertakings with relatively simple business models.[78]

7.3.5.5 The Key Function Holders in a Decentralized Structure of Key Functions

Issues concerning key function holders within the meaning of the insurance supervisory regime likewise emerge when the key functions are decentralized. The director of the capital investment area, for example, may also be responsible for compliance with investment provisions; or similarly, the head of an area charged

---

[75] See *Bürkle*, "Die rechtliche Dimension von Solvency II" [in English: The Legal Dimension of Solvency II], VersR (2007), 1595 (1599 f.); id., n. 26 above, at ref. 99; *Dreher*, "Das Risikomanagement nach sec. 64 a VAG und Solvency II" [in English: Risk Management under Sec. 64a German Insurance Supervision Act and Solvency II], VersR (2008), 998 (1004).

[76] A differing view *Grote/Schaaf*, VersR (2012), 17 (21).

[77] Assuming the directorship of a function in this case would be incompatible with the "full independence" required under art. 47, para. 2 of the Solvency II Directive and art. 258 SG6, para. 1 sent. 1, para. 2 of the DVO [Draft Implementing Measures Solvency II].

[78] See also Recital 32 of the Solvency II Directive.

with the prevention and control of money laundering may also have compliance responsibility for tasks that fall under the compliance function if the individual in question is subject to oversight—and concomitantly to any guidance associated with the function-specific responsibility—by the director of the compliance function for these tasks.

Even a decentralized key function culminates in the responsibility of one individual. The individual in question cannot, according to the principle of functional segregation under art. 41, para. 1, subpara. 2 of the Solvency II Directive and art. 258 SG6, para. 1 of the DVO, essentially[79] bear added responsibility for a different key function. So, for example, the head of the legal department can simultaneously be director of the compliance function.[80] To begin with, this does not infringe on the principle of functional segregation. This is so because the legal department—surprisingly—is not counted among the governance functions. There is also essentially no conflict with the principle of functional independence, since this relates to the other functions and only indirectly to supplementary operating activities. In the end, what applies to the compliance function is only the standard of "independent" and not that of "fully independent" as set forth in art. 258 SG6, para. 1 of the DVO.[81] Whichever person at the top of a decentralized organization holds responsibility for a key function is thus in effect, as with a deputy director,[82] a key function holder as set forth in the insurance supervisory regime.

Whether additional persons within decentralized key functions also fall into this group of key function holders in the legal sense is determined on a case-by-case basis according to the criteria individual to the undertaking and the relevant activities as discussed earlier.[83] For the heads of a capital investment area or the prevention of money laundering put forth as examples at the beginning of this section, who—in relation to their compliance activities—tare subject to oversight and possible guidance by the director of the compliance function, this classification is likely, at least in very large insurance undertakings. For these, it becomes apparent that every recourse to persons with a leadership role in the important areas of the insurance undertaking, in situations where the key functions are decentralized, can elevate the number of key function holders as defined in the insurance supervisory regime compared to a centralized organization where staff members subordinate to the director of a key function can hold multiple responsibilities. This could offset the goal of reducing the burden with respect to personnel

---

[79] On exceptions for small and medium-size insurance undertakings, see Recital 32 of the Solvency II Directive and art. 258 SG6, para. 2 of the DVO.

[80] See *Dreher* according to discussion report by *Thomas*, ZGR (2010), 591 (594) in the context of the principle of the independence of procedure of the functions stipulated by MaRisk VA [Minimum Requirements for Risk Management (Insurance Supervision)].

[81] See above, 7.3.5.3.

[82] See above section "The Deputy Director of a Function as Key Function Holder".

[83] See above section "Subordinate Staff Members of a Function Director as Key Function Holders".

and organizational expense sought through a decentralized structure of key functions.

7.4 Summary

1. The Solvency II Directive uses the term "key function" several times. It links to numerous rules related, for example, to the fit-and-proper requirements for persons with responsibilities in these areas, the insurance undertaking's duties of notice and disclosure to the supervisory authority or the public, and to specific supervisory intervention powers.
2. The choice of terminology in the system of rules found in Solvency II, even with sometimes differing use of terms in the Solvency II Directive and its various language versions, clearly shows in the final analysis that the uniformity of the key function concept must be assumed. The term "key function" is therefore identical in meaning with other terms that substitute for it in the Solvency II rules such as "key task" or (in German) "Fundamentalfunktion" [in English: fundamental function].
3. The terminological dual-tracking deviating from this with the use of both the term "key function" and "key task" in the German language version of the Solvency II Directive and the VAG 2012 [German Insurance Supervision Act 2012] does not produce a different understanding of the concept, but rather a terminological confusion that is unnecessary in all respects. The term "key task" in the VAG 2012 [German Insurance Supervision Act 2012], then, does not have its own unique legal meaning.
4. The key functions are exhaustively regulated in the Solvency II system. The four functions are the risk-management function, the compliance function, the internal audit function, and the actuarial function. The meaning of "key function" cannot be expanded by the national insurance supervisory regime. In view of the associated legal implications under the insurance supervisory regime, adding functions other than the four governance functions to the key functions, as the government draft of the VAG 2012 [German Insurance Supervision Act 2012] provides in its Statement of Reasons, would signify an enormous intervention into an undertaking's freedom of internal organization and a step backward to the earlier general supervision according to the principles of abusiveness, which is excluded under Solvency II.
5. The regulatory Levels 1 and 2 of Solvency II use numerous terms, which are not always consistent with one another, when referring to persons who perform work in the area of the four key functions. They nevertheless clearly differentiate between persons who are legally differentiated by the Solvency II Directive and the DVO. To this is added the equalization under supervision law of "persons who effectively run the undertaking or hold other key functions". Therefore, the Solvency II system refers only to persons who perform tasks of distinctive importance as part of a key function. Excluded are persons who may

also perform tasks in the area of a key function, but not in this distinctive way. The distinction between a holder of a key function and the staff members in a key function who are subordinate to this individual is also mirrored in the Solvency II provisions on duty of notice and qualification requirements for the persons working in key function areas.

6. Only natural persons can be key function holders. Legal persons or other groups of persons cannot be key function holders.
7. The concrete identification of key function holders as laid down in the insurance supervisory regime assumes an institutional determination supplemented by a functional view. A further point to consider is that the key functions may be either centrally organized in the form of separate departments or decentralized in the form of an integrated management structure. Such a decentralized exercise of duties is possible notwithstanding the reference to independence of procedure in the government's draft of the VAG 2012 [German Insurance Supervision Act 2012]. This widely understood criterion does not accord with the provisions concerning independence as they are constructed under the European Law for the activities of key functions.
8. With centralized key functions, the key function holders as defined by the insurance supervisory regime are the director of the key function, the deputy director of the key function, and—depending on the circumstances characterizing the individual company and its activities, such as the size of the undertaking—those subordinate staff members in the key function with distinct job descriptions and decisional authority.
9. In a decentralized structure, aside from the director and deputy director of a key function, subordinate staff members may meet the legal requirements for key function holders, again based on the circumstances of the individual company and with the requirement of distinct job descriptions and decision authority. Decentralized organization will lead to a larger group of persons in the key function than would be the case for a centralized structure.
10. Insurance undertakings must determine the key function holders as defined by the insurance supervisory regime by self-assessment in the guidelines on key functions, for which the managing board bears the overall responsibility. This assessment is subject to review by the insurance supervisory authority.
11. Managing board members in principle cannot be key function holders as defined by the insurance supervisory regime.

Chapter 8
Supervisory Review of Key Functions

Contents

8.1 Introduction 244
8.2 The "Fit" Requirement for Key Function Holders and Their Subordinate Staff Members in Key Functions 245
  8.2.1 The Two-Tier Qualification Structure in General 245
  8.2.2 The Special Rules 247
  8.2.3 The Fitness of Key Function Holders 249
  8.2.4 The Fitness of Subordinate Staff to Key Function Holders 257
8.3 The "Proper" Requirement for Key Function Holders and Their Subordinate Staff Members in Key Functions 258
  8.3.1 The Two-Tier Structure of the Proper Requirement and the Proceduralization of the Proper Requirement as Starting Point 258
  8.3.2 The Proper Requirement of Key Function Holders 259
  8.3.3 The "Proper" Requirement for Staff Members Subordinate to Key Function Holders 264
8.4 The Remuneration of Key Function Holders 264
8.5 The Duties of Notice and Public Disclosure for Key Function Holders 265
  8.5.1 The Duties of Notice to Supervisory Authorities 265
  8.5.2 The Duties of Public Disclosure 268
8.6 Supervisory Recall and Prohibition of Exercise of Function for Key Function Holders in Cases of Fit-and-Proper Deficiencies and Supervisory Right to Direct Information from Key Function Holders 268
  8.6.1 Solvency II 268
  8.6.2 VAG-RegE [Government's Draft of a Tenth Act Amending the German Insurance Supervision Act] 269
8.7 Summary 271

First published as "Die aufsichtsbehördliche Kontrolle der Inhaber von Schlüsselfunktionen nach Solvency II und künftigem VAG" [in English: Review by Supervisory Authorities of the Holders of Key Functions under Solvency II and the Future VAG [German Insurance Supervision Act]], VersR (2012), 1061 ff.

M. Dreher, *Treatises on Solvency II*, DOI 10.1007/978-3-662-46290-4_8

Abstract Picking up from the Chap. 7 examination of the term "key functions" and of the key function holders, this chapter undertakes an examination of the supervisory review of key functions. In particular, this inquiry involves the areas of supervision of the key function holders as to fit-and-proper monitoring, the issue of remuneration of key function holders, the duties of notice and disclosure attendant on a change in key function holders, and the powers of insurance supervisory authorities in the supervision of key function holders.

8.1 Introduction

The Solvency II Directive[1] at Level 1, the DVO implementing it at Level 2, currently in draft form,[2] as well as the CEIOPS Consultation Paper "Draft proposal for Level 3 Guidelines on the System of Governance" of December 2010[3] and the future VAG [German Insurance Supervision Act] at Level 4[4] often name the holders of key functions as the addressees of the rule or, in the case of the Governance Guidelines, their object. Since neither the term "key function holder" or even the term "key function" are specifically defined by law, and since numerous legal questions arise from the clarification of the legal requirements for both, clarity with respect to these legal requirements is a precondition for application of the legal rules addressed to key function holders.[5] Building on this, the individual rules of the new insurance supervisory regime are then discussed with a focus on their relevance to key function holders in insurance undertakings.[6] Among these, the requirements that such persons be "fit" (below, 8.2) and also "proper" (below, 8.3) have especially significant weight. Issues surrounding remuneration come to the fore as well since the new insurance supervisory regime also addresses remuneration in the area of key functions (below, 8.4). Finally, the examination turns to the duties of notice and disclosure that exist with respect to the supervisory authority and the public in connection with key function holders and their

[1] Directive 2009/138/EG of the European Parliament and of the Council of 25 Nov. 2009, OJEU L 335, p. 1, of 17 Dec. 2009.

[2] The abbreviation DVO when used here and after in reference to the Level 2 DRA signifies the EU Commission draft known as Draft Implementing Measures Solvency II, 31 Oct. 2011.

[3] Hereafter: Governance Guidelines.

[4] RegE eines Zehnten Gesetzes zur Änderung des VAG [Government's Draft of a Tenth Act Amending the German Insurance Supervision Act] of 15 Feb. 2012, BT-Drucks. [Document of the German Bundestag] 17/9342; also, BR-Drucks [Document of the German Bundesrat] 90/12 (hereafter: VAG-RegE) 90/12.

[5] See on this point *Dreher*, "Begriff und Inhaber der Schlüsselfunktionen nach Solvency II und VAG 2012" [in English: Concept and Holders of Key Functions under Solvency II and the German Insurance Supervision Act 2012 (Draft)], VersR (2012), 933 (Chap. 7, above).

[6] Any mention of insurance undertakings in this chapter includes reinsurance undertakings.

subordinate staff members (below, 8.5), and whether the supervisory authority may recall these persons or restrict their activity, and if the authority is entitled to obtain information directly from them (below, 8.6).

8.2 The "Fit" Requirement for Key Function Holders and Their Subordinate Staff Members in Key Functions

8.2.1 The Two-Tier Qualification Structure in General

Recital 34 of the Solvency II Directive requires: "All persons that perform key functions should be fit and proper".[7] Art. 258 SG6, para. 3 of the DVO takes up this very general requirement with the following sentence: "The persons performing a function ... shall have the necessary ... expertise ... to carry out their responsibilities". Thus, the rules apply to all persons who engage in work included within the scope of a key function, irrespective of their position within the hierarchy of the key function. The European insurance supervisory regime rightly presumes that all staff members who are part of a key function must possess the knowledge and skills necessary to properly meet their responsibilities.

But art. 42, para. 1 of the Solvency II Directive goes further, formulating more than just general qualifications for all persons who hold key functions.[8] Rather, the provision defines "fitness" as follows: "their professional qualifications, knowledge and experience are adequate to enable sound and prudent management." This is mirrored in art. 263 SG11, para. 2 of the DVO, which defines still further the special fitness criterion applicable only[9] to key function holders within the meaning of art. 263 SG11, para. 1 of the DVO.

Thus the two-tier qualification structure is clear in the very wording of the rules, according to which the special qualification requirements for key function holders are differentiated from the general qualification requirements that apply to all staff of the undertaking who work in such functions. A systematic analysis of the framework of regulations fully supports the assumption of this two-level qualification structure. To start with, the special qualification requirements are restricted to key function holders, as these individuals are understood in the insurance supervisory regime. The background for this, in turn, is the telos of the equivalence

---

[7] Other language versions of the Solvency II Directive hold likewise. See *Dreher*, VersR (2012), 933 (936 f.) (Chap. 7, above, at 7.3.1).

[8] Concerning the irrelevance of using the term "key task" in place of "key function" in the German language version of the Solvency II Directive, see *Dreher*, VersR (2012), 933 at II 2 (Chap. 7, above, at 7.2.2).

[9] However, in art. 42, para. 1 of the Solvency II Directive, these are prefixed by "persons who effectively run the undertaking", which brings clear definition to the group that constitutes the addressees of the law. See *Dreher*, VersR (2012), 933 (934 f.) (Chap. 7, above, at 7.2.2).

between the key function holders and the persons who effectively run the undertaking. This equivalence of key function holders to the members of the governing body, which generally means the members of the managing board, is justified exclusively by the distinctive nature of the position of key function holder.[10] This is the sole basis upon which enables art. 42, para. 1 of the Solvency II Directive to equate the holders of key functions with the management of the business even with respect to the special qualification requirements.[11] These further requirements consequently pertain only to the key function holders as laid down in the insurance supervisory regime and defined in more detail previously.[12] They do not, however, affect all other subordinate staff members in one of the key functions.

In addition, the qualification requirements themselves also demonstrate that they are directed exclusively toward these distinct key function holders. Thus art. 42, para. 1 a of the Solvency II Directive refers overall to "sound and prudent management". For one thing, this cannot be required of all subordinate staff members in the key functions of an insurance undertaking. Such staff members have no influence on the management of the insurance undertaking and its business policies, especially on its appetite for risk. If the triad of "professional qualifications, knowledge and experience", which is supposed to ensure sound and prudent management, were actually to extend to all subordinate staff members, then excluded from working in key functions would be graduates of an institution of higher education at the commencement of their careers, all persons moving between key functions within the insurance undertaking as well as those moving from another business area within the insurance undertaking into a key function, and those coming from another undertaking altogether. Extending these far-reaching qualification requirements to all staff in the key functions of an insurance undertaking would therefore both fail of its purpose and be incompatible with the principle of proportionality applicable under, i.a., art. 29, para. 3 of the Solvency II Directive in a general sense and Recital 31, sent. 3 of the Solvency II Directive for the organization of the key functions more specifically.

The system of qualification requirements under the Solvency II Directive includes the Level 2 rules in art. 263 SG11 of the DVO, referred to previously, which govern the implementation of art. 42, para. 2 of the Solvency II Directive. The requirements for fitness found therein go still further than those in art. 42, para. 1 a of the Solvency II Directive. Art. 263 SG11, para. 1 of the DVO requires "documented policies and adequate procedures" in order to ensure the fitness of key function holders at all times. Para. 2 provides numerous criteria for fitness that pertain only to holders of other key functions within the meaning of para. 1, as separate rules are provided for the members of governing bodies in para. 3.

In detail, art. 263 SG11, para. 2 of the DVO provides that the insurance undertaking would have to assess the occupational and professional qualifications

[10] See *Dreher,* VersR (2012), 933 (937 f.) (Chap. 7, above, at 7.3.2).

[11] See *Dreher,* VersR (2012), 933 (938) (Chap. 7, above, at 7.3.4).

[12] See *Dreher,* VersR (2012), 933 (938 f.) (Chap. 7, above, at 7.3.5).

of a person as well as his or her knowledge and relevant professional experience within and outside of the insurance sector. It would also have to take account of the particular responsibilities and duties assigned to this person. Since art. 42 of the Solvency II Directive applies only to key function holders as laid down in the insurance supervisory regime, the implementation rules are also applicable only to key function holders as laid down in the insurance supervisory regime, and not to all staff members that work in a key function. Aside from this unambiguous conclusion from the perspective of the legal system, the area of personal application of the provision also reveals a contextual underpinning of stringent requirements for processes and qualifications that cannot and should not apply to all staff in a key function.

Finally, from a legal systematic perspective, and with art. 42, para. 1 of the Solvency II Directive and art. 263 SG11, paras. 1 and 2 of the DVO as background, Recital 35 of the Solvency II Directive confirms that the two-tier qualification structure applies to the qualification requirements for persons who operate in an area of a key function. According to the Recital, "the purpose of assessing the required level of competence, professional qualifications and experience of those who effectively run the undertaking or have other key functions should be taken into consideration as additional factors". This means that the issuers of the Directive themselves assume that the qualifications level at the top of the undertaking—that is, the management and holders of other key functions—in part determines the qualifications level of subordinate staff members within a key function. In other words, Recital 35 of the Solvency II Directive pertaining to the qualifications of subordinate staff in key functions makes explicit the rather obvious notion that, with consideration given to the tasks and undertaking involved, a level of qualification lower than that required of key function holders is sufficient for the staff subordinate to them.

8.2.2 *The Special Rules*

8.2.2.1 The Actuarial Function

The general two-tier qualification structure is supplemented in the Solvency II Directive by special rules.[13] To start with, there are special, function-specific rules in art. 48, para. 2 of the Solvency II Directive that apply to the actuarial function. They prescribe the following for this function:

[13] These special rules cannot be examined in-depth in the present context.

> The actuarial function shall be carried out by persons who have knowledge of actuarial and financial mathematics, commensurate with the nature, scale and complexity of the risks inherent in the business of the insurance or reinsurance undertaking, and who are able to demonstrate their relevant experience with applicable professional and other standards.[14]

Although the DVO contains no concrete details with respect to these function-specific rules, the opposite is found with the detailed rules in the Level 3 drafts.

8.2.2.2 The Outsourcing of Key Functions

Special rules also apply to the *outsourcing* of key functions. The *outsourcing* of key functions[15] is permitted under art. 49 of the Solvency II Directive.[16] Art. 264 SG12 of the DVO contains numerous implementation regulations in this regard. In this text, the DVO correctly presumes that outsourcing shall not be allowed to alter the obligations of an insurance undertaking arising from the Solvency II Directive.[17] The following also applies to an insurance undertaking under art. 264 SG12, para. 6 a of the DVO:

> The insurance undertaking ... shall ... verify ... that all staff of the service provider ... are sufficiently qualified and reliable.

At Level 3, Guideline 11 of the Governance Guidelines stipulates that the fit-and-proper requirements for holders of key functions in cases of *outsourcing* apply to those staff members of the service providers who assume the respective responsibilities.[18] According to Explanation No. 3.33 to these Guidelines, the responsibility for the determination that staff members of the service provider satisfy these requirements falls to the insurance undertaking.

---

[14] For the somewhat flawed implementation legislation, see sec. 31, para. 3 VAG-RegE [Government's Draft of a Tenth Act Amending the German Insurance Supervision Act].

[15] Regarding supervision in the case of outsourcing see art. 38 of the Solvency II Directive.

[16] Regarding implementation, see sec. 32 of the VAG-RegE [Government's Draft of a Tenth Act Amending the German Insurance Supervision Act].

[17] See also *Bürkle*, in: Fahr/Kaulbach/Bär/Pohlmann, VAG [in English: The German Insurance Supervision Act] (5th ed. 2012), in Solvabilität II [in English: Solvency II], ref. 97.

[18] See also the relevant explanation at No. 3.33 ff. and the explanation at No. 1.11, sent. 3 of the Governance Guidelines.

8.2.3 The Fitness of Key Function Holders

8.2.3.1 The Requirements

Solvency II

The general qualification requirements already discussed apply to all persons who perform work in a key function, regardless of their level in the hierarchy.[19] There are, however, special requirements in addition to these which arise from the higher qualifications demanded of the key function holders under the insurance supervisory regime. According to art. 42 para. 1 a of the Solvency II Directive, key function holders as laid down in the insurance supervisory regime must meet the following specific requirements for professional qualifications:

> Their professional qualifications, knowledge, and experience are adequate to enable sound and prudent management (fitness requirement).

Art. 263 SG11 para. 2 of the DVO concretizes these rules at Level II with the following wording:

> The assessment of whether a person is "fit" shall include an assessment of the person's professional and formal qualifications, knowledge and relevant experience within the insurance sector, other financial sectors or other businesses and shall take account of the respective duties allocated to that person and, where relevant, the insurance, financial, accounting, actuarial and management skills of the person.

Guideline 12 then follows at Level 3, along with explanations.[20] However, unlike other guidelines and explanations on this matter, this applies only to members of governing bodies.[21] Other staff in the functions are covered only under the general explanations in No. 3.37 f.

The individual criteria of art. 263 SG11, para. 2 of the DVO are rather widely drawn. They require both professional and formal qualifications as well as relevant knowledge and experience. At the same time, however, they permit reasonable distinctions and the transfer of qualifications. This can be seen in the inclusion of qualifications from the overall financial sector and other areas of business in the criteria. It is also reflected in the consideration given to the specific responsibilities of a key function holder and the person's skills in relation to the responsibilities.

In contrast, art. 263 SG11, para. 2 of the DVO does not provide detailed specifications for the legal requirement "sound and prudent management" as

---

[19] See above, 8.2.1 and in detail below, 8.2.4.

[20] Governance Guidelines Nos. 2.12 and 3.39 ff.

[21] See on this point also Governance Guidelines No. 3.1.

mandated under art. 42, para. 1 a of the Solvency II Directive.[22] The skills required for management pertain mainly to members of the managing board as contained in art. 42, para. 1 of the Solvency II Directive. This is understandable, as the corporate management has to run the undertaking on its own responsibility set forth under sec. 76, para. 1 AktG [German Stock Corporation Act]. Thus the criterion of prudence in art. 42 of the Solvency II Directive should not be separately interpreted to be, as may first appear, an implied limitation on the undertaking's freedom to act in accordance with its own appetite for risk.[23] This becomes readily apparent in a comparative analysis of the various language versions of this directive.[24]

VAG-RegE [Government's Draft of a Tenth Act Amending the German Insurance Supervision Act]

Sec. 25, para. 1, sent. 1 of the VAG-RegE [Government's Draft of a Tenth Act Amending the German Insurance Supervision Act] requires that persons who "have other key functions" are not only proper but also fit. Fitness is defined in sec. 25, para. 1 of the VAG-RegE [Government's Draft of a Tenth Act Amending the German Insurance Supervision Act] as follows:

> Fitness is contingent on the professional qualifications, knowledge and experience that ensure sound and prudent management of the undertaking. This requires adequate theoretical and practical knowledge of the insurance business and, in cases where management duties are performed, sufficient leadership experience.

The text of sec. 25 of the VAG-RegE [Government's Draft of a Tenth Act Amending the German Insurance Supervision Act] clearly goes beyond the fitness criteria laid down in the European requirements for key function holders. The Statement of Reasons for the government's draft reflects this only indirectly by providing for the implementation of art. 42 of the Solvency II Directive and by presuming that sec. 25 of the VAG-RegE [Government's Draft of a Tenth Act Amending the German Insurance Supervision Act] "integrates the specific rules of sec. 7 a para. 1 of the VAG [German Insurance Supervision Act], earlier version".[25] Nevertheless, and in agreement with art. 263 SG11, para. 2 of the DVO in this

---

[22] See on this point 8.2.1, above.

[23] For a different view see *Bürkle*, "Europarechtliche Vorgaben für die interne Governance im Versicherungssektor" [in English: Requirements for Internal Governance in the Insurance Sector], WM (2012), 878 (881).

[24] See, e.g., the English language version: "sound and prudent management" and the French language version "gestion saine et prudente".

[25] VAG-RegE [Government's Draft of a Tenth Act Amending the German Insurance Supervision Act], id. n. 4 above, at Statement of Reasons for sec. 25 VAG [German Insurance Supervision Act] at 272.

respect, the Statement of Reasons for the VAG-RegE [Government's Draft of a Tenth Act Amending the German Insurance Supervision Act] also points out that the specific requirements are based "on the respective key task and the responsibilities a person has while executing it". "In addition, the nature, scale and complexity of the risks with which the business operations of the undertaking are associated have influence on the fitness requirement".[26]

The legal requirements of "professional qualification", "knowledge and experience" are also found in art. 42, para. 1 of the Solvency II Directive. The explanation of the requirement of "knowledge" in sec. 25, para. 1, sent. 3 of the VAG-RegE [Government's Draft of a Tenth Act Amending the German Insurance Supervision Act] with its reference to "adequate theoretical and practical knowledge" is not only an appropriate amplification of fitness but is also consistent with the corresponding requirement in art. 263 SG11, para. 2 of the DVO.

Sec. 25, para. 1 of the VAG RegE [Government's Draft of a Tenth Act Amending the German Insurance Supervision Act] deviates, however, from art. 42, para. 1 of the Solvency II Directive and art. 263 SG11, para. 2 of the DVO in sentence 3 by specifying the requirement of "management experience" instead of simply "experience" as rendered in the Directive and the DVO, and then again in sentence 4 by requiring "a managerial position held with an insurance undertaking of comparable size and type of business for three years" in order to meet such management experience. Indeed, this is supposed to apply—continuing with the presumption of sec. 7 a, para. 1 sent. 3 of the current VAG [German Insurance Supervision Act][27]—only for the "performance of management duties", meaning that by contrary inference it does not apply to those specified later who have "other key tasks". Nonetheless, there could be spillover effects.[28] Overall, sec. 25, para. 1, sent. 4 of the VAG-RegE [Government's Draft of a Tenth Act Amending the German Insurance Supervision Act] sets the fitness standard at a very high level. Especially significant here is the trio of "three years", "insurance undertaking" and "comparable size and type of business". It is clear at the outset that the rule is incompatible with moves made by personnel between different sectors as well as with the current one-year orientation period for management positions in the banking sector, which has the approval of BaFin [Federal Financial Supervisory Authority]. And if one were to take the last of the three requirements literally, even the "advancement" of a person from a smaller to a relatively larger undertaking—regardless of the actual magnitude of the undertaking—would hardly be possible in the future.

---

[26] VAG-RegE [Government's Draft of a Tenth Act Amending the German Insurance Supervision Act], id. n. 4 above, at Statement of Reasons for sec. 25 VAG [German Insurance Supervision Act] at 272.

[27] See on this point *Dreher*, "Die Kontrolle der Geschäftsleiter von Versicherungsunternehmen" [in English: The Monitoring of Managers of Insurance Undertakings], ZVersWiss (2006), 375 (396 f., 401 f.) (Supplement, Annual Conference 2006).

[28] On this methodical approach, see in detail *Dreher*, "Ausstrahlungen des Aufsichtsrechts auf das Aktienrecht" [in English: Effects of Supervisory Law on Corporation Law], ZGR (2010), 496.

The fixed 3-year requirement for management experience is as excessive an application of the Solvency II rules as the stipulation of insurance undertakings of comparable size and business type. Under the principle of full harmonization,[29] these have no justification in national implementation law and—particularly after the DVO takes effect—have no legal effect due to the primacy of European law. This holds true even more so for the one other stipulation in the triad: that the experience must be in connection with an "insurance undertaking". Art. 263 SG11, para. 2 of the DVO directly provides for consideration of "knowledge and relevant experience within the insurance sector, other financial sectors or other businesses". Ultimately, this means that the staff in question may come to an insurance undertaking from another part of the financial services sector—or even from another field of business altogether[30]—much the same as they can move to a larger insurance undertaking from a relatively smaller undertaking. And no rigid 3-year restrictions apply. Now, if this is the case even for the managing board members, meaning the persons who effectively run the business, it is certainly no different for the key function holders who are subordinate to them. Consequently, the direct reference to "insurance businesses" in sec. 25, para. 1, sent. 3 of the VAG-RegE [Government's Draft of a Tenth Act Amending the German Insurance Supervision Act], where key function holders are expressly mentioned, is not compatible with the Solvency II rules. Exclusively relevant, and sufficient in the final analysis, are knowledge and experience within the meaning of art. 263 SG11, para. 2 of the DVO.

Earlier, under the VAG [German Insurance Supervision Act] then in effect, the question arose as to whether knowledge of the German language was a necessary component of fitness for managing board members of insurance undertakings. While the literature in insurance supervisory law sometimes supported this idea, it was rejected from a number of perspectives, including as an interpretation of the relevant criteria—namely, knowledge of the substantive requirements of the responsibilities assumed and actual communication skill in the German language with the aid of language mediators.[31] This applies even more so today following the completion of harmonization of insurance supervision by the Solvency II project for the time being. The outcome is also a product of basic European freedoms as well as the uniform applicability of supervisory law to insurance groups and other cross-border undertakings of relevance to insurance. Applicability to key function holders proceeds from the fact that they cannot be subject to different rules based on

[29] See on this point *Dreher/Lange*, "Die Vollharmonisierung der Versicherungsaufsicht durch Solvency II" [in English: Full Harmonization of Insurance Supervision under Solvency II], VersR (2011), 825 (831 f.) (Chap. 1, above, at 1.4.2); *Bürkle*, "Die Zukunft der materiellen Versicherungsaufsicht in Deutschland" [in English: The Future of Substantive Insurance Supervision in Germany] VersR (2011), 1469 (1472 ff.); *Bürkle/Grote*, "Die aufsichtsbehördlichen Eingriffsbefugnisse nach Solvency II" [in English: Supervisory Intervention Powers under Solvency II] in: Dreher/Wandt, eds., Solvency II in der Rechtsanwendung [in English: Solvency II in Legal Application], (Karlsruhe: Verlag Versicherungswirtschaft 2009), 191 ff. and 225 ff.

[30] See, on sec. 7 a, para. 1, sent. 3 VAG *Dreher*, ZVersWiss (2006), 375 (401 f.).

[31] *Dreher*, ZVersWiss (2006), 375 (397 f.) with further references.

their equivalence in terms of fitness requirements with managing board members of insurance undertakings under the Solvency II Directive. If overall governance is assigned in the future to financial supervision, as provided in sec. 289, para. 3 of the VAG-RegE [Government's Draft of a Tenth Act Amending the German Insurance Supervision Act],[32] it would mean that BaFin could apply its legal view on German language proficiency even to the general agents and management in the offices of German insurance undertakings in other EU/European Economic Area countries outside Germany in accordance with sec. 54, para. 2, sent. 1 of the VAG-RegE [Government's Draft of a Tenth Act Amending the German Insurance Supervision Act].

BaFin laid out its view of expertise requirements for supervisory board members in a non-binding notice dated Feb. 22, 2010.[33] The standards described were met with enormous criticism due, for example, to their low qualification requirements, erroneous assumptions on corporate law, and certain implied ways to meet the requirements.[34] The notice will be entirely obsolete when the new standards of the Solvency II system take effect. It can therefore have no legal significance for key function holders, even indirectly.

8.2.3.2 Proceduralization

The Policies

Under art. 41, para. 3, subpara. 1 of the Solvency II Directive, insurance undertakings "shall have written policies in relation to at least risk management, internal control, internal audit and, where relevant, *outsourcing*". It must therefore encompass three of the key functions: risk management[35] and compliance—which is included by virtue of its membership in the internal control system under art. 46, para. 1, subpara. 2 of the Solvency II Directive—and internal audit. Regarding the actuarial function, the Directive recognizes an obligation to establish policies

---

[32] For a critical view of the alignment with the European insurance supervisory regime, see *Dreher/ Ballmaier*, "Das aufsichtliche Überprüfungsverfahren nach Art. 36 Solvency II-Richtlinie und § 289 VAG-RegE" [in English: The Supervisory Review Process under art. 36 of the Solvency II Directive and Sec. 289 of the Government's Draft of a Tenth Act Amending the German Insurance Supervision Act] in: Dreher/Wandt, eds., Solvency II in der Rechtsanwendung [in English: Solvency II in Legal Application], Frankfurt Edition, Volume 26, Karlsruhe (2012) 73ff. (Chap. 2, above).

[33] BaFin [German Federal Financial Supervisory Authority], "Merkblatt zur Kontrolle der Mitglieder von Verwaltungs- und Aufsichtsorganen gemäß KWG und VAG" [in English: Guidance Notice on Vetting Members of Administrative and Supervisory Bodies in accordance with the Banking Act and the Insurance Supervision Act] dated Feb. 22, 2010; the draft of a new version of the notice dated May 3, 2012 is currently in the consultation phase. The new notice contains no changes with respect to the matter discussed above.

[34] See *Dreher/Lange*, "Die Qualifikation der Aufsichtsratsmitglieder von Versicherungsunternehmen nach VAG und Solvency II" [in English: Qualifications of Supervisory Board Members of Insurance Undertakings under VAG and Solvency II] ZVersWiss (2011), 211 (218 f.) (Chap. 6, above, at 6.3.2).

[35] See also, on the risk management policies, art. 44, para. 2, subpara. 3 of the Solvency II Directive.

only indirectly, namely in art. 48, para. 1 i along with art. 41, para. 3, subpara. 1, sent. 2 of the Solvency II Directive. Added to these are further rules in the Solvency II system that also have implications for the need of policies of insurance undertakings. They proceed, i.a., from art. 263 SG11, para. 1, of the DVO, which states that insurance undertakings must establish, implement, and maintain "documented policies".[36]

Under art. 41, para. 3, subpara. 2, sent. 2 of the Solvency II Directive, the policies "shall be subject to prior approval by the administrative, management or supervisory body". For German law, it is not entirely clear whether or not the supervisory board, as positioned in the German dual organizational structure of managing board and supervisory board, is addressed by this. The uncertainly arises from the role of the managing board, which, under sec. 76 of the AktG [German Stock Corporation Act], is fully responsible for the management of the company and thus also for enacting essentially all company policies. The supervisory board can therefore "approve" neither the policies of the undertaking, nor its reports (as suggested by art. 55, para. 2 of the Solvency II Directive), nor any internal model (as suggested by art. 35, para. 5 and 116, para. 1 of the Solvency II Directive). Rather, the policies and reports etc. are directly attributable to managing board. It alone bears the responsibility, and not some other board upstream from it. The text of the Directive in other language versions and the objective pursued by the issuer of the Directive in assigning policy responsibility support the fundamental accountability of the managing board for the policies extensively discussed in the Solvency II Directive. Excluded however, are policies concerning the fit-and-proper requirements for managing board members under art. 263 SG11 of the DVO. The same applies to policies concerning the qualification requirements for supervisory board members[37] if the intention is to view supervisory board members as key function holders.[38] For the policies affecting members of the managing board, the supervisory board of each company holds sole responsibility. This on its own impedes the use of predetermined, standardized qualification policies across the group for all persons who effectively run the insurance undertaking or hold key functions in it as laid down in the insurance supervisory regime.

The reverse holds true for the managing board, which bears responsibility for policies affecting subordinate staff members in their capacity as key function holders under the insurance supervisory regime. With these policies the managing board can and must govern the basic responsibilities and powers of each key function. Thus, in order to comply with the requirements of art. 263 SG11 of the DVO, it must also identify the group of key function holders under the insurance supervisory regime for the particular undertaking either abstractly or based on job descriptions. Further, it must establish the fit-and-proper requirements for these persons and their subordinate staff. Finally, the DVO also specifies, as mandatory in

[36] See on this point *Dreher,* VersR (2012), 933 (940) (Chap. 7, above, at 7.3.5.4).

[37] See on this point, e.g., art. 263 SG11, para. 3 of the DVO.

[38] See *Dreher*, VersR (2012), 933 (937 f.) (Chap. 7, above, at 7.3.2.3).

the subject-matter of such policies, the procedures that must be provided for and followed in order to enforce these requirements within the insurance undertaking.

The Establishment and Documentation of Fitness ("Assessment")

Art. 263 SG11 of the DVO and the Level 3 Governance Guidelines place particular emphasis on the "assessment" as to whether key function holders meet the fit-and-proper requirements. Guideline 14 (b) and (c) of the Governance Guidelines thus expressly requires that the policies include "a description of the procedure of assessing fitness ... both initially and on an ongoing basis" and "a description of the minimum situations that give rise to a reassessment of fitness".[39] Thus an initial assessment of fitness must be made using a specific procedure, as well as reviews—whether regular or initiated by certain events—of assessments already made. This procedure must be included in the policies related to the key functions.[40] Consequently, numerous issues must be addressed by the policies, such as who is responsible for assessing which key function holder, what procedure must be followed in doing so, what evidence of formal qualifications must be submitted and in what executed form, how often or on what occasion is a review or recall of a current qualifications assessment necessary,[41] and what form of professional training is appropriate and necessary.[42]

The increasing importance of formalized processes under Solvency II and the flood of documentation requirements for insurance undertakings that comes with it,[43] also extends to the assessment of fitness for key function holders. It is only by documenting these internal assessment processes that the managing board can be relieved with respect to have both provided for the necessary organizational processes and induced their actual implementation—as required by art. 263 SG11, para. 1, of the DVO. This may include acts of delegation throughout the operational structure.[44] However, the managing board itself must always form

[39] See nos. 2.14 and 3.2.4 of the Governance Guidelines.

[40] See explanation to Guideline 14 of the Governance Guidelines at No. 3.55: "The policies and procedures describe how the undertakings will assess the persons".

[41] See the three examples in No. 3.56 of the Governance Guidelines.

[42] On this point see 8.2.3.3, below.

[43] See on this point *Dreher*, "Die Solvenzanforderungen in der Versicherungsaufsicht nach Solvency II und VAG-RegE" [in English: Solvency Requirements in Insurance Supervision under Solvency II and VAG-RegE [Government's Draft of a Tenth Act Amending the German Insurance Supervision Act]], at 4.2.3, ZVersWiss (2012), 381 (Chap. 6, above).

[44] See on the significance of management responsibility in general and the associated limits on delegation authority from a corporate law view *Dreher*, "Nicht delegierbare Geschäftsleiterpflichten" [in English: Non-delegable Duties of Business Managers] in Festschrift für [Publication in Honor of] Klaus J. Hopt on his 70th Birthday on Aug. 24, (2010), 517 (518 ff.) with further references, and with respect to horizontal or vertical delegation as viewed by insurance supervisory law *Dreher* id., n. 43, above, at 4.1.1.

its own impression in assessing the fitness of the functional leaders and their deputies because key function holders are often very close to the managing board as a result of their distinctive job description and decision-making powers.

8.2.3.3 Timing and Retention of Qualification

Art. 41, para. 1 of the Solvency II Directive mandates that key function holders must meet the fitness requirements at all times. Art. 263 SG11, para. 1 of the DVO repeats this, once again with the words "at all times". And at Level 3, the Governance Guidelines expressly provide as follows in explanation No. 3.38:

> The fitness assessment . . . includes arranging for further professional training as necessary, so that staff is also able to meet changing or increasing requirements of their particular responsibilities.

In other words, the fitness qualifications that the Solvency II system demands of key function holders must be present not only at the time an individual assumes the role, but permanently.[45] To ensure this, insurance undertakings are required—according to the Level 3 explanations—to provide the appropriate and necessary professional training based on the "assessment"[46] stressed earlier. The government's draft of the VAG [German Insurance Supervision Act], on the other hand, does not speak to the matter of qualification timing or duration in either sec. 25 or in the Statement of Reasons.

The view, which is suggested and to some extent represented—including by BaFin in its notice dated February 22, 2010[47]—in the context of the German insurance supervisory regime concerning the qualifications of supervisory board members, that such qualifications can be attained through additional training after the assumption of duties is inconsistent with corporate, liability, and supervision law[48] and is not an issue with respect to the qualifications of key function holders in light of the Solvency II requirements. The question it presents, which has clear implications on liability, may be easily confused with another question but, from a strictly legal standpoint, must be kept separate. The question is, what supervisory consequences can a qualification have that, in the view taken here, is required from the very start, but missing at the time, and only earned while a supervisory or subsequent judicial proceeding is taking place? This is not a matter of liability arising from decisions made in the absence of the necessary qualifications. Rather, it concerns the relevant point in time for the legal assessment of supervisory

[45] See on this point section "The Establishment and Documentation of Fitness ("Assessment")", above.

[46] See above, section "The Establishment and Documentation of Fitness ("Assessment")".

[47] See above, n. 33.

[48] See *Dreher/Lange*, ZVersWiss (2011), 211 (218 f.) (Chap. 6, above, at 6.3.2).

measures or, in other words, whether it is actually possible to have an after-the-fact cure for deficient qualifications that had no impact in terms of legal liability.[49]

8.2.4 *The Fitness of Subordinate Staff to Key Function Holders*

8.2.4.1 Solvency II

Under the two-tier qualification structure that underlies the Solvency II system, general qualification requirements also apply to the subordinate staff of key function holders.[50] As discussed previously, the Solvency II Directive in Recital 34—"fit and proper"—and the DVO in art. 258 SG6, para. 3—"necessary expertise"—rightly presume that all staff members who perform work in key functions possess the knowledge and skills necessary to properly carry out their duties.[51] The same applies pursuant to No. 3.31 of the Governance Guidelines for "all persons working within a key function". This underscores a difference between the general qualification requirements for all staff members in key functions[52] and the special qualifications that apply only to key function holders. From Recital 35 of the Solvency II Directive[53] and No. 3.37 of the Governance Guidelines it also proceeds that the special level of qualification required of the key function holder in each individual case partly determines the lower, general level of qualification related to the tasks and the undertaking that are required of the subordinate staff in key functions, and that the qualifications and experience of other staff members in the undertaking must be taken into account in determining the qualification requirements for staff members in key functions.

It follows that an undertaking's internal policies on key functions must, in accordance with these requirements and in consideration of the principle of proportionality, provide specific details not only on the required qualification profile of key function holders but also that of staff members in key functions. Added to this as further subject-matter of the policies are all of the other questions previously discussed in connection with the proceduralization of fitness and the qualification

[49] See in detail on this point *Dreher*, ZVersWiss (2006), 357 (411 f.) with numerous references as well as, recently, "VGH München" [in English: Munich High Administrative Court], NJW (2011), 2822.

[50] See above, at 8.2.1.

[51] See above, at 8.2.1.

[52] See as a parallel *WpHG [German Securities Trading Act]*-WpHGMaAnzV [German Securities Trading Act Employee Notice Regulations] of BaFin [German Federal Financial Supervisory Authority], BGBl. [German Federal Law Gazette] (2011), I 3116 ff. with abstract rules on the expertise and fit and proper criteria for staff members within the scope of the WpHG.

[53] See on this point 8.2.1, above.

dates and content for holders of key functions[54] if they also apply at the level of their subordinate staff members. The matter of professional development, i.a., through internal or external training, has material significance here. Guideline 14 (d) of the Governance Guidelines requires that the written policies for key function holders also include: "a description of the procedure of assessing fitness and proper requirements of other personnel, both initially and on an ongoing-basis".

8.2.4.2 VAG-RegE [Government's Draft of a Tenth Act Amending the German Insurance Supervision Act]

The government's draft of the VAG [German Insurance Supervision Act] itself does not address the matter of qualifications for staff members who are subordinate to key function holders. Only the Statement of Reasons for sec. 25 touches on it as follows: "All persons who are engaged in tasks identified as key tasks are subject to the requirements of sec. 24 of the VAG-E[55]". If this rule is taken literally, then any staff member who performs work for a key function is an addressee of sec. 25 of the VAG-RegE [Government's Draft of a Tenth Act Amending the German Insurance Supervision Act]. But this would not be consistent with the wording of the rule, which appropriately speaks only to those persons "who effectively run the insurance undertaking or hold other key tasks". Further, and most importantly, such excessive qualification requirements would be compatible neither with the two-part qualification structure of the Solvency II system nor with the principal of proportionality that underlies it. Thus, the Statement of Reasons for sec. 25 of the VAG-RegE [Government's Draft of a Tenth Act Amending the German Insurance Supervision Act], despite its broadly formulated wording, has no ultimate legal significance in the present issue of qualification requirements for subordinate staff members of key function holders.

8.3 The "Proper" Requirement for Key Function Holders and Their Subordinate Staff Members in Key Functions

8.3.1 The Two-Tier Structure of the Proper Requirement and the Proceduralization of the Proper Requirement as Starting Point

In addition to fitness, the proper requirement of key function holders plays a significant role in the management of insurance undertakings. Under Solvency II, the two elements of the fit-and-proper requirements are of equal importance and

[54] See above, 8.2.3.2 and 8.2.3.3.

[55] The reference to sec. 24 is an editing error; sec. 25 is meant.

rank under the law. The chairman of the European Insurance Occupational Pensions Authority (EIOPA) stresses repeatedly that problems at insurance undertakings are primarily "attributable to the failure of management and not unmet capital requirements".[56] With the personal proper requirement now brought to bear in addition to fitness, the issues[57] that emerge are essentially the same. At the outset, it concerns the two-tier structure of qualifications—repeated here in a two-tier structure of proper requirement—and the proceduralization of the proper requirement under the sub-topics of policies, assessment, and documentation as well as timing and maintenance of the proper requirement. The parallel starting points proceed from what are fundamentally similar legal rules governing the fit-and-proper requirements in the Solvency II system. For example, CEIOPS Guideline 14 on *Policies and Procedures* applies to both areas.

8.3.2 The Proper Requirement of Key Function Holders

8.3.2.1 Solvency II

Under the overarching term "proper", art. 42, para. 1 b of the Solvency II Directive requires that key function holders be "of good repute and integrity".[58] Art. 43 of the Solvency II Directive also provides detailed rules on the mutual recognition of proof of good repute or proof of no previous bankruptcy among the Member States by submission of the equivalent documents or assurance under oath. Recital 99 of the DVO expands on this in Level 2 as follows:

> The past conduct of that person should be examined to see whether that person may not be able to effectively discharge his duties in accordance with the applicable rules, regulations and guidelines. Information regarding past conduct may be information sourced from criminal or financial records. A person's past business conduct could provide indications as to that person's integrity.

Along with this is art. 263 SG11, para. 4 of the DVO, according to which the assessment of the proper requirement includes the following:

> An assessment of that person's honesty and financial soundness based on evidence regarding their character, personal behaviour and business conduct including any criminal, financial, supervisory aspects and relevant for the purpose assessment.

[56] Statement by *Bernardino* according to a report in the Börsenzeitung [in English: Stock Market Journal] dated Feb. 11, 2012.

[57] See above, at 8.2.1 and 8.2.3.

[58] Recital 34, sent. 2 of the Solvency II Directive addresses only the necessary proper requirement.

Guideline 13 of the Governance Guidelines provides further requirements that are again accompanied by very detailed explanatory text.[59]

The actual criteria for good repute and integrity are found under the overarching term chosen in art. 42, para. 1 b of the Solvency II Directive. But the distinction is not always applied at the three levels, where one invariably finds the term "reputation" or "character" in place of the term "integrity". The intent of the Solvency II legislator, however, is adequately described only with the overarching term of proper requirement. A central problem with evaluation under supervisory law of a person's reliability, integrity, reputation, or character—to use the terms of the Solvency II system—is in designing an assessment that can be documented and legally enforced. In this respect, Recital 99 of the DVO provides guidance by stating a person's past conduct can provide indications of future fulfillment of the proper requirement. Documents associated with criminal background or finances should be reviewed for this purpose. Art. 263 SG11, para. 4 of the DVO in fact requires that an assessment of "honesty and financial soundness" be based on evidence regarding the person's character, personal behavior, and business conduct.

Governance Guideline 14 picks up the frequent reference to criminal conduct in the past and expands it to disciplinary or administrative offenses. As in art. 263 SG11, para. 4 of the DVO, Guideline 14 and its explanatory text stress that the offenses must be relevant to the purposes of supervision. Yet based on the aims of the Solvency II Directive and the scope of the law on supervision of insurance undertakings, the explanatory text for the relevant requirements overreaches by, for example, stating that the entirety of consumer protection and corporate law are deemed relevant. The explanatory text is also unacceptable in consideration of the presumption of innocence as it would take account of ongoing investigations or enforcement measures outside of court proceedings—even in cases where these originate simply from professional associations. It also lists "honesty" as a component of the proper requirement. The important question in this respect is whether any conflicts of interest[60] exist which would necessitate, for example, consideration of an individual's financial situation.

As is the case with a number of terms used—such as character assessment under art. 263, para. 4 of the DVO—this requirement reveals that the Solvency II rules have lost sight of the principle of proportionality when it comes to assessing the proper requirement. Unless the aim is to have "see-through key function holders"—with the same as members of the managing board and supervisory board—and if one respects the fundamental right to the protection of one's own privacy and informational self-determination as required by law, then the assessment of the proper requirement cannot extend to a person's private relationships.

The full focus of the proper requirement assessment is therefore on an individual's professional and business affairs. For the reasons stated, there are just two

[59] No. 3.46 to 3.54 Governance Guidelines; see also the general Explanation No. 3.32, sent. 2 of the Governance Guidelines.

[60] On this point generally see art. 249 SG1, para. 5 of the DVO.

avenues through which the proper requirement assessment can reach into the private sphere, be it for personal character or financial soundness. The first would be an assessment of objective, formally accessible data such as register abstracts, and the second would be consideration of any determinations made in relation to specific events, such as a personal bankruptcy for the head of risk management. Art. 43 of the Solvency II Directive itself makes clear that, under normal circumstances, meaning aside from essential additional findings related to certain events, "proof of good repute" in the form of an "extract from the judicial record" or equivalent document suffices. This is so because under para. 1 of this rule, a Member State that requires "of its own nationals proof of good repute ... shall accept ... as sufficient evidence in respect of nationals of other Member States the production" of such documents.[61] It then stands to reason that art. 263 SG11, para. 4 of the DVO and the elaborate Governance Guidelines each require significant correction prior to adoption and should be restricted to standards that are constitutionally acceptable and legally practicable.

The determination as to whether and to what extent any facts related to professional matters or to private matters that either impact the assessment of the proper requirement or constitute an occasion for further assessment can generally be made through questionnaires.[62] Using such questionnaires, information can be gathered regarding professional conduct (i.e., about violations of external or internal rules and policies in the past, even from previous superiors under certain circumstances) and also regarding private conduct, based on the position being filled or assessed for continuation (i.e. about special circumstances with professional relevance such as a personal bankruptcy or excessive personal debt with an individual's overall net asset balance[63]).

Conclusions about present and future proper requirement drawn from past conduct have enormous significance in the present context. As much as an impeccable past indicates current and future fulfillment of the proper requirement, past supervisory offenses are hardly a monocausal indicator of current or future nonfulfillment of the proper requirement. Specifically, a weighting of the circumstances at play in the past is needed. Of relevance to this are, for example the severity and duration of a legal infringement, the instance of the officials or judicial institution taking account of the right to appeal, as well as subsequent reviews of the facts and/or legal aspects, the length of time since the infringement and the "self-cleaning" of the person in question, especially through subsequent unblemished conduct.[64] Against this background, Explanation No. 3.52 Governance Guidelines

[61] According to para. 2, even submission of a declaration under oath is sufficient in cases where a Member State does not issue such documentation.

[62] Computer simulation could also be considered, involving, for example, decision-making in situations where conflict of interest or legal infringement plays a role.

[63] Of course, this "personal balance sheet" is not to be disclosed to the insurance undertaking.

[64] See in this regard, e.g., relevant methods in cartel procurement law of restoring the reliability of a public contracting entity within the meaning of sec. 97, para. 4, of the GWB [Act Against Restraints of Competition], *Dreher*, "Die "Selbstreinigung" zur Rückgewinnung der

rightly establishes that there can be no automatic designation of non-fulfillment of the proper requirement based on past supervisory infringements.[65] Instead, each determination of the proper requirement must be made on a case-by-case basis.

Up to now, the notion of proper requirement found in trade law was always applied in the context of the control of the proper requirement with regard to managing board or supervisory board members, or of those who hold a significant interest. Already the past, this has been fundamentally objectionable due to the European origin of the proper requirement and the autonomous interpretation of terms in European law if the contours of such a term were discernible.[66] Under the DVO and the Governance Guidelines, the situation is now not only prevailing but also especially important. This is so because both regulatory levels define and concretize the concept of the proper requirement in European law through art. 42 of Solvency II Directive to a far greater extent than before. Thus, the interpretation of the term "proper requirement" must now be made within the requirements and—to the extent they apply—without regard to German trade case law and literature.

8.3.2.2 VAG-RegE [Government's Draft of a Tenth Act Amending the German Insurance Supervision Act]

The Statement of Reasons for sec. 25 of the VAG-RegE [Government's Draft of a Tenth Act Amending the German Insurance Supervision Act] presumes that "with respect to the personal proper requirement the same requirements apply for all persons within the scope of sec. 25 of the VAG-RegE [Government's Draft of a Tenth Act Amending the German Insurance Supervision Act] regardless of the individual risk profile of an undertaking".[67] This statement draws a distinction between proper requirement and the requirements for fitness. The German legislator does not provide a basis for the uniform treatment apparently necessary for managing and supervisory board members and key function holders. It is unpersuasive in its substance and stands in contradiction to the European insurance supervisory regime.

Substantively, there is no common basis of evaluation for a uniform inquiry into the proper requirement for all persons. Managing board members, for example, are different from supervisory board members in their influence on the decisions of the undertaking. Unofficially, this leads to a higher standard of proper requirement for

kartellvergaberechtlichen Zuverlässigkeit" [in English: The 'Self-Cleaning' for Restoration of reliability under Cartel Procurement Law] in Festschrift für [Publication in Honor of] Horst Franke on his 60th Birthday, (2009), 31 ff.; *Dreher/Hoffmann*, NZBau (2012), 265.

[65] See as well, previously, *Dreher*, ZVersWiss (2006), 375 (389).

[66] See *Dreher*, ZVersWiss (2006), 375 (385 ff.).

[67] VAG-RegE [Government's Draft of a Tenth Act Amending the German Insurance Supervision Act], id. n. 4 above, at Statement of Reasons for sec. 25 VAG [German Insurance Supervision Act] at 272.

the former. For example, while the proper requirement of a managing board member comes under scrutiny for a past infringement of competition law resulting in a fine,[68] such offense cannot carry the same significance for supervisory board members because it cannot impact the future functioning of the business in the same way. And, looking at past insider trading as an example, one must surely make distinctions within the managing board between a capital investment manager and a human resources or IT manager. With respect to the key function holders, these persons are subordinate to the managing board that runs the undertaking within the meaning of sec. 76, para. 1 of the AktG [German Stock Corporation Act] and thus do not have the same level of responsibility and decision-making power for the actions of the undertaking. Prior tax arrears of a specific undertaking, for example, would have different significance for each managing board member than for a key function holder such as the director of the actuarial function.

Setting aside the absence of a substantive foundation for the uniformity proposition for proper requirements in the VAG [German Insurance Supervision Act], the concept is also inconsistent with art. 263 SG11, para. 4 of the DVO. At this regulatory level, the test of whether a key function holder is proper takes place specifically on the following terms: "an assessment of that person's ... based on evidence regarding their". In the same manner the explanations for Guideline 13 of the Governance Guidelines frequently emphasize the circumstances that shape the proper requirement assessment of the individual. Then, however, Explanation No. 3.53 cites nearly word-for-word the passage in the Statement of Reasons to the VAG-RegE [Government's Draft of a Tenth Act Amending the German Insurance Supervision Act] that was cited at the beginning of this section. On this matter, it suffices to point out that Level 3 provisions, which are essentially non-binding, cannot expand the law laid down in the Directive and DVO.[69]

Why the government draft of the VAG [German Insurance Supervision Act] does not implement art. 43 of the Solvency II Directive[70] even though it would ease the testing of the proper requirement enormously, is simply inexplicable. The simplified documentation of the proper requirement under this rule could be directly significant for personnel changes or movements between large insurance undertakings within the EU/European Economic Area Member States. From a legal view non-implementation also brings up a matter of basic freedoms. This concerns limitations on the free movement of labor under art. 45 of the AEUV [Treaty on the Functioning of the European Union] in cases where an individual from another EU/European Economic Area country intends to move to an insurance undertaking headquartered in Germany and the proof of the proper requirement issued by his or her current home country is not recognized in Germany.

---

[68] See *Dreher*, ZVersWiss (2006), 375 (389 f.).

[69] See *Dreher*, VersR (2012), 933 (935 f.) (Chap. 7, above, at 7.2.3).

[70] See on this point 8.3.2.1, above.

8.3.3 The "Proper" Requirement for Staff Members Subordinate to Key Function Holders

8.3.3.1 Solvency II

As with the fitness, the two-tier structure of the Solvency II system continues in the proper requirements. Thus, it is already required in Recital 34, sent. 1 of the Solvency II Directive that "all persons who perform key functions" be "proper". This category includes subordinate staff to key function holders. That this affects all staff in a key function also arises from the contrast with the duty of notice to supervisory officials that explicitly applies "only to key function holders" under Recital 34, sent. 2 of the Solvency II Directive. Explanation No. 3.31 of the Governance Guidelines also expressly repeats the validity of the "proper" criterion for all staff that work in a key function. Going far beyond the regulatory context, Explanation No. 3.53 even adds that the proper requirement applies to all employees of an insurance undertaking. The only correct pronouncement in connection with this is that individual graduated inquiries into repute and integrity based on specific responsibilities and authority must be conducted for other staff members—meaning also those in key functions.

8.3.3.2 VAG-RegE [Government's Draft of a Tenth Act Amending the German Insurance Supervision Act]

The government's draft of the VAG [German Insurance Supervision Act] makes no specific statement on fit-and-proper requirements for the subordinate staff members of key function holders. Nothing other than the issue already discussed is found here,[71] this issue being that the Statement of Reasons, in contrast to the text in sec. 25 of the VAG-RegE [Government's Draft of a Tenth Act Amending the German Insurance Supervision Act], wrongly seeks to encompass all persons working in key functions in the same manner as the key function holders themselves.

8.4 The Remuneration of Key Function Holders

Secs. 26 and 34 of the VAG-RegE [Government's Draft of a Tenth Act Amending the German Insurance Supervision Act] provide remuneration rules and a legal basis for a corresponding regulation in furtherance of sec. 64 b of the VAG [German Insurance Supervision Act]. They do not explicitly address key function holders on this matter. Although the "general governance requirements" under art. 41 of the Solvency II Directive and the associated legal basis in art. 50, para. 1 a of the

[71] See above, at 8.2.4.2.

Solvency II Directive do not go into the subject of remuneration at insurance undertakings, the EU Commission in art. 249 SG1, para. 1 l of the DVO requires that the undertaking adopt written principles on their remuneration policy. Art. 265 SG13, para. 1 c of the DVO concretizes this, stating, i.a., that the remuneration policy applies to key function holders and must take into account their tasks and performance.

Art. 265 SG13, para. 2 of the DVO provides a total of seven remuneration principles that insurance undertakings must follow in establishing and implementing remuneration policies. These expressly apply to key function holders. They even include, under (b), the requirement that the variable part of remuneration for staff members in key functions—that is, not only that of the key function holders—must be independent of the performance of the operating units and areas they control. This has significance particularly when formulating the remuneration principles for key function holders and their subordinate staff members when the key functions are organized in a decentralized manner.[72] The Governance Guidelines, which are to be revised with respect to remuneration policies after the DVO is adopted, currently contain no further information specific to the remuneration of key function holders.[73]

8.5 The Duties of Notice and Public Disclosure for Key Function Holders

8.5.1 The Duties of Notice to Supervisory Authorities

8.5.1.1 Solvency II

As indicated earlier,[74] there are particular duties of notice to supervisory authorities that affect key function holders. According to art. 42, para. 2 of the Solvency II Directive—as seen generally in Recital 34 of the Solvency II Directive as well as, with respect to outsourcing, art. 297 SRS4, para. 2 a of the DVO—any "change to the identity" of key function holders must be reported to the supervisory authority. Additionally, "all information needed to assess whether . . . the persons are fit and proper" must be transmitted. Under art. 297 SRS4, para. 1 b of the DVO, the supervisory authority must be informed of the undertaking's policies and processes to ensure compliance with the fit-and-proper requirements. Under art. 42, para. 3 of the Solvency II Directive, the supervisory authority must also be notified if a key function holder has been "replaced" because he or she "no longer fulfills these requirements".

[72] See *Dreher*, VersR (2012), 933 (939, 941) (Chap. 7, above, at 7.3.5.3 and 7.3.5.5).

[73] See Governance Guidelines, Guideline 10 and Explanation No. 3.28 f.

[74] See *Dreher*, VersR (2012), 933 (938) (Chap. 7, above, at 7.3.3).

Even the wording of the Solvency II rules shows that this is not a requirement for notice of a prospective transfer of the position of key function holder, but for notice of a transfer already accomplished. This is seen in the words "changes to the identity" and "replacement" of such a person, which denote past action. They refer to an event that has already occurred. Recital 98, sent. 2 of the DVO confirms this with the following passage:

> However, acknowledging the need to avoid undue burden on insurance or reinsurance undertakings or supervisors, a notification by insurance and reinsurance-undertakings should not imply pre-approval by the supervisory authority.

But, if there is no basis for checking in advance and obtaining pre-approval or rejection of an individual designated by the insurance undertaking to become a key function holder, then precisely such duty of pre-notice that fails of its purpose would cause an undue burden on insurance undertakings and supervisors that Recital 98, sent. 2 of DVO wishes to avoid. This obvious result of not requiring insurance undertakings to provide advance notice to the supervisory authority is also not in question in the contradictory Explanation No. 3.57 (a) of the Governance Guidelines,[75] according to which a duty of notice exists "when a person . . . who is responsible for a key function is going to be or has been appointed". This explanation is also inconsistent with Explanation No. 1.11 of the Governance Guidelines, according to which the notice pertains to "persons . . . being key function holders".

Ultimately, further excessive rules attached to the duties of notice at Level 3 have no legal significance. Such can be seen in the requirement in Explanation No. 3.60 (c) of the Governance Guidelines in that a rationale for the person's nomination as a key function holder be submitted in addition to the information the insurance undertaking must already provide to the supervisory authority under art 42 para. 2 of the Solvency II Directive. Nor do the facts substantiate that Explanation No. 3.63 of the Governance Guidelines should make a key function holder responsible for the content, completeness, and accuracy of the notice,[76] while at the same time making the insurance undertaking responsible for its timeliness. Governance Guideline 14 (a) further requires[77] that the undertaking's policies describe the notification procedure to the supervisory authority, including the extent to which it involves the key function holders.

[75] See, on this issue, the hierarchy of the regulatory language in the Solvency II system, above, at 8.3.2.2.

[76] It is noteworthy that only in this place the Explanation uses the term "application" instead of "notification".

[77] See on this point section "The Policies", above.

8.5.1.2 VAG-RegE [Government's Draft of a Tenth Act Amending the German Insurance Supervision Act]

Sec. 44, no. 1 of the VAG-RegE [Government's Draft of a Tenth Act Amending the German Insurance Supervision Act] currently includes a duty of notice for "the planned appointment . . . of other persons responsible for key tasks . . . including the information relevant to the evaluation of their qualification (sec. 25, para. 1)". Continuation of the current legal situation is the only rationale cited in the Statement of Reasons of the VAG-RegE [Government's Draft of a Tenth Act Amending the German Insurance Supervision Act][78] for this advance notice demand; and this demand contravenes the European insurance supervisory regime and must not be heeded should it survive unamended. There is also the requirement, according to sec. 44, no. 2 of the VAG-RegE [Government's Draft of a Tenth Act Amending the German Insurance Supervision Act], to give notice of "the retirement. . . of any of the persons named under No. 1 including information as to the reasons if this is relevant to the evaluation of his or her qualification (sec. 25, para. 1)". This obligation to state reasons for the replacement of a key function holder is also found in Explanation no. 3.62 (b) of the Governance Guidelines.

In contrast to the notice that a person has become a key function holder,[79] this sort of requirement to state the rationale for the replacement of a key function holder by an insurance undertaking can be justified.[80] Only such statement of rationale can occasion any necessary inquiry by the supervisory authority, which had prior opportunity to evaluate the qualifications and proper requirement of the person in question in the context of the duty of notice, into whether the replacement was based on reasons that are irrelevant rather than founded grounds such as retirement or promotion. The Statement of Reasons for the VAG-RegE [Government's Draft of a Tenth Act Amending the German Insurance Supervision Act], however, justifies the requirement for submitting the rationale by stating that the quitting persons "can be expected to seek a comparable position at another insurance undertaking" and thus the supervisory authority will be "in a position to conduct a particularly thorough examination when evaluating the qualifications of an applicant that has separated from another undertaking".[81] This particular Statement of Reasons is not only the basis of an unsubstantiated prejudice against those

[78] VAG-RegE [Government's Draft of a Tenth Act Amending the German Insurance Supervision Act], id. n. 4 above, at Statement of Reasons for sec. 44 at 278.

[79] See 8.5.1.1, above.

[80] See regarding the current equivalent practice of the BaFin [Federal Financial Supervisory Authority] with the retirement of a managing board member *Hasse*, "Informations- und Offenlegungspflichten der Versicherungsunternehmen nach Solvency II" [in English: Information and Disclosure Obligations for Insurance Undertakings under Solvency II] in: Dreher/Wandt, eds., Solvency II in der Rechtsanwendung [in English: Solvency II in Legal Application], (Karlsruhe: Verlag Versicherungswirtschaft 2009), 61 (79) with further references.

[81] VAG-RegE [Government's Draft of a Tenth Act Amending the German Insurance Supervision Act], id. n. 4 above, at Statement of Reasons for sec. 44 at 279.

who change employers and in doing so often climb the corporate ladder simply by virtue of their qualifications. Far more, it assigns the Supervisory Authority with a review of the qualifications of these persons that is not provided for in the Solvency II system, independent of any specific new responsibilities assigned to the current key function holder.

8.5.2 The Duties of Public Disclosure

Art. 51 of the Solvency II Directive requires that insurance undertakings publish a very extensive "report on solvency and financial condition".[82] This report shall also include a description of the system of governance. Based on this, art. 285 PDS4 of the DVO requires the following in the report: under para. 1 a, a description of the significant roles and responsibilities of key functions; under para. 1 c iii—factually unjustifiable—a description of the main characteristics of the system of occupational pensions and early retirement for key function holders, unless the remuneration report expressly excludes information on staff member remuneration; under para. 2, a description of both the fit-and-proper requirements and the procedure for assessing these requirements for key function holders. Sec. 50 of the VAG-RegE [Government's Draft of a Tenth Act Amending the German Insurance Supervision Act] correctly says nothing on this matter since the DVO becomes directly applicable law in each Member State when it takes effect.

8.6 Supervisory Recall and Prohibition of Exercise of Function for Key Function Holders in Cases of Fit-and-Proper Deficiencies and Supervisory Right to Direct Information from Key Function Holders

8.6.1 Solvency II

Art. 34, para. 2 of the Solvency II Directive grants power to the supervisory authorities to take measures "with regard to insurance or reinsurance undertakings, and the members of their administrative, management or supervisory body". There is no supervisory authority to intervene with the subordinate staff of the managing

[82] On this point, in detail, see *Dreher/Schaaf*, "Die Veröffentlichungspflichten von Versicherungsunternehmen gegenüber der Allgemeinheit nach Solvency II" [in English: Insurance Undertakings' Duty of Disclosure to the Public under Solvency II] in: Dreher/Wandt, eds., Solvency II in der Rechtsanwendung, [in English: Solvency II in Legal Application], Verlag Versicherungswirtschaft, Karlsruhe (2009), 129 ff. (Chap. 13, below).

board, such as key function holders, found here or anywhere else. On the contrary, Recital 98, sent. 3 of the DVO confirms that the only addressees regarding measures with respect to key function holders are the insurance undertakings:

> In the event that a supervisory authority concludes that a person does not comply with the fit and proper requirements set out in directive 2009/138/EC it should have the power to require the undertaking to replace that person.

Thus the supervisory authorities must direct their demand to replace a key function holder with another person exclusively to the managing board of the insurance undertaking. And this alone accords with the general rule regarding the key functions found in art. 258 SG6, para. 1, sent. 2 DVO, according to which each key function operates under the ultimate responsibility of the managing board.

8.6.2 VAG-RegE [Government's Draft of a Tenth Act Amending the German Insurance Supervision Act]

In contrast to the Solvency II rules, the VAG-RegE [Government's Draft of a Tenth Act Amending the German Insurance Supervision Act] directs in sec. 297 sent. 1 no. 1 that the BaFin [Federal Financial Supervisory Authority] shall not only demand the recall of a key function holder in an insurance undertaking but also "directly prohibit this person from the exercise of office" if "facts are present from which it ensues that the person does not meet the requirements of sec. 25". In view of the Solvency II requirements, the latter is inconsistent with European law. In another inconsistency with the system, it deviates from the new provision added for compliance officers, taking effect on November 1, 2012, in sec. 34 d, para. 4, sent. 1, no. 1 of the WpHG [German Securities Trading Act],[83] which provides the BaFin only with the authority "to prohibit the investment services enterprise from entrusting that staff member with the reported activity for so long as he does not satisfy the statutory requirements". Considering the relevance to basic rights of the BaFin measures affecting the key function holders, the comparison between the VAG [German Insurance Supervision Act] and the WpHG requirements also highlights the deficiencies present in sec. 297, sent. 1, no. 1 of the VAG-RegE [Government's Draft of a Tenth Act Amending the German Insurance Supervision Act] with respect to the proportionality of the supervisory power it provided for.[84] This is so not only because of the missing "so long as" clause in the VAG-RegE [Government's Draft of a Tenth Act Amending the German Insurance Supervision

[83] See art. 1 no. 9 and 9 Gesetz vom [Law of] 5 Apr. 2011 BGBl (2011) I 538 and with this WpHGMaAnzV [German Securities Trading Act Employee Notice Regulations] n. 52.

[84] See in more detail on the supervisory interventions frequently graduated in accordance with the principle of proportionality *Dreher*, ZVersWiss (2006), 396 (408 f.).

Act], but also based on a comparison of sent. 1, no. 1 to the expressly required prior "warning" by the supervisory authority when it intends to recall managing board or supervisory board members or to prohibit their exercise of the office in accordance with sec. 297 sent. 1, nos. 2 and 3 of the VAG-RegE [Government's Draft of a Tenth Act Amending the German Insurance Supervision Act].

The criticism of the recall, in contrast, applies only to the terminology. A recall is a reversal of an appointment. But unlike managing board and supervisory board members, who are also included in sec. 297 of the VAG-RegE [Government's Draft of a Tenth Act Amending the German Insurance Supervision Act], key function holders are not appointed. They are assigned responsibility by the managing board. Thus they must be relieved of the responsibility if necessary, and dismissed without regard to this responsibility, if this is also required, or relieved of such duties in the insurance undertaking in advance of the effective date of such termination.

For the first time, sec. 299, para. 1, no. 1 of the VAG-RegE [Government's Draft of a Tenth Act Amending the German Insurance Supervision Act][85] gives the BaFin [Federal Financial Supervisory Authority] a right to information from all "employees" of insurance undertakings and therefore from key function holders and their subordinate staff members. All employees are expressly obligated to provide information in such inquiries. To start with, this requirement is inconsistent with the European insurance supervisory regime for the reason stated earlier, namely that the Solvency II requirements provide no legal basis for such procedures to be conducted by the supervisory authorities with respect to the subordinate staff of the managing board. There is also the fact, specifically with regard to the informational duties of the insurance undertaking to the supervisory authority ("supervisory reporting"), that these duties according to art. 35 of the Solvency II Directive likewise extend only to the insurance undertaking and to the third parties named, none of which includes the subordinate employees to the managing board of the insurance undertaking. The implementation table attached to the VAG-RegE [Government's Draft of a Tenth Act Amending the German Insurance Supervision Act] for sec. 299, para. 1 no. 1 of the VAG-RegE [Government's Draft of a Tenth Act Amending the German Insurance Supervision Act], therefore, can also only refer to the stipulations of the Solvency II Directive, which simply do not justify this direct right of inquiry and a corresponding duty to provide information.

It must also be considered that a request for information directed by the BaFin [Federal Financial Supervisory Authority] directly to key function holders could lead to substantial conflicts of interest for them. The difference between a key function holder acting essentially under instruction in the interest of the company and an enterprise official implanted in the company in the public interest and not bound by instruction[86] would become very apparent through this duty to provide

[85] See currently sec. 83, para. 1, sent. 1, no. 1 of the VAG, in which the duty to provide information does not extend to employees of insurance undertakings.

[86] See in detail *Rittner/Dreher*, Europäisches und deutsches Wirtschaftsrecht [in English: European and German Economic Law] (3rd ed. 2008) sec. 12, ref. 22 f.

information. The duty to provide information on the part of key function holders to the insurance supervisory authority would ultimately almost amount to the partially existing reporting duty of the enterprise officials. Finally, key function holders would be severely affected by this sort of indirect reporting duty in that they would have be apprehensive about a recall or a prohibition of exercise of function any time information requested by the supervisory authority is withheld.

8.7 Summary

1. The distinction between key function holders and subordinate staff members in key functions remains meaningful in the qualification requirements of the Solvency II Directive in a two-tier qualification structure. Accordingly, more narrowly regulated qualification requirements apply to key function holders particularly in the Solvency II Directive and the DVO. In contrast, for subordinate staff members working in key functions, more general and lower qualification requirements related to the specific responsibilities and undertaking apply.
2. Special rules in the area of qualification requirements are seen in the Solvency II Directive for the actuarial function and for the outsourcing of key functions.
3. The qualification requirements for key function holders under the Solvency II Directive and the DVO are based on both professional and formal qualifications as well as relevant knowledge and experience. They allow for reasonable distinctions and the transfer of qualifications. Sec. 25 of the VAG-RegE [Government's Draft of a Tenth Act Amending the German Insurance Supervision Act], on the other hand, carries the current German standards forward. It is therefore more strict relative to the Solvency II requirements and inconsistent with European law in this respect. This is seen in the requirements trio of "three years", "insurance undertaking" and "comparable size and type of business". Indeed these criteria are supposed to apply only in the context of the "performance of management duties", meaning primarily to members of the managing board. But they could spill over to key function holders in the insurance supervisory regime. Sec. 25 of the VAG-RegE [Government's Draft of a Tenth Act Amending the German Insurance Supervision Act] also expressly requires "theoretical and practical knowledge of the insurance business" for key function holders. These far-reaching requirements are legally impermissible and excessive in substance for both groups because they would hinder persons from changing industries and rising in the hierarchy of an undertaking—including in the course of a change from one insurance undertaking to another. The Solvency II rules, on the other hand, expressly take account of knowledge and experience from other parts of the financial services sector and from other fields of business. They do not apply a rigid 3-year restriction and are not based on experience and knowledge from undertakings of comparable size and business type.

4. Knowledge of the German language is not a qualification requirement for key function holders if they know the substantive requirements of the responsibilities assumed and communication skill in the German language can be insured with the aid of language mediators.
5. In addition to fitness, the Solvency II Directive also requires the fulfillment of the proper requirement for key function holders. The two-tier approach of a distinction between key function holders and their staff members also applies here. Regardless of the use of numerous additional terms in the Solvency II system such as integrity, reputation, and character, the term proper is the only relevant legal term. This term proper in the European law is essentially autonomous, which means it is independent of the German proper criteria under trade law.
6. When assessing the proper requirement, documents regarding past conduct such as register abstracts should be relevant for the determination. However, the Level 2 and 3 text of Solvency II is excessive in terms of the details it seeks from the private sphere of the addressees of the rule. This can be seen in the documentation requirements, the relevance of certain conduct in the past, and the relevance of certain proceedings before administrative authorities, courts, or even professional associations. The requirements are based on the concept of a fully transparent key function holder which is blind to basic rights. It loses sight of a fundamental principle of the Solvency II system: the principle of proportionality. This constitutional deficiency is found not only in the inquiry into repute and integrity for key function holders but also for members of the supervisory and managing boards since the Solvency II text encompasses all addressees of the fit-and-proper requirements essentially to the same degree.
7. It is not sustainable either factually or under European law if the government's draft of the VAG [German Insurance Supervision Act] assumes a uniform concept of proper requirement for all addressees of the rule. The failure to implement art. 43 of the Solvency II Directive in the VAG-RegE [Government's Draft of a Tenth Act Amending the German Insurance Supervision Act] is also unsustainable on the facts and leads to avoidable legal problems in the free movement of labor in cases where key function holders engage in cross-border activity.
8. The Solvency II rules require an extensive proceduralization of the fit-and-proper requirements. This applies both to the policies required for the first time for key functions and to assessing and documenting that the requirements for the key functions under the insurance supervisory regime are complied with.
9. The insurance undertaking must establish, implement, and maintain documented policies in which they describe all significant aspects related to the key functions, the key function holders, and the subordinate staff in key functions. Because of the numerous topics to be addressed in the policies, they have an enormous scope and corresponding complexity. The policies that apply to the key function holders and the staff subordinate to them in key functions are the ultimate responsibility of the managing board. However, the supervisory board of the given insurance undertaking is responsible for the requirements

aimed at managing board members. This prevents the adoption by the managing board of an ultimate parent company of the group of group-wide fit-and-proper standards for all addressees of the rule.

10. The assessment and documentation of the fit-and-proper requirements for key function holders is the subject-matter of detailed rules in the Solvency II provisions. For this purpose, numerous process-oriented rules, i.a., are required in the policies of insurance undertakings; and these policies must be observed in practice. Professional training of key function holders and their staff is of special significance in this concern. As a rule, the managing board itself is required to assess the fit-and-proper requirement of key function holders.
11. The fitness and personal proper requirement of key function holders must be present "at all times" and permanent. From this it follows not only that post-hoc qualification following the assumption of duties as a key function holder is not countenanced but also that an obligation exists for continuous professional training in order to maintain the required fitness.
12. The DVO includes requirements for the remuneration of key function holders that especially affect the variable part of remuneration of key function holders in a decentralized structure of key functions.
13. The Solvency II requirements provide for certain duties on the part of insurance undertakings to notify the supervisory authority with respect to information on key function holders. This includes, i.a., after-the-fact information concerning the assumption of the responsibilities of a key function holder by an individual or the relief from responsibilities in the case of a current key function holder. The VAG-RegE [Government's Draft of a Tenth Act Amending the German Insurance Supervision Act], on the other hand, imposes an inconsistent duty on insurance undertakings to notify the BaFin [Federal Financial Supervisory Authority] even that such an event is intended.
14. In their "report on solvency and financial position", insurance undertakings must disclose certain information to the general public concerning the organization of their key functions, the corresponding fit-and-proper requirements and their proceduralization as well as, in some cases, even the retirement benefits of key function holders.
15. Under the Solvency II requirements, the insurance supervisory authority can take measures solely against the insurance undertaking for the purpose of removing key function holders. In contrast, in addition to the supervisory authority's recall demands to insurance undertakings, the VAG-RegE [Government's Draft of a Tenth Act Amending the German Insurance Supervision Act] also provides the supervisory authority with the direct power towards a person to prohibit the exercise of responsibilities as a key function holder if the fit-and-proper requirements are not, or no longer, met. Assignment of such power contravenes European law. It is also inconsistent with the principal of proportionality simply in consideration of basic rights and their relevance to these measures. Finally, it is not compatible with the financial services supervisory system.

16. The right to information provided for the first time in sec. 299, para. 1, no. 1 of the VAG-RegE [Government's Draft of a Tenth Act Amending the German Insurance Supervision Act] with respect to all employees of insurance undertakings, and therefore with respect to the key function holders and their subordinate staff members, is inconsistent with European law.

Chapter 9
'Senior Management' of Insurance Undertakings

Contents

9.1 Introduction 275
9.1.1 The Normative Rules 276
9.2 'Senior Management' in the Solvency II System 277
9.3 Summary 281

Abstract This chapter treats the subject of senior management in insurance undertakings. This subject comes into view because this category appears in the nomenclature of the Solvency II Level 3 draft rules. This then leads to the question whether there is a fit-and-proper-review above and beyond the limits drawn in art. 42 of the Solvency II Directive, a question ultimately answered in the negative.

9.1 Introduction

The new insurance supervisory regime under the Solvency II Directive,[1] the planned DVO[2] and the RegE-VAG,[3] are directed mainly, as with current supervisory law, at the management of insurance undertakings,[4] which generally means the

First published as "Das 'senior management' der Versicherungsunternehmen und das künftige Versicherungsaufsichtsrecht" [in English: The 'Senior Management' of Insurance Undertakings and the Future Insurance Supervisory Regime], VersR (2013), 35 ff.

[1] Directive 2009/138/EC of the European Parliament and of the Council of 25 Nov. 2009, OJEU L 335, p. 1, of 17 Dec. 2009.

[2] The abbreviation DVO when used here and after in reference to the Level 2 DVO signifies the EU Commission draft known as Draft Implementing Measures Solvency II, 31 Oct. 2011.

[3] RegE eines Zehnten Gesetzes zur Änderung des VAG [Government's Draft of a Tenth Act Amending the German Insurance Supervision Act] of 15 Feb. 2012, BT-Drucks. [Document of the German Bundestag] 17/9342; also, BR-Drucks [Document of the German Bundesrat] 90/12.

[4] Any mention of insurance undertakings in this chapter includes reinsurance undertakings.

M. Dreher, *Treatises on Solvency II*, DOI 10.1007/978-3-662-46290-4_9

managing board members,[5] and at key function holders.[6] Supervisory board members are included in the Solvency II Directive only for undertakings that are part of a group and for insurance holding companies. More specifically, supervisory board members are not among the persons who "hold other key functions" within the meaning of art. 42 of the Solvency II Directive.[7] Nor does the DVO add anything further in this area. General monitoring of the fit-and-proper standard for supervisory board members is conducted only in a broad sense under company law, as provided for currently and in the future at the national level, for the supervisory board members of financial services institutions.[8]

However, sec. 25, para. 2, sent. 1 of the RegE-VAG does not limit fit-and-proper supervision to managing board members, persons equivalent to them such as de facto members of management, supervisory board members, and key function holders. It goes further, and provides that all persons "authorized to make significant decisions for the undertaking" are subject to supervision. This leads to an important practical question for insurance undertakings: Is "senior management" of the insurance undertaking also subject to fit-and-proper supervision and all of the legal implications that ensue?

9.1.1 The Normative Rules

The starting point for answering this question is art. 42, para. 1 of the Solvency II Directive, which applies to "all persons who effectively run the undertaking or have other key tasks".[9] Neither the Solvency II Directive nor the DVO refers to "senior management" in connection with this. Aside from the subordinate staff members in

[5] See in detail on this point *Dreher*, "Die Kontrolle der Geschäftsleiter von Versicherungsunternehmen" [in English: The Monitoring of Managers of Insurance Undertakings], ZVersWiss (2006), 375 (Supplement, Annual Conference 2006).

[6] On this point see *Dreher*, "Begriff und Inhaber der Schlüsselfunktionen nach Solvency II und VAG 2012" [in English: Concept and Holders of Key Functions under Solvency II and the German Insurance Supervision Act 2012], VersR (2012), 933 (Chap. 7, above); id., "Die aufsichtsbehördliche Kontrolle der Inhaber von Schlüsselfunktionen nach Solvency II and künftigem VAG" [in English: Review by Supervisory Authorities of the Holders of Key Functions under Solvency II and the Future German Insurance Supervision Act], VersR (2012), 1061 (Chap. 8, above).

[7] See in detail *Dreher/Lange*, "Die Qualifikation der Aufsichtsratsmitglieder von Versicherungsunternehmen nach VAG und Solvency II" [in English: Qualifications of Supervisory Board Members of Insurance Undertakings under the German Insurance Supervision Act and Solvency II], ZVersWiss (2011), 211 (Chap. 6, above); disputed.

[8] See *Dreher*, VersR (2012), 933 (937 f.) (Chap. 7, above, at 7.3.2.3).

[9] The difference between the terms "key task" and "key function" in the legal provisions is ultimately irrelevant. The term "key function" predominates in the Solvency II system and is also used exclusively hereafter. See *Dreher*, VersR (2012), 933 (934 f.) (Chap. 7, above, at 7.2.2).

key functions, staff members of insurance undertakings below the managing board[10] are addressed only in art. 249 SG1, paras. 1 e and f of the DVO. This rule mandates, as a requirement for proper governance and thus a duty of the managing board, that the undertaking employs only persons who are suited to the tasks assigned to them. There is no reference to "senior management" in the provision, yet key function holders are unambiguously designated as addressees in the regulation. Therefore, "senior management" would have to fall under persons who "effectively run the undertaking", at best.

The draft of the CEIOPS Consultation Paper "Draft Proposal for Level 3 Guidelines on the System of Governance" of December 2010 describes this group of persons in ref. 1.9 as follows:

> Persons effectively running the undertaking cover the administrative, management or supervisory body as well as senior management. The latter includes persons employed by the undertaking who are responsible for high level decision making and implementing strategies devised and the policies approved by the management body.[11]

The text of sec. 25, para. 2, sent. 1 of the RegE-VAG[12] currently accords with this, as does the subsequent Statement of Reasons for sec. 25 of the RegE-VAG, which states the following:

> Persons who effectively run the undertaking are those who, in addition to the management, have substantial effect on the decisions of the undertaking below the level of management. Whether such lower levels of management are present in an undertaking and which persons are classified under positions are matters subject to evaluation of the individual case.[13]

9.2 'Senior Management' in the Solvency II System

Ultimately, senior management and holders of "key functions", among which are counted only subordinate staff members to the managing board, are placed on obligatory equal footing only under the future VAG [German Insurance

---

[10] See *Dreher*, VersR (2012), 1061 (1066 f. and 1069) (Chap. 8, above, at 8.2.4 and 8.3.3).

[11] Hereafter cited as the Governance Guidelines.

[12] "Persons who effectively run the undertaking are those who, in addition to the management, are authorized to make significant decisions for the undertaking".

[13] VAG-RegE [Government's Draft of a Tenth Act Amending the German Insurance Supervision Act], id. n. 3 above, at Statement of Reasons for sec. 25 VAG [German Insurance Supervision Act] at 272.

Supervision Act]. Indicators of the distinction between senior management and other staff members include being given responsibility for particularly important decisions and implementing the strategies and requirements of the managing board. This would mean that all staff members in the various areas of the undertaking who have any sort of distinctive responsibility would be encompassed by the Solvency II Directive and the DVO simply based on the legal qualifier, "persons who effectively run the undertaking".

This proposition, which is found only at Level 3 and in the RegE-VAG, contains a significant inconsistency with respect to the treatment of key function holders, regardless of whether the Solvency II Directive and the DVO intended to include senior management in fit-and-proper supervision and despite the lack of evidence for this. The inconsistency is seen in the detailed rules concerning key function holders, which would not at all be necessary if senior management were an addressee of the rule on the basis of "effectively running the business". This is because key function holders are always part of the senior management of an undertaking and as such would be addressees of the rule in any case, even without the detailed rules. Conversely, if this singled-out senior management were in fact included in fit-and-proper supervision because it meets the condition necessary of "effectively running the undertaking", then an open term "key function", such as found only at Level 3 and in the RegE-VAG would miss the mark.[14] It would mean that the same group of individuals would now be named twice as addressees of the law, additionally through the condition of "other key functions". From the apparent alignment of the RegE-VAG both in its regulations and statement of reasons to the Governance Guidelines it can be assumed that in formulating the VAG [German Insurance Supervision Act] government draft, not only was the non-binding nature of CEIOPS (now EIOPA)[15] guidelines overlooked, but also, and most significantly, the date of submission of the Governance Guidelines. The draft of these guidelines specifically dates from the time before dissemination of the DVO draft. Since the concept of "senior management" is not taken up at Level 1 and the DVO made no changes to this with respect to the fit-and-proper requirements, such action is also excluded at Level 3 in the future. The VAG [German Insurance Supervision Act] draft would have needed to take this into account and ought not to have been based on the non-binding regulatory wishes of CEIOPS, which are superseded by binding regulations, now published in draft form.

The individual regulations of the Solvency II system also demonstrate that a vertical extension of the fit-and-proper requirements to staff members subordinate to the managing board of the undertaking applies only to the key function holders and not to all of senior management. Art. 249 SG1, para. 1 e and f of the DVO requires—as discussed earlier—that the insurance undertaking employ suitable personnel. Under supervision law, the Level 1 and 2 rules encompass those staff

[14] See *Dreher*, VersR (2012), 933 (935 f.) (Chap. 7, above, at 7.2.3).

[15] On this point see *Sasserath-Alberti/Hartig*, "EIOPA-Verordnung: Herausforderungen für die Praxis" [in English: EIOPA Regulation: Challenges for Practitioners], VersR (2012), 524 (530 ff.).

members subordinate to the managing board only in their capacity as key function holders. And it is only in this same capacity that the fit-and-proper requirements for them are regulated in detail. There is nothing in any way equivalent to this for senior management. But most importantly, the DVO itself distinguishes between "holders of key functions and other categories of staff whose professional activities have a material impact on the undertaking's risk profile".[16] It expressly mandates where it intends to encompass the latter, that being senior management and in particular the risk-takers or, in the words of the RegE-VAG, "persons who have substantial influence on the decisions of the undertaking".[17] A separate subjugation of senior management under national insurance supervision law is not provided for in the Solvency II system. This is especially true in the context of the (chief) underwriters or risk-takers being considered as distinct staff members subordinate to the managing board with significant relevance to risk. As the previous quoted language from the DVO shows, these persons are addressees of the Solvency II rules in specific circumstances and entirely separate from key function holders. This is seen, for example, both under art. 265 SG13, para. 1 c, para. 2 of the DVO in the juxtaposition of the two different groups of persons and under art. 265 SG13, para. 1 d of DVO for the specific inclusion of risk-takers.

The inclusion of senior management in sec. 25, para. 2, sent. 1 of the RegE-VAG would therefore be carried out without a legal basis for competence at Levels 1 and 2 of Solvency II. There would be no criteria defined by European law and—as the VAG draft demonstrates with its legal requirement of "decisions with substantial influence"—any pertinent criteria would be entirely uncertain. In the end the identification of the addressee group of the regulation would fall to the respective supervisory authorities. This would not only be a recidivism to supervision according to the principles of abusiveness[18] which is no longer permissible under Solvency II. It would also be incompatible with the principles of full

---

[16] See art. 265 SG13, para. 1 c, para. 2 of the DVO.

[17] Under existing law, see also risk-takers within the meaning of sec. 4, para. 1 VersVergV [Remuneration Regulation for the Insurance Industry], "whose activities have a material impact on the undertaking's risk profile".

[18] See *Dreher/Lange*, "Die Vollharmonisierung der Versicherungsaufsicht durch Solvency II" [in English: Full Harmonization of Insurance Supervision under Solvency II], VersR (2011), 825 (831 f.) (Chap. 1, above, at 1.4.2); *Bürkle*, "Die Zukunft der materiellen Versicherungsaufsicht in Deutschland" [in English: The Future of Substantive Insurance Supervision in Germany], VersR (2011), 1469 (1472 ff.); id.,"Die aufsichtsbehördlichen Eingriffsbefugnisse nach Solvency II – Legalitätskontrolle statt materieller Aufsicht" [in English: Supervisory Intervention Powers under Solvency II – Control of Legality in place of Substantive Supervision] and *Grote*, "Die aufsichtsbehördlichen Eingriffsbefugnisse nach Solvency II – Die besonderen Eingriffsbefugnisse" [in English: Supervisory Intervention Powers under Solvency II – Special Intervention Powers] in: Dreher/Wandt, eds., Solvency II in der Rechtsanwendung [in English: Solvency II in Legal Application], (Karlsruhe: Verlag Versicherungswirtschaft 2009) 191 ff. and 225 ff.; *Kaulbach,* in Bähr, ed., Handbuch des Versicherungsaufsichtsrechts [in English: Manual of Insurance Supervision Law] (2011), sec. 8, ref. 46.

harmonization[19] and the creation of "supervisory convergence" within the meaning of Recital 40 of the Solvency II Directive.[20]

Finally, it must be emphasized that only the managing board within the meaning of sec. 76, para. 1 of the AktG [Stock Corporation Act] is required to "manage the company under its own responsibility". This organization of responsibilities is mirrored throughout the Solvency II system based on the basic provision in art. 40 of the Solvency II Directive.[21] The responsibility of senior management, on the other hand, is always derived from the managing board and exists exclusively in relation to it.[22] If senior management notionally were to "effectively run" the company, not only the group of addressees of the law would not be defined or definable with legal certainty, but the actual organizational structure of the insurance undertaking would be thrown into doubt. This is so because it assumes that senior management is responsible to the managing board[23] and (only) the managing board is responsible internally to the supervisory board and externally to the BaFin [Federal Financial Supervisory Authority].[24] Ultimately, the inclusion of senior management as an addressee of the fit-and-proper requirements can be ruled out from a legal point of view.

---

[19] In detail *Dreher/Lange*, VersR (2011), 825 (Chap. 1, above); *Bürkle*, VersR (2011), 1469 (1472 f.); *Wandt/Sehrbrock*, Regelungsziele der Solvency II-Rahmenrichtlinie [in English: Regulatory Objectives of the Solvency II Framework Directive], ZVersWiss (2011), 193 (200). On an unclear basis – "The Directive does not prescribe full harmonization in all areas" – and inconsistent with continuing the VAG's [German Insurance Supervision Act's] existing law, RegE [Government's Draft], id., n. 3 above, p. 255. Contrary to that, the German Bundesrat assumes full harmonization in its opinion to the RegE [Government's Draft], BR-Drucks. [Document of the German Bundesrat] 90/12 at 2 f. in substance and at 13 explicitly. Also in support of full harmonization – although confusing the terms full harmonization and maximum harmonization – staff member of the Austrian Federal Ministry of Finance *Wagner*, "Solvabilität II und VAG neu: Was bleibt, was ändert sich"? [in English: Solvency II and the New German Insurance Supervision Act: What is Unchanged? What is Changed?], VersRdsch (9/2010), 23 (24, 26); FMA [Financial Market Authority (Austria)] – Österreichische Finanzmarktaufsicht Solvency II Handbuch [in English: Austrian Financial Market Authority Solvency II Manual] (2012), 1, 5 in reference to the "new rules" under Solvency II.

[20] See on this point *Dreher/Lange*, VersR (2011), 825 (827 f.) (Chap. 1, above, at 1.3.1.2).

[21] Contrary to *Weber-Rey*, ("Leitungsfunktion des Aufsichtsrates bei Versicherern anerkennen" [in English: Acknowledging the Management Function of the Supervisory Board] in the Börsenzeitung, 5 Mar. 2012, p. 4), the supervisory board of an insurance undertaking does not participate in management, and the imposition of such responsibility would be incompatible both with European and German corporate law and with European and German insurance supervision law.

[22] Likewise, explicitly, art. 258 SG6, para. 1 sent. 2 of the DVO for the key functions.

[23] Thus the criterion of "sound and prudent management" in art. 42, para. 1 a of the Solvency II Directive aimed at members of the managing board would not be suitable for senior management; see *Dreher*, VersR (2012), 1061 (1063) (Chap. 8, above, at 8.2.3.1).

[24] The RegE-VAG also opens the floodgates – including for senior management – in sec. 299, para. 1, no. 1 with BaFin's [Federal Financial Supervisory Authority] first-ever entitlement, impermissible under European law, to information directly from all "employees" of the insurance undertaking; see in detail *Dreher*, VersR (2012), 1061 (1071) (Chap. 8, above, at 8.6.2).

9.3 Summary

1. The Solvency II Directive at Level 1 and the draft of the DVO at Level 2 do not provide for monitoring the fit-and-proper standard by the supervisory authority over "senior management". To the contrary, the DVO draft takes account of "senior management" only in other contexts.
2. Only in the earlier version of the CEIOPS *Governance Guidelines*, which became invalid with the submission of the DVO, is such fit-and-proper monitoring of senior management provided for.
3. At the same time, the RegE-VAG standardizes fit-and-proper monitoring of senior management. This would include all persons below the level of the managing board who "are authorized to make significant decisions for the undertaking". The supervisory authority itself would then be able to determine the group of addressees of their own supervision, which would also mean a recidivism to general supervision according to the principles of abusiveness, a result no longer allowed under the Solvency II system.
4. The RegE-VAG's extension of fit-and-proper monitoring to senior management is not only inconsistent with European law for numerous reasons. It is also incompatible with the organizational structure of insurance undertakings. Under this structure, only the management board is externally responsible to the BaFin [Federal Financial Supervisory Authority], with explicit exceptions such as those related to fit-and-proper monitoring of key function holders under the Solvency II Directive. In the final analysis, it can therefore be concluded that senior management is not an addressee for monitoring of the fit-and-proper standard in the Solvency II system.

Chapter 10
Definition, Tasks and Legal Nature of the Compliance Function

Contents

10.1 Introduction 284
10.2 The Legal Bases of Compliance Under the Insurance Supervisory Regime 286
10.2.1 The Relationship of Compliance Under the Insurance Supervisory Regime to Compliance Under General Company Law 286
10.2.2 The Solvency II Directive 287
10.2.3 The Draft of the Solvency II Implementing Regulation 288
10.2.4 The CEIOPS Guidelines on the System of Governance 290
10.2.5 The EIOPA Guidelines on the System of Governance 291
10.2.6 The VAG-RegE [Government's Draft of a Tenth Act Amending the Insurance Supervision Act] 292
10.2.7 The Government's Draft of the German Banking Ringfencing Act 293
10.2.8 MaRisk BA [Minimum Requirements for Risk Management (Banking Supervision)] 294
10.2.9 MaComp VA [Minimum Requirements for the Compliance Function (Insurance Supervision)]? 294
10.3 The Definition of "Compliance Under the Insurance Supervisory Regime" 296
10.4 The Task of Compliance Under the Insurance Supervisory Regime and the Compliance-Related Requirements 299
10.4.1 Underlying Principles 299
10.4.2 General Legal Monitoring 306
10.4.3 Advising the Managing Board 313
10.4.4 Evaluation of Risks from Changes in the Legal Environment 316
10.4.5 Evaluation of the Compliance Risk 317
10.5 The Legal Nature of Compliance Under the Insurance Supervisory Regime 318
10.5.1 The Long Arm of the Insurance Supervisory Authority? 318
10.5.2 Company Officials? 319
10.5.3 Statutorily Prescribed and Designed Functions of Undertakings 321
10.6 Summary 322

First published as "Begriff, Aufgaben und Rechtsnatur der versicherungsaufsichtsrechtlichen Compliance nach Solvency II" [in English: Definition, Tasks, and the Legal Nature of Compliance under the Insurance Supervisory Regime of Solvency II], VersR (2013), 929 ff.

M. Dreher, *Treatises on Solvency II*, DOI 10.1007/978-3-662-46290-4_10

Abstract This chapter addresses the compliance function under art. 46, para. 1 of the Solvency II Directive. The first items to be addressed here are the normative bases of compliance under the insurance supervisory regime and its conceptual content. Then, the tasks and relevant requirements for compliance under the insurance supervisory regime are identified. The chapter concludes by examining the function of compliance under the insurance supervisory regime of the Solvency II system.

10.1 Introduction

"If you think compliance is expensive, try non-compliance". This well-known statement[1] demonstrates on the one hand the necessity of compliance by and within undertakings in general and thus also by and within insurance undertakings.[2] On the other hand it discloses the potentially boundless nature of compliance and similarly the threat potential—particularly as to legal liability—posed to the implementation of the concept of compliance and does so evidently more than existing and quite convincing factual arguments. In this context of sometimes exaggerated perceptions of compliance, it is understandable that concerns would arise within the business community, culminating in the view that any person active in business practically would need to have a compliance officer peering over his or her shoulder.[3] The dispositive response, however, is to establish a culture of compliance in undertakings that is conjoined with its opportunities and outcomes. This is so because these permit none but a positive picture.[4]

An overview of this positive view of compliance leads first to the recognition that the economic activity of the undertakings and their employees is conditioned

---

[1] The statement is attributed to former U. S. Deputy Attorney General *Paul McNulty*.

[2] In this chapter, the term "insurance undertaking" includes reinsurance undertakings. See on compliance in the insurance industry, e.g., *Bürkle*, ed., "Compliance in Versicherungsunternehmen" [in English: Insurance Undertakings' Compliance] (2009); *Müller*, "Compliance-Management – Dargestellt am Beispiel der Versicherungswirtschaft" [in English: Compliance Management: A Representative View in the Insurance Industry] (2007); *Preusche*, sec. 37: "Compliance-Organisation in der Versicherungswirtschaft" [in English: Compliance Organization in the Insurance Industry] in: Hauschka, ed., Corporate Compliance (2nd. ed. 2010).

[3] See for this tendency, if not precisely for this image, *Hemeling*, "Organisationspflichten des Vorstands zwischen Rechtspflicht und Opportunität" [in English: The Managing Board's Organizational Duties: Between Legal Duty and Opportunity], ZHR 175 (2011), 368 (369 ff.).

[4] See also e.g., *Bürkle*, id., n. 2 at sec. 1, ref. 70 f. and recently id., "Compliance in (deutschen) Versicherungsunternehmen" [in English: Compliance in (German) Insurance Undertakings], VersRdsch 1–2/2012, 45 (46) as well as from the economic point of view, e.g., *Wöhle*, "Ökonomische Grundlagen von Compliance" [in English: The Economic Bases of Compliance] in: Braumüller/Ennöckl/Gruber/Raschauer, eds., Compliance & Finanzmarktrecht [in English: Compliance and the Law of Financial Markets] (2011), 1 (10 ff.).

upon a system of open markets, markets based on freedom and equality of all who participate in the economy. This means, in other words, acting within the bounds established by law. Since compliance aims at action in accordance with the law, it contributes to values-oriented business management. This is so for two reasons: First, compliance ensures the concrete business model of the undertaking, including consistent compliance with the undertaking's own internal rules. Second, it ensures entrepreneurial freedom, which otherwise would be increasingly hemmed in with remedial legislation brought on by a growing number of infringements in commerce. Action in accordance with the law not only protects employees themselves, for example, from the employment and legal liability consequences of avoidable errors on the job. In addition, such action protects and preserves the reputation of the undertaking. Note the familiar statement of *Warren Buffet*:

> It takes more than 20 years to build up a reputation, but only 5 minutes to ruin it.

And finally, more and more undertakings subjected to infringements by other undertakings are discovering a new, reversed role for compliance. First, compliance can become a tool for settling up for damages that have occurred. In addition, future harm can be prevented or at least financially minimized by a forward-looking strategy in contracts, such as an integrity clause or a liquidated damages provision.

From a beginning in general company law,[5] the concretization of duties and limits for compliance has quickly found application to supervised undertakings in the financial services fields, i.e., to insurance undertakings, lending institutions, and

[5] See on this point recently, e.g., *Dreher*, "Vorstandsverantwortung im Geflecht von Risikomanagement, Compliance und interner Revision" [in English: Managing Board Responsibility within the Web of Risk Management, Compliance, and Internal Review] in Festschrift für [Publication in Honor of] Uwe Hüffer on his 70th Birthday (2010), 161; *Hüffer*, "Compliance im Innen- und Außenrecht der Unternehmen" [in English: Compliance of Undertakings in Domestic and Foreign Law] in Festschrift für [Publication in Honor of] Günter H. Roth on his 70th Birthday (2011), 299 ff.; *Goette*, "Organisationspflichten in Kapitalgesellschaften zwischen Rechtspflicht und Opportunität" [in English: Organizational Duties in Corporations: Between Legal Duty and Opportunity], ZHR 175 (2011), 388; *Kindler*, "Pflichtverletzung und Schaden bei der Vorstandshaftung wegen unzureichender Compliance" [in English: Managing Board Liability for Breach of Duty and Damages on Account of Inadequate Compliance] in Festschrift für [Publication in Honor of] Günter H. Roth on his 70th Birthday (2011), 367 ff.; *Kort*, "Rechtsfragen der Compliance-Organisation von Unternehmen außerhalb spezialgesetzlich geregelter Branchen im deutschen Recht" [in English: Legal Issues of Undertakings' Compliance Organization Outside Specially Regulated Areas in German Law] in Festschrift für [Publication in Honor of] Günter H. Roth on his 70th Birthday (2011), 408 ff.; *Reichert/Ott*, "Non Compliance in der AG – Vorstandspflichten im Zusammenhang mit der Vermeidung, Aufklärung und Sanktionierung von Rechtsverstößen" [in English: Corporate Non-compliance – Managing Board Duties in the Context of Avoiding, Settling, and Sanctioning Breaches of the Law], ZIP (2009), 2173; *Bachmann*, "Compliance – Rechtsgrundlagen und offene Fragen" [in English: Compliance – Legal Bases and Open Issues] in: VGR [Corporate Law Association], ed., Gesellschaftsrecht in der Diskussion 2007 [in English: Discussion on Company Law 2007] (2008), 66 ff.

bond/securities services undertakings.[6] This is so because compliance within these sectors was and is deemed particularly necessary on account of their significance for the economy in general.

The different aspects of compliance in the financial services sector leads to numerous legal questions. This article examines three basic compliance questions pertaining to the insurance supervisory regime. A preliminary matter is to ascertain how mandatory compliance under the insurance supervisory regime is placed (10.2, below). Proceeding upon this basis, the discussion turns to delineating the term "compliance under the insurance supervisory regime" (10.3, below). Such discussion will not, however, complete the description of compliance under the insurance supervisory regime. Therefore, the task of compliance under the insurance supervisory regime and the pertinent requirements will be delineated (10.4, below). Finally, against the foregoing background, this article will examine the legal nature of compliance under the insurance supervisory regime (10.5, below).

10.2 The Legal Bases of Compliance Under the Insurance Supervisory Regime

10.2.1 The Relationship of Compliance Under the Insurance Supervisory Regime to Compliance Under General Company Law

There is fundamental agreement, although controversial as to its provenance, that under general company law a legal duty of compliance for all undertakings already exists independently of the special law relating to supervised undertakings. There is, however, dispute about the provenance of this duty.[7] Such a duty derives above all from the managing board's duty under sec. 91 para. 2 of the AktG [German Stock Corporation Act]

> to establish a monitoring system such that developments that threaten the continued existence of the company may be identified at an early stage,[8]

---

[6] Of many examples from the literature, see *Lösler*, "Die Mindestanforderungen an Compliance und die weiteren Verhaltens-, Organisations- und Transparenzpflichten nach §§ 31 f. WpHG (MaComp)" [in English: Minimum Requirements for Compliance and Further Conduct, Organizational, and Transparency Duties under secs. 31 f. of the WpHG [German Securities Trading Act (MaComp)]], WM 2010, 1917.

[7] The same applies basically to public insurance undertakings under a differing legal basis.

[8] On this point see *Dreher*, id., n. 5 above, at 168 ff. id., "Ausstrahlungen des Aufsichtsrechts auf das Aktienrecht" [in English: Effects of Supervisory Law on Corporation Law], ZGR (2010), 496 (519 f.); *Spindler*, "Compliance in der multinationalen Bankengruppe" [in English: Compliance in Multinational Banking Groups], WM 2008, 905 (906 f.).

from the managing board's general leadership responsibility under secs. 76 and 93 of the AktG [German Stock Corporation Act],[9] or from the overall rules pertaining to organization and supervision of undertakings.[10] The provenance is therefore of great but unfortunately largely overlooked practical significance, since only placement of the duty of compliance in sec. 91, para. 2 of the AktG [German Stock Corporation Act] would lead to inclusion of compliance in audit and reporting according to sec. 317, para. 4 and sec. 321, para. 4 of the HGB [German Commercial Code].[11] In the present context the issue concerning the basis in company law for a duty of compliance can be left open as well is the generally disputed issue of a company-law-based duty to create a compliance organization.[12] The same accounts to the issue of the scope of certain rules of the DCGK [German Corporate Governance Code] relating to compliance, namely no. 4.1.3 and no. 5.3.2, if the special insurance supervisory regime is superimposed on general company-law rules irrespective of their debatable scope.[13]

10.2.2 The Solvency II Directive

The Solvency II Directive is central to compliance under the insurance supervisory regime.[14] Under Recital 30 and art. 13, no. 29 of the Solvency II Directive, "the

---

[9] On this point see *Hüffer*, id., n. 5 above, at 304; *Goette*, ZHR 175 (2011), 388 (392); *Kindler*, id., n. 5 above, at 370 f.; *Wundenberg*, "Compliance und die prinzipiengeleitete Aufsicht über Bankengruppen" [in English: Compliance and Principles-directed Supervision of Banking Groups] (2012) 142 f.; *Koch*, "Compliance-Pflichten im Unternehmensverbund?" [in English: Compliance Duties in an Undertaking Group?], WM (2009), 1013 (1014); *Reichert/Ott*, ZIP (2009), 2173 (2174); *Bachmann*, id., n. 5 above, at 73 f.; *Bürkle*, "Corporate Compliance – Pflicht oder Kür für den Vorstand der AG?" [in English: Corporate Compliance – Duty or Choice for a Corporate Managing Board?], BB (2005), 565 (568 ff.); *Fleischer*, "Vorstandsverantwortlichkeit und Fehlverhalten von Unternehmensangehörigen – Von der Einzelüberwachung zur Errichtung einer Compliance-Organisation" [in English: Managing Board Responsibility and Employee Error or Misconduct – from Individual Monitoring to Establishment of a Compliance Organization], AG (2003), 291 (299).

[10] On this point see *Schneider*, "Die Überlagerung des Konzernrechts durch öffentlich-rechtliche Strukturnormen und Organisationspflichten" [in English: The Superimposition of Company Law by Public Form Rules and Organization Duties], ZGR (1996), 225 (230); id., "Compliance als Aufgabe der Unternehmensleitung" [in English: Compliance as a Task of Company Management], ZIP (2003), 645 (649) and elsewhere.

[11] See *Dreher*, id., n. 5 above, at 169.

[12] See on this point, e.g., *Dreher*, id., n. 5 above, at 168 ff.; *Bachmann*, id., n. 5 above at 67 ff.; *Kort*, id., n. 5 above, at 408 f.; all with further references.

[13] On this point see 10.4.2.3, below.

[14] Directive 2009/138/EU of the European Parliament and of the Council of 25 Nov. 2009, OJEU L 335, p. 1, of 17 Dec. 2009.

system of governance includes... the compliance function".[15] Art. 40 of the Solvency II Directive—in German company-law terminology in substance also sec. 76, para. 1 of the AktG [German Stock Corporation Act]—imposes upon the managing board "the ultimate responsibility for compliance, by the undertaking concerned, with the laws, regulations, and administrative provisions adopted pursuant to this Directive". Art. 46, para. 1 of the Solvency II Directive requires further, i.a., "an effective internal control system" (ICS), that includes, from the German-language version, "a function for compliance with the requirements ('compliance function')".[16] Individual tasks of the compliance function are addressed in art. 46, para. 2 of the Solvency II Directive in the following language:

> The compliance function shall include advising the administrative, management or supervisory body on compliance with the laws, regulations and administrative provisions adopted pursuant to this Directive. It shall also include an assessment of the possible impact of any changes in the legal environment on the operations of the undertaking concerned and the identification and assessment of compliance risk.

10.2.3 *The Draft of the Solvency II Implementing Regulation*

Art. 260 SG8 of the draft of an implementing regulation (hereafter: DVO)[17] contains the following rules relating to the compliance function for the insurance supervisory undertakings:

1. The compliance function of insurance and reinsurance undertakings shall include a compliance policy and a compliance plan. The compliance policy shall define the responsibilities, competencies and reporting duties of the compliance function. The compliance plan shall set out the planned activities of the compliance function which take into account all relevant areas of the activities of insurance and reinsurance undertakings and their exposure to compliance risk.

---

[15] This passage corresponds to the expectations in Chapter II B 3 of the OECD Guidelines Insurer Governance 2011 and ICP8 IAIS Insurance Core Principles, Standards, Guidance and Assessment Methodology of 1 Oct. 2011 with Supplement of 12 Oct. 2012.

[16] This is handled differently in credit institutions, where "risk management" stands as an overarching concept comprising, i.a., an ICS, internal audit, a risk-monitoring function, and a compliance function. See sec. 25 a, para. 1, sent. 3, clause 2, no. 3 c of CRD [Capital Requirements Directive] IV, Implementing Act, Government's Draft, BT-Drucks. [Document of the German Bundestag] 17/10974.

[17] EU Commission, Draft Implementing measures Solvency II of 31. Oct. 2011.

2. The duties of the compliance function shall include assessing the adequacy of the measures adopted by the insurance or reinsurance undertaking to prevent non-compliance.

In the context of the report on solvency and financial condition, as specified in art. 51 of the Solvency II Directive,[18] art. 285 PDS4, para. 5 d of the DVO draft adds the obligation to describe how the compliance function is implemented. Following a parallel track, and in conformity with the required supervisory reporting to the supervisory authority under art. 35 of the Solvency II Directive,[19] art. 297 SRS4, para. 5c of the DVO draft requires reporting on the undertaking's internal compliance guidelines prepared pursuant to art. 260 SG8 of the DVO draft, on the process for reviewing these guidelines, on the frequency of review, and on all significant changes pertaining to the guidelines.

Independently of the compliance function, art. 258, para. 3, SG8 of the DVO draft sets up a rule for all key functions. The rule affects the right for access to information and reads as follows:

> The persons performing a function shall be able to communicate at their own initiative with any staff member and shall have the necessary authority, resources and expertise and that they have unrestricted access to all relevant information necessary to carry out their responsibilities.

In addition, art. 258, para. 4 of the DVO draft requires all persons performing a key function—in this context the compliance function—to report any major problem in their area of responsibility to their managing board. The area of responsibility is determined with the German dual system.

Group supervision with centralized risk management under art. 236 of the Solvency II Directive is subject to further requirements under art. 335 CRM1, para. 1 b and para. 2 c of the DVO draft. These requirements address the exercise of the compliance function by the parent undertaking in respect of the subsidiary. A number of undertaking groups, however, have their head offices outside the EU.

---

[18] On this point see *Dreher/Schaaf*, "Die Veröffentlichungspflichten von Versicherungsunternehmen gegenüber der Allgemeinheit nach Solvency II" [in English: Insurance Undertakings' Duties of Disclosure to the Public under Solvency II] in: Dreher/Wandt, eds., "Solvency II in der Rechtsanwendung", [in English: Solvency II in Legal Application], (Verlag Versicherungswirtschaft, Karlsruhe 2009) 129 ff. (Chap. 13, below).

[19] On this point see *Dreher*, "Die Veröffentlichungspflichten von Versicherungsunternehmen gegenüber der BaFin" [in English: Insurance Undertakings' Duties of Disclosure to the BaFin [Federal Financial Supervisory Authority]], ZVersWiss (2009), 187 (Chap. 12, below); *Dreher/Ballmaier*, "Das aufsichtliche Überprüfungsverfahren nach Art. 36 Solvency-II-Richtlinie und § 289 VAG-RegE" [in English: The Supervisory Review Process under art. 36 of the Solvency II Directive and Sec. 289 of the Government's Draft of a Tenth Act Amending the German Insurance Supervision Act], in: Dreher/Wandt, eds., Solvency II in der Rechtsanwendung 2012 [in English: Solvency II in Legal Application 2012], (Karlsruhe: Verlag Versicherungswirtschaft 2012) 73 ff. (Chap. 2, above).

In such cases, under art. 260 of the Solvency II Directive, supervision of the insurance undertakings licensed in the EU is limited to a review of equivalence relating to supervision. There is an exception for situations in which the Commission previously has made a general determination concerning the equivalence of the supervisory system in the outside country. The criteria applicable to a review of equivalence are found in art. 368 GTCE1 of the DVO draft. Under para. 1 j, one of the criteria is whether the undertaking group is required to establish and maintain a compliance function. And finally, art. 358 RTCE1, para. 1 h of the DVO draft, concretizing art. 172 of the Solvency II Directive, also sets rules for the equivalence requirements for reinsurance undertakings headquartered in outside countries to the extent the compliance function is involved.

10.2.4 The CEIOPS Guidelines on the System of Governance

In December 2010, CEIOPS, the predecessor of EIOPA, presented a "Draft proposal for Level 3 Guidelines on the System of Governance".[20] These so-called Level 3 rules on the insurance supervisory regime in the Solvency system contain numerous specifics relating to compliance under the insurance supervisory regime and the Solvency II Directive. Consideration of this text, however, must be guided by a dual recognition: first, that this text appeared before the issuance of the DVO draft; and, second, Level 3 Guidelines cannot alter the substance of the DVO draft, inasmuch as it is a Level 2 scheme.[21]

At the outset, in point no. 1.14, the Governance Guidelines describe the compliance function as follows:

> The compliance function has to perform a number of compliance-activities to promote the undertaking's compliance with applicable laws and regulatory requirements and enhancing staff awareness.

This supplements no. 3.155 of the Governance Guidelines, under which the compliance function is to identify, assess, monitor, and report the compliance risk exposure of the undertaking. In no. 3.156, the Governance Guidelines define compliance risk

---

[20] Hereafter denoted as Governance Guidelines.

[21] On this point see *Dreher*, "Begriff und Inhaber der Schlüsselfunktionen nach Solvency II und VAG 2012" [in English: Concept and Holders of Key Functions under Solvency II and the German Insurance Supervision Act 2012], VersR (2012), 933 (936) (Chap. 7, above, at 7.2.3); id., "Versicherungsaufsichtsrecht und Verbraucherschutz im Solvency-II- und EIOPA-System" [in English: The Insurance Supervisory Regime and Consumer Protection in the Solvency II and EIOPA System], VersR (2013), 401 (408) (Chap. 3, above, at 3.3.2.2); *Sasserath-Alberti/Hartig*, "EIOPA-Verordnung: Rechtliche Herausforderungen für die Praxis" [in English: EIOPA Regulation: Legal Challenges for Practitioners], VersR (2012), 524 (531).

as the risk of legal or regulatory sanctions, material financial loss or loss to reputation an undertaking may suffer as a result of not complying with laws, regulations and administrative provisions as applicable to its activities.

No. 3.157 of the Governance Guidelines notes that compliance activities focus on examining and promoting the undertaking's compliance with applicable laws and regulatory requirements. This is followed in no. 3.158 by a list of representative activities for the compliance function of an insurance undertaking. Among these, no. 3.158 g requires at least annual reporting to the "management body" on compliance issues.

Further, Guideline 8 of the Compliance Guidelines presupposes that undertakings will devise written company guidelines[22] that will set out the obligation of the organizational units to inform the governance function, including the compliance function, of all facts relevant for the discharge of their duties.[23] Guideline 40 likewise addresses compliance policy. Besides the requirement to have such compliance guidelines in insurance undertakings, it directs that the compliance policy should comply with the undertaking's General Governance—Written policies.

Guideline 41 addresses the compliance plan. Insurance undertakings should produce such a plan annually, which should describe the compliance work to be undertaken. The plan shall ensure that all relevant areas of the undertaking are appropriately covered, taking into account their susceptibility to compliance risk.

10.2.5 The EIOPA Guidelines on the System of Governance

On 27 March 2013, EIOPA issued the Proposal for "Guidelines on the System of Governance". These serve expressly as preparation for the application of Solvency II in the transition before the Directive takes effect. The Guidelines do not provide a detailed layout of the compliance function, such as they do for the other key functions. In nos. 1.21, 1.22, and 1.28, the Guidelines mention only the duty to establish a compliance function at the level of the individual undertaking and of the group, to the extent group supervision is applicable. In addition, the Guidelines require that the undertaking's guidelines in turn require the other units to inform the compliance function of all facts material to the performance of its duties, thus repeating superfluously a rule already prescribed in the DVO draft. The Explanatory Text accompanying the proposed Guidelines goes no further. It includes in no. 1.199 only the statement that a single incidence of external support for

[22] On this point see *Dreher*, "Die aufsichtsbehördliche Kontrolle der Inhaber von Schlüsselfunktionen nach Solvency II and künftigem VAG" [in English: Review by Supervisory Authorities of the Holders of Key Functions under Solvency II and the Future German Insurance Supervision Act], VersR (2012), 1061 (1065) (Chap. 8, above, at 8.2.3.2).

[23] For the undertaking guidelines see further ref. 3.20 f. of the Governance Guidelines.

compliance under the insurance supervisory regime will "ordinarily" not constitute outsourcing under the insurance supervisory regime.

10.2.6 The VAG-RegE [Government's Draft of a Tenth Act Amending the Insurance Supervision Act]

The VAG-RegE [Government's Draft of a Tenth Act Amending the German Insurance Supervision Act][24] includes rules on compliance under the insurance supervisory regime initially in sec. 8, no. 11, with the definition of functions. In agreement with the Solvency II Directive, among these functions is the compliance function.[25] Sec. 24, para. 1, sent. 1, the VAG-RegE [Government's Draft of a Tenth Act Amending the German Insurance Supervision Act] specifies "a business organization" that, i.a., will ensure "compliance with the laws, regulations, and supervisory requirements which insurance undertakings must observe". Further, sec. 29 of the VAG-RegE [Government's Draft of a Tenth Act Amending the German Insurance Supervision Act] implements the requirement of art. 46, para. 1 of the Solvency II Directive. Paragraph 1 identifies the compliance function as an element of the Internal Control System (hereafter: ICS). Sec. 29, para. 2 of the VAG-RegE [Government's Draft of a Tenth Act Amending the German Insurance Supervision Act] then governs the tasks of the compliance function as follows:

> The compliance function includes advising the managing board on compliance with the laws and regulations applicable to the operation of the insurance business. In addition, the compliance function shall assess the possible impact of any changes in the legal environment on the undertaking and shall identify and assess the risk (compliance risk) associated with infringement of legal requirements.

In accordance with the principle of proportionality,[26] the rules of the Directive shall be "applied proportionately" to small insurance undertakings. This is controlled by art. 29, para. 4 of the Solvency II Directive.

Art. 4 of the Solvency II Directive defines insurance undertakings of limited economic significance and excludes them from the scope of its coverage. This definition is implemented in German law by sec. 198 of the VAG-RegE

---

[24] RegE eines Zehnten Gesetzes zur Änderung des VAG [Government's Draft of a Tenth Act Amending the German Insurance Supervision Act] of 15 Feb. 2012, BT-Drucks. [Document of the German Bundestag] 17/9342; also, BT-Drucks [Document of the German Bundestag] 90/12 (hereafter: VAG-RegE) 90/12.

[25] See, however, on the absent mention of the term "key functions" in the VAG-RegE [Government's Draft of a Tenth Act Amending the German Insurance Supervision Act], *Dreher*, VersR (2012), 933 (934) (Chap. 7, above, at 7.2.2.2).

[26] See 10.3, below.

[Government's Draft of a Tenth Act Amending the German Insurance Supervision Act]. Section 199, para. 3, no. 7 of the VAG-RegE [Government's Draft of a Tenth Act Amending the German Insurance Supervision Act] excludes "small insurance undertakings" from the provisions of sec. 29, paras. 1 and 2 of the VAG-RegE [Government's Draft of a Tenth Act Amending the German Insurance Supervision Act], to the extent that these "need not maintain a compliance function".

The VAG-RegE [Government's Draft of a Tenth Act Amending the German Insurance Supervision Act] as conceived gives the same treatment to insurance holding companies, a treatment not supported by European law. This is expressed in the government's draft through the omission of any reference to sec. 29 in sec. 276, para. 1.[27]

10.2.7 The Government's Draft of the German Banking Ringfencing Act

In February 2013, the German Federal Government presented the "Government's Draft of an Act on Shielding against Risks and on Planning for Reorganization and Winding-up of Credit Institutions and Financial Groups".[28] In the interim, this Act has been passed. This Act contains a new sec. 64 a, para. 7 of the German Insurance Supervision Act, which in part raises the MaRisk VA [Minimum Requirements for Risk Management (Insurance Supervision)] to the level of a statute. This has raised numerous issues, as has the corresponding penal provision of the government's draft with a new sec. 142[29] of the German Insurance Supervision Act. Yet independently of these issues, according to sec. 64 a, para. 7, no. 2 a of the German Insurance Supervision Act (Draft), "the organizational structure as a rule should provide for a clear demarcation of functions between the establishment of fundamental risk positions and their review and monitoring". This has an impact as well on compliance under the insurance supervisory regime.

---

[27] See the Statement of Reasons for secs. 29 and 276 of the VAG-RegE [Government's Draft of a Tenth Act Amending the German Insurance Supervision Act].

[28] BR-Drucks. [Document of the German Bundesrat] 94/13 of 8 Feb. 2013; also, BT-Drucks. [Document of the German Bundestag] 17/12601 of 4 Mar. 2013 and the substantially amended proposed decision of the German Bundestag Finance Committee, BT-Drucks. [Document of the German Bundestag] 17/13523.

[29] On the original version of sec. 142 of the German Insurance Supervision Act, defanged by the proposed decision cited at n. 28 above, see *Dreher*, "Die Kriminalisierung von Banken- und Versicherungsvorständen" [in English: Criminalizing Banking and Insurance Managing Boards], FAZ no. 97 (26 April 2013), 24.

10.2.8 MaRisk BA [Minimum Requirements for Risk Management (Banking Supervision)]

On 14 December 2012, the BaFin [Federal Financial Supervisory Authority] presented new MaRisk BA, which for the first time contain a submodule AT [General Part] 4.4.2 on the compliance function and which took effect on 1 January 2013.[30] In seven points, the MaRisk BA address numerous issues whose parallel is also to be found in the insurance arena.

10.2.9 MaComp VA [Minimum Requirements for the Compliance Function (Insurance Supervision)]?

In the area of securities supervision, the BaFin [Federal Financial Supervisory Authority] published Circular 4/2010 (WA) "Minimum Requirements for the Compliance Function and Additional Requirements Governing Rules of Conduct, Organization and Transparency pursuant to Sections 31 et seq. of the Securities Trading Act (Wertpapierhandelgesetz – WpHG) for Investment Services Enterprises". The present MaComp WA contain in BT 1 requirements "directed to the compliance function of the bond/securities services enterprise".[31] This is a second revised version of 31 August 2012 consisting of 24 closely printed pages. In this context it is questionable whether the BaFin should also fashion minimum requirements for compliance under the insurance supervisory regime, to be called, presumably, MaComp VA.

In BT 1, the MAComp WA spend three pages dealing with three subject areas, all under the general heading "Position and Tasks of Compliance": first, under the main heading "Status", the individual subjects "Independence", "Effectiveness", and "Permanence". Then under the main heading "Responsibilities of the compliance function" are listed eleven points on this subject. Finally, they briefly address the "Relationship with the BaFin [Federal Financial Supervisory Authority]".

Applying differential diagnostic analysis to the insurance supervisory regime shows that neither an occasion, a competence, nor a need exists for a corresponding MaComp VA. To begin with, there is no comparable point of departure. Investment services enterprise personnel charged with the compliance function under the WpHG [German Securities Trading Act] and the corresponding European law requirements are oriented toward combating insider trading[32] and thus have a

---

[30] BaFin [Federal Financial Supervisory Authority] Circular 10/2012 (BA): MaRisk BA of 14 Dec. 2012.

[31] See MaComp WA AT 1, no. 6.

[32] See MaComp WA AT 1, no. 6.1 and BT 1.1.2 at 3 and BT 1.2 at 3.

differing function and status[33] from those who exercise the compliance function in insurance undertakings. In addition, the MaComp WA address only bond/securities trading out of the entire field of activity of bond/securities services enterprises.[34] Added to this is the fact that beyond its legal provisions, the Solvency II Directive expressly presumes the right of insurance undertakings to organize key functions themselves and thus also their compliance function.[35] In addition, particularly for compliance under the insurance supervisory regime, art. 260 SG8, para. 1, sent. 2 of the DVO draft confers on insurance undertakings themselves autonomy in forming their own internal compliance policy. This power is granted subject to mandatory requirements such as those found in art. 258 SG6, para. 3 of the DVO draft.[36] Since the DVO draft here means the "responsibilities, competencies, and reporting duties of the compliance function", insurance undertakings generally have the freedom to provide the concrete content relative to their own operations. Their employment of this freedom can of course be monitored after the fact in the Supervisory Review Process.[37] Any additional curtailing of this operational freedom by BaFin [Federal Financial Supervisory Authority] circulars on compliance under the insurance supervisory regime would thus be inconsistent with this freedom and with Directive requirements.

Further, the BaFin [Federal Financial Supervisory Authority] would lack competence to issue a circular on MaComp VA. This is so because the content of the MaComp WA does not deal with the self-description of individual administrative practices, but with concrete, detailed requirements to addressees of the circular, such as was the case with the previously issued MaRisk VA. The Solvency II Directive allows disclosure only of "the general criteria and methods...used in the Supervisory Review Process as set out in art. 36". This restriction appears in the

[33] See on this point but with no explanation of the insurance supervisory regime, e.g., *Casper*, "Der Compliance-Beauftragte" [in English: The Compliance Officer] in Festschrift für [Publication in Honor of] Karsten Schmidt on his 70th Birthday (2009), 199 ff. *Harm*, "Compliance in Wertpapierdienstleistungsunternehmen und Emittenten von Finanzinstrumenten" [in English: Compliance in Bond/Securities Services and Issuers of Financial Instruments] (2008), 76 ff.; *Lösler*, WM (2010), 1917.

[34] See on this point *Bürkle*, "Vorgaben der Richtlinie Solvabilität II für die Compliance in Versicherungsunternehmen" [in English: Requirements of the Solvency II Directive for Compliance in Insurance Undertakings] in "Düsseldorfer Vorträge zum Versicherungsrecht 2010" [in English: Dusseldorf Lectures on Insurance Law 2010], (Karlsruhe: Verlag Versicherungswirtschaft 2011) 1 (3).

[35] See Recital 31 of the Solvency II Directive and the Statement of Reasons for sec. 24 of the VAG-RegE [Government's Draft of a Tenth Act Amending the German Insurance Supervision Act], id., at n. 24 above, at 271. On the relationship of self-organization to the growing process orientation of the insurance supervisory regime in this context, see *Dreher*, "Solvenzanforderungen in der Versicherungsaufsicht nach Solvency II und künftigem VAG" [in English: Solvency Requirements in Insurance Supervision under Solvency II and the Future German Insurance Supervision Act], ZVersWiss (2012), 381 (Chap. 4, above).

[36] On the undertakings' guidelines for key functions, see *Dreher*, VersR (2012), 1061 (1065) (Chap. 8, above, at 8.2.3.2); on the requirements of the Governance Guidelines, see 10.2.4, above.

[37] On this point see in detail *Dreher/Ballmaier*, id., n. 19, above.

Directive at art. 31, para. 2 b and is implemented in sec. 312, paras. 1 and 2, no. 2 of the VAG-RegE [Government's Draft of a Tenth Act Amending the German Insurance Supervision Act]. Providing concrete content to art. 46 of the Solvency II Directive on the compliance function by national supervisory authorities below the fourth regulatory level, "national implementing act", in the form of a fifth regulatory level, "national supervisory directives", is thus not permissible in the Solvency II system. In addition, such a procedure would impugn the creation of "supervisory convergence. . .also in respect of supervisory practices", as required by Recital 40 of the Solvency II Directive and likewise by art. 71, para. 2, sent. 1 of the Solvency II Directive.[38]

Finally, there also would be no corresponding need for MaComp VA. Subjects such as the tasks and independence of the compliance function, the duty of notice, fit-and-proper requirements as to staff members, and reporting lines have already received detailed treatment in the proposals for Level 2 and Level 3 rules. Thus, the specific elements of compliance under the insurance supervisory regime as demanded by full harmonization[39] have now been fully addressed by the European legislator to the limit of that legislator's intent. It is now up to the national legislator to implement these requirements. Tertium non datur.

10.3 The Definition of "Compliance Under the Insurance Supervisory Regime"

The phrase "compliance under the insurance supervisory regime" is not defined in the Solvency II system. It is often primarily understood from an organizational point of view. While diverging somewhat at the level of concrete descriptions, a

---

[38] On this point see for more detail *Dreher/Ballmaier*, id., n. 19 above, at 89 ff.

[39] On this point see in detail *Dreher/Lange*, "Die Vollharmonisierung der Versicherungsaufsicht durch Solvency II" [in English: Full Harmonization of Insurance Supervision under Solvency II], VersR (2011), 825 (Chap. 1, above); *Bürkle*, "Die Zukunft der materiellen Versicherungsaufsicht in Deutschland" [in English: The Future of Substantive Insurance Supervision in Germany], VersR (2011), 1469 (1472 f); *Wandt/Sehrbrock*, "Regelungsziele der Solvency-II-Rahmenrichtlinie" [in English: Regulatory Objectives of the Solvency II Framework Directive], ZVersWiss (2011), 193 (200). On an unclear basis – "The Directive does not prescribe full harmonization in all areas. . ." – and inconsistent with continuing the VAG's [German Insurance Supervision Act's] existing law in RegE eines Zehnten Gesetzes zur Änderung des VAG [Government's Draft of a Tenth Act Amending the German Insurance Supervision Act] of 15 Feb. 2012, BT-Drucks. [Document of the German Bundestag] 17/9342, p. 255. On the contrary, affirming the principle of full harmonization, BR-Drucks. [Document of the German Bundesrat] 90/12 at 2 f in substance and at 13 explicitly. Also in support of full harmonization, *Wagner*, "Solvabilität II und VAG neu: Was bleibt, was ändert sich"? [in English: Solvency II and the New German Insurance Supervision Act: What is Unchanged? What is Changed?], VersRdsch 9/2010, 23 (24, 26) and FMA-Österreichische Finanzaufsicht, Solvency II Handbuch [in English: Financial Market Supervision: Austrian Financial Supervision, Solvency II Manual] (2012), 1 (5) in reference to the "new rules" under Solvency II.

prevalent view holds that compliance is "the sum of the organizational precautionary provisions put in place by an organization to ensure continuing effective conduct in accordance with the law by the undertaking and by any persons acting on behalf of the undertaking".[40] Compliance under the insurance supervisory regime is thus located within the law concerning the organization of undertakings.[41] Indeed, this is reflected in the fact that compliance is part of the "business organization" by virtue of sec. 64, para. 1, sent. 1 of the VAG [German Insurance Supervision Act]. The VAG [Insurance Supervision Act], however, does not content itself in the present law on rules for business organizations, but goes on to emphasize the rules' substantive objective, namely, "compliance with the laws, regulations, and supervisory requirements that they [viz., the insurance undertakings] are bound to observe".

Art. 46, para. 1, subpara. 2 of the Solvency II Directive makes it clear that compliance under the insurance supervisory regime is likewise part of the undertaking's organizational system, namely, the ICS. The Solvency II Directive, however, like the applicable portion of the VAG [German Insurance Supervision Act] singles out the task of the mandatory compliance function.[42] This is, under art. 46, para. 1, subpara. 2 of the Solvency II Directive, "monitoring compliance with the requirements".[43] Under paragraph 2 of this provision, the compliance function also "shall include advising the administrative, management or supervisory body" on matters of compliance. Under the German corporate law dual system this means advising the managing board.

> Further, the compliance function includes an assessment of the possible impact of any changes in the legal environment on the operations of the undertaking concerned and the identification and assessment of the risk arising from non-compliance with the requirements of the law (compliance risk).[44]

[40] As formulated by *Bürkle*, id., n. 2 above, at sec. 1 ref. 4 and recently *Bürkle*, id., n. 34 above, at 2; *Bürkle*, VersRdsch 1-2/2012, 45 and *Bürkle*, "Compliance und Revision im Versicherungsbereich nach Solvency II" [in English: Compliance and Review in the Insurance Industry under Solvency II], CCZ (2012), 220. Taking an approach based on the law of organizations for the insurance supervisory regime are, e.g., *Reese/Ronge*, "Aufgaben und Charakter der Compliance-Funktion im Versicherungsunternehmen unter besonderer Berücksichtigung von Solvency II" [in English: Tasks and Character of the Compliance Function in Insurance Undertakings with Particular Regard for Solvency II], VersR (2011), 1217 (1220 f.) and for compliance in bond/securities services undertakings, *Casper*, id., n. 33 above, at 201 and for general company law, e.g., *Spindler*, WM (2008), 905; *Reichert/Ott*, ZIP (2009), 2173 and *Kort*, "Verhaltensstandardisierung durch Corporate Compliance" [in English: Standardization of Conduct through Corporate Compliance], NZG (2008), 81.

[41] *Bürkle*, id., n. 34 above, at 2; id., VersRdsch 1-2/2012, 45.

[42] And see 10.4.1.1, below.

[43] See in detail 10.4.2, below.

[44] See in detail 10.4.3–10.4.5, below.

The very wording of this provision in its listing shows that the term "compliance under the insurance supervisory regime" even under the Solvency II Directive must be understood not only in terms of the law concerning organizations, but also as having equal weight in matters affecting tasks and powers, i.e., matters of substantive law.[45] This means that the compliance function is assigned to the legality duty of the undertaking's management.[46] But the insurance supervisory regime does not contend with a perfect organization for compliance under the insurance supervisory regime. After all, the organization is but a means to an end, with the end being performing the function which from a legal point of view is set for the task of compliance under the insurance supervisory regime. There is another continuing contested issue at work here: whether under general company law a managing board is under an organization-law duty with respect to compliance, contrasted with the question of the existence of a substantive compliance duty.[47] Even if the Solvency II requirements resolve this question in favor of establishing the duty of compliance as a matter of organization law with respect to insurance undertakings, the controversy discloses under general company law both the distinction between and the independence of the two aspects of the term "compliance under the insurance supervisory regime".

Seen against this background, the term "compliance under the insurance supervisory regime" contains a combination of both organizational and substantive law requirements. Thus, the definition of the term must take account of both elements and is properly stated as compliance by insurance undertakings with the requirements of the law on the basis of organizational measures appropriate and adequate to the purpose. The characteristic of adequacy follows from the effective operation of the principle of commensurability or proportionality. This principle in the form of a horizontal clause arises from Recital 19 and art. 29, para. 3 of the Solvency II

---

[45] Thus in essence also, *Hemeling*, "Compliance im Erst- und Rückversicherungsunternehmen" [in English: Compliance in Direct Insurance and Reinsurance Undertakings], CCZ (2010), 21; also appearing in GDV-Leitfaden, "Compliance im Erst- und Rückversicherungsunternehmen" [in English: Compliance in Direct Insurance and Reinsurance Undertakings] (Nov. 2009) 6, in which here – id., 22 and 10 – respectively, contrary to the term "function" in the Solvency II Directive, "a clear difference between the compliance function and a compliance organization" is postulated; on the term "function" under the insurance supervisory regime see for a detailed treatment *Dreher* VersR (2012), 933 (Chap. 7, above); and similarly for general company law see *Goette*, ZHR 175 (2011), 388 (391); *Hüffer*, n. 5 above, at 301 f.; *Hauschka* in: Hauschka, ed., Corporate Compliance (2nd ed. 2010) sec. 1, ref. 2; "Arbeitskreis externe und interne Überwachung der Unternehmung" [in English: Working Group for External and Internal Audit] (AKEIÜ), "Compliance: 10 Thesen für die Unternehmenspraxis" [in English: Compliance: 10 Subjects for Business Management], DB (2010), 1509 (1510); *Kremer/Klahold*, "Compliance-Programme in Industriekonzernen" [in English: Compliance Programs in Industrial Concerns], ZGR (2010), 113 (116).

[46] On the term "business manager", see in detail *Dreher*, "Nicht delegierbare Geschäftsleiterpflichten" [in English: Non-delegable Duties of Business Managers] in Festschrift für [Publication in Honor of] Klaus J. Hopt on his 70th Birthday (2010) 517 (518 ff.).

[47] See, e.g., *Dreher*, id., n. 5 above, at 168 ff.; *Hüffer*, id., n. 5 above, at 303 f.

Directive and controls the totality of the insurance supervisory regime.[48] The principle is thus directly applicable to compliance under the insurance supervisory regime. This is true both for the organization of compliance under the insurance supervisory regime and for the fulfillment of its task.[49]

10.4 The Task of Compliance Under the Insurance Supervisory Regime and the Compliance-Related Requirements

10.4.1 Underlying Principles

10.4.1.1 The Area of Operation of Compliance Under the Insurance Supervisory Regime and Its Hierarchy

Previously in this chapter,[50] four areas have been identified in which compliance under the insurance supervisory regime is operational under the Solvency II Directive[51]: These areas may be conceptually categorized as general legal monitoring, advice of management, evaluation of the risks arising from changes in the law,[52]

---

[48] See *Dreher*, ZVersWiss (2012), 381 (393, 418 ff.) (Chap. 4, above, at 4.3.2.3 and 4.4.2.5); *Wandt/Sehrbrock*, "Die Umsetzung des Verhältnismäßigkeitsgrundsatzes der Solvency-II-Richtlinie im VAG-Regierungsentwurf" [in English: Implementation of the Solvency II Directive's Principle of Proportionality in the Government's Draft of a Tenth Act Amending the Insurance Supervision Act], VersR (2012), 802, also reprinted in: Dreher/Wandt, eds., Solvency II in der Rechtsanwendung [in English: Solvency II in Legal Application], (Karlsruhe: Verlag Versicherungswirtschaft 2012) 21 ff. *Wandt*, "Prinzipienbasiertes Recht und Verhältnismäßigkeitsgrundsatz im Rahmen von Solvency II" [in English: Principles-based Law and the Principle of Proportionality in the Context of Solvency II] (Karlsruhe: Verlag Versicherungswirtschaft 2012); *Dröse/Littmann*, "Der Verhältnismäßigkeitsgrundsatz im Anwendungsbereich des Solvency-II-Regimes unter besonderer Berücksichtigung firmeneigener (Rück-)Versicherungsunternehmen" [in English: The Principle of Proportionality as Applied within the Framework of Solvency II with Particular Attention to In-house Insurance and Reinsurance Undertakings], ZVersWiss (2012), 339; and generally on the principle of proportionality in European Union law *Trstenjak/Beysen*, Das Prinzip der Verhältnismäßigkeit in der Unionsrechtsordnung [in English: The Principle of Proportionality in European Union Law], EuR (2012), 265.

[49] On this point see 10.4.1.3, below.

[50] See 10.3, above.

[51] With respect to credit institutions, there is a differing function description, consistent with the EBA [European Banking Authority] Guidelines on Internal Governance, not in the text of the Act, but only in the Statement of Reasons for sec. 25 a, para. 1, sent. 3, cl. 2, no. 3 c CRD [Capital Requirements Directive] IV, Implementing Act, Government's Draft, id., n. 16 above, at 108.

[52] To the extent that *Bürkle*, id., n. 2 above, at sec. 1, ref. 141 f. and id., n. 34 above, at 16 and elsewhere, who was most likely the first to undertake a conceptual and content-based systemization of the compliance function tasks, characterizes the evaluation of risks arising from changes in

and evaluation of the compliance risk.[53] The areas of operation of the compliance function, however, are not of equal import and are not exhaustive. Rather, the Solvency II Directive itself arranges them in hierarchical order and supplies a non-exhaustive list. This has not been recognized, however, in previous legal treatises on compliance under the insurance supervisory regime, which treatises rather took an early, undifferentiated approach to the "four subfunctions" of the compliance function[54] and thenceforward uncritically conformed to this classification.[55] This issue also has significant practical import for the extent and depth of activities in the compliance function of the insurance supervisory regime.

The ICS, under art. 46, para. 1, subpara. 2, of the Solvency II Directive includes within the compliance function the general tasks of "monitoring compliance with the requirements". Thus, from the legal point of view, compliance under the insurance supervisory regime has only this one central task. But as shown in art. 46, para. 2 of the Solvency II Directive, this can be separated out into several subtasks. In this provision, the Directive identifies three subtasks: advising the management body, assessment of the possible effect of changes in the legal environment, and the assessment of compliance risk. By including the phrases "zählt auch" and "umfasst ebenfalls" in the German language version, art. 46, para. 2 of the Solvency II Directive demonstrates that these three subtasks serve only as examples. Other official language versions of the Directive support this view. Thus, the English language version has "shall include" and the French has "dans le cadre de cette fonction" and "comprend également". Along with the subtasks given as examples in the Directive, compliance under the insurance supervisory regime also includes such further subtasks as the identification and assessment of legal risks and advising management on methods and means to avoid or mitigate such risks.[56]

the law as an "early warning function", his use of terminology lacks a concrete legal point of reference.

[53] The term chosen by *Bürkle*, id., n. 34 above, at 18 – "risk monitoring function" – likewise encounters difficulty through lacking a concrete legal point of reference and runs the hazard of conceptual fuzziness with regard to risk management under art. 44 of the Solvency II Directive.

[54] This traces back to *Bürkle*, id., n. 2 above, at sec. 1, ref. 141 ff. id., n. 34 above, at 16 and elsewhere; see recently, id., CCZ (2012), 220 (222) and VersRdsch 1–2/2012, 45 (49).

[55] See, e.g., *Korinek/Schadler-Liebl*, "Versicherungsaufsichtsrechtliche Compliance nach Solvency II" [in English: Compliance under the insurance supervisory regime under Solvency II], VersRdsch 9/2011, 30 (32 ff.) and *Wolf*, "Zur Aufgabenverteilung zwischen den Governance-Funktionen von Versicherungsunternehmen nach der Solvency II-Richtlinie – Überlegungen am Beispiel der Funktionen Compliance, Risikomanagement und interne Revision" [in English: On the Division of Tasks between the Governance Functions of Insurance Undertakings under the Solvency II Directive – Thoughts on the Functions of Compliance, Risk Management, and Internal Audit], VersR (2013), 678 (680).

[56] For a detailed treatment, see *Schaaf*, "Risikomanagement und Compliance in Versicherungsunternehmen" – aufsichtsrechtliche Anforderungen und Organverantwortung", [in English: Risk Management and Compliance in Insurance Undertakings – Supervisory Requirements and Institutional Responsibility], (Karlsruhe: Verlag Versicherungswirtschaft 2010) 135 ff.

The Solvency II Directive is limited to identifying the central task of compliance under the insurance supervisory regime and giving examples of certain tasks included in that function. Thus quite properly there is no comprehensive concrete description of how the function is to be performed. And on the one hand, the Directive takes account of the freedom of internal organization emphasized by Recital 31 in conjunction with the elaboration of the key functions. On the other hand, there has arisen in the interim a series of tools generally recognized as efficacious for performing compliance functions for any compliance, i.e., independently of assignment to category of the insurance supervisory regime. It is therefore not apparent that this need be taken up into the Directive. Even though expressed in varying terminology, these tools are analyzable in the triad of instruction, preventive monitoring (including advice), and coercive sanctions.[57] For example, in the subtasks advice and evaluation of compliance risk, the Solvency II Directive manifestly operates within this system.

10.4.1.2 The Principle of Materiality and the Task of Compliance Under the Insurance Supervisory Regime

The principle of materiality is a prime characteristic of the new supervisory system under the Solvency II Directive in those areas where it applies. In reference to the previously mentioned task of compliance under the insurance supervisory regime, concretized in the Solvency II Directive itself, the question arises whether the principle of materiality applies also to performance of the compliance task. An additional consideration is that the principle of legality per se requires unconditional application. Thus upon initial consideration, it might appear that application of the principal of materiality consigns the compliance function and the principle of legality to a relative status not provided for in the Solvency II system. Along with the principle of proportionality[58] to be addressed below and the potential for a decentralized compliance organization,[59] it is precisely the principal of materiality that is put forward as a means to address the oft-feared hypertrophy of compliance under the insurance supervisory regime.[60]

---

[57] For more detail see *Dreher*, "Kartellrechtscompliance" [in English: Competition Law Compliance], ZWeR (2004), 75 (93 ff.); id. in: Krieger/Schneider, eds., Handbuch Managerhaftung [in English: Manual of Managerial Liability] (2nd. ed. 2010) sec. 31 ref. 61 ff. *Bürkle*, id., n. 2 above, at sec. 1; *Hauschka*, id. at n. 45 above, at sec. 1, ref. 24 ff. *Inderst*, in: Görling/Inderst/Bannenberg, eds., Compliance (2010) 103 ff.; *Moosmayer*, Compliance (2nd. ed. 2012) 33 ff.

[58] See 10.4.1.3, below.

[59] See on this point *Dreher*, VersR (2012), 933 (939, 941) (Chap. 7, above, at 7.3.5.3 and 7.3.5.5). Likewise for the lending sector, now the new MaRisk BA, id., n. 30 above, at no. 4; and explicitly BaFin [Federal Financial Supervisory Authority], MaRisk-Novelle [Amended] 2012 – Correspondence to the associations of 14 Dec. 2012 in the section on the compliance function.

[60] See on this point 10.1, above.

In the Solvency II system,[61] the principle of materiality means that any applicable supervisory requirements are not applied dogmatically, but in a qualitative fashion with a view to the essence of the particular matter at issue. This applies not only for side issues, but also for core issues, such as orientation to risk, the quality of the system of governance, and compliance with the Solvency Capital Requirement.[62] Thus, unlike the principle of proportionality discussed below,[63] the principle of materiality is not a legal requirement in the sense of a horizontal clause overarching the insurance supervisory regime. Rather it is related to matters of fact, i.e., its application is restricted to the 19 particular places in the text of the Directive where it is included.[64] The implication of this for compliance under the insurance supervisory regime is that the principle of materiality is a prior consideration to the "compliance with the requirements" as a task, to the extent it affects definite requirements. General legal monitoring by the compliance function of the insurance undertakings cannot exceed the requirements themselves.

Essentially, the principle of materiality restricts the task of compliance under the insurance supervisory regime not generally, but only selectively. It is of no importance for the function of compliance under the insurance supervisory regime whether legal requirements for the insurance industry are material or non-material. Cafeteria health regulations are an example of non-materiality often mentioned by those in the industry. Restriction of the task to monitoring only "material" deficiencies with regard to legal requirements is to be found only in the instances enumerated in the statutes. Beyond this, there is no legal obligation in compliance under the insurance supervisory regime for a highly inclusive degree of monitoring, one that purports to cover all legal requirements. Such a degree of monitory is frequently abhorred in the insurance industry and, further, would be neither reasonable nor achievable. Only the principle of proportionality and not the principle of materiality can form the basis for a proper concretization of tasks.

10.4.1.3 The Principle of Proportionality and the Function of Compliance Under the Insurance Supervisory Regime

The principle of proportionality affects the overall insurance supervisory regime in the Solvency II system other than the principle of materiality. It constitutes thereby an insurance supervisory regime horizontal clause, which also forms a substantive

[61] See in detail on this point *Dreher*, ZVersWiss (2012), 381 (417 f.) (Chap. 4, above, at 4.4.2.5).

[62] See *Dreher*, ZVersWiss (2012), 381 (417) (Chap. 4, above, at 4.4.2.5) with other references.

[63] These two insurance supervisory regime principles can be differentiated under the parameters of the insurance supervisory regime. Therefore, they may also be differentiated in connection with compliance under the insurance supervisory regime; to this extent ambiguous, *Reese/Ronge*, VersR (2011), 1217 (1221) und *Saria*, "Compliance nach Solvency II" [in English: Compliance under Solvency II], VersRdsch 11/2011, 21 (24): "Principle of materiality, which...can claim general application as an expression of the principle of proportionality".

[64] There is in addition a mention in Recital 38.

part of compliance under the insurance supervisory regime and its performance.[65] The starting point here is that in accordance with Recital 18, sent. 2 of the Solvency II Directive not only the "actions taken by the supervisory authorities" with the objective of "effectiveness of supervision", but in a consistent manner also the internal monitoring activities already put in place by the insurance undertakings[66] must "be proportionate to the nature, scale and complexity of the risks inherent...". This alone shows, taking up again the discussion relating to the cafeteria example which is prevalent in the industry,[67] that monitoring of such requirements by compliance under the insurance supervisory regime despite the unrestricted application of the principle of legality in all areas cannot and should not be on a par with legal requirements, such as those for capital investment[68] or solvency capital.[69]

An additional foundation for the principle of proportionality is to be found in Recital 19 and art. 29, para. 3 of the Solvency II Directive. Under this authority, the "requirements" of the Directive should not "be too burdensome for small and medium-sized insurance undertakings". Further, in alignment with Recital 18, sent. 2 of the Solvency II Directive the strictures of the Directive generally shall be "applied in a manner which is proportionate to the nature, scale and complexity of the risks inherent in the business of an insurance or reinsurance undertaking". And ultimately the principle of commensurability applies as well in the general area of company law compliance, where despite conceptual differences in the present context, the effect is the same. The significance of this principle is that only legally and factually suitable, feasible, required, and adequate measures and action shall be undertaken.[70]

The principle of proportionality entails concrete consequences for the task of compliance under the insurance supervisory regime. These consequences relate to the performance of this task with respect to factual situations as well as to time and location. Each of these three dimensions requires that the performance of the task be concretely designed for the individual undertakings, on the basis of the principle of proportionality. From the factual perspective, this signifies ranking the subjects monitored according to their exposure to risk. This is to be combined with the impact of a risk occurrence on maintaining "continuity and regularity" in insurance

[65] See 10.3, above.

[66] Under art. 46, para. 1, subpara. 2 of the Solvency II Directive, compliance under the insurance supervisory regime is a part of the ICS of the insurance undertakings.

[67] See 10.4.1.2, above.

[68] On this point see *Dreher*, ZVersWiss (2012), 381 (405 f.) (Chap. 4, above, at 4.4.1.1).

[69] On this point see *Dreher*, ZVersWiss (2012), 381 (385 ff.) (Chap. 4, above, at 4.2.3).

[70] See BGH [in English: Federal Court of Justice], 11 Mar. 1986 – KRB 7/85 – WuW/E 2262, 2264 – file notes: "what is realistically reasonable"; *Dreher*, id., n. 5 at 174; id., ZWeR (2004), 75 (94 f.); *Spindler*, WM (2008), 905 (909); *Fleischer*, AG (2003), 291 (300); *Reichert/Ott*, ZIP (2009), 2173 (2174); *Bürkle*, "Corporate Compliance als Standard guten Unternehmensführung des DCGK" [in English: Corporate Compliance as a Standard of Good Business Management of the DCGK [German Corporate Governance Code]], BB (2007), 1797 (1798); *Bachmann*, id., n. 5 above, at 78 f.

undertakings' performance,[71] as emphasized and required by the Solvency II Directive[72] for general governance requirements. This is illustrated by the example already given of legal requirements for the various performance areas of an insurance undertaking. This required hierarchical approach, then, covers the extent of the performance of compliance under the insurance supervisory regime, ranging from monitoring the totality of legal requirements for insurance undertakings in the area of their subject matter to monitoring requirements in particular areas highly susceptible to risk only.

In similar fashion, however, this task of hierarchical ranking gives something up to the insurance undertakings with respect to the thoroughness of their performance of compliance. This spectrum may range from compliance measures directed toward complete monitoring to mere plausibility checks on the one hand and from unannounced monitoring measures to such measures as would always be fixed far in advance on the other hand. And further, where time considerations are involved, the period of regular monitoring procedures must be established, as must the occasion for additional ad hoc measures.

Ultimately, the managing board of the insurance undertaking is principally responsible for this task description and for establishing the monitoring measures. The appropriate place for these provisions to be recorded is in the undertakings' guidelines,[73] which are also compliance-related, and in the concrete compliance plan.[74]

10.4.1.4 The Task-Related Requirements for the Holder of the Compliance Function in the Insurance Undertakings and for the Managing Board as Monitoring Body

Key function holders in the Solvency II system must be not only personally reliable ("proper") but also factually suitable ("fit").[75] The task of general legal monitoring, which the holder of the compliance function must perform, is of broad extent. This task has repercussions also for the subject-specific profile requirements for the occupant of such a position. Improper filling of such a position has legal consequences not only for the individual involved, but also for the managing board which filled the position. In the case of an obviously poor choice, the "fitness" of the hiring board members may justly be called into question. The same applies to later negligent monitoring.

---

[71] See art. 41, para. 4 of the Solvency II Directive.

[72] Likewise now explicit in MaRisk BA, id., at n. 30, AT 4.4.2 no. 2, and BaFin [Federal Financial Supervisory Authority], Correspondence to the associations, id., n. 59 above, in the relevant chapter.

[73] On this point see *Dreher*, VersR (2012), 1061 (1065) (Chap. 8, above, at 8.2.3.2).

[74] On this point see 10.2.4, above.

[75] See in detail *Dreher*, VersR (2012), 1061 (Chap. 8, above).

It strongly appears that the task of general legal monitoring requires that the holder of the compliance function must have completed a legal education and have an aptitude for the legal profession.[76] Individual subtasks such as the required advice of the managing board in matters pertaining to the insurance supervisory regime further outline the profile requirements. These differentiate the profile for the holder of the task of compliance within undertakings subject to the insurance supervisory regime from the profile requirements applicable to a compliance officer under general company law. In this latter area, there is some sentiment that exclusively lawyers should serve[77] and other views that at least "legal guidance"[78] from outside parties is required, with such legal guidance being sought based on the compliance officer's own legal knowledge. The background, then, is first the core task of "general legal monitoring" and the subtasks emphasized in the Directive of advising the managing board concerning the insurance supervisory regime. The holder of the function of compliance under the insurance supervisory regime is ultimately responsible for performing these duties. A further background feature is evaluating risks arising from changes in the legal environment. Against this background, it appears that compliance under the insurance supervisory regime is significantly more marked by legal features than general company-law derived compliance already is. Consequently, the result is that, contrary to the latter, the former compels the requirement to assign the task to an individual with an appropriate legal education.

To the extent, however, that they may be required to have a "comprehensive competence in the insurance supervisory regime",[79] this would miss the mark as to what is actually achievable and legally to be expected. If this criterion were to be applied, for want of appropriate legal experts in Germany only a very few insurance undertakings would be able to find suitable holders of the compliance function, i.e., individuals possessing "comprehensive" insurance supervisory regime expertise. In fact, the principle of proportionality has an effect also upon the insurance supervisory regime profile requirements for holders of the insurance supervisory regime compliance function. Pars pro toto, i.e., transferable to other legal competence areas, this means two things: First, the amount of prescribed supervisory knowledge and experience is likewise characterized by the triad of "nature, scale and complexity" of the risks[80] existing in the insurance undertaking. And second, resort may

[76] Such as an attorney-at-law.

[77] See, e.g., *J. Hüffer/U. H. Schneider*, "Juristen an die Compliance-Front!" [in English: Lawyers to the Compliance Front!], ZIP (2010), 55.

[78] See, e.g., *Moosmayer*, "Modethema oder Pflichtenprogramm guter Unternehmensführung? – Zehn Thesen zu Compliance" [in English: Fashion Subject or Obligatory Program of Good Business Management? – Ten Theses on Compliance], NJW (2012), 3013 (3014); somewhat vague in its conclusion, AKEIÜ [in English: Working Group for External and Internal Audit], DB (2010), 1509 (1516 f.).

[79] See *Bürkle*, id., n. 34 above, at 15; id., n. 2 above, at sec. 1, ref. 147.

[80] See for more detail 10.4.2.3, below.

be had at need to outside (insurance supervisory) legal advice, as follows from the potential of continuing and far-reaching outsourcing of the compliance function.

In sum, the qualification profile for a holder of the insurance supervisory regime compliance function appears as follows: First, with respect to the job description and the related fitness criterion it is imperative but also sufficient to require a full legal education.[81] If there are multiple holders of the insurance supervisory regime compliance function, it will suffice that one of them meets this criterion. Second, it is to be expected that all holders will possess knowledge and skills in the insurance supervisory regime, in insurance contract law in the areas of law where the insurance undertaking is particularly exposed to compliance risks. Third, these holders must possess sufficient familiarity with other legal areas so that they can identify risks to the extent that they recognize when outside counsel is required and they then arrange to acquire that counsel. One may presume generally that a fully trained lawyer serving as a holder of the insurance supervisory regime compliance function will possess such knowledge and skills.

But well-grounded legal knowledge and skills are not enough in themselves to constitute a completely sufficient basis of subject-specific suitability. Thus the fourth requirement comprises a general understanding of the insurance business and the business model of the particular insurance undertaking at issue and its own business process. And for a fifth and last point, because of interfacing with the other three insurance supervisory regime functions, namely risk management, internal audit, and actuarial, the holder of the compliance function also must have a basic command of these areas. This is so because only in this way can the holder perform the activity monitoring required by supervisory law for these areas.

10.4.2 General Legal Monitoring

10.4.2.1 The Insurance Supervisory Regime or Legal Requirements in General as a Subject of Monitoring?

The Solvency II Directive outlines only minimally the central task of general legal monitoring. For example, the English, French, and Dutch versions of art. 46, para. 1, subpara. 2 of the Solvency II Directive do not contain the task description "monitoring compliance with the requirements" such as is found in the German language version [in German: "Überwachung der Einhaltung der Anforderungen"]. These language versions go no further than to require a "compliance function", "fonction de vérification de la conformité", or a "compliance functie". As rendered back into German, these phrases are but the term "Compliance-Funktion". So the

[81] Somewhat vaguely as to the conclusion, *Korinek/Schadler-Liebl*, VersRdsch 9/2011, 30 (37), would require "in any case well-grounded legal knowledge and skills" and, though referring to the "necessary legal education", do not give concrete details on the point.

question then arises as to how the task of general legal monitoring is to be concretized.

The answer cannot come from the advice task area, because the compliance function "shall include" the advising task. Therefore it cannot fully describe this task. The "laws, regulations and administrative provisions adopted pursuant to this Directive" with regard to the advice task do not therefore essentially limit the subject-matter of the monitoring task of the compliance function. In art. 46, para. 2 of the Solvency II Directive, the issuer of the Directive in regard to the subject-matter and objective of the Directive was apparently solely concerned with emphasizing the particular significance of the insurance supervisory regime in the advice of the managing board by the compliance function, as required by the insurance supervisory regime. In addition, the narrow construction of the advice task in the Solvency II Directive comports with art. 40 of the Solvency II Directive. This is so because, consistent with this construction, this provision assigns ultimate responsibility "for the compliance...with the laws, regulations and administrative provisions adopted pursuant to this Directive" to the usual organizational triad of "administrative, management or supervisory bodies". As with the issue of advice of the managing board by the compliance function under art. 46, para. 2 of the Solvency II Directive, the European legislator in art. 40 of the Solvency II Directive by emphasizing the managing board's "ultimate responsibility" for compliance with the insurance supervisory regime was concerned with fundamentally clarifying the objective of the rules scheme: The insurance supervisory regime provides the imperative guideline for insurance undertakings. The managing board itself, therefore, retains "ultimate" responsibility for following this guideline. And this includes compliance.

There is no warrant in arts. 40 and 46, para. 2 of the Solvency II Directive for restricting the task of "general legal monitoring" of the compliance function to the insurance supervisory law.[82] This would fail not only in view of the previously noted telos of the rules.

[82] See *Schaaf*, id., n. 56 above, at 20, 131 f. and recently *Korinek/Schadler-Liebl*, VersRdsch 9/2011, 30 (34) and *Reese/Ronge*, VersR (2011), 1217 (1224); contra, *Bürkle*, id., n. 34 above, at 5 ("it depends upon the European supervisory regime source of the given legal requirements") and at 14 ("the totality of the requirements of the internal control system"), id., VersRdsch 1-2/2012, 45 (48) ("Insurance supervisory regime compliance is primarily concerned with compliance with regulatory rules particularly relating to insurance activities.") and again id., n. 2 above, at sec 1, ref. 142, but not resolving the contradiction to the two subtasks offered as examples, i.e., evaluation of risks arising from changes in the legal environment and compliance risks, a contradiction not restricted to the insurance supervisory regime according to *Bürkle*, id., n. 34 above, at 17 f. To the extent that *Wolf*, VersR (2013), 678, would restrict compliance under the insurance supervisory regime "in the undertakings' areas classified as not relevant to risk" generally "to overarching inquiries and structural aspects" and proceeds from the premise that "monitoring in reference to factual, content-oriented subjects to the contrary will not occur for the present", this view has no support in the Solvency II Directive and would lead to substantial legal uncertainty in the fringes of the two areas.

More than that, it would lead to an absurd interpretation of arts. 40 and 46, para. 2 of the Solvency II Directive. This is so because these provisions point to "regulations and administrative provisions adopted" "pursuant to this Directive" or "in accordance with this Directive" as the basis for the managing board's responsibility for compliance and the advice of the managing board by the compliance function. In other words, the issue is exclusively the "future European insurance supervisory regime".[83] Such an interpretation of arts. 40 and 46, para. 2 of the Solvency II Directive would mean that not even compliance with the Solvency II Directive would be covered, for example in the case of its direct or supplementary application. This absurd result could be countered, however, by noting that only the given national insurance supervisory regime would be affected because of the implementation of the Solvency II Directive. Nevertheless, the Directive does not differentiate in other places along these lines, in particular not in the governance functions, between its own terms and those of future national implementation law "pursuant to this Directive".

Completely independently and first and foremost, the language of the Solvency II Directive itself indicates that the insurance supervisory regime duty of compliance is not thus restricted as to subject matter. As a first point, other official language versions of the Directive besides the German do not recognize a subject-matter restriction in art. 46, para. 1, subpara. 2 of the Solvency II Directive, which is the primary provision for compliance under the insurance supervisory regime. Nor does the German version in its supplementary "monitoring of compliance with the requirements" recognize any such limitation.[84] Further in this context, there is the "shall include" legal requirement of art. 46, para. 2 of the Solvency II Directive, as noted above. This factor bars any attempt to limit the monitoring task of the insurance supervisory regime compliance function to the insurance supervisory law. Furthermore, art. 46, para. 2 of the Solvency II Directive refers to the "legal environment" and "legal requirements" in general while addressing the other tasks of the compliance function, with no reference to the insurance supervisory regime. This cannot be glossed over with a reference to the formulation of the

[83] Explicitly, *Bürkle*, id., n. 34 above, at 5.

[84] The explanations of *Saria*, VersRdsch 11/2011, 21 (27 ff.), suffer from failure to consider the core provision para. 1 of art. 46 of the Solvency II Directive and from sole focus on para. 2 of the Directive, which identifies subtasks of compliance under the insurance supervisory regime only by way of example. She arrives, therefore, above all on the basis of general considerations of the telos of the Directive, at the conclusion that the compliance duty "clearly at least" pertains to the insurance supervisory regime. Further, however, "those legal provisions that exhibit a particular reference to the actual business of insurance" are included. VersRdsch 11/2011, 21 (29). Thus "the general provisions of law on companies, taxation, crime, labor, and social services,. . .etc." should be "excluded". This delineation fails to persuade for lack of clarity. This can be seen in the simplistic examples: drawn from the criminal law, participation of an insurance undertaking in a bidding cartel (punishable under sec. 298 of the StGB [German Criminal Code]) with respect to calls for proposal for insurance services; based on the likewise excluded general company law, non-compliance with the requirements applicable to managing board compensation by an insurance undertaking, which requirements are separate from the insurance supervisory regime rules.

advice task, even if this task were not subject to the legal requirement "shall include", not the least because of the equivalence of the three areas of operation named as examples in paragraph 2.

Ultimately, the broad view put forward here on the subject of compliance under the insurance supervisory regime flows also from the legal structuring of the ICS itself. Under art. 46, para. 1, subpara. 2 of the Solvency II Directive, this includes, i. a., "administrative and accounting procedures". The legal requirements for accounting, however, basically do not partake of the nature of an insurance supervisory regime. Nonetheless, they are included within the legal "requirements" for an insurance undertaking.[85] If the insurance supervisory regime compliance function were limited to monitoring the "regulations and administrative provisions" "adopted pursuant" the Solvency II Directive, then this regime could not find fault even with a complete absence of accounting and thus also not with a fundamentally flawed ICS. This is so even though the compliance function itself is a part of the ICS.[86] Art. 46, para. 1, subpara. 1 of the Solvency II Directive contains no subject-matter limitations with respect to the ICS. Thus, in principle, what can be monitored must be monitored, to the extent requirements of a legal nature are involved. From the perspective of the Solvency system, it is true, compliance under the insurance supervisory regime includes especially monitoring whether the insurance undertaking and its employees are in compliance with the insurance supervisory law. But of equal rank and importance is, for example, monitoring compliance with insurance contract law and all other legal requirements. Explanation no. 3.157 of the Governance Guidelines proceeds directly from the same principle, with its formulation "compliance with applicable laws and regulatory requirements". Nor is harm done by the fact that in addition a convergent supervisory practice essentially cannot occur within the meaning of Recital 40 and art. 71, para. 2, sent. 1 of the Solvency II Directive concerning the monitoring of requirements other than those of supervision law because of areas characterized in part by national law, such as insurance contract law. This is so because from the very outset the directive on convergence can cover only those legal areas characterized by European law.

In sum, therefore, the general legal monitoring task of the compliance function extends not only to compliance with the insurance supervisory law,[87] but also to compliance with the legal requirements for the insurance undertaking as a whole. In this setting, the subject matter of insurance supervisory monitoring under art. 34 of the Solvency II Directive does not play a role with respect to the subject matter of

---

[85] It is not relevant to determining the subject matter of compliance under the insurance supervisory regime that the European insurance supervisory regime in supplementing the Insurance Accounts Directive – RL [of DVO] 91/674/EWG ABlEG 1991 L 374, sent. 7 by later amendment – contains no substantive provisions, but only procedural ones. This is so because the Solvency II Directive does not distinguish in this respect among the "requirements" to be monitored. Insofar as *Wolf*, VersR (2013), 678 (684), largely excludes accounting from the monitoring by compliance under the insurance supervisory regime, he ignores the contexts adduced here.

[86] See above, at 10.2.2.

[87] See for the opposing view the references in n. 82, above.

compliance under the insurance supervisory regime. Because of its very broad language, which requires a correspondingly narrow interpretation,[88] the Directive is to the effect that

> the supervisory authority shall ensure that the insurance and reinsurance undertakings comply with the regulations and administrative provisions imposed upon them in each Member State.

10.4.2.2 Internal Directives as Subject of Monitoring?

The internal directives of an insurance undertaking[89] are therefore included within the legal requirements that are the subject matter of compliance under the insurance supervisory regime. This applies, for example, to underwriting guidelines or general ethics guidelines, concerning acceptance of gifts, invitations, and hospitality from other persons. They constitute also legal rules in the form of internal law of insurance undertakings. Infringements of such guidelines could in fact ultimately have consequences under labor law.

10.4.2.3 The Relationship of Compliance Under the Insurance Supervisory Regime to Compliance Under Company Law

In the context of what has been set forth above, one may answer the question already raised[90] concerning the relationship of compliance under the insurance supervisory regime to compliance under general company law. If compliance under the insurance supervisory regime is engaged with compliance with legal requirements for the insurance undertaking as a whole and with the creation of a compliance organization, then it includes the compliance demanded by company

---

[88] See *Dreher/Ballmaier*, id., n. 19 above, at 108 f., 114 f.

[89] Accord *Bürkle*, id., n. 34 above, at 14; *Saria*, VersRdsch 11/2011, 21 (31); *Korinek/Schadler-Liebl*, VersRdsch 9/2011, 30 (32) and for general company law, no. 4.1.3 DCGK [German Corporate Governance Code] since July 2007; for a different view see *Hüffer*, id., n. 5 above, at 302 f., misjudging the legal nature of internal company guidelines and regarding only governmental law provisions as compatible with compliance. The GDV [German Insurance Association] discussion paper "Governance-Funktionen unter Solvency II: Kernaufgaben um Schnittstellenfragen" [in English: Governance Functions under Solvency II: Core Functions in Interface Areas] (2012), 13 f. designates the "internal requirements" as subjects of monitoring, not for the compliance function, but only for the internal audit. Id. at 19.

[90] See above, at 10.2.1.

law. Thus, the insurance supervisory regime is superimposed as *lex specialis*[91] upon company law, which is the applicable associations law for public insurance undertakings.

Under company law, there is likewise a basic obligation to create a compliance function.[92] Under this view, the distinctive feature of the duty of compliance in the insurance supervisory regime is that this duty, not explicitly set forth in company law, is established by law in the insurance supervisory regime. Furthermore there is this: With respect to organizing the compliance function, under general company law the managing board has broad discretion in determining what is required and reasonable.[93] Insurance undertakings, on the other hand, are subject to supervisory requirements at all regulatory levels of the Solvency II system. These contain in part detailed requirements, for example, for the tasks of the compliance function, the requirements as to directors and staff members,[94] and supervisory monitoring.[95]

If, however, one is of the view that compliance under the insurance supervisory regime is limited to monitoring the national implementation in law of the Solvency II Directive,[96] a host of further questions and consequences arises, some of them thorny. One issue is the boundary between compliance under the insurance supervisory regime and compliance under company law. The issue already noted[97] concerning monitoring the ICS as a whole is an example. Further, substantial consequences arise, for example, in reference to the scope of supervisory monitoring of managing board responsibility for compliance and of the actions of the compliance function. A further example would be supervisory monitoring of whether the holders of this function and their staff members meet the fit-and-proper requirements. This is so because, in any given case, the responsibilities and actions of these persons would be subject to supervisory monitoring only insofar as compliance with the insurance supervisory regime were at issue. Outside this scenario, the insurance supervisory authorities would have no competence toward

---

[91] On this point generally, see *Dreher*, ZGR (2010), 496 (502); *Saria*, VersRdsch 11/2011, 21 (32 f.), initially argues contra for a special feature of company law compliance which would assume "parallel and mutually independent" existing obligations. *Ludwig*, in: Branchenspezifische Wirtschaftsaufsicht und Corporate Governance [in English: Sector-specific Economic Supervision and Corporate Governance] (2012) 258 f. writes of "internal audit focused on compliance with timely identification of legal risks". Unfortunately and astonishingly, his description is completely uninfluenced by the impact of supervisory law on compliance law nor does it reflect the impact of the current literature on the subject.

[92] See *Dreher*, id., n. 5 above, at 171 ff. with further references, disputed.

[93] See, e.g., *Bürkle*, BB (2007), 1797 (1799); *Fleischer*, "Corporate Compliance im aktienrechtlichen Unternehmensverbund" [in English: Corporate Compliance Groups Formed under Company Law], CCZ (2008), 1 (3); *Spindler*, WM (2008), 905 (909); *Dreher*, id., n. 5 above, at 172; id., ZWeR (2004), 75 (94) on concretizing bases on competition law compliance.

[94] See as to their determination, *Dreher*, VersR (2012), 933 (936 ff.) (Chap. 7, above, at 7.3) and VersR (2012), 1061 (Chap. 8, above), on "fit-and proper" supervision.

[95] See *Dreher*, VersR (2012), 1061 (1069 ff.) (Chap. 8, above, at 8.5 and 8.6).

[96] See for this view in the literature 10.4.2.1, above.

[97] See above, at 10.4.2.1.

these persons. This would, for example, affect compliance with the rules on prevention of money laundering to a very great extent. This is so because these rules are based on their own directive.[98] The Solvency II Directive addresses them only in art. 59, para. 1 c in connection with supervisory monitoring of procurement of qualified investments in insurance undertakings.

10.4.2.4 The Relationship of Compliance Under the Insurance Supervisory Regime to Compliance Foreseen by Special Laws

The number of areas sought to be protected by special laws has undergone a rapid and voluminous increase. Along with this trend has come a commensurate increase in officially required company officials.[99] This development includes insurance undertakings. At the least, this applies to data security officers under secs. 4 f and 4 g of the BDSG [German Federal Data Protection Act], money-laundering officers under secs. 2, para. 1, no. 4, and 9, para. 2, no. 1 of the GwG [German Money-Laundering Act] and claim adjustment officers under sec. 7 b of the VAG [German Insurance Supervision Act] and sec. 150 of the VAG-RegE [Government's Draft of a Tenth Act Amending the German Insurance Supervision Act], and also the responsible actuary under sec. 11 a VAG [German Insurance Supervision Act] and sec. 132 VAG RegE [Government's Draft of a Tenth Act Amending the German Insurance Supervision Act]. Inasmuch as it falls to each of these officers as a legal obligation to ensure compliance with certain likewise legally prescribed standards, the question arises whether compliance under the insurance supervisory regime also includes this kind of compliance areas regulated by special law.

The starting point here is the conclusion previously arrived at that general legal monitoring, by virtue of the compliance demanded by the insurance supervisory regime, in principle extends to compliance with the legal requirements for insurance undertakings as a whole, even though to a different degree of intensity. There is, therefore, no exception for the legal areas as to which insurance undertakings must install company officials and in which these company officials assume certain verification tasks. To the contrary, the statutory and internal company requirements for their part constitute "requirements" within the meaning of art. 46, para. 1, subpara. 2 of the Solvency II Directive. The general legal monitoring duty of compliance under the insurance supervisory regime thus applies, i.a., to the issues of whether the company officials required by special law are present, whether they meet the requirements of the law, and whether they are actually acting in accordance with legal requirements.[100]

[98] Directive 2005/60/EC, OJEU L 309, 25 Nov. 2005 at 15.

[99] See in detail on this point and on the individual legal questions for the company officials *Rittner/ Dreher*, Europäisches und deutsches Wirtschaftsrecht [in English: European and German Economic Law] (3rd. ed. 2008) sec. 12.

[100] Of a differing view is *Saria*, VersRdsch 11/2011, 21 (34), excluding from the factual ambit of compliance under the insurance supervisory regime those legal areas covered by company officials under special laws but paying no regard to the job description, which in part is wholly divergent

10.4.2.5 Implementation of the General Legal Monitoring Task in the VAG-RegE [Government's Draft of a Tenth Act Amending the German Insurance Supervision Act]

The coming implementation of the Solvency II Directive's compliance rules in the VAG-RegE [Government's Draft of a Tenth Act Amending the German Insurance Supervision Act] pertains to "the laws, regulations, and supervisory requirements to be observed by insurance undertakings" for the general monitoring task.[101] This broad language of the core task of compliance under the insurance supervisory regime coincides with the present result established for the requirements of the Solvency II Directive.

By contrast, to the extent that concretizing the core task "general legal monitoring" by the three subtasks of the compliance function noted as examples in the Solvency II Directive is involved, sec. 29, para. 2, of the VAG-RegE [Government's Draft of a Tenth Act Amending the German Insurance Supervision Act] deviates in part from the Directive. This affects the task of advising the managing board by the compliance function. Whereas the directive refers to "compliance with the laws, regulations and administrative provisions adopted pursuant to this Directive", the VAG-RegE [Government's Draft of a Tenth Act Amending the German Insurance Supervision Act] extends the advice task generally to "compliance with the laws and administrative provisions applicable to the conduct of the insurance business". In the context of the broad understanding presented here of the general legal monitoring task of compliance under the insurance supervisory regime, and further based on the terms of the Solvency II Directive, such an expanded implementation scheme is permissible and reasonable. This is so even if the particular emphasis on the insurance supervisory regime desired by the European issuer of directives for concrete subtasks gets lost with such a legislative formulation.

10.4.3 Advising the Managing Board

Under art. 46, para. 2 of the Solvency II Directive, one of the first instances noted of a subtask of the insurance supervisory regime compliance function is advice of the managing board. This has been especially prescribed for the insurance supervisory regime by the Directive. At the same time, this area is thus emphasized from among all potential subtasks. And independently of this, it applies generally to the legal requirements for insurance undertakings.[102]

from compliance under the insurance supervisory regime. Consistent pursuit of this view would necessarily require her to view even the issue of the presence of a money-laundering official in an insurance undertaking as not compatible with compliance.

[101] See above, at 10.2.5.

[102] See above, at 10.4.2.1. Likewise essentially, MaRisk BA, id., n. 30 above, at no. 1.

In sum, advice of the managing board by the compliance function under by the insurance supervisory regime can be shielded from liability as well as be the basis for liability. This latter situation will obtain to the extent that the managing board is responsible for adhering to the principle of legality under company law principles on the one hand[103] and under insurance supervisory regime principles on the other.[104] Advice from the compliance function concerning legal principles that is contrary to intended actions could lead to bad faith on the part of the managing board members. By the same token, appropriate advice can avoid breaches of duty by managing board members. This applies particularly in the realm of the business judgment rule (hereafter: BJR), found in sec. 93, para. 1, sent. 2 of the AktG [German Stock Corporation Act] by reason of the legal requirement of action "on the basis of appropriate information". To the extent that insurance supervisory regime advice is adduced in this setting,[105] it is probable that the field for applying the BJR would be rather rarely established, in the absence of a "management decision" as prescribed by sec. 93, para. 1, sent. 2 of the AktG [German Stock Corporation Act].[106] This is so because principle-based decisions are to be legally

[103] See above, at 10.2.1.

[104] See above, at 10.2.2.

[105] See *Bürkle*, id., n. 34 above, at 15.

[106] The issue of the managing board's duty to act and the application of the BJR in the realm of a principles-based supervisory regime is as yet not clear. Based on the supervisory regime Legal Judgment Rule, *Bürkle*, in "Aufsichtsrechtliches Legal Judgment: Sachlicher Anwendungsbereich und prozedurale Voraussetzungen" [in English: Supervisory Regime Legal Judgment: Factual Realm of Application and Procedural Requisites], VersR (2013), 792, arrives at a very broad application of the BJR in the insurance supervisory regime with respect to the "how" of an action. To this extent also in favor of "at least a suitable application" of the BJR is *Louven/Raapke*, in "Aktuelle Entwicklungen in der Corporate Governance von Versicherungsunternehmen" [in English: Current Developments in Corporate Governance of Insurance Undertakings], VersR (2012), 257 (264). For a view against transference of the BJR into principles-based insurance supervision with a reference to decisions bound by law despite "a certain discretionary scope with respect to concrete implementation", see *Armbrüster*, "Aufsichtsrecht überlagert Aktienrecht" [in English: The Supervisory Regime Imposed on Corporate Law], KSzW (2013), 10 (14) and id. in: Bähr, ed., Handbuch des Versicherungsaufsichtsrechts [in English: Manual of Insurance Supervision Law] (2011) sec. 11, ref. 66. According to the *view presented here*, in this context the issue is likewise not the application of the BJR but on the one hand the criteria for the concretization of the insurance supervisory regime principles set up as guidelines for the managing board's actions on behalf of the undertaking. And on the other hand, the issue is the scrutiny, initially supervisory but thereafter judicial, when these sorts of principles-based decisions are involved. Whereas, as a consequence of the prohibition on optimization in supervisory review proceedings, see *Dreher*, VersR (2013), 401 (405) (Chap. 3, above, at 3.3.2.1); *Dreher/Ballmaier*, id. n. 19 above, at 95, (108 f.), the supervisory authority can test the management decisions only as to reasonableness, the supervisory decision itself is subject to full judicial review, see *Dreher*, ZVersWiss (2012), 381 (416 f. 422 f.) (Chap. 4, above, at 4.4.2.5 and 4.4.3.1); *Dreher/Häußler*, "Die Aufsicht über Versicherungsunternehmen durch die BaFin und die Überwachungsaufgabe des Aufsichtsrats" [in English: Supervision of Insurance Undertakings by BaFin [Federal Financial Supervisory Authority] and the Monitoring Task of the Supervisory Board], ZGR (2011), 471 (490 f.), in which the limitation of review by the supervisory authority continues to be restricted to the reasonableness of the management decision. On the other side of the fence,

concretized by the individual undertaking and therefore are characterized by legal issues. This is the case even if individual preconditions for application of the BJR—for example, the requirement of appropriate information—apply in the same manner in the area of principles-based decisions, but on other legal bases, namely action in the interest of the undertaking.

The term "monitoring" suggests at first blush a post hoc task and scarcely seems consistent with prior advice tasks.

Nonetheless, monitoring does in fact include preventive advice. It has long been recognized in company law that the monitoring task of the supervisory board under sec. 111 of the AktG [German Stock Corporation Act] includes advice of the managing board in the sense of "forward-looking monitoring".[107] But also in the context of the special rules on compliance under the insurance supervisory regime no other arrangements could exist. General legal monitoring as a task will have to extend conceptually to the coming legal requirements to ensure that these requirements are met within undertakings in a proper and appropriate manner. In like manner, it is a part of monitoring, if the compliance function not only identifies legal deficiencies that have come to light, but also analyzes them, draws conclusions, and makes action proposals to avoid future occurrences of the same. Monitoring is therefore at all times an anticipatory activity. And the subtask of advising the managing board identified by the Solvency II Directive is necessarily bound up with monitoring. Understandably, the Directive keeps in view the subject-matter of the rules pars pro toto only with reference to the insurance supervisory regime.

As is the case with all compliance tasks, by virtue of the insurance supervisory regime compliance function, advice of the managing board is selectively subject to the principle of materiality[108] and generally subject to the principle of proportionality.[109] Even if the former principle in a particular case does not extend to a subject for which there should be advice of the managing board, the latter principle requires examining whether a subject requires legal advice by the compliance function by reason of its general relevance and its value to internal company operations.

The Solvency II Directive mentions the subtask "advice of the managing board" on the basis as set forth above, in particular the managing board's responsibility for legality with respect to undertaking as whole, but nevertheless only by means of

Langenbucher, "Vorstandshaftung und Legalitätspflicht in regulierten Branchen" [in English: Managing Board Liability and the Duty of Legality in Regulated Sectors], ZBB (2013), 16 (22 f.) argues for an optimization directive as follows: "In any case, principles-based supervisory rules require that every effort be made to effectuate the legislatively formulated supervisory principle as optimally as possible".

[107] Accord BGHZ [in English: Decisions of the Federal Court of Justice in Civil Matters] (Ger.) (hereafter, BGHZ) 114, 127 (130); *Dreher/Häußler*, ZGR (2011), 471 (474 f.); *Hüffer*, AktG [in English: German Stock Corporation Act] (10th ed. 2012) sec. 111, ref. 5; *Hopt/Roth*, AktG [in English: German Stock Corporation Act], v. 4 (4th ed. 2006) sec. 111, refs. 56, 58 f.; *Lutter/Krieger*, "Rechte und Pflichten des Aufsichtsrats" [in English: Rights and Obligations of the Supervisory Board] (5th ed. 2008) sec. 3, ref. 94 ff.

[108] See above, at 10.4.1.2.

[109] See above, at 10.4.1.3.

example in concretizing the general compliance task "monitoring of compliance with the requirements". This does not, however, warrant a contrary inference. Thus, compliance under the insurance supervisory regime is tasked with advising all insurance undertaking staff members working in the respective risk areas.[110] This follows inherently from the training and instruction tasks conjoined with any and every compliance activity.[111]

The task of "advice of the managing board" in legal matters by the company's own compliance function demonstrates at the same time that the legislator regards such in-house advice as adequate and sufficient. Thus in the normal situation, there is no occasion either for additional and deeper inquiry obligations on the part of the managing board or for resort to outside legal advisers, where no question arises concerning the qualifications and professionalism of the in-house adviser and his or her advice, with reference to the subject-matter of advice by the compliance function.[112,113] At the same time, however, the supervisory duty of the compliance function to advise the managing board raises a distinct question with regard to the rulings of the BGH [German Federal Court of Justice][114] and the European Court of Justice,[115] which have denied corporate counsel—though often assuming the compliance function—equivalence in the law with outside counsel.

10.4.4 Evaluation of Risks from Changes in the Legal Environment

By use of examples, art. 46, para. 2 of the Solvency II Directive emphasizes the second subtask, evaluation of risks from changes in the legal environment, in the context of compliance under the insurance supervisory regime. Like advice of the managing board, this task constitutes a part of the core task of general legal monitoring in the sense of anticipatory monitoring through observation and assessment.

An example of this is assessment of risks connected with the July 2012 ruling of the BGH [German Federal Court of Justice] regarding the examination of general

---

[110] Accord also *Korinek/Schadler-Liebl*, VersRdsch 9/2011, 30 (33) and previously in detail *Schaaf*, id., n. 56 above, at 141 ff. *Bürkle*, id., n. 2 above, at sec. 1, ref. 173 f.

[111] See 10.3, above.

[112] Some particular situations, such as cases of sharpening crisis or especially risk-threatened positions, cannot be regarded as normal.

[113] On this point see, independently of compliance under the insurance supervisory regime, BGH AG 2011, 876 (ISION) and from the literature, e.g., *Junker/Biederbick*, AG (2012), 898; *Strohn*, ZHR 176 (2012), 137; *Krieger*, ZGR (2012), 496; *Binder*, AG [in English: The Corporation] (2012), 885; *Fleischer*, KSzW (2013), 3.

[114] BGH [German Federal Court of Justice], NJW (2011), 1517 pnt. 6.

[115] EuGH [European Court of Justice], NJW (2010), 3557, pnt. 49 (Akzo Nobel).

insurance conditions in life insurance, risks that continue to exist because of unresolved vagueness.[116] This ruling will subject insurance undertakings to extremely high expenses, not accounted for when the insurance policies were issued. Therefore, it has to be a subtask of an insurance undertaking's compliance function to perceive such developments from the very beginning, to evaluate them, and if possible draw the legal conclusions, e.g., by identifying the risks for which provisions for liabilities and charges might be required, in order to recommend these to the managing board. To give a concrete example, an already extant compliance function, because of its exceptionally significant economic importance, would have watched and analyzed the development from its inception in the insurance law literature and in the corresponding lower court decisions. And this would have been done with steadily increasing intensity.

10.4.5 Evaluation of the Compliance Risk

Evaluation of the compliance risk is a third subtask of compliance under the insurance supervisory regime according to art. 46 of the Solvency II Directive.[117] Under art. 260 SG8, para. 2 of the DVO draft, an explicit part of this is also the evaluation of whether the measures employed by the insurance undertaking to avoid non-compliance are adequate.

Number 3.155 of the Governance Guidelines explicates the compliance function in regard to the compliance risk. This provision describes the compliance function as identification, evaluation, monitoring, and reporting with respect to the compliance risks of the insurance undertaking. No. 3.156 of the Governance Guidelines in turn defines the compliance risk in the manner already cited,[118] i.e., as the risk of legal or supervisory sanctions, substantial financial losses, or losses to reputation.

The Solvency II Directive identifies some chief risks and defines them in art. 13, nos. 30 through 35. Among these the operational risk, except for its tie to the internal audit task, is most closely tied to the compliance task. This is so because "the risk of loss arising from inadequate or failed internal processes, personnel or systems, or from external events" is the definition of operational risk given in art. 13, no. 33 of the Solvency II Directive. In art. 107, paras. 2 and 3, the Solvency II Directive, the standard model describes operational risk in terms of flat rate

[116] See "BGH" [in English: German Federal Court of Justice], VersR (2012), 1149 and also *Armbrüster*, "Konsequenzen des Urteils zu unwirksamen Klauseln" [in English: Consequences of the Judgment on Ineffective Clauses], VW 19/2012, 1434; id., "Kehrtwende des BGH bei der AGB-Kontrolle in der Lebensversicherung" [in English: The Federal Court of Justice Makes an About-face in Monitoring of General Terms and Conditions for Life Insurance], NJW (2012), 3001; *Präve*, VersR (2012), 1159 (1163) and VersR (2012), 657.

[117] See in detail on this point, but without reference to the insurance industry, *Moosmayer*, id., n. 57 above, at 25 ff.

[118] See above, at 10.2.4.

calculations. In counterbalance, the ORSA process under art. 45 of the Solvency II Directive[119] and risk avoidance through the procedural and systemic examinations of internal audit take the operational risk fully into account as well. In the context of the compliance risk, which to a great extent is allocated under the operational risk, the emphasis in the Solvency II Directive on the subtask "evaluation of the compliance risk" by compliance under the insurance supervisory regime at the same time can be seen as a further balancing of the blanket inclusion of the operational risk in the standard formula.[120]

10.5 The Legal Nature of Compliance Under the Insurance Supervisory Regime

10.5.1 The Long Arm of the Insurance Supervisory Authority?

The legal nature of compliance under the insurance supervisory regime is problematic. It could be considered that the compliance function would operate in insurance undertakings as "the long arm" of the insurance supervisory authority, would be in the nature of company officials, or would merely perform a function within the undertaking, even if that function is mandated and contoured by law.

As set forth above,[121] the managing board bears the ultimate responsibility for compliance with the insurance undertaking's duty of legality. With reference to the insurance supervisory regime, art. 40 of the Solvency II Directive expressly assigns this responsibility to the managing board. By contrast, the Solvency II system contains no rules that would assign the activity of compliance under the insurance supervisory regime to the insurance supervisory authorities. Rather, the insurance supervisory regime is limited to categorizing the establishment of a compliance function as part of the ICS from an organizational point of view and to assigning that function certain tasks as a matter of substantive law.[122] Conversely, there is no legal basis for compliance-specific interventions by the insurance supervisory authority beyond the prescribed legal consequences for breach of certain legal duties, such as notice of newly designated holders of the compliance function.[123] Thus the pertinent national insurance supervisory authority cannot require the

---

[119] See on this point in detail *Dreher/Ballmaier*, "Die unternehmenseigene Risiko- und Solvabilitätsbeurteilung (ORSA) nach Solvency II und VAG 2012" [in English: Risk and Solvency Assessment (ORSA) by Undertakings under Solvency II and the German Insurance Supervision Act 2012], VersR (2012), 129 (Chap. 5, above).

[120] See *Saria*, VersRdsch 11/2011, 21 (24).

[121] See above, at 10.2.2.

[122] See above, at 10.2.2 and 10.2.3.

[123] See *Dreher* VersR 2012, 1061 (1069 f.) (Chap. 8, above, at 8.5.1).

managing board of an insurance undertaking to provide, e.g., ad hoc or on a periodical basis, a statement that the insurance undertaking has met its compliance-related obligations. Thus, the compliance-specific compliance function ultimately is not the "long arm" of the insurance supervisory authority.

10.5.2 Company Officials?

Nonetheless, the holders of the compliance function[124] may occupy the position of public company officials.[125] The number of company officials under European or German law has become excessive. And there are differences among them with respect to their positions within companies or with regard to the authorities.[126] Of particular note in the financial services sector has been the compliance officer under sec. 33, para. 1, sent. 2, nos. 1 and 5 and sec. 34 d, para. 3, sent. 1 of the WpHG [German Securities Trading Act] along with sec. 12, para. 4, sent. 1 of the WpDVerOV [German Investment Services Conduct of Business and Organization Regulation]. This compliance officer, however, is not a company official.[127] There are company officials, however, also in the insurance industry as, for example, claim adjustment officers, responsible actuaries, or money-laundering officials show.[128]

The point of departure for the rules on company officials is the freedom of internal organization accorded the company owners, which is curtailed by the normative requirement requiring installation of company officials for certain tasks. Further, all the rules relating to company officials share an acceptance of the duty by private undertakings to implement matters of public interest. Originally, this concerned only matters deemed particularly worthy of safeguarding from hazards. Since company officials, as per the rules applicable to them, constitute a legal addition within the undertaking's organization and have the objective as a rule

[124] See as to the determination of the group of key function holders *Dreher*, VersR (2012), 933 (Chap. 7, above).

[125] This is a different issue from that of the relationship of the insurance supervisory regime compliance function to company officials required by special law in general and especially in insurance undertakings. This issue resolves into two areas: the respectively assigned tasks – see 10.4.2.4, above – and whether the holder of a compliance function can serve at the same time as a company official under the special laws.

[126] See on this point and the following in detail *Rittner/Dreher*, id., n. 99 above, at sec. 12 with further references.

[127] See, e.g., *Lösler*, "Zur Rolle und Stellung des Compliance-Beauftragten" [in English: On the Role and Position of the Compliance Officer], WM (2008), 1098 (1099); *Casper*, id., n. 33 above, at 214; for a different view *Veil*, "Compliance-Organisationen in Wertpapierdienstleistungsunternehmen im Zeitalter der MiFiD" [in English: Compliance Organizations in Bond/Securities Services Undertakings in the Age of the MiFiD [Markets in Financial Services Directive]], WM 2008, 1093 (1097); *Harm*, id., n. 33 above, at 170.

[128] See above, at 10.4.2.4.

of internal monitoring of the organization, their actions are parallel to those of the pertinent supervisory authority. They supplement the supervisory authority. They do not replace it.

As such, company officials constitute foreign matter within undertakings. At the same time, however, they are designed to be an internal part of the undertaking. The tasks and rights typically mandated by law for company officials do not cast doubt on this. Examples of the foregoing are duties, especially those concerning rights of information, monitoring, and initiative. Further examples are other privileges and powers, in particular freedom of action, right of proposal and report and the right of consultation, and independent decisional authority.[129] A different situation obtains only in those few instances where company officials have a direct or indirect right of appeal to the supervisory authority, as under sec. 4 g, para. 1, sent. 2 of the BDSG [German Federal Data Protection Act] and sec. 32, para. 2, sent. 2 of the Verordnung über den Schutz vor Schäden durch ionisierende Strahlen [German Regulation on Protection against Harm from Ionizing Radiation] (StrlSchV). This, however, is strictly limited to the statutorily prescribed cases. It cannot be expanded as done by voices in the literature into a "right of self-defense" by company officials if they experience resistance to their views within the undertakings.[130]

The holder of the compliance function within the meaning of compliance under the insurance supervisory regime has no such right of appeal to the insurance supervisory authorities.[131] Rather, for the holders of the key function compliance and far below this threshold, the insurance supervisory regime does not recognize the previously mentioned tasks and powers that are normal for company officials. The only special position in this sense is constituted by the right of information and right to report for all key functions relating to the undertaking, pursuant to the DVO draft.[132] But by itself this right does not mean the legal posture of the persons affected is comparable to that of regular company officials. There is a further point: Even in a true emergency, where an objection to substantial illegal actions or omissions by the holders of the compliance function does not move the managing board to undertake a remedy or the managing board even participates in the actions or omissions, the contact for the compliance function under this emergency

[129] See for more detail the systematization in *Rittner/Dreher*, id., n. 99 above, at sec. 12, ref. 15 ff.

[130] On this point see also *Rittner/Dreher*, id., n. 99 above, at sec. 12, ref. 34 and *Dreher, id.*, "Unternehmensbeauftragte und Gesellschaftsrecht" [in English: Company Officials and Company Law] in Festschrift für [Publication in Honor of] Carsten Peter Claussen on his 70th birthday (1997) 69 (83 ff.).

[131] For two possible, general exceptions – independent of compliance under the insurance supervisory regime –, in which the compliance officer shall be entitled to the information from the authority even absent special statutory basis, see *Bürkle*, "Grenzen der Garantenstellung des Compliance Officers" [in English: Limits of the Penal Guarantor Position of the Compliance Officer], CCZ 2010, 4 (10). The exceptions relate to cases involving the risk of personal criminal liability for failure to provide information and cognizable collusion between the supervisory board and the managing board.

[132] See above, at 10.2.3.

information obligation is not an insurance supervisory authority, but solely the supervisory board.[133] Thus, from the legal point of view, the holders of the compliance function in the scheme of compliance under the insurance supervisory regime are not company officials.[134]

10.5.3 Statutorily Prescribed and Designed Functions of Undertakings

In its legal nature, compliance under the insurance supervisory regime is simply a statutorily prescribed and designed function of an undertaking.[135] It sets forth certain special statutory requirements for holders of the function, with respect to qualifications and fit-and-proper criteria.[136]

In reference to the use of "compliance function" as a term, the Statement of Reasons for sec. 29 of the VAG-RegE [Government's Draft of a Tenth Act Amending the German Insurance Supervision Act][137] notes that a statutorily prescribed function can be performed by several persons.[138] "Therefore the term 'compliance function' will be given preference here over the term "compliance officer". This position of the VAG-RegE [Government's Draft of a Tenth Act Amending the German Insurance Supervision Act] is an immediate occasion for wonder, because the German language recognizes a plural for the term "compliance officer" and the basis of the statute is thus not sound by its own terms. Even apart from such semantic deficiencies, it is above all unpersuasive in the context of the preceding to jostle the holders of the compliance function into the vicinity of the

[133] See generally on this point *Dreher*, ZGR (2010), 496 (520 f.) with further references; *Bürkle*, "Neues Aufsichtsrecht für Aufsichtsräte durch den Regierungsentwurf zum 10. VAG-Änderungsgesetz" [in English: A New Supervisory Regime in the Government's Draft on the Tenth VAG [German Insurance Supervision Act] Amended Act], ZVersWiss (2012), 493 (504); and from the perspective of the supervisory board for direct contact to staff of the undertaking, *Dreher*, "Antikorruptionsuntersuchungen durch den Aufsichtsrat – Compliance und Bildung eines Antikorruptionsausschusses" [in English: Anti-corruption Investigations by the Supervisory Board – Compliance and Establishment of an Anti-corruption Commission] in Festschrift für [Publication in Honor of] Wulf Goette on his 65th Birthday (2011) 43 (48 ff.) and for voluntarily appointed compliance officers, *Bürkle*, CCZ (2010), 4 (9 f.).

[134] See, id., *Dreher*, VersR (2012), 1061 (1071) (Chap. 8, above, at 8.6.2); likewise since, *Bürkle*, CCZ (2012), 220 (223) and for compliance officers in insurance undertakings under existing law, *Schaaf*, id., n. 56 above, at 147 f.

[135] On the questions of waiving compliance under the insurance supervisory regime from an organizational point of view in smaller insurance undertakings, see *Dreher*, VersR (2012), 933 (939) (Chap. 7, above, at 7.3.5.3).

[136] See in detail *Dreher*, VersR (2012), 1061 (Chap. 8, above).

[137] VAG-RegE [Government's Draft of a Tenth Act Amending the German Insurance Supervision Act], n. 24 above, at 275 f.

[138] See on this point in more detail *Dreher*, VersR (2012), 933 (940) (Chap. 7, above, at 7.3.5.4).

company officials. In addition, the Statement of Reasons to the draft act is likewise inapposite to the extent that it draws a parallel to sec. 33, para. 1, sent. 1, no. 1 of the WpHG [German Securities Trading Act] and the mention of the compliance function there, although sec. 34 d, para. 3, sent. 1 of the WpHG [German Securities Trading Act] actually characterizes as "compliance officers" those staff members whom the undertakings "entrust with responsibility for the compliance function".

10.6 Summary

1. Compliance under the insurance supervisory regime, like compliance in general, is not based primarily on the liability threat potential of omitted compliance measures, but rather on its contribution to a free economic system in the sense of maintaining open markets, on fostering values-oriented business management, and on guarding members of management as well as staff members from illegal activity and its consequences.
2. The legal bases of compliance under the insurance supervisory regime are to be found especially in the Solvency II Directive as regulatory level one, in the draft of the implementing regulation corresponding to the Directive at regulatory level two, and in the draft of the Governance Guidelines of regulatory level three.
3. The German legislator must reenact the requirements of regulatory level one in a new VAG [German Insurance Supervision Act]. The VAG-RegE [Government's Draft of a Tenth Act Amending the German Insurance Supervision Act] of February 2012 and new sec. 64 a, para. 7 of the VAG [German Insurance Supervision Act] based on the German Bank Ringfencing Act in this respect do not represent legislative implementation that follows European law exclusively. Rather, they deviate in part from mandatory European requirements.
4. As the new Solvency II system comes into effect, missing are the factual impetus and the actual need as well as the legal competence for an insurance supervisory regime compliance rules system in the form of MaRisk VA—corresponding to the compliance rules system applicable only since 1 January 2013 in the MaRisk BA—or in the form of MaComp VA—corresponding to the compliance rules system of the MaComp WA.
5. Like the term "compliance" in all its uses, the term "compliance under the insurance supervisory regime" has two dimensions. Up until now, the widespread understanding in respect to compliance under the insurance supervisory regime also has been focused on organizational law. This understanding has been to assign compliance with the supervisory regime to the law concerning organization of undertakings and to emphasize the organizational precautionary provisions an undertaking employs to ensure conduct in conformity with the law. But "compliance" and concomitantly "compliance under the insurance supervisory regime" must be understood not only from the point of view of organizational law, but also in a substantive law sense. Under this view, within

an undertaking the managing board's leadership obligation involves a legal duty. Thus, the definition of "compliance under the insurance supervisory regime" is properly stated as compliance by insurance undertakings with the requirements of the law on the basis of organizational measures suitable for and adequate to the purpose.

6. The Solvency II Directive identifies four areas of operation within the task of compliance under the insurance supervisory regime. Contrary to the previously common classification, however, these first of all are not of equal import, but are ranked hierarchically by the Solvency II Directive itself; and second of all, the listing is non-exhaustive. The one core task of compliance under the insurance supervisory regime is thus—as expressed in the German-language version of the Solvency II Directive—"monitoring of compliance with the requirements" and—as expressed by the Solvency II Directive in many other language versions—general legal monitoring. By way of example only, the Directive identifies the three subtasks: advising the managing body on matters concerning the insurance supervisory regime, assessment of risks arising from changes in the legal environment, and the assessment of compliance risk.
7. Consistent with the task of general legal monitoring, the subject-matter of compliance under the insurance supervisory regime is not limited to the preservation of the insurance supervisory regime. Rather, the task of compliance under the insurance supervisory regime extends to compliance with the legal requirements for the insurance undertaking as a whole. Also included within this are the internal directives of an insurance undertaking.
8. In some legal areas—for example money-laundering and data security—insurance undertakings are subject to compliance regulated by special law. In such cases, compliance devolves upon company officials. Also in these areas, compliance with legal requirements is included within the tasks of compliance under the insurance supervisory regime.
9. In contrast to the principle of proportionality, the principle of materiality does not constitute a horizontal clause within the insurance supervisory regime. Thus, the principle of materiality restricts the task of compliance under the insurance supervisory regime not generally, but only selectively in the areas included.
10. But even beyond this, there is no legal obligation for comprehensive compliance under the insurance supervisory regime such as would include all legal requirements for an insurance undertaking, embracing, for example, the oft-mentioned cafeteria health regulations. This follows from the principle of proportionality in accordance with the insurance supervisory regime. Compliance under the insurance supervisory regime must therefore be in reasonable proportion to the nature, scale, and complexity of the risks. Furthermore, only what is legally and factually suitable, feasible, required, and appropriate to a given case is warranted. Thus, the principle of proportionality both allows and requires significant distinctions in compliance under the insurance supervisory regime with respect to potential compliance measures. The distinction pertains to extent, i.e., as to facts, time and location, as well as to depth.

11. General legal monitoring as a task of compliance under the insurance supervisory regime characterizes the profile requirements for the holder of the insurance supervisory regime compliance function. The subtasks of compliance with the supervisory regimes identified in the Solvency II Directive by way of example delineate this task as one far more characterized by legal considerations than general compliance under company law already is. It is therefore mandatory for the holder of the insurance supervisory regime compliance function to have a complete legal education, given the nature of his or her job description and the related supervisory criterion of subject-specific suitability. Additionally and equally imperatively, the individual must possess knowledge and skills in the insurance supervisory regime, in insurance contract law, and in the areas of law where the insurance undertaking is particularly exposed to compliance risks. Further, these holders must possess sufficient familiarity with the law to enable them to identify risks at least to the extent of recognizing the need for outside counsel and acquiring that counsel. And finally, the holder of the insurance supervisory regime compliance function must have an understanding of how the insurance industry operates and of the business model of the particular insurance undertaking at issue. Further, the holder must have a basic understanding of the activity of the three other key functions.
12. The task of compliance under the insurance supervisory regime includes such compliance as is required under general company law. The insurance supervisory regime in this respect is *lex specialis* with regard to general company law.
13. The Solvency II Directive identifies advice of the managing board regarding the insurance supervisory regime as a subtask of compliance under the insurance supervisory regime, thus emphasizing the importance of this advice. The duty of advice with respect to insurance supervisory regime matters is, however, only pars pro toto for the overall advice task of the insurance supervisory regime compliance function. Depending upon the individual circumstances, such advice may shield the managing board from liability or itself be the basis for its liability.
14. Assessment of risks from changes in the legal environment constitutes the second example of a subtask of compliance under the insurance supervisory regime given by the Solvency II Directive.
15. The third portion of the task of general legal monitoring appears in the Solvency II Directive as assessment of compliance risk. In the Solvency II Directive, this risk is largely assigned under the operational risk. The draft of the Governance Guidelines at the third regulatory level defines it as the risk of legal or supervisory sanctions, substantial financial losses, or reputational losses.
16. The legal nature of the insurance supervisory regime compliance function neither is that of a long arm of the insurance supervisory authority in insurance undertakings nor does it partake of the character of a public company official. Rather, it represents a statutorily required and designed undertaking function.

Chapter 11
Integrating the Compliance Function into the Legal Department

Contents

11.1 Introduction 326
11.2 Combining the Legal Department and the Compliance Function as a Legal Problem 327
11.3 Combining the Legal Department and the Compliance Function in Light of Their Respective Responsibilities 328
11.3.1 Crossover in Tasks 328
11.3.2 Advisement of Insurance Undertakings' Staff Members as an Area of Potential Conflict 330
11.3.3 Advisement of an Insurance Undertaking's Managing Board as an Area of Potential Conflict 331
11.3.4 Formation of Law by the Legal Department as an Area of Potential Conflict 333
11.4 Combining the Legal Department and the Compliance Function in Light of the Special Rules Aimed at the Compliance Function as a Key Function 334
11.4.1 Particular Competencies 334
11.4.2 Special Qualifications 335
11.5 Combining the Legal Department and the Compliance Function in Light of the Principle of Functional Segregation 336
11.6 Combining the Legal Department and the Compliance Function in Light of the Principle of Functional Independence 337
11.7 Combining the Legal Department and the Compliance Function in Light of the Principles of Freedom of Internal Organization and of Proportionality 338
11.8 Summary 340

First published as "Die Zusammenlegung von Rechtsabteilung und Compliance-Funktion bei Versicherungsunternehmen im Solvency-II-System" [in English: Combining the Legal Department and the Compliance Function of Insurance Undertakings in the Solvency II System], in: Wandt et al., Versicherungsrecht, Haftungs- und Schadensrecht, Festschrift für Egon Lorenz zum 80. Geburtstag [in English: Publication in honor of Prof. Dr. Egon Lorenz on his 80th birthday], Karlsruhe (2014), 119 ff.

M. Dreher, *Treatises on Solvency II*, DOI 10.1007/978-3-662-46290-4_11

Abstract This chapter addresses a governance issue: whether it is permissible under the insurance supervisory regime of Solvency II for an insurance undertaking to merge its compliance function with its legal department. The Solvency II provisions in fact do not address the legal department of an insurance undertaking. But the tasks and powers of a legal department are in part the same as those of the compliance function under art. 46, para. 1 of the Solvency II Directive. The conclusion is thus: General insurance supervisory regime principles such as functional segregation and functional independence do not prohibit such a merger. Indeed, such a merger would seem to be advisable in many instances in light of the supervisory law principles of freedom of internal organization and of proportionality.

11.1 Introduction

The Solvency II provisions do not address the legal department of an insurance undertaking. This is somewhat surprising in view of the internal status and position of a legal department as well as in consideration of the responsibilities imposed on such a department. The legal department is directly attached to the managing board and advises the board with regard to all basic issues relating to company law. By contrast, art. 46, para. 2 of the Solvency II Directive places the task of advising the managing board within the compliance function, with emphasis on advisement concerning insurance supervisory law.[1] Along with this posture, the Solvency II Directive has made the compliance function a component of the system of governance. Pursuant to Recital 33 of the Solvency II Directive, the compliance function is a "key function [. . .] and consequently also [an] important and critical function [. . .]".[2]

The importance of the legal department of an insurance undertaking suggests that it could well have been identified as a key function. This might have clarified a number of issues relating to interface and compatibility with the key functions as identified by the Solvency II Directive. At any rate, the Solvency II system simply ignores the existence of insurance undertakings' legal departments.[3] This raises numerous issues touching the position and activity of the legal department within an insurance undertaking under the Solvency II system. One of these issues has

[1] See on this point in detail *Dreher*, "Begriff, Aufgaben und Rechtsnatur der versicherungsaufsichtsrechtlichen Compliance" [in English: Concept, Tasks, and Legal Nature of Compliance with the Insurance Supervisory Regime], VersR (2013), 929 (937 ff., 940 ff.) (Chap. 10, above, at 10.4.2 and 10.4.3).

[2] Certain particular requirements are the legal consequence of this characterization. An example is found in the outsourcing provisions of art. 49, para. 2 of the Solvency II Directive.

[3] So far as may be discovered, the legal department is addressed only by no. 1.203 (p. 54) of the 27 March 2013 EIOPA Explanatory Text On the Proposal for Guidelines on the System of Governance in connection with outsourcing, and then only indirectly. That passage reads: "The following activities cannot be considered critical or important operational functions or activities: a) the provision of advisory services to the undertaking, and other services which do not form part of the undertaking's insurance or reinsurance activities, such as legal advice, [. . .]".

considerable practical significance: whether the compliance function and the legal department of an insurance undertaking can be combined. Although not previously closely examined, such a merger has been regarded as legally permissible[4] and also logical in view of the tasks and objectives of the two functions and as a means of efficiently using resources. The question now is whether such a merger would face legal obstacles.

With this in mind, the first inquiry is to ascertain where, from a supervisory law point of view, the difficulty lies with respect to combining the legal department and the compliance function in an insurance undertaking (11.2, below). The article then discusses the merger of the legal department and the compliance function in light of their respective tasks (11.3, below), the particular provisions aimed at the compliance function as a key function (11.4, below), the principles of functional segregation (11.5, below), of functional independence (11.6, below) and of self-organization and proportionality (11.7, below).

11.2 Combining the Legal Department and the Compliance Function as a Legal Problem

Since the legal department is not directly addressed in the Solvency II system, such department for its part would only be incompatible with the compliance function if thereby its integrity and task performance were put at risk. There is, however, no fundamental reason to make such an assumption. Rather, the activities of the compliance function are likewise rights-based and subject to upholding the principle of legality.

Thus, the criteria applicable to the compliance function under the Solvency II provisions come to the fore. Of first import in characterization is the special task description for the compliance function in art. 46 of the Solvency II Directive.[5] Next in consideration are certain legal principles applicable to all four key functions. These are: the "fit and proper" requirements for those exercising the compliance function as a key function under Recital 35, art. 42 of the Solvency II Directive, and art. 263 SG11 DVO[6]; a right to be informed with respect to any

[4] This has already been noted by: *Bürkle*, "Die Compliance-Praxis im Finanzdienstleistungssektor nach Solvency II" [in English: Compliance Practice in the Financial Services Sector under Solvency II], CCZ (2008), 50 (53); *Dreher*, "Das Risikomanagement nach § 64a VAG und Solvency II" [in English: Risk Management under Sec. 64 a of the German Insurance Supervision Act and Solvency II], VersR (2008), 998 (1004); and *Reese/Ronge*, "Aufgaben und Struktur der Compliance-Funktion im Versicherungsunternehmen unter besonderer Berücksichtigung von Solvency II" [in English: Tasks and Structure of the Compliance Function in Insurance Undertakings with Particular Regard for Solvency II], VersR (2011), 1217 (1232). The same is true for undertakings not subject to supervisory requirements: see, e.g., *Kort*, in: Publication in Honor of G.H. Roth (2011), 407 (414 f.).

[5] On this point see below, at 11.3.

[6] On this point see below, at 11.4. The abbreviation DVO when used here and below in reference to the Level 2 DVO signifies the EU Commission draft known as Draft Delegated Acts Solvency, 20 Dec. 2013.

staff member under art. 258, para. 3 SG6 DVO; a duty to inform of the compliance function with respect to the managing board under art. 258, para. 4 DVO of any major problem in its area of responsibility; and requirements on variable remuneration under art. 265 SG13, para. 1 (c) and para. 2 (b) DVO. In addition, the principles of functional segregation under art. 41, para. 1, subpara. 2 of the Solvency II Directive and art. 258 SG6, para. 1 DVO and of functional independence under Recital 107, sent. 1 and art. 258 SG6, para. 1, sent. 1 DVO are of particular importance.

11.3 Combining the Legal Department and the Compliance Function in Light of Their Respective Responsibilities

11.3.1 Crossover in Tasks

The activity of a legal department in an insurance undertaking—especially in an insurance undertaking that is the parent of an insurance group[7]—depends on the task imposed on it by the managing board in its leadership role. The normal complement of such tasks includes all law-related processes excepting matters of tax, labor, and insurance law. These are consigned to the appropriate operating department. The primary tasks, then, are: legal advisement of the managing board, which normally has a corporate law emphasis; advisement of staff members; analyzing procedures for legality; and designing structures, procedures, and transactions from a legal perspective in liaison with the pertinent departments. Here, the primary concern is avoidance of legal hazards and formation of law in the interest of the undertaking.

Art. 46 of the Solvency II Directive imposes general legal monitoring on the compliance function as a core task. The compliance function specifically encompasses the insurance supervisory regime, but is correctly considered also to include compliance with the legal requirements imposed on insurance undertakings in general.[8] Thereafter, art. 46 of the Solvency II Directive sets forth three subtasks of the compliance function by way of example. These are in the areas of: advisement of the managing board, where the directive notes only the insurance supervisory regime but generally includes the legal requirements for insurance undertakings; evaluation of risks due to changes in the legal environment; and the evaluation of compliance risk.

---

[7] See in detail on supervision of undertaking groups *Dreher/Ballmaier*, Solvency II und Gruppenaufsicht [in English: Solvency II and Group Supervision], in: Dreher/Wandt, (eds.), Solvency II in der Rechtsanwendung [in English: Solvency II in Legal Application] (2013, 2014), 45 ff.

[8] See in detail on this point and the following, with numerous references, *Dreher*, n. 1, above, at 934 f., 937 ff.

Compliance function tasks under the Solvency II Directive thus exhibit on the one hand partial alignment with the tasks of the legal department of an insurance undertaking, for instance, in providing the undertaking's managing board and staff members with legal advisement. Also, these functions share the objective of complying with the principle of legality in the exercise of their responsibilities. On the other hand, however, their respective tasks part ways in that the compliance function is not tasked with generating legal formulations. If one starts by taking the term "compliance" to mean action by insurance undertakings in conformity with the legal requirements based on suitable and adequate organizational measures,[9] then merging the legal department with the compliance function would not appear to generate the potential for conflict. This is so because both are concerned with meeting the legal requirements directed at insurance undertakings and their staff members. An activity may involve advisement, formulation, or monitoring. It may be performed upon request, as in the legal department, or as part of an ongoing task, as in the compliance function. Irrespective of these variable conditions, the principle of legality is the common point of reference. Nevertheless, this area receives closer examination below in view of particular areas of activity in the legal department and the tasks of the compliance function.

At the outset, it does not appear problematic in the present context to evaluate legal risks and compliance risk, which are subtasks of the compliance function and also are emphasized in the Solvency II Directive.[10] Ascertainment and evaluation of changes in the law and the risks associated therewith clearly constitute a central task of the legal department, as a part of the general task of handling the legal matters of an insurance undertaking. In this respect, the work of the legal department and the compliance function overlap. Under art. 260 SG8, para. 2 DVO, the subtask of evaluating compliance risk consists in evaluating the adequacy of the measures instituted to comply with the legal requirements imposed on an insurance undertaking. This provision is further concretized in no. 3.155 EIOPA Governance Guidelines. A legal department experiences this as but the obverse of its core task of complying with the principle of legality. Thus it is likewise not apparent that there should be a potential conflict arising from the simultaneous performance of tasks by the legal department and the compliance function of an insurance undertaking so far this particular subtask is concerned. The same is ultimately true insofar as the literature on the relationship between the legal department and the compliance function is concerned, where the focus with respect to the compliance function is on organizational issues.[11]

---

[9] See on this point in detail *Dreher*, n. 1, above, at 933 f.

[10] See in detail on this task *Dreher*, n. 1, above, at 941 f.

[11] See, e.g., *Bürkle*, *id.*, (ed.) Compliance in Versicherungsunternehmen [in English: Insurance Undertakings' Compliance], (2009) sec. 1, ref. 165 and generally *Hauschka/Spiekermann*, in: Hauschka (ed.), Corporate Compliance (2nd ed. 2010) sec. 15, ref. 27.

11.3.2 Advisement of Insurance Undertakings' Staff Members as an Area of Potential Conflict

The opposite may be the case, however, if staff members openly present legally questionable circumstances to a legal department combined with the compliance function and require appropriate advisement. The same would be true if the information about such practices arrives anonymously. It is, of course, true that advising, informing, and training staff members are tasks in the ambit of both the legal department and the compliance function. Only the compliance function, however, is responsible for the triad of instruction, preventive monitoring—including counseling—and coercive sanctions.[12] Whereas coercive procedures in the sense of an incentive to employ labor law measures, or the threat or exercise of such measures, are a portion of the compliance function, the legal department is fundamentally not occupied with coercive matters. This is so because such an aspect would have the tendency to undermine the vital trust of staff members, who must be allowed to resort openly to the legal department for advisement concerning critical matters. This approach serves both the interest of the undertaking and compliance with the principle of legality because the legal department can thus operate to protect the interest of the undertaking while also effectuating the duty of legality. To the extent staff members convey "major problems" within the meaning of the Solvency II DVO to the compliance function or the compliance function learns of such through other means, the compliance function must fulfill its previously mentioned duty to inform the managing board.[13] And further, the compliance function must then activate coercive measures in accordance with its previously mentioned job description, if necessary. In this context reference should be made to the decision practice of the BGH [German Federal Court of Justice], under which, indicatively for fulfilling the compliance obligation, "it may also be significant whether the affected party, i.e., the party subject to supervision, employed the threatened measures following infringement of its directives".[14]

In view of this, one could presume combining the legal department with the compliance function would be bound to lead to conflicts because staff members would be hesitant to trust the legal department in the same measure that they would if it were a stand-alone department. This view is contradicted, however, in that the Solvency II system sets forth no requirement that insurance undertakings maintain

---

[12] See for a fuller discussion *Dreher*, "Kartellrechtscompliance" [in English: Competition Law Compliance], ZWeR (2004), 75 (93 ff.) and, particularly on the coercive aspect of compliance, 100 f.; *id.*, "Kartellrechtscompliance in der Versicherungswirtschaft" [in English: Competition Law Compliance in the Insurance Industry] VersR (2004), 1 ff.; *id.* in: Krieger/Schneider (eds.), Handbuch Managerhaftung [Manual of Managerial Liability] (2nd ed. 2010) Sec. 31, ref. 61 ff.; *Bürkle*, n. 11, above, at Sec. 1, ref. 24 ff.; *Inderst*, in: Görling/Inderst/Bannenberg (eds.), Compliance (2010) 103 ff.; *Moosmayer*, Compliance (2nd ed. 2012) 33 ff.

[13] See 11.2, above.

[14] Accord, BGH [German Federal Court of Justice], WuW/E BGH (2202), 2204 – Brückenbau Hopener Mühlenbach.

their own legal departments. Legal department tasks thus can be assigned to an entity within an insurance group or even outsourced to outside firms. In cases of outsourcing, there would exist no in-house legal department at all for staff members to bring confidential matters to, which they otherwise might do because the department resides in their own company or because some legal department personnel might be personally known to the staff members. Thus, as a rule the additional existence of a legal department with accessible contact persons does not legally preclude combining the legal department and the compliance function. Furthermore, such combining may at need facilitate handling staff member concerns by a legal department and compliance function appropriately structured as to content and personnel, under the leadership of its director[15] or the one exercising the function.[16] In the previously mentioned instances of "major problems" within the meaning of the DVO, experience shows that staff members encountering such problems generally turn first to outside counsel or, to the extent staff members are not themselves involved, submit appropriate information anonymously. For all that, it is ultimately not warranted to take a closer look to the fact that the staff members of the legal department also have the obligation pursuant to their employment contracts to notify the managing board about major legal problems that they become aware of. As a result, there arises no contradiction between confidential advisement by the legal department and coercive monitoring by the compliance function.

11.3.3 Advisement of an Insurance Undertaking's Managing Board as an Area of Potential Conflict

Both the legal department and the compliance function are tasked with advising the managing board regarding legal matters.[17] These entities might seem to have different viewpoint and thus a potential for conflict if, for example, advisement by the legal department focuses on what is legally possible for the undertaking, i.e., an examination of discretionary scope, but advisement by the compliance function looks at what is objectively risk-free from a legal point of view. Yet such an observation would rest upon assumptions as unrealistic as they are legally

[15] The director of the legal department should most often be a part of senior management. See *Dreher*, "Das 'senior management' der Versicherungsunternehmen und das künftige Versicherungsaufsichtsrecht" [in English: Senior Management of Insurance Undertakings and the Future Insurance Supervisory Regime], VersR (2013), 35 ff. (Chap. 9, above).

[16] See on the requirements for holders of the compliance function as a key function *Dreher*, "Die aufsichtsbehördliche Kontrolle der Inhaber von Schlüsselfunktionen nach Solvency II und künftigem VAG" [in English: Review by Supervisory Authorities of the Holders of Key Functions under Solvency II and the Future German Insurance Supervision Act], VersR (2012), 1061 ff. (Chap. 8, above).

[17] See 11.3.1, above; and in detail on this responsibility of the compliance function *Dreher*, n. 1, above, at 940 f.

inapposite. Thus it is not the prime office of a legal department to found its legal advice on what is but marginally legally defensible. Rather, any measure recommended in the undertaking's interest must be legally defensible. This can entail legal risks, as seen in nearly all litigation before the courts, since such cases in their progress through the stages of appeal often put forward widely disparate legal positions taken by the courts. Likewise, a compliance function cannot exclude the possibility that its legal advice can entail legal risks. In addition, it is not the mandate of the compliance function to avoid legal risks in the undertaking's interest with such counsel as "payment makes peace" in the context of claims by third parties or "good conduct makes peace" in the context of disputes over largely unsettled issues, such as those arising under the Solvency II insurance supervisory regime. Rather, the compliance function is acting in the undertaking's interest and fulfills its responsibility to ensure that the insurance undertaking complies with the legal requirements whenever the insurance undertaking proposes pursuing a course that is legally defensible. This can include the knowing assumption of legal risks.[18] It is likewise the office of every insurance undertaking's legal department to recommend precisely this course to the managing board.

In some highly important cases where, considering the risk status, the usual level of certitude is not sufficiently provided by the responsible staff member of the legal department, the obligations attendant on all dealings in the undertaking's interest require the further adherence to the two-person rule. In the typical operational structure this will generally lead to further engagement with the matter at issue at a higher level in the hierarchy of the legal department. If an insurance undertaking has only one legal specialist or if the whole legal department consists of one person, then the undertaking has an obligation to confer with outside counsel. Otherwise, this obligation exists only in the especially critical cases described in the following.

In those especially critical cases involving, for example, factually, financially, or legally significant circumstances with corresponding risk appetite or—particularly as in competition law or in the insurance supervisory regime—an especially difficult self-assessment by an insurance undertaking arising from special legal circumstances—in both examples: supervision of legality based on principles-based rules—is mandated, both the legal department and the compliance function would have to come to the further conclusion that their own legal counsel should be supported and verified by means of one or more neutral outside legal opinions.[19] A part of the responsibility of counsel would be to advise the managing board of this.

---

[18] See *Schaaf*, Risikomanagement und Compliance in Versicherungsunternehmen – aufsichtsrechtliche Anforderungen und Organverantwortung [in English: Risk Management and Compliance in Insurance Undertakings – Supervisory Requirements and Institutional Responsibility] (2010), 143.

[19] Obtaining outside legal counsel generally requires particular attention in view of the ISION ruling of the BGH [German Federal Court of Justice], NZG (2011), 1271 – see on this point, e.g., *Decker*, GmbHR (2014), 72 ff.; *Sander/Schneider*, ZGR (2013), 725 ff.; *Kremer*, in: VGR (ed.), Gesellschaftsrecht in der Diskussion [in English: Discussion on Company Law] (2012, 2013) 171 ff.; *Klöhn*, DB (2013), 1535 ff.; *Fleischer*, KSzW (2013), 3ff.; *Strohn*, ZHR, 176 (2012),

Ultimately, only the merging of the legal department with the compliance function of an insurance undertaking can achieve the result that the director or position holder of the combined function can bring the individual perspectives of both areas to the table in advising the managing board. This leads directly to added validity and objectivity of legal advice due to a corresponding self-assessment of the counselor considering both areas of activity. This can lead to the result that in cases where several positions are legally defensible advisement of the managing board of the diverse options in a given situation may resolve to a single, well-founded legal position. This outcome serves the interest of the undertaking both in the managing board's acceptance of the legal appraisals and in the advisement to be expected from a combined legal department and compliance department.

11.3.4 Formation of Law by the Legal Department as an Area of Potential Conflict

The legal department of an insurance undertaking is constantly engaged with legal formulation. As this relates to insurance supervision, this may involve preparing an outsourcing contract compliant with arts. 38 and 49 of the Solvency II Directive or the corresponding implementing provisions of national law and the DVO or it may touch on participation in an internal model in the context of the solvency supervision requirements.[20] Further, the legal department of an insurance undertaking is regularly called upon to give its approval to legally relevant documents or processes before these may be given effect or instituted. By contrast, the compliance function has no responsibility for legal formulation,[21] nor does it answer for rights-based elucidation of normal business procedures within the insurance undertaking.

Seen against this background, one might erect a hypothetical contradiction between the accretion of risk through formation of law or through assumption of responsibility in matters of law by the legal department and the monitoring of risk through legal monitoring by the compliance function. To do so, however, would be to assess the situation incorrectly at the outset. This is so because it would imply a different legal assessment for formation of law or other assumption of responsibility in legal matters relating to ongoing business by the legal department from the legal assessment for the dealings of the compliance function. As set forth above,[22] the

137 ff. and on reliance on expert legal opinion, BGH [German Federal Court of Justice] (4 April 2013) – 3StR521/12 – and especially for competition law with reference to the Schenker ruling of the EuGH WuW/E EU-R 2754 ff. – see on this point, e.g., *Dreher*, EWiR (2013), 470 f.; *von Danwitz*, JECLAP (2013), 389 f.; *Brettel/Thomas*, ZWeR (2013), 272 ff.

[20] See on this point *Dreher*, "Solvenzanforderungen in der Versicherungsaufsicht nach Solvency II und künftigem VAG" [in English: Solvency Requirements in Insurance Supervision under Solvency II and the Future Insurance Supervision Act], ZVersWiss (2012), 381 ff. (Chap. 4, above).

[21] See on this point 11.3.1, above.

[22] See 11.3.3, above.

actions of both the legal department and the compliance function are subject to the principle of legality and the requirement of a legally defensible course of conduct in the interest of the undertaking. This posture leads to the result that both are obligated in critical cases to adhere to the two-person rule and, further, in especially critical cases to obtain outside legal counsel in advising the managing board. Thus, the construct of contradiction between accretion of risk and risk monitoring rests on an inapposite foundation. Nor do legal formulation and assumption of responsibility in matters of law for ongoing business activities by the legal department therefore ultimately lead to a task-related area of potential conflict.

11.4 Combining the Legal Department and the Compliance Function in Light of the Special Rules Aimed at the Compliance Function as a Key Function

11.4.1 Particular Competencies

A further question arises as to whether the particular provisions of Solvency II for the compliance function as a key function could impede the combining of the compliance function and the legal department. To begin with, these provisions include those establishing particular rights for the compliance function as a key function. These refer to the right to information with respect to all staff members and the obligation of direct managing board involvement with any major problem within its area of responsibility.[23] The managing board's involvement with significant issues of the insurance undertaking, in particular such as might include substantial legal, and thus reputational, risks, demonstrates clearly that the managing board bears ultimate responsibility for complying with the principle of legality. Art. 40 of the Solvency II Directive stipulates this in particular for the insurance supervisory regime. In so doing, however, the Directive regulates in a merely declaratory manner the sole responsibility that the managing board bears in any case for leading the business, as set forth under sec. 76 of the AktG [German Stock Corporation Act].[24] The special rules on the compliance function's duty to inform the managing board likewise express in a declaratory manner what the compliance function, but also the legal department, is bound to do with respect to the managing board.

---

[23] See 11.2, above.

[24] See on this point with numerous references *Dreher*, "Die Vorstandsverantwortung im Geflecht von Risikomanagement, Compliance und interner Revision" [in English: Managing Board Responsibility within the Web of Risk Management, Compliance, and Internal Review] in: Publication in Honor of Hüffer (2010) 161 ff.; *id.*, "Nicht delegierbare Geschäftsleiterpflichten" [in English: Non-delegable Duties of Business Managers] in: Publication in Honor of Hopt (2010) 517 ff.

On the basis of the Solvency II system, only the compliance function as a key function has an unmediated right to information with respect to all staff members. The legal department does not. To the extent the same persons staff the compliance function and the legal department-this is the case in larger legal departments, at least at the top-the relevant person can assert the special right to information solely in his or her capacity as holder or staff member of the compliance function. While this requires the one acting to have awareness of the role he or she is taking on, nevertheless it will not lead to an impairment of the compliance function under Solvency II, even in the case of reversal or arrogation of roles. In such a case, the person involved would simply be overreaching his or her rights as a staff member of the legal department. The exercise of compliance function tasks would, however, be unaffected.

11.4.2 Special Qualifications

The holders of the four key functions, and their deputies,[25] are subject to special "fit" and "proper" requirements in the Solvency II system.[26] The holder of the compliance function is thus also the addressee of the rule, while the European insurance supervisory regime describes no special qualification for the legal department. If this individual is also the holder of the compliance function, he or she must satisfy the applicable special insurance supervisory regime requirements. There is no vestigial qualification level, not even in reference to the fitness required beyond the mandatory proper requirement. It may be presumed, however, that in the ordinary course the director of the legal department of an insurance undertaking would in any case meet these requirements.[27] Alternatively, this must be so because of the additional assumption of the role of holder of the compliance function. There are therefore likewise no apparent indications that the insurance supervisory "fit" and "proper" special qualifications for the holder of a compliance function could impede its merger with the legal department.

---

[25] Thus, *Dreher*, "Begriff und Inhaber der Schlüsselfunktionen nach Solvency II und VAG 2012" [in English: Concept and Holders of Key Functions under Solvency II and the German Insurance Supervision Act 2012], VersR (2012), 933 (938, 940) (Chap. 7, above, at 7.3.5); accord, *Pohlmann*, in: Düsseldorfer Vorträge zum Versicherungsrecht 2012 [in English: Dusseldorf Lectures on Insurance Law 2012] (2013) 29 (46).

[26] See in detail *Dreher*, n. 16, above, at 1063 ff.; *Pohlmann*, n. 25, above, at 60 ff.

[27] See on the five-part qualification profile for the holder of the compliance function in an insurance undertaking *Dreher*, n. 1, above, at 937. A divergence of qualifications may arise, however, if one should require, along with *Bürkle*, in: Düsseldorfer Vorträge zum Versicherungsrecht [in English: Dusseldorf Lectures on Insurance Law] (2010) 1 (15), that every holder of the compliance function must have a "comprehensive knowledge of the insurance supervisory regime"; contra, *Dreher*, n. 1, above, at 937.

11.5 Combining the Legal Department and the Compliance Function in Light of the Principle of Functional Segregation

Combining the legal department and the compliance function could concern the principle of functional segregation. Art. 47, para. 2 of the Solvency II Directive and arts. 258 SG6, para. 1, sent. 1 and 261 SG9, para. 1 DVO require such segregation from other key functions precisely for the key function of internal audit. This is so because in this area segmented task performance is a part of the required independence, which is particularly emphasized because it is described as "complete". Art. 41, para. 1, subpara. 2, of the Solvency II Directive and art. 258 SG6, para. 1, sent. 1 DVO apply to the other three key functions and thus also to the compliance function. These require, i.a., "an adequate transparent organisational structure with a clear allocation and appropriate segregation of responsibilities." This is concretized in art. 258 SG6, para. 1, sent. 1 DVO. Paragraph 2 of this provision, depending on the nature, scope, and complexity of the business risk in an insurance undertaking, allows the undertaking the option to assign more than one key function to a single person or unit within the undertaking. This recast version of the DVO proposal of 20 December 2013 stands as the first instance of an implementing provision of the Solvency II Directive requirements to depart from the Directive. This is so because Recital 32 of the Solvency II Directive, which European law essentially considers central to construing the Directive, addresses by way of exception only "smaller and less complex undertakings". The 31 October 2011 version of the DVO contains a similar provision.[28]

Quite apart from the change in the EU Commission's legal theory, in this view the principle of functional segregation does not impede combining the legal department and the compliance function in an insurance undertaking.[29] Solvency II does not characterize the legal department as a key function. Therefore from the outset, the legal department is not part of the constellations to which the principle of functional segregation applies.

Somewhat anticipating Solvency II in the Bank Ringfencing Act, the German legislator enacted in sec. 64a, para. 7, no. 2 of the VAG [German Insurance Supervision Act] a provision that addresses functional segregation. Under that provision, "managers must see to it that a) tasks and responsibilities within the management structure are clearly defined and segregated from one another and that conflicts of interest are averted, generally by means of a clear functional segregation between establishment of material risk positions and the supervision and monitoring of the same". The Legal Department is a staff department. The same

[28] With regard to the hierarchy of basic legal act and implementing regulation, surprisingly in any case for excessive regulation, not present here, of a permissible approach, see *Dreher/Lange*, "Die Vollharmonisierung der Versicherungsaufsicht durch Solvency II" [in English: Full Harmonization of Insurance Supervision under Solvency II], VersR (2011), 825 (829) (Chap. 1, above, at 1.3.2).

[29] See *Dreher*, n. 25, above, at 941.

applies to the compliance function. Both units thus fulfill the legal requirement "supervision and monitoring", but not, however, that of "establishment of material risk positions".[30] Therefore, also the segregation of functions required by sec. 64a, para. 7, no. 2 of the VAG [German Insurance Supervision Act], which moreover would have to be scrutinized on the basis of its use of the term "function" compared to the usage of that term in the Solvency II Directive, does not run counter to combining the legal department and the compliance function in an insurance undertaking.

11.6 Combining the Legal Department and the Compliance Function in Light of the Principle of Functional Independence

Besides the principle of functional segregation, the Solvency II Directive also recognizes the principle of functional independence. Pursuant to Recital 32 along with art. 41, para. 1, subpara. 2 of the Solvency II Directive and Recital 107 along with art. 258 SG6, para. 1, sent. 1 DVO, this principle applies to all key functions. The European legislator requires complete independence only for the key function internal audit. The pertinent provisions are found in Recital 32 along with art. 41, para. 2 of the Solvency II Directive and in Recital 107, sent. 2 along with art. 258 SG6, para. 1, sent. 1 DVO. The legal requirement of independence in effect signifies that the compliance function shall not be exposed to conflicts of interest by virtue of its organization and activity.[31] To be sure, the Solvency II system encompasses only the relationship of the four key functions to each other. Nevertheless, the postulate of independence must also apply in relation to the other divisions of the undertaking, if there may arise a danger of conflicts of interest from their intersection. Combining the legal department and the compliance function creates an interface with respect to the structure and personnel of an undertaking's functions. This is therefore to be valued also in light of the principle of independence for the compliance function.

The basic starting point for conflicts of interest is the link between operational and monitoring activity. This is so because in this realm accretion of risk and risk monitoring could reside in the same person or unit. Nevertheless, the recognition has gradually crystallized that a decentralized organization in the sense of an

---

[30] See in reference to the lack of conflict in accretion of risk 11.3.4, above.

[31] See in detail on the compliance function *Dreher*, n. 1, above, at 939, 941 and *id.*, "Ausstrahlungen des Aufsichtsrechts auf das Aktienrecht" [in English: Effects of Supervisory Law on Corporation Law], ZGR (2010), 496 (537 f.) with the example of the risk management function. Independence notwithstanding, the compliance function is subject to the instruction right belonging to the managing board. See *Fletzberger*, "Compliance und Aufsichtsrecht" [in English: Compliance and Supervisory Law] in: Braumüller/Ennöckl/Gruber/Raschauer (eds.), Compliance & Finanzmarktrecht [in English: Compliance and the Law of Financial Markets] (2011) 23 (31).

integrated management structure can be adopted for the compliance function.[32] Because of the independence required under supervisory law, one condition of such a decentralized organization for the compliance function is that the holder of the compliance function must be free of conflicts of interest both in his or her own compliance activities as well as in monitoring and guiding the activities of the decentralized compliance staff.

If nevertheless a risk of conflict of interest should arise in particular cases with regard to the holder or to individual staff members of the compliance function, where these latter are also staff members of the legal department, in the course of their activities and if the potential conflict does not arise solely from permissible decentralized task performance, as previously described, then there exist various options to prevent the conflict of interest from actually coming into existence. One option is for the insurance undertaking to provide a system for responsibilities in the compliance guidelines for certain compliance-related situations within the combined unit for larger undertakings below the rank of the holder of the compliance function and the head of the legal department. This system would be structured with a view to permanently preventing the risk of conflicts of interest in regard to the tasks of one who is also a staff member of the legal department. There is also the option, as previously noted,[33] of resort to outside expert counsel and internally to establish a two-person rule. Finally, the remuneration guidelines of an insurance undertaking under arts. 41, 50, para. 1a of the Solvency II Directive in conjunction with arts. 249 SG1, para. 1 (l), 265 SG13, para. 1 (c) DVO must apply to the holder of the compliance function; and under art. 265 SG13, para. 2 (b) DVO, the variable portion of his or her remuneration and that of the staff members must be independent of the performance of operational units and areas subject to monitoring by them.[34]

11.7 Combining the Legal Department and the Compliance Function in Light of the Principles of Freedom of Internal Organization and of Proportionality

Recital 31, sent. 2 of the Solvency II Directive grants every insurance undertaking that establishes a compliance function the right of "freely deciding how to organise that function in practice save where otherwise specified in this Directive". This is more than just a further proof of permission for decentralized performance of key

[32] See only *Dreher*, n. 25, above, at 939, 941 f.; *Bürkle*, n. 27, above, at 6 f.; *Wolf*, "Zur Aufgabenverteilung zwischen den Governance-Funktionen von Versicherungsunternehmen nach der Solvency II-Richtlinie" [in English: On the Division of Tasks between the Governance Functions of Insurance Undertakings under the Solvency II Directive], VersR (2013), 678 (683 f.).

[33] See 11.3.4, above.

[34] See in more detail *Dreher*, n. 16, above, at 1069.

functions. Rather, in consideration of the principles-based mandates, this asserts a general principle of freedom of internal organization to the effect that: "Everything which is not forbidden is allowed".[35] This applies with equal effect to the combining of the legal department and the compliance function of an insurance company.

A further principle that characterizes the dutiful exercise of the managing board's directorial discretion is the principle of proportionality in the insurance supervisory regime. This principle is expressed, i.a., in Recitals 18, sent. 2, 19, and 29, sent. 3 and art. 29, para. 3 of the Solvency II Directive. In these provisions the legislator intended to express the significance of the "nature, scope, and complexity of the risks" of an insurance undertaking for the requirements imposed upon it and the exercise of the supervisory powers of the insurance supervisory authorities.[36] This applies also in the context of insurance undertakings' right under Solvency II system to structure their own organizations. For these reasons, the managing board is obliged to evaluate combining the legal department and the compliance function in light of the three factors just mentioned: nature, scope, and complexity of risk. This does not mean, however, that in a particular case these considerations actually could lead to a mandate to disjoint the two areas. Rather, these criteria should lead the decision-maker to determine in what configuration and with what resources the tasks of the compliance function shall be performed, insofar as these tasks are merged with those of a legal department.

To the extent this decision might affect, say, preserving the independence of the compliance function, the managing board of an insurance undertaking is free to employ additional measures that go beyond merely avoiding conflicts of interest.[37] A part of such a move might be to appoint a director or deputy director of the compliance function under the insurance supervisory regime for a certain minimum

---

[35] See on the principle of self-organization *Dreher*, n. 1, above, at 933 and *id.*, n. 20, above, at 412 f.; *Wolf*, n. 32, above, at 681.

[36] See on this point *Dreher*, n. 20, above, at 393, 418 ff.; *Wandt/Sehrbrock*, "Die Umsetzung des Verhältnismäßigkeitsgrundsatzes der Solvency II-Richtlinie im VAG-Regierungsentwurf" [in English: Implementation of the Solvency II Directive's Principle of Proportionality in the Government's Draft of a Tenth Act Amending the Insurance Supervision Act], VersR (2012), 802 ff., also in: Dreher/Wandt (eds.), Solvency II in der Rechtsanwendung [in English: Solvency II in Legal Application] (2012) 21 ff.; *Wandt*, "Prinzipienbasiertes Recht und Verhältnismäßigkeitsgrundsatz im Rahmen von Solvency II" [in English: Principles-based Law and the Principle of Proportionality in the Context of Solvency II], Mannheimer Verträge zur Versicherungswirtschaft [in English: Mannheim Lectures on the Insurance Industry] (2012) 91; *Dröse/Littmann*, "Der Verhältnismäßigkeitsgrundsatz im Anwendungsbereich des Solvency II-Regimes unter besonderer Berücksichtigung firmeneigener (Rück-)Versicherungsunternehmen" [in English: The Principle of Proportionality as Applied within the Framework of Solvency II with Particular Attention to In-house Insurance and Reinsurance Undertakings], ZVersWiss (2012), 339 ff., and generally on the principle of proportionality in European Union law, *Trstenjak/Beysen*, "Das Prinzip der Verhältnismäßigkeit in der Unionsrechtsordnung" [in English: The Principle of Proportionality in European Union Law], EuR (2012), 265 ff.

[37] See concerning the already existing deficiencies in protection for voluntarily appointed compliance officers *Bürkle*, "Grenzen der strafrechtlichen Garantenstellung des Compliance-Officers" [in English: Limits of the Penal Guarantor Position of the Compliance Officer], CCZ (2010), 4 (5).

period, a period, however, that should not be set for too short a time.[38] Also to be considered would be an extension of the period of termination notice.[39] In employing such measures, to the extent the managing board of an insurance undertaking selects them because of the merging of the compliance function with the legal department, good sense would dictate that this be done with full consideration given to all four governance functions and not just to the compliance function.

11.8 Summary

1. An insurance company's legal department and its operations are unexplored territory on the map of the Solvency II system. This accords neither with its responsibilities nor with its position within the undertaking.
2. The integrity of the legal department and its performance of its responsibilities are as little affected by combining it with the compliance function as are by turn the same aspects in the compliance function.
3. The compliance function is subject to numerous special provisions under the insurance supervisory regime. These are chiefly a consequence of its role as key function in the Solvency II system. And thus these constitute the criteria against which to judge whether a merger with the legal department is permissible under supervisory law.
4. To the extent that the respective responsibilities of the legal department and the compliance function are involved, the following applies:

    a) Both areas are essentially responsible in the interest of the undertaking for maintaining the principle of legality and for complying with the legal requirements imposed on insurance undertakings. There are peripheral distinctions: The compliance function is governed by supervisory law, while it is the managing board of an insurance undertaking that determines the responsibilities of the legal department in the interest of the undertaking; the legal department is generally solely assigned responsibility for formation of law; the compliance function is occupied with substantial legal questions permanently, not only upon request, and its occupation is marked by a decided emphasis in the undertaking's organization on complying with the principle of legality. The concurrent exercise of these disparate responsibilities by the legal department and the compliance function does not, however, give rise to potential conflicts.

[38] The MaComp (WA), BT 1.1.1 at 6 assume a minimum period for the compliance officer of 24 months, under the WpHG [German Securities Trading Act].

[39] The MaComp (WA), BT 1.1.1 at 6 assume a minimum termination notice period for the compliance officer of 12 months, under the WpHG [German Securities Trading Act].

b) Both the legal department and the compliance function are responsible for providing legal counseling to staff members of an insurance undertaking when staff members come to them with critical matters. One could perhaps envision a contrary posture between the confidential advisement of the legal department and the coercive actions of the compliance function, but no such contradiction exists.
c) Likewise, both the legal department and the compliance function bear responsibility for providing the managing board of the insurance undertaking with advice on legal issues. Standing for this general principle, the Solvency II Directive has explicitly provided this for the compliance function under the insurance supervisory regime. Any attempt to create an opposition between risk-oriented examination of legal possibilities by the legal department and risk-averse monitoring by the compliance function misses the point of what is legally mandated and actually possible for these two functions.
d) Both entities are bound to observe the principle of legality and the criterion of a legally defensible course of conduct in the interest of the undertaking. The legal department bears sole responsibility for formation of law. By virtue of the alignment of operational mandates for both units, there is no conflict between accretion of risk arising from legal formulation on the one hand and risk monitoring by the compliance function on the other.

5. The Solvency II Directive's special rules for key functions and thus also for the compliance function do not constitute a hindrance to combining it with the legal department.
6. The same is true for the principle of functional segregation under Solvency II and new sec. 64a, para. 7, no. 2 VAG [German Insurance Supervision Act].
7. Further, combining the legal department and the compliance function can be harmonized with the supervisory law principle of functional independence.
8. Finally, combining the legal department and the compliance function appears not only legally permissible, but in fact in many cases mandated in the interest of the undertaking in light of the supervisory law principles of freedom of internal organization and of proportionality.

Part IV
Disclosure

Chapter 12
Supervisory Reporting

Contents

12.1 Introduction ... 346
12.2 The Obligations to Notify Based on Formal Grounds ... 347
12.2.1 The Term "Obligations to Notify Based on Formal Grounds" ... 347
12.2.2 Obligations to Notify Based on Formal Organizational Grounds ... 348
12.2.3 Reporting Duties Related to Tariffs and General Policy Conditions ... 351
12.3 The Disclosure Obligations of Financial Reporting ... 352
12.3.1 The Disclosure Obligations for Financial Reporting Based on Formal Organizational Grounds ... 352
12.3.2 The Disclosure Obligations for Substantive Financial Reporting ... 357
12.4 The Disclosure Obligations for Risk Reporting ... 364
12.5 Disclosure Obligations at the Group Level ... 366
12.5.1 The Obligations to Notify Based on Formal Grounds at the Group Level ... 366
12.5.2 The Disclosure Obligations of Financial Reporting at the Group Level ... 368
12.5.3 The Disclosure Obligations of Risk Reporting at the Group Level ... 371
12.6 The Disclosure Obligations for Financial Conglomerates ... 372
12.7 Further Implications ... 373
12.7.1 The Function of the Reporting and Disclosure Obligations ... 373
12.7.2 The Scope of the Reporting and Disclosure Obligations ... 375
12.7.3 The Relationship Between the VAG [German Insurance Supervision Act] and Solvency II Directive Regarding Reporting and Disclosure Obligations ... 377
12.7.4 The Concretization and Practical Management of Reporting and Disclosure Obligations ... 380
12.8 Summary ... 382

Abstract The third pillar of Solvency II is disclosure. This chapter discusses supervisory reporting against the background of the insurance supervisory regime disclosure rules in Germany. Insurance undertakings are under a duty to disclose a large amount of information to the insurance supervisory authority. The same holds

First published as "Die Veröffentlichungspflichten von Versicherungsunternehmen gegenüber der BaFin" [in English: The Duty of Disclosure of Insurance Undertakings with respect to the BaFin], ZVersWiss (2009), 187 ff.

M. Dreher, *Treatises on Solvency II*, DOI 10.1007/978-3-662-46290-4_12

true for other corporations in the financial market, such as insurance holding companies. This chapter analyzes and systematizes the insurance related disclosure scheme. It then turns to legal questions pertaining to reporting requirements under the German Insurance Supervision Act and the prospective effect of the Solvency II Directive. Finally it draws several conclusions as to the scale and the limits of insurance-related disclosure requirements.

12.1 Introduction

As part of the 9th amendment to the VAG [German Insurance Supervision Act], sec. 55c of the Act took effect on 1 January 2008. Paragraph 1 of this section requires insurance undertakings periodically to provide the BaFin [Federal Financial Supervisory Authority] with copies of the risk report prepared in accordance with sec. 64a, para. 1, sent. 4, no. 3 (d) of the VAG [German Insurance Supervision Act] as well as with the internal audit report.[1] The provision thus anticipates the rules of the third pillar of the framework directive for Solvency II, the adoption of which—despite the ever-emerging protests of individual Member States on particular points—is still expected under the Czech Presidency of the EU prior to the EU parliamentary elections in 2009.[2] Even before the 9th amendment to the VAG [German Insurance Supervision Act] took effect, the list of disclosure obligations to the BaFin [Federal Financial Supervisory Authority] under the insurance supervisory regime was extensive and difficult to comprehend. At the group level, there were easily 70–80 notifications to the BaFin [Federal Financial Supervisory Authority] in the course of a fiscal year. Violations of these disclosure obligations can be very costly for an insurance undertaking. In many cases, they constitute administrative offenses sanctionable by the BaFin [Federal Financial Supervisory Authority] with severe fines.[3]

In light of the further expansion of the list of disclosure obligations to the BaFin [Federal Financial Supervisory Authority] under the insurance supervisory regime through sec. 55c of the VAG [German Insurance Supervision Act] it is necessary to systematize the individual obligations. An overview of the content and cycle of the

[1] As a result of a waiver by the BaFin [Federal Financial Supervisory Authority], the submission requirement takes effect in 2009. During 2008, however, both reports could have been submitted to the BaFin [Federal Financial Supervisory Authority] on a voluntary basis. See on this point *Wehling/Treber*, VW (2008), 178 (179).

[2] On the objections specifically related to group supervision, see Börsenzeitung dated 22 Oct. 2008, p. 4 as well as, with a positive projection for the adoption of Solvency II, Financial Times Deutschland, dated 19 Nov. 2008, p. 1, and in general on group supervision under Solvency II, *Sehrbrock*, ZVersWiss (Supplement, Annual Conference 2008), 27 ff.

[3] See, for example, sec. 144, para. 1a, no. 2 or 2b of the VAG [German Insurance Supervision Act], and for the level of fines, sec. 144, para. 2 of the VAG [German Insurance Supervision Act].

disclosure obligations is associated with this. At the same, the second draft of a framework directive for Solvency II[4] must be taken into account when explaining the individual obligations. Current information indicates it will apply only to direct insurance and reinsurance undertakings and not to pension and retirement funds. Thus an area to be examined is whether and to what extent additions or changes to content affecting the former can be expected in the near future. This article does not address the duty of disclosure to the general public intended as a product of the third pillar of Solvency II for supervisory purposes.[5] Further, this article is limited to the discussion of disclosure obligations in ongoing business operations.[6]

Against this background, the following outline is presented for the analysis: the disclosure obligations under insurance supervision law can be roughly divided into obligations to notify based on formal grounds (below, 12.2), disclosure obligations for financial reporting (below, 12.3), and those for risk reporting (below, 12.4). The treatment of disclosure obligations at the group level is separate and discussed in its own chapter (below, 12.5). The article concludes with a concise presentation of the disclosure obligations for financial conglomerates (below, 12.6), followed by several conclusions regarding the reporting and disclosure requirements under the VAG [German Insurance Supervision Act] and the Solvency II Directive (below, 12.7) as well as a summary (below, 12.8).

12.2 The Obligations to Notify Based on Formal Grounds

12.2.1 The Term "Obligations to Notify Based on Formal Grounds"

Disclosure obligations that fall into the category of obligations to notify based on formal grounds are differentiated in the negative from financial and risk reporting in that their fulfillment, taken in isolation, does not enable the BaFin [Federal Financial Supervisory Authority] to draw conclusions about the insurance undertaking's net asset, financial, and earnings position or the effectiveness of its risk management.

The obligations to notify based on formal grounds, stipulated primarily in sec. 13d of the VAG [German Insurance Supervision Act], can be divided into two

[4] Proposal for a Directive of the European Parliament and of the Council on the taking-up and pursuit of the business of Insurance and Reinsurance (Solvency II) of 26 Feb. 2008, (COM(2008) 119 final), (2nd Draft), and concerning this, Council, Common Position of 25 Nov. 2008; First Draft of 10 Jun. 2007, COM(2007) 361 final = BR-Drucks. [Document of the German Bundesrat] 510/07 (1st Draft).

[5] See on this point *Dreher/Schaaf*, "Die Veröffentlichungspflichten von Versicherungsunternehmen gegenüber der Allgemeinheit nach Solvency II" [in English: Insurance Undertakings' Duty of Disclosure to the Public under Solvency II] in: Dreher/Wandt (eds.), Solvency II in der Rechtsanwendung [in English: Solvency II in Legal Application] (2009), 129 ff. (Chap. 13, below).

[6] Some reference will be made to the extensive disclosure obligations in the admission procedure to provide clarification.

groups. The first group concerns disclosure of changes in the undertakings' organization. Thus, the disclosures categorized in this first group are referred to below as obligations to notify based on formal organizational grounds. The second group is concerned with the structure of insurance contract terms. Since the majority of these disclosure obligations are in the context of rate-making, this article summarizes all obligations of the second group as tariff obligations, using the majority as a generic term for the whole group.

12.2.2 *Obligations to Notify Based on Formal Organizational Grounds*

12.2.2.1 Appointments to Key Offices

Many of the obligations to disclose organizational form are related to appointments to key offices. This specifically includes the reporting duties under sec. 13d, nos. 1 and 2 of the VAG [German Insurance Supervision Act] designed to inform the supervisory authority of changes—planned or executed in the past—in the persons occupying management positions or to the power of representation of the managers. According to no. 1, direct insurance undertakings must inform the BaFin [Federal Financial Supervisory Authority] without delay of their intention to appoint a member of their management and provide the information relevant to an assessment of the individual's fit-and-proper qualification under sec. 7a, para. 1 of the VAG [German Insurance Supervision Act].[7] According to no. 2 the same applies with regard to the separation of a member of management or the withdrawal of the power of representation given to a member of management. By references in sec. 121a, para. 1, sent. 1 and sec. 113, para. 1 of the VAG [German Insurance Supervision Act], reinsurance undertakings and pension funds are also subject to sec. 13d, nos. 1 and 2 of the VAG [German Insurance Supervision Act]. All of these notifications to the insurance supervisory authority enable it to conduct the management monitoring as required under law.[8]

Sec. 11a, para. 2, sent. 1 and sent. 4 of the VAG [German Insurance Supervision Act] currently contain reporting duties with respect to the responsible actuary that functionally correspond to sec. 13d, no. 1 and no. 2, first instance. This is directly

[7] Unlike sec. 13e, para. 1, sent. 1 of the VAG [German Insurance Supervision Act] concerning the holding-company level, sec. 13d, no. 1 of the VAG [German Insurance Supervision Act] has no reporting obligation for the actual appointment – that is, for the execution of the plan to appoint a member of management. On sec. 13e, para. 1 of the VAG [German Insurance Supervision Act], see below, at 12.5.1.2.

[8] See on this point in detail *Dreher*, "Die Kontrolle der Geschäftsleiter von Versicherungsunternehmen" [in English: The Monitoring of Managers of Insurance Undertakings], ZVersWiss (Supplement, Annual Conference 2006), 375 ff. and on the notification duties themselves, id. 402 and, below, at 12.7.4; on the new requirements for management monitoring with respect to risk management see *Dreher/Schaaf*, WM (2008), 1765 (1768).

applicable to life insurance undertakings and, by reference, to certain accident, liability, and health insurance undertakings as well as pension funds.[9] Further, sec. 71, para. 2, sent. 1 in conjunction with. sec. 79 of the VAG [German Insurance Supervision Act] requires that direct insurance undertakings engaged in the business of life insurance, substitute health insurance, or private long-term care insurance, and who must therefore appoint a trustee under the law, notify the BaFin [Federal Financial Supervisory Authority] as to the proposed trustee prior to the appointment.[10] In contrast, there is generally no reporting duty for the separation of a trustee. However, as an exception, the supervisory authority must be informed if the supervisory authority itself appointed the trustee in accordance with sec. 71, para. 2, sent. 3 of the VAG [German Insurance Supervision Act] and the insurance undertaking intends to terminate the appointment.[11] Termination requires the supervisory authority's consent in this case only. Internally, in accordance with sec. 71, para. 1 of the VAG [German Insurance Supervision Act], the supervisory board—or the managing board, if none exists—is responsible for the termination.[12]

A look at art. 42 of the Draft Solvency II suggests that the number of obligations to notify based on formal organizational grounds affecting the appointment of key offices will grow in the future. Art. 42, para. 1 of the Draft Solvency II requires that all persons who effectively run the insurance undertaking or have other key functions satisfy a certain suitability and integrity profile. The disclosure obligation in art. 42, para. 2 of the Draft Solvency II accompanies this "fit-and-proper test". It requires direct insurance and reinsurance undertakings to notify the supervisory authority of any change to the occupants of key offices. The insurance undertaking must also send all information needed to assess the suitability and integrity of all persons proposed for the respective offices.[13] The CEIOPS Issues Paper of 17 Jul.

---

[9] See references in secs. 11d, 11e, 12, para. 2, sent. 1 of the VAG [German Insurance Supervision Act] for the specified accident, liability, and health insurance undertakings; the applicability to pension funds proceeds from sec. 113, para. 1 of the VAG [German Insurance Supervision Act]. Funeral expense funds must also appoint an actuary. But the actuary in this case has only a limited range of responsibilities under sec. 11a, para. 5 sent. 1 of the VAG [German Insurance Supervision Act].

[10] Under sec. 79a of the VAG [German Insurance Supervision Act], sec. 71 of the VAG [German Insurance Supervision Act] does not apply to public insurance undertakings.

[11] There is no duty to report, however, if the trustee's appointment ends due to lapse of time or the trustee itself terminates in accordance with sec. 621 of the BGB [German Civil Code].

[12] In detail *Lipowsky*, in: Prölss (ed.), VAG [German Insurance Supervision Act], (12th ed. 2005), sec. 71, ref. 9.

[13] See as parallel to the term "key staff" in European competition law, which the EU Commission defines in the context of accepting commitments according to art. 6, para. 2, subpara. 2 and art. 8, para. 2, subpara. 2 of the Merger Control Regulation – see EU Commission, 17 Jun. 2008, file 32008/M5075, OJEU 2008, no. C 229, p. 13 – as follows: "all staff necessary to sustain the existence and competitiveness of the business [being sold]".

CEIOPS goes still further into review requirements in its document of 25 Feb. 2009, Draft CEIOPS' Advice for Level 2 Implementing Measures on Solvency II: Reporting Requirements, pnt. 3.57 sub A.2: "An undertaking should provide details of process and procedures it has established to ensure that it is satisfied that those persons that effectively run the undertaking or have other key functions are fit and proper."

2007[14] indicates that the understanding of key offices under EU law whose tenure may only proceed after notification and evidence of the suitability of the person proposed is submitted to the supervisory authority could extend further than that on which insurance supervision law is currently based. Under number 2.2., pnt. 21 of the Issues Paper, CEIOPS states that, in addition to executive management and senior staff,[15] key persons in an insurance undertaking specifically include "independent non-executive directors", meaning the supervisory board members of an Aktiengesellschaft (German stock corporation) or the non-executive administrative board members of a monistic insurance SE (European public limited company).[16,17] CEIOPS is closely integrated with the four-level Lamfalussy process[18] used in the Solvency II initiative. It can therefore be expected that, in the near future, the legislator will stipulate, at least for direct and reinsurance undertakings, corresponding reporting duties in sec. 13d, no. 1 and no. 2 of the VAG [German Insurance Supervision Act] to the BaFin [Federal Financial Supervisory Authority] for changes to the supervisory board—which are currently mentioned only in sec. 13d, no. 2a of the VAG [German Insurance Supervision Act] in the context of submitting internal rules of procedure.[19] This is also true for rules pertaining to the supervisory board that would parallel sec. 7a, para. 1 of the VAG [German Insurance Supervision Act] for a future check on supervisory board members regarding the applicable form of fitness[20] and properness.

---

[14] CEIOPS, Issues Paper "Risk Management and Other Corporate Issues" of 17 Jul. 2007, available for download on the Internet at http://www.ceiops.eu/content/view/236/154/.

[15] See on this point *Dreher/Schaaf*, n. 5, C. III.

[16] It must also be true for administrative board members of public insurance undertaking, even if CEIOPS did not have them in view.

[17] See on this point and on the risk-related responsibilities of the supervisory board of an insurance AG (German stock corporation) or SE (European public limited company) *Schaaf*, ZVersWiss, (2009), 613 ff. (Lecture at the Annual Conference of the Deutscher Verein für Versicherungswissenschaft [in English: German association for insurance academics] in March 2009). In addition to management and supervisory board members, the "fit-and-proper-test" under Solvency II indirectly extends to the senior staff subordinate to management that are heads of the staff functions of risk control, compliance, and internal audit as well as the actuarial function. See on this point in detail CEIOPS, Advice to the European Commission on Supervisory Reporting and Public Disclosure in the Framework of the Solvency II Project, March 2007, pnt. 4.8; CEIOPS, Issues Paper dated 3 Nov. 2008, Implementing Measures on System of Governance, pnt. 5.2, and CEIOPS, Consultation Paper No. 33 of 26 Mar. 2009, Draft CEIOPS' Advice for Level 2 Implementing Measures on Solvency II: System of Governance, pnt. 3.31 and 3.43.

[18] On the four levels of the Lamfalussy process, see *Dreher/Rittner*, Europäisches und deutsches Wirtschaftsrecht [in English: European and German Economic Law], (3rd ed. 2008), sec. 32, ref. 8 and sec. 33, ref. 5; *Schmolke*, NZG (2005), 912 (913 f.); *id.*, EuR (2006), 432 (433 ff.); *Wandt*, VW (2007), 473; *Mürkle*, VersR (2007), 1595 (1596 f.); *id.*, CCZ (2008), 50.

[19] And also below, 12.2.2.2.

[20] On the requirements from a corporate law view, see *Dreher*, "Die Qualifikation der Aufsichtsratsmitglieder" [in English: The Qualification of Supervisory Board Members], in: FS [Publication in Honor of] Boujong, 1996, p. 71 ff.

Within art. 42 of the Draft Solvency II, it must be further emphasized that paragraph 3 provides for an immediate reporting duty in the event a person holding a key office no longer has the integrity required under paragraph 1 (b).[21] In contrast, the loss of professional qualification—conceivable in exceptional cases—within the meaning of paragraph 1 (a) has no associated reporting duty. Here as well, the list of disclosure requirements under insurance supervisory law can be expected to grow longer with respect to holding key offices. Add to this that factors such as personal "integrity" or "properness" are difficult to define objectively as a matter of legal certainty. They are therefore inadequate as basis for additional disclosure requirements of this type in the future. This reporting duty also demonstrates by example that such duties often have their starting point in the area of obligation to notify based on formal organizational grounds. They are, however, substantive in nature and thus far more significant than their systematic legal classification currently suggests.

12.2.2.2 Other Obligations to Notify Based on Formal Organizational Grounds

Sec. 13d, no. 2a of the VAG [German Insurance Supervision Act] requires direct insurers and, by reference in sec. 113, para. 1 of the VAG [German Insurance Supervision Act], pension funds to report the entry into force as well as later amendments of the internal rules of procedure of the managing board and supervisory board immediately to the supervisory authority. Based on sec. 121a, para. 1, sent. 1 of the VAG [German Insurance Supervision Act], this reporting duty does not apply to reinsurance undertakings.

Lastly, sec. 13d, no. 9 of the VAG [German Insurance Supervision Act] contains an additional obligation to notify based on formal organizational grounds. Direct insurers in motor vehicle liability insurance must report the name and address of the designated claims adjustment officer in accordance with sec. 7b, para. 1, sent. 1 of the VAG [German Insurance Supervision Act] to the supervisory authority.

12.2.3 Reporting Duties Related to Tariffs and General Policy Conditions

Sec. 13d, no. 6 of the VAG [German Insurance Supervision Act] requires direct insurance undertakings in life and accident insurance with guaranteed premium

[21] On proof of integrity to supervisory authorities, see art. 299 of the Draft Solvency II. The provision refers only to the proof of the "proper" criteria and not to the proof of "fit" criteria. In the estimation of the Council, Common Position of 25 Nov. 2008, the provision should be "brought forward" in the future to the governance rules as art. 42a of the Draft Solvency II due to its factual relationship to art. 42 of the Draft Solvency II.

refunds limited to the embedded life insurance component, and likewise pension funds by reference in sec. 113, para. 1 of the VAG [German Insurance Supervision Act] to disclose their bases for calculating premiums and insurance reserves to the supervisory authority.[22] A corresponding rule is found in sec. 13d, no. 8 of the VAG [German Insurance Supervision Act] for substitute health insurance. The reporting duty added only recently under sec. 13d, no. 10 of the VAG [German Insurance Supervision Act] directly affects the rate policy of insurance undertakings in pension funds.[23] According to this, tariffs that provide for varying premiums or benefits according to gender must be reported immediately to the BaFin [Federal Financial Supervisory Authority]. The underlying actuarial and statistical data to be disclosed in accordance with sec. 10a, para. 2a, sent. 1 of the VAG [German Insurance Supervision Act] must be included.

Furthermore, direct insurance undertakings that offer substitute health insurance and compulsory insurance, in accordance with sec. 13d, no. 7 of the VAG [German Insurance Supervision Act], must include the intended use of new or amended general policy conditions. The future of the reporting duty under sec. 13d, no. 7 of the VAG [German Insurance Supervision Act] for substitute health insurance appears "certain" in consideration of Solvency II. Indeed, art. 179, para. 1 of the Draft Solvency II forbids the systematic submission of general and special policy conditions to the supervisory authority. Exceptions are made only for compulsory insurance in art. 179, para. 2 of the Draft Solvency II. However, in art. 204, para. 1 (b) and Recital 57 of the Draft Solvency II provides Member States the option to require submission of the general policy conditions to the supervisory authority for substitute health insurance.

12.3 The Disclosure Obligations of Financial Reporting

12.3.1 The Disclosure Obligations for Financial Reporting Based on Formal Organizational Grounds

12.3.1.1 Term and Distinction

The disclosure obligations described below for financial reporting based on formal organizational grounds are distinctive from the obligations to notify

[22] On the restrictive interpretation in alignment with the directive of sec. 13, no. 6 VAG [German Insurance Supervision Act] with regard to art. 8, para. 3, subpara. 2 of the First Council Directive on non-life insurance, which contains a prohibition without exception of systematic submission of tariffs for indemnity insurance *Präve*, in: Prölss (ed.), VAG [German Insurance Supervision Act], (12th ed. 2005), sec. 13d, ref. 14.

[23] Sec. 13d, no. 10 VAG [German Insurance Supervision Act] was added with effect from 2 Jun. 2007 by legislation of 28 May 2007, BGBl. [German Federal Law Gazette] I, p. 923.

based on formal organizational grounds in that they provide the supervisory authority with information about the net asset, financial and earnings position of an insurance undertaking, at least indirectly. In content, the obligations concern organizational actions in an insurance undertaking such as changes to the shareholder structure, restructuring measures, or the development of the business. Unlike the disclosure obligations for substantive financial reporting, however, the duties of financial reporting based on formal organizational grounds do not enable the BaFin [Federal Financial Supervisory Authority] to quantify the net asset, financial and earnings position of an insurance undertaking and judge on a reliable basis how financially viable the undertaking is. The information provided to the supervisory authority merely presents indicators of financial stability of an insurance undertaking.

12.3.1.2 The Disclosure of Shareholder Structure and Close Ties

Direct and reinsurance undertakings and pension funds must disclose their shareholder structure and close ties to third parties to the BaFin [Federal Financial Supervisory Authority] in accordance with sec. 13d, no. 4 and 5 of the VAG [German Insurance Supervision Act].[24] They are also required, under sec. 13d, no. 4 of the VAG [German Insurance Supervision Act], to report, immediately upon becoming aware, any change to a significant ratio of ownership interest[25] in the undertaking itself, the attainment, surpassing, or shortfall of certain qualifying holdings (namely, 20, 33 and 50 %), as well as the fact that the undertaking will become a subsidiary of another undertaking within the meaning of the legal definition of sec. 7a, para. 2, sent. 6 of the VAG [German Insurance Supervision Act].[26] Under sec. 13d, no. 5 of the VAG [German Insurance Supervision Act], the names and addresses of those with significant holdings, along with the amount of their holding, must be disclosed annually to the BaFin [Federal Financial Supervisory Authority]. The primary meaning and purpose of these disclosures is first and foremost to enable an assessment by the supervisory authority of the good repute of holders of a significant ownership interest who have a considerable ability to influence the stability and continuity of an insurance undertaking. With

[24] The applicability of sec. 13d, no. 4 and 5 of the VAG [German Insurance Supervision Act] to reinsurance undertakings proceeds from sec. 121a, para. 1, sent. 1 of the VAG [German Insurance Supervision Act], and to pension funds from sec. 113, para. 1, of the VAG [German Insurance Supervision Act].

[25] The term significant interest is defined in sec. 7a, para. 2, sent. 3 of the VAG [German Insurance Supervision Act].

[26] The disclosure by the insurance undertaking of ownership interests in the undertaking itself is complemented by the corresponding reporting duty of a potential holder of significant ownership interest under sec. 104, para. 1 of the VAG [German Insurance Supervision Act] and art. 56 of the Draft Solvency II.

sec. 13d, no. 4 and 5 VAG [German Insurance Supervision Act], the insurance supervision law should correspond to the requirements of art. 60 in conjunction with art. 56 of the Draft Solvency II and there is no apparent need for adjustment here.[27]

Sec. 13d, no. 4a of the VAG [German Insurance Supervision Act] concerns the disclosure of close ties under sec. 8, para. 1, sent. 4 of the VAG [German Insurance Supervision Act] to another natural person or undertaking. With sec. 13d, no. 4a of the VAG [German Insurance Supervision Act], the legislator intends to prevent the emergence of a non-transparent holdings structure that could significantly impair effective supervision and thus the protection of the interests of insured persons.[28] The potential to impair the holdings network arises at the threshold of 20 % of the shares or voting rights. Additionally, under sec. 8, para. 1, sent. 4, no. 2 of the VAG [German Insurance Supervision Act], the legislator always assumes a close tie in the case of parent, subsidiary, or affiliate relationships. The disclosure obligations in sec. 13d, no. 4a of the VAG [German Insurance Supervision Act] should also satisfy the requirements of art. 60 of the Draft Solvency II that expressly refer to direct and indirect holdings.

12.3.1.3 The Disclosure of Restructuring Measures

Additional disclosure obligations for direct insurance undertakings are mandated in secs. 14 and 14a of the VAG [German Insurance Supervision Act] with regard to restructuring measures. These also apply to pension funds in accordance with sec. 113, para. 1 of the VAG [German Insurance Supervision Act], but not to reinsurance undertakings, which are subject to separate rules under sec. 121a, para. 3 and sec. 121f of the VAG [German Insurance Supervision Act].[29] The new sec. 14 of the VAG [German Insurance Supervision Act] encompassed in the 9th amendment to the VAG [German Insurance Supervision Act] codifies—if not expressly, then certainly indirectly—the obligation to submit portfolio transfer agreements. A portfolio transfer does not represent a conversion within the meaning of the German Law Regulating the Transformation of Companies. Rather, it is an option available to the insurance undertaking in addition to a fusion, splitting-up, sale of assets, and

---

[27] This also applies to the qualifying holdings specified in sec. 13d, no. 4 of the VAG [German Insurance Supervision Act]. In fact, art. 56 of the Draft Solvency II essentially provides for reporting duties triggered by qualifying holdings of 20, 30, and 50 percent. However, under art. 56, para. 2, sent. 3 of the VAG [German Insurance Supervision Act], Member States may waive application of the 30 percent threshold if they apply a threshold of one-third in accordance with art. 9, para. 3 (a) of Directive 2004/109/EC.

[28] The existence of a close tie can provide grounds under sec. 8, para. 1, sent. 2, no. 1 of the VAG [German Insurance Supervision Act] for the BaFin [Federal Financial Supervisory Authority] to deny an insurance undertaking the license to operate.

[29] See also on this point *Bürkle*, VersR (2008), 1590 ff.

change of legal form.[30] According to sec. 14, para. 1, sent. 1 of the VAG [German Insurance Supervision Act] the portfolio transfer agreement requires supervisory approval in order to take effect.[31] The approval requires application by both the transferring and receiving undertaking.[32] A copy of the portfolio transfer agreement, which must be in writing in accordance with sec. 14, para. 6 of the VAG [German Insurance Supervision Act], and a declaration that no ancillary agreements have been made must be included with the application. In consideration of art. 39, para. 1 of the Draft Solvency II, changes are scarcely to be expected.

The rules of sec. 14a of the VAG [German Insurance Supervision Act] subject any conversion of an insurance undertaking to the condition of supervisory approval. Here, too, it is a precondition for validity. Approval requires application by all undertakings participating in the conversion. To be submitted with the application is the relevant transformation agreement, which means the fusion, splitting-up and takeover agreement, the transfer agreement, or, for a change of legal form, a transformation report in which both the change of form and the future holdings of the shareholders in the legal entity are described and justified.[33] Disclosure obligations in connection with conversions of direct insurance and reinsurance undertakings are not provided for in Solvency II.

12.3.1.4 The Disclosure of Establishment of Business in Foreign Countries

Under sec. 13b, para. 1, sent. 1, domestic direct insurance undertakings must notify the BaFin [Federal Financial Supervisory Authority] of the intended establishment of offices outside of Germany in the EU and European Economic Area, indicating the relevant countries. The content of this notice must satisfy the requirements in sec. 13b, para. 1, sent. 2 of the VAG [German Insurance Supervision Act].

---

[30] On the high degree of practical relevance of a portfolio transfer and the financial advantages of this compared to conversions within the meaning of the German Law Regulating the Transformation of Companies as well as the distinction between a portfolio transfer and the individual species of transformation, see *Hübner*, in: Lutter (ed.), UmwG [in English: German Law Regulating the Transformation of Companies], vol. II, (3rd ed. 2004), Appendix 1, sec. 189, ref. 6 ff.

[31] On the assignment to supervisory approval as a precondition to taking effect see *Präve*, in: Prölss (ed.), VAG [German Insurance Supervision Act], (12th ed. 2005), sec. 14, ref. 39; *Kaulbach*, in: Fahr/Kaulbach/Bähr, VAG [German Insurance Supervision Act], (4th. ed. 2007), sec. 14, ref. 8.

[32] See *Präve*, in: Prölss (ed.), VAG [German Insurance Supervision Act], (5th ed. 2005), sec. 14, ref. 21; *Hübner*, in: Lutter (ed.), UmwG [German Law Regulating the Transformation of Companies], vol. II, (3rd ed. 2004), Appendix 1, sec. 189, ref. 83.

[33] On the content of the transformation report see *Semler/Schwanna*, in: Semler/Stengel (eds.), UmwG [German Law Regulating the Transformation of Companies], (2nd ed. 2007), sec. 190, ref. 14 f. Accordingly, the transformation report must include a transformation resolution with minimum content under law in accordance with sec. 194, para. 1 of the UmwG [German Law Regulating the Transformation of Companies].

Accordingly, the notice must include estimate of expenses for the expansion of administrative capacity, the network of representatives, and projected premium income as well as information about the organizational structure. In addition, an appropriate general agent with powers of representation must be named. Any changes to the information required under sec. 13b, para. 1, sent. 2, nos. 1–4 of the VAG [German Insurance Supervision Act] are also subject to reporting requirements under paragraph 4, sentence 1.

Corresponding disclosure obligations are found in sec. 13c, para. 1, sent. 1 of the VAG [German Insurance Supervision Act] for cases in which a domestic direct insurance undertaking intends to engage in services in foreign EU and European Economic Area countries. The undertaking must also notify the BaFin [Federal Financial Supervisory Authority] accordingly if it intends to operate additional insurance lines there, cover additional risks, or appoint a different representative for claims settlement. The requirements of secs. 13b and 13c of the VAG [German Insurance Supervision Act] do not apply to pension funds and reinsurance undertakings.[34] This will change in the future, at least with regard to reinsurance undertakings, against the background of arts. 143 and 145 of the Draft Solvency II, which contain the corresponding disclosure obligations for the development of business in foreign countries.

12.3.1.5 Disclosure Related to Outsourcing

In sec. 13, para. 1a, the insurance supervisory law contains the duty of advance notice to the BaFin [Federal Financial Supervisory Authority] with regard to the outsourcing of important functions as defined by sec. 5, para. 3, no. 4 of the VAG [German Insurance Supervision Act].[35] Submission of the outsourcing contracts to the BaFin [Federal Financial Supervisory Authority] is even a precondition for their validity under civil law according to sec. 13, para. 1a, sent. 2–6 of the VAG [German Insurance Supervision Act]. With its duty of advance notice, sec. 13, para. 1a of the VAG [German Insurance Supervision Act] corresponds to the advice in Recital 20 of the second draft of Solvency II recommended to the Member States to standardize a disclosure obligation with respect to outsourcing that informs the supervisory authority about the plan for the outsourcing contract prior to its execution.

In contrast, art. 48, para. 3 of the Draft Solvency II requires only that insurance undertakings headquartered in Germany inform the BaFin [Federal Financial Supervisory Authority] "in a timely manner" of an executed outsourcing of important

[34] See sec. 113, para. 3 and sec. 121a, para. 1, sent. 1 of the VAG [German Insurance Supervision Act].

[35] In detail on the outsourcing of the risk management function under insurance supervision law, and in particular on the paradigm shift of the BaFin [Federal Financial Supervisory Authority] with regard to the ability to outsource internal audit see *Dreher/Schaaf*, WM (2008), 1765 (1770 f.).

functions as well as all important developments relating to the outsourced functions.[36] Since the proposed directive has no notification deadline, a strong argument can be made that the term "in a timely manner" should not be understood as having a technical meaning, but rather in the general sense of "immediately, without undue delay". In this respect, art. 48, para. 3 of the Draft Solvency II would entail changes to the VAG [German Insurance Supervision Act] as, in the future, even important developments related to the outsourced functions that occur after execution of the contract would need to be cause for reporting duties. Added to this is the preliminary work by CEIOPS for the implementing regulations at Level 2 requiring that a significant amount of information with regard to outsourcing be disclosed by undertakings to the supervisory authority. In the future, for example, undertakings must document how they determine the competence of external service providers ("a detailed due diligence checking process"), how they monitor the same, and how they ensure that their organization is not adversely impacted by the outsourcing.[37] Further, the disclosure obligations with respect to outsourcing in the future must also apply to reinsurance undertakings, which currently have no such obligations.[38]

12.3.2 The Disclosure Obligations for Substantive Financial Reporting

12.3.2.1 The Disclosure of Solvency

At the center of substantive financial reporting—in addition to the disclosure obligations for assessment of the structure of own funds—are the disclosure obligations that enable the supervisory authority to assess the solvency of the undertaking.[39] Direct insurance undertakings are required under sec. 53c,

[36] The European Council, in its Common Position of 25 Nov. 2008, seeks to encompass even the outsourcing of "critical" functions, which it sees as distinct from "important operating" functions, in the term "outsourcing" as it relates to the insurance supervisory regime in the future. It thus proposes that the outsourcing of staff functions for the prevention of crises should be included in supervision. On the admissibility of outsourcing the risk control function, compliance function, and internal audit, see *Dreher/Schaaf*, WM (2008), 1765 (1770 f.).

[37] See CEIOPS, Issues Paper of 3 Nov. 2008, Implementing Measures on System of Governance, pnt. 10.1 ff.; CEIOPS of 25 Feb. 2009, Draft CEIOPS' Advice for Level 2 Implementing Measures on Solvency II: Reporting Requirements, pnt. 3.57 sub A.7.

[38] Sec. 121a, para. 1 of the VAG [German Insurance Supervision Act] provides no corresponding applicability of sec. 13 of the VAG [German Insurance Supervision Act] to reinsurance undertakings. Thus with respect to functional outsourcing, the reinsurance supervision in secs. 119, para. 2, no. 6, and 121a, para. 4, sent. 3 of the VAG [German Insurance Supervision Act] differs from the direct insurance supervision in secs. 5, para. 3, no. 4; 81, para. 4 (a); 83, para. 5, no. 2; and 53d of the VAG [German Insurance Supervision Act].

[39] Even as part of its business plan, a direct insurance undertaking must prove under sec. 5, para. 4, sent. 1 and 2 of the VAG [German Insurance Supervision Act] that it has a level of own funds

para. 4 of the VAG [German Insurance Supervision Act] to submit a calculation of their solvency margin annually to the BaFin [Federal Financial Supervisory Authority] and to document the underlying own funds as part of their regular business operations. The calculation of the solvency margin is governed by the German Capital Resources Regulation,[40] and enacted through sec. 53c, para. 2, no. 1 VAG [German Insurance Supervision Act]. Specifications as to the form of the notice and calculation of the solvency margin are provided in the BaFin [Federal Financial Supervisory Authority] Circular 4/2005 (VA) of 1 Mar. 2005.[41] Equivalent obligations exist for reinsurance undertakings in accordance with sec. 121a, para. 1, sent. 2 in conjunction with sec. 53c, para. 4 of the VAG [German Insurance Supervision Act], and for pension funds in accordance with sec. 4, para. 1 of the PKAustV [German Pension Fund Capital Resources Regulation].[42] Based on the information disclosed, the BaFin [Federal Financial Supervisory Authority] reviews whether the undertaking has met its solvency requirements and, in the event of insufficient funds, takes the necessary measures under sec. 81b of the VAG [German Insurance Supervision Act][43] or sec. 121a, para. 1, sent. 3 of the VAG [German Insurance Supervision Act].

The draft of a framework directive for Solvency II makes clear that the scope of disclosure duties for the purpose of supervisory assessment of solvency will notably increase when the new supervisory regime takes effect. This is due primarily to complexity but also to greater individualization in the future solvency system. The solvency system is the subject-matter of the first pillar of Solvency II. At its center are the rules for the calculation of quantitative Solvency Capital Requirements, the Minimum Capital Requirement, and the Target Solvency Capital Requirement.[44] The Target Solvency Capital Requirement is the decisive solvency figure under

available that corresponds to the minimum amount of the guarantee fund under sec. 53c, para. 2 VAG [German Insurance Supervision Act]. It must also submit the composition of these funds. The law provides equivalent obligations for reinsurance undertakings in sec. 119, para. 3, sent. 1 in conjunction with sec. 121d of the VAG [German Insurance Supervision Act], and for pension funds in sec. 113, para. 2, no. 2 in conjunction with sec. 114, para. 2 of the VAG [German Insurance Supervision Act].

[40] Regulation on the capital resources of insurance undertakings (German Capital Resources Regulation) of 13 Dec. 1983, BGBl. [German Federal Law Gazette] I, p. 1261.

[41] Based on sec. 53c, para. 4 of the VAG [German Insurance Supervision Act].

[42] German Pension Fund Capital Resources Regulation of 20 Dec. 2001 (BGBl. [German Federal Law Gazette] I, p. 4180), amended through article 5 of the law of 28 May 2007 (BGBl. [German Federal Law Gazette] I, p. 923). The legal basis is found in sec. 114, para. 2, no. 4 of the VAG [German Insurance Supervision Act].

[43] For pension funds, sec. 81b, para. 4 of the VAG [German Insurance Supervision Act] applies only according to the standard in sec. 113, para. 2, no. 8a of the VAG [German Insurance Supervision Act].

[44] In detail on this point, for example, *Dreher*, VersR (2008), 998 (1001 f.); *Nguyen*, Handbuch der wert- und risikoorientierten Steuerung von Versicherungsunternehmen [in English: Handbook of Value and Risk-based Management of Insurance Undertakings] (2008), 293 f. *Romeike*, in: Romeike/Müller-Reichart (eds.), Risikomanagement in Versicherungsunternehmen [in English: Risk Management in Insurance Undertakings] (2008), 115 (135).

Solvency II. It reflects the actual risk profile of an insurance undertaking. Undertakings essentially have the choice of calculating their Target solvency capital requirement using a universal standard model or an internal model requiring approval. In contrast, the Minimum Capital Requirement serves as a simple, robust measure of the level of own funds below which the issuer of the directive views the interests of the insured as seriously endangered.[45]

A minimum framework for disclosure for the purpose of supervisory assessment of solvency is provided in art. 35, para. 1, sent. 1, 2 (a) in conjunction with art. 36 of the Draft Solvency II.[46] Accordingly, the Member States must require that insurance and reinsurance undertakings, as part of regular business operations, provide the supervisory authority with the information needed by the supervisor to assess their "valuation principles applied for solvency purposes" and "their [solvency] capital ... needs", at a minimum.[47,48] Indeed, only the implementation regulations of the Commission, expected at the second level of the Lamfalussy process, will provide complete certainty as to which information specifically requires disclosure.[49] However, arts. 102, para. 1, sent. 1 and 127, para. 2 of the Draft Solvency II contain special, concrete disclosure obligations for the supervisory assessment of the "[solvency] capital needs" within the meaning of art. 35, para. 1, sent. 1, 2 (a) in conjunction with art. 36, para. 2 (c) of the Draft Solvency II. According to these, insurance and reinsurance undertakings must calculate and report to the supervisory authority their Target Solvency Capital Requirement at least annually and their Minimum Capital Requirement quarterly.[50] If the Minimum Capital Requirement is below 20 % of the Target Solvency Capital Requirement or exceeds half of it, the undertaking must report this to the supervisory authority and provide the reasons for it.[51]

---

[45] As a condition for their license to operate, direct insurance and reinsurance undertakings under art. 18, para. 1 (e) and (f) of the Draft Solvency II must prove that they are in a position of holding sufficient own funds to meet the Solvency Capital Requirement and the Minimum Capital Requirement. Further, under art. 18, para. 1 (d) they must prove that, at the time of their application, they have basic own funds to cover the absolute lower limit of minimum capital (see art. 127, para. 1 (d) of the Draft Solvency II).

[46] On the objectives of the disclosure obligations that support the supervisory assessment of solvency, and on the function of the supervisory authority in the context of Pillar 3 of Solvency II, see *Nguyen*, WPg (2008), 651 (653 ff.).

[47] Parentheses added by author.

[48] See also Recital 15 of the framework directive.

[49] See CEIOPS of 25 Feb. 2009, Draft CEIOPS' Advice for Level 2 Implementing Measures on Solvency II: Reporting Requirements, pnt. 3.60. The legal basis is found in art. 35, para. 6, sent. 1 of the Draft Solvency II; on the Lamfalussy process see above, n. 18.

[50] On the content to be disclosed in detail see CEIOPS, Issues Paper of 15 Aug. 2008, Supervisory Review Process and Undertakings' Reporting Requirements, pnt. 5.20 ff. and CEIOPS of 25 Feb. 2009, Draft CEIOPS' Advice for Level 2 Implementing Measures on Solvency II: Reporting Requirements, pnt. 3.45 sub (ii).

[51] See art. 127, para. 4, sent. 2 of the Draft Solvency II in the version of the Council, Common Position of 25 Nov. 2008.

The evaluation principles for the purpose of solvency are primarily reflected in the internal model for calculation of the Target Solvency Capital Requirement, if the undertaking uses this. With regard to internal models, whose compliance with the law requires supervisory review under art. 36, para. 2 (f) of the Draft Solvency II, special disclosure obligations are stipulated in art. 110, para. 7 as well as arts. 116 and 118 Draft Solvency II.[52] For the calculation of the Target solvency capital requirement based on an internal model, art. 110, para. 7 of the Draft Solvency II additionally requires that the undertaking submit an estimate based on the standard formula for the first 2 years following issuance of the license to operate. Under art. 116, para. 1 of the Draft Solvency II, direct insurance and reinsurance undertakings must notify the supervisory authority if a previously approved internal model is either no longer used or no longer meets the legal requirements. They must simultaneously submit a plan to restore compliance or demonstrate that the effect of non-compliance is immaterial. They must also provide evidence to the supervisory authority under art. 118 of the Draft Solvency II that the internal model is used in the business "for other purposes". This means that the internal model is used for risk capital allocation, in particular for the internal assessment of risks and solvency within the meaning of art. 44 of the Draft Solvency II, and integrated into the risk management system of the undertaking under art. 43 of the Draft Solvency II. In cases where an undertaking uses a partial internal model, it must also demonstrate to the supervisory authority that the model is used to calculate individual factors specified in art. 110, para. 2 of the Draft Solvency II.[53]

12.3.2.2 Disclosure of the Structure of Own Funds

A general obligation on insurance undertakings to periodically disclose the structure of their own funds to the BaFin [Federal Financial Supervisory Authority] is not currently part of insurance supervisory law. Only sec. 13d, no. 3 of the VAG [German Insurance Supervision Act] stipulates a disclosure obligation related to own-funds structure. It requires direct insurance undertakings and, by reference in sec. 113, para. 1 of the VAG [German Insurance Supervision Act], pension funds in the legal form of a stock corporation, including the SE,[54] to immediately notify the BaFin [Federal Financial Supervisory Authority] of amendments concerning capital increases to the

[52] For the admission procedure, art. 110, para. 3 of the Draft Solvency II requires direct insurance and reinsurance undertakings to submit the necessary documentation to the BaFin [Federal Financial Supervisory Authority] for assessing the legal compliance of an internal model with their application for a license to operate.

[53] See on this point art. 43, para. 5 and art. 44 of the Draft Solvency II.

[54] The option of a capital increase is available only to insurance corporations, including those organized as an SE. Mutual insurance associations and public insurance companies must rely on their operating revenue to generate needed capital.

articles of incorporation. The requirement does not apply to reinsurance undertakings. The implementation of a capital increase gives the supervisory authority information about the—amended—amount of own funds held by the insurance undertaking. Under sec. 181, para. 3 of the AktG [German Stock Corporation Act], amendments to the articles of incorporation take effect only after entry in the commercial register. Thus, the notification to the BaFin [Federal Financial Supervisory Authority] must occur immediately following the entry.

The Solvency II regime will introduce various disclosure obligations to enable supervisory review of the own-funds structure of direct insurance and reinsurance undertakings. The basic framework in art. 35, para. 1, sent. 1, 2 (a) in conjunction with art. 36 of the Draft Solvency II requires the Member States to require that direct insurance and reinsurance undertakings provide the supervisory authority with the information needed by the supervisor to assess "their [own] capital structure".[55] With regard to art. 36, para. 2 (e) of the Draft Solvency II, it can be assumed that the implementation regulations expected at the second level of the Lamfalussy process will require direct insurance and reinsurance undertakings to disclose the quality and quantity of their own funds periodically.[56]

12.3.2.3 The Disclosure Relating to Accounting

Under sec. 55, para. 2, sent. 1 of the VAG [German Insurance Supervision Act], insurance undertakings must submit their annual financial statement as prepared by their legal representative, followed later by the adopted financial statement, to the supervisory authority along with the management report. Sec. 55, para. 2, sent. 1 of the VAG [German Insurance Supervision Act] is supplemented by secs. 58, para. 2, sent. 1 and 59, sent. 1 of the VAG [German Insurance Supervision Act].[57] Under this rule, insurance undertakings must immediately advise the BaFin [Federal Financial Supervisory Authority] of the auditor appointed by the supervisory board and submit a copy of the audit report immediately upon adoption of the annual financial statement. In view of this extensive regimen of accounting disclosure obligations, the requirements pending under EU law in art. 33, para. 1 and para. 3, sent. 1 of the Draft Solvency II—apart from the textual references to new solvency regulations—would hardly require anything new.

[55] Parentheses added by author.

[56] See the corresponding list by CEIOPS of 25 Feb. 2009, Draft CEIOPS' Advice for Level 2 Implementing Measures on Solvency II: Reporting Requirements, pnt. 3.61.

[57] Secs. 58, para. 2, sent. 1, and 59, sent. 1 of the VAG [German Insurance Supervision Act] are not applicable to public insurance undertakings subject to supervision by the federal states according to sec. 60 of the VAG [German Insurance Supervision Act], nor to smaller mutual insurance associations that are exempt from the requirement of an annual financial statement audit, according to sec. 64 VAG [German Insurance Supervision Act].

12.3.2.4 The Disclosure of Investment Activity

Under sec. 54d, sent. 1 of the VAG [German Insurance Supervision Act], insurance undertakings must report their total investments to the BaFin [Federal Financial Supervisory Authority], broken down by new and existing investments. The disclosure obligations include periodic recurring reports as well as notifications based on certain events. They encompass both restricted and unrestricted assets as well as the use of derivative financial instruments. In accordance with the powers assigned to it in sec. 54d, sent. 1 of the VAG [German Insurance Supervision Act], the BaFin [Federal Financial Supervisory Authority] has regulated the form and timing of the disclosures in detail in Circulars 30/2002, 1/2004 and 11/2005.[58] The disclosure obligations in sec. 54d, sent. 1 of the VAG [German Insurance Supervision Act] are also applicable to pension funds under sec. 113, para. 1 of the VAG [German Insurance Supervision Act] and to reinsurance undertakings under sec. 121a, para. 1, sent. 1 of the VAG [German Insurance Supervision Act].

Under sec. 66, para. 1 of the VAG [German Insurance Supervision Act] direct insurance undertakings must establish a minimum level of guarantee assets as indicated in paragraph 1a for coverage of their technical provisions. They are required, in addition to the obligations under sec. 54d, sent. 1 of the VAG [German Insurance Supervision Act], to inform the supervisory authority of the nature of custody for these assets under sec. 66, para. 5, sent. 2 of the VAG [German Insurance Supervision Act]. At the close of each financial year, insurance undertakings are required under sec. 66, para. 6, sent. 6 of the VAG [German Insurance Supervision Act] to submit a copy of the list of assets disclosing the individual items of the guarantee assets to the BaFin [Federal Financial Supervisory Authority]. Sec. 66, paras. 5 and 6 of the VAG [German Insurance Supervision Act] are likewise applicable to pension funds through sec. 113, para. 1 of the VAG [German Insurance Supervision Act], but not to reinsurance undertakings.

Further disclosure obligations relating to the investment activity of direct insurance undertakings are provided in sec. 54, para. 4 of the VAG [German Insurance Supervision Act]. According to sec. 54, para. 4, sent. 1, no. 2 in conjunction with sent. 2 of the VAG [German Insurance Supervision Act], insurance undertakings must notify the BaFin [Federal Financial Supervisory Authority] of interests they acquire—for stock holdings or other shares, however, only if the holding threshold of 10 % is exceeded—by the end of the month following the transaction.[59] The equivalent applies under sec. 54d, para. 4, sent. 1, no. 3 in conjunction with

---

[58] The power granted in sec. 54d, sent. 1 of the VAG [German Insurance Supervision Act] is sometimes viewed as unconstitutional because of its vagueness – see *Bähr/Kaulbach*, in: Fahr/Kaulbach/Bähr, VAG [German Insurance Supervision Act], (4th ed. 2007), sec. 54d, ref. 4.

[59] Disclosure obligations to the BaFin [Federal Financial Supervisory Authority] under securities supervision law that may pertain to insurance undertakings as institutional investors, specifically those in secs. 21, para. 1 and, para. 1a, 25, para. 1 of the WpHG [German Securities Trading Act] on the disclosure of holdings as well as the relevant issuer obligations in secs. 26, para. 2 and 26a sent. 1 of the WpHG [German Securities Trading Act] are not addressed in the present context. On

sent. 2 of the VAG [German Insurance Supervision Act] for investments in an affiliated company as defined by sec. 15 of the AktG [German Stock Corporation Act]. Sec. 54, para. 4 of the VAG [German Insurance Supervision Act] applies in accordance with sec. 113, para. 1 of the VAG [German Insurance Supervision Act] to pension funds but not to reinsurance undertakings.

Comparable disclosure obligations with respect to investment activity are not found in the proposed Solvency II directive. However, art. 35, para. 1, sent. 1, 2 (a) in conjunction with art. 36 of the Draft Solvency II prescribes an obligation for disclosure of information on the supervisory assessment of "capital management". Details on the content of the disclosure can be expected at the second level of the Lamfalussy process, according to the explanatory text.[60] Since compliance with the investment requirements within the meaning of Chapter VI, Section 6 in art. 36, para. 2 (d) of the Draft Solvency II is explicitly mentioned as a subject-matter of insurance supervision, the specifics in the Commission's implementation regulations—based on previous experience with the Lamfalussy process[61]—will in all likelihood be extensive.[62]

12.3.2.5 Disclosure of the Threat of Insolvency

Sec. 88, para. 2 of the VAG [German Insurance Supervision Act] requires the managing board of an insurance undertaking to notify the supervisory authority immediately of the inability to make payment or of over-indebtedness of the undertaking. The disclosure obligation gains justification from the particular point of insolvency law for insurance undertakings which, under sec. 88, para. 1 of the VAG [German Insurance Supervision Act], in deviation from sec. 113, para. 1 of the German Bankruptcy Act, sets forth that only the BaFin [Federal Financial Supervisory Authority]—and not management—can petition for the insolvency proceeding. The rule applies accordingly to re-insurance undertakings and pension funds under sec. 121a, para. 1 and sec. 113, para. 1, respectively, of the VAG [German Insurance Supervision Act].[63]

---

this point in the current problem of "hidden ownership" see recently *Fleischer/Schmolke*, ZIP (2007), 1501; *U. H. Schneider*, NZG (2007), 888.

[60] See explanatory text (sub 4.) for art. 35 of the Draft Solvency II.

[61] On a tendency to over-regulate in connection with the Lamfalussy process see *Rittner/Dreher*, Europäisches und deutsches Wirtschaftsrecht [in English: European and German Economic Law], (3rd ed. 2008), sec. 32, ref. 8; *Schmolke*, NZG (2005), 916; *id.*, EuR (2006), 432 (446); *Wandt*, VW (2007), 473 (474); in reference to the experience in connection with the MIFID (Markets in Financial Instruments Directive) *Weber-Rey* AG (2007), R396 (R398).

[62] See the corresponding list by CEIOPS of 25 Feb. 2009, Draft CEIOPS' Advice for Level 2 Implementing Measures on Solvency II: Reporting Requirements, pnt. 3.61.

[63] With regard to the application of sec. 88, para. 1 and 2 of the VAG [German Insurance Supervision Act] to pension funds, it must be pointed out that the list in sec. 113, para. 3 of the VAG [German Insurance Supervision Act] contains a drafting error: the referenced provision "sec. 88, para. 1, sent. 2 of the VAG [German Insurance Supervision Act]", which is not supposed to

The pending requirements in the seventh chapter of the framework directive for Solvency II will shift the timing forward for the current requirement for disclosure of a basis for insolvency by the insurance undertaking to the supervisory authority. Under art. 136, para. 1 of the Draft Solvency II, insurance and reinsurance undertakings must inform the supervisory authority immediately upon ascertaining that the Solvency Capital Requirement is no longer covered, or if a threat exists that such a situation could arise within the next 3 months. Art. 137, para. 1 contain stipulations with identical wording with regard to insufficient funds for the Minimum Capital Requirement. The future situation, in which even an over-extension with the mere capability to bring about insolvency for the undertaking within 3 months would be cause for mandatory disclosure to the supervisory authority, could empower the supervisory authority to avert an actual insolvency of the undertaking through supervisory reorganization measures. In contrast, under the current disclosure concept, notification is not likely to reach the BaFin [Federal Financial Supervisory Authority] until "the horse has already bolted from the stable".

12.4 The Disclosure Obligations for Risk Reporting

Sec. 55c, para. 1 of the VAG [German Insurance Supervision Act] requires insurance undertakings to periodically submit copies of the risk report prepared in accordance with sec. 64a, para. 1, sent. 4, no. 3 (d) of the VAG [German Insurance Supervision Act] as well as the internal audit report.[64] According to sec. 55c, para. 5, the risk report must be submitted to the BaFin [Federal Financial Supervisory Authority] no later than 1 month after it is filed with management, and the internal audit report must be submitted along with the prepared financial statement. Sec. 55c of the VAG [German Insurance Supervision Act] also applies to pension funds based on sec. 113, para. 1 of the VAG [German Insurance Supervision Act] and reinsurance undertakings based on sec. 121a, para. 1, sent. 2 of the VAG [German Insurance Supervision Act].

The content of both reports[65] has not yet been fully clarified. The legal requirements are vague and indeterminate. The requirements of the MaRisk VA

apply to pension funds, does not exist. But sec. 88, para. 1 and 2 of the VAG [German Insurance Supervision Act] must also apply to pension funds. Otherwise, the application of sec. 88, para. 3, sent. 3 of the VAG [German Insurance Supervision Act] and, most importantly, sec. 88, para. 5 of the VAG [German Insurance Supervision Act] would not make sense.

[64] The only exceptions, according to sec. 55c, para. 6 of the VAG [German Insurance Supervision Act], are funeral expense funds and small mutual insurance associations as specified in sec. 64a, para. 5, sent. 1 of the VAG [German Insurance Supervision Act] as well as undertakings exempted by application in accordance with sentence 2.

[65] See on this point *Dreher/Schaaf*, "Inhalt und Organisation des Risiko- sowie des Revisionsberichts" [in English: Content and Organization of the Risk Report and Internal Audit Report], VersR (2009), 1151 (1168).

[Minimum Requirements for Risk Management (Insurance Supervision)], which—at least for the risk report—are also found throughout the entire circular,[66] offer only a limited contribution to the clarification. The following example may illustrate the legal uncertainty in insurance practice with respect to the content of the risk report: under sec. 64a, para. 1, sent. 4, no. 3 (d), first indent of the VAG [German Insurance Supervision Act], the risk report must state "what the major objectives of risk management" are. This is bewildering since the primary addressee of the risk report, according to sec. 64a, para. 1, sent. 4, no. 3 (d) of the VAG [German Insurance Supervision Act], is management. And management itself determines the major goals of risk management and its overarching limits. Thus the question: what major goals of risk management could be unknown to the undertaking's management body, and thus require periodic reporting to it?

The risk report[67] largely makes reference to the risk management process as laid down in sec. 64a, para. 1, sent. 4, no. 3 (b) of the VAG [German Insurance Supervision Act], meaning the processes of risk identification, risk analysis and assessment, and risk management and monitoring. It includes a presentation of the overall risk profile, a description of the methods used for identification and assessment, an explanation of deliberate risk management measures taken, and the result of a review of effectiveness of these measures.

The audit report under sec. 55, para. 1, no. 2 of the VAG [German Insurance Supervision Act] must indicate the significant findings from the review by internal audit in the past fiscal year as well as the planned areas of audit for the current fiscal year. Pursuant to the legislative materials, the audit findings should inform the BaFin [Federal Financial Supervisory Authority] in particular about the functional capacity of risk management at the undertaking as well as circumstances that hinder efficient implementation of the business strategy or conceal organizational risks.[68] In accordance with the MaRisk VA [Minimum Requirements for Risk Management (Insurance Supervision)], the audit report should advise with respect to corrective measures in addition to recording the descriptions of defects found.[69] The selection of areas of audit for the current fiscal year must be based on a risk-oriented audit plan, which is updated annually.

---

[66] Specifically, detail on the content of the risk report in the MaRisk VA [Minimum Requirements for Risk Management (Insurance Supervision)] is found in the explanatory text for 5., under 2.; the explanatory text for 7., under 1.; at 7.2.1, under 2. (b) including the additional explanatory text; at 7.3.1, under 5. and 8.; at 7.3.2.3, under 4. and 6.; at 7.3.4 and the explanatory text for 10., under 1.

[67] See on this point *Dreher*, VersR (2008), 998 (1005).

[68] Since the content of the risk report clearly extends further than the statements specific to risk management in the management report submitted to the BaFin [Federal Financial Supervisory Authority] in accordance with sec. 55, para. 2, sent. 1 of the VAG [German Insurance Supervision Act] (see sec. 289, para. 2 (a) and (b) in conjunction with sec. 341a of the HGB [German Commercial Code]), the latter appears to be of lesser significance from a supervisory perspective, at least for risk reporting.

[69] See MaRisk VA [Minimum Requirements for Risk Management (Insurance Supervision)], at 7.4, under 7.

With sec. 55c of the VAG [German Insurance Supervision Act], which must always be viewed in the context of sec. 64a of the VAG [German Insurance Supervision Act], the legislator has anticipated art. 35, para. 1, sent. 1 in conjunction with sent. 2 (a) in conjunction with art. 36 of the Draft Solvency II. According to this passage, Member States must mandate that direct insurance and reinsurance undertakings submit information to the supervisory authority to enable assessment of the system of governance, and the risk management system, in particular.[70] Sec. 55c of the VAG [German Insurance Supervision Act] would already satisfy the pending requirements under EU law to a large extent. Nevertheless, the impending implementation of the new solvency requirements in insurance supervisory law will necessitate supplementation with regard to the content of the reports.[71]

12.5 Disclosure Obligations at the Group Level

12.5.1 The Obligations to Notify Based on Formal Grounds at the Group Level

12.5.1.1 No Group-Specific Reporting Duties for Shareholding Direct Insurance and Reinsurance Undertakings

Shareholding undertakings, meaning direct insurance and reinsurance undertakings who are parent companies of a direct insurance or reinsurance undertaking, have a qualified holding in such in accordance with paragraph 2, number 1, or belong to a horizontal business group, are subject to additional supervision, known as "solo-plus supervision", under sec. 104a, para. 1, no. 1 of the VAG [German Insurance Supervision Act]. It does not, however, require any formal, group-specific disclosures for shareholding direct insurance and reinsurance undertakings. This is due to the fact that all undertakings that are part of a group in the configurations described are individually required to make disclosures.

---

[70] In detail on the risk reporting information to be disclosed to the supervisory authority see CEIOPS, Advice to the European Commission on Supervisory Reporting and Public Disclosure in the Framework of the Solvency II Project, March 2007, pnt. 4.12 and CEIOPS of 25 Feb. 2009, Draft CEIOPS' Advice for Level 2 Implementing Measures on Solvency II: Reporting Requirements, pnt. 3.57, sub A.3.

[71] Thus the current content required in a risk report under the law and MaRisk VA [Minimum Requirements for Risk Management (Insurance Supervision)] will expand in the risk management system as set forth in sec. 64a VAG [German Insurance Supervision Act], for example, with the inclusion of internal models for the calculation of the Target Solvency Capital Requirement, since the risk report will need to provide information through the audits of this element as an important component of risk management.

12.5.1.2 The Reporting Duties of Insurance Holding Companies with Respect to Appointments to Management Positions

Different rules apply to domestic insurance holding companies with respect to the appointment and separation of members of management.[72] The term insurance holding company is—even if not entirely congruent[73]—given legal definition in sec. 1b, para. 1, sent. 1 of the VAG [German Insurance Supervision Act] and in sec. 104a, para. 2, no. 4 of the VAG [German Insurance Supervision Act]. If an insurance holding company does not operate the insurance business itself, the requirements for direct insurance and reinsurance undertakings do not apply.[74] Only those subsidiary undertakings subject to solo-plus supervision under sec. 104a, para. 1, no. 2 of the VAG [German Insurance Supervision Act] have a reporting obligation at the level of the individual undertaking. Sec. 13e of the VAG [German Insurance Supervision Act] closes the regulation gap with regard to disclosure by insurance holding companies. According to sec. 13e, para. 1, sent. 1, no. 1 of the VAG [German Insurance Supervision Act], insurance holding companies must inform the BaFin [Federal Financial Supervisory Authority] immediately of their intention to appoint a manager as well as of the following execution of this intention and must provide the information relevant for an assessment of the individual's fit-and-proper qualification. Sec. 13e, para. 1 S. 1, no. 2 VAG [German Insurance Supervision Act] also stipulates disclosure to the BaFin [Federal Financial Supervisory Authority] upon the separation of a manager. The fit-and-proper requirements for managers of insurance holding companies referred to in sec. 13e, para. 1, sent. 1, no. 1 of the VAG [German Insurance Supervision Act] have—unfortunately, from a legislative perspective—a double origin in the VAG [German Insurance Supervision Act], namely through sec. 1b, para. 2 in conjunction with sec. 7a, para. 1, sent. 1 of the VAG [German Insurance Supervision Act] and again independently through sec. 7a, para. 3 of the VAG [German Insurance Supervision Act]. Furthermore, there are differences in the content of these two regulatory areas. While sec. 7a, para. 1 of the VAG [German Insurance Supervision Act] refers to

[72] See on management monitoring at insurance holding companies especially *Dreher*, ZVersWiss (Supplement, Annual Conference 2006), 375 (380 f.).

[73] Sec. 1b of the VAG [German Insurance Supervision Act] was introduced as part of the VAG [German Insurance Supervision Act] amendment of 2004. Sec. 104a, para. 2, no. 4 of the VAG [German Insurance Supervision Act] is based on implementation of the Insurance Group Directive 98/78/EC of the European Parliament and of the Council of 27 Oct. 1998, OJEC L 330 of 5 Dec. 1998, p. 1 through the VAG [German Insurance Supervision Act] amendment of 2000. On the varying definitions of insurance holding company in the VAG [German Insurance Supervision Act] see BT-Drucks. [Document of the German Bundestag] 15/3418, p. 19; on this point *Bürkle*, VersR (2005), 458 (459 f.); *Bähr*, in: Fahr/Kaulbach/Bähr, VAG [The German Insurance Supervision Act], (4th ed. 2007), sec. 1b, ref. 2.

[74] See sec. 1b, para. 1, sent. 2 of the VAG [German Insurance Supervision Act]. On the danger that undertakings that are not supervised but are affiliated with insurance undertakings under a legal group structure could defeat supervisory measures see BT-Drucks. [Document of the German Bundestag] 15/3418, p. 17.

managers, sec. 7a, para. 3 of the VAG [German Insurance Supervision Act] includes those persons who "effectively run" the business of an insurance holding company.

Unlike the situation with independent direct insurance and reinsurance undertakings, no expansion at the group level of the disclosure obligations related to a change in the occupant of a key office in the course of implementing the framework directive of Solvency II is expected. The relevant provision for insurance holding companies is art. 261 of the Draft Solvency II, which refers in sentence 2 to both the "fit-and-proper test" as well as the disclosure obligations of art. 42 of the Draft Solvency II. This provision expressly relates to their management bodies only. Other persons that occupy key offices in a holding company, for example, supervisory board members, are not included in art. 261 of the Draft Solvency II in accordance with its title.

12.5.2 The Disclosure Obligations of Financial Reporting at the Group Level

12.5.2.1 The Disclosure Obligations for Financial Reporting Based on Formal Organizational Grounds at the Group Level

The Disclosure of Internal Group Transactions. Under sec. 104e, para. 3, sent. 1 of the VAG [German Insurance Supervision Act] shareholding direct insurance and reinsurance undertakings as well as subsidiaries of an insurance holding company within the meaning of sec. 104a, para. 1, nos. 1 and 2 of the VAG [German Insurance Supervision Act] must produce an annual report for the BaFin [Federal Financial Supervisory Authority] on significant transactions conducted within the group.[75] The reason for disclosure of internal group transactions is that a group can exploit these to conceal its financial position.[76] Neither sec. 104e, para. 3 of the VAG [German Insurance Supervision Act] nor art. 8 of the Insurance Group Directive[77] specifies the conditions under which internal group transactions qualify as significant. At the delegated level of legislation, the BaFin [Federal Financial Supervisory Authority] Circular 3/2004 is instructive. According to the Circular, the transactions enumerated in sec. 104e, para. 2, nos. 1–6 of the VAG [German

[75] On the form and content of the disclosure see Circular 3/2004, A. III. and on the time frame for the details within it, under B. Also subject to the reporting duty under sec. 104e, para. 1, sent. 1 of the VAG [German Insurance Supervision Act] are transactions with natural persons who have holdings in one or more group businesses.

[76] On the potential influence of the controlling company within an insurance group see *Dreher/ Schaaf*, WM (2008), 1765 (1772 f.).

[77] Directive 98/78/EC of the European Parliament and of the Council on the supplementary supervision of insurance undertakings in an insurance group of 27 Oct. 1998, OJEC L 330 of 5 Oct. 1998, p. 1.

Insurance Supervision Act], which include loans, guarantees, and reinsurance transactions, are considered significant when they exceed certain thresholds.[78] In terms of form, the disclosure under sec. 104e, para. 3, sent. 1 of the VAG [German Insurance Supervision Act] must satisfy the detailed supervisory requirements presented in the Circular and occur within 4 months after the end of a fiscal year. An ad-hoc disclosure obligation for internal group transactions within the meaning of paragraph 1 is stipulated in sec. 104e, para. 4, sent. 2 of the VAG [German Insurance Supervision Act] if a threat to solvency appears likely.[79] The disclosure should put the supervisory authority in a position where it can take measures in accordance with sec. 104h in conjunction with secs. 81, para. 2 and 81b, para. 1 and 2 of the VAG [German Insurance Supervision Act].

Thus, German insurance supervision law already corresponds with the impending regulation in art. 249, para. 2 Draft Solvency II to a large degree. In sentence 1, the regulation requires periodic disclosure of all significant internal group transactions, supplemented in sentence 2 by an equivalent ad-hoc requirement. A small number of conceptual differences is found only for insurance groups that have an insurance holding company as the ultimate parent. According to sec. 104e, para. 3, in conjunction with para. 1, sent. 1, first indent, in conjunction with sec. 104a, para. 1, no. 2 of the VAG [German Insurance Supervision Act], the subsidiary of the holding company is the addressee of the disclosure obligation. In contrast, art. 249, para. 2, sent. 3 of the Draft Solvency II names the insurance holding company at the top of the group as the undertaking required to report in this configuration. It also remains to be seen how the Commission, which is empowered under art. 249, para. 4 of the Draft Solvency II to adopt corresponding implementation regulations, will define the threshold for significant transactions against the background of the new solvency requirements.

The Disclosure of Group, Shareholder, and Holdings Structure. For direct insurance and reinsurance undertakings as well as pension funds in a group, there are no group-specific disclosure obligations related to the structure of the group, shareholders, or holdings. On the other hand, for insurance holding companies that do not run the actual insurance business, there are numerous such obligations. For one, sec. 1b, para. 2 of the VAG [German Insurance Supervision Act] declares the disclosure obligations in sec. 13d, no. 4a and no. 5 of the VAG [German Insurance

[78] See Circular 3/2004, A. II. A bar level of 10 % is given consistently as the threshold for the transactions listed by the legislator. For example, group internal loans, guarantees, and off-balance-sheet transactions are considered significant if they represent 10 % of the required solvency margin (solo-solvency); capital investments are considered significant if they exceed 10 % of the total capital investment of the direct insurance or reinsurance undertaking subject to the additional supervision; reinsurance transactions are significant if they represent at least 10 % of the written premiums from the transaction underwritten (for reinsurance assumed) or the total transaction rendered (for reinsurance ceded).

[79] According to *Lipowsky*, in: Prölss (ed.), VAG [The German Insurance Supervision Act], (12th ed. 2005), sec. 104e, ref. 8, the term "likelihood" referred to in Circular 3/2004, A. IV. does not require the presence of a specific danger.

Supervision Act] as applicable.[80] For another, under sec. 13e, para. 1, sent. 1, no. 3 of the VAG [German Insurance Supervision Act] insurance holding companies must immediately disclose to the BaFin [Federal Financial Supervisory Authority] any changes to the group structure through which the group engages in cross-sector activity.[81] Further, insurance holding companies are required, under sec. 13e, para. 2, sent. 1 of the VAG [German Insurance Supervision Act], to submit a collective notice of their holdings annually to the BaFin [Federal Financial Supervisory Authority]. Insurance holding companies must report the establishment, change, or surrender of holdings to the BaFin [Federal Financial Supervisory Authority] without delay, according to sec. 13e, para. 2, sent. 2 of the VAG [German Insurance Supervision Act]. Such obligations are not part of group supervision under Solvency II.

12.5.2.2 The Disclosure Obligations for Substantive Financial Reporting at the Group Level

The Disclosure of Solvency at the Group Level. The current version of the German Insurance Supervision Act has no requirement for disclosure for the purpose of supervisory assessment of group solvency. In contrast, the draft of a framework directive for Solvency II, which will fundamentally alter the conception of insurance group supervision, includes such requirements.[82] Under Solvency II, group supervision will no longer be exercised as a "solo-plus approach" added on to individual supervision, but rather take its place to a substantial degree. This paradigm shift is evidenced by art. 211, para. 1, sent. 2 of the Draft Solvency II. Accordingly, the provisions for individual supervision of insurance undertakings apply only to group configurations to the extent Title III does not specify otherwise. Art. 216, para. 2 and 3 of the Draft Solvency II introduces a new key indicator for solvency in supervisory law with the consolidated target solvency capital requirement, which is calculated using a standard model or internal model and takes account of diversification effects. Under art. 217, para. 1 of the Draft Solvency II the consolidated Target Solvency Capital Requirement must be calculated at least annually. The direct insurance or reinsurance undertaking at the top of the respective group structure, or the insurance holding company, or the particular undertaking as specified by the supervisory authority is required to submit the result of the calculation, along with the relevant underlying data, to the competent group

[80] On the content of the disclosure obligations under sec. 13d, no. 4a and no. 5 of the VAG [German Insurance Supervision Act] see above, at 12.3.1.2.

[81] Based on the style and scope of changes to group structure, the undertaking at the top of the structure either technically remains an insurance holding company within the meaning of secs. 1b, para. 1, sent. 1 and 104a, para. 2, no. 4 of the VAG [German Insurance Supervision Act], or it becomes a mixed insurance holding company within the meaning of sec. 104a, para. 2, no. 5 of the VAG [German Insurance Supervision Act].

[82] In detail on the changes to group supervision *Krämer*, ZVersWiss (2008), 319 (330 ff.).

supervisory authority.[83] In cases where the risk profile since the last report has undergone considerable change, art. 217, para. 2, sent. 2 of the Draft Solvency II further requires that the Target Solvency Capital Requirement be entirely recalculated and disclosed to the competent supervisory authority.

The Group-specific Disclosure Obligations with respect to Accounting. Sec. 55, para. 2, sent. 2 of the VAG [German Insurance Supervision Act] requires insurance undertakings that prepare group financial statements or group management reports to submit these immediately to the BaFin [Federal Financial Supervisory Authority]. The rule applies accordingly, based on sec. 113, para. 1 and sec. 121a, para. 1, sent. 1 of the VAG [German Insurance Supervision Act], to pension funds and re-insurance undertakings. However, the framework directive for Solvency II contains no submission requirement corresponding to art. 33 at the group level. The submission of the group financial statement to the supervisory authority can still be indirectly assumed from art. 217, para. 1, sent. 2 in conjunction with art. 228, para. 1, sent. 1 of the Draft Solvency II.

12.5.3 The Disclosure Obligations of Risk Reporting at the Group Level

Under sec. 55c, para. 4, sent. 1 of the VAG [German Insurance Supervision Act], direct insurance and reinsurance undertakings that are shareholding undertakings within the meaning of sec. 104a, para. 1, no. 1 of the VAG [German Insurance Supervision Act] are also required to submit risk and audit reports at the insurance group level to the BaFin [Federal Financial Supervisory Authority].[84] Sec. 55, para. 4, sent. 2 of the VAG [German Insurance Supervision Act] further stipulates a submission at the group level for insurance holding companies structured as the parent of an insurance group.

The general reference in art. 258, para. 2, sent. 2 of the Draft Solvency II to art. 35 of the Draft Solvency II has primary relevance to risk reporting at the group level. Under art. 258, para. 2, sent. 2 in conjunction with art. 35, para. 1, sent. 1, 2 (a) in conjunction with art. 36 of the Draft Solvency II, the Member States must standardize the disclosure obligation for risk reporting at the group level in order to provide the competent authorities with information needed for a review of the risk management

[83] On the appropriate supervisory authority for group supervision see art. 210, para. 1 (d) in conjunction with art. 251, para. 1 of the Draft Solvency II.

[84] As with independent insurance undertakings, the risk report mandated under commercial law as part of the management report is of lesser significance from the supervisory perspective. See sec. 55, para. 2, sent. 2 of the VAG [German Insurance Supervision Act] in conjunction with secs. 315, para. 2, no. 2 (a) and 341i of the HGB [German Commercial Code].

structure on a group-wide basis.[85,86] Additionally, art. 248, para. 2, sent. 1 of the Draft Solvency II mandates a specific disclosure obligation on the concentration of risk in the group. Under this provision, the ultimate parent of a direct insurance or reinsurance undertaking, an insurance holding company, or undertaking designated by the supervisory authority must report any significant concentration of risk at the group level to the supervisory authority at least annually.

12.6 The Disclosure Obligations for Financial Conglomerates

Insurance undertakings that are part of a financial conglomerate within the legal definition of sec. 104k, no. 4 of the VAG [German Insurance Supervision Act] or subordinate to a mixed financial holding company as defined by sec. 104k, no. 3 of the VAG [German Insurance Supervision Act] are subject to the additional supervision described in arts. 104k to 104w of the VAG [German Insurance Supervision Act], which contains special disclosure obligations for financial conglomerates.[87] Since the supervision of financial conglomerates is performed through a cooperation between the BaFin [Federal Financial Supervisory Authority] and the German Bundesbank in accordance with standards in sec. 104l of the VAG [German Insurance Supervision Act], all of the disclosures described in the following must be made to both of these organizations.

The current German Insurance Supervision Act includes obligations to notify based on formal organizational grounds with respect to financial conglomerates in sec. 13e, para. 1, sent. 2 of the VAG [German Insurance Supervision Act], which makes reference to sentence 1, numbers 1 and 2. Accordingly, mixed financial holding companies must report the intention to appoint a member of management and the execution of such an appointment as well as the separation of any member of management. Additionally, mixed financial holding companies that are the ultimate parent of a financial conglomerate must submit an annual collective notice reporting the undertakings belonging to the conglomerate.

For financial reporting, secs. 104r and 104q of the VAG [German Insurance Supervision Act] mandate a range of disclosure obligations to the supervisory authority incumbent upon financial conglomerates. With respect to organizational form, sec. 104r, para. 1, 2nd instance, of the VAG [German Insurance Supervision Act] requires parent companies of financial conglomerates within the meaning of sec. 104q, para. 3, sent. 6–8 or para. 4 of the VAG [German Insurance Supervision

[85] See on this point *Dreher/Schaaf*, WM (2008), 1765 (1772 f.).

[86] See on this point art. 250, para. 1 and 252, para. 1 (d) of the Draft Solvency II.

[87] On the supervision of financial conglomerates see *Rittner/Dreher*, Europäisches und deutsches Wirtschaftsrecht [in English: European and German Economic Law], (3rd ed. 2008), sec. 31, ref. 44 ff.

Act] to submit notice of significant internal group transactions within the financial conglomerate. Substantive financial reporting, on the other hand, is found in sec. 104q, para. 2, sent. 2 of the VAG [German Insurance Supervision Act]. According to this passage, parent companies of financial conglomerates must submit to the supervisory authorities all documentation required for a review of own funds sufficiency. In order to avoid the duplication of supervision, both obligations are subject to the condition that no equivalent disclosure requirement exists under the German Credit Services Act.

In contrast, a requirement comparable in scope to sec. 55c, para. 4 of the VAG [German Insurance Supervision Act] for risk reporting by financial conglomerates to the supervisory authorities is not present in the German Insurance Supervision Act. This is surprising given that financial conglomerates must satisfy the requirements for risk management in sec. 104s of the VAG [German Insurance Supervision Act], which contains risk management requirements similar to those in sec. 64a VAG [German Insurance Supervision Act], and that the circular MaRisk VA [Minimum Requirements for Risk Management (Insurance Supervision)] explicitly extends to financial conglomerates in its scope of application.[88] Thus far, the disclosure obligations for risk reporting by financial conglomerates are limited to sec. 104r, para. 1, 1st instance, of the VAG [German Insurance Supervision Act], requiring mixed financial holding companies to immediately report significant concentrations of risk[89] at the level of the conglomerate.

12.7 Further Implications

12.7.1 *The Function of the Reporting and Disclosure Obligations*

Reporting and disclosure obligations in general can be justified only if they legitimately serve the objectives of insurance supervision. The objective of ongoing supervision of insurance undertakings, according to sec. 81, para. 2, sent. 1 of the VAG [German Insurance Supervision Act], is to "avoid or eliminate irregularities". In the context of licensing supervision under sec. 5, para. 2 of the VAG [German Insurance Supervision Act], there is an emphasis on permitting insurance operations only for those undertakings that can be viewed as "able to meet their future liabilities consistently". This corresponds to the objective of ongoing supervision in the context of financial supervision in sec. 81, para. 1, sent. 5 of the VAG [German

[88] See MaRisk VA [Minimum Requirements for Risk Management (Insurance Supervision)], at 2 below 1, as well as the relevant explanatory text.

[89] See on this point the legal definition in sec. 104k, no. 9 of the VAG [German Insurance Supervision Act].

Insurance Supervision Act].[90] Thus, for example, direct insurance and reinsurance undertakings as well as pension funds are required to submit the calculation of their solvency margin to the BaFin [Federal Financial Supervisory Authority] and to provide documentation of the underlying own funds.[91] It is on the basis of this information that the insurance supervisory authority then exercises its powers of financial supervision. However, regulatory intensity differs by the various types of insurance operations. For example, the VAG [German Insurance Supervision Act] differentiates among direct insurance undertakings, reinsurance undertakings, insurance groups, financial conglomerates, insurance holding companies, and pension funds as well as insurance special purpose vehicles.[92]

It is therefore not surprising that the reporting and disclosure obligations are also aligned with these distinctions. The result is a different set of disclosure obligations to the BaFin [Federal Financial Supervisory Authority] for each addressee of insurance supervision. The criteria for each of these duties of disclosure would have to be whether it serves to fulfill a supervisory objective and is consistent with the desired regulatory intensity for a particular type of business activity in the field of insurance. Measured on this basis, however, and with a view to the reporting and disclosure obligations as a whole, the requirements appear to have emerged more as historical accident than systematic design. This can be illustrated by two examples in existing law from the more recent rules related to group supervision: insurance holding companies within the meaning of sec. 1b of the VAG [German Insurance Supervision Act], which have been subject to supervision only since 2004, are required to submit a "collective notice of their holdings" to the BaFin [Federal Financial Supervisory Authority] each year in accordance with sec. 13e, para. 2, sent. 1 of the VAG [German Insurance Supervision Act]. However, sec. 13e, para. 2, sent. 2 of the VAG [German Insurance Supervision Act] requires "immediate notice" of each "establishment, change, or surrender of holdings".[93] The regulation concerning management monitoring at insurance holding companies is also entirely inconsistent and isolated from a broader system.[94] And conversely, with Solvency II, it could happen that in the future important events currently subject to reporting no longer require automatic disclosure. The conversion of a direct insurance or reinsurance undertaking provides an illustration.[95]

Each reporting and disclosure obligation requires not only a factual connection to the objective of supervision. It must also be consistent in its legal consequences with

[90] On the supervision of insurance undertakings see the overview in *Rittner/Dreher*, Europäisches und deutsches Wirtschaftsrecht [in English: European and German Economic Law], (3rd ed. 2008), sec. 31, ref. 19 ff., 93 ff.

[91] See above, 12.3.2.1.

[92] See in detail *Rittner/Dreher*, Europäisches und deutsches Wirtschaftsrecht [in English: European and German Economic Law] (3rd ed. 2008), sec. 31, ref. 38 ff.

[93] See 12.5.2.1, above (second section).

[94] See 12.5.1.2, above.

[95] See 12.3.1.3, above.

the significance of the obligation to insurance supervision. Thus, for example, an outsourcing contract made by an insurance undertaking is valid only if the contract is submitted in advance to the BaFin [Federal Financial Supervisory Authority] in accordance with sec. 13, para. 1a of the VAG [German Insurance Supervision Act].[96] The validity or invalidity of the contract under civil law as a consequence of compliance with the disclosure obligation may, in fact, be still convincing. The opposite is true, however, for the timing under which this legal consequence arises. Three months are supposed to elapse following submission of the contract before it is actually valid under civil law if the contract is concluded with a non-insurance undertaking and the BaFin [Federal Financial Supervisory Authority] does not oppose it. This length of time must be startling, at least in consideration of German and European competition law according to which the significant decisions on the opening of the in-depth proceeding under merger control must be made within 1 month or 25 business days, even in the most difficult cases.[97]

Ultimately, the reporting and disclosure obligations must be consistent with the objective of supervision not only in their requirements but also in their legal consequences. Implementation of the Solvency II Directive would entail a major amendment of the VAG [German Insurance Supervision Act]. Thus, a detailed assessment of the old and new reporting and disclosure obligations to the BaFin [Federal Financial Supervisory Authority] would need to be performed at the latest possible point in time. This is the only way the requirements can be evaluated according to the criterion of consistency with the supervisory objective discussed above, as well as the following criteria, and formulated accordingly in law.

12.7.2 The Scope of the Reporting and Disclosure Obligations

A review of these criteria requires an examination of the scope of reporting and disclosure obligations. The range of such obligations—still excluding the requirements for disclosure to the public in Solvency II[98]—is difficult to capture even under a systematic approach. Nevertheless, insurance undertakings are typically responsible for several, at times extremely extensive, reports on a weekly basis. This raises the question of which factors can be adjusted such that reporting and disclosure obligations are established by law only with factual justification and in keeping with the principle of proportionality.

One adjustable factor can be found in the decision of whether a report or disclosure is required based on an occasion or as a periodic duty. The former places

[96] See 12.3.1.5, above.

[97] See sec. 40, para. 1 of the GWB [Act Against Restraints of Competition] and art. 10, para. 1 Regulation No. 1/2003.

[98] See on this point *Dreher/Schaaf*, n. 5.

an obligation on the insurance undertaking only when certain events occur. Much of the draft of the Solvency II Directive takes this approach. It would apply, for example, to certain developments in the area of outsourcing[99] or solvency capital formation.[100] The current VAG [German Insurance Supervision Act] contains a multitude of periodic reporting duties, such as the annual list of significant shareholders[101] and the collective notice of undertakings constituting a conglomerate.[102] These periodic reporting and disclosure obligations demand a particularly close scrutiny. In each case, the question must be asked, why would an occasion-based obligation not suffice? The tendency toward a large number of periodic reports—which all addressees of the law are specifically required to produce—simply becomes a filing process for an excessive number of voluminous documents rather than a source of insight or even analysis. A factual justification for a deviation from the occasion-based approach would therefore be needed for each periodic reporting and disclosure obligation. That such justification exists, for example, in the area of solvency[103] is obvious. It is highly questionable, however, for the annual collective notice of conglomerate undertakings.[104] Why would it not suffice to report only changes to the group companies?

The critical analysis proposed here for reporting and disclosure obligations applies all the more so when there are both periodic and occasion-based obligations pertaining to the same facts. It is not apparent on any level, for example, why reporting to the BaFin [Federal Financial Supervisory Authority] on significant shareholdings in a direct insurance undertaking, reinsurance undertaking, or pension fund is necessary both annually as well as on the occasion of any changes.[105]

A second adjustable factor that helps determine the scope of reporting and disclosure obligations under insurance supervisory law is the selection of those who would be required to meet these obligations. Staying with the example, the reporting obligation related to significant shareholders in insurance undertakings extends not only to these current shareholders but even to such future shareholders in advance.[106] The reasoning of such rules in the VAG [German Insurance Supervision Act] could be described as "better safe than sorry". But the principle of proportionality and the objective of bureaucracy reduction were probably not among the guiding principles of the rules.

The same is true when leaving the realm of the national insurance supervisory regime, which is ever more frequent due to the internationalization and

[99] See 12.3.1.5, above.
[100] See 12.5.2.2, above (first section).
[101] See 12.3.1.2, above.
[102] See 12.6, above.
[103] See 12.3.2.1, above.
[104] See 12.6, above.
[105] See 12.3.1.2, above.
[106] See 12.3.1.2, above.

Europeanization of the insurance business and financial markets. In the current legal environment, there are often reporting obligations to meet in numerous EU and European Economic Area countries, also for undertakings that belong to insurance groups.[107] Apart from the fundamental matter of how group supervision is resolved at the European level, relief is sorely needed in conjunction with the implementation of the Solvency II Directive from the multiple reporting and disclosure duties, most likely through the bundling of the information flow to a single receiver.

An additional, third adjustable factor influencing the scope of reporting and disclosure obligations specifically concerns undertakings that not only operate insurance businesses but also have a presence in other supervised sectors such as financial services. The legislator is endeavoring to avoid parallel reporting duties under the VAG [German Insurance Supervision Act] and KWG [German Credit Services Act][108] and should continue on this path. Just as with double supervision, double reporting and disclosure obligations would also be disproportionate.

Ultimately the scope of the reporting and disclosure obligations must satisfy the principle of proportionality on the points of suitability, necessity and adequacy. Since 2006, when the German Regulatory Control Council was created, an estimate of the costs specifically associated with information duties of undertakings must be added to the draft legislation of every amendment—irrespective of insurance industry—as "bureaucracy costs".[109] Following the decades-long "enrichment" of the VAG [German Insurance Supervision Act] with such duties, its reform through the implementation of the Solvency II Directive presents a good opportunity to apply these cost/benefit analyses not only in isolated connection with individual reporting and disclosure obligations, but rather as a whole to all continuing and new obligations.

12.7.3 *The Relationship Between the VAG [German Insurance Supervision Act] and Solvency II Directive Regarding Reporting and Disclosure Obligations*

Against this background, it is to ask what influence Solvency II will have on the reporting and disclosure obligations in the VAG [German Insurance Supervision Act]. The assessment of the current set of such obligations in the previous sections

---

[107] See on the example of multi-jurisdictional monitoring of management *Dreher*, ZVersWiss (Supplement, Annual Conference 2006), 375 (413 f.).

[108] See 12.6, above.

[109] See on debureaucratization and in connection with deregulation *Rittner/Dreher*, Europäisches und deutsches Wirtschaftsrecht [in English: European and German Economic Law], (3rd ed. 2008), sec. 7, ref. 120.

suggests four areas in which the rules in the VAG [German Insurance Supervision Act] and Solvency II can be variously contrasted. First is the area in which the Solvency II rules are congruent with the existing VAG [German Insurance Supervision Act] rules or expressly allow for an existing national rule. This includes the reporting duties related to qualifying holding and close ties, for example.[110] Second is the area in which the VAG [German Insurance Supervision Act] contains more obligations than the Solvency II Directive. Examples of this are the duties contained only in the VAG [German Insurance Supervision Act] for disclosure in connection with conversion of direct insurance and reinsurance undertakings,[111] with the investment activity of direct insurance undertakings,[112] and with accounting at the group level.[113] Conversely, a third area comprises the reporting and disclosure rules in the draft Solvency II Directive that are not currently found in the VAG [German Insurance Supervision Act]. Examples are the newly created disclosure obligations in the area of (own) capital structure at the level of the individual insurance undertaking[114] and at group level.[115] These obligations can be attributed to the new solvency approach in the directive. Added to this are numerous reporting and disclosure obligations for reinsurance undertakings that are also planned for introduction in the directive.[116] The fourth and final area is where the rules differ between the VAG [German Insurance Supervision Act] and Solvency II.[117] This can be the case with regard to the subject-matter or the addressees, for example in disclosures of internal group transactions, currently made by the subsidiaries of an insurance holding company, made in the future under Solvency II by the insurance holding company itself.[118]

Against this background, there are certain demands on the European and German legislators. For the final version of the Solvency II Directive, the European legislator must raise the question of whether the reporting and disclosure obligations are based on a coherent system or simply constitute the greatest common denominator of all member state requirements as the result of an add-on process. This question arises, for example, in the fit-and-proper test under art. 42, para. 1 of the draft Solvency II Directive, which extends not only to the members of management also to "all persons who ... have other key functions". An immediate consequence of this passage is extensive reporting duties to enable an assessment of

[110] See 12.3.1.2, above.

[111] See 12.3.1.3, above.

[112] See 12.3.2.4, above.

[113] See 12.5.2.2, above (second section).

[114] See 12.3.2.2, above.

[115] See 12.5.2.2, above (first section).

[116] See, for example, 12.3.2.2, above.

[117] A further distinction can be drawn in this area between mandatory and voluntary Solvency II regulations.

[118] See 12.5.2.1, above (first section).

the suitability and integrity of these persons.[119] Art. 42, para. 2 of the draft Solvency II Directive expressly requires the submission of "all information" in this respect. Since the expression "persons with key functions" in insurance undertakings is very unclear, and the directive is explicitly limited to management in its regulations for group structures,[120] it can be expected that senior staff and supervisory board members of insurance undertakings will also become subjects of management monitoring.[121] Initial pronouncements by CEIOPS confirm this assumption.[122] It is thus demonstrated that the Lamfalussy process[123] will at times afford an exceptional responsibility for the formulation of the implementing measures to the EU Commission and the "technical committees" at Levels 2 and 3 that are subordinate to the framework legislation at Level 1. Particularly in view of the fact that the directive's new approach to solvency will bring a notable increase in the reporting and disclosure requirements for this area,[124] an expansion of equivalent obligations in other regulatory areas of the directive can only be considered with urgent factual justification.

This is also true for the German legislator when implementing the directive, as the draft contains only a minimum stipulation in the central rule of art. 35 under the heading "Information to be provided for supervisory purposes" in paragraph 1, sentence 1.[125] It states the following: "Member States shall require insurance and reinsurance undertakings to submit to the supervisory authorities the information which is necessary for the purposes of supervision. That information shall include at least the information necessary for the following when performing the process referred to in Article 36". For the German legislator—and the BaFin [Federal Financial Supervisory Authority] as its certainly central incentive and advising body—this leads to the question of whether it will limit the reporting and disclosure obligations to those defined in the European law or extend beyond that with the additional stipulations. Even if it does refrain from "piling on" in the implementation, legislative self restraint is also needed prior to that. Where the VAG [German Insurance Supervision Act] currently contains reporting and disclosure duties that are not found in the Solvency II Directive, an effort must be made not just to refrain from "piling on", but to actually reduce the pile in question. In any event, it becomes clear once again that the reporting and disclosure obligations are in need of a complete check-up if they are to become a proportionate and consistent framework of regulations.

---

[119] See 12.2.2.1, above.

[120] See 12.5.1.2, above.

[121] See in opposition to such monitoring of supervisors *Dreher*, ZVersWiss (Supplement, Annual Conference 2006), 375 (382).

[122] See 12.2.2.1, above.

[123] See on this point, 12.2.2.1 and 12.3.2.1, above.

[124] See 12.3.2.1, above.

[125] See on this point 12.2.2.1 and 12.2.2.2, above.

12.7.4 The Concretization and Practical Management of Reporting and Disclosure Obligations

As has just been demonstrated in connection with the Solvency II rules, the rules themselves often remain undefined, ceding the detail of the reporting and disclosure obligations to the level below the framework directive. Thus with respect to solvency supervision, art. 35 of the draft Solvency II Framework Directive requires that insurance undertakings submit "the information which is necessary for the purposes of supervision". Likewise, according to art. 42 of the draft Solvency II Framework Directive, insurance undertakings must provide to the insurance supervisory authority "all information" that they themselves possess for the assessment of fitness in the context of monitoring management and persons with key functions. Thus the scope of required information cannot be derived solely from the Solvency II Directive.

The situation today is often similar in the VAG [German Insurance Supervision Act]. It provides specifics on reporting duties only in a few cases, such as in sec. 13b, para. 1, sent. 2 of the VAG [German Insurance Supervision Act] concerning the intention to establish an office in a foreign EU/European Economic Area state. Beyond this, the BaFin [Federal Financial Supervisory Authority] generally establishes the details of reporting and disclosure obligations through circulars, such as it has for the reporting and disclosure obligations related to the solvency margin[126] and the numerous reporting duties related to investment assets.[127]

However, a legal basis does not always appear to be sufficient or even present. An example is reporting for internal group transactions according to Circular 3/2004 (VA).[128] There is no basis for this in either sec. 104e, para. 3 of the VAG [German Insurance Supervision Act] or in sec. 104g of the VAG [German Insurance Supervision Act]. Instead, sec. 55a, para. 1, sent. 1, no. 1 (b) of the VAG [German Insurance Supervision Act] in conjunction with the Regulation on the Transfer of Competence to adopt Regulations on the basis of sec. 55a, para. 1 VAG [German Insurance Supervision Act] dated 10 Jul. 1986 enables the BaFin [Federal Financial Supervisory Authority] to issue an equivalent regulation. However, in the Circular—now 18 years from the adoption of the legal basis to the issuance of a regulation—the BaFin [Federal Financial Supervisory Authority] writes that the regulation "is planned for a later time. Prior to that, experience with the reporting should be gained in accordance with the present circular".[129] From a legal point of

[126] See above, at 12.3.2.1 on Circular 4/2005 (VA) based on sec. 53c, para. 4 of the VAG [German Insurance Supervision Act].

[127] On the circular issued based on sec. 54d of the VAG [German Insurance Supervision Act] see *Lipowsky*, in: Prölss, VAG [The Insurance Supervision Act], (12th ed. 2005), sec. 54d, ref. 2; *Bähr*, in: Fahr/Kaulbach/Bähr, VAG [The German Insurance Supervision Act], (4th ed. 2007), sec. 54d, ref. 2.

[128] See 12.5.2.1, above (first section).

[129] See A. I. of Circular 3/2004 (VA).

view, therefore, the Circular is a nullity. Due to its abuse of form, it can be considered only as a non-binding inducement for insurance undertakings to provide the relevant information.[130]

Likewise, for the duty of notice for management monitoring under sec. 7a, para. 1 of the VAG [German Insurance Supervision Act], Circular 6/97[131] shall continue to apply. The legislator actually created a legal basis for the notice regulation long ago with sec. 5, para. 6 of the VAG [German Insurance Supervision Act]. The adoption of such a regulation only would be constitutional. In this respect, the notice regulation in the lending sector serves as a model, albeit an old one. It is not an isolated case that the supervisory authority is empowered to issue a regulation, but details are nevertheless governed only on the basis of legally inadmissible circulars. In this regard, too, the need emphasized several times earlier is confirmed: With the implementation of the Solvency II Directive, to review—and if necessary to re-regulate—all reporting and disclosure obligations under the VAG [German Insurance Supervision Act] in a factually coherent manner using clear criteria and with particular emphasis on the fulfillment of supervisory objectives, sufficient empowerment, and proportionality in the requirements, legal consequences, and sanctions. The concept of a single notice regulation for all reporting and notice duties to be governed by administrative regulation is obvious in this respect.

From the point of view of the addressees of the rule, this need for a coherent system of reporting and disclosure obligations unleashed by a melange of European and German laws that are hardly more understandable, in addition to delegated legislation and "simple official practice", is self-evident. But this is especially true from the standpoint of the numerous small and medium-size insurance undertakings. For all undertakings in the insurance industry, but particularly for small and medium-size insurance businesses, the reporting and disclosure obligations not only lead to a costly list of duties that must be worked through in accordance with requirements set by non-legislative rules. An additional phenomenon is emerging as well. This lies in the design of reporting and disclosure obligations in a way that forces the undertakings into a state of constant self-analysis, based on sometimes extremely unclear criteria, possibly with the results of the existing reporting and disclosure obligations. Increasingly, causes for required reporting and disclosure are not just certain events or dates prescribed under supervisory law. Instead, individual rules are attached to developments in the "inner workings" of the insurance undertaking. For example, as part of the solvency supervision under Solvency II, insurance undertakings are required to make disclosure even if an approved model no longer meets requirements.[132] Likewise, under art. 42, para. 3 of the draft Solvency II Directive, a reporting duty arises if a manager or person in

[130] On the non-binding nature of a supervisory circular see also decision of the administrative court of the State of Hessen (Hessischer VGH) of 31 May 2006 – 6 UE 3256/05 (rkr), WM (2007), 392 (393); *Bürkle*, VersR (2007), 1595 (1597).

[131] VerBAV (1997), 311 f.

[132] See above, 12.3.2.1.

a key function no longer meets the fit-and-proper requirements and has therefore been released from the function. However, the extremely indeterminate criteria for this are "excellent reputation and integrity", according to art. 42, para. 1 (b) of the draft Solvency II Directive, in the version already softened by the Common Position of the Council of 24 November 2008. The constant monitoring of the managing board and possibly also supervisory board members and senior staff for their compliance with these terms for the purpose of being able to comply with reporting duties that arise in the event of changes will be a particularly delicate task within an insurance undertaking or insurance group in the future once the directive is adopted and subsequently implemented in the VAG [German Insurance Supervision Act].

12.8 Summary

1. The range of disclosure obligations to the BaFin [Federal Financial Supervisory Authority] under insurance supervisory law can be divided into three main categories, namely, obligations to notify based on formal grounds, disclosure obligations for financial reporting, and disclosure obligations for risk reporting.
2. The scope of disclosure obligations under insurance supervisory law related to changes in the occupancy of "key offices"—mainly, management and members of the supervisory or administrative board—will increase under Solvency II. At least at the level of the individual undertaking, an expansion of key offices subject to disclosure to include the supervisory board and senior staff can be expected.
3. The reporting duty in sec. 13d, no. 7 of the VAG [German Insurance Supervision Act] for new or amended general policy conditions in health and compulsory insurance continues to be permissible under art. 179, para. 2 and art. 204, para. 1 (b) of the Draft Solvency II. Still, the rules give the Member States freedom of choice in this respect.
4. For the disclosure of shareholder structure, the VAG [German Insurance Supervision Act] and Solvency II prescribe a doubling of the reporting duty. On the other hand, Solvency II requires no disclosure of restructuring measures, in deviation from the VAG [German Insurance Supervision Act].
5. With regard to outsourcing of important functions, the disclosure obligations under insurance supervisory law no longer terminate with the execution of the outsourcing for ongoing business operations. Subsequent major developments in the outsourced area will trigger separate reporting duties.
6. With Solvency II, the number of disclosure obligations for the purpose of supervisory assessment of the solvency of direct insurance and reinsurance undertakings will rise sharply. The first pillar of Solvency II allows discretion in structuring through the option of using an internal model for the calculation of the Target Solvency Capital Requirement. The price of this is greater disclosure requirements for the undertaking.

7. Under Solvency II, the disclosure obligations for reinsurance undertakings are more sharply aligned to those for direct insurance undertakings. In particular, reinsurance undertakings will need to adjust to new disclosure obligations in connection with the development of business in foreign countries and the outsourcing of important functions.
8. The requirements in terms of content for the risk and audit reports that have been submitted since 2009 in accordance with sec. 55, para. 1 of the VAG [German Insurance Supervision Act] have not yet been fully clarified even a full year after the regulation took effect. For financial conglomerates, in contrast with parent undertakings in an insurance group, there are at present no disclosure obligations for risk reporting.
9. At the group level, as part of the conceptual modifications to group supervision as a result of Solvency II, the introduction of a consolidated Target Solvency Capital Requirement as a group-specific key solvency indicator can be expected along with the expansion of disclosure requirements in the area of financial reporting.
10. Taken as a whole, the reporting and disclosure obligations under the VAG [German Insurance Supervision Act] cannot be called a closed system. Rather, it proves to be a diverse collection that has arisen over time with considerable differences in the regulatory requirements, intensity, and type for the various addressees of the rules. The same is true of the occasions that trigger reporting and disclosure duties as well as the legal consequences associated with the fulfillment of these duties or sanctions in the event of non-fulfillment.
11. At the latest, the implementation of the Solvency II Directive once it has been adopted must be an inducement to converting the proliferation of reporting and disclosure obligations in the VAG [German Insurance Supervision Act] and the new obligations under the Directive into a consistent system. The following concrete criteria hold primary significance in this effort, in addition to the principle of proportionality in general: the contribution that a reporting and disclosure obligation makes to fulfilling the objectives of supervision in accordance with the VAG [German Insurance Supervision Act]; the review to determine if an event-based reporting and disclosure requirement would suffice in place of regular periodic reporting; the least possible duplication in the format of event-based and periodic duties; likewise no duplication of the obligations through the designation of multiple reporting entities for the same facts; the bundling of reporting and disclosure obligations for undertakings in insurance groups with operations in multiple EU/European Economic Area countries and for undertakings in financial conglomerates that are subject not only to insurance supervision; lastly, the avoidance of reporting and disclosure duties with no clear conditions that are associated with developments in the "inner workings" of insurance undertakings and force them into constant and unmanageable self-analysis.
12. A comparison of the VAG [German Insurance Supervision Act] and the draft Solvency II Directive shows that the reporting and disclosure obligations are only partially aligned. Outside of this, they diverge, or stated differently, the

draft Solvency II Directive brings—to a large extent—new obligations. It also contains an extensive range of minimum rules. In such cases, the German legislator should avoid "piling on" and, in much the same way, he should reduce the pile to the greatest extent possible in those areas where the VAG [German Insurance Supervision Act] now goes further than the Directive in reporting and disclosure obligations.

13. The "enrichment" of reporting and disclosure duties required under law as the result of non-legislative provisions is in particular need of attention. This is true at the European level for the implementation measures at the second and third levels of the Lamfalussy process with regard to the highly indefinite rules in the directive—for example, "all information"—and at the national level for the practice of circulars from the BaFin [Federal Financial Supervisory Authority] circumventing constitutional regulation as codified in the VAG [German Insurance Supervision Act] through recourse to circulars with no basis in law.

Chapter 13
Public Disclosure

Contents

13.1 Introduction 386
13.2 The Objectives and Addressees of the Duties of Public Disclosure 388
13.3 Minimum Content of the Report on Solvency and Financial Condition 391
13.3.1 Overview 391
13.3.2 Financial Reporting 392
13.3.3 Information Related to Formal Organizational Aspects 397
13.3.4 The Information on Risk Reporting 398
13.4 The Duty to Update in the Event of Significant Changes to Published Information 400
13.5 The Duty of Disclosure for Direct Insurance and Reinsurance Undertakings in the National Context 401
13.5.1 Disclosure Duties Under Capital Market Law 401
13.5.2 Disclosure Duties Under Commercial Law 404
13.6 Comparison of the Report on Solvency and Financial Condition Under Solvency II and Publication Required Under National Commercial and Capital Market Law 407
13.6.1 The Equal Rank of the Disclosure Duties of Solvency II and Disclosure Duties Under Capital Market and Commercial Law 407
13.6.2 Content Overlap Between the Report on Solvency and Financial Condition Under Solvency II and the Annual Financial Statement and Management Report 408
13.6.3 Content Overlap Between the Report on Solvency and Financial Condition Under Solvency II and Publications Under Capital Market Law 410
13.7 Disclosure Duties at Group Level 410
13.7.1 Disclosure Duties at Group Level Under Solvency II 410
13.7.2 Disclosure Duties at Group Level in National Context 412
13.7.3 Content Overlap Between the Report on Solvency and Financial Condition at Group Level Under Solvency II and the Annual Financial Statement, Management Report, and Financial Reports Under Capital Market Law 413

First published as "Die Veröffentlichungspflichten von Versicherungsunternehmen gegenüber der Allgemeinheit nach Solvency II" [in English: Insurance Undertakings' Duty of Disclosure to the Public under Solvency II], in: Dreher/Wandt, (eds.), Solvency II in der Rechtsanwendung [in English: Solvency II in Legal Application], Frankfurt Edition, Volume 17, Karlsruhe (2009), 129 ff. with *Martin Schaaf* as coauthor. *Martin Schaaf* was at that time a research assistant at the Law School of Johannes Gutenberg University in Mainz.

M. Dreher, *Treatises on Solvency II*, DOI 10.1007/978-3-662-46290-4_13

13.8 Form of Disclosure in the Report on Solvency and Financial Condition 414
13.9 Protection of Business and Trade Secrets in Public Disclosure Duties 415
13.10 Further Conclusions 416
13.10.1 Regulatory Approach in Public Disclosure Duties 416
13.10.2 Potential Synergies in Fulfillment of Public Disclosure Duties 418
13.10.3 Selection of Publication Date for the Report on Solvency and Financial Condition 419
13.10.4 Relief at Group Level and the Principle of Proportionality 420
13.10.5 Less Favorable Protection of Confidentiality Interests for Direct Insurance and Reinsurance Undertakings Compared to Basel II 421
13.11 Summary 423

Abstract This chapter treats public disclosure, focusing primarily on the Report on Solvency and Financial Condition under art. 51, para. 1 of the Solvency II Directive. Thus, the first subjects to be addressed are the objectives and addressees of public disclosure. Then the required content of the report is examined. This part concludes by addressing the duty to update the report when information changes significantly. Further inquiry is undertaken into the relationship between such public disclosure and the duty of public disclosure as existing in national capital market and commercial law. Next, the duty of public disclosure for groups and the form of the reports are examined. Finally, some general conclusions concerning public disclosure are set forth, based on the determinations reached.

13.1 Introduction

Following the passage of the Solvency II Framework Directive by the European Parliament on 22 April 2009 and its adoption by the European Council on 10 November 2009, legislation at the first stage of the Lamfalussy process concludes with announcement in the official journal scheduled for the last quarter of 2009.[1] Thus far, preparations for the new supervisory regime by the direct insurance and reinsurance undertakings covered under the Directive, as well as the insurance academic literature, have focused almost exclusively on the solvency and governance requirements of the first and second pillars. By contrast, the third pillar—namely, the public disclosure requirements of interest in this chapter—has

[1] A current schedule for the process of implementation into law is available on the homepage of the Commission at http://ec.europa.eu/internal_market/insurance/docs/solvency/solvency2/annex1_timetable_en.pdf.

received very little attention.[2] This is surprising since, with arts. 51 ff. of Solvency II,[3] the issuer of the Directive ultimately imposes a significant change on direct insurance and reinsurance undertakings with respect to disclosure requirements.

As a consequence of the recent international developments in the financial services sector, the insurance supervisory regime in the future will no longer rely solely on disclosure duties on the part of the undertaking to supervisory authorities.[4] Instead, Solvency II expands these present duties—which will still be numerous, partly modified in content, and more extensive—with the addition of comprehensive disclosure obligations to the public.[5] At the center is the "Report on Solvency and Financial Condition", to be published annually by all direct insurance and reinsurance undertakings in accordance with art. 51, para. 1, subpara. 1 of Solvency II.

The present article explores questions associated with this report from a legal perspective. In matters where the draft of the Directive remains general, specific details from the working papers of CEIOPS are drawn upon to facilitate an evaluation of the expected legal landscape based on current information. The analysis first looks at the objectives and addressees of the new duties of public disclosure (Sect. 13.2, below). It then turns to the content required in the Report on Solvency and Financial Condition (Sect. 13.3, below). Related to the report content, the duty to update in accordance with art. 54, para. 1, subpara. 1 of Solvency II will also be discussed (Sect. 13.4, below). An inventory of disclosure duties under current commercial and capital market law in the national context then follows (Sect. 13.5, below). Building on this analysis, the article examines the alignment in content between the emerging disclosure duties in the insurance supervisory regime under Solvency II and the current publication duties in national law (Sect. 13.6, below). The particularities in connection with the corresponding disclosure obligations at the group level are treated separately (Sect. 13.7, below). Following this, the article discusses the formal requirements of publication of the Report on Solvency

---

[2] Apparently thus far, a discussion of the content of public disclosure duties can be found from an economic viewpoint only and briefly in *Nguyen*, WPg (2008), 651 (655 ff.).

[3] The Directive of the European Parliament and of the Council on the taking-up and pursuit of the business of Insurance and Reinsurance – Solvency II in the version of 19 Oct. 2009, available on the Internet at http://register.consilium.europa.eu/pdf/en/09/st03/st03643-re01.en09.pdf; see also the proposal for an amended Directive of 30 Mar. 2009, the second draft of 26 Feb. 2008, COM (2008) 119 final, and concerning the latter, Council, Common Position of 25 Nov. 2008, as well as the first draft of 10 Jun. 2007, COM(2007) 361 final = BR-Drucks. [Document of the German Bundesrat] 510/07. Unless expressly noted otherwise, subsequent statements refer to the version of 19 Oct. 2009, cited as Solvency II.

[4] See in detail on the emerging disclosure duties to supervisory authorities under Solvency II and the current obligations under the VAG [German Insurance Supervision Act] *Dreher*, ZVersWiss (2009), 187 ff. (Chap. 12, above).

[5] Currently, disclosure to the public required by insurance supervisory regime appears only in the specific case of the disclosure of "actuarial and statistical data from which the consideration of gender as a factor in risk assessment is derived", as found in sec. 10a, para. 2a VAG [German Insurance Supervision Act] and likewise provided for in European law.

and Financial Condition (Sect. 13.8, below) and the protection of trade secrets (Sect. 13.9, below). It closes with a number of conclusions, including the potential for synergies and achieving proportionality in the public disclosure duties required under Solvency II (Sect. 13.10, below). Omitted from the subject-matter of this article is the question of which legal requirements arise in terms of organizational measures for meeting the public disclosure duties Solvency II.[6]

13.2 The Objectives and Addressees of the Duties of Public Disclosure

In legislating the public disclosure requirements, the Directive aims to capitalize on the dynamics of the European internal insurance market for supervisory purposes based on the model of banking supervisory law.[7,8] Such public disclosure can increase transparency in the insurance market and remove informational imbalances. Current, reliable information on the financial condition, solvency, and corporate governance of direct insurance and reinsurance undertakings, particularly with respect to risk management, could encourage the addressees of publication, in the process of making economic decisions, to reward risk-conscious businesses that deploy rigorous systems for managing risk, and conversely, to sanction those who do not. This market behavior as intended by the issuer of the Directive could be even further intensified by the option presented in art. 54, para. 2 of Solvency II. Undertakings that make use of this option in the future and thereby voluntarily disclose certain information exceeding the minimum requirements for the Report on Solvency and Financial Condition[9] would set new standards for transparency. A corresponding reward in the marketplace could force other businesses to follow suit. In practice, however, such behavior on the part of individual undertakings should not be expected. This is so because the mandatory information is already very highly detailed; and additional information must not be reselected each year. Rather, under arts. 51, para. 1, subpara. sent 1, and 35, para. 4 of Solvency II, which should also apply in this case, information would need to be "consistent over a longer period of time" and, under art. 55, para. 1 of Solvency II, "ensure the ongoing appropriateness of any information disclosed".

[6] See art. 54 of Solvency II and in this regard *Dreher/Schaaf*, VersR (2009), 1151 (1166 f.).

[7] See the third pillar of Basel II, namely arts. 146 ff. of Directive 2006/48/EC of the European Parliament and of the Council of 14 Jun. 2006 relating to the taking up and pursuit of the business of credit institutions, OJEU No. L 177 of 30 Jun. 2006, p. 1.

[8] See also CEIOPS, Advice to the European Commission on Supervisory Reporting and Public Disclosure in the Framework of the Solvency II Project, March 2007, pnt. 5.2.

[9] The decision for or against voluntary disclosure of additional information is part of the disclosure strategy to be documented in writing in accordance with art. 54, para. 1, 2nd clause of Solvency II. On the disclosure strategy see CEIOPS of 25 Feb. 2009, Draft CEIOPS' Advice for Level 2 Implementing Measures on Solvency II: Reporting Requirements, pnt. 3.22 ff.

At issue, however, is who the addressee of publication is from a legal point of view. The answer to this specific question is the basis for the legal assessment of whether—and to what level of depth and differentiation—the duties to inform are factually justified, and whether they are proportional in their impact on the insurance undertakings they pertain to. Opinions on this matter from a legal point of view have thus far not been forthcoming. From an economic perspective, on the other hand, all persons and institutions that may have a potential interest related to insurance undertakings, with no differentiation among them, have been elevated to addressees of publication with respect to the public disclosure duties incumbent on insurance undertakings.[10] Interest in information from an economic point of view and legal duties to inform or rights to be informed, however, must be strictly separated in consideration of the material and personnel expense associated with disclosure as well as the concomitant interference with secrecy and confidentiality interests. Consequently, from a legal standpoint, the legal addressees of publication must be specifically defined. The objectives of the Solvency II Directive and its specific rules on public disclosure duties are to be used as the relevant criterion,

According to Recital 16, the "main objective" of the Solvency II Directive is the "adequate protection of policy holders and beneficiaries" defined as "any natural or legal person who is entitled to a right under an insurance contract". As "other objectives", meaning secondary objectives, Recital 16 names "financial stability and fair and stable markets", referring to insurance markets. Art. 27 of Solvency II makes reference to this fundamental objective under the heading, "Main objective of supervision" as follows: "Member States shall ensure that the supervisory authorities are provided with the necessary means, and have the relevant expertise, capacity, and mandate to achieve the main objective of supervision, namely the protection of policy holders and beneficiaries". Art. 27 is the introductory paragraph to Chapter 3 of Solvency II, which bears the heading, "Supervisory authorities and general rules". Thus, the subsequent specific rules must be interpreted on the basis of these "general rules". This applies with particular meaning to "public disclosure" in arts. 51, 52, 54 of Solvency II, which indicate no sub-objectives of their own, but instead explicitly stipulate in art. 51, para. 1, subpara. 1 that "the principles set out in paragraph 3 and 4 of Article 35" must also be taken into account for the rules on public disclosure duties. For its part, art. 35 of Solvency II refers directly and correctly to "information to be provided for supervisory purposes". Even in this respect, but independently of it as well, each rule in the

[10]For example, according to *Nguyen*, Rechnungslegung in Versicherungsunternehmen [in English: Accounting in Insurance Undertakings], (2008), p. 928, figure 7–29, included as addressees of publication of insurance undertakings are investors, creditors, shareholders, competitors, ratings agencies, brokers, and government officials. Similarly – although with special emphasis on the policyholder – CEIOPS of 25 Feb. 2009, Draft CEIOPS' Advice for Level 2 Implementing Measures on Solvency II: Reporting Requirements, pnt. 3.32 f. On the other hand, according to CEIOPS of 2 Jul. 2009, Draft CEIOPS' Advice for Level 2 Implementing Measures on Solvency II: Supervisory Reporting and Public Disclosure Requirements, pnt. 3.58, policyholders clearly bring up the rear among the listed addressees of publication.

Directive harks back to the underlying objectives of the Directive. From a legal view, therefore, each must also be evaluated on this basis when the assessment and specification of its content in a rule is at issue.

Consequently, based on the main objective of the Directive, the primary addressees of public disclosure can only be policyholders and insured parties as well as other entitled persons such as beneficiaries. The broader public—such as competitors and shareholders of the insurance undertaking, insurance brokers, the press, and ratings agencies—can only be considered secondary addressees of publication. Nevertheless, Recital 38 of Solvency II must be taken into consideration, as it relates to public disclosure duties. The introductory phrase is of sole interest in this passage: "In order to guarantee transparency . . .". Recital 38 and the disclosure rules themselves provide no other points of reference for the transparency requirement, as seen elsewhere in the Directive. This is logical when considering that each rule in the Directive must be able to contribute to achievement of the objective, as discussed. The European Economic and Social Committee (ESC)[11] and CEIOPS[12] presume that disclosure duties serve "to reinforce market discipline". But this creates no deviation because such statements by the ESC and CEIOPS represent only an analysis of means and consequences with regard to the disclosure mandates found in the actual Directive. Thus market discipline as such is not an objective of the Directive against which the result of public disclosure duties would be gauged from a legal standpoint. Rather, the legal benchmark for evaluating these disclosure rules is formed by the objectives of the Directive, which sees policyholders, insured parties, and others with entitlements arising from insurance contracts as the primary addressees of disclosure, with recognition of any broader public even as a secondary addressee of disclosure under Solvency II as a subordinate aim.

Against this background, the information disclosed in the Report on Solvency and Financial Condition must, on one hand, be sufficiently detailed to motivate economically rational action on the part of the relevant addressees. But the content may neither overload the disclosure addressees with information[13] nor unduly

---

[11] ESC, Opinion on the Proposal for the Solvency II Directive, OJEU (2008), no. C 224 of 30 Aug. 2008, pp. 11, 17.

[12] See CEIOPS, Issues Paper of 1 Nov. 2007, Policy on harmonisation of contents and formats for public disclosure and supervisory reporting, item 6.2. and CEIOPS, Issues Paper of 15 Aug. 2008, Supervisory Review Process and Undertakings Reporting Requirements, pnt. 6.4 (b) as well as CEIOPS of 25 Feb. 2009, Draft CEIOPS' Advice for Level 2 Implementing Measures on Solvency II: Reporting Requirements, pnt. 3.6: "Information required for public disclosure shall [...] support market transparency and market discipline."

[13] See CEIOPS, Issues Paper of 1 Nov. 2007, Policy on harmonisation of contents and formats for public disclosure and supervisory reporting, item 7.2. and similarly CEIOPS, Issues Paper of 15 Aug. 2008, Supervisory Review Process and Undertakings Reporting Requirements, pnt. 6.14 (a) as well as CEIOPS of 25 Feb. 2009, Draft CEIOPS' Advice for Level 2 Implementing Measures on Solvency II: Reporting Requirements, pnt. 3.6.: "Information should be relevant, accessible, meaningful, reliable and readily understandable." On the parallel problem of excessive information by financial market participants from the number of publications issued in the banking

burden the undertakings required to make disclosure.[14] With a view to the high wire act the European legislator must perform, CEIOPS proposes in a catch phrase that each element of the information disclosed be "fit for purpose".[15] Stated plainly, the new disclosure duties are an additional organizational and financial burden on the affected direct insurance and reinsurance undertakings, a burden that it is difficult to overestimate. They must internally collect and process the information needed for disclosure—possibly group-wide. This requires considerable human and material resources. From the perspective of the undertaking, the urgent question arises of whether and to what extent the new disclosure duties under insurance supervisory regime brought on by Solvency II overlap with existing commercial and capital market legal disclosure requirements,[16] creating synergistic opportunities as a result.[17]

13.3 Minimum Content of the Report on Solvency and Financial Condition

13.3.1 Overview

Under art. 51, para. 1, subpara. 1 of Solvency II, the publication of a Report on Solvency and Financial Condition by direct insurance or reinsurance undertakings must proceed in accordance with the principles specified in art. 35, para. 3 and 4 of Solvency II. Under these principles, the information to be disclosed comprises a mix of quantitative and qualitative elements. With regard to time, it can be historic, current, or prospective in nature. The information may originate from internal or

sector see the critique by the German Central Credit Committee, Opinion of 21 Jul. 2006 on the draft of the Solvency Regulation of 31 Mar. 2006, p. 151, which in this respect can also be seen as criticism of the European requirements under Basel II, and on this point *Kemmer*, in: Ballwieser/ Grewe (eds.), Wirtschaftsprüfung im Wandel [in English: Auditing in Transition], (2008), pp. 189, 198.

[14] The issuer of the Directive essentially anticipated this risk: See the reference in art. 51, para. 1, subpara. 1 of Solvency II to art. 35, para. 4 (a) of Solvency II, according to which the information submitted to the supervisory authorities must "reflect the nature, scale and complexity of the business of the undertaking concerned". The same applies with regard to CEIOPS, Issues Paper of 15 Aug. 2008, Supervisory Review Process and Undertakings' Reporting Requirements, pnt. 6.2.

[15] See CEIOPS, Issues Paper of 11 Nov. 2007, Policy on harmonisation of contents and formats for public disclosure and supervisory reporting, items 2. and 7. and referring to this, CEIOPS, Issues Paper of 15 Aug. 2008, Supervisory Review Process and Undertakings' Reporting Requirements, pnt. 4.2. It requires that the "fit for purpose" test has "a clear understanding of why the information is needed and what it will be used for".

[16] On this point see below, at 13.6.

[17] On this point see below, at 13.10.2.

external sources. Its representation must be complete, verifiable, and consistent over a long period of time.

Art. 51, para. 1, subpara. 2 of Solvency II provides a list of the minimum required content for the annual Report on Solvency and Financial Condition. The list is apparently based on the information undertakings must disclose to the supervisory authority for supervisory purposes in accordance with art. 35, para. 1 in conjunction with art. 36 of Solvency II.[18] However, as a result of the different purposes of disclosure, it does not fully match the overall scope and depth of this information.[19]

Although the Commission will provide further substance for the content of the Report on Solvency and Financial Condition through implementation measures at the second level of the Lamfalussy process,[20] the foundation of the report's content is already apparent from the Framework Directive. It can be roughly divided into financial reporting information, information on organizational form, and risk reporting information.[21] The financial reporting information allows the addressees of publication to draw conclusions about the net asset, financial, and earnings position of the undertaking in question. The information on organizational form reveals the design and operational structure of a direct insurance or reinsurance undertaking including information on staff holding key functions. Risk reporting information describes risk management at the undertaking.

13.3.2 Financial Reporting

13.3.2.1 The Description of the Business and Performance

Art. 51, para. 1, subpara. 2 (a) of Solvency II first requires a description of the business and performance of the respective undertaking. The description of the business must start with a presentation of the corporate structure of the undertaking, including the nature and purpose of the undertaking, its legal form, and—if

[18] See in detail on this point *Dreher*, ZVersWiss (2009), 187 (202 ff.) (Chap. 12, above, at 12.4).

[19] On the various supervisory purposes see CEIOPS, Advice to the European Commission on Supervisory Reporting and Public Disclosure in the Framework of the Solvency II Project, March 2007, pnt. 1.8 and CEIOPS of 2 Jul. 2009, Draft CEIOPS' Advice for Level 2 Implementing Measures on Solvency II: Supervisory Reporting and Public Disclosure Requirements, pnt. 3.28.

[20] The legal basis for the implementation measures can be found in art. 56 of Solvency II. On the four levels of the Lamfalussy process see *Rittner/Dreher*, Europäisches und deutsches Wirtschaftsrecht [in English: European and German Economic Law], (3rd ed. 2008), sec. 32, ref. 8 and sec. 33, ref. 5; *Schmolke*, NZG (2005), 912 (913 f.); *id.*, EuR (2006), 432 (433 ff.); *Wandt*, VW (2007), 473; *Bürkle*, (VersR) 2007, 1595 (1596 f.); *id.*, CCZ (2008), 50.

[21] Due to the different content and supervisory purposes, the system of information categories proposed in the literature for disclosures to the supervisory authority – see *Dreher*, ZVersWiss (2009), 187 (189) (Chap. 12, above, at 12.2.1) – cannot be fully applied to the disclosure duties to the public. But the categories align to a large extent.

applicable and along general lines—its shareholder composition.[22,23] It must also provide addressees with the business policy objectives of the insurance undertaking as well as the strategies and time frame under which it pursues them.[24] Here, any changes and adjustments to the business strategy compared to the prior year must be explained. Also required here is the main constituent internal and external business data as well as risks[25] or developments that could positively or negatively influence attainment of the stated objectives.

The description of the performance of an insurance undertaking should provide a portrait to the addressee of economic results during the reporting period.[26] This must be quantified by the inclusion of performance-related figures and the data on key indicators customary in industry practice. Performance-related figures include in particular the profit and loss statement, verifiable cash flow calculations, and presentation of the largest income and expense items in the market segments covered by the undertaking.[27] Common key indicators are the claims ratio,[28] expense ratio[29] or combined claims/expense ratio.[30] These provide the addressee with insight as to the adequacy of an insurance undertaking's premium structure.

[22] For mutual insurance associations, the disclosure of all members who are also policyholders is apparently excluded for reasons of confidentiality. Thus, the disclosure of shareholder composition mainly affects the insurance Aktiengesellschaft (German stock corporation – AG) and Societas Europaea (European Company – SE). It is aimed in particular at the disclosure of shareholders whose influence can be relevant to the development of an undertaking. Therefore, the disclosure of all shareholders known by name is likewise excluded for this reason alone.

[23] See CEIOPS, Advice to the European Commission on Supervisory Reporting and Public Disclosure in the Framework of the Solvency II Project, March 2007, pnt. 4.4 and CEIOPS of 2 Jul. 2009, Draft CEIOPS' Advice for Level 2 Implementing Measures on Solvency II: Supervisory Reporting and Public Disclosure Requirements, pnt. 3.96.

[24] See CEIOPS, Advice to the European Commission on Supervisory Reporting and Public Disclosure in the Framework of the Solvency II Project, March 2007, pnt. 4.8.

[25] Financial and risk reporting overlap at this point.

[26] See also CEIOPS, Advice to the European Commission on Supervisory Reporting and Public Disclosure in the Framework of the Solvency II Project, March 2007, pnt. 4.7 and CEIOPS of 25 Feb. 2009, Draft CEIOPS' Advice for Level 2 Implementing Measures on Solvency II: Reporting Requirements, pnt. 3.38, where a separation between "performance from investment activities" and "performance from underwriting activities" is proposed.

[27] On segmentation see art. 80 of Solvency II.

[28] The claims ratio for a financial year is the ratio of the undertaking's expense for insured events (deducting for the reinsurance share) to its earned premiums.

[29] The expense ratio describes the ratio of expenses for insurance operations to earned premiums.

[30] The combined claims/expense ratio is relevant only for indemnity insurance and not the insurance of persons. It compares the combination of insurance claims and operational expenses to earned premiums.

13.3.2.2 The Description of the Bases of Valuation for Solvency Purposes

In addition, under art. 51, para. 1, subpara. 2 (d) of Solvency II, the report by the undertaking must provide separate descriptions of the bases and methods used in the valuation of assets, technical provisions, and other liabilities recognized for solvency purposes. All significant differences from the valuation required under commercial law performed in preparation of the annual financial statement must be explained. With regard to the valuation of assets for solvency purposes, differences from the valuation required under commercial law, such as those related to accounting for hidden reserves, may arise from art. 75 of Solvency II.[31] Deviations requiring explanation in the valuation of technical provisions maybe based, for example, on the methods used for solvency calculations, which conceptually differ, sometimes significantly, from the methods allowed under commercial law. While the valuation of technical provisions under arts. 76 ff. of Solvency II are essentially based on their fair market value, the valuation methods under commercial law are characterized by the principle of caution.[32]

With respect to the valuation of technical provisions, the Report on Solvency and Financial Condition must contain, above all, the total amount as well as the amount in each provision category.[33,34] The "best estimate" and risk margin components, under art. 77, para. 1 of Solvency II, must be shown separately. The report must also explain the method used in determining both the "best estimate" and the risk margin. And it must provide information to the addressees with regard to the assets designated for coverage of the technical reserves as well as the target and Minimum Capital Requirements. The structure of the capital investment portfolio, at a minimum, must also be described along with an explanation of concentrations in particular sectors, regions or with certain counterparties.[35] Finally, insurance

---

[31] Referring to the second draft (see n. 3), the general explanatory text for art. 74 of Solvency II, requires – in conjunction with implementation measures by the Commission adopted on the basis of the authority in paragraph 2 – valuation standards for solvency purposes for all assets based on the consideration of fair value.

[32] See sec. 341e, para. 1 of the HGB [German Commercial Code]. On financial accounting for technical provisions under secs. 341e to 341h of the HGB [German Commercial Code] in conjunction with the Regulation on Insurance Accounting (RechVersV) and the underlying valuation methods see, as one example among many, *Nguyen*, Rechnungslegung von Versicherungsunternehmen [in English: Accounting in Insurance Undertakings], (2008), p. 331 ff. with further references.

[33] In the terminology of the HGB [German Commercial Code], technical reserves are divided into excess premium, coverage provisions, provisions for outstanding claims, provisions performance-related and non-performance-related premium refunds, equalization and similar provisions as well as other technical provisions.

[34] See CEIOPS, Advice to the European Commission on Supervisory Reporting and Public Disclosure in the Framework of the Solvency II Project, March 2007, pnt. 4.9.

[35] See CEIOPS, Advice to the European Commission on Supervisory Reporting and Public Disclosure in the Framework of the Solvency II Project, March 2007, pnt. 4.10.

undertakings subject to disclosure must describe other liabilities relevant to solvency, such as pension provisions or provisions for currency risks.[36]

13.3.2.3 The Description of Capital Management

A focus of financial reporting to the public is the description of capital management of an insurance undertaking under art. 51, para. 1, subpara. 2 (e) of Solvency II.[37] The description must include at least the structure and amount of own funds as well as their quality level[38] (i). According to art. 51, para. 2, subpara. 1 of Solvency II, the most important differences with respect to the value of these elements in the annual financial statement must be explained and their capital transferability[39] must be briefly described. Differences in the amount of Solvency II own funds as compared with their corresponding balance sheet items may arise in particular from the full-fair-value approach for all assets and liabilities required under Solvency II, but also from the consideration of "ancillary own funds" for solvency purposes within the meaning of art. 89 Solvency II. With the exception of the unpaid share capital or initial funds as specified in art. 89, para. 1, subpara. 2 (a) of Solvency II, ancillary own funds are specifically not own funds as meant in sense of a balance sheet.[40] Under art. 50, para. 2 of Solvency II, major changes in comparison to the prior year must be described and analyzed.

The amount of the Minimum Capital Requirement and the Target Solvency Capital Requirement must also be provided (ii).[41] According to art. 51, para. 2, subpara. 2 of Solvency II, if an insurance undertaking uses an internal model

---

[36] See CEIOPS, Advice to the European Commission on Supervisory Reporting and Public Disclosure in the Framework of the Solvency II Project, March 2007, pnt. 4.11.

[37] See in detail on the individual requirements CEIOPS of 25 Feb. 2009, Draft CEIOPS' Advice for Level 2 Implementing Measures on Solvency II: Reporting Requirements, pnt. 3.45; CEIOPS of 2 Jul. 2009, Draft CEIOPS' Advice for Level 2 Implementing Measures on Solvency II: Supervisory Reporting and Public Disclosure Requirements, pnt. 3.99.

[38] On the quality classification of own funds under Solvency II see second draft (n. 3), explanatory text for arts. 86 to 90 of Solvency II.

[39] Capital transferability refers to the capacity of an undertaking, in the event it incurs internal losses limited to a particular area, to move capital to where it is specifically needed.

[40] Thus ancillary own funds specifically include liabilities that direct insurance and reinsurance undertakings can call on for the purpose of increasing their own capital, for example, supplementary contributions and letters of credit. These require supervisory approval prior to their consideration as own funds in accordance with art. 90, para. 1 of Solvency II.

[41] On the (Target) Solvency Capital Requirement and Minimum Capital Requirement see art. 100 ff. and art. 128 ff. Solvency II and from the literature, for example, *Romeike*, in: Romeike/Müller-Reichart (eds.), Risikomanagement in Versicherungsunternehmen [in English: Risk Management in Insurance Undertakings], (2nd ed. 2008), pp. 115, 135 ff.; *Nguyen*, Handbuch der wert- und risikoorientierten Steuerung von Versicherungsunternehmen [in English: Handbook of Value and Risk-based Management of Insurance Undertakings], (2008), p. 293; *Dreher*, VersR (2008), 998 (1000).

to calculate the Target Solvency Capital Requirement, the report must indicate, for comparative purposes, the hypothetical amount of Target Solvency Capital Requirement that would have resulted from use of the standard formula within the meaning of art. 103 of Solvency II.[42] Additionally, significant differences resulting from use of the internal model versus the standard formula must be explained, particularly with regard to the methods applied to the identification, analysis, and valuation of risk, the consideration of diversification effects among individual risks, simulated stress tests, and model validation (iii).[43] A more expansive disclosure duty based on the amendment proposed by the Council of November 25, 2008 in connection with the Target Solvency Capital Requirement appears under art. 51, para. 1, subpara. 2 (e) (iii) of Solvency II. It obligates an undertaking to disclose if it made use of the disputed—confined to the pensions business—Member State option under art. 304 of Solvency II, in the valuation of equity price risk.[44]

If the supervisory authority has imposed a capital add-on in accordance with art. 37 of Solvency II, the report must disclose this information and provide a summary of the supervisory authority's reasons for the action.[45] Any non-compliance with the target or Minimum Capital Requirement during the reporting period must be described, even if the problem has since been resolved. The origin and consequences of the non-compliance must be explained along with any remedial measures taken (iv).

---

[42] Under art. 51, para. 2, subpara. 2, sent. 4 of Solvency II, public disclosure of the Solvency Capital Requirement may transpire under notice that the final amount is still subject to supervisory assessment.

[43] See CEIOPS, Advice to the European Commission on Supervisory Reporting and Public Disclosure in the Framework of the Solvency II Project, March 2007, pnt. 4.23 and CEIOPS of 2 Jul. 2009, Draft CEIOPS' Advice for Level 2 Implementing Measures on Solvency II: Supervisory Reporting and Public Disclosure Requirements, pnt. 3.79.

[44] The optional approach for valuation of equity risk regulated in art. 304 of Solvency II ("duration-based equity risk sub-module") is a value-at-risk approach as described in art. 106 in conjunction with 104, para. 4 of Solvency II. In the financial services sector, value-at-risk is a traditional method for measuring market and interest-rate risk. It represents the negative change in the value measured in monetary units that will not be exceeded at a given probability (confidence level) within a certain period of time. See in general on value-at-risk *Nguyen*, Handbuch der wert- und risikoorientierten Steuerung von Versicherungsunternehmen [in English: Handbook of Value and Risk-based Management of Insurance Undertakings], (2008), p. 18; *Müller-Reichart/Romeike*, in: Romeike/Müller/Reichert (eds.), Risikomanagement in Versicherungsunternehmen [in English: Risk Management in Insurance Undertakings], (2nd ed. 2008), pp. 47, 78. The standard approach assumes a fixed one-year time frame at a confidence level of 99.5 %. The alternative approach, presented in art. 304 of Solvency II, is available to undertakings at the outset only if it is recognized in Member State law. If it is so recognized, undertakings may choose a value-at-risk approach based on the usual duration of an equity investment rather than a rigid one-year time frame. However, it is valid only if the confidence level insures that policyholders and beneficiaries are protected to the same extent required by art. 101 of Solvency II.

[45] See, however, the opening clause to art. 51, para. 2, subpara. 3 of Solvency II.

13.3.3 Information Related to Formal Organizational Aspects

Art. 51, para. 1, subpara. 2 (b) of Solvency II stipulates that a description of the system of governance of the insurance undertaking shall be set forth in the Report on Solvency and Financial Condition. CEIOPS requires a detailed description of the organizational structure in this regard.[46] This description includes the composition of management, the allocation of duties among its members, the composition of the supervisory body as well as the responsibilities of senior staff from the operating areas—to at least the level directly below management in the undertaking's hierarchy. These also always include the heads of the staff functions mandated under arts. 41 ff. of Solvency II, risk management, compliance, and internal audit, in addition to the actuary.[47]

An explanation of the fitness and integrity for each of these key function holders in the undertaking is likewise required.[48] These explanations should enable the addressees of the publications to judge whether the functional staff members entrusted with key tasks in the undertaking satisfy the "fit and proper" requirement in art 42, para. 1 of Solvency II. According to CEIOPS, however, a brief "statement of compliance" should suffice. With regard to the design and operating structure of the undertaking, the allocation of tasks and responsibilities as well as organization of staff functions involved in crisis prevention—risk management, compliance, and internal audit—must be presented.[49] Their activities must be delineated by the responsibilities of the operating areas[50] Lastly, the report must provide a brief description of internal reporting to management, and specifically, the reporting lines.

---

[46] See CEIOPS, Advice to the European Commission on Supervisory Reporting and Public Disclosure in the Framework of the Solvency II Project, March 2007, pnt. 4.8.

[47] See Recitals 30, 33, 34; CEIOPS, Advice to the European Commission on Supervisory Reporting and Public Disclosure in the Framework of the Solvency II Project, March 2007, pnt. 4.8 (b); CEIOPS, Issues Paper of 11 Mar. 2008, Implementing Measures on System of Governance, pnt. 5.2 as well as – especially clear – CEIOPS, Consultation Paper No. 33 of 26 Mar. 2009, Draft CEIOPS' Advice for Level 2 Implementing Measures on Solvency II: System of Governance, pnts. 3.31 and 3.43: "The other 'key functions' are those considered important and critical in the system of governance and include risk management, compliance, internal audit [...] functions. Additional key functions may be relevant".

[48] See only CEIOPS of 2 Jul. 2009, Draft CEIOPS "Advice for Level 2 Implementing Measures on Solvency II: Supervisory Reporting and Public Disclosure Requirements", pnt. 3.113.

[49] See CEIOPS, Advice to the European Commission on Supervisory Reporting and Public Disclosure in the Framework of the Solvency II Project, March 2007, pnt. 4.12.

[50] On the organizational segregation of the risk-management, compliance, and internal audit functions see *Dreher*, VersR (2008), 998 (1003); *Bürkle*, VersR (2007), 1595 (1599 f.); *id.* CCZ (2008), 50 (55).

13.3.4 The Information on Risk Reporting

In part, the information on risk reporting to be disclosed under art. 51, para. 1, subpara. 2 (b) and (c) of Solvency II is closely connected to the information on financial reporting and organizational form. The core aim of risk reporting is to enable the addressees of disclosure to reliably assess whether the risk management employed is adequate for undertaking's risk profile. With the obligatory disclosure of "the risk exposure, concentration, mitigation and sensitivity" in the Report on Solvency and Financial Condition in accordance with art. 51, para. 1, subpara. 2 of Solvency II, the Directive casts a very wide net in terms of content. Moreover, this disclosure must be made "separately for each category of risk". With the six risk categories specified in art. 13, nos. 30–35 of Solvency II (underwriting risk, market risk, credit risk, operational risk, liquidity risk, and concentration risk), precisely 24 disclosure duties with respect to risk instantly result by multiplying these with the four reporting elements named in the Directive.[51]

Against this background, it is not surprising that the relevant CEIOPS papers address all risk related areas of an insurance undertaking, including risk strategy, the risk management process, and the risk management organization.[52] The methods and procedures for risk identification, assessment, management, and monitoring must be discussed for each risk category.[53] The report is structured and designed to devote significant attention to diversification and concentration effects. The report must also describe the cooperation between the risk management function and the business operating areas that are required to practice risk management.[54] If the direct insurance or reinsurance undertaking uses an internal model to

[51] On the extensive scope of risk-related disclosure duties see the requirements extending over nearly 5 pages on CEIOPS of 25 Feb. 2009, Draft CEIOPS' Advice for Level 2 Implementing Measures on Solvency II: Reporting Requirements, pnt. 3.41. According to this, for example, the report on risk exposure for each the six risk categories should include the development of the risks over the past financial years and a projection by management for the coming financial years; it should describe the products and investments underlying the respective risks, disclose at least the upper limit, and include a statement on risk tolerance and risk-bearing capacity. Special requirements are added for "financial instruments".

[52] See CEIOPS, Advice to the European Commission on Supervisory Reporting and Public Disclosure in the Framework of the Solvency II Project, March 2007, pnt. 4.12; especially clear, CEIOPS of 25 Feb. 2009, Draft CEIOPS' Advice for Level 2 Implementing Measures on Solvency II: Reporting Requirements, pnt. 3.39 sub B.3. as well as CEIOPS of 2 Jul. 2009, Draft CEIOPS Advice for Level 2 Implementing Measures on Solvency II: Supervisory Reporting and Public Disclosure Requirements, pnts. 3.114 to 3.116.

[53] See CEIOPS, Advice to the European Commission on Supervisory Reporting and Public Disclosure in the Framework of the Solvency II Project, March 2007, pnt. 4.12.

[54] See CEIOPS, Advice to the European Commission on Supervisory Reporting and Public Disclosure in the Framework of the Solvency II Project, March 2007, pnt. 4.12. The delineation of tasks and responsibilities between the risk-management, compliance, and internal audit functions was addressed under organizational form; see above, at 13.3.3. In view of the significance to risk management of organizational separation at direct insurance and reinsurance undertakings of the staff functions involved in crisis prevention, the delineation of inter-functional tasks and

calculate the Target Solvency Capital Requirement, the report must describe its integration with the risk management system.[55] In several places, CEIOPS also emphasizes the need to present the key points of regular and ad hoc internal reporting to the undertaking's management.

Nevertheless, although "enrichment" of risk reporting to the public is expected in secondary law despite the already broadly drafted disclosure mandates in art. 51, para. 1, subpara. 2 (b) and (c) of Solvency II, the comparison of the rules by which insurance supervisory authorities must be informed—which, in Germany, is the BaFin [Federal Financial Supervisory Authority]—and those by which the public must be informed, is surprising. The duties to inform the insurance supervisory authorities with respect to risk are laid down in art. 35, para. 1 sent. 1 and 2, and in art. 36 of Solvency II. In anticipation of this, the German legislator enacted secs. 55c and 64a of the VAG [German Insurance Supervision Act] as part of the 9th VAG [German Insurance Supervision Act] amendment, in effect since 1 January 2008.[56]

Under sec. 55c, para. 3 of the VAG [German Insurance Supervision Act], insurance undertakings may "submit a summary" in place of the full risk and audit reports to the supervisory authority if these reports contain such summary. For this rule, the German legislator could in the future invoke the admissibility under the Directive of the submission of limited reports by referring to the power under art. 36, para. 6 of Solvency II, given even to the supervisory authority, to mandate the structure of the report. However, for disclosure to the public, the obligations described above with the 24-part structure are firm due to the mandatory Directive rules in this respect. Ultimately, this can only mean that risk reporting to the supervisory authority may be limited to submission of a summary risk report while the reporting by an insurance undertaking to the public must meet risk disclosure standards that are significantly more detailed and in-depth. The most recent policy documents from CEIOPS on implementation measures at the second level of the Lamfalussy process confirm this impression. In these papers, CEIOPS requires—for policyholders, specifically—an easily understandable summary of the main statements in the Report on Solvency and Financial Condition.[57] Notably, the summary is not intended to replace the detailed disclosures in the report, but rather supplement these as a separate, additional part.

---

responsibilities can also be counted as risk reporting information. In this respect, the two information categories are hardly distinct from one another.

[55] On integration of the internal model with risk management see art. 44, para. 5 of Solvency II.

[56] See, on the entirety, *Dreher/Schaaf*, VersR (2009), 1151 ff.; *Dreher*, VersR (2008), 998 ff.; *id.*, ZVersWiss (2009), 187 (202 ff.) (Chap. 12, above, at 12.4).

[57] See CEIOPS of 25 Feb. 2009, Draft CEIOPS' Advice for Level 2 Implementing Measures on Solvency II: Reporting Requirements, pnt. 3.33; CEIOPS of 2 Jul. 2009, Draft CEIOPS' Advice for Level 2 Implementing Measures on Solvency II: Supervisory Reporting and Public Disclosure Requirements, pnts. 3.91 to 3.94.

13.4 The Duty to Update in the Event of Significant Changes to Published Information

If major developments occur involving substantial change to the information published in the Report on Solvency and Financial Condition, art. 54, para. 1, subpara. 1 of Solvency II requires direct insurance and reinsurance undertakings to disclose these changes, including the relevant information as to their nature and impact. As examples, art. 54, para. 1, subpara. 2 of Solvency II names two potential developments: the first is any non-compliance with the Minimum Capital Requirement if the supervisory authority holds the view that the relevant undertaking cannot present a recovery plan within 3 months, (a)[58]; the second is any material non-compliance with the Target Solvency Capital Requirement if the supervisory authority does not receive a reasonable recovery plan within 2 months (b).[59] Upon the respective request by the supervisory authority, and in accordance with art. 54, para. 1, subpara. 3 and 4 of Solvency II, the undertaking concerned must disclose the amount of non-compliance with the capital requirement in such cases, together with an explanation of its origins and consequences as well as any remedial measures.[60] Other "major developments" not specifically mentioned in the Directive that could require an update to the Report on Solvency and Financial Condition include an unexpected drop in share price on the equity market and material changes to legal conditions.

[58] In this respect, lit. (a) makes reference to art. 139, para. 1 of Solvency II. Accordingly, direct insurance and reinsurance undertakings must notify the supervisory authority immediately when the Minimum Solvency Capital Requirement is no longer covered or they see a risk that such a situation could arise within three months. On the submission of a recovery plan see art. 139, para. 2 of Solvency II.

[59] In this respect, lit. (b) makes reference to art. 138, para. 1 of Solvency II. Accordingly, direct insurance and reinsurance undertakings must notify the supervisory authority immediately when the Target Solvency Capital Requirement is no longer covered or they see a risk that such a situation could arise within three months. On the submission of a recovery plan see art. 138, para. 2 of Solvency II.

[60] On this authority by the supervisory authority to induce the leadership of a direct insurance or reinsurance undertaking to inform the public of critical developments and the proposal by CEIOPS for "naming and shaming" see *Wandt*, VW (2007), 473 (476); *Nguyen*, WPg (2008), 651 (656).

13.5 The Duty of Disclosure for Direct Insurance and Reinsurance Undertakings in the National Context

13.5.1 Disclosure Duties Under Capital Market Law

13.5.1.1 Area of Application

The current German Insurance Supervision Act does not contain public disclosure duties for direct insurance and reinsurance undertakings.[61] However, disclosure duties under supervisory law that may also have direct relevance for insurance undertakings are stipulated in capital market law. Of primary interest in the present context are the disclosure duties under the WpHG [German Securities Trading Act].[62] Of course, these do not extend to all insurance undertakings. They affect only those insurance undertakings that fall under the legal definition of domestic issuers in sec. 2, para. 7 of the WpHG [German Securities Trading Act].[63] Domestic issuers are essentially defined here as issuers whose country of origin is the Federal Republic of Germany. But, under sec. 2, para. 7, no. 1 of the WpHG [German Securities Trading Act], it does not apply if the securities issued[64] are admitted for trading exclusively on an organized market in a country outside of Germany but within the EU/European Economic Area and, in that country, the undertaking must comply with disclosure and reporting duties under the Transparency Directive.[65] Such issuers are not subject to the additional domestic disclosure duties and the associated supervision by the BaFin [Federal Financial Supervisory Authority] under securities supervisory law. Inversely, issuers whose country of origin is not Germany but another country within the EU/European Economic Area whose securities are admitted for trading on an organized market exclusively in Germany also fall under the definition of domestic issuer in sec. 2, para. 7, no. 2 of the WpHG [German Securities Trading Act]. These issuers are subject to the disclosure rules of

---

[61] On the duty under sec. 55, para. 3 of the VAG [German Insurance Supervision Act] see below, n. 78.

[62] On the individual disclosure duties under the German Securities Acquisition and Takeover Act (WpÜG) see the section immediately following, under 3.5.2.

[63] See for a critique of conformity under European law of the limitation of the regular disclosure duties – reviewed below – incumbent on domestic issuers *Mülbert/Steup*, NZG (2007), 761 (765 f.).

[64] The legal definition of "securities" is found in sec. 2, para. 1 of the WpHG [German Securities Trading Act].

[65] Directive 2004/109/EC on the harmonisation of transparency requirements for information about issuers whose securities are admitted to trading on a regulated market and amending Directive 2001/34/EC of 15 Dec. 2004, OJEU no. L 390 of Dec. 31, 2004, p. 38; on implementation in Germany see *Rittner/Dreher*, Europäisches und deutsches Wirtschaftsrecht [in English: European and German Economic Law], (3rd ed. 2007), sec. 33 ref. 4, n. 21 with further references.

the German Securities Trading Act and to supervision by the BaFin [Federal Financial Supervisory Authority] under German securities supervisory law.

13.5.1.2 Disclosure Duties with Respect to Ownership Structure Based on Certain Events

The first group of disclosure duties under capital market law pertains to the event-based duties incumbent upon stock issuers. Under sec. 26, para. 1, sent. 1 of the WpHG [German Securities Trading Act], a domestic issuer of stock must disclose, within 3 days of receiving the information, when certain holdings thresholds requiring notification of the issuer by the relevant shareholder or derivative beneficiary[66] have been met, not met, or exceeded. Sentence 2 prescribes a comparable disclosure duty with respect to shares held by the issuer itself. Under sec. 26a of the WpHG [German Securities Trading Act], a domestic issuer must disclose the total number of voting rights at the end of any calendar month in which an increase or decrease in voting rights took place.

There may also be additional publication duties in connection with acquisition of a controlling position in a target company under sec. 35 WpÜG [German Securities Acquisition and Takeover Act].[67]

13.5.1.3 Regular Financial Reporting to the Public

The Annual Financial Report

A second group of disclosure duties under security supervisory law pertains to periodic financial reporting. According to sec. 37v, para. 1 of the WpHG [German Securities Trading Act] an undertaking that qualifies as a domestic issuer of securities[68] is required to publish an annual financial report no later than 4 months after the conclusion of each financial year. The annual report is composed of an auditing financial statement, a management report, and a related statement of

[66] In this respect, the requirement refers to sec. 21 of the WpHG [German Securities Trading Act], which itself establishes a disclosure duty to the issuers and the BaFin [Federal Financial Supervisory Authority] but not to the public. The relevant holdings thresholds are 3 %, 5 %, 10 %, 15 %, 20 %, 25 %, 30 %, 50 % and 75 % of total voting rights. On the disclosure obligation under sec. 21 WpHG [German Securities Trading Act] see, among many such references, *Weber-Rey*, in: Habersack/Mülbert/Schlitt (eds.), Handbuch der Kapitalmarktinformation [in English: Guide to Capital Market Information], (2008), sec. 23 ref. 65 ff.

[67] See in detail on this point, particularly on the parallels in the rules of secs. 21 ff. WpHG [German Securities Trading Act] and sec. 35 WpÜG [German Securities Acquisition and Takeover Act], *Weber-Rey*, in: Habersack/Mülbert/Schlitt (eds.), Handbuch der Kapitalmarktinformation [in English: Guide to Capital Market Information], (2008), sec. 23 ref. 154 ff.

[68] See, however, the restriction in sec. 37z, para. 1 of the WpHG [German Securities Trading Act].

compliance (financial statement affidavit) in accordance with secs. 264, para. 2, sent. 3, 289, para. 1 sent. 5 of the HGB [German Commercial Code].[69] Thus, sec. 37v, para. 1 of the WpHG [German Securities Trading Act] forms a constituent part, however, only when the undertaking is not already required to disclose the accounting documentation in the annual financial report under commercial law, and in particular under sec. 325 HGB [German Commercial Code].[70] This is specifically the case for domestic issuers registered in Germany. For such undertakings, only the disclosure duties under commercial law are relevant.

The Interim Reports

For this reason, more individual significance may be assigned to the interim disclosure duties of secs. 37w, para. 1, sent. 1 and 37x, para. 1, sent. 1 of the WpHG [German Securities Trading Act]. Under sec. 37w, para. 1, sent. 1 of the WpHG [German Securities Trading Act], mainly the issuers of stock as well as issuers of debt securities within the meaning of sec. 2, para. 1 sent. 1 of the WpHG [German Securities Trading Act] must publish a semi-annual report.[71] The semi-annual report is composed of a condensed financial statements, the interim management report, and a financial statement affidavit with respect to these.[72] In accordance with sec. 37w, para. 4, sent, 1 of the WpHG [German Securities Trading Act], the interim management report must include, at a minimum, the "significant events" during the reporting period and their impact on the condensed financial statements as well as the major opportunities and risks expected in the 6 months following reporting period. Specific details can be found in this respect in the German Accounting Standard (DRS) no. 16.[73]

---

[69] In detail on the content of the annual financial report see *Goetze/Wunderlich*, in: Habersack/ Mülbert/Schlitt (eds.), Handbuch der Kapitalmarktinformation [in English: Guide to Capital Market Information], (2008), sec. 9, ref. 20; *Mülbert/Steup*, NZG (2007), 761 (764).

[70] See BT-Drucks. [Document of the German Bundestag] 16/2498, p. 43.

[71] Excluded from the disclosure obligation under sec. 37w, para. 1 S. 1, 2nd clause of the WpHG [German Securities Trading Act] are issuers whose equity securities are debt titles that fall under sec. 2, para. 1, sent. 1, no. 2 of the WpHG [German Securities Trading Act] or that establish at least a conditional right to acquire securities in accordance with sec. 2, para. 1, sent. 1, no. 1 or 2 of the WpHG [German Securities Trading Act]. Additional reference is made to the exceptions under sec. 37z, para. 1 of the WpHG [German Securities Trading Act].

[72] The condensed balance sheet and the condensed profit and loss statement within the condensed financial statements must contain the same headings and subtitles as the prior full-year financial statements. Additional line items must be included only if their omission from the report would render it misleading. The interim management report must provide at least the important events within the reporting period and their impact on the issuer. The major opportunities and risks for the six months of the financial year following the reporting period must be described; see BT-Drucks. [Document of the German Bundestag] 16/2498, p. 44 f.

[73] German Accounting Standard no. 16 took effect on 5 May 2008. It is directly applicable only to undertakings that are subject to semi-annual or interim reporting and at the same time are parent

Sec. 37x, para. 1, sent. 1 of the WpHG [German Securities Trading Act] requires the management of domestic issuers that do not publish quarterly reports to prepare and publish an "interim statement" no sooner than 10 weeks after the beginning and no later than 6 weeks before the end of the first and respectively the second half of the financial year.[74,75] This statement must allow an assessment of how the operations of the issuers business have developed since the end of the most recent published annual or semi-annual financial report. At a minimum, under sec. 37x, para. 2, sent. 2 of the WpHG [German Securities Trading Act], the "significant events and transactions" of the period of the statement must be described and their implications on the financial position of the issuer presented.[76]

13.5.2 Disclosure Duties Under Commercial Law

13.5.2.1 Area of Application and Scope of Publication Requirements Under Commercial Law

Under sec. 341a, para. 1, sent. 1 of the HGB [German Commercial Code] all direct insurance and reinsurance undertakings[77] regardless of legal form must issue annual financial statements including annex and a management report in accordance with the requirements for large corporations laid down in secs. 264–289 of the HGB [German Commercial Code]. The annual financial statements and management report must be submitted in electronic form to the publisher of the electronic Federal Gazette in accordance with sec. 341l, para. 1, sent. 1 in

companies subject to group accounting. Nevertheless, application of the standard is also explicitly recommended for individual undertakings subject to reporting. DRS [German Accounting Standard] no. 16, pnt. 41 contains a non-exhaustive listing of possible major events. These may be of an external nature, such as in the case of changes to legal conditions, developments in the economy, or interest rates. Alternatively, they may be internal in nature, including, for example, restructuring measures, the introduction of new products, or the development of new markets.

[74] Regardless of the ambiguous wording of sec. 37x, para. 2, sent. 1, 2nd clause of the WpHG [German Securities Trading Act], the period represented by the interim statement is not necessarily restricted to three months but depends rather on the date of publication and can vary between two and a half months and four and half months; see BT-Drucks. [Document of the German Bundestag] 16/3644, p. 77.

[75] Thus the duty is primarily incumbent upon issuers that are not already required to publish quarterly reports for the first three quarters of financial year under the rules of the Frankfurt stock exchange due to their listing in the particular segment of the official or regulated market that has additional requirements for admittance (Prime Standard) on the Frankfurt Stock exchange; also according to *Hutter/Kaulamo*, NJW (2007), 550 (552).

[76] DRS [German Accounting Standard] no. 16, pnts. 61 ff. and 41 may also be consulted for specifics in this respect.

[77] On the term "insurance undertaking" within the meaning of German commercial law see the legal definition in secs. 341, para. 1 and 2 of the HGB [German Commercial Code].

conjunction with sec. 325, para. 2 of the HGB [German Commercial Code] and published immediately following the submission.[78]

13.5.2.2 Content of the Annual Financial Statements

The annual financial statements within the meaning of secs. 242, para. 1, and 264, para. 1, sent. 1 of the HGB [German Commercial Code] consist of the balance sheet and the profit and loss statement. The annex explains the annual financial statement and forms an integral unit with it. The minimum content of the annex is specified in secs. 284, para. 2, and 285 of the HGB [German Commercial Code]. In particular, it must explain the accounting and valuation methods used and also itemize liabilities and revenue. The annual financial statements provide the addressees of publication with a view of the financial, earnings, and economic position of an undertaking as of a particular reporting date. They mainly impart financial reporting information to public and contain little information on organizational form. This can be seen, for example, in the information required under sec. 285, sent. 1, nos. 9 and 10 of the HGB [German Commercial Code] as to the names and professions[79] of managing board and supervisory board members as well as their total remuneration.

13.5.2.3 Content of the Management Report

Separately from the items reported in the financial statements, the management report discloses the business performance and the situation of the entity required to make disclosure. It contains financial reporting information, but centers on risk reporting. Information on formal organizational aspects provided to addressees in the management report is rudimentary at best.[80] The financial reporting includes, in

[78] In addition, in accordance with sec. 55, para. 3 VAG [German Insurance Supervision Act], direct insurance and reinsurance undertakings must send the annual financial statements and management report to any insured person upon demand in the fiscal year that follows the reporting year.

[79] With respect to the description of the profession, sec. 285, sent. 1, no. 10 of the HGB [German Commercial Code] does not refer to one's professional training but to the actually practiced main profession. It is likely that this requirement is directed mainly at the supervisory board since the office of supervisory board member is designed under the legal model as a secondary position. For the managing board, the requirement can only mean that the area assigned to each managing board member is stated in the framework of a distribution of operating responsibilities. On the whole see *Lange*, in: Münchener Kommentar HGB [in English: Munich Commentary on the German Commercial Code], (2nd ed. 2008), volume IV, sec. 285, ref. 199 ff.; *Merkt*, in: Baumbach/Hopt, HGB [in English: The German Commercial Code], (33rd ed. 2008), sec. 285, ref. 10.

[80] Thus, for example, human resources developments (see the following section) in this context refer to purely economic factors such as the change in the number of employees in the undertaking; see on this point sec. 285, sent. 1, no. 7 of the HGB [German Commercial Code]. In consideration of the inferences that can be drawn about the financial position of an undertaking from changes in

particular, information on the economic and legal environment, sales and earnings performance including the major performance indicators, information on financing and on developments in social commitment and human resources.[81]

The disclosure of risk reporting information is first laid out in sec. 289, para. 1, sent. 4 of the HGB [German Commercial Code]. Accordingly, the management report must describe the company's opportunities and risks and assess the expected development of the company in consideration of them. DRS [German Accounting Standard] no. 5–20 on risk reporting by insurance undertakings can be consulted for the specific information in this requirement. Although it is only directly applicable to the group management report, corresponding application is expressly recommended for the management reports of individual entities.[82] DRS [German Accounting Standard] 5–20 requires an "overall analysis" as of the reporting date of the actuarial risks, the risks from default on underwriting receivables, risks from capital investments as well as operational and other risks. Diversification effects must be taken into account and changes compared to the prior year must be described. It requires—to the extent technically possible—a quantification of the risks including an explanation of the valuation method applied. On this basis, the undertaking must make a projected estimate of its overall risk profile.

Sec. 289, para. 2, no. 2 (a) and (b) of the HGB [German Commercial Code] is also relevant to risk reporting. The explanations it requires, however, do not pertain to the overall risk management of an insurance undertaking under sec. 64a VAG [German Insurance Supervision Act] and sec. 91, para. 2 of the AktG [German Stock Corporation Act].[83] They are limited to the use of financial instruments and hedge transactions in particular.[84] Thus only in this respect is the management report required to address the company's risk-management goals and methods, its

the number of employees, the corresponding information is allocated here to the area of financial reporting. Additionally, information about the legal environment can have organizational relevance, for example, if the outsourcing of significant business functions is reported within the meaning of sec. 5, para. 3, no. 4 of the VAG [German Insurance Supervision Act]. On the outsourcing of internal audit and elements of risk management see *Dreher/Schaaf*, WM (2008), 1765 (1770 f.).

[81] In this respect, sec. 289, para. 1 of the HGB [German Commercial Code] contains hardly any specific requirements; the information specified corresponds to the general opinion in auditing and law; see, for example, the compilation by *Lange*, in: Münchener Kommentar HGB [in English: Munich Commentary on the German Commercial Code], (2nd ed. 2008), vol. IV, sec. 289, ref. 60; *Ballwieser*, in: FS [Publication in Honor of] Baetge, 2007, p. 153, 160 f.; *Merkt*, in: Baumbach/Hopt, HGB [in English: The German Commercial Code], (33rd ed. 2008), sec. 289, ref. 1.

[82] See the reference to sec. 289, para. 1, sent. 4 of the HGB [German Commercial Code] in DRS [German Accounting Standard] 5–20, pnt. 2.

[83] In detail on risk management under sec. 64a of the VAG [German Insurance Supervision Act] see *Dreher*, VersR (2008), 998.

[84] See *Wiedmann*, in: Ebenroth/Boujong/Joost/Strohn, HGB [in English: The German Commercial Code], vol. I, (2nd ed. 2008), sec. 289, ref. 29; *Lange*, in: Münchener Kommentar HGB [in English: Munich Commentary on the German Commercial Code], vol. IV, (2nd ed. 2008), sec. 289, ref. 108; *Baumbach/Hopt*, HGB [in English: The German Commercial Code], (33rd ed. 2008), sec. 289, ref. 2.

risks pertaining to price changes, default, and liquidity, or the risks from fluctuations in payment streams to which the company is exposed.

13.6 Comparison of the Report on Solvency and Financial Condition Under Solvency II and Publication Required Under National Commercial and Capital Market Law

13.6.1 The Equal Rank of the Disclosure Duties of Solvency II and Disclosure Duties Under Capital Market and Commercial Law

According to the draft of the Solvency II Framework Directive, the obligation to publish a Report on Solvency and Financial Condition is parallel to the disclosure duties under commercial and capital market law. The duties are therefore cumulative and independent of one another.[85] Nevertheless, the issuer of the directive has acknowledged potential overlap in the content of the different disclosure requirements. The nearly identical wording of the rules in arts. 51, para. 1, subpara. 2 and 53, para. 3 of Solvency II provide evidence of this. The purpose of these passages is to avoid the disproportionate duplication of reports. Thus the direct insurance and reinsurance undertakings that must report may, in the Report on Solvency and Financial Condition, refer to "equivalent information [...] disclosed publicly under other legal or regulatory requirements". This congruence, supported by the issuer of the Directive, between the Report on Solvency and Financial Condition on one hand and the annual financial statements, management report as well as financial reports under capital-market law on the other is evaluated in the following discussion.

[85] The duty to issue financial statements providing information on the financial position, solvency and the risks in class 18 of part a of Annex I is still anchored in art. 33, para. 1 of the draft of the Directive dated 26 Feb. 2008 (n. 3). However, the Council, Common Position of 25 Nov. 2008, deleted the substantial portions of the provision. The new version of art. 33 now refers only to the information exchange between supervisory authorities for the purposes of supervision.

13.6.2 Content Overlap Between the Report on Solvency and Financial Condition Under Solvency II and the Annual Financial Statement and Management Report

13.6.2.1 Congruence in Content with Respect to Financial Reporting

With regard to the description of the business and performance, the content of the Report on Solvency and Financial Condition is largely the same as the content of the annual financial statements and management report. Required here as well as in financial reporting are disclosure of the profit and loss statement, information on key performance indicators and an analysis of sales and earnings performance. But the content is not completely identical. An example of the differences would be in the presentation of the undertaking's internal objectives and strategies. This is obligatory—limited to key elements—only in the Report on Solvency and Financial Condition but not for the management report.[86] Indeed, in an early draft, the German Accounting Law Reform Act (BilReG) still contained a specific requirement that the undertaking discuss "significant objectives and strategies" in the management report separately from the risks and opportunities of future progress.[87] The relevant passage was deleted, however, in the ministerial draft for a BilReG [German Accounting Law Reform Act] since it was not indicated in European law[88] and it was also expected that undertakings would not or could not provide specific information.[89]

On the other hand, the Report on Solvency and Financial Condition requires an extensive disclosure of information not contained in the annual financial statements or management report in the description of valuation principles for solvency purposes and the description of capital management. It also requires explanations of deviations from the annual financial statements and management report. This is due primarily to the new solvency regime of the first pillar. Much of the additional information in the Report on Solvency and Financial Condition compared to publications for accounting is directly connected with the calculation of the Minimum and Target Solvency Capital Requirements and with the optional use of an internal model for the calculation of the Target Solvency Capital Requirement in particular. Other additional information arises from the consideration of hidden reserves in the valuation of "basic own funds" and in the justification of accounting

[86] Of a different opinion, with regard to the management report, *Merkt* in: Baumbach/Hopt (eds.), HGB [The German Commercial Code], (33rd. ed. 2008), sec. 289, ref. 1.

[87] For a discussion on this point see *Lange*, in: Münchener Kommentar HGB [in English: Munich commentary on the German Commercial Code], (2nd ed. 2008), vol. IV, sec. 289, ref. 83. On overlap with the major content in the risk strategy see section below at 3.

[88] See Bundesministerium der Justiz [German Federal Ministry of Justice – BMJ], Ministerial Draft of BilReG [German Accounting Law Reform Act] of 13 Dec. 2003, p. 25.

[89] See also *Pfitzer/Oser/Orth*, DB (2004), 2593 (2597).

liabilities as "ancillary own funds".[90] The description of the composition of the entire capital investment portfolio in terms of its significant characteristics and the description of capital transferability are also not required in the management report.

13.6.2.2 Congruence in Content with Respect to Information Related to Formal Organizational Aspects

As part of the Report on Solvency and Financial Condition, insurance undertakings will also need to publish information on organizational form that is not currently part of the annual financial statements or management report. This information primarily concerns the design and operational structure, as for example the delineation of tasks and responsibilities among staff functions that oversee crisis prevention. From an organizational perspective, the required personnel information is no longer limited to the members of governing bodies, meaning the members of the managing board and—also new in the report—members of the supervisory or administrative board of an insurance undertaking. Even senior staff members directly subordinate to management that perform "key functions"[91] must be disclosed together with information as to their fitness.

13.6.2.3 Congruence in Content with Respect to Information on Risk Reporting

The Report on Solvency and Financial Condition provides the public with a more comprehensive insight into the risk management of an insurance undertaking then can be obtained from the management report. The management report is required to contain almost no information on the major content of the risk strategy. Only the "risk management goals" in connection with the management of risks from financial derivatives transactions must be provided. The management report is also not required to provide an explanation of how risk management is embedded in the undertaking's organization, and specifically how the cooperation between the business functional operating areas and internal audit is arranged or how internal risk reporting is structured in relation to management, including lines of reporting, key content, and cycles. However, there are parallels in content in the areas of risk identification and risk valuation, at least in the reliance on the requirements in DRS [German Accounting Standard] 5–20. Both the Report on Solvency and Financial Condition and the management report require an explanation of the risk categories, the primary methods and procedures used, and a description of diversification effects. It should nevertheless be noted that the requirements of DRS [German Accounting Standard] 5–20 are not binding on individual undertakings.

---

[90] On ancillary own funds see above, 13.3.2.3.

[91] See on this point *Dreher*, ZVersWiss (2009), 187 (190 f.) (Chap. 12, above, at 12.2.1).

13.6.3 Content Overlap Between the Report on Solvency and Financial Condition Under Solvency II and Publications Under Capital Market Law

The content overlap of the Report on Solvency and Financial Condition and the annual financial statements management report is largely equivalent to the overlap with the reports under capital market law, namely the annual financial report and—apart from the diverging reporting period—the semi-annual financial report.

There is further parallel content between the Report on Solvency and Financial Condition and the interim reports under capital-market law with regard to "important events" within the meaning of art. 54, para. 1, subpara. 1 of Solvency II. Such events will require not only an update to the Report on Solvency and Financial Condition. They generally also will constitute "important events" within the meaning of sec. 37w, para. 4, sent. 1 of the WpHG [German Securities Trading Act] or "material events" within the meaning of sec. 37x, para. 2, sent. 2 of the WpHG [German Securities Trading Act] and are therefore included in the interim reports under capital market law.

For insurance undertakings that issue stock and fall under the legal definition of a domestic issuer in accordance with sec. 2, para. 7 of the WpHG [German Securities Trading Act], there may be additional overlap in content between the Report on Solvency and Financial Condition and the event-induced publications under secs. 26 and 26a of the WpHG [German Securities Trading Act]. All such publications in this respect relate to the disclosure of shareholder composition or portions thereof. Differences exist only insofar as the disclosures stipulated in the WpHG [German Securities Trading Act] are required only in the event certain holdings thresholds are met, not met, or exceeded.

13.7 Disclosure Duties at Group Level

13.7.1 Disclosure Duties at Group Level Under Solvency II

13.7.1.1 The Report on Solvency and Financial Condition at Group Level

Art. 256, para. 1, sent. 1 of Solvency II stipulates that shareholding direct insurance and reinsurance undertakings[92] as well as insurance holding companies,[93] must

[92] See the legal definition in art. 212, para. 1 (a) of Solvency II, which refers to art. 12, para. 1 of Directive 83/349/EEC of 13 Jun. 1983 concerning consolidated accounts, OJEC no. L 193 of 18 Jul. 1983, p. 1, and thus to the criteria for unified management or identification of management body members.

[93] See the legal definition in art. 212, para. 1 (f) of Solvency II.

publish an annual Report on Solvency and Financial Condition at the group level. The Directive thus establishes the disclosure duty at the level of the ultimate parent company of a group. For the content of the group report, art. 256, para. 1, sent. 2 of Solvency II refers to art. 51 of Solvency II, which applies accordingly.[94] All information to be disclosed must therefore be compiled from the group perspective. For example, the description of the business must describe the entire group, which means that the group structure must be included in the report, and in particular, the level of holdings in the entities.[95] The same applies with respect to information on the design of the group and the operational structure.[96] Specifically, these must encompass the organization of group internal audit, group risk management, and group-wide reporting. The information on risk reporting at the group level is the subject matter of group risk management. Primarily, this information must describe the group risk strategy as well as the coordination within the group of risk identification, valuation, management, and monitoring.

13.7.1.2 Comparison of Reports by the Individual Undertaking and the Group

The duty to publish a report on the group's solvency and financial condition by the ultimate parent company raises the question of whether all direct insurance and reinsurance undertakings that are part of the group must also publish individual reports. Art. 256, para. 2 and 3 of Solvency II addresses this question. According to para. 2, a group report by the parent company releases the direct insurance and reinsurance undertakings in the group from the duty of individual publication under three conditions. First, the content of the group report of the parent company must satisfy the minimum requirements of art. 256, para. 1 in conjunction with art. 51, para. 1, subpara. 2 of Solvency II. Second, it must include all information that the direct insurance and reinsurance undertakings that belong to the group would have to disclose in individual reports.[97] Third, the supervisory authority responsible for group supervision must consent to the waiver of individual report preparation by the group's companies.[98] Paragraph 3 authorizes the supervisory authority

---

[94] In detail on the content requirements of art. 50 of Solvency II see above, at 13.3.

[95] See CEIOPS, Advice to the European Commission on Supervisory Reporting and Public Disclosure in the Framework of the Solvency II Project, March 2007, pnt. 4.4; CEIOPS of 2 Feb. 2009, Draft CEIOPS' Advice for Level 2 Implementing Measures on Solvency II: Reporting Requirements, pnt. 3.39 sub B.1 (d) and CEIOPS of 2 Jul. 2009, Draft CEIOPS' Advice for Level 2 Implementing Measures on Solvency II: Supervisory Reporting and Public Disclosure Requirements, pnt. 3.97.

[96] See CEIOPS, Advice to the European Commission on Supervisory Reporting and Public Disclosure in the Framework of the Solvency II Project, March 2007, pnt. 4.8.

[97] See implications on this point below, 13.10.4.

[98] Art. 256, para. 2, subpara. 2 of Solvency II requires that the supervisory authority responsible for group supervision consult and coordinate with the supervisory authorities referred to in art. 248, para. 1 of Solvency II prior to issuing consent.

responsible for group supervision to require subsequent publication by the ultimate group parents of missing information or additional information if the information omitted in the group report is material.

13.7.1.3 The Deleted Obligation to Disclose Group Support

Article 241, as it still appeared in the second draft of the Solvency II Framework Directive, required additional disclosures at the group level in connection with "group support". However, as a result of sustained resistance by some EU Member States, all regulations on group support were deleted without replacement, including the rules concerning special disclosure duties.[99]

13.7.2 Disclosure Duties at Group Level in National Context

While the disclosure duties at the level of the individual undertaking under capital market law are based on the issuer, nevertheless there are some specific requirements on the corporate group. For example, under sec. 37y, no. 2, sent. 1 of the WpHG [German Securities Trading Act], the legal representative of an ultimate group parent company is responsible for preparing and publishing semi-annual financial reports not only for the group entity itself but also for the other companies belonging to the group. Under sec. 37y, no. 3 of the WpHG [German Securities Trading Act], the parent company's information presented in the interim statement on "important events" and their impact refers to the entirety of all companies within the group and not just to the parent entity itself.

Irrespective of their legal form, insurance undertakings that are a ultimate parent company in an insurance group as well as insurance holding companies[100] must prepare group financial statements and a group management report[101] in accordance with sec. 341i, para. 1, sent. 1 and para. 2 of the HGB [German Commercial Code].[102] According to sec. 341j, para. 1, sent. 1 of the HGB [German Commercial Code] in conjunction with sec. 297, para. 1, sent. 1 of the HGB [German Commercial Code], the group financial statements consist of the group balance sheet, group profit and loss statement, group annex, cash-flow statement, and statement of changes in equity. The net asset, financial and earnings position in the group

[99] See Council, Common Position of 25 Nov. 2008; also, on the discussion concerning group support and its deletion, the report in the Financial Times of Germany dated 10 Dec. 2008, p. 25.

[100] On the criterion defining unified management as well as the concept of control see sec. 341j, para. 1, sent. 1 of the HGB in conjunction with sec. 290, para. 1 to 3 of the HGB.

[101] DRS [German Accounting Standard] 5–20 is directly applicable in this respect; see above at 13.5.2.3.

[102] On scope of consolidation see secs. 294 ff. of the HGB [German Commercial Code].

financial statements must represent the consolidated undertakings as if these undertakings were a single overall entity.[103] Accordingly, the requirements for the group management report in sec. 315, para. 1, sent. 5, and para. 2, no. 2 (a) and (b) of the HGB [German Commercial Code], which apply to insurance undertakings regardless of legal form under sec. 341j, para. 1, sent. 1 of the HGB [German Commercial Code], are identical in their wording to those of sec. 289, para. 1, sent. 4, and para. 2, no. 2 (a) and (b) of the HGB [German Commercial Code].

13.7.3 Content Overlap Between the Report on Solvency and Financial Condition at Group Level Under Solvency II and the Annual Financial Statement, Management Report, and Financial Reports Under Capital Market Law

13.7.3.1 Content Overlap Between the Report on Solvency and Financial Condition at Group Level and the Annual Financial Statement and Management Report

The overlap with the annual financial statements and management report and the content reported at the level of the individual undertaking in the Report on Solvency and Financial Condition corresponds to the overlap in the group-specific publications required of the ultimate group parent company. In addition, there are two further parallels in content at the group level.[104] First, both the Report on Solvency and Financial Condition and the group annex require a presentation of the group structure and, in cases of de facto group formation, the inclusion of information on the respective holdings.[105] Second, there are close correlations in content between the cash flow statement and the valuation of liquidity risk published in the Report on Solvency and Financial Condition. Unlike the balance sheet, which provides a view to an undertaking's liquidity as of the reporting date only, the cash flow statement helps the addressees of disclosure to evaluate the ability of the undertaking to

---

[103] See sec. 297, para. 3, sent. 1 of the HGB [German Commercial Code].

[104] The parallels in the specifics of group accounting that arise under IAS/IFRS (International Accounting Standards/International Financial Reporting Standards) are outside the scope of this article. According to sec. 315a, para. 1 and 2 of the HGB [German Commercial Code], Capital Market-based undertakings are required to issue group financial statements that comply with IAS/IFRS. An overview of the accounting standards of the IASB (International Accounting Standards Board) applicable to group accounting for insurance undertakings is provided in *Nguyen*, Rechnungslegung in Versicherungsunternehmen [in English: Accounting in Insurance Undertakings], (2008), p. 616 f.

[105] On the notes to the group financial statements see sec. 341j, para. 1, sent. 1 of the HGB [German Commercial Code] in conjunction with sec. 313, para. 2 of the HGB [German Commercial Code] concerning disclosures on the scope consolidation.

generate excess income in the future and thus meet its payment obligations.[106] In this respect, the cash flow statement—as with the Report on Solvency and Financial Condition—enables conclusions to be drawn about the overall liquidity risk at the group level.

13.7.3.2 Content Overlap Between the Report on Solvency and Financial Condition at Group Level and Control Messages of the Ultimate Group Parent Under Section 35 of the WpÜG [German Securities Acquisition and Takeover Act]

In cases where a de facto group is established, the overlap in content may exist between the Report on Solvency and Financial Condition and control messages as required by sec. 35 of the WpÜG [German Securities Acquisition and Takeover Act]. For example, if a direct insurance or reinsurance undertaking acquires a majority holding in another direct insurance or reinsurance undertaking, the holding must not only be reported in the description of the group structure in the group Report on Solvency and Financial Condition, but also must be disclosed to the public simultaneously in accordance with sec. 35 of the WpÜG [German Securities Acquisition and Takeover Act].

13.8 Form of Disclosure in the Report on Solvency and Financial Condition

Arts. 50 ff. of Solvency II contain no requirements on the format of publication for the Report on Solvency and Financial Condition. In this matter, the Member States are required to specify acceptable disclosure media or leave the choice of medium to the direct insurance and reinsurance undertakings subject to disclosure.[107] Guidance for such decisions can be found in the solvency regulation adopted for banking based on sec. 26a, para. 1, sent. 3 in conjunction with sec. 10, para. 1, sent. 9, no. 7 of the KWG [German Credit Services Act]. According to sec. 320, para. 1 of the SolvV [Regulation governing the capital adequacy of institutions, groups of institutions and financial holding groups], the undertakings "own Internet site" or "other suitable media" constitute allowable disclosure media. Reference there can

[106] The cash-flow statement centers on the three elements of cash flow from operations, cash flow from financing activity, and cash flow from investment activity. See in detail on this *Busse von Colbe*, in: Münchener Kommentar HGB [in English: Munich Commentary on the German Commercial Code], (2nd. ed. 2008), vol. IV, sec. 297, ref. 18 ff.; *Nguyen*, Rechnungslegung von Versicherungsunternehmen [in English: Accounting in Insurance Undertakings], (2008), p. 621 ff.

[107] There are also no format requirements in the parallel rules under Basel II; see art. 148, para. 1 of Directive 2006/48/EC: The choice of disclosure medium is generally left to the credit institutions.

also be made to other information published in the scope of legal disclosure.[108] Under sec. 320, para. 2, sent. 1 of the SolvV [Regulation governing the capital adequacy of institutions, groups of institutions and financial holding groups], the fact of publication together with notice of the disclosure medium must be announced in the electronic version of the German Federal Gazette. The responsible supervisory authorities, the BaFin [Federal Financial Supervisory Authority], and the German Bundesbank must be notified of the announcement. Analogous requirements are expected for the insurance industry. However, the Council has recently amended the draft of the Solvency II Directive, explicitly incorporating disclosure to the public in either print or electronic form into Recital 38.

13.9 Protection of Business and Trade Secrets in Public Disclosure Duties

From the perspective of the undertaking, there is a considerable amount of information subject to disclosure by direct insurance and reinsurance undertakings in the Report on Solvency and Financial Condition that requires confidentiality. This is true, for example, with respect to publication of important content in the operating or risk strategy, or information on risk assessment in connection with the introduction of new products or development of new business areas. Such information could be of great interest to competitors, investors, and lenders in equal measure.

Art. 53 of Solvency II, which also applies to group reports under art. 256, para. 1, sent. 2 of Solvency II, regulates the protection of business and trade secrets. According to para. 1, direct insurance and reinsurance undertakings are not required to disclose sensitive information if competitors of the undertaking would gain a significant undue advantage as a result of the disclosure (a). The same applies when the undertakings subject to disclosure are bound by obligations of secrecy or confidentiality to policyholders or based on other counterparty relationships (b). In both cases, however, the competent supervisory authority or group supervisory authority must consent to the nondisclosure. If the consent to nondisclosure is granted, the undertaking must indicate this in the Report on Solvency and Financial Condition along with the reasons. But a further limitation on protection of the confidentiality interests of direct insurance and reinsurance undertakings—above and beyond the consent requirement—is set forth in art. 53, para. 4 of Solvency II. This paragraph stipulates that information on the undertaking's capital management must always be disclosed. Such information is generally exempted from the protection of art. 53, para. 1 of Solvency II.

[108] On the option to refer under arts. 51, para. 1, subpara. 2 and 53, para. 3 of Solvency II see above, at 13.6.1.

13.10 Further Conclusions

13.10.1 Regulatory Approach in Public Disclosure Duties

The objective of the new duties of disclosure to the public by insurance undertakings established in Solvency II is to create transparency and reduce asymmetries in the publicly available company information from the insurance industry primarily for policyholders, insured persons, and beneficiaries—and secondarily for other interested parties.[109] The means to achieve this are the comprehensive disclosure duties themselves. Recital 38 of Solvency II places clear emphasis on the public as the addressee of the information in three places. At the same time, contrary to the objectives of Solvency II,[110] it is only the group of secondary addressees of disclosure,[111] specifically, the professional public—such as the financial press, other insurance undertakings, analysts or ratings agencies—that can be meant here. The audience first considered by the directive in its aim for transparency and informational symmetry, namely policyholders and insureds, is scarcely considered in the approach and implementation of the public disclosure duties that insurance undertakings are to fulfill in the future.

Evidence of this can be seen by way of example in the obligation under art. 51, para. 1, subpara. 2 (e) (iii) of Solvency II. The report is required to contain "information allowing a proper understanding of the main differences" between the underlying assumptions of the standard formula and those of any internal model used by the undertaking for the calculation of its Solvency Capital Requirement.[112] There is a flawed assumption here that the typical policyholder or insured knows the meaning of or difference between a standard model and internal model, or would be willing or even be in a position to deal with the underlying assumptions in these models. For this reason alone, the information disclosed in accordance with art. 51, para. 1, subpara. 2 (e) (iii) of Solvency II would not pass the "fit for purpose" test[113] stipulated by CEIOPS. But the professional public also presents an issue here, since it is already in a position to filter out many elements of the future mandatory public information through analyst conferences, benchmarking, evaluation of the extensive publications required by commercial and capital market law, and other means. Thus the question of who actually benefits becomes just as pressing as the question of proportionality posed by the new disclosure duties.

---

[109] See above, 13.2.

[110] See on this point above, 13.2.

[111] See on this point also above, 13.2.

[112] The scope of information is still largely uncertain. In this respect, CEIOPS of Feb. 25, 2009, Draft CEIOPS' Advice for Level 2 Implementing Measures on Solvency II: Reporting Requirements, pnt. 3.45 sub (iii) states only that the information "could include a justification of differing key assumptions from the standard formula if appropriate." On the information concerning the Solvency Capital Requirement requiring disclosure see above, 13.3.2.3.

[113] See above, 13.2.

Based on both the scope and degree of differentiation in the information to be published as well as the expense it entails, the matter of proportionality is certainly not clear at the outset.

This question can only be fully answered—also with regard to the special situation of small and medium-sized insurance undertakings—when the detailed rules at the second level of the Lamfalussy process have concretized the disclosure duties. With the undifferentiated reference in art. 51, para. 1, subpara. 1 to the principle of proportionality anchored in art. 35, para. 4 (a) of Solvency II, small and medium-sized insurance undertakings are confronted with the problem, which can hardly be assessed ex ante, of whether and, most importantly, where they may waive the submission of particular points of information in their reports, and the level of detail at which they are required to disclose various items.[114] Conversely, this means that this concretization process requires particular attention, as does that with respect to disclosure duties to insurance supervisory authorities[115]—to the same extent as the earlier process of designing the Solvency II Directive itself as it relates to disclosure duties. Once the delegated legislation is adopted, any criticism of the design of disclosure duties by insurance undertakings will come too late in the process of creating the national implementing law. Good reason therefore exists to perform a thorough legal assessment, which thus far seems to be missing, with respect to excessive public disclosure duties under arts. 51 ff. of Solvency II prior to the promulgation of the Directive and subsequently at the next regulatory level.

In addition to the principle of proportionality, the primary criteria for this are the constitutional requirements regarding the legal certainty of the norms. The more specific the disclosure duties are made in advance at level of the Directive, the less potential exists for dispute in the rules later in their legal application and in their national implementation. Staying with the example of the standard model versus an internal model, however, the legal requirement for "information" referring to "proper understanding of underlying assumptions" of the most complex capital requirement systems does not meet this criterion.

---

[114] CEIOPS has fully acknowledged this problem: see CEIOPS of Feb. 25, 2009, Draft CEIOPS' Advice for Level 2 Implementing Measures on Solvency II: Reporting Requirements, pnt. 3.30. However, it does not provide the undertakings with the distinct criteria between essential and non-essential information. The definition of materiality, closely aligned with the work of the IASB, appears to be only slightly helpful from the point of view of an undertaking. According to this definition, information is significant and must be included in the Report on Solvency and Financial Condition if it has the ability to influence the economic decisions of the addressees of publication. Because the very next sentence directly predicates significance on the size of the undertaking, on the one hand, and on the potential for any non-disclosure to be misleading to the addressee on the other, the definition becomes highly adulterated. The same applies to the imprecise treatment from CEIOPS, Issues Paper of Nov. 1, 2007, Policy on harmonisation of contents and formats for public disclosure and supervisory reporting, number 7. 1 at the end: "Moreover, particular care should be taken to ensure that the harmonisation of contents and formats is not too burdensome for small and medium-sized insurance undertakings, by applying the proportionality principle to the utmost extent possible."

[115] See in detail on this point *Dreher*, ZVersWiss (2009), 187 ff. (Chap. 12, above).

Further, the regulatory approach of Solvency II takes no account of the organization and information responsibilities under corporate law. This has implications on the fulfillment of informational duties by the ultimate parent company of a group, particularly in a de facto group. The Directive simply presumes[116] that the undertaking at the top of an insurance group would be fully entitled to obtain information and intervene in the affairs of any insurance undertaking in the group. This undifferentiated assumption is at odds with the legal reality of a very detailed framework of corporate regulation which obligates the managing boards of subsidiaries that are not bound to instruction in group law under sec. 76, para. 1 AktG [German Stock Corporation Act] to the independent control of the respective company. Consequently, a review must be conducted in each case based on the specific group situation as to whether the group disclosure duties under supervisory law can even be satisfied by the organization and information responsibilities under corporate law in view of the flow of information required.[117] The relationship between the insurance supervisory regime on one hand and corporate law—particularly group law—on the other is thus put to a test by the Solvency II Directive, which, implicitly and possibly without due consideration, assumes the primacy of the supervisory regime. In view of the mandatory nature of the corporate and group law applicable to the permissible legal forms of insurance undertakings, this approach could lead to considerable friction in the course of implementation at the national level, if not sooner.

13.10.2 Potential Synergies in Fulfillment of Public Disclosure Duties

Uncertainty in multiple respects also appears in the relationship between the future insurance supervisory regime and accounting law. Taken as a whole, the Report on Solvency and Financial Condition extends clearly beyond the annual financial statements and the management report under commercial law. This is mainly attributable to the fact that numerous additional information is associated with the solvency regime under the first pillar of Solvency II, including, for example, the new methods and approaches to valuation for solvency purposes and information related to the new capital requirements. As a result, it will be virtually impossible to simultaneously meet all public disclosure duties under the insurance supervisory regime through the publication of the annual financial statements and management report or the interim reports under capital market law. On the contrary, the obligatory explanations of material differences in the item-by-item valuations between

[116] See above, 13.7.

[117] See on this point, based on the group-wide risk management of credit institutions, *Schneider*, Options and limits in the implementation of the risk management requirements under corporate and banking supervisory law at group level, Dissertation, Mainz (2009).

the Report on Solvency and Financial Condition and the publications under commercial and capital market law require additional effort.

Conversely, however, it may be that some of the content disclosed in the Report on Solvency and Financial Condition will also meet the respective publication requirements under commercial and capital market law.[118] In November 2007, CEIOPS announced a forthcoming specification of parallel content that would enable undertakings to exploit the potential for synergies in their disclosures.[119] To date, however, this has not been issued. There is, in fact, potential for synergies relating primarily to the information gathered for financial and risk reporting, such as that in the profit and loss statement, the description of the business, or the risk identification and valuation processes. In this respect, direct insurance and reinsurance undertakings can readily achieve synergy effects in gathering and preparing their information.[120] In addition, they may utilize the referral option in the Report on Solvency and Financial Condition as provided for in art. 51, para. 1, subpara. 2 and art. 53, para. 3 of Solvency II and make references to congruent information in the annual financial statements, management report, and—at the group level—the cash-flow statement. Direct insurance or reinsurance undertakings that issue shares can take advantage of some additional synergy potential in publishing or updating their Report on Solvency and Financial Condition and in fulfilling their event-based capital market issuer duties pertaining to their holding structure.

13.10.3 Selection of Publication Date for the Report on Solvency and Financial Condition

Because of the indicated synergy opportunities, synchronizing the publication of the Report on Solvency and Financial Condition with publication of the annual financial statements and annual report is advisable. Arts. 51 ff. of Solvency II give no specific deadline for publication of the Report on Solvency and Financial Condition. Thus, for individual undertakings, publication in conjunction with the annual report and management report in the first 4 months of the new financial year can be recommended.[121] At the group level, publication within the time frame defined in sec. 341i, para. 3, sent. 1 of the HGB [German Commercial Code] is

---

[118] On a parallel situation in banking supervision see *Hillen*, in: Boos/Fischer/Schulte-Mattler, KWG [The German Credit Services Act], (3rd ed. 2008), sec. 26a, ref. 6.

[119] See CEIOPS, Issues Paper of Nov. 1, 2007, Policy on harmonisation of contents and formats for public disclosure and supervisory reporting, no. 6.1.

[120] See on this point CEIOPS, Issues Paper dated Nov. 1, 2007, Policy on harmonisation of contents and formats for public disclosure and supervisory reporting, no. 6.1: "If undertakings can produce the same figures for regulatory purposes and financial accounting, the cost burden will be significantly reduced."

[121] See sec. 341a, para. 1, sent. 1, 2nd clause of the HGB [German Commercial Code], which waives the three month period in sec. 264, para. 1, sent. 2 of the HGB [German Commercial Code].

advisable, which would be within 2 months of the issuing deadline for the last (individual) statement to be issued and included in the group statement.[122]

13.10.4 Relief at Group Level and the Principle of Proportionality

The waiver in art. 256, para. 2 of Solvency II of individual reports prepared by group undertakings in addition to the group Report on Solvency and Financial Condition should, in principle, be welcomed. It takes account of the situation where, with respect to its economic decisions, a group is perceived by the public as a single entity and market discipline can only be achieved in this respect through Reports on Solvency and Financial Condition at the group level. At the same time, it avoids a disproportionate additional burden on the undertaking. This is so because the additional publication of individual reports brings no gains to market transparency.[123]

The question clearly arises in this respect as to whether market transparency actually improves if a group report, regardless of the group structures present, must always and in each individual case indicate all information that group companies would need to disclose at the individual-undertaking level. More to the point: Does a group report really need to explain to its addressees the reporting lines through which the risk reporting function of a contractually controlled insurance stock corporation carries out risk reporting to "its" managing board, which is subject to the instruction of the group parent company? Or would the explanation of group risk reporting—that is, the description of the lines of reporting to group management—be sufficient in this respect? In any event, a good deal of the information disclosed under art. 51, para. 1, subpara. 2, sent. 2 of Solvency II would be at least similar, if not identical, at the individual and group levels. This is true, for example, with regard to the methods used in risk identification and valuation and to risk classification.

Against this background, a more flexible formulation of art. 256, para. 2, subpara. 1 (b) of Solvency II would be preferred from a legislative perspective in order to achieve proportionality but also to avoid overloading the addressees of publication with unnecessary duplicate information. Certainly of interest in connection with

[122] The deadline can be no later than twelve months after the reporting date of the group financial statement. In compliance with sec. 290, para. 1, sent. 2 of the HGB [German Commercial Code], sec. 341i, para. 3, sent. 2 HGB [German Commercial Code] limits the latest deadline to four months for corporations that are subject to the requirements of sec. 325, para. 4, sent. 1 of the HGB [German Commercial Code], but not simultaneously to the relief provision of sec. 327a of the HGB [German Commercial Code].

[123] For a parallel situation in banking supervision, namely in sec. 26a, para. 4 of the KWG [German Credit Services Act], see *Hillen*, in: Boos/Fischer/Schulte-Mattler, KWG [in English: The German Credit Services Act], (3rd ed. 2008), sec. 26a, ref. 20.

this is that the implementation rule for credit institutions under Basel II has already blazed the trail in the right direction. Sec. 319, para. 2 of SolvV [Regulation governing the capital adequacy of institutions, groups of institutions and financial holding groups] states the following: "In the case of a group of institutions or financial holding group, the disclosure requirements apply only to the group's superordinated company. The information it gives shall relate to the group".

13.10.5 Less Favorable Protection of Confidentiality Interests for Direct Insurance and Reinsurance Undertakings Compared to Basel II

There are three ways in which Solvency II provides less protection for the confidentiality interests of the disclosing direct insurance and reinsurance undertakings than Basel II provides for the protection of the confidentiality interests of banks.[124] For one, there are no specific per se exemptions to the protection of confidentiality and secrecy in the disclosure duties of credit institutions. This is relevant in particular to the description of the structure of own funds.[125]

Second, the protection of confidentiality and secrecy under banking supervisory law is guided by a fundamentally different concept of supervision which is more advantageous from an undertaking's perspective. Using a self-assessment, credit institutions must weigh whether non-disclosure of particular information is justified on the basis of confidentiality or in the interest of avoiding an undue competitive disadvantage. If certain information is not published, credit institutions are required to justify this in their report and to provide general information with respect to the required disclosure.[126] Following publication of the report, if the supervisory authority determines that the non-disclosure was improper, it may specifically order the publication of supplementary information. In contrast, the requirement for the supervisory authority's consent under art. 53, para. 1 of Solvency II can delay the publication of the entire Report on Solvency and Financial Condition, particularly in the case of assessments in dispute between undertakings and the supervisory authority of confidentiality or the need for secrecy. Such delays can easily engender mistrust among investors, creditors, and ratings agencies especially in times of economic crisis.

---

[124] On protection of the confidential interests of banks in connection with public disclosures under Basel II see art. 146 of Directive 2006/48/EC.

[125] Banks are also required to describe their own funds structure under Basel II; see on this point Annex XII, Part 2, 3, and at a national level, secs. 324 f. of SolvV [Regulation governing the capital adequacy of institutions, groups of institutions and financial holding groups].

[126] See art. 146, para. 3 of Directive 2006/48/EC as well as sec. 26a, para. 2 of the KWG [German Credit Services Act].

In addition, in administrative processes involving the non-disclosure of presumably confidential or secret information, direct insurance and reinsurance undertakings are in a weaker position than credit institutions. When credit institutions proceed to appeal an order by the BaFin [Federal Financial Supervisory Authority] for the relevant disclosure following their publication of a report that omits certain information for confidentiality reasons,[127] the Authority must prove its basis for ordering the encumbering administrative measure if the merits of the case are unclear.[128] In contrast, if a direct insurance or reinsurance undertaking wishes in the future to sue for the consent that the BaFin [Federal Financial Supervisory Authority] has withheld by petitioning for a writ of mandamus, the burden of proof is reversed. If the merits of the case are unclear, the direct insurance or reinsurance undertaking, as the complainant, bears the burden of substantive proof for all facts that support its petition regarding the obligation.[129]

This weakening in the position of insurance undertakings compared to banks with respect to the protection of confidentiality interests raises issues of proportionality in the emerging rules. It indicates an effort on the part of the issuer of the Directive to prevent frequent publication by direct insurance and reinsurance undertakings of "redacted" reports. If undertakings withhold large amounts of ostensibly confidential information from their published Reports on Solvency and Financial Condition, disclosure of which must be enforced by the supervisory authority—through the courts if necessary—it would hardly be conducive to increasing market transparency and reducing information asymmetries.[130] To be sure, the ex ante consent approach of art. 53, para. 1 of Solvency II is better suited than the bank supervision approach to preventing an abusive distortion of the boundaries that define the disclosure duties and to achieving the core aims of the third pillar of Solvency II. Nevertheless, the consent approach in art. 53, para. 1 of Solvency II appears to be disproportional. Thus far, such danger has neither come to fruition in the credit institution supervision, nor are there any indications that they could come to fruition in the field of insurance supervision. The Community

[127] Under sec. 55 of the VwGO [Administrative Court Procedures Code] in conjunction with sec. 172, no. 2 of the GVG [Courts Constitution Act], the public can be excluded for the protection of important business and trade secrets.

[128] See *Hüttenbrink*, in: Kuhla/Hüttenbrink, Der Verwaltungsprozess [in English: Administrative Procedure], (3rd ed. 2002), ref. 233; generally, on the principle of official investigation in administrative procedure, *Garloff*, in: Posser/Wolf (eds.), Beckscher Online-Kommentar VwGO, [in English: Beck Online Commentary – VwGO [Administrative Court Procedures Code]], as of October, 2008; *Dawin*, in: Schoch/Schmidt-Assmann/Pietzner (eds.), VwGO [in English: The Administrative Court Procedures Code], 15th supplemental issue, as of September 2007, vol. I, sec. 86 ref. 6 ff.

[129] See *Hüttenbrink*, in: Kuhla/Hüttenbrink, Der Verwaltungsprozess [in English: Administrative Procedure], (3rd ed. 2002), ref. 235. In such cases it does not matter whether the consent of the supervisory authority constitutes an administrative measure – which seems obvious – since the substantive burden of proof in a proceeding for injunctive relief and in a mandamus proceeding is identical.

[130] See, on the objectives of the disclosure duties, above, 13.2.

legislator should therefore consider adapting a concept similar to banking supervision in the area of insurance supervisory regime as well.

Proportionality also appears questionable with regard to art. 53, para. 4 of Solvency II, which is concerned with capital management. There is no apparent factual reason that information on the structure of own funds would require confidentiality in individual cases for credit institutions but not for direct insurance and reinsurance undertakings. Nor is the mandatory ex post transparency under art. 53, para. 4 of Solvency II with regard to solved problems with the target or Minimum Solvency Capital Requirements persuasive in this area. Under art. 54, para. 1, subpara. 2 of Solvency II, a duty has already been defined to issue updates to the Report on Solvency and Financial Condition if the solvency capital requirement is not adhered to and there is no sound recovery plan or its targets are not achieved by a certain deadline. With this, the public is already notified of fundamental changes concerning the Solvency Capital Requirements. Publishing other developments in this area, or publishing the same developments again, is not called for either on its own account or based on the level of detail required—such as origins, consequences, and remedial measures.

13.11 Summary

1. As a tangible result of legislating the disclosure duties to the public under the third pillar of Solvency II, the issuer of the Directive hopes to achieve greater transparency in the insurance market and to reduce information asymmetry. A primary means to this end is an annual "Report on Solvency and Financial Condition", the content of which has comprehensive minimum requirements defined in the Directive. According to the objectives expressly pursued by the Directive, the primary addressees of these publications are policyholders, insured parties, and all other legal persons such as beneficiaries who may have rights under an insurance contract. Competitors, brokers, the press, ratings agencies, and other interested parties are taken together from a legal view only as secondary addressees of the information.
2. The minimum content of the Report on Solvency and Financial Condition under Solvency II can be roughly classified as financial reporting information, formal organizational information, and risk reporting information.
3. Taken as a whole, the Report on Solvency and Financial Condition extends clearly beyond the publications required under commercial and capital market law. In this respect, it will bring about a notable increase in cost and resources expended by the direct insurance and reinsurance undertakings subject to the disclosures. Such expenditure can also be seen in the requirement to explain differences by individual line item in the valuation for solvency purposes as compared to the evaluation principles and methods under commercial law.
4. The minimum content of the Report on Solvency and Financial Condition under Solvency II is often inconsistent in terms of size and complexity with the

regulatory approach to informing policyholders and insureds as the primary segments of the public whose interest the Directive is supposed to protect. At the same time, it is doubtful whether the Reports on Solvency and Financial Condition will lead to any notable increase in the amount of information available to the professional public as the secondary addressee of publication. However, an exhaustive assessment on this matter as well as the question that arises immediately thereafter as to the proportionality of the disclosure duties can only be completed once substance has been provided at the second level of the Lamfalussy process. So that the assessment does not turn out poorly, these questions should be considered as early as possible and appropriate legal review should be performed on all public disclosure duties required in the draft.

5. There is partial overlap between the Report on Solvency and Financial Condition on one hand and the periodic capital market and commercial law publications on the other. The overlap is primarily related to financial and risk reporting. References can be made in this respect in the Report on Solvency and Financial Condition to the respective publication under commercial or capital market law, thus taking advantage of the potential for synergies.
6. Direct insurance and reinsurance undertakings that fall under the legal definition of domestic issuers may be able to benefit from a number of additional synergy opportunities. These opportunities may arise from the overlapping content between the Report on Solvency and Financial Condition and the event-based disclosure duties for issuers under capital market law.
7. Synergies may also be exploited by coordinating the timing of the disclosures required under insurance supervisory, commercial, and capital market law.
8. The waiver provided in the Directive for the preparation of Reports on Solvency and Financial Condition at the individual undertaking level by direct insurance and reinsurance undertakings that are part of a group in favor of a single group report should, in principle, be welcomed. However, a significantly more flexible formulation of art. 256, para. 2, subpara. 1 (b) of Solvency II is needed both for proportionality and in the interest of increasing market transparency.
9. With regard to the protection of confidentiality interests, the public disclosure duties under Solvency II put direct insurance and reinsurance undertakings in a less favorable position than the banks that are subject to parallel disclosure requirements under Basel II. Concerns with regard to the proportionality of the rules in the insurance area arise both from a fundamental perspective in view of the regulatory approach and specifically from the general exclusion of information on the capital management of direct insurance and reinsurance undertakings from the Directive's secrecy protections—particularly with respect to the structure of own funds.

List of Rules

List of Legal Rules	
Level 1	
A. EU	
I. Primary legislation	
1. "CFREU", Charter of the Fundamental Rights of the European Union	174
art. 15	174
art. 15, para. 1	225
art. 16	37, 174, 177
art. 38	78
art. 52	174
2. "TEC", Treaty establishing the European Community	76
art. 47, para. 2	76
art. 55	76
3. "TFEU", Treaty on the Function of the European Union	76, 78
art. 45	263
art. 101	134
art. 101, para. 1	40
art. 102	134
art. 114	76
art. 114, para. 3	78
art. 114, para. 4	78
art. 114, para. 6	78
art. 114, para. 9	78
art. 114, para. 10	76
art. 169, para. 1	76

(continued)

M. Dreher, *Treatises on Solvency II*, DOI 10.1007/978-3-662-46290-4

List of Legal Rules	
art. 169, para. 2	76
art. 169, para. 2 (a)	76
art. 169, para. 4	78
art. 263	148
art. 267	147
art. 289, para. 3	119
art. 290	118
art. 290, para. 1	8, 15
art. 290, para. 1, subpara. 2, sent. 2	118
art. 296	84
II. Secondary legislation	
1. Regulation	
a) Council Regulation (EC) No 2157/1001 of 8 October 2001 on the Statute for a European company (SE)	
art. 39, para. 1, sent. 1	176
b) Council Regulation (EC) No 1/2003 of 16 December 2002 on the implementation of the rules on competition laid down in Articles 81 and 82 of the Treaty	
art. 10, para. 1	375
c) Merger Control Regulation, EU Commission of 17 Jun. 2008, file 32008/M5075, OJEU 2008, no. C 229, p. 13	
art. 6, para. 2, subpara. 2	349
art. 8, para. 2, subpara. 2	349
d) "EIOPA Regulation", Regulation (EU) No 1094/2010 of the European Parliament and of the Council of 24 Nov. 2010, OJEU L 331 of 15 Dec. 2010, p. 48 ff.	5, 14, 67, 68, 69, 70, 71, 74, 75, 76, 78, 85, 86, 88, 90, 94, 95, 96
Recital 7	14
Recital 8	14
Recital 10	14, 85
Recital 10, sent. 3	69
Recital 21	14
Recital 31	14
Recital 47, sent. 3	70
Recital 50, sent. 4	70
Recital 66	70
art. 1	14
art. 1, para. 2	14
art. 1, para. 3	14, 84, 85, 95
art. 1, para. 6	95
art. 1, para. 6, subpara. 1, sent. 1	69, 88
art. 1, para. 6, subpara. 1, sent. 2	75
art. 1 para. 6, subpara. 1, sent. 2 (a)	76
art. 1, para. 6, subpara. 1, sent. 2 (f)	68, 75, 76, 83, 86
arts. 8 ff.	14

(continued)

List of Legal Rules	
art. 8, para. 1 (b)	14
art. 8, para. 1 (i)	69
art. 8, para. 1 (j)	69
art. 8, para. 1 (h)	75
art. 8, para. 2 (i)	69, 75
art. 9	69, 70, 76
art. 9, para. 1	69
art. 9, para. 1 (a)	87, 96
art. 9, para. 3	70
art. 9, para. 4	70
art. 9, para. 5	70
art. 10	85
art. 15	85
art. 16	82, 83, 84, 164
art. 16, para. 1	83
art. 17, para. 6	14
art. 21	78
art. 22	78
art. 23	78
art. 24	78
art. 25	78
art. 26	78
art. 29	14
art. 29, para. 2	87, 95
art. 38	70
art. 38, para. 5	70
art. 61	148
2. Directive	
a) Directive 83/349/EEC of 13 Jun. 1983 concerning consolidated accounts, OJEC L 193 of 18 Jul. 1983, p. 1 ff.	
art. 12, para. 1	410
b) Directive 85/577/EEC of the Council of 20 Dec. 1985 to protect the consumer in respect of contracts negotiated away from business premises, OJEC L 372 of 31 Dec. 1985, p. 31 ff.	5
c) Council Directive 91/674/EEC of 19 December 1991 on the annual accounts and consolidated accounts of insurance undertakings, OJEC L 374 of 31. Dec. 1991	309
d) "Third non-life insurance Directive", Council Directive 92/49/EEC of 18 Jun. 1992, OJEC L 228 of 11. Aug. 1992, p. 1 ff.	17
e) "Third life assurance Directive", Council Directive 92/96/EEC of 10 Nov. 1992, OJEC L 360 of 9. Dec. 1992, p. 1 ff.	17

(continued)

List of Legal Rules	
f) Directive 93/13/EC of 5 Apr. 1993 on abusive terms in consumer contracts, OJEC L 95 1993, p. 29 ff.	5
g) Directive 97/7/EC of the European Parliament and of the Council of 20 Apr. 1997 on the protection of consumers in respect of distance contracts, OJEC L 144 of 4 Jun. 1997, p. 19 ff.	5
h) Insurance Group Directive 98/78/EC of the European Parliament and of the Council of 27 Oct. 1998, OJEC L 330 of 5 Dec. 1998, p. 1 ff.	367, 368
art. 8	368
i) Directive 99/44/EC of the European Parliament and of the Council of 25 May 1999, on certain aspects of the sale of consumer goods and associated guarantees, OJEC L 171 of 7 Jul. 1999, p. 12 ff.	6
j) Directive 2002/65/EC on the distance marketing of consumer financial services, OJEU L 271 of 9 Oct. 2002, p. 16 ff.	80
Recital 13	7
art. 2d	80
k) Directive 2002/83/EC of the European Parliament and of the Council of 5 Nov. 2002 on life insurance, OJEU L 345 of 19. Dec. 2002, p. 1 ff.	
art. 13, para. 3 (b)	20
l) Directive 2002/92/EC on Insurance Mediation	
aa) Proposal for a directive of the European Parliament and of the council on insurance mediation, COM(2012) 352 (final); also at BR-Drucks. 388/12 of 4 Jul. 2012	76
Recitals 5 ff.	76
bb) final version, OJEU L 9 of 15. Jan. 2003, p. 3 ff.	76
Recital 8	76
Recital 17	76
Recital 18	76
Recital 22	76
Recital 23	76
m) Directive 2004/39/EC of 21 April 2004 on markets in financial instruments amending Council Directives 85/611/EEC and 93/6/EEC and Directive 2000/12/EC of the European Parliament and of the Council and repealing Council Directive 93/22/EEC, OJEU L 145 of 30 April 2004	13, 72, 363
n) Directive 2004/109/EC on the harmonisation of transparency requirements for information about issuers whose securities are admitted to trading on a regulated market and amending Directive 2001/34/EC of 15 Dec. 2004, OJEU L 390 of 31. Dec. 2004, p. 38 ff.	401

(continued)

List of Legal Rules	
art. 9, para. 3 (a)	354
o) "UCP Directive", Directive 2005/29/EC of 11 May 2005 concerning unfair business-to-consumer practices in the internal market, OJEU L 149/22 of 11 June 2005	90
Recital 18	90
p) Directive 2005/60/EC of the European Parliament and of the Council of 26 Oct. 2005 on the prevention of the use of the financial system for the purpose of money laundering and terrorist financing, OJEU L 309/15 of 25 Nov 2005	312
q) "Banking directive", Directive 2006/48/EC of the European Parliament and of the Council of 14 Jun. 2006 relating to the taking up and pursuit of the business of credit institutions, OJEU L 177 of 30 Jun. 2006, p. 1 ff. (recast) of 14 June 2006 relating to the taking up and pursuit of the business of credit institutions (recast)	182
arts. 146 ff.	388
art. 146	421
art. 146, para. 3	421
art. 148, para. 1	414
r) Solvency II Framework Directive	
aa) drafts/proposals	
(i) Proposal for a Directive of the European Parliament and of the Council on the taking-up and pursuit of the business of Insurance and Reinsurance - Solvency II of 10 Jul. 2007, COM(2007) 361 (final) (1st draft)	347, 387
(ii) Proposal for a Directive of the European Parliament and of the Council on the taking-up and pursuit of the business of Insurance and Reinsurance - Solvency II of 26 Feb. 2008, COM(2008) 119 (final) (2nd Draft)	347, 360, 369, 370, 387
Recital 15	359
Recital 20	356
Recital 57	352
art. 18, para. 1 (d)	359
art. 18, para. 1 (e)	359
art. 18, para. 1 (f)	359
art. 33	407
art. 35	363, 371, 379, 380
art. 35, para. 1, sent. 1	363, 366, 371, 379
art. 35, para. 1, sent. 2 (a)	359, 361, 363, 366, 371
art. 35, para. 6, sent. 1	359

(continued)

List of Legal Rules	
art. 36	359, 361, 363 366, 371, 379
art. 36, para. 2 (c)	359
art. 36, para. 2 (d)	363
art. 36, para. 2 (f)	360
art. 36, para. 2 (e)	361
art. 39, para. 1	355
art. 42	349, 351, 368, 380
art. 42, para. 1	349, 378
art. 42, para. 1 (a)	351
art. 42, para. 1 (b)	351, 382
art. 42, para. 2	349, 379
art. 42, para. 3	351, 381
art. 42a	351
art. 43	360
art. 43, para. 5	360
art. 44	360
art. 48, para. 3	357
art. 56	353, 354
art. 60	354
art. 102, para. 1, sent. 1	359
art. 110, para. 2	360
art. 110, para. 3	360
art. 110, para. 7	360
art. 116	360
art. 116, para. 1	360
art. 118	360
art. 127, para. 1 (d)	359
art. 127, para. 2	359
art. 136, para. 1	364
art. 137, para. 1	364
art. 143	356
art. 145	356
art. 179, para. 1	352
art. 179, para. 2	352, 382
art. 204, para. 1 (b)	352, 382
art. 210, para. 1 (d)	371
art. 211, para. 1, sent. 2	370
art. 216, para. 2	370
art. 216, para. 3	370
art. 217, para. 1	370
art. 217, para. 1, sent. 2	371
art. 217, para. 2, sent. 2	371
art. 228, para. 1, sent. 1	371

(continued)

List of Legal Rules	
art. 248, para. 2, sent. 1	372
art. 249, para. 2	369
art. 249, para. 2, sent. 1	369
art. 249, para. 2, sent. 2	369
art. 249, para. 2, sent. 3	369
art. 249, para. 4	369
art. 250, para. 1	372
art. 251, para. 1	371
art. 252, para. 1 (d)	371
art. 258, para. 2, sent. 2	372
art. 261	368
art. 299	351
(iii) Draft Solvency II in the version of the Council, Common Position of 25 Nov. 2008	
art. 127, para. 4, sent. 2	359
bb) final version	
(i) Directive 2009/138/EC of the European Parliament and of the Council of 25 Nov. 2009 on the taking-up and pursuit of the business of Insurance and Reinsurance (Solvency II), OJEU L 335, 17 Dec. 2009	
Recital 2	4, 8, 9
Recital 5	113
Recital 6	10
Recital 9	10
Recital 11	9, 10
Recital 15	133
Recital 16	9, 30, 71, 77, 79, 83, 102, 175, 389
Recital 17	33, 71, 80, 103, 143
Recital 18, sent. 2	303, 339
Recital 19	113, 114, 136, 143, 161, 298, 303, 339
Recital 20	143
Recital 21	143
Recital 26, sent. 4	114
Recital 28	53
Recital 29, sent. 1	133
Recital 29, sent. 3	339
Recitals 30 ff.	208
Recital 30	287, 397
Recital 31	85, 135, 136, 295, 301
Recital 31, sent. 2	234, 239, 338
Recital 31, sent. 3	246
Recital 31, sent. 4	239
Recital 32	113, 234, 239, 240, 336, 337
Recital 33	206, 219, 221, 223, 224, 326, 397
Recital 34	206, 221, 227, 231, 245, 257, 265, 397
Recital 34, sent. 1	264

(continued)

List of Legal Rules	
Recital 34, sent. 2	259, 264
Recital 35	206, 221, 227, 228, 232, 247, 257, 327
Recital 36	160, 163, 179
Recital 38	140, 302, 390, 415, 416
Recital 40	9, 39, 280, 296, 309
Recital 45	101
Recital 46	9
Recital 53	10
Recital 54	9, 115
Recital 59	113
Recital 60	179
Recital 64	103
Recital 65	103
Recital 66	113
Recital 67	133
Recital 68	133
Recital 75	10
Recital 79	79
Recital 81	10
Recital 83	10
Recital 85	10
Recital 86	10
Recital 87	10
Recital 93	10
Recital 96	10
Recital 98	77, 79
Recital 99	10
Recital 104	219
Recital 105	80
Recital 113	9
Recital 114	9
Recital 115	9
Recital 127	10
Recital 141	79
art. 4	292
art. 13, no. 29	219, 236, 287
art. 13, no. 30	134, 317, 398
art. 13, no. 31	117, 120, 134, 317, 398
art. 13, no. 32	134, 317, 398
art. 13, no. 33	32, 134, 317, 398
art. 13, no. 34	134, 317, 398
art. 13, no. 35	134, 317, 398
art. 18, para. 1 (a)	23

(continued)

List of Legal Rules	
art. 18, para. 1 (b)	23
art. 24	102
art. 26, para. 3	227, 228
art. 27	30, 35, 71, 102, 175, 389
art. 28	30, 35, 71, 102, 175
art. 28, para. 2	123, 124
art. 29, para. 1	28, 40, 54
art. 29, para. 3	136, 161, 246, 298, 303, 339
art. 29, para. 4	113, 143, 292
art. 30, para. 1	34
art. 30, para. 2, subpara. 1	34
art. 31, para. 1	40, 62
art. 31, para. 2, subpara. 1 (b)	39
art. 31 para. 2 (b)	295
art. 33	407
art. 34	59, 309
art. 34, para. 1	38, 43, 53, 54, 55, 58, 59, 225
art. 34, para. 1, sent. 1	20
art. 34, para. 2	58, 59, 206, 268
art. 34, para. 5	33, 36, 60
art. 35	33, 162, 170, 180, 186, 189, 289, 379, 389
art. 35, para. 1	392
art. 35, para. 1, sent. 1	12, 190, 399
art. 35, para. 1, sent. 2	399
art. 35, para. 1, sent. 2 (a)	187, 188, 189
art. 35, para. 2	60
art. 35, para. 2 (a)	187
art. 35, para. 2 (c)	33, 35, 36, 61
art. 35, para. 2 (i)	187
art. 35, para. 2 (iii)	189
art. 35, para. 3	389, 391
art. 35, para. 4	388, 389, 391
art. 35, para. 4 (a)	391, 417
art. 35, para. 5	254
art. 36	27, 28, 31, 32, 33, 38, 39, 44, 59, 60, 77, 101, 108, 225, 295, 379, 392, 399
art. 36, para. 1	32, 34, 38, 54, 63, 77
art. 36, para. 1, subpara. 1	30, 31, 37, 38
art. 36, para. 1, subpara. 2	30, 31, 32, 38, 39
art. 36, para. 2	31, 32, 34, 37, 38, 77, 108
art. 36, para. 2 (a)	32, 34, 43, 63, 190, 191
art. 36, para. 3	31, 32, 35, 48, 108, 109
art. 36, para. 4	31, 32, 39
art. 36, para. 5	32, 40, 53, 54, 55, 58, 59, 61, 64, 65, 108, 191

(continued)

List of Legal Rules	
art. 36, para. 6	31, 34, 399
art. 36, para. 6, subpara. 2	32, 59
art. 37	60, 101, 139, 168, 172, 179, 180, 181, 182, 183, 396
art. 37, para. 1, sent. 1	63
art. 37, para. 1, sent. 2 (a)	62, 180, 183, 184, 192
art. 37, para. 1, sent. 2 (b)	180, 183, 184, 192
art. 37, para. 1, sent. 2 (c)	53, 62, 63, 172
art. 37, para. 1 (a)	172
art. 37, para. 1 (b)	172
art. 37, para. 2, subpara. 2	140
art. 38	248, 333
art. 40	38, 124, 125, 206, 237, 280, 288, 307, 308, 318, 334
arts. 41 ff.	41, 42, 44, 135, 219, 397
art. 41	83, 206, 264, 338
art. 41, para. 1	41, 42, 225, 256
art. 41, para. 1, subpara. 1	207
art. 41, para. 1, subpara. 2	42, 125, 233, 238, 240, 328, 336, 337
art. 41, para. 2	337
art. 41, para. 3	237
art. 41, para. 3, subpara. 1	253
art. 41, para. 3, subpara. 1, sent. 2	254
art. 41, para. 3, subpara. 2	141, 206
art. 41, para. 3, subpara. 2, sent. 2	254
art. 41, para. 4	143, 304
art. 41, para. 5	135
art. 41, para. 5, subpara. 2	236
arts. 42 ff.	42
art. 42	41, 42, 130, 131, 206, 208, 209, 221, 222, 230, 232, 233, 236, 247, 250, 262, 275, 276, 327
art. 42, para. 1	21, 22, 206, 207, 208, 209, 210, 215, 220, 221, 227, 228, 245, 246, 247, 250, 251, 276, 349, 378, 397
art. 42, para. 1 (a)	206, 207, 208, 246, 249, 250, 280
art. 42, para. 1 (b)	72, 259, 260
art. 42, para. 2	220, 221, 227, 228, 231, 246, 265, 266
art. 42, para. 3	265
art. 43	259, 261, 263, 272
art. 43, para. 1	261
art. 43, para. 2	261
art. 44	125, 129, 221, 300
art. 44, para. 1, subpara. 1	43
art. 44, para. 1, subpara. 2	221, 227, 228

(continued)

List of Legal Rules	
art. 44, para. 2	125, 160, 161
art. 44, para. 2, subpara. 2	129
art. 44, para. 2, subpara. 2 (b)	129
art. 44, para. 2, subpara. 2 (e)	32
art. 44, para. 2, subpara. 3	253
art. 44, para. 5	399
art. 44, para. 5 (c)	136
art. 44, para. 5 (e)	238
art. 45	125, 137, 158, 159, 163, 164, 167, 170, 173, 174, 182, 317
art. 45, para. 1	110, 159, 162
art. 45, para. 1, subpara. 2 (a)	160, 163, 166
art. 45, para. 1, subpara. 2 (b)	163
art. 45, para. 1, subpara. 2 (c)	166, 168, 170, 172, 180, 182, 183, 185
art. 45, para. 2	159, 166, 168, 186
art. 45, para. 2, sent. 1	168
art. 45, para. 2, sent. 2	166, 169
art. 45, para. 3	159
art. 45, para. 4	159, 162, 163, 173, 176, 178
art. 45, para. 5	49, 141, 159, 160, 173, 189
art. 45, para. 6	159, 162, 169, 186, 187, 188, 189
art. 45, para. 7	159, 169, 179
art. 46	83, 296, 317, 327, 328
art. 46, para. 1	284, 288, 292, 326
art. 46, para. 1, subpara. 1	309
art. 46, para. 1, subpara. 2	172, 237, 253, 297, 300, 303, 306, 308, 309, 312
art. 46, para. 2	206, 238, 288, 297, 300, 307, 308, 309, 313, 316, 326
art. 47, para. 1, subpara. 2	173
art. 47, para. 2	233, 238, 239, 336
art. 47, para. 3	206, 238
art. 48	41, 148, 170, 237
art. 48, para. 1 (e)	206, 238
art. 48, para. 1 (i)	43, 166, 170, 254
art. 48, para. 2	247
art. 49	248, 333
art. 49, para. 2	326
art. 49, para. 2 (a)	141
arts. 50 ff.	414
art. 50	411
art. 50, para. 1 (a)	264, 338
art. 50, para. 1 (b)	227
art. 50, para. 1 (c)	230

(continued)

List of Legal Rules	
art. 50, para. 2	158, 395
arts. 51 ff.	387, 417, 419
art. 51	80, 110, 136, 186, 268, 289, 389, 411
art. 51, para. 1	386
art. 51, para. 1, subpara. 1	387, 389, 391, 417
art. 51, para. 1, subpara. 1, sent. 1	388
art. 51, para. 1, subpara. 2	190, 392, 398, 407, 411, 416, 419
art. 51, para. 1, subpara. 2, sent. 2	420
art. 51, para. 1, subpara. 2 (a)	392
art. 51, para. 1, subpara. 2 (b)	190, 397, 398, 399
art. 51, para. 1, subpara. 2 (c)	398, 399
art. 51, para. 1, subpara. 2 (d)	394
art. 51, para. 1, subpara. 2 (e)	395
art. 51, para. 1, subpara. 2 (e) (i)	395
art. 51, para. 1, subpara. 2 (e) (ii)	395
art. 51, para. 1, subpara. 2 (e) (iii)	396, 416
art. 51, para. 1, subpara. 2 (e) (iv)	396
art. 51, para. 1, subpara. 2 (e) (v)	141
art. 51, para. 2, subpara. 1	395
art. 51, para. 2, subpara. 2	395
art. 51, para. 2, subpara. 2, sent. 4	396
art. 51, para. 2, subpara. 3	396
art. 51, para. 3	411
art. 52	389
art. 53	415
art. 53, para. 1	190, 415, 421, 422
art. 53, para. 3	191, 407, 415, 419
art. 53, para. 4	415, 423
art. 54	191, 388, 389
art. 54, para. 1	191, 388
art. 54, para. 1, subpara. 1	387, 400, 410
art. 54, para. 1, subpara. 2	400, 423
art. 54, para. 1, subpara. 2 (a)	400
art. 54, para. 1, subpara. 2 (b)	141, 400
art. 54, para. 1, subpara. 3	400
art. 54, para. 1, subpara. 4	141, 400
art. 54, para. 2	388
art. 55, para. 1	388
art. 55, para. 2	254
art. 56	392
art. 59, para. 1 (c)	312
art. 62	60
art. 71	11

(continued)

List of Legal Rules	
art. 71, para. 2	381
art. 71, para. 2, sent. 1	296, 309
art. 71, para. 2, sent. 2	222
art. 72, para. 1	33, 35, 49
art. 72, para. 1, subpara. 1 (a)	38
art. 73	32
art. 74	394
art. 75	45, 107, 111, 115, 394
art. 75, para. 1	44, 115, 127
arts. 76 ff.	46, 394
art. 76, para. 1	127
art. 76, para. 2	45
art. 76, para. 3	45, 117
art. 76, para. 4	45
art. 77, para. 1	45, 394
art. 77, para. 2	117
art. 77, para. 2, subpara. 1	45
art. 77, para. 2, subpara. 2	45, 47, 148
art. 77, para. 3	45
art. 77, para. 4	45
art. 77, para. 5, subpara. 2	112
art. 78	46
art. 79	46
art. 80	393
art. 81	46
art. 82	45
art. 83	45
art. 84	46
art. 85	46, 61
arts. 86 ff.	395
arts. 87 ff.	103, 135
art. 87	103
art. 88, no. 1	115
art. 88	51, 103
art. 89	103, 395
art. 89, para. 1, subpara. 1	52
art. 89, para. 1, subpara. 2 (a)	395
art. 90	52, 103
art. 90, para. 1	395
art. 91	103
art. 92	103
arts. 93 ff.	111
art. 93	51, 103, 120

(continued)

List of Legal Rules	
art. 93, para. 1	51
art. 93, para. 2	51
art. 93, para. 2, subpara. 1, sent. 2	52
art. 94	52, 103
art. 95	103
art. 96	103
art. 97	52, 103
arts. 98 ff.	111
art. 98	52, 103, 120
art. 99	103
art. 99, sent. 1 (a)	52
arts. 100 ff.	104, 395
art, 100, para. 1	104
art. 100, para. 1, subpara. 1	105
art. 101	48, 105, 396
art. 101, para. 3	184
art. 101, para. 3, subpara. 1	48
art. 101, para. 3, subpara. 2	116
art. 101, para. 4	125
art. 102, para. 1	170
art. 102, para. 1, subpara. 1	105
art. 102, para. 1, subpara. 2	104
art. 103	396
art. 104, para. 4	396
art. 104, para. 4, subpara. 1	116
art. 104, para. 5	112
art. 104, para. 7	114
art. 105, para. 3, subpara. 2 (a)	119
art. 105, para. 3, subpara. 2 (b)	119
art. 105, para. 3, subpara. 2 (c)	119
art. 105, para. 3, subpara. 2 (d)	119
art. 105, para. 3, subpara. 2 (e)	119
art. 105, para. 3, subpara. 2 (f)	119
art. 105, para. 4, subpara. 2 (a)	119
art. 105, para. 5	119
art. 105, para. 5, subpara 2 (d)	117
art. 106	396
art. 106, para. 2	112
art. 106, para. 3	120
art. 107, para. 2	317
art. 107, para. 3	317
art. 109	114
art. 110	114, 134

(continued)

List of Legal Rules	
art. 111, para. 1	112
art. 111, para. 2	128
art. 112	100
art. 112, para. 2, subpara. 2	130
art. 112, para. 7	113
art. 116	125
art. 116, para. 1	254
art. 118, para. 1	141
art. 119	60, 114, 134, 181, 182, 183, 192
arts. 120 ff.	53
art. 120	141
art. 120, para. 1	125, 129
art. 120, para. 1 (b)	103
art. 120, para. 3	125, 137
art. 121	141
art. 121, para. 2, subpara. 3	137, 141
art. 121, para. 4, subpara. 2	125
art. 122	141
art. 122, para. 1	116
art. 122, para. 2	116
art. 123	130, 141
art. 124	141
art. 124, subpara. 2	137
art. 125	136, 141
arts. 128 ff.	395
art. 128	105
arts. 129 ff.	48
art. 129	105
art. 129, para. 1 (b)	105
art. 129, para. 1 (c)	116
art. 129, para. 4, subpara. 1	105
art. 130	105
art. 131	105
art. 132	128
art. 132, para. 1	49
art. 132, para. 2	50, 163
art. 132, para. 2, subpara. 3	50
art. 132, para. 4, subpara. 2	50
art. 132, para. 4, subpara. 3	50
art. 132, para. 4, subpara. 4	50
art. 133, para. 1	49
art. 135, para. 2	50
art. 136	109

(continued)

List of Legal Rules	
art. 137	109
arts. 138 ff.	55
art. 138	60, 109
art. 138, para. 1	60, 400
art. 138, para. 2	61, 400
art. 138, para. 3	61
art. 138, para. 4	124
art. 138, para. 4, subpara. 2	61
art. 138, para. 5	61
art. 139	61, 109
art. 139, para. 1	400
art. 139, para. 2	400
art. 140	109
art. 141	55, 61, 109
art. 141, para. 2	143
art. 142	102, 109
art. 143	109
art. 144	109
art. 163	102
art. 172	290
art. 181, para. 1, subpara. 2, sent. 1	73
art. 182, para. 2, sent. 1	73
art. 183	83, 84
art. 183, para. 1, subpara. 2	84
art. 183, para. 2	71
art. 185	83, 84
art. 185, para. 2 (d)	81
art. 185, para. 3 (l)	84
art. 186, para. 2 (b)	71
arts. 212 ff.	106
art. 212, para. 1 (a)	106, 410
art. 212, para. 1 (c)	106
art. 212, para. 1 (e)	78
art. 212, para. 1 (f)	106, 410
arts. 213 ff.	11
art. 213, para. 1, sent. 2	11, 106
art. 213, para. 2	106
art. 214, para. 2	12
arts. 218 ff.	106
art. 218, para. 1	106
art. 218, para. 2	106, 116
art. 218, para. 3	106, 116
art. 218, para. 4	28, 106
art. 218, para. 5	107

(continued)

List of Legal Rules	
art. 219, para. 1, subpara. 1	106
art. 220	107
art. 220, para. 2	107
arts. 221 ff.	107
art. 221	107
art. 222	107, 111
art. 223	107, 111
art. 224	107, 111, 115
art. 230, para. 1, subpara. 2 (a)	106, 116
art. 232	101
art. 233, para. 1 (a)	106, 116
art. 233, para. 2	106, 116
art. 233, para. 6, subpara. 2	101
art. 233, para. 6, subpara. 3	101
arts. 236 ff.	107
art. 236	289
art. 241	412
arts. 244 f.	107
arts. 247 ff.	28, 106
art. 248	206, 229
art. 248, para. 1	411
art. 248, para. 1 (d)	206, 208
art. 248, para. 2	78
art. 250	208
art. 256	110
art. 256, para. 1	411
art. 256, para. 1, sent. 1	400, 410
art. 256, para. 1, sent. 2	411, 415
art. 256, para. 2	411, 420
art. 256, para. 2, subpara. 1 (b)	420, 424
art. 256, para. 2, subpara. 2	411
art. 256, para. 3	411
art. 257	206, 208, 209, 229
art. 260	290
art. 304	11, 396
art. 310	76
art. 310, para. 1, sent. 1	12
cc) amending Solvency II	
(i) Proposal for a Directive of the European Parliament and of the Council amending Directives 2003/71/EC and 2009/138/EC in respect of the powers of the European Insurance and Occupational Pensions Authority and the European Securities and Markets Authority, COM (2011) 8 (final)	
art. 2, para. 7	158
art. 2, para. 72	159
art. 2, para. 74	159

(continued)

List of Legal Rules	
(ii) Response of the European Economic and Social Committee to the "Proposal for a directive of the European Parliament and of the Council amending Directives 2003/71/EC and 2009/138/EC in respect of the powers of the European Insurance and Occupational Pensions Authority and the European Securities and Markets Authority", 2011/C 218/15	164
s) Directive 2007/64/EC of the European Parliament and of the Council of 13 Nov. 2007 on payment services in the internal market amending Directives 97/7/EC, 2002/65/EC, 2005/60/EC, and 2006/48/EC and repealing Directive 97/5/EC, OJEC L 319 of 5 Dec. 2007, p. 1 ff.	7
t) Directive 2008/48/EC of the European Parliament and of the Council of 23 Apr. 2008, on credit agreements for consumers and repealing Council Directive 87/102/EEC, OJEU L 133 of 22 May 2008, p. 66 ff.	
Recital 10	7
Recital 11	7
art. 22	7
u) Directive 2009/14/EC of the European Parliament and of the Council of 11 Mar. 2009, amending Directive 94/19/EC on deposit-guarantee schemes as regards the amount insured and payout delay, OJEU L 68 of 13 Mar. 2009, p. 3 ff.	
Recital 3	6
art. 1, no. 3 (a)	6
art. 7, para. 1 (a)	6
v) "CRD IV", Capital Requirements Directive IV	
aa) Proposal for a regulation of the European Parliament and of the Council on prudential requirements for credit institutions and investment firms, COM(2011) 452 (final)	
art. 109, para. 4	117
bb) final version	
Statement of Reason for sec. 25a, para. 1, sent. 3, clause 2, no. 3 (c)	299
sec. 25a, para. 1, sent. 3, clause 2, no. 3 (c)	288
3. Decision	
Decision 2009/79/EU of the Commission of 23 Jan. 2009 establishing the Committee of European Insurance and Occupational Pensions Supervisors, OJEU L 25 of 29 Jan. 2009, p. 28 ff.	9
4. Recommendations und opinions	
Recommendation of the Commission for a comprehensive directive on consumer rights of 8 Oct. 2008, COM(2008) 614 (final)	7

(continued)

List of Legal Rules	
5. Other texts	
a) Basel II	30, 388, 391, 414, 421, 424
Annex XII, Part 2, 3	421
b) Basel III	11, 30
c) CEIOPS	
aa) Advice to the European Commission on Supervisory Reporting and Public Disclosure in the Framework of the Solvency II Project of March 2007	
no. 1.8	392
no. 4.4	393, 411
no. 4.7	393
no. 4.8	350, 393, 397, 411
no. 4.8 (b)	397
no. 4.9	394
no. 4.10	394
no. 4.11	395
no. 4.12	366, 397, 398
no. 4.23	396
no. 5.2	388
bb) Issue Paper, New Risk Management and Other Corporate Issues of 17 Jul. 2007	229
no. 2.2, pnt. 21	350
pnt. 2.2	206
cc) Issues Paper, Policy on harmonisation of contents and formats for public disclosure and supervisory reporting of 1 Nov. 2007	
no. 2	391
no. 6.1	419
no. 6.2	390
no. 7	391
no. 7.1	417
no. 7.2	390
dd) Internal Governance, Supervisory Review and Reporting Expert Group Issues Paper on ORSA Feedback Statement 2008 CEIOPS-IGSRR-26/08	179
ee) Issues Paper, Implementing Measures on System of Governance of 11 March 2008	
no. 5.2	397
ff) "IP ORSA", Issues Paper on Own Risk and Solvency Assessment (ORSA) of 27 May 2008	160
no. 3 (b)	179
no. 3 (c)	181
no. 8	160
no. 9	160
no. 9.47	163
no. 11	160
no. 51	187

(continued)

List of Legal Rules	
gg) Issues Paper, Supervisory Review Process and Undertakings Reporting Requirements of 15 Aug. 2008	
no. 1.1	31
no. 1.3	31
no. 3.6	39
no. 4.2	39
no. 4.4	33
nos. 4.9. ff.	36
no. 4.12	36
no. 4.22	36
no. 4.25	36
no. 4.27	36
no. 4.29 f.	36
nos. 4.35 ff.	33
no. 4.38	49
no. 4.39	49
no. 4.40	49
no. 4.42	56
no. 4.43	40, 56
no. 4.45	56, 60, 61
nos. 5.20 ff.	359
no. 6.2	391
no. 6.4 (b)	390
no. 6.14 (a)	390
hh) Issues Paper, Implementing Measures on System of Governance of 3 Nov. 2008	
pnt. 5	206
pnt. 5.2	206, 350
pnts. 10.1 ff.	357
ii) Draft Advice for Level 2 Implementing Measures on Solvency II: Reporting Requirements of 25 Feb. 2009	
no. 3.6	390
nos. 3.22 ff.	388
no. 3.30	417
nos. 3.32 f.	389
no. 3.33	399
no. 3.38	393
no. 3.39	398, 411
no. 3.41	398
no. 3.45	359, 395, 416
no. 3.57	349, 357, 366
no. 3.60	359
no. 3.61	361, 363

(continued)

List of Legal Rules	
jj) Consultation Paper No. 33, Draft Advice for Level 2 Implementing Measures on Solvency II: System of Governance of 26 Mar. 2009	350
no. 3.31	350, 397
no. 3.43	350, 397
kk) Advice for Level 2 Implementing Measures on Solvency II: Supervisory Reporting and Public Disclosure Requirements	
(i) draft, 2. Jul. 2009	
no. 3.28	392
no. 3.58	389
no. 3.79	396
no. 3.91	399
no. 3.92	399
no. 3.93	399
no. 3.94	399
no. 3.96	393
no. 3.97	411
no. 3.99	395
no. 3.113	397
no. 3.114	398
no. 3.115	398
no. 3.116	398
(ii) final Version, October 2009	
no. 3.25	186
nos. 3.30. ff	186
no. 3.2.5	29
no. 3.48	189
no. 3.50	184
no. 3.3.2	184
no. 3.62	81
no. 3.70	40
no. 3.71	191
no. 3.315	189
no. 3.371	189
ll) Advice for Level 2 Implementing Measures on Solvency II: System of Governance of October 2009	12
mm) "Governance Guidelines", Consultation Paper, Draft Proposal for Level 3 Guidelines on the System of Governance of December 2010	72, 85, 222, 224, 225, 226, 231, 232, 244, 255, 261, 262, 265, 277, 278, 281, 290, 322
explanations to Guideline 13	72
no. 1.11	248, 266
no. 1.11, sent. 2	231
no. 1.11, sent. 3	248

(continued)

List of Legal Rules	
no. 1.14	290
no. 2.12	249
no. 2.14	255
no. 3.1	249
no. 3.155	290, 317, 329
no. 3.156	290, 317
no. 3.157	291, 309
no. 3.158	291
no. 3.158g	291
no. 3.2.4	255
nos. 3.28 f.	265
no. 3.31	257, 264
no. 3.32, sent. 2	260
no. 3.33	248
nos. 3.33 ff.	248
no. 3.37	249, 257
no. 3.38	249
nos. 3.39 ff.	249
nos. 3.46 ff.	260
no. 3.52	261
no. 3.53	263
no. 3.56	255
no. 3.57	231
no. 3.57 (a)	266
no. 3.57 (c)	225
no. 3.60 (c)	266
no. 3.62 (b)	267
no. 3.63	266
ref. 1.9	277
ref. 1.10	224
ref. 2.5	246
ref. 2.10	132
refs. 3.2.8. f.	132
ref. 3.46	72
ref. 3.48	72
Guideline 1	225
Guideline 5	225
Guideline 8	291
Guideline 10	265
Guideline 11	248
Guideline 12	249
Guideline 13	260
Guideline 14	225, 260

(continued)

List of Legal Rules	
Guideline 14 (a)	266
Guideline 14 (b)	255
Guideline 14 (c)	255
Guideline 14 (d)	258
Guideline 40	291
Guideline 41	291
d) EBA [European Banking Authority]	
aa) Guidelines on Internal Governance	299
bb) Consultation paper on draft Guidelines for assessing the suitability of members of the management body and key function holders of a credit institution of 18 Apr. 2012	230
e) EIOPA	
aa) "Level 3 Proposal", Draft Proposal for Level 3 Guidelines on Own Risk and Solvency Assessment (Article 45), 2010	
no. 3.25	189
no. 3.27	189
no. 3.7	162
bb) QIS 5: Relevant risk-free interest rate term structures of 6 Jul. 2010	118
cc) "Consultation Paper", Consultation Paper on the Proposal for Guidelines on Own Risk and Solvency Assessment, 2011	158, 163, 168
no. 3.2	159
no. 3.5	158
no. 3.15	186
no. 4.1	160
no. 4.3	171
no. 4.6	169
no. 4.15	187
no. 4.16	186
no. 4.34	183
no. 4.40	163
nos. 4.49 ff.	185
no. 4.50	185
no. 4.52	185
no. 4.53	183
no. 4.64	185
nos. 4.69 ff.	163, 178
no. 4.70	176, 178
no. 4.71	178
no. 4.72	178
Guideline 1	165
Guideline 2	165

(continued)

List of Legal Rules	
Guideline 3	187
Guideline 4	186, 187
Guideline 5	186, 187
Guideline 6	186, 187
Guideline 8	160
Guideline 13	185
Guideline 14	163, 176
Guideline 15	160
dd) "Report on the fifth quantitative impact study" (QIS 5) for Solvency II of 14 Mar. 2011	113
ee) Report on Financial Literacy and Education Initiatives by Competent Authorities of 16 Dec. 2011	69
ff) Initial Overview of Key Consumer Trends in the EU of 1 Feb. 2012	87
gg) CCPFI Mandate of 29 Mar. 2012	70, 71
sent. 1.	71
hh) Working paper: Public Consultation on the Guidelines and Best Practices Report on Complaints-Handling by Insurance Undertakings Summary of the responses received of 14 Jun. 2012, p. 5	82, 83, 84, 86, 87, 95
ii) Impact Assessment on Guidelines on complaints-handling by insurance undertakings of 14 Jun. 2012	82, 83
jj) 27 June 2012 press release/EIOPA Newsletter, 27 Jun. 2012	83, 84
kk) "EIOPA Guidelines", Guidelines on complaints-handling by insurance undertakings of 27 Jun. 2012	38, 82, 83, 84, 85, 86, 94, 95
point 9 in the introduction	87
Guideline 2	86
Guideline 2, point 1	83
Guideline 4, point 9	87
ll) Methodology Report for Collecting, Analysing and Reporting on Consumer Trends of November 2012 (published in December 2012)	87
mm) Board of Supervisors, EIOPA procedures for issuing warnings, temporary prohibitions and restrictions of 12 Nov. 2012 (published on 6 Dec. 2012)	69
Recital 2	69
nn) EIOPA Work Program 2013, 13, n. 1	88
oo) Proposal for "Guidelines on the System of Governance" of 27 March 2013	
no. 1.21	291

(continued)

List of Legal Rules	
no. 1.22	291
no. 1.28	291
no. 1.199	291
f) European Commission	
aa) Notice of the Commission on consumer policy strategy, COM(2002) 208 (final), OJEU C 137 of 8 Jun. 2002	7
bb) QIS 5 Technical Specifications of 5 July 2010	117, 118, 119, 120, 122
SCR.5.88	117
cc) Proposal for a directive of the European Parliament and of the Council on the access to the activity of credit institutions and the prudential supervision of credit institutions and investment firms and amending Directive 2002/87/EC of the European Parliament and of the Council on the supplementary supervision of credit institutions, insurance undertakings and investment firms in a financial conglomerate of 20. Jul. 2011, COM(2011) 453 (final), also at BR-Drucks. 424/11	30
dd) "DVO", Draft Implementing measures Solvency II of 31. Oct. 2011	42, 47, 72, 86, 103, 112, 122, 123, 145, 147, 152, 221, 224, 227, 229, 230, 231, 232, 234, 241, 244, 248, 252, 254, 262, 263, 265, 268, 271, 275, 276, 278, 279, 281, 291, 320, 327, 330, 331, 333, 336
Recital 20	118
Recital 22	123
Recitals 24 ff.	122
Recital 97, sent. 1	234
Recital 97, sent. 2	234
Recital 98	224, 231
Recital 98, sent. 1	227, 228
Recital 98, sent. 2	266
Recital 98, sent. 3	269
Recital 99	224, 227, 228, 259, 260
Recital 107	328, 337
Recital 107, sent. 2	337
arts. 5 ff.	115
art. 7 V3, para. 1	115
art. 7 V3, para. 2	115
art. 7 V3, para. 4	115
art. 7 V3, para. 5	115
arts. 12 TPS1 ff.	46
arts. 19 TP6 ff.	47
art. 19 TP6, para. 1	47

(continued)

List of Legal Rules	
art. 19 TP6, para. 2	47
art. 19 TP6, para. 3	47
art. 19 TP6, para. 4	47
art. 19 TP6, para. 5	47
art. 19 TP6, para. 6	47
art. 19 TP6, para. 7	47
art. 37 IR 1, no. 1 (b)	122
art. 37 IR1, para. 1 (c)	122
art. 38 IR2 ff.	47
art. 39 IR4	47, 118
art. 39 IR4, para. 4	118
art. 40 IR 5	47, 118
art. 40 IR 5, para. 2	118
art. 41 IR6	122
art. 41 IR6, para. 1	123
art. 41 IR6, para. 1, sent. 2 (c)	123
art. 41 IR6, para. 6	123
art. 42bis	122
art. 42ter	122
arts. 47 TPS1 ff.	46
art. 47 TPS1, para. 1	46
art. 47 TPS1, para. 2	46
art. 47 TPS1, para. 3	46
art. 47 TPS1, para. 4	46
art. 47 TPS1, para. 5	46
arts. 51 ff.	103
arts. 51 AOF1 ff.	52
art. 57 AOF 7	52
arts. 58 COF1 ff.	52
art. 72 EOF1	52
arts. 75 ff.	104
art. 163 SR7, para. 3 (b)	117
arts. 244 RL2 ff.	50
arts. 211 TSIM1 ff.	53
arts. 226 ff.	105
arts. 244 RL2 ff.	50
art. 244 RL2, para. 1	50
art. 244 RL2, para. 2	50
art. 244 RL2, para. 3	51
art. 244 RL2, para. 4	51
art. 247 RL5, para. 1	51
art. 249, no. 1 (c)	230
art. 249 SG1, para. 1 (e)	277, 278

(continued)

List of Legal Rules	
art. 249 SG1, para. 1 (f)	277, 278
art. 249 SG1, para. 1 (l)	265, 228
art. 249 SG1, para. 5	260
art. 251 SG3	227, 228
art. 251 SG3, para. 3	169
art. 258, para. 1, sent. 2	237
art. 258, para. 4	289, 328
art. 258 SG6	225, 227
art. 258 SG6, para. 1	233, 234, 238, 240, 328
art. 258 SG6, para. 1, sent. 1	239, 328, 336, 337
art. 258 SG6, para. 1, sent. 2	238, 239, 269, 280
art. 258 SG6, para. 2	234, 239, 240
art. 258 SG6, para. 3	227, 245, 257, 295, 328
art. 258 SG6, para. 4	227, 238, 238
art. 258, para. 3, SG8	289
art. 259 SG7, para. 1 (b)	173
art. 260 SG8	288, 289
art. 260 SG8, para. 1, sent. 2	295
art. 260 SG8, para. 2	317, 329
art. 261, para. 1	233
art. 261 SG9, para. 1	336
art. 262 SG 10, para. 8	238
art. 263, para. 1	237
art. 263 SG 11	246, 254, 327
art. 263 SG 11, para. 1	227, 228, 245, 246, 247, 254, 255, 256
art. 263 SG 11, para. 2	245, 246, 247, 249, 250, 252
art. 263 SG11, para. 2, sent. 3	251
art. 263 SG11, para. 2, sent. 4	251
art. 263 SG 11, para. 3	230, 254, 255
art. 263 SG 11, para. 4	259, 260, 261, 263
art. 264 SG12	248
art. 264 SG12, para. 6 (a)	248
art. 265	132
art. 265 SG13, para. 1 (c)	227, 228, 265, 279, 328, 338
art. 265 SG13, para. 1 (d)	279
art. 265 SG13, para. 2	265, 279
art. 265 SG13, para. 2 (b)	265, 328, 338
art. 265, para. 2 (c)	133
art. 268 CA3	184
art. 268 CA3, para. 3	184
art. 271 CA6	184
arts. 282 PDS1 ff.	190
art. 282 PDS1, para. 1	190

(continued)

List of Legal Rules	
art. 282bis PDS1bis	186
art. 283 PDS2, para. 2	48
art. 284 PDS3, para. 1 (g)	48
art. 285, para. 2 (a)	228
art. 285, para. 2 (b)	228
art. 285 PDS4	268
art. 285 PDS4, para. 1 (a)	268
art. 285 PDS4, para. 1 (c) (iii)	268
art. 285 PDS4, para. 2 (a)	228
art. 285 PDS4, para. 2 (b)	228
art. 285 PDS4, para. 4	188, 190
art. 285 PDS4, para. 5 (d)	289
art. 288 PDS7	48
art. 293 PDS13	191
art. 293 PDS13, para. 1	481
art. 294 SRS1	187
art. 294 SRS1, para. 1 (a)	48, 188
art. 294 SRS1, para. 1 (c)	188
art. 294 SRS1, para. 3	188
art. 294bis SRS1bis	186
art. 294, para. 1 (c)	187
art. 294, para. 3	187
art. 296 SRS3	49
art. 297, para. 4	187
art. 297 SRS4, para. 1 (b)	265
art. 297 SRS4, para. 2 (a)	227, 231, 265
art. 297 SRS4, para. 4 (a)	189
art. 297 SRS4, para. 5 (c)	289
art. 300 SRS7	49
arts. 321 ff.	106
art. 335 CRM1, para. 1 (b)	289
art. 335 CRM1, para. 2 (c)	289
art. 358 RTCE1, para. 1 (h)	290
art. 368 GTCE1	290
art. 368 GTCE1 para 1 (j)	290
Annex PD1	190
ee) Proposal for a Regulation of the European Parliament and of the Council on key information documents for investment products, COM(2012) 352 (final), BR-Drucks. 388/12 of 4 Jul. 2012.	72, 94
art. 2 (a)	72
art. 4 (c)	72

(continued)

List of Legal Rules	
g) OECD	
aa) Guidelines on Insurer Governance of 2010	212, 213
h) IAIS, International Association of Insurance Supervisors	
aa) Insurance Core Principal (Enterprise Risk Management) 2010	
no. 16.1.10	167
bb) Insurance Core Principles, Standards, Guidance and Assessment Methodology of 1 Oct. 2011 with Supplement of 12 Oct. 2012	288
B. German	
I. Act	
1. Constitution [Basic Law]	138, 150
art. 12	37
art. 12, para. 1	174
art. 17	89
art. 19, para. 4	58
art. 20, para. 1	92
art. 101, para. 1, sent. 2	148
2. Non-constitutional Law	
a) Act on Shielding against Risks and on Planning for Reorganization and Winding-up of Credit Institutions and Financial Groups [Gesetz zur Abschirmung von Risiken und zur Planung der Sanierung und Abwicklung von Kreditinstituten und Finanzgruppen]	
aa) Governments Draft, BR-Drucks. 94/13 of 8 Feb. 2013	293
bb) Governments Draft, BT-Drucks. 17/12601 of 4 Mar. 2013	293
cc) amended proposed decision of the German Bundestag Finance Committee, BT-Drucks. 17/13523 of 15 May 2013	293
b) Act to Strengthen German Financial Supervision [Gesetz zur Stärkung der deutschen Finanzaufsicht]	
aa) draft	
(i) Governments Draft, BT-Drucks. 16/12783 of 27 April 2009	200
Statement of Reason	200
(ii) Recommended Resolution and the Report of the Finance Commission, BT-Drucks. 16/13684 of 1. July 2009	200
Statement of Reason	200
(iii) Governments Draft, BT-Drucks. 17/10040 of 19 Jun. 2012	74, 89, 92
Statement of Reason	89, 92
(iv) response to the position of the German Federal Council, BT-Drucks. 17/10252 of 4. Jul. 2012	80
bb) final version, BGBl I 2305 of 29 Jul. 2009	21, 196

(continued)

List of Legal Rules	
c) AktG [German Stock Corporation Act]	125, 207
sec. 15	263
sec. 76	127, 176, 254, 287, 334
sec. 76, para. 1	237, 250, 263, 280, 288, 418
sec. 90, para. 1, sent. 1, no. 1	128
sec. 90, para. 1, sent. 1, no. 4	128
sec. 91, para. 2	201, 286, 287, 406
sec. 93	287
sec. 93, para. 1, sent. 2	176, 314
sec. 100	197, 199
sec. 100, para. 4	197
sec. 100, para. 5	197, 213
sec. 103	203
sec. 103, para. 3, sent. 1	203
sec. 109, para. 1, sent. 2	214
sec. 111	315
sec. 124, para. 3, sent. 1	212
sec. 161	199
sec. 181, para. 3	361
d) BDSG [German Federal Data Protection Act]	
sec. 4f	312
sec. 4g	312
sec. 4g, para. 1, sent. 2	320
e) BGB [German Civil Code]	125
sec. 621	349
f) "CRD IV Implementing-Act", Governments Draft [RegE Gesetzes zur Umsetzung der Richtlinie 2012//EU über den Zugang zur Tätigkeit von Kreditinstituten und die Beaufsichtigung von Kreditinstituten und Wertpapierfirmen und zur Anpassung des Aufsichtsrechts an die Verordnung (EU) Nr. /2012 über die Aufsichtsanforderungen an Kreditinstitute und Wertpapierfirmen (CRD IV-Umsetzungsgesetz)], BT-Drucks. 17/10974	
sec. 25a, para. 1, sent. 3, clause 2, no. 3 (c)	288, 299
g) Third Law implementing directives of the Council of the European Communities on insurance law [Drittes Gesetz zur Durchführung versicherungsrechtlicher Richtlinien des Rates der Europischen Gemeinschaften], BGBl I 1630 of 21 Jul. 1994	171
h) FinDAG [Financial Services Supervisory Act]	88
sec. 4, para. 4	88
i) GenTG [Genetic Engineering Act]	58
j) GVG [Courts Constitution Act]	
sec. 172, no. 2	422
k) GWB [Act Against Restraints of Competition]	
sec. 40, para. 1	375
sec. 97, para. 4	261

(continued)

List of Legal Rules	
l) GwG [German Money-Laundering Act]	
sec. 2, para. 1, no. 4	312
sec. 2, para. 1, no. 9	312
sec. 2, para. 2, no. 1	312
m) HGB [German Commercial Code]	125, 394, 404
sec. 242, para. 1	405
secs. 264 ff.	404
sec. 264, para. 1, sent. 1	405
sec. 264, para. 1, sent. 2	419
sec. 264, para. 2, sent. 3	403
sec. 264d	115
sec. 284, para. 2	405
sec. 285	405
sec. 285, sent. 1, no. 7	405
sec. 285, sent. 1, no. 9	405
sec. 285, sent. 1, no. 10	405
sec. 289	191
sec. 289, para. 1	406
sec. 289, para. 1, sent. 4	406, 413
sec. 289, para. 1, sent. 5	403
sec. 289, para. 2, no. 2 (a)	265, 406, 413
sec. 289, para. 2, no. 2 (b)	265, 406, 413
sec. 290	115
sec. 290, para. 1	412
sec. 290, para. 1, sent. 2	420
sec. 290, para. 2	412
sec. 290, para. 3	412
secs. 294 ff.	412
sec. 297, para. 1, sent. 1	412
sec. 297, para. 3, sent. 1	413
sec. 313, para. 2	413
sec. 314a	365
sec. 315, para. 1, sent. 5	413
sec. 315, para. 2, no. 2 (a)	413, 371
sec. 315, para. 2, no. 2 (b)	413
sec. 315a	115
sec. 315a, para. 1	413
sec. 315a, para. 2	413
sec. 317, para. 4	201, 287
sec. 321, para. 4	287
sec. 325	403
sec. 325, para. 2	405
sec. 325, para. 4, sent. 1	420

(continued)

List of Legal Rules	
sec. 327a	420
sec. 341, para. 1	404
sec. 341, para. 2	404
sec. 341a	365
sec. 341a, para. 1, sent. 1	404, 419
sec. 341e	394
sec. 341e, para. 1	394
sec. 341f	394
sec. 341g	394
sec. 341h	394
sec. 341i	371
sec. 341i, para. 1, sent. 1	412
sec. 341i, para. 2	412
sec. 341i, para. 3, sent. 1	420
sec. 341i, para. 3, sent. 2	420
sec. 341j, para. 1, sent. 1	412
sec. 341l, para. 1, sent. 1	404
n) InvG [German Investment Act]	
sec. 6, para. 3	205
o) KWG [German Credit Services Act]	
sec. 10, para. 1, sent. 9, no. 7	414
sec. 25a	182
sec. 26a, para. 1, sent. 3	414
sec. 26a, para. 2	421
sec. 26a, para. 4	420
sec. 36, para. 3	200, 201
p) SGG [Social Court Act]	
art. 258	167
q) StGB [German Criminal Code]	
sec. 298	308
r) TKG [Telecommunications Act]	58
s) VAG [German Insurance Supervision Act]	
aa) draft	
(i) Governments Draft of a Ninth Act Amending the German Insurance Supervision Act, BT-Drucks. 16/6518 of 24 Sep. 2007	165, 346
Statement of Grounds	164
sec. 55c, para. 1	346
(ii) Governments Draft of a Tenth Act Amending the German Insurance Supervision Act, BT-Drucks. 17/9342; also BR-Drucks. 90/12 of 15 Feb. 2012	28, 29, 33, 34, 35, 38, 43, 51, 57, 68, 73, 94, 100, 162, 167, 168, 217, 218, 226, 223, 235, 244, 250, 251, 258, 262, 264, 269, 273, 275, 291, 292, 293, 296, 313, 321
Statement of Reason	104, 112, 189, 223, 224, 234, 235, 241, 251, 256, 263, 267, 278, 321

(continued)

List of Legal Rules	
Statement of Reason General Part	170
Statement of Reason	34, 102, 170, 182
Statement of Reason for sec. 24	135, 295
Statement of Reason for sec. 25	222, 223, 224, 226, 230, 250, 251, 258, 262, 277
Statement of Reason for sec. 27	234
Statement of Reason for sec. 28	159, 160, 161, 162, 168, 170, 171, 176, 177, 178, 182
Statement of Reason for sec. 29	236, 321
Statement of Reason for sec. 44	267
Statement of Reason for sec. 69	102
Statement of Reason for sec. 87	103
Statement of Reason for sec. 101	182
Statement of Reason for sec. 125	124
Statement of Reason for sec. 276	293
Statement of Reason for sec. 289	24, 35
Statement of Reason for sec. 311	73
sec. 1	73, 108
sec. 1, para. 1	73
sec. 1, para. 2	88
sec. 8, no. 6	106
sec. 8, no. 11	219, 220, 221, 292
sec. 8, no. 24	106
sec. 8, no. 25	134
sec. 8, no. 26	117, 120, 134
sec. 8, no. 27	134
sec. 8, no. 28	134
sec. 8, no. 29	134
sec. 8, no. 30	134
secs. 24 ff.	41, 42, 44
sec. 24	42, 111, 166, 258
sec. 24, para. 1, sent. 1	234, 292
sec. 24, para. 1, sent. 2	42, 233, 292
sec. 24, para. 3	232, 237
sec. 24, para. 3, sent. 3	141
sec. 24, para. 4	143
secs. 25 ff.	42
sec. 25	41, 42, 111, 131, 137, 222, 223, 226, 230, 236, 250, 256, 258, 262, 264, 269, 271, 277
sec. 25, para. 1	60, 250, 251, 267
sec. 25, para. 1, sent. 1	222, 250
sec. 25, para. 1, sent. 3	251
sec. 25, para. 1, sent. 4	251
sec. 25, para. 2, sent. 1	276, 277

(continued)

List of Legal Rules	
sec. 26	132, 264
secs. 27 ff.	161
sec. 27	125, 129
sec. 27, para. 1, sent. 1	43
sec. 27, para. 1, sent. 2	168
sec. 27, para. 2	179
sec. 27, para. 3	125
sec. 27, para. 3, sent. 1, no. 1	129
sec. 27, para. 3, sent. 1, no. 2	129
sec. 27, para. 3, sent. 1, no. 3	129
sec. 27, para. 3, sent. 1, no. 4	129
sec. 27, para. 3, sent. 1, no. 5	129
sec. 27, para. 3, sent. 1, no. 6	129
sec. 27, para. 5	167, 220, 238
sec. 27, para. 5, sent. 1	234
sec. 28	125, 159, 167, 168, 169, 170, 192
sec. 28, para. 1, sent. 1	49, 141, 178
sec. 28, para. 1, sent. 2	163, 178,
sec. 28, para. 2	110
sec. 28, para. 2, no. 3	167, 170
sec. 28, para. 3	168, 169
sec. 28, para. 3, sent. 2	169
sec. 29	292, 293, 321
sec. 29, para. 1	172, 292
sec. 29, para. 2	110, 125, 238, 292
sec. 30	173
sec. 30, para. 2	233, 234, 238
sec. 31	41, 148, 220, 237
sec. 31, para. 1, no. 5	238
sec. 31, para. 2	170
sec. 31, para. 2, sent. 2	43
sec. 31, para. 3	248
sec. 32	248
sec. 34	264
sec. 34, para. 1	132
sec. 42, para. 3	141
sec. 43	33
sec. 43, para. 1	189
sec. 44, no. 1	236, 267
sec. 44, no. 2	267
sec. 44, no. 8	49, 159, 160, 169, 170, 189, 236
sec. 45, para. 2	35, 102, 110
sec. 45, para. 4, no. 4	49

(continued)

List of Legal Rules	
sec. 47, para. 2	35, 102, 110
sec. 50	33, 80, 136, 186, 190, 268
sec. 50, para. 4	141
sec. 50, para. 7	191
sec. 51	190
sec. 52	191
sec. 52, para. 1, sent. 2, no. 2	141
sec. 52, para. 2, sent. 1, no. 2	141
sec. 54, para. 2, sent. 1	253
sec. 64a, para. 7	293, 322
sec. 64a, para. 7, no. 2 (a)	293
sec. 64b	264
sec. 69	35, 44, 45, 107, 111
sec. 69, para. 1	127
sec. 69, para. 1, sent. 1	102
sec. 69, para. 1, sent. 2	110
sec. 69, para. 2	115
sec. 69, para. 3	115
secs. 70 ff.	46
sec. 70, para. 1	127
sec. 70, para. 2, sent. 2	45
sec. 70, para. 3	45, 117
sec. 70, para. 4	45
sec. 72, para. 1	45, 117
sec. 72, para. 2	45
sec. 72, para. 2, sent. 2	148
sec. 73, para. 1	45
secs. 77 f.	45
sec. 79, para. 1	46
sec. 79, para. 2	46, 61
secs. 80 ff.	103, 135
sec. 80	103
sec. 80, para. 1, sent. 1	104
sec. 80, para. 3	51
sec. 80, para. 4	52
sec. 80, para. 5	52
sec. 81	52, 103
secs. 82 ff.	111
sec. 82	51, 103, 120
sec. 83	52, 103
sec. 84	103
secs. 85 f.	52, 103, 111, 120
secs. 85	103

(continued)

List of Legal Rules	
sec. 86	48, 103
secs. 87 ff.	104
sec. 87, para. 2	114, 134, 192
sec. 88	48, 105
sec. 88, para. 2	48
sec. 88, para. 2, sent. 1	48
sec. 88, para. 2, sent. 4	116
sec. 89, para. 1	105
sec. 91, para. 3, sent. 1	116
sec. 93	120
sec. 95, para. 2, sent. 1, no. 4	117
sec. 97, para. 3	120
sec. 100, para. 1	114
sec. 100, para. 2	114
sec. 101	114, 134
sec. 102	100
sec. 102, para. 7	113
sec. 103, para. 1, sent. 2	130
sec. 104	125
sec. 104, para. 1	137
sec. 105, para. 1	141
secs. 106 ff.	53, 141
sec. 106	141
sec. 106, para. 1	129
sec. 106, para. 1, no. 2	103
sec. 106, para. 3	141
sec. 107	141
sec. 107, para. 2	137, 141
sec. 108	141
sec. 109	141
sec. 109, para. 2, sent. 2	116
sec. 110	130, 141
sec. 111	141
sec. 111, para. 2	137
sec. 112	136, 141
sec. 113, para. 1	105
sec. 114, para. 1	105
sec. 115, para. 1	50
sec. 115, para. 1, no. 1	50, 163
sec. 115, para. 1, no. 3	50
sec. 115, para. 1, no. 5, clause 1	50
sec. 115, para. 1, no. 6	50
sec. 115, para. 1, no. 7	50

(continued)

List of Legal Rules	
sec. 115, para. 1, no. 8	50
sec. 123	109
sec. 124	109
sec. 125	109
sec. 125, para. 1	60
sec. 125, para. 2	61
sec. 125, para. 3, sent. 1	61
sec. 125, para. 3, sent. 3	132
sec. 125, para. 3, sent. 5	61
sec. 125, para. 4	124
sec. 125, para. 4, sent. 2	61
sec. 126	61, 109
sec. 127	109
sec. 128	61, 109, 143
sec. 132	312
sec. 142	293
sec. 150	312
sec. 175, sent. 2	176
sec. 198	291
sec. 199, para. 3, no. 7	293
secs. 213 f.	105
sec. 231, para. 1, sent. 2	106
sec. 231, para. 2	106
secs. 236 ff.	106
sec. 236	116
sec. 236, para. 1	106
sec. 236, para. 2	106
sec. 236, para. 3	106
sec. 237, para. 1, sent. 1	106
sec. 238	107
secs. 239 ff.	107
sec. 239	107
secs. 240 f.	111
sec. 240	107
sec. 241	107
sec. 247	116
sec. 247, para. 1, sent. 2	106
sec. 251	116
sec. 250	101
sec. 251	116
sec. 251, para. 1, no. 1	106
sec. 251, para. 2	106
sec. 251, para. 6	101

(continued)

List of Legal Rules	
secs. 253 ff.	107
sec. 257, para. 2, sent. 5	34
secs. 259 f.	107
secs. 261 ff.	106
sec. 266, para. 3	107
sec. 269	110
sec. 276, para. 1	293
sec. 289	27, 77, 101, 108
sec. 289, para. 1	34
sec. 289, para. 1, sent. 2	55
sec. 289, para. 1, sent. 4	123, 124
sec. 289, para. 2	31, 34, 35, 108
sec. 289, para. 3	31, 34, 41, 253
sec. 289, para. 3, sent. 2	31, 33, 37, 38, 63, 64
sec. 289, para. 4	31, 34, 41, 63, 192
sec. 289, para. 4, sent. 1	38
sec. 290	136, 143, 161, 190
sec. 292	64, 73, 101, 108
sec. 292, para. 1	192
sec. 292, para. 1, sent. 3	34, 55, 108, 109
sec. 292, para. 2, no. 3	108, 109
sec. 295	101, 179, 183
sec. 295, para. 1	63, 139, 180
sec. 295, para. 1, sent. 1, no. 1	62, 192
sec. 295, para. 1, sent. 1, no. 2	192
sec. 295, para. 1, sent. 1, no. 3	62, 63
sec. 295, para. 1, sent. 2	172
sec. 295, para. 2	139, 140
sec. 297	236, 270
sec. 297, sent. 1, no. 1	269
sec. 297, sent. 1, no. 2	270
sec. 297, sent. 1, no. 3	270
sec. 299	36
sec. 299, para. 1, no. 1	189, 270, 274, 280
sec. 300, para. 1	36
sec. 312, para. 1	296
sec. 312, para. 2, no. 2	39, 62, 296
sec. 319, para. 2, sent. 2	73
sec. 324, para. 1, sent. 2	222
sec. 326	146
sec. 327	146
bb) German Act To Strengthen the Financial Market and Insurance Supervision of 29 July 2009, BGBl. 2009 I, p. 2305	22, 74, 77, 88, 99, 105, 140, 146, 147, 158, 165, 166, 167, 169, 189, 196, 200, 202, 204, 214, 220, 220, 235, 252, 263, 269, 272, 278, 297, 346, 347, 357, 374, 375, 376, 377, 378, 379, 381, 382, 383, 384, 399

(continued)

List of Legal Rules	
sec. 1b	367, 374
sec. 1b, para. 1, sent. 1	367
sec. 1b, para. 1, sent. 2	367
sec. 1b, para. 2	367, 369
sec. 1b, para. 4, no. 3	20
sec. 1b, para. 6	20
sec. 5, para. 2	373
sec. 5, para. 3, no. 4	356, 357, 406
sec. 5, para. 4, sent. 1	357
sec. 5, para. 4, sent. 2	357
sec. 5, para. 5, no. 9	202
sec. 5, para. 6	202, 381
sec. 7, para. 2, sent. 1	22
sec. 7, para. 2, sent. 3, clause 1	22, 24
sec. 7a, para. 1	250, 348, 350, 367, 381
sec. 7a, para. 1, sent. 1	367
sec. 7a, para. 1, sent. 3	251, 252
sec. 7a, para. 2, sent. 3	353
sec. 7a, para. 2, sent. 6	353
sec. 7a, para. 3	367, 368
sec. 7a, para. 4	21, 22, 24, 197, 200, 201, 202, 203, 207, 230
sec. 7a, para. 4, sent. 1	196, 200, 202, 207, 210, 214, 215
sec. 7a, para. 4, sent. 2	201
sec. 7b	312
sec. 7b, para. 1, sent. 1	351
sec. 8, para. 1, sent. 1, no. 3	55, 77
sec. 8, para. 1, sent. 1, no. 5	203
sec. 8, para. 1, sent. 2, no. 1	354
sec. 8, para. 1, sent. 4	354
sec. 8, para. 1, sent. 4, no. 2	354
sec. 10	73
sec. 10a	73
sec. 10a, para. 2 (a)	387
sec. 10a, para. 2 (a), sent. 1	352
sec. 11a	312
sec. 11a, para. 2, sent. 1	348
sec. 11a, para. 2, sent. 4	348
sec. 11a, para. 5, sent. 1	349
sec. 11d	349
sec. 11e	349
sec. 12, para. 2, sent. 1	349
sec. 13	357
sec. 13, para. 1 (a)	356, 375

(continued)

List of Legal Rules	
sec. 13, para. 1 (a), sent. 2	356
sec. 13, para. 1 (a), sent. 3	356
sec. 13, para. 1 (a), sent. 4	356
sec. 13, para. 1 (a), sent. 5	356
sec. 13, para. 1 (a), sent. 6	356
sec. 13b	356
sec. 13b, para. 1, sent. 1	355
sec. 13b, para. 1, sent. 2	355, 380
sec. 13b, para. 1, sent. 2, no. 1	356
sec. 13b, para. 1, sent. 2, no. 2	356
sec. 13b, para. 1, sent. 2, no. 3	356
sec. 13b, para. 1, sent. 2, no. 4	356
sec. 13c	356
sec. 13c, para. 1, sent. 1	356
sec. 13d	347
sec. 13d, no. 1	348, 350
sec. 13d, no. 2	348, 350
sec. 13d, no. 2 (a)	350, 351
sec. 13d, no. 3	360
sec. 13d, no. 4	353, 354
sec. 13d, no. 4 (a)	354, 369, 370
sec. 13d, no. 5	353, 354, 369, 370
sec. 13d, no. 6	351
sec. 13d, no. 7	352, 382
sec. 13d, no. 8	352
sec. 13d, no. 9	351
sec. 13d, no. 10	352
sec. 13d, no. 12	202
sec. 13e	367
sec. 13e, para. 1, sent. 1	348
sec. 13e, para. 1, sent. 1	348
sec. 13e, para. 1, sent. 1, no. 1	367, 372
sec. 13e, para. 1, sent. 1, no. 2	367, 372
sec. 13e, para. 1, sent. 1, no. 3	370
sec. 13e, para. 1, sent. 2	372
sec. 13e, para. 2, sent. 1	370, 374
sec. 13e, para. 2, sent. 2	370, 374
sec. 14	354
sec. 14, para. 1, sent. 1	355
sec. 14, para. 6	355
sec. 14a	354, 355
sec. 28	159
sec. 35, para. 3	199, 203

(continued)

List of Legal Rules	
sec. 36	212
sec. 53c	100
sec. 53c, para. 2	358
sec. 53c, para. 2, no. 1	358
sec. 53c, para. 4	357, 358, 380
sec. 53d	357
sec. 54, para. 4	358, 362, 379
sec. 54, para. 4, sent. 1, no. 2	362
sec. 54, para. 4, sent. 2	362
sec. 54d	380
sec. 54d, sent. 1	362
sec. 54d, para. 4, sent. 1, no. 3	362
sec. 54d, para. 4, sent. 2	363
sec. 55, para. 1	383
sec. 55, para. 1, no. 2	365
sec. 55, para. 2, sent. 1	361, 365
sec. 55, para. 2, sent. 2	371
sec. 55, para. 3	401, 405
sec. 55, para. 4, sent. 2	371
sec. 55a, para. 1	380
sec. 55a, para. 1, sent. 1, no. 1 (b)	380
sec. 55c	346, 364, 365, 366, 399
sec. 55c, para. 1	346, 364
sec. 55c, para. 3	399
sec. 55c, para. 4	373
sec. 55c, para. 4, sent. 1	371
sec. 55c, para. 5	364
sec. 55c, para. 6	364
sec. 56, para. 2, sent. 3	354
sec. 58, para. 2, sent. 1	361
sec. 59, sent. 1	361
sec. 64	361
sec. 64, para. 1, sent. 1	297
sec. 64a	134, 161, 164, 165, 166, 167, 192, 201, 235, 366, 373, 406
sec. 64a, para. 1	164, 166
sec. 64a, para. 1, sent. 3	166
sec. 64a, para. 1, sent. 4, no. 1	179
sec. 64a, para. 1, sent. 4, no. 3 (a)	165, 166
sec. 64a, para. 1, sent. 4, no. 3 (b)	167, 365
sec. 64a, para. 1, sent. 4, no. 3 (d)	346, 364, 365
sec. 64a, para. 2	164, 166
sec. 64a, para. 5, sent. 1	364
sec. 64a, para. 5, sent. 2	364

(continued)

List of Legal Rules	
sec. 64a, para. 7	293, 322
sec. 64a, para. 7, no. 2	293, 336, 337, 341
sec. 64b	264
sec. 66, para. 1	362
sec. 66, para. 5	362
sec. 66, para. 5, sent. 2	362
sec. 66, para. 6	362
sec. 66, para. 6, sent. 6	362
sec. 71	349
sec. 71, para. 1	349
sec. 71, para. 2, sent. 1	349
sec. 71, para. 2, sent. 3	349
sec. 79	349
sec. 79a	349
sec. 81	202
sec. 81, para. 1, sent. 2	17, 18
sec. 81, para. 1, sent. 3	18, 88
sec. 81, para. 1, sent. 4	18
sec. 81, para. 2	18, 369
sec. 81, para. 2, sent. 1	18, 24, 373
sec. 81, para. 4 (a)	357
sec. 81, para. 1, sent. 5	373
sec. 81b	358
sec. 81b, para. 1	369
sec. 81b, para. 1 (a)	132
sec. 81b, para. 2	369
sec. 81b, para. 4	358
sec. 83, para. 1, sent. 1, no. 1	270
sec. 83, para. 5, no. 2	357
sec. 83a, para. 1, no. 4	203
sec. 87, para. 1, no. 1	203
sec. 87, para. 8	203
sec. 87, para. 8, sent. 1	202
sec. 87, para. 8, sent. 2	203
sec. 87, para. 8, sent. 3	203
sec. 88, para. 1	363, 364
sec. 88, para. 1, sent. 2	363
sec. 88, para. 2	363, 364
sec. 88, para. 3, sent. 3	364
sec. 88, para. 5	364
sec. 104, para. 1	353
sec. 104a, para. 1, no. 1	366, 368, 371
sec. 104a, para. 1, no. 2	367, 368, 369

(continued)

List of Legal Rules	
sec. 104a, para. 1, sent. 1	369
sec. 104a, para. 2, no. 4	367, 370
sec. 104a, para. 2, no. 5	370
sec. 104e, para. 1	369
sec. 104e, para. 1, sent. 1	368
sec. 104e, para. 2, no. 1	368
sec. 104e, para. 2, no. 2	368
sec. 104e, para. 2, no. 3	368
sec. 104e, para. 2, no. 4	368
sec. 104e, para. 2, no. 5	368
sec. 104e, para. 2, no. 6	368
sec. 104e, para. 3	368, 369, 380
sec. 104e, para. 3, sent. 1	368, 369
sec. 104e, para. 4, sent. 2	369
sec. 104g	380
sec. 104h	369
secs. 104k ff.	372
sec. 104k, no. 3	372
sec. 104k, no. 4	372
sec. 104k, no. 9	373
sec. 104l	372
sec. 104q	372
sec. 104q, para. 2, sent. 2	373
sec. 104q, para. 3, sent. 6	372
sec. 104q, para. 3, sent. 7	372
sec. 104q, para. 3, sent. 8	372
sec. 104q, para. 4	372
sec. 104r	372
sec. 104r, para. 1	372, 373
sec. 104s	373
sec. 110a, para. 4, no. 3 (a)	18
sec. 113, para. 1	348, 349, 351, 352, 353, 354, 360, 362, 363, 364, 371
sec. 113, para. 2, no. 2	358
sec. 113, para. 2, no. 8 (a)	358
sec. 113, para. 3	356, 363
sec. 114, para. 2	358
sec. 114, para. 2, no. 4	358
sec. 119, para. 2, no. 6	357
sec. 119, para. 3, sent. 1	358
sec. 121, para. 1, no. 4	204
sec. 121a, para. 1	357, 363
sec. 121a, para. 1, sent. 1	348, 351, 353, 356, 362, 371
sec. 121a, para. 1, sent. 2	358, 364

(continued)

List of Legal Rules	
sec. 121a, para. 1, sent. 3	358
sec. 121a, para. 3	354
sec. 121a, para. 4, sent. 3	357
sec. 121c	202
sec. 121c, para. 2, no. 1	203
sec. 121c, para. 6	202, 203
sec. 121c, para. 6, sent. 1	202
sec. 121c, para. 6, sent. 2	203
sec. 121c, para. 6, sent. 3	203
sec. 121c, para. 6, sent. 4	203
sec. 121d	358
sec. 121f	354
sec. 121g, para. 2	202
sec. 121g, para. 2, sent. 1	196
sec. 142	293
sec. 144, para. 1 (a), no. 2	346
sec. 144, para. 1 (a), no. 2 (b)	346
sec. 144, para. 2	346
sec. 157 para. 1, sent. 2	73
t) VVG [Insurance Contracts Act]	
sec. 167	91
u) VwGO [Code of Administrative Court Procedure]	
sec. 55	422
sec. 114	147
v) WpHG [Securities Trading Act]	257, 269, 294, 340, 401
sec. 2, para. 1	401
sec. 2, para. 1, sent. 1	403
sec. 2, para. 1, sent. 1, no. 1	403
sec. 2, para. 1, sent. 1, no. 2	403
sec. 2, para. 7	401, 410
sec. 2, para. 7, no. 1	401
sec. 2, para. 7, no. 2	401
secs. 21 ff.	402
sec. 21	402
sec. 21, para. 1	362
sec. 21, para. 1 (a)	362
sec. 25, para. 1	362
sec. 26	410
sec. 26, para. 1, sent. 1	402
sec. 26, para. 1, sent. 2	402
sec. 26, para. 2	362
sec. 26a	402, 410
sec. 26a, sent. 1	362

(continued)

List of Legal Rules	
sec. 31	286, 294
sec. 32	286, 294
sec. 33, para. 1, sent. 1, no. 1	322
sec. 33, para. 1, sent. 2, no. 1	319
sec. 33, para. 1, sent. 2, no. 5	319
sec. 34d, para. 3, sent. 1	319, 322
sec. 34d, para. 4, sent. 1, no. 1	269
sec. 37v, para. 1	402
sec. 37w, para. 1, sent. 1	403
sec. 37w, para. 4, sent. 1	403, 410
sec. 37x, para. 1, sent. 1	403, 404
sec. 37x, para. 2, sent. 1	404
sec. 37x, para. 2, sent. 2	404, 410
sec. 37y, no. 2, sent. 1	412
sec. 37y, no. 3	412
sec. 37z, para. 1	402, 403
w) WpG [German Securities Acquisition and Takeover Act]	401, 414
sec. 35	402, 414
II. Regulation	
1. InhKontrollV [Holder Control Regulation]	207
sec. 15, para. 1, sent. 6, no. 2	207
sec. 15, para. 1, sent. 7, no. 2	218
2. KapAusstV [German Capital Resources Regulation] Regulation on the capital resources of insurance undertakings	358
3. MaKonV [Market Manipulation Definition Ordinance]	
sec. 2, para. 3, no. 5	218
4. PKAustV [German Pension Fund Capital Resources Regulation]	
sec. 4, para. 1	358
5. RechVersV [Regulation on Insurance Accounting]	394
6. SolvV [Regulation governing the capital adequacy of institutions, groups of institutions and financial holding groups]	
sec. 319, para. 2	421
sec. 320, para. 1	414
sec. 320, para. 2, sent. 1	415
sec. 324	421
sec. 325	421
7. StrlSchV [German Regulation on Protection against Harm from Ionizing Radiation]	
sec. 32, para. 2, sent. 2	320
8. VersVergV [German Remuneration Regulation for the Insurance Industry]	132
sec. 4, para. 1	279

(continued)

List of Legal Rules	
9. WpDVerOV [German Investment Services Conduct of Business and Organization Regulation]	
sec. 12, para. 4, sent. 1	319
10. WpHGMaAnzV [German Securities Trading Act Employee Notice Regulation]	257, 269
III. Others	
1. BaFin	
a) Circular	
6/97	21, 381
30/2002	362
1/2004	362
3/2004	368, 369, 380
4/2005 (VA)	358, 380
11/2005	262
"MaRisk VA", Minimum Requirements for Risk Management (Insurance Supervision), 3/2009	20, 129, 134, 161, 164, 165, 166, 167, 192, 235, 240, 293, 295, 322, 364, 365, 366, 373
no. 4 (1)	165
no. 6 (1)	165
no. 7.2.2	129
no. 7.3.2.2 (1)	165
no. 7.3.1 (1)	166
no. 7.3.1 (4)	166
no. 7.4	365
"MaComp WA", Minimum Requirements for the Compliance Function (Securities Supervision), 4/2010	
version - published 7 June 2010	294
version - published 31 August 2012	294, 295, 322
AT 1, no. 6	294
AT 1, no. 6.1	294
BT 1	294
BT 1.1.1	340
BT 1.1.2	294
BT 1.2	2994
"MaComp VA", Minimum Requirements for the Compliance Function (Insurance Supervision)	294, 295, 296
"MaRisk BA", Minimum Requirements for Risk Management (Banking Supervision), 10/2012 (BA)	294, 300, 304, 313, 322
AT 4.4.2 no. 2	294, 304
b) Issuer Guideline	
IV.2.2.4	206
IV.2.2.11	206
c) Journal	
May 2009, 8	131

(continued)

List of Legal Rules	
March 2011, 9	181
October 2011, 3	74
April 2012, 13	80, 89
June 2012, 3	89
August 2012, 12	83, 86
d) Results of the Fifth Quantitative Impact Study on Solvency II (QIS 5), (2011) [Ergebnisse der fünften quantitativen Auswirkungsstudie zu Solvency II (QIS 5)]	110, 118, 119, 120, 122
e) Supervisory Directive [Aufsichtsrichtlinie] of 21 Feb. 2008	
Preamble	30
2. German Federal Council	
a) Advice of the Committee on the Draft of a Tenth Act Amending the German Insurance Supervision Act [Empfehlungen der Ausschüsse zu dem Entwurf eines Zehnten Gesetzes zur Änderung des VAG], BR-Drucks. 90/1/12 of 16 Mar. 2012	102, 146
b) Response to the VAG-RegE [Governments Draft of a Tenth Act Amending the German Insurance Supervision Act], BR-Drucks. 90/12 sent. 4	222
3. German Federal Government	
a) Answer to a parliamentary question on "Consumer organizations and market monitoring functions as part of the consumer-oriented supervision of the financial markets" ["Verbraucherorganisationen und ihre Marktwächterfunktion als Teil der systematischen verbraucherorientierten Beobachtung des Finanzmarkts"], BT-Drucks. 17/11751	74
b) Answer to a parliamentary question on the topic: "Exercise of the Supervisory and Monitoring Function of the State as Shareholder" ["Wahrnehmung der Aufsichts- und Kontrollfunktion des Staats als Anteilseigner"], BT-Drucks. 16/11536 of 29 Dec. 2008	205
c) Answer to parliamentary question, BT-Drucks. 17/8225 of 19 Dec. 2011	117, 129, 192
4. German Federal Ministry of Justice – BMJ [Bundesministerium der Justiz], Ministerial Draft of BilReG [German Accounting Law Reform Act] of 13 Dec. 2003, p. 25	408

(continued)

List of Legal Rules	
5. Political parties	
a) Bündnis 90/Die Grünen (German Green Party) per a report in VW 17 (2011), 1207: "Consumer Protection Watchdogs Seek to Become Financial Market Guardians" ["Verbraucherschützer wollen Finanzmarktwchter werden"]	75
b) Motion of the CDU/CSU and FDP factions, BT-Drucks. 17/6456	114, 119
6. Others	
German Government Commission German Corporate Governance Code	
a) DCGK [German Corporate Governance Code]	199, 287
no. 4.1.3	287, 310
no. 5.3.2	287
no. 5.3.3	212
no. 5.4.1	199, 201, 213
b) press release, 10 Feb. 2010, to be found at http://www.corporate-governance-code.de/ger/download/Qualifizierung_von_Aufsichtsraeten_10_02_2010.pdf.	199
b) DRS [German Accounting Standard]	
no. 5-20	406
no. 16	406, 409, 412
pnt. 41	403, 404
pnts. 61 ff.	404
c) Financial Reporting Enforcement Panel [Deutsche Prüfstelle für Rechnungslegung e. V.], Activity Report 2011	116
d) German Central Credit Committee, Opinion of 21 Jul. 2006 on the draft of the Solvency Regulation of 31 Mar. 2006, p. 151	391

Index

A

Abusiveness, 17ff., 43, 53, 73, 146, 241
Actuarial function, 170, 220, 247, 253, 263
Administrative offenses, 260, 346
Asset-liability management system (ALM), 50, 129, 151
Audit report, 134f., 346, 361ff., 371, 383, 399

B

Back door supervision, 43
Basic own funds, 51ff., 103ff., 359, 408
Behavioral economics, 90f. *See also* Consumer protection/profile
Best Practices Report, 82ff., 95
Business judgment rule (BJR), 176, 314 *See also* Compliance
Business organization, 34ff., 42ff., 130, 173, 220, 235, 297
Business performance, 36, 49, 405

C

Calculation, 115, 119ff., 135ff., 181ff., 358
Capital requirement, 100ff., 117ff., 135ff., 180ff., 359ff., 382, 395ff., 400, 408, 416ff., 423 *See also* Solvency II Directive
  business performance, 36, 49, 405
  financial guarantees, 46
  future looking approach, 47, 63
  market value, 48, 101, 115, 394
  minimum, 105, 359ff.
  monitoring system, 48, 286
  special purpose vehicles, 196, 202, 374
  technical provisions, 31, 45ff., 61, 74, 108, 117, 127, 148, 362, 394
Capital transferability, 395, 409
CEIOPS, 189ff., 206ff., 222ff., 244ff., 259, 277, ff., 290, 350ff., 367ff., 379ff., 390ff. *See also* Compliance
Centralized structure, 236, 241, 273
Classification, 52f., 58ff., 86, 120, 208, 220, 240, 300, 351
Collective consumer protection, 67, 88ff.
College of supervisors, 78 *See also* Solvency II Directive
Committee of European Insurance and
Occupational Pensions Supervisors. *See* (CEIOPS)
Committee on Consumer Protection
and Financial Innovation (CCPFI), 10, 70ff.
Communications system, 42
Company law, 86, 197ff., 214ff., 228ff., 276
  German Commercial Code (HGB), 124, 191, 365, 403ff., 413ff., 420ff.
  German Corporate Governance Code (DCGK), 199ff., 212ff., 287, 303
  legal duty, 212, 285
  officials, 264, 312ff., 319ff.
Competence-based rationale, 88
Complaints-handling, 82ff.
Compliance, 136f., 159ff., 173ff., 206ff., 229ff., 239ff., 254ff., 286ff., 317ff., 326ff., 358ff., 397ff.
  business judgment rule (BJR), 176, 314f.
  CEIOPS, 189ff., 206ff., 222ff., 244ff., 259, 277ff., 290, 350ff., 367ff., 379ff., 390ff.

M. Dreher, *Treatises on Solvency II*, DOI 10.1007/978-3-662-46290-4

Compliance (*cont.*)
  duty of notice, 220, 231ff., 264ff., 296, 381
  fit (*see* Fit)
  Government's Draft of a Tenth Act Amending the German Insurance Supervision Act, 101, 340
  Government's Draft of the German Banking Ringfencing Act, 293
  guidelines, 38ff., 68, 75, 82, 157, 290ff.
  key functions (*see* Key functions)
  legal nature, 318ff.
  monitoring (*see* Monitoring)
  officer, 269, 305, 319ff., 340
  proper (*see* Proper)
  values-oriented business management, 285
Comply-or-explain, 164, 341, 382
Concept of fairness, 75
Constitutional law, 6, 18, 73, 91, 121
Consultation paper, 73, 116, 158ff., 176, 185, 230, 244, 298
Consumer profile, 88ff.
  reasonably well-informed, 90
  reasonably observant, 90
Consumer protection, 69ff., 75ff., 88ff.
  best practice report, 83ff., 95
  collective consumer protection, 67, 88ff.
  competence-based rationale, 88ff.
  complaints-handling, 94ff.
  concept of fairness, 75f.
  consumer profile, 88f.
  EIOPA Regulation, 14ff., 33, 85ff., 278, 290
  financial market supervision, 74f.
  free movement of service, 18, 76
  German insurance supervisory regime, 33, 88
  high level of protection, 77ff.
  indemnification payments, 75ff., 175
  indirect, 80ff.
  market discipline, 81, 390, 420
  private insurance law, 92
  separation of responsibility, 88
  social insurance law, 92
  Solvency and Financial Condition Report (SCFR), 33, 80, 94, 186
  travel cancellation insurance, 93
  warnings, 69ff.
Consumer trends, 69, 87ff., 96
  payment protection insurance, 87
Control messages, 414
Control of legality, 21, 279
Corporate governance, 42, 85, 95, 165, 199ff., 287, 303, 311, 388
Criterion of prudence, 250

D

de facto group, 414, 418
de facto members of management body, 228, 233
Deputy director, 232, 237, 240
Directive. *See* Harmonization; Solvency II Directive
Disclosure obligation, 352ff., 364ff., 372ff.
  accounting, 361, 371, 378
  establishment of business in foreign countries, 355ff.
  financial conglomerates, 372ff.
  financial reporting, 352ff., 368ff., 392ff.
  group level, 366ff., 371ff.
  internal group transactions, 369ff.
  investment activity, 362ff., 378
  outsourcing, 265ff., 356f (*see also* Key functions)
  periodic recurring reports, 362
  public (*see* Public disclosure)
  restructuring measures, 354ff.
  risk reporting, 364ff., 392, 398ff.
  significant ownership interest, 353
  structure of own funds, 357, 360ff.
  substantive financial reporting, 353, 357ff., 373
  threat of insolvency, 363ff.
Discretionary power, 119, 145 *See also* Solvency II Directive; Supervisory authority
Domestic insurance holding companies, 367
Dual structure, 228
Dual-tracking, 220 *See also* Key functions
Duty of notice. *See* Compliance
  duty of advance notice, 356ff.

E

Economic freedom. *See* Harmonization
Efficient portfolio management, 50
EIOPA. *See* Solvency II Directive
EIOPA regulation. *See* Consumer protection
Equalization, 228ff.
Equity price risk, 396ff.
European Commission, 8, 17, 159
European Economic and Social Committee, 390

European Insurance and Occupational Pensions Authority. *See* Solvency II Directive
Evaluation. *See* Key functions
Explanatory notices, 39

F
Factually suitable. *See* Fit
Failure of purpose, 88
Federal Financial Supervisory Authority (BaFin), 74ff., 120, 131, 368ff.
Financial reporting information, 392ff., 405
  annual financial report, 402ff.
  capital management, 363, 395ff., 408, 423
  cash flow calculation, 393
  Commercial Law, 393, 403, 404ff.
  interim reports, 410, 418
  key indicators, 393
  shareholder composition, 393, 410
Financial market supervision. *See* Consumer protection
Fit, 43, 131, 195ff., 220ff., 232ff., 244, 249ff., 268ff., 304, 321, 335, 348ff., 367, 382, 397
Fitness requirement, 126, 249, 251, 253, 256
Follow-up assessment, 36
Formation of law, 333ff., 340
Framework of regulations, 245, 379
Free movement of service. *See* Consumer protection
Full harmonization. *See* Harmonization
Functional view, 233, 242
Funds items, 51ff.
  ancillary, 51f.
  basic, 51f.
Future looking approach, 47

G
German Commercial Code (HGB). *See* Company law
German Corporate Governance Code (DCGK). *See* Company law
German Insurance Supervision Act, 312ff., 321ff., 337, 350ff., 377ff.
  constitutional law (*see* Constitutional law)
  principle of abusiveness (*see* Principle of abusiveness)
  self-generated administrative practices, 24
German insurance supervisory regime. *See* Consumer protection
Governance Guidelines, 225, 231, 244ff., 264, 290ff.
Government's Draft of a Tenth Act Amending the German Insurance Supervision Act, 101, 299
Government's Draft of the German Banking Ringfencing Act, 293ff.
Group level, 106ff., 115 *See also* Disclosure obligations
  controlled insurance stock corporation, 420
  protection of confidentiality, 421ff.
  relief, 420ff.
  risk management, 388, 392, 397f., 409ff.
  risk strategy, 398, 409, 415
Group specific disclosure, 369, 371
Group supervision, 78 *See also* Solvency II Directive

H
Harmonization, 5ff., 16ff., 226, 252
  absolute sectorial harmonization, 6
  discretionary power (*see* Discretionary power)
  economic freedom, 4, 19
  full, 231, 252, 280, 296
  internal market, 7, 9, 14, 19, 69f., 112, 119
  legal, 5, 9
  level playing field, 7, 13ff., 23, 79
  maximum, 5ff.
  minimum, 5ff.
  pan-European, 4, 8, 10, 19, 23
  reverse discrimination, 18f., 24
  supererogatory implementation, 5
  unification, 7
High level protection. *See* Consumer protection
Holder Control Regulation, 207
Holder of key functions
  fit and proper (*see* Fit; Proper)
  level of competence, 247
  outsourcing (*see* Outsourcing)
  sound and prudent management, 245, 249f.
  subordinate staff member, 227ff., 245ff., 258ff., 270, 276
  two-level qualification structure, 245
Holder of the compliance function, 242, 304ff., 320, 324, 336ff.
Horizontal business group, 366

I
Implementation table, 270
Indemnification payments. *See* Consumer protection
Institutional analysis, 232f.
Instruction right, 337

Insurance holding companies, 22, 210, 276, 367ff., 410ff.
Insurance supervisory regime, 10, 30ff., 200ff., 387, 418, 423
  information documents for investment products, 72
  Markets in Financial Instruments Directive (MIFID), 72
  national insurance supervisory regime, 74, 308
Integration, 53, 137, 148, 158, 179, 187, 191, 399
Internal audit report, 346, 364
Internal directives, 310ff.
Internal market. *See* Harmonization; Consumer protection
Investment rules, 31, 108
Investment provisions, 48ff., 64, 239
  absence of incentives to redeem, 51
  asset-liability management system, 50
  efficient portfolio management, 50
  funds items, 51
  mandated prudent person principle, 49
  permanent availability and subordination, 51
  principle of freedom of investment, 49
  sufficient duration, 51f.
  tier, 51f., 74, 245ff., 258ff.
  qualitative rules, 50
Item-by-item valuation, 418

K

Key function, 42, 158, 196, 206, 218ff., 227ff., 245ff., 258ff., 264ff., 289, 295, 331ff., 379, 409
  actuarial, 211ff., 237
  deputy director (*see* Deputy director)
  dual-tracking (*see* Dual-tracking)
  duty of notice and public disclosure, 265ff.
  equalization (*see* Equalization)
  evaluation, 260ff.
  internal audit, 346, 364
  outsourcing, 248ff.
  risk-management, 43ff., 125, 219ff.
  subordinate staff members (*see* Subordinate staff members)
Key offices, 348ff., 368

L

Labor representatives, 205, 207
Lamfalussy process, 350, 359ff., 379, 384, 392, 417, 424
Legal department, 226, 240, 327ff., 333ff.
  compliance function, 327ff.
  key function (*see* Key function)
  principle of freedom of internal organization and of proportionality, 338ff.
  principle of functional independence, 337
  principle of functional segregation, 336
Legal duty. *See* Company law
Legality. *See* Principle of legality
Legal nature. *See* Compliance
Legal principles. *See* Solvency II Directive
Level playing field. *See* Harmonization
Lex specialis, 59, 188, 311, 324
Limited economic significance. *See* Solvency II Directive

M

Management advising, 288, 292, 297ff., 305, 313ff.
Management body, 208, 228, 230, 277, 300, 365, 410
Managing board, 125ff., 178ff., 286ff., 297ff., 305ff., 314ff., 327ff., 349ff., 382, 405ff.
Mandatory law, 91
Market discipline. *See* Consumer protection
Markets in Financial Instruments Directive (MIFID). *See* Insurance supervisory regime
Materiality. *See* Principle of legality
Minimum level of guarantee assets, 362
Minimum Requirement for Risk Management (MaRisk), 164ff., 294ff.
Minimum Requirement for the Compliance Function (MaComp), 294ff.
Monistic system, 230
Monitoring, 22, 31ff., 85ff., 172, 175, 180, 196ff., 211ff., 218ff., 230ff., 244, 276, 304ff., 337ff., 348ff., 365ff., 381f., 398, 411
Multiplicity of terms, 227

N

National insurance supervisory regime, 74, 308

O

Officials. *See* Company law
ORSA. *See* Own risk and solvency assessment
Outsourcing. *See* Disclosure obligation; Key functions
Own risk and solvency assessment (ORSA), 158ff., 180ff.
Own-funds structure, 361

P

Payment protection insurance, 87
Permanent availability and subordination, 52
Personally reliable, 305
Portfolio transfer agreement, 355
Principle-based, 314
Principle of abusiveness, 17ff *See also* Abusiveness
Principle of commensurability, 298, 303
Principles of freedom of internal organization and of proportionality, 338
Principle of freedom of investment, 49
Principle of functional independence, 234, 240, 337
Principle of functional segregation, 234, 336
Principle of legality, 301, 303, 314, 329f.
Principle of materiality, 29, 136, 164, 189, 301ff.
Principle of proportionality, 301ff., 339, 375f.
Private insurance law. *See* Consumer protection
Prohibition of exercise of function, 268ff.
Prohibition on borrowing, 22ff.
Proper, 43, 131, 195ff., 220ff., 232ff., 244, 249ff., 268ff., 304, 321, 335, 348ff., 367, 382, 397
  good repute and integrity, 260
  private sphere, 261, 272
  two-tier structure, 258ff.
Proportionality. *See* Principle of legality
Public disclosure, 386ff., 415ff.
  disclosure media, 414
  duty to update, 400ff.
  event-based duties, 419, 424
  nondisclosure, 415
  organizational form, 348, 392, 398
  policyholders, 122ff., 390, 400, 416
  risk reporting information, 406
  secondary addressees, 416
  qualitative elements, 391
  ultimate parent company, 412, 418

Q

Qualification requirements, 22ff., 197ff., 206ff., 231
Quantitative requirement, 29, 36, 61, 133, 208

R

Regulatory arbitrage. *See* Solvency II Directive
Remedy of deficiencies, 5ff., 268ff.
Remedy of weaknesses, 32, 37, 53ff., 109
Remuneration, 132, 264ff., 338, 405
Reporting procedure, 30ff., 54, 77, 108
Reservation of materiality. *See* Solvency II Directive
Reverse discrimination. *See* Harmonization
Risk evaluation, 166
Risk management, 41ff., 166ff. *See also* Group level
Risk report, 346ff., 366ff.
  concentration effects, 399
  diversification, 370, 398, 406, 409
  risk management function, 108, 173, 219f., 235ff.
Rule-based. *See* Solvency II Directive

S

Scrutiny, 28ff.,57ff., 147, 263, 376
Second regulatory level (Level 2). *See* Solvency II Directive
Secrecy interest, 389, 421
Selected management structure, 234ff., 338, 372
Self-generated administrative practices. *See* German Insurance Supervision Act
Separation of responsibility. *See* Consumer protection
Significant ownership interest, 353
Significant undue advantage, 415
Social insurance law. *See* Consumer protection
Solo-plus supervision, 367
Solvency and Financial Condition Report (SCFR). *See* Consumer protection
Solvency II Directive, 8ff., 31ff., 68ff., 71ff., 158ff., 181ff., 206ff., 287ff., 346ff., 377ff.
  capital requirement, 44ff., 60ff.
  College of Supervisors, 9f.
  control of legality, 21
  discretionary power (*see* Discretionary power)
  draft of an implementing regulation (DVO), 47ff., 86ff., 220ff., 245ff.
  EIOPA *See* European Insurance and Occupational Pensions Authority
  European Insurance and Occupational Pensions Authority (EIOPA), 14ff., 69ff., 259, 291ff.
  group supervision, 10ff.,24, 78ff., 210, 291, 346, 370ff., 411f.
  Lamfalussy process (*see* Lamfalussy process)

Solvency II Directive (*cont.*)
limited economic significance, 293
principle-based (*see* Principle based)
principle of commensurability (*see* Principle of commensurability)
principle of legality (*see* Principle of legality)
principle of materiality (*see* Principle of materiality)
principle of proportionality (*see* Principle of proportionality)
regulatory arbitrage, 14, 19, 112
reservation of materiality, 8, 15
rule-based, 10
second regulatory level (Level 2), 11ff., 72
stand-alone provision, 11
Spillover effect, 252
Stand-alone department, 331
Stand-alone provision. *See* Solvency II Directive
Substantive compliance duty, 298
Supererogatory implementation. *See* Harmonization
Supervising insurance mediation, 71
Supervisory authority, 60ff., 74ff., 103ff.
Act to Strengthen the Financial Market and Insurance Supervision, 22, 196, 200
assessment, 135ff (*see also* Own risk and solvency assessment)
business experience, 197
company law overall responsibility, 213
criteria for good repute and integrity, 260
deficiencies, 194, 214, 233, 268ff.
discretion, 10ff., 29, 39, 46, 62, 115, 120, 311, 339
exchange-listed companies, 199ff.
expert requirement, 200ff.
expertise, 211ff.
fit and proper (*see* Fit; Proper)
Hertie case, 197
labor representatives, 205
minimum requirements, 197ff.
OECD guidelines, 213
personal prerequisites, 197
principle of abusiveness (*see* Principle of abusiveness)
recall, 203f., 236, 268ff.
supervisory board, 21, 124ff., 195ff., 211ff.
three-year requirement, 251
timing and retention, 256
weaknesses (*see* Remedy of weaknesses)
Supervisory convergence, 9ff., 39, 280
Supervisory monitoring, 310ff.
Supervisory review process, 27ff., 37ff., 107ff., 289, 295, 391
investment provisions, 49ff., 239
principle of abusiveness (*see* Principle of abusiveness)
reporting procedure (*see* Reporting procedure)
supervisory authority (*see* Supervisory authority)
technical provisions, 31, 45ff., 108, 127, 187, 362, 394
weaknesses (*see* Remedy of weaknesses)
Supervisory system. *See* Solvency II Directive
System of governance, 108, 125, 132, 135, 141, 173, 206ff., 220ff., 244, 268, 277, 290ff.

T
Target solvency capital requirement, 359ff., 396, 400, 408
Tariff obligation, 348
Technical provisions, 31, 45ff., 61, 74, 108, 117, 127, 148, 362, 394
Travel cancellation insurance, 93
Two-level qualification structure. *See* Holder of key functions
Two-person rule, 333f., 338
Two-tier structure. *See* Proper

U
Unification. *See* Harmonization
Unit-linked life insurance policies, 87

V
Values-oriented business management. *See* Compliance

W
Warnings. *See* Consumer protection
Weaknesses. *See* Remedy of weaknesses

MIX
Papier aus verantwortungsvollen Quellen
Paper from responsible sources
FSC® C105338

If you have any concerns about our products,
you can contact us on
ProductSafety@springernature.com

In case Publisher is established outside the EU,
the EU authorized representative is:
Springer Nature Customer Service Center GmbH
Europaplatz 3, 69115 Heidelberg, Germany

Printed by Libri Plureos GmbH
in Hamburg, Germany